NTC's Dictionary of RUSSIAN COGNATES Thematically Organized

NTC's Dictionary of RUSSIAN COGNATES Thematically Organized

Rose Nash, Ph.D.

NTC Publishing Group

Library of Congress Cataloging-in-Publication Data

Nash, Rose.
NTC's dictionary of Russian cognates : thematically organized / Rose Nash.
p. cm.
ISBN 0-8442-0459-5
1. Russian language—Cognate words—English—Dictionaries.
2. English language—Cognate words—Russian—Dictionaries.
I. National Textbook Company. II. Title. III. Title: Dictionary of Russian Cognates.
PG2640.N37 2000
491.73'21—dc21 99-39590
CIP

Typeset by Varda Graphics, Inc.

Published by NTC Publishing Group
A division of NTC/Contemporary Publishing Group, Inc.
4255 West Touhy Avenue, Lincolnwood (Chicago), Illinois 60712-1975 U.S.A.

Printed in the United States of America
International Standard Book Number: 0-8442-0459-5
00 01 02 03 04 HP 14 13 12 11 10 9 8 7 6 5 4 3 2 1

Contents

The Russian Alphabet

Letter	Approximate sound
а	*a* as in *are*
б	*b* as in *be*
в	*v* as in *vine*
г	*g* as in *go*
д	*d* as in *day*

Note: In Russian, *d* is a dental consonant—the tip of the tongue touches the back of the upper teeth.

е	*ye* as in *yes*
ё	*yo* as in *yore*

Note: Russian ë is always stressed.

ж	*s* as in *pleasure*, *z* as in *azure*
з	*z* as in *zone*
и	*ee* as in *eel*
й	*y* as in *boy*
к	*k* as in *kite*
л	*l* as in *look*
м	*m* as in *map*
н	*n* as in *nap*
о	*o* as in *ore*
п	*p* as in *pet*
р	*r* as in *roll*

Note: Russian *r* is always trilled.

с	*s* as in *say*, *c* as in *cent*
т	*t* as in *top*

Note: In Russian, *t* is a dental consonant—the tip of the tongue touches the back of the upper teeth.

у	*u* as in *put*
ф	*f* as in *fine*
х	*ch* as in German *ich*—no equivalent English sound
ц	*ts* as in *cats*
ч	*ch* as in *check*
ш	*sh* as in *ship*
щ	*shch* as in *fresh cheese*
ъ	hard sign—no sound
ы	*i* as in *bill*
ь	soft sign—palatalizes the preceding consonant
э	*e* as in *egg*
ю	*yu* as in *yule*
я	*ya* as in *yard*

Abbreviations

aj = adjective
av = adverb
BR = British spelling
impf = imperfective
indecl = indeclinable
intj = interjection
nf = feminine noun
nfpl = feminine plural noun
nm = masculine noun
nmf = masculine and feminine nouns
nmpl = masculine plural noun
nn = neuter noun
nnpl = neuter plural noun
npl = plural noun
nplsv = plural noun, singular verb
nsg = singular noun
[obs] = obsolete
[pej] = pejorative
pf = perfective
pl = plural
pref = prefix
prep = preposition
vi = intransitive verb
vr = reflexive verb
vt = transitive verb
vt(i) = transitive or intransitive verb
vt(r) = transitive or reflexive verb

Introduction

WHAT IS A COGNATE?

This is a book about words in English and Russian that (1) are similar in form and (2) have the same meanings. Its purpose is to enable you to learn a large amount of bilingual vocabulary quickly, whether you are a beginning, intermediate, or advanced language student.

It is generally believed that English and Russian have few if any cognates compared to English and other European languages, such as Spanish and French. In fact, Russian and English have thousands of similar words, but their similarity is obscured behind the unfamiliar Cyrillic alphabet used by written Russian. This visual handicap prevents easy recognition of Russian words by speakers of English (which uses the Latin alphabet) and has led to the false impression that the two vocabularies are completely different and that Russian words are very difficult to learn.

The cognates in this dictionary come from five main sources. First, although not close on the family tree (English is on the Germanic branch, Russian on the Slavic branch), both languages are Indo-European, and have related words for the most basic concepts, such as kinship terms and numbers. Many of these words still retain some formal evidence of their common prehistoric origin:

mama (ма́ма), papa (па́па), son (сын), daughter (дочь), two (два), three (три), six (шесть), seven (семь), no (нет)

A second source of cognates is the historical, geographical, economic, political, and social contact with other European languages sharing Latin- and Greek-based cognates with English that began with the reign of Peter the Great in the seventeenth century. This is the basic vocabulary of Western civilization, and through centuries of usage these borrowed words have completely assimilated into Russian phonetic, orthographic, and grammatical patterns:

athlete (атле́т), center (це́нтр), crisis (кри́зис), energy (эне́ргия), hotel (оте́ль), information (информа́ция), machine (маши́на), museum (музе́й), police (поли́ция), restaurant (рестора́н), system (систе́ма)

A third source of cognates is direct borrowing of cultural concepts between the two languages. Traditional Russian has contributed to English such words as:

balalaika (балала́йка), borscht (борщ), dacha (да́ча), samovar (самова́р), steppe (степь), troika (тро́йка), tsar (царь), vodka (во́дка)

Loanwords into English from the more recent twentieth-century Russian of the Soviet era reflect the importance of politics and outer space:

cosmonaut (космона́вт), glasnost (гла́сность), kolkhoz (колхо́з), mir (мир), perestroika (перестро́йка), sputnik (спу́тник), tovarishch (това́рищ)

In the other direction, a look at direct borrowings from English into Russian also provides an interesting mirror of contemporary history. During the seventy years of communism and the Cold War era, when contact with the West was sharply limited, many borrowings from English were negative stereotypes promoted by propaganda and movie characters:

boss (босс), businessman (бизнесме́н), cowboy (ковбо́й), gangster (га́нгстер), hooligan (хулига́н), racket (рэ́кет), sex symbol (секс-си́мвол), snob (сноб), Uncle Sam (Дя́дя Сэм)

A rich period of Russian vocabulary development began in 1991 when the former Soviet Union was dismantled. In its effort to reap the rewards of capitalism as quickly as possible, the new post-Soviet Russian government eagerly solicited investment from multinational companies. As a result, the larger cities of Russia are now amply supplied with American-style businesses, American-style entertainment, and American-style advertising. Because of this influence on daily life, dozens of older English loanwords have become an integral part of the standard language, and new words enter the language daily. The infusion of English vocabulary into contemporary Russian is so rapid and widespread that many recent loanwords in common everyday use still do not appear in published dictionaries. Here is an up-to-date sampling of the cognates that you will find in this book:

clothing
jeans (джи́нсы), pullover (пуло́вер), shorts (шо́рты), sweater (сви́тер)

entertainment
disk jockey (диск-жоке́й), sex shop (секс-шоп), show (шо́у), striptease (стрипти́з), weekend (уикэ́нд), Western (ве́стерн)

sports
bodybuilding (бо́ди-би́лдинг), crawl (кроль), drive (драйв), knockout (нока́ут), surfing (сёрфинг)

business
business lunch (би́знес-ланч), dealer (ди́лер), know-how (но́у-ха́у), leasing (ли́зинг), manager (ме́неджер), marketing (ма́ркетинг), raider (ре́йдер), shopping (шо́пинг)

computers
computer (компью́тер), diskette (диске́та), display (диспле́й), fax (факс), file (файл), hacker (ха́кер), Internet (Интерне́т), joystick (джо́йстик), microchip (микрочи́п), multimedia (мультиме́дия), printer (при́нтер), scanner (ска́нер), software (со́фтвер), virus (ви́рус)

A fourth source of cognates is international cultural contact. English and Russian have borrowed words not only from each other, but directly or indirectly from other languages as well. Here are cognates from some of the languages that have enriched both vocabularies:

French
aperitif (аперити́в), boudoir (будуа́р), boutique (бути́к), chauffeur (шофёр), chef (шеф), chic (шик), eclair (экле́р), ensemble (анса́мбль), menu (меню́), negligee (неглиже́), rendevous (рандеву́), souvenir (сувени́р)

German
Blitzkrieg (блицкри́г), Erzatz (эрза́ц), Führer (фю́рер), Glockenspiel (гло́кеншпиль), Leitmotiv (лейтмоти́в), Putsch (путч), Schnapps (шнапс), Strudel (штру́дель), Wunderkind (вундерки́нд)

Japanese
geisha (ге́йша), haiku (ха́йку), hara-kiri (харaки́ри), kamikaze (камика́дзе), karate (карате́), kimono (кимоно́), shiatsu (сиацу́), sushi (су́си or су́ши), tatami (тата́ми)

Spanish
fiesta (фие́ста), gaucho (га́учо), hacienda (гасие́нда), lasso (лассо́), machete (мачете), plaza (пла́за), siesta (сие́ста), sombrero (сомбре́ро)

Hebrew
amen (ами́нь), cherub (херуви́м), kibbutz (кибу́ц), matzo (маца́), sabra (са́бра), seraph (серафи́м), shibboleth (шибболе́т)

Hindi
guru (гу́ру), karma (ка́рма), raja (ра́джа), sari (са́ри), sitar (сита́р), swami (сва́ми), yogi (йог)

Italian
bandit (банди́т), cappuccino (капучи́но), fresco (фре́ска), ghetto (ге́тто), opera (о́пера), piazza (пья́цца), soprano (сопра́но), vendetta (венде́тта)

Turkish
caftan (кафта́н), dervish (де́рвиш), fez (фе́ска), halvah (халва́), pasha (паша́), turban (тюрба́н), yogurt (йо́гурт)

The spelling of the borrowed word as it appears in English or Russian may be an exact transliteration or a modified spelling assimilated to the host language patterns. In some cases, there are two variant spellings, one of them more closely representing its form in the original language. For example, Japanese, which has no "sh" sound, gave English the word spelled *sushi*. It was then borrowed by Russian, where it has two variant spellings: ***су́ши***, influenced by English, and ***су́си***, which reflects the original Japanese pronunciation.

Finally this dictionary includes, as a useful fifth source of shared cognate vocabulary, proper nouns of several different kinds:

personal names
Anna (А́нна), Michael (Миха́ил)

place names
America (Аме́рика), Russia (Росси́я)

historical figures
Cleopatra (Клеопа́тра), Napoleon (Наполео́н)

religious figures
Buddha (Бу́дда), Christ (Христо́с)

artists
Picasso (Пика́ссо), Rembrandt (Рембра́ндт)

writers
Pushkin (Пу́шкин), Shakespeare (Шекспи́р)

composers
Bach (Бах), Tchaikovsky (Чайко́вский)

scientists
Einstein (Эйнште́йн), Pavlov (Па́влов)

philosophers
Confucius (Конфу́ций), Socrates (Сокра́т)

fictional characters
Don Quixote (Дон-Кихо́т), Dracula (Драку́ла)

folklore
Aladdin (Аладди́н), Santa Claus (Са́нта Клаус)

mythology
Apollo (Аполло́н), Zeus (Зевс)

MEANING AND TRANSLATION

The great American linguist Leonard Bloomfield defined the meaning of a word as all the contexts in which it is used. A good monolingual dictionary distinguishes these contexts by describing the senses of the word separately and providing paraphrases, examples, labels, synonyms, and so on, all in the same language as the word being defined. If the word is part of the common everyday vocabulary and not a purely technical or scientific term, it is probably used in many different contexts with many different meanings. *Webster's New World College Dictionary*, Third Edition (Macmillan, 1997), lists thirty-two main senses for the word ***line*** as a noun, not including its uses as a verb or adjective and in idioms.

Dealing with multiple contexts can be problematic in a bilingual dictionary because the various meanings of a word may not have the same translation. For example, ***line*** = ***ли́ния*** [línia] in geometry, but a line for hanging clothes is ***верёвка***; a line for fishing is ***ле́ска***; a line on the face is ***скла́дка***; a line in a drawing or painting is ***штрих***; a line of print or writing is ***строка́***; a dividing line is ***черта́***; a waiting line is ***о́чередь***, and one's line of work is ***профе́ссия***.

Bilingual dictionaries use various methods for defining the senses of words that have more than one meaning. Some bilingual dictionaries simply list all the possible translations, separating each sense group with a semicolon. Others may number the senses, give labels, add associated words such as subjects and objects, or provide usage examples. In all these cases, the purpose is to identify the contexts in which the word appears so that the user can choose the correct translation.

In this dictionary, the contexts are defined by topic, and the meaning of every pair of cognates appearing in that particular list is identical. If cognates have the same meaning in more than one context, they will appear in more than one topic list. For example, ***line*** and ***ли́ния*** are translational equivalents not only in mathematics but also in topics that deal with geography, dance, electricity, communications, politics, the military, transportation, and sports.

The cognate is not always the only possible translation, and in some cases it may not even be the most common one, but it is certainly the one easiest for language learners to remember and use for expressing oneself in the nonnative language. For example, under the topic business, there is the entry ***commerce*** = ***комме́рция***. Some Russian speakers may use the noncognate synonym ***торго́вля*** in this context, but they will always recognize and understand ***комме́рция***. A cognate dictionary is a very useful bridge between two languages, but it cannot give all possible translations. Noncognate synonyms of the words in this dictionary, if they exist, can be found in a thesaurus.

Frequency of usage also plays a role in correct translation. If both the English and Russian look-alike words are high frequency, it is logical for a language learner to assume that they have the same meaning in all contexts. While this is true in a majority of cases, there are exceptions that may cause translation errors. For example, English ***magazine*** (= Russian ***журна́л***) and Russian ***магази́н*** (= English ***shop***, ***store***), both high-frequency words, are often confused. Word pairs like these are called "false friends" or "deceptive cognates." Since this dictionary focuses on words that do have the same meanings, false cognates are excluded.

Every language has its own unique way of expressing meanings, and sometimes translational equivalents do not correspond exactly. For example, in English, language names may be expressed either as single words or as phrases, but in Russian they are always phrases: ***Russian*** (the Russian language) = ***ру́сский язы́к***. Sometimes the noncorresponding translational equivalents in both languages are phrases with different grammatical structures: ***to call it quits*** = ***быть кви́тым***. Multiword expressions important to the topic are included in this dictionary if at least one of the English words and one of the Russian words are cognates.

DICTIONARY INFORMATION

1. accent marks

Russian orthography, like English orthography, does not have written accent marks, and, as in English, correct pronunciation must be learned along with the word. In the topic lists the stressed vowel is indicated in all Russian words of more than one syllable except for *ë*, which is always stressed.

2. English spellings

Irregular and/or double English plural forms are given in parentheses with the abbreviation *pl* for plural:

crisis (*pl* crises)
dogma (*pl* dogmas, dogmata)
echo (*pl* echoes)

Spellings that are exclusively British are given in parentheses with the abbreviation BR for British:

honor (BR honour)
meter (BR metre)
pajamas (BR pyjamas)

Alternate spellings are indicated either by parentheses around the optional letters or as complete separate words: dialog(ue); tsar, czar.

3. things not translated

Words in brackets following the English word are explanatory or informational:

cobalt [Co]	(chemical symbol)
DOS [= disk operating system]	(expansion of abbreviation)
Kathmandu [Nepal]	(location)
kilohertz [= kHz]	(abbreviation)
minstrel [obs]	(obsolete)
muscular [muscle-bound]	(clarification of meaning)
muscular [relating to muscles]	

Words in parentheses are optional added words:

crossword (puzzle)	кроссво́рд *nm*
documentary (film)	документа́льный фильм *nm*
permanent (wave)	перманéнт *nm*

4. part-of-speech and gender labels

If the English and Russian cognates are the same part of speech and number, labels are given only for the Russian words:

applause *nsg*	аплодисмéнты *nmpl*
park	парк *nm*
sports *npl*	спорт *nm*

Gender is indicated for all Russian nouns except for plural nouns that have no singular form:

clavichord *nsg*	клавико́рды *npl*
jungle *nsg*	джу́нгли *npl*

In noun + noun phrases, two gender labels are given following the phrase:

beauty secret	секре́т красоты́ *nm, nf*
dictatorship of the proletariat	диктату́ра пролетариа́та *nf, nm*

5. gender of place names

Place names used with an identifying noun take the gender of the identifying noun:

Lake Michigan	о́зеро Мичига́н *nn*
(the city of) Oslo	го́род О́сло *nm*
Yangtze River	река́ Янцзы́ *nf*

The grammatical gender of place names used without an identifying noun is usually predictable by its ending in the same way as other nouns:

Baikal	Байка́л *nm*
Congo	Ко́нго *nn*
Moscow	Москва́ *nf*

These rules are somewhat subjective, since the identifying word may be understood rather than expressed and still determine grammatical gender. In fact, Russian speakers do not always agree on the gender of place names, and many dictionaries that include place names list these words in a separate section without gender labels.

6. animate nouns that refer to persons

At the end of most topics, there is a list of persons associated with that topic. In these lists, the generic masculine form is used for nouns that include both sexes but do not have well-established separate sex-distinguishing feminine forms. These are often general categories, titles, or names of professions:

critic	кри́тик *nm* (male or female)
professor	профе́ссор *nm* (male or female)
reporter	репортёр *nm* (male or female)

Corresponding feminine forms, if commonly used, follow the masculine form:

student	студе́нт *nm*, -ка *nf*
partner	партнёр *nm*, -ша *nf*

American	америка́нец *nm*, америка́нка *nf*
Catholic	като́лик *nm*, католи́чка *nf*

Theoretically, a corresponding feminine form can be created for any masculine animate noun that does not refer specifically to a male, either by adding to or replacing the suffix as in the examples above. However, Russian speakers differ widely in their acceptance of these words, and standard dictionaries do not agree on their usage. Some feminine forms are used only colloquially (e.g., ***профе́ссорша* = *lady professor***), and a few pairs (as in English) have quite different meanings for the masculine and feminine forms (e.g., ***губерна́тор*** *nm* = ***governor***, ***губерна́нтка*** *nf* = ***governess***).

In this book, the chief authority for inclusion of these feminine forms, as well as for other questions of grammatical gender, spelling, and stress pattern, was the *Oxford Russian Dictionary* (Oxford University Press, 1997).

PRONUNCIATION GUIDE

Modern Russian is based on the Cyrillic alphabet, a writing system developed for Slavic peoples in the ninth century A.D. by Saint Cyril, a missionary of the Eastern Orthodox church. It is still used in several other languages including Bulgarian, Serbian, and Ukrainian. The original alphabet, which had forty-three letters, has been reformed and simplified several times, and now contains only thirty-three letters. (See the complete alphabet on page vii.)

At first glance, words written in Russian look strange and incomprehensible. However, the Russian alphabet is not difficult to learn. Most of its letters are derived from the Greek alphabet, and correspond basically to the letters and sounds of our familiar Latin-based English alphabet. Russian spelling is much more phonetic than English spelling, which means that once you have learned to recognize the Russian letters and their sound values, you will be able to pronounce Russian words quite accurately, although, of course, you will probably not sound like a native speaker until you have taken a course in Russian phonetics. Here is a brief summary of the main similarities and differences between the Russian and English alphabets.

Five letters in the Russian alphabet are identical to letters in the English alphabet:

Russian	**English**	**Phonetic Symbol**
А а	A a	[a]
К к	K k	[k]
М м	Mm	[m]
О о	O o	[o]
Т т	T t	[t]

Seven Russian letters *look* like English letters but have different sounds:

В в	V v		[v]
Н н	N n		[n]
Р р	R r		[r] (trilled)
С с	S s		[s]
У у	U u	(p*u*t)	[u]
Е е	E e	(*ye*t)	[ye]
Х х	—		[x] (guttural fricative, no equivalent in English)

Nine unfamiliar Russian letters correspond to letters and sounds in English:

Б б	B b		[b]
Д д	D d		[d]
Г г	G g		[g]
З з	Z z		[z]
Л л	L l		[l]
П п	P p		[p]
Ф ф	F f		[f]
Э э	E e	(*e*gg)	[e]
Ю ю	U u	(*u*se)	[yu]

Three single Russian consonant letters correspond to two-letter combinations in English:

Ч ч	ch	[č]
Ш ш	sh	[š]
Ф ф	ph (or f)	[f]

Three Russian consonant letters and five Russian vowel letters not in the English alphabet represent sounds or sound combinations that exist in English, spelled in various ways:

Ж ж	azure, plea*s*ure	[ž]
Щ щ	fre*sh ch*eese	[šč]
Ц ц	ca*ts*	[ts]
Ё ё	*yo*ke	[yo]
Я я	*ya*cht	[ya]
И и	*see*, mach*i*ne	[iy]
Й й	bo*y*	[y]
ы	b*i*ll	[I]

The last letter has no capital form as it never appears at the beginning of a word.

Finally, two Russian letters not in the English alphabet are merely pronunciation signals for the preceding consonant letters, and have no sound value of their own. Since they always follow another letter and never appear at the beginning of a word, they too have no capital forms:

ъ "hard sign"	объект	object
ь "soft sign"	культ	cult

There are a few English letters and letter combinations that have no equivalent in the Russian alphabet. The most frequent correspondences are these:

English letter *h* becomes Russian *г* (pronounced like *g*)

harmony	гармо́ния
Havana	Гава́на
hero	геро́й
horoscope	гороско́п
humanism	гумани́зм

English letter *j* becomes Russian *дж*, *ж*, or *ю*:

j = *дж* (pronounced like *j* in the word *jet*):

jazz	джаз
jeans	джи́нсы
jeep	джип
jig	джи́га
jungle	джу́нгли

j = *ж* (pronounced like *s* in the word *pleasure*):

jacket	жаке́т
jargon	жарго́н
jelly	желе́
jockey	жоке́й
journal	журна́л

j = *ю* (pronounced like *you*):

jeweler	ювели́р
jubilee	юбиле́й
Jupiter	Юпи́тер
jurist	юри́ст
justice	юсти́ция

English letters *qu* become Russian *кв* (pronounced like *k* + *v*):

quadrant	квадра́нт
Quaker	ква́кер
quart	ква́рта
quintet	квинте́т
quota	кво́та

English letters *th* become Russian *т* or *ф*:

th = *т* (pronounced like *t*):

theater	теáтр
theme	тéма
theory	теóрия
thermostat	термостáт
throne	трон

th = *ф* (pronounced like *f*):

anathema	анáфема
Athena	Афи́на
logarithm	логари́фм
myth	миф
Thomas	Фомá

English letters *w* and *wh* become Russian *в* (pronounced like *v*):

waffle	вáфля
waltz	вальс
watt	ватт
whisky	ви́ски
wine	винó

English letter *x* becomes Russian *кс* (pronounced like *k* + *s*):

boxing	бокс
deluxe	люкс
excursion	экскýрсия
taxi	такси́
xylophone	ксилофóн

The Russian letter *ц* represents the English sound combination *ts* as in ca*ts*. Words may start with this consonant in Russian, but not in English. The most frequent English correspondence is the letter *c* (pronounced like *s*):

cement	цемéнт
center	центр
ceremony	церемóния
civilization	цивилизáция
cynic	ци́ник

The only Russian letter that has no phonetic equivalent in English is the letter *x*, a guttural consonant that sounds like the *ch* in the German word *ich*. The most frequent English letter correspondence is *ch* (pronounced like *k*):

chaos	ха́ос
character	хара́ктер
charisma	хари́зма
chemistry	хи́мия
Christ	Христо́с

Among the thousands of cognates shared by Russian and English we can find numerous word pairs that are mirror images of each other—exact transliterations, letter for sound and sound for letter. With a bit of practice they are easy to recognize and pronounce, even though the stressed syllable in longer words is not always in the same place. Here are fifty of them:

one-syllable words

act	акт
bank	банк
class	класс
fact	факт
front	фронт
park	парк
plan	план
risk	риск
stop	стоп
test	тест

two-syllable words

canal	кана́л
cosmos	ко́смос
drama	дра́ма
era	э́ра
gala	га́ла
organ	о́рган
picnic	пикни́к
student	студе́нт
tractor	тра́ктор
verdict	верди́кт

three-syllable words

aspirin	аспири́н
camera	ка́мера
director	дире́ктор
element	элеме́нт
instrument	инструме́нт
minimum	ми́нимум
ornament	орна́мент
period	пери́од
radio	ра́дио
veteran	ветера́н

four-syllable words

agitator	агита́тор
kaleidoscope	калейдоско́п
linoleum	лино́леум
melodrama	мелодра́ма
opportunist	оппортуни́ст
panorama	панора́ма
protozoa	протозо́а
radiator	радиа́тор
supermarket	суперма́ркет
terrorism	террори́зм

five-syllable words

accompaniment	аккомпанеме́нт
cannibalism	каннибали́зм
fundamentalist	фундаментали́ст
impresario	импресса́рио
instrumentalist	инструментали́ст
nitroglycerine	нитроглицери́н
pedophilia	педофили́я
perpendicular	перпендикуля́р
videocamera	видеока́мера

ORGANIZATION OF THE DICTIONARY

The dictionary has twenty separate theme groups subdivided into ninety-six topics. The groups in the first part of the book deal with subjects of general interest such as recreation, sports, daily life, and work while the later groups deal with more specialized fields such as politics, flora and fauna, science, technology, geography, and history. Each topic list has its own appropriate format. A complex topic like mathematics needs many headings and subheadings to properly organize all the terms used in that field, while a simpler topic like personal names needs very few. However many headings and subheadings there are, they are arranged so that the general terms for that topic appear first, followed by more specific categories. At the end of each topic list are cross-references to other topics or parts of topics that have related vocabulary. The topics within a theme group often share terminology, and to obtain a complete picture of the cognate vocabulary for that subject area, all the topics included in the theme group should be consulted.

The form of the cognate given in the topic lists is the one most frequently used in that context, usually a noun. At the end of the dictionary is a Supplementary Vocabulary list of approximately 2,500 additional related words not included as entries in the topic lists. Most of these are adjectives and verbs derived from the noun form.

This dictionary can help you learn Russian vocabulary quickly in two ways. If you are primarily a language student, start at the beginning with the first topic, everyday vocabulary.

Here you will find familiar, easy-to-remember words that you can put to use immediately, including a basic list of over one hundred very high-frequency cognates.

If you are a specialist or have a particular interest, scan the Contents for your subject area. You will also find helpful the Alphabetical List of Topics that immediately follows this Introduction.

ACKNOWLEDGMENTS

The model used for *NTC's Dictionary of Russian Cognates* was the author's earlier work, *NTC's Dictionary of Spanish Cognates* (1997). Many experts contributed to the preparation of that dictionary, and their knowledge of the subject matter is reflected in this book. Among those who contributed directly to the preparation of the present work, the author is especially grateful to Eduardo Bianchi, Dr. Edward Levine, Dr. Eugene V. Mohr, and Tatiana Ivanova. The arduous task of copyediting the Russian entries for accuracy was admirably performed by Bella Kalisher Freedman in the early stages of preparation and in the final stages by Arcadiy and Natalia Skatchkov.

Alphabetical List of Topics

The Wide World of Words

EVERYDAY VOCABULARY ◆ DICTIONARIES ◆ BOOKS AND LIBRARIES ◆ JOURNALISM ◆ LITERATURE ◆ FICTION AND FOLKLORE

EVERYDAY VOCABULARY

100-PLUS HIGH-FREQUENCY WORDS

absolute	абсолю́тный *aj*
act	акт *nm*
alternative	альтернати́ва *nf*
analysis (*pl* analyses)	ана́лиз *nm*
aspect	аспе́кт *nm*
atmosphere	атмосфе́ра *nf*
automatic	автомати́ческий *aj*
bar	бар *nm*
barrier	барье́р *nm*
base	ба́за *nf*
basis	ба́зис *nm*
center (BR centre)	центр *nm*
central	центра́льный *aj*
chaos	хао́с *nm*
characteristic	характери́стика *nf*
check (BR cheque)	чек *nm*
civilization	цивилиза́ция *nf*
class	класс *nm*
combination	комбина́ция *nf*
company	компа́ния *nf*
control	контро́ль *nm*
copy	ко́пия *nf*
credit	креди́т *nm*
crisis (*pl* crises)	кри́зис *nm*
culture	культу́ра *nf*
curious	курьёзный *aj*
cycle	цикл *nm*
detail	дета́ль *nf*
echo (*pl* echoes)	э́хо *nn*
effect	эффе́кт *nm*
energy	эне́ргия *nf*
fact	факт *nm*
figure	фигу́ра *nf*
filter	фильтр *nm*
focus (*pl* foci)	фо́кус *nm*
form	фо́рма *nf*
general	генеральный *aj*
group	группа *nf*
hero (*pl* heroes)	геро́й *nm*
hotel	оте́ль *nm*
humor (BR humour)	ю́мор *nm*, юмори́стика *nf*
idea	иде́я *nf*
individual	индивидуа́льный *aj*
industry	инду́стрия *nf*
information	информа́ция *nf*
interest	интере́с *nm*
interview	интервью́ *nn*, *indecl*
line	ли́ния *nf*
logic	ло́гика *nf*
machine	маши́на *nf*
magic	ма́гия *nf*
mask	ма́ска *nf*
mass	ма́сса *nf*
matter	мате́рия *nf*
metal	мета́лл *nm*
method	ме́тод *nm*, мето́дика *nf*
model	моде́ль *nf*
moment	моме́нт *nm*
nervous	нерво́зный *aj*
normal	норма́льный *aj*
operation	опера́ция *nf*
organ	о́рга́н *nm*
original	оригина́льный *aj*
park	парк *nm*
party [political]	па́ртия *nf*
pause	па́уза *nf*
period	пери́од *nm*
plan	план *nm*
popular	популя́рный *aj*
position	пози́ция *nf*
practical	практи́ческий, практи́чный *aj*
practice (BR practise)	пра́ктика *nf*
principle	при́нцип *nm*
product	проду́кт *nm*
protest	проте́ст *nm*
public	пу́блика *nf*
reaction	реа́кция *nf*
real	реа́льный *aj*
reform	рефо́рма *nf*
result	результа́т *nm*
role	роль *nf*
secret	секре́т *nm*
serious	серьёзный *aj*
sex	секс *nm*

signal	сигна́л *nm*
situation	ситуа́ция *nf*
social	социа́льный *aj*
special	специа́льный *aj*
sports *npl*	спорт *nm*
standard	станда́рт *nm*
stop	стоп *nm*
strategy	страте́гия *nf*
structure	структу́ра *nf*
style	стиль *nm*
surprise	сюрпри́з *nm*
symbol	си́мвол *nm*
system	систе́ма *nf*
technology	техноло́гия *nf*
tendency	тенде́нция *nf*
term	те́рмин *nm*
theory	тео́рия *nf*
tone	тон *nm*
type	тип *nm*
typical	типи́чный, типи́ческий *aj*
universal	универса́льный *aj*

CONVERSATIONAL FORMS

clipped words

auto	авто́ *nn, indecl*
deli	магази́н деликате́сов *nm, nm*
demo	демонстра́ция *nf*
disco	ди́ско *nn, indecl*
gas	газоли́н *nm*
gym	гимнасти́ческий зал *nm*
hi-tech	высокосло́жная техноло́гия *nf*
hippo	гиппопота́м *nm*
lab	лаборато́рия *nf*
limo	лимузи́н *nm*
math	матема́тика *nf*
mayo	майоне́з *nm*
memo	мемора́ндум *nm*
mike	микрофо́н *nm*
phone	телефо́н *nm*
photo	фо́то *nn, indecl*
polio	полиомиели́т *nm*
porn, porno	порногра́фия *nf*
pro	профессиона́л *nmf*
prof	профе́ссор *nm*
rhino	носоро́г *nm*
sax	саксофо́н *nm*
schizo	ши́зик *nm*
sync, synch	синхрониза́ция *nf*
taxi	такси́ *nn, indecl*

greetings and exclamations

ah!	а!, ах! *intj*
aha!	ага́! *intj*
ahchoo!	апчхи́! *intj*
ahem!	гм! *intj*
alleluia!, hallelujah!	аллилу́йя! *nf, indecl*
bah!	ба! *intj*
bravo!	бра́во! *intj*
bye-bye!	бай-бай! *intj*
eureka!	э́врика! *intj*
ha-ha!	ха-ха! *intj*
hello! [answering telephone]	алло́! *intj*
hey!	эй! *intj*
hip, hip, hooray!	гип-гип, ура́! *intj*
hm!	гм! *intj*
hooray, hurrah, hurray!	ура́! *intj*
hosanna!	оса́нна *nf, intj*
oh!	о! *intj*
oho!	ого́! *intj*
ow!, oy!	ой! *intj*
phew!	фу! *intj*
phooey!	фу! *intj*
pooh!	фу! *intj*
sh!	шш! *intj*
tee-hee!	хи-хи! *intj*
yah!	ха! *intj*
yum yum!	ням-ням! *intj*

imitation and baby talk

ding-dong	динь-дон *nm*
miaow, miaou	мя́у *intj*
mommy, mummy	мама́ша, ма́мочка *nf*
pee, peepee	пи-пи́ *nn, indecl*
ticktock	тик-та́к *nm*

COMMON PREFIXES

aero-	а́эро-
Afro-	а́фро-
anti-	а́нти-
astro-	а́стро-
auto-	а́вто-
bio-	би́о-
contra-	ко́нтра-
deci-	де́ци-
electro-	эле́ктро-
Euro-	е́вро-
ex-	экс-
exo-	э́кзо-
extra-	э́кстра-
ferro-	фе́рро-

gyro-	ги́ро-
hecto-	ге́кто-
hem- (BR haem-)	ге́мо-
hydro-	ги́дро-
hyper-	ги́пер-
infra-	и́нфра-
iso-	и́зо-
macro-	ма́кро-
maxi-	ма́кси-
mega-	ме́га-
meta-	ме́та-
micro-	ми́кро-
milli-	ми́лли-
mini-	ми́ни-
mono-	мо́но-
neo-	не́о-
neuro-	не́вро-
ortho-	о́рто-, о́рфо-
para-	па́ра-
patho-	па́то-
peri-	пе́ри-
photo-	фо́то-
poly-	по́ли-
pro-	про-
pseudo-	псе́вдо-
psycho-	пси́хо-
quasi-	ква́зи-
radio-	ра́дио-
retro-	ре́тро-
schizo-	ши́зо-
Sino-	си́но-
socio-	со́цио-
spectro-	спе́ктро-
super-	су́пер-
tele-	те́ле-
trans-	транс-
ultra-	у́льтра-
vice-	ви́це-

LATIN EXPRESSIONS

a posteriori	апостерио́ри *av*
a posteriori	апостерио́рный *aj*
a priori	априо́ри *av*
a priori	априо́рный *aj*
ad absurdum	до абсу́рда
alma mater	а́льма-ма́тер *nf, indecl*
casus belli	ка́зус бе́лли *nm*
de facto	де-фа́кто *av*
de jure	де-ю́ре *av*
ex post facto	пост фа́ктум *aj, av*
homo sapiens	хо́мо са́пиенс *nm, indecl*
lingua franca (*pl* linguae francae)	ли́нгва фра́нка *nf*
modus vivendi	мо́дус виве́нди *nm, indecl*
persona non grata	персо́на нон гра́та *nf, indecl*
pro forma	профо́рма *nf*
status quo	ста́тус-кво́ *nn, indecl*

FRENCH EXPRESSIONS

bon mot	бонмо́ *nn, indecl*
carte blanche	карт-бла́нш *nm*
en masse	в ма́ссе *av*
force majeur	форс-мажо́р *nm*
nouveau riche	нувори́ш *nm*
passe-partout	паспарту́ *nn, indecl*
table d'hote	табльдо́т *nm*
tête-à-tête	тет-а-те́т *nm, av*
vis-à-vis	визави́ *av*

See also **MEDICAL PRACTICE** *(common medical prefixes)*, **USING LANGUAGE**

DICTIONARIES

GENERAL TERMS

alphabetical	алфави́тный *aj*
glossary	глосса́рий *nm*
idiom study	идиома́тика *nf*
lexical	лекси́ческий *aj*
lexicographic	лексикографи́ческий *aj*
lexicography	лексикогра́фия *nf*
lexicology	лексиколо́гия *nf*
lexicon [book]	лексико́н *nm*
lexicon [words]	ле́ксика *nf*
paronymy	парони́мия *nf*
synonymy	синономи́я *nf*
term	те́рмин
terminology	терминоло́гия *nf*

KINDS OF DICTIONARIES

biographical	биографи́ческие *aj*
dialectal	диале́ктный *aj*
encyclopedic	энциклопеди́ческий *aj*
etymological	этимологи́ческий *aj*
geographical	географи́ческий *aj*
idiomatic	идиомати́ческий *aj*
phraseological	фразеологи́ческий *aj*
rhetorical	ритори́ческий *aj*

technical	техни́ческий *aj*
terminological	терминологи́ческий *aj*
thematic	темати́ческий *aj*

DICTIONARY INFORMATION

kinds of information

definition	дефини́ция *nf*
etymology	этимоло́гия *nf*
grammatical	граммати́ческий *aj*
orthographic	орфографи́ческий *aj*
phonetic	фонети́ческий *aj*
semantic	семанти́ческий *aj*

words and word combinations

antonym	антони́м *nm*
forms	фо́рмы *nmpl*
idiom	идио́ма *nf*
paronym	парони́м *nm*
synonym	сино́ним *nm*
variants	вариа́нты *nmpl*

usage labels

archaic	архаи́ческий *aj*, архаи́чный *aj*
euphemism	эвфеми́зм *nm*
figurative	фигура́льный *aj*
formal	форма́льный *aj*
historical	истори́ческий *aj*
informal	неформа́льный *aj*
literary	литерату́рный *aj*
neologism	неологи́зм *nm*
poetic	поэти́ческий *aj*
proverbial	провербиа́льный *aj*
vulgar	вульга́рный *aj*

PERSONS

etymologist	этимо́лог *nm*
lexicographer	лексико́граф *nm*
lexicologist	лексико́лог *nm*

See also **USING LANGUAGE**, **WRITING**

BOOKS AND LIBRARIES

ASPECTS OF BOOKS

types of books

album	альбо́м *nm*
almanac	альмана́х *nm*
anthology	антоло́гия *nf*
atlas	а́тлас *nm*
autobiography	автобиогра́фия *nf*
bestseller	бестсе́ллер *nm*
bibliography	библиогра́фия *nf*
biography	биогра́фия *nf*
catalog(ue)	катало́г *nm*
codex [obs]	ко́декс *nm*
comic book	кни́жка с ко́миксами *nf, nmpl*
compendium	компе́ндиум *nm*
dissertation	диссерта́ция *nf*
encyclopedia (BR encyclopaedia)	энциклопе́дия *nf*
geographic(al)	географи́ческий *aj*
humor collection	юмори́стика *nf*
hymnal	сбо́рник ги́мнов *nm, nmpl*
pharmacopeia, pharmacopoeia	фармакопе́я *nf*
psalmody	псалмо́дия *nf*
psalter, Psalter	псалты́рь *nf*
telephone directory	телефо́нная кни́га *nf*
thesaurus (*pl* -es or thesauri)	теза́урус *nm*
thriller	три́ллер *nm*
trilogy	трило́гия *nf*

parts of books

bibliography	библиогра́фия *nf*
folio	фо́лио *nn, indecl*
illustration	иллюстра́ция *nf*
rubric	ру́брика *nf*
text	текст *nm*
title page	ти́тульный лист *nm*

book preparation

compilation	компиля́ция *nf*
correction	корректу́ра *nf*
pagination	пагина́ция *nf*
revision	реви́зия *nf*

other terms

card index	картоте́ка *nf*
coauthorship	соа́вторство *nn*
publication	публика́ция *nf*
published	опублико́ванный *aj*
titled	ти́тульный *aj*
tome	том *nm*
unpublished	неопублико́ванный *aj*

LIBRARIES

tools and equipment

card catalog	ка́рточный катало́г *nm*
microfiche reader	ри́дер *nm*

microfiche	микрофи́ша, микроплёнка *nf*
microfilm	микрофи́льм *nm*
photocopier	фотокопирова́льный аппарат *nm*

other terms

public library	публи́чная библиоте́ка *nf*
register	реги́стр *nm*

PERSONS

anthologist	состави́тель антоло́гии *nm, nf*
author	а́втор *nm*
autobiographer	автобио́граф *nm*
bibliographer	библио́граф *nm*
bibliophile	библиофи́л *nm*
biographer	био́граф *nm*
cataloguer	каталогиза́тор *nm*
coauthor	соа́втор *nm*
compiler	компиля́тор *nm*
corrector	корре́ктор *nm*
redactor	реда́ктор *nm*

See also **LITERATURE**, **PRINTING**

JOURNALISM

GENERAL TERMS

bulletin	бюллете́нь *nm*
communique	коммюнике́ *nn, indecl*
free press	свобо́дная пре́сса *nf*
information	информа́ция *nf*
mass media	сре́дства ма́ссовой информа́ции *nnpl, nf*
national press	общенациона́льная пре́сса *nf*
news agency	информацио́нное аге́нтство *nn*
periodical press	периоди́ческая печа́ть, перио́дика *nf*
photojournalism	фотожурнали́стика *nf*
press	пре́сса *nf*
press agency	аге́нтство печа́ти *nn, nf*
press bureau	пресс-бюро́ *nn, indecl*
press center	пресс-це́нтр *nm*
press conference	пресс-конфере́нция *nf*
press organ	о́рган печа́ти
publication	публика́ция *nf*
publicly	публи́чно *av*
publish	публикова́ть *impf*, опубликова́ть *pf*
Pulitzer Prize	Пу́литцеровская пре́мия *nf*
reporting	репорта́ж *nm*
sensationalism	сенсационали́зм *nm*
tabloid press	бульва́рная пре́сса *nf*

ASPECTS OF JOURNALISM

news media

chronicle	хро́ника *nf*
gazette	газе́та *nf*
journal	журна́л
pamphlet	памфле́т *nm*
periodical	периоди́ческое изда́ние *nn*
radio	ра́дио *nn, indecl*
tabloid	табло́ид *nm*
TASS [obs]	ТАСС *nn, indecl*
television	телеви́дение *nn*

newspaper sections

comics	ко́миксы *nmpl*
financial	фина́нсовый *aj*
sports *npl*	спорт *nm*

kinds of articles

digest	да́йджест *nm*
documentary	документа́льный *aj*
exclusive	эксклюзи́вный *aj*
exposé	экспозе́ *nn, indecl*
factual	факти́ческий, факти́чный *aj*
informational	информацио́нный *aj*
interview	интервью́ *nn, indecl*
report	репорта́ж *nm*

news-gathering and reporting

actuality	актуа́льность *nf*
briefing	бри́финг *nm*
censorship	цензу́ра *nf*
confidentiality	конфиденциа́льность *nf*
confidentially	конфиденциа́льно *av*
illustration	иллюстра́ция *nf*
objectivity	объекти́вность *nf*
photography	фотогра́фия *nf*
sensational	сенсацио́нный *aj*
uncensored	неподцензу́рный *aj*

other terms

issue number	нóмер журнáла *nm*, *nm*
printed matter	печáтный материáл *nm*
publicity	паблúсити *nn*, *indecl*, публúчность *nf*
sensation	сенсáция *nf*
series (*pl* series)	сéрия *nf*
special edition	специáльный вы́пуск *nm*

PERSONS

censor	цéнзор *nm*
correspondent	корреспондéнт, -ка *nmf*
film critic	кинокрúтик *nm*
interviewer	интервьюéр *nm*
journalist	журналúст, -ка *nmf*
pamphleteer	памфлетúст *nm*
photographer	фотóграф *nm*
photojournalist	фотожурналúст, -ка *nmf*
press attaché	пресс-атташé *nm*, *indecl*
press corps	корреспондéнтский кóрпус *nm*
public, the	пýблика *nf*
publicist	публицúст *nm*
reporter	репортёр *nm*

See also **COMMUNICATIONS**, **USING LANGUAGE**

LITERATURE

GENERAL TERMS

authorship	áвторство *nn*
belles-lettres *npl*	беллетрúстика *nf*
classic	клáссик *nm*
classic(al)	классúческий *aj*
classical literature	классúческая литератýра *nf*
classics, the *npl*	клáссика *nf*
criticism	крúтика *nf*
dramatic	драматúческий *aj*
factual	фактúческий, фактúчный *aj*
figure of speech	риторúческая фигýра *nf*
folklore studies *npl*	фольклорúстика *nf*
folklore	фольклóр *nm*
form and content	фóрма и содержáние *nf*, *nn*
genre	жанр *nm*
humanities	гуманитáрные наýки *nfpl*
legend	легéнда *nf*
legendary	легендáрный *aj*
literary	литературовéдческий *aj*
literature	литератýра *nf*
lyric (poetry)	лúрика *nf*
lyrical	лирúческий, лирúчный *aj*
plagiarism	плагиáт *nm*
poem [long]	поэ́ма *nf*
poetic quality	поэтúчность *nf*
potpourri	попуррú *nn*, *indecl*
Pushkin studies	пушкиновéдение *nn*
reading material	материáл для чтéния *nm*, *nn*
tetrology	тетралóгия *nf*
titled	титулóванный *aj*
trilogy	трилóгия *nf*
work of genius	гениáльное произведéние *nn*

ASPECTS OF LITERATURE

genres

allegory	аллегóрия *nf*
drama	дрáма *nf*
epic poetry	э́пика *nf*
epic, epic poem	эпопéя *nf*, эпúческая поэ́ма *nf*
erotica	эрóтика *nf*
escapism	эскапúзм *nm*
legend	легéнда *nf*
poetry	поэ́зия *nf*
prose	прóза *nf*

elements

character	харáктер *nm*
dialog(ue)	диалóг *nm*
dramatic situation	драматúчная ситуáция *nf*
form	фóрма *nf*
intrigue	интрúга *nf*
lyricism	лирúзм *nm*
moral (of the story)	морáль *nf*
structure	структýра *nf*
style	стиль *nm*
theme	тéма *nf*

styles and themes

adventure	авантю́ра *nf*
avant-garde	авангáрд *nm*

bucolic	буколи́ческий *aj*
Byronic	байрони́ческий *aj*
classicism	классици́зм *nm*
didactic	дидакти́ческий *aj*
epistolary	эпистоля́рный *aj*
Faustian	фа́устовский *aj*
Gothic (novel)	готи́ческий *aj*
historical	истори́ческий *aj*
humorous	юмористи́ческий *aj*
imagism	имажини́зм *nm*
Kafkaesque	кафкиа́нский *aj*
modernism	moderни́зм *nm*
naturalism	натурали́зм *nm*
neoclassicism	неоклассици́зм *nm*
pastorale	пастора́ль *nf*
Rabelaisian	раблезиа́нский *aj*
realism	реали́зм *nm*
romanticism	романти́зм *nm*, рома́нтика *nf*
socialist realism	социалисти́ческий реали́зм *nm*
surrealism	сюрреали́зм *nm*
symbolism	символи́зм *nm*
Utopianism	утопи́зм *nm*

parts of a work

analects	анале́кты *nmpl*
bibliography	библиогра́фия *nf*
citation	цита́та *nf*
epilog(ue)	эпило́г *nm*
episode	эпизо́д *nm*
exposition	экспози́ция *nf*
prolog(ue)	проло́г *nm*

humor in literature

comedy	коме́дия *nf*
farce	фарс *nm*
humor (BR humour)	ю́мор *nm*, юмори́стика *nf*
irony	иро́ния *nf*
parody	паро́дия *nf*
sarcasm	сарка́зм *nm*
satire	сати́ра *nf*

FORMS OF FICTION

adventure novel	авантю́рный рома́н *nm*
bucolic literature	буко́лика *nf*
detective novel	детекти́вный рома́н
fable	фа́була *nf*
fantasy	фанта́зия *nf*
fantasy literature	фанта́стика *nf*
folklore	фолькло́р *nm*
Gothic novel	готи́ческий рома́н *nm*
heroic epic	герои́ческий э́пос *nm*
historical novel	истори́ческий рома́н *nm*
novella, novelette	нове́лла *nf*
romance	рома́н *nm*
saga	са́га *nf*

FORMS OF DRAMA

melodrama	мелодра́ма *nf*
miracle play	мира́кль *nm*
morality play	моралите́ *nn, indecl*
tragedy	траге́дия *nf*
tragicomedy	трагикоме́дия *nf*

FORMS OF POETRY

ballad	балла́да *nf*
couplet	купле́т *nm*
eclogue	экло́га *nf*
elegy	эле́гия *nf*
epithalamium	эпитала́ма *nf*
epode	эпо́д *nm*
epos	э́пос *nm*
haiku	хайку́ *nn, indecl*
idyll, idyl	иди́ллия *nf*
octave	окта́ва *nf*
ode	о́да *nf*
paean	пеа́н *nm*
Pindaric ode	пинда́рская о́да *nf*
rondeau, rondel	рондо́ *nn, indecl*
sonnet	соне́т *nm*
triolet	триоле́т *nm*

FORMS OF FACTUAL PROSE

autobiography	автобиогра́фия *nf*
biography	биогра́фия *nf*
chrestomathy	хрестома́тия *nf*
critique	кри́тика *nf*, крити́ческая статья́ *nf*
dissertation	диссерта́ция *nf*
ephemera	эфемери́ды *nfpl*
essay	эссе́ *nn, indecl*
exegesis	экзеге́за *nf*
literary criticism	литерату́рная кри́тика *nf*
memoirs	мемуа́ры *nmpl*

monograph	моногра́фия *nf*
reading material	материа́л для чте́ния *nm, nn*
samizdat [obs]	самизда́т *nm*
synopsis (*pl* synopses)	сино́псис *nm*
thesis (*pl* theses)	те́зис *nm*

SHORT FORMS OF WIT OR WISDOM

aphorism	афори́зм *nm*
bon mot	бонмо́ *nn, indecl*
epigram	эпигра́мма *nf*
epigraph	эпи́граф *nm*
epitaph	эпита́фия *nf*
epithet	эпи́тет *nm*
limerick	лиме́рик *nm*
maxim	ма́ксима *nf*

TERMS IN POETRY

basic terms

meter (BR metre)	метр *nm*
metrics *nplsv*	ме́трика *nf*
nuance	нюа́нс *nm*
pause	па́уза *nf*
poetics *nplsv*	поэ́тика *nf*
prosody	просо́дия *nf*
rhythm	ритм *nm*
rhythmics *nplsv*	ри́тмика *nf*
scansion	сканди́рование *nn*
versification	версифика́ция *nf*

kinds of verse

Alexandrine verse	александри́йский стих *nm*
antistrophe	антистрофа́ *nf*
strophe	строфа́ *nf*
trope	троп *nm*

kinds of rhythm

amphibrach	амфибра́хий *nm*
anapest	ана́пест *nm*
choriambic	хориямби́ческий *aj*
dactyl	да́ктиль *nm*
distich	ди́стих *nm*
hexameter (BR -metre)	гекза́метр *nm*
iamb, iambus (*pl* iambuses, iambi)	ямб *nm*
pentameter (BR -metre)	пента́метр *nm*
pyrrhic (foot)	пирри́хий *nm*
spondee	спонде́й *nm*
tercet	терце́т *nm*
terza rima	терци́на *nf*
tetrameter (BR -metre)	тетра́метр *nm*
trimeter (BR -metre)	триме́тр *nm*
trochaic	трохеи́ческий *aj*

figures of speech

hyperbole	гипе́рбола *nf*
metaphor	мета́фора *nf*
metonymy	метони́мия *nf*
oxymoron	оксю́морон *nm*
personification	персонифика́ция *nf*
synecdoche	сине́кдоха *nf*
zeugma	зе́вгма *nf*

sound patterns

acrostic	акрости́х *nm*
alliteration	аллитера́ция *nf*
anacrusis (*pl* anacruses)	анакру́са *nf*
anaphora	ана́фора *nf*
assonance	ассона́нс *nm*
consonance	консона́нс *nm*
echo (*pl* echoes)	э́хо *nn*
onomatopoeia	ономатопе́я *nf*
rhyme	ри́фма *nf*

PERSONS

writers and storytellers

anonymous writer	анони́м *nm*
author	а́втор *nm*
autobiographer	автобио́граф *nm*
bard [obs]	бард *nm*
bibliographer	библио́граф *nm*
biographer	био́граф *nm*
dramatist	драмату́рг *nm*
epic poet	э́пик *nm*
fantasy writer	фанта́ст *nm*
futurist	футури́ст *nm*
humorist (BR humourist)	юмори́ст *nm*
imagist	имажини́ст *nm*
lyric poet	ли́рик *nm*
minstrel [obs]	менестре́ль *nm*
novelist	новелли́ст, -ка *nmf*
parodist	пароди́ст *nm*
plagiarist	плагиа́тор *nm*
poet	поэ́т *nm*, поэте́сса *nf*
poet laureate	по́эт-ла́уреат *nm*
poetess [obs]	поэте́сса *nf*

prose writer — прозаик *nm*
romanticist — романтик *nm*
satirist — сатирик *nm*
stylist — стилист *nm*
troubadour [obs] — трубадур *nm*
versifier — версификатор *nm*

scholars and specialists

classicist — классик *nm*
folklorist — фольклорист *nm*
literary man/woman — литератор *nm*
literary critic/scholar — литературовед *nm*
literati — литераторы *nmpl*
Pushkin scholar — пушкинист *nm*
Shakespeare scholar — шекспировед *nm*

See also **FAMOUS FIGURES OF YESTERDAY AND TODAY** *(writers)*, **ANCIENT CIVILIZATIONS** *(literature and music)*, **FICTION AND FOLKLORE**

FICTION AND FOLKLORE

GENERIC ROLES

anti-hero — антигерой *nm*
detective — детектив *nm*
evil genius — злой гений *nm*
hero — герой *nm*
heroine — героиня *nf*
ingenue, ingénue — инженю *nf, indecl*
personage — персонаж *nm*
protagonist — протагонист *nm*

science-fiction

humanoid — гуманоид *nm*
Martian — марсианин *nm*
robot — робот *nm*
Superman — супермен *nm*
Venusian — венерианец *nm*

FAMOUS CHARACTERS

– fictional –

Don Quixote — Дон-Кихот *nm*
Dracula — Дракула *nm*
Falstaff — Фальстаф *nm*
Faust — Фауст *nm*
Frankenstein — Франкенштейн *nm*
Gargantua — Гаргантюа *nm*
Hamlet — Гамлет *nm*
Jekyll and Hyde — Джекилл и Хайд *nmpl*
King Lear — Король Лир *nm*
Lilliputian — лилипут, -ка *nmf*
Lolita — Лолита *nf*
Macbeth — Макбет *nm*
Mephistopheles — Мефистофель *nm*
Othello — Отелло *nm*
Peter Pan — Питер Пэн *nm*
Pollyanna — Поллиана *nf*
Quasimodo — Квазимодо *nm*
Rip Van Winkle — Рип Ван Винкль *nm*
Romeo — Ромео *nm*
Scrooge — Скрудж *nm*
Sherlock Holmes — Шерлок Холмс *nm*
Shylock — Шейлок *nm*
Simon Legree — Саймон Легри *nm*
Svengali — Свенгали *nm*
Tartuffe — Тартюф *nm*
Tom Sawyer — Том Сойер *nm*

– legendary –

Aladdin — Аладдин *nm*
Don Juan — Дон-Жуан *nm*
Lancelot — Ланселот *nm*
Lilith — Лилит *nf*
Merlin the Magician — Мерлин *nm*
Mother Hubbard — матушка Хаббард *nf*
Peeping Tom — любопытный Том *nm*
Prince Charming — прекрасный принц *nm*
Robin Hood — Робин Гуд *nm*
Santa Claus — Санта Клаус *nm*
Scheherezade — Шахерезада *nf*
William Tell — Вильгельм Телль *nm*

human-like beings and spirits

Azrael — Азраил *nm*
Baba-Yaga — баба-яга *nf*
dybbuk — диббук *nm*
Eblis — иблис *nm*
elf (*pl* elves) — эльф *nm*
fairy — фея *nf*
genie (*pl* genies, genii) — джинн *nm*
gnome — гном *nm*
houri (*pl* houris) — гурия *nf*
jinn, jinni (*pl* jinns, jinn) — джинн *nm*
Lorelei — Лорелея *nf*
peri — пери *nf, indecl*
Pinocchio — Пиноккио *nm*
troll — тролль *nm*
vampire — вампир *nm*
Yeti, yeti — йети *nm, indecl*

creatures and things

Cheshire cat — Чеширский кот *nm*
dragon — дракон *nm*
Excalibur — Экскалибур *nm*

monster	монстр *nm*
phoenix, phenix	фе́никс *nm*
roc	пти́ца Рух *nf*
time machine	маши́на вре́мени *nf, nn*

imaginary places

Avalon	Авало́н *nm*
Camelot	Камело́т *nm*
El Dorado	Эльдора́до *nn*
Gotham City	Го́там *nm*
Lilliput	Лиллипу́тия *nf*
Ruritania	Рурита́ния *nf*
Shangri-la	Ша́нгри-ла *nf*
Utopia	Уто́пия *nf*

See also **THE BIBLE** *(creatures, things, supernatural beings)*, **CLASSICAL MYTHOLOGY**

Pleasures and Pastimes

ENTERTAINMENT ◆ SPORTS ◆ GAMES AND TOYS ◆ TV, VIDEO, AND RADIO ◆ MOVIES ◆ PHOTOGRAPHY ◆ TOURISM

ENTERTAINMENT

FORMS OF ENTERTAINMENT

participatory

amateur radio	люби́тельское ра́дио
ballroom dancing *nsg*	ба́льные та́нцы *nmpl*
camping	ке́мпинг *nm*
collecting	коллекциони́рование *nn*
cruising	круи́з *nm*
excursion	экску́рсия *nf*
exotica *npl* [collecting]	экзо́тика *nf*
hobby	хо́бби *nm, indecl*
karaoke	карао́ки *nn, indecl*
numismatics *nplsv*	нумизма́тика *nf*
philately	филатели́я *nf*
photography	фотогра́фия *nf*
picnic	пикни́к *nm*
playing cards	игра́льные ка́рты *nfpl*
sensation	сенса́ция *nf*
show business	шоу-би́знес *nm*
tourism	тури́зм *nm*

spectator / listener

acrobatics	акроба́тика *nf*
attraction	аттракцио́н *nm*
ballet	бале́т *nm*
card trick	ка́рточный фо́кус *nm*
cinema	кино́ *nn, indecl*
circus	цирк *nm*
comics	ко́миксы *nmpl*
computer	компью́тер *nm*
cyclorama	циклора́ма *nf*
derby [horse racing]	де́рби *nm, indecl*
figure skating	фигу́рное ката́ние *nn*
fireworks *npl*	фейерве́рк *nm*
opera	о́пера *nf*
pantomime	пантоми́ма *nf*
pomp	по́мпа *nf*
pyrotechnics *nplsv*	пироте́хника *nf*
radio program	радиопостано́вка *nf*
revue	ревю́ *nn, indecl*
rodeo	роде́о *nn, indecl*
show	шоу *nn, indecl*
spectacle	спекта́кль *nm*
striptease	стрипти́з *nm*
television	телеви́дение *nn*
theater	теа́тр *nm*
variety show	варьете́ *nn, indecl*
vaudeville	водеви́ль *nf*
video	ви́део *nn, indecl*

participatory or spectator / listener

dance	та́нец *nm*
hypnotism	гипноти́зм *nm*
juggling, jugglery	жонглёрство *nn*, жонгли́рование *nn*
magic	ма́гия *nf*
masquerade	маскара́д
music	му́зыка *nf*
sports *npl*	спорт *nm*
theater (BR theatre)	теа́тр *nm*

events and celebrations

banquet	банке́т *nm*
benefit performance	бенефи́с *nm*
carnival	карнава́л *nm*
cavalcade	кавалька́да *nf*
cocktail party	копте́йль *nm*
costume ball	бал-маскара́д *nm*
exposition	экспози́ция *nf*
festival	фестива́ль *nm*
fiesta	фие́ста *nf*
gala	га́ла *aj, indecl*
jubilee	юбиле́й *nm*
parade	пара́д *nm*

humor

absurd	абсу́рдный *aj*
absurdity	абсу́рдность *nf*
April Fools' joke	первоапре́льская шу́тка *nf*
black humor	чёрный ю́мор *nm*
buffoonery	буффона́да *nf*
burlesque	бурле́ск *nm*
clowning	клоуна́да *nf*
comic effect	коми́чность *nf*
comical	коми́чный, коми́ческий *aj*

mimicry	ми́мика *nf*
parody	паро́дия *nf*

PLACES

amusement park	лу́на-парк *nm*
art gallery	карти́нная галере́я *nf*
ballroom	ба́льный зал
broadcasting studio	радио-сту́дия *nf*
cabaret	кабаре́ *nn, indecl*
casino	казино́ *nn, indecl*
clubhouse	клуб *nm*
dance hall	танцева́льный зал *nm*
disco	ди́ско *nn, indecl*
hippodrome	ипподро́м *nm*
museum	музе́й *nm*
music hall	мю́зик-хо́лл *nm*
night club	ночно́й клуб *nm*
park	парк *nm*
radio station	радиоста́нция *nf*
stadium (*pl* stadiums or stadia)	стадио́н *nm*
television studio	телесту́дия *nf*
theater (BR theatre)	теа́тр *nm*
theme park	темати́ческий па́рк *nm*
zoo, zoological garden/park	зооса́д, зоопа́рк, зоологи́ческий парк/сад *nm*

TOOLS AND EQUIPMENT

binoculars *npl*	бино́кль *nm*
camcorder	камко́рдер *nm*
camera	ка́мера *nf*
carousel	карусе́ль *nf*
confetti	конфетти́ *nn, indecl*
klaxon	кла́ксон *nm*
marionette	марионе́тка *nf*
mask	ма́ска *nf*
megaphone	мегафо́н *nm*
model airplane	моде́ль самолёта *nf*
Roman candle	ри́мская свеча́ *nf*
stamp album	альбо́м для ма́рок *nm, nfpl*
stand [for display]	стенд *nm*
trampoline	трампли́н *nm*
trapeze	трапе́ция *nf*

PERSONS

entertainment characters

buffoon	буффо́н *nm*
Charlie Chaplin	Ча́рли Ча́плин *nm*
circus performer	цирка́ч *nm*
clown	кло́ун *nm*
comedian	комедиа́нт, -ка *nmf*
comedic actor	комеди́йный актёр *nm*
comedienne	коми́ческая актри́са *nf*
comic, comedian	ко́мик *nm*
comic actor	коми́ческий актёр *nm*
geisha	ге́йша *nf*
Harlequin	Арлеки́н *nm*
humorist (BR humourist)	юмори́ст *nm*
illusionist	иллюзиони́ст *nm*
imitator	имита́тор *nm*
juggler	жонглёр *nm*
local talent *nsg*	ме́стные тала́нты *nmpl*
master of ceremonies [= MC]	церемонийме́йстер *nm*
Mickey Mouse	Ми́кки Ма́ус *nm*
mimic	мим *nm*
musician	музыка́нт *nm*
parodist	пароди́ст *nm*
Pierrot [obs]	Пьеро́ *nm, indecl*
Pulchinello [obs]	Полишине́ль *nm*
Punch [obs]	Панч *nm*
troupe	тру́ппа *nf*

other persons

collector (as a hobby)	коллекционе́р *nm*
numismatist	нумизма́т *nm*
philatelist	филатели́ст *nm*
radio ham	радиолюби́тель *nm*
radio listener	радиослу́шатель *nm*
television viewer	телезри́тель, -ница *nmf*

See also **DANCE**; **MAGIC** *(entertainment)*; **MOVIES**; **TV, VIDEO, AND RADIO**; **MUSIC**; **SPORTS**; **GAMES AND TOYS**; **THEATER PERFORMANCE**; **VISUAL ARTS**

SPORTS

GENERAL TERMS

athletic	атлети́ческий *aj*
athletics *nplsv*	атле́тика *nf*
championship (title)	чемпиона́т *nm*
chance	шанс *nm*
equipping, equipment	экипиро́вка *nf*
form	фо́рма *nf*
league	ли́га *nf*
line	ли́ния *nf*
physical culture	физи́ческая культу́ра, физкульту́ра *nf*

record	реко́рд *nm*
record (-breaking)	реко́рдный *aj*
sport *nsg*, sports *npl*	спорт *nm*
sports medicine	спорти́вная медици́на *nf*
sportsmanlike	спортсме́нский *aj*
sportsmanship	спорти́вный дух *nm*
training	трениро́вка *nf*
unsportsmanlike	неспорти́вный *aj*

ASPECTS OF SPORTS

types

indoor sport(s)	спорт в за́лах *nm*, *nmpl*
nonprofessional	непрофессиона́льный *aj*
outdoor sport(s)	спорт на откры́том во́здухе *nm*, *nm*
professional	профессиона́льный *aj*
spectator sport(s)	зре́лищный спорт *nm*
winter sport(s)	зи́мний спорт *nm*

places

arena	аре́на *nf*
ballpark	бейсбо́льное по́ле *nn*
basketball court	баскетбольная площа́дка *nf*
boxing ring	боксёрский ринг *nm*
campsite	ке́мпинг *nm*
coliseum	колизе́й *nm*
golf course	площа́дка для го́льфа *nf*, *nm*
gymnasium (*pl* gymnasiums or gymnasia)	гимнасти́ческий зал *nm*
hippodrome	ипподро́м *nm*
Olympic village	олимпи́йская дере́вня *nf*
racetrack	трек *nm*
roller-skating rink	роликодро́м *nm*
sports complex	спорти́вный ко́мплекс *nm*
stadium (*pl* stadiums or stadia)	стадио́н *nm*
tennis court	те́ннисный корт *nm*
velodrome	велодро́м *nm*

contests

championship	чемпиона́т *nm*
favorite [horse-racing] (BR favourite)	фаври́т, -ка *nmf*
Grand Prix	гран-при́ *nn*, *indecl*
match	матч *nm*
Olympic medal	олимпи́йская меда́ль *nm*
Olympic games	олимпи́йские и́гры *nfpl*
photo finish	фотофи́ниш *nm*
prize	приз *nm*
prize money *nsg*	призовы́е де́ньги *npl*
rematch	матч-рева́нш *nm*, повто́рный матч
revenge match	рева́нш *nm*
set	сет *nm*
tennis match	те́ннисный матч *nm*
tournament	турни́р *nm*
trophy	трофе́й *nm*

COMMON SPORTS

ball/racket sports

badminton	бадминто́н *nm*
baseball	бейсбо́л *nm*
basketball	баскетбо́л *nm*
football	(америка́нский) футбо́л *nm*
golf	гольф *nm*
handball	гандбо́л *nm*
hockey	хокке́й *nm*
ice hockey	хокке́й на льду́ *nm*, *nm*
jai alai	хау-ала́й *nm*
lacrosse	лакро́сс *nm*
polo	по́ло *nn*, *indecl*
rugby	ре́гби *nn*, *indecl*
tennis	те́ннис *nm*
volleyball	волейбо́л *nm*
water polo	ватерпо́ло, во́дное по́ло *nn*, *indecl*

water sports

regatta	рега́та *nf*
scuba	ску́ба *nf*
surfing	сёрфинг *nm*
windsurfing	виндсе́рфинг *nm*
yachting	я́хтенный спорт *nm*

other sports

acrobatics *npl*	акроба́тика *nfsg*
cross-country (race)	кросс *nm*
figure skating	фигу́рное ката́ние *nn*
parachute-jumping	парашюти́зм *nm*

Olympic events

biathlon	биатло́н *nm*
discus throw	мета́ние ди́ска *nn*
marathon race	марафо́нский бег *nm*

martial arts

aikido	айкидó *nn*
boxing	бокс *nm*
judo	дзюдó *nn, indecl*
juijitsu, jujitsu	джи́у-джи́тсу *nn, indecl*
karate	каратэ́ *nn, indecl*
kendo	ке́ндо *nm, indecl*
kung fu	кун-фу́ *nn, indecl*
sumo wrestling	сумó *nn, indecl*

fitness

aerobics *nplsv*	аэрóбика *nf*
bodybuilding	бóди-би́лдинг *nm*
gymnastics *nplsv*	гимна́стика *nf*
hatha yoga	ха́тха-йóга *nf*
jogging	джóггинг *nm*
physical culture	физи́ческая культу́ра, физкульту́ра *nf*
tai chi	тай-чи́ *nn, indecl*
yoga	йóга *nf*

RULES AND ACTIONS IN SPORTS

specific actions

balance, to regain one's	сбаланси́ровать *pf*
balance (oneself), to keep one's balance	баланси́ровать *impf*
body block	блок *nm*
break!	брейк! *intj*
butterfly stroke	баттерфля́й *nm*
crawl	кроль *nm*
dribbling	дри́блинг *nm*
drive	драйв *nm*
feint	финт *nm*
knockdown	нокда́ун *nm*
knockout	нока́ут *nm*
nelson	не́льсон *nm*
parachute jump	прыжóк с парашю́том *nm, nm*
pass	пас *nm*
slalom	сла́лом *nm*
smash	смэш *nm*
spinning	спиннинг *nm*
sprint	спринт *nm*
technical knockout [= TKO]	техни́ческий нока́ут *nm*
uppercut	апперкóт *nm*

other terms

disqualification	дисквалифика́ция *nf*
distance	диста́нция *nf*
false start	фальста́рт *nm*
finals *npl*	фина́л *nm*
finish	фи́ниш *nm*
finish line	ли́ния фи́ниша *nf*
finish line	фи́нишная черта́ *nf*
forward	фóрвард *nm*
foul	фол *nm*
goal	гол *nm*
goal line	ли́ния ворóт *nf*
handicap	гандика́п *nm*
heat [racing]	гит *nm*
lead, to be in the	лиди́ровать *impf*
line of sight	ли́ния прице́ла *nf, nm*
penalty	пена́льти *nn, indecl*
period	пери́од *nm*
point	пункт *nm*
position	пози́ция *nf*
qualifying	квалификациóнный *aj*
quarterfinal	четвертьфина́л *nm*
round	ра́унд *nm*
semifinal	полуфина́л *nm*
sideline	бокова́я ли́ния *nf*
start, starting line	старт *nm*, ли́ния ста́рта
starting signal	ста́ртовый сигна́л *nm*
strategy	страте́гия *nf*
telemark	телема́рк *nm*
chance	шанс *nm*

EQUIPMENT

boats and vehicles

canoe	канóэ *nn, indecl*
catamaran	катамара́н *nm*
go-cart	карт *nm*
kayak	кая́к *nm*
motorboat	мотóрная лóдка *nf*
motorcycle	мотоци́кл *nm*

other equipment

alpenstock	альпенштóк *nm*
aqualung	аквала́нг *nm*
basketball	баскетбóльный мяч *nm*
bat	би́та *nf*
binoculars *npl*	бинóкль *nm*
catgut	кетгу́т *nm*
discus	диск *nm*
floor mat	мат *nm*
football	футбóльный мяч *nm*
gymnastic apparatus *nsg*	гимнасти́ческие снаря́ды *nmpl*

hula hoop	ху́ла-хуп *nm*
mask	ма́ска *nf*
niblick	ни́блик *nm*
parallel bars	паралле́льные бру́сья *nmpl*
racket, racquet	раке́тка *nf*
roller skates	ро́лики *nmpl*
skateboard	скейтбо́рд *nm*
snorkel	шно́ркель *nm*
tennis racket	те́ннисная раке́тка *nf*
tennis ball	те́ннисный мяч *nm*
toboggan	тобогга́н *nm*
trampoline	трампли́н *nm*
trapeze	трапе́ция *nf*
traverse	тра́верс *nm*
yacht	я́хта *nf*

PERSONS

athletes and sportsmen

ace	ас *nm*
acrobat	акроба́т *nm*
aerobicist	аэроби́ст, -ка *nmf*
Alpinist	альпини́ст *nm*
aquanaut	акванáвт *nm*
athlete	атле́т *nm*
badminton player	бадминтони́ст, -ка *nmf*
baseball player	бейсболи́ст *nm*
basketball player	баскетболи́ст, -ка *nmf*
biathlete	биатлони́ст, -ка *nmf*
bobsleigh rider	бобслеи́ст *nm*
boxer	боксёр *nm*
butterfly swimmer	баттерфляи́ст *nm*
canoeist	каноэи́ст *nm*
center forward	центр-фо́рвард *nm*
cross-country runner	кроссме́н *nm*
discus-thrower	дискобо́л *nm*
figure skater	фигури́ст, -ка *nmf*
finalist	финали́ст *nm*
football player [American]	футболи́ст *nm*
golfer	игро́к в гольф *nm, nm*
gymnast	гимна́ст, -ка *nmf*
handball player	гандболи́ст, -ка *nmf*
hockey player	хоккеи́ст *nm*
jockey	жоке́й *nm*
jogger	джо́ггер *nm*
judoist	дзюдои́ст, -ка *nmf*
linesman	судья́ на ли́нии *nm, nf*
marathon runner	марафо́нец *nm*
matador	матадо́р *nm*
medalist (BR medallist)	медали́ст, -ка *nmf*
motorcyclist	мотоцикли́ст *nm*
Olympian	олимпи́ец *nm*, олимпи́йка *nf*
opponent	оппоне́нт *nm*
outsider [in race]	аутса́йдер *nm*
parachutist	парашюти́ст, -ка *nmf*
picador	пикадо́р *nm*
pro, professional	профессиона́л, -ка *nmf*
record holder	рекордсме́н, -ка *nmf*
rugby player	регби́ст *nm*
second [in a duel]	секунда́нт *nm*
semifinalist	полуфинали́ст *nm*
sportsman (*pl* sportsmen)	спортсме́н *nm*
sportswoman (*pl* sportswomen)	спортсме́нка *nf*
sprinter	спри́нтер *nm*
surfer	сёрфинги́ст *nm*
tennis player	теннси́ст, -ка *nmf*
toreador	тореадо́р *nm*
volleyball player	волейболи́ст, -ка *nmf*
water polo player	ватерполи́ст *nm*
windsurfer	виндсёрфинги́ст *nm*

other persons

arbiter, arbitrator	арби́тр *nm*
captain	капита́н *nm*
champion	чемпио́н, -ка *nmf*
fan	фэн *nm*
goalkeeper	голки́пер *nm*
jury	жюри́ *nn, indecl*
manager	ме́неджер *nm*
marker (of scores)	маркёр *nm*
nonprofessional	непрофессиона́л *nm*
prizewinner	призёр, -ша *nmf*
referee	ре́фери́ *nm, indecl*
sparring partner	спа́рринг-партнёр *nm*
sportscaster	спорти́вный коммента́тор *nm*
starter	ста́ртер *nm*
trainer	тре́нер *nm*

See also **ENTERTAINMENT, GAMES AND TOYS, BOATS AND SHIPS, LAND TRANSPORTATION, PERSONAL GROOMING**

GAMES AND TOYS

GENERAL TERMS

match	матч *nm*
rematch	матч-рева́нш *nm*

tournament	турни́р *nm*

NAMES OF GAMES

board and table games

billiards *npl*	билья́рд *nm*
cards	ка́рты *nfpl*
darts *npl*	дарт *nm*
lotto	лото́ *nn, indecl*
mah-jongg	маджо́нг *nm*
Monopoly	Монопо́лия *nf*
pachisi, parchesi	пачи́си *nnpl*
ping-pong	пинг-по́нг *nm*
pool	билья́рд *nm*
snooker	сну́кер *nm*
table tennis	насто́льный те́ннис *nm*

casino games

baccarat	баккара́ *nn, indecl*
blackjack	блэкдже́к *nm*
keno	ке́но *nn*
roulette	руле́тка *nf*

other card games

bridge	бридж *nm*
canasta	кана́ста *nf*
contract bridge	бридж-контра́кт *nm*
cribbage	кри́ббидж *nm*
faro	фарао́н *nm*
poker	по́кер *nm*
rummy	ра́мми *nn, indecl*
solitaire	солите́р *nm*
whist	вист *nm*

word games

acrostic	акрости́х *nm*
anagram	анагра́мма *nf*
charades *npl*	шара́да *nf*
crossword (puzzle)	кроссво́рд *nm*
cryptogram	криптогра́мма *nf*
logogriph (puzzle)	логогри́ф *nm*
rebus	ре́бус *nm*
Scrabble	скрэбл *nm*
telestich	телести́х *nm*

other games

checkers	ша́шки *npl*
computer game	компью́терная игра́ *nf*
cricket	кри́кет *nm*
croquet	кроке́т *nm*
dominoes *npl*	домино́ *nn, indecl*
lottery	лотере́я *nf*
pachinko	пачи́нко *nn, indecl*
pall-mall [obs]	пэл-мэл *nm*
pinball	пинбо́л *nm*
video game	видеоигра́ *nf*

RULES AND ACTIONS

general

bank	банк *nm*
pass	пас *nm*
position	пози́ция *nf*
strategy	страте́гия *nf*

chess

check	шах *nm*
chess match	ша́хматный матч *nm*
end game	э́ндшпиль *nm*
gambit	гамби́т *nm*
mate	мат *nm*

bridge

double	дубль *nm*
grand slam	большо́й шлем *nm*
pass *vi*	пасова́ть *impf*
rubber	ро́ббер *nm*
slam	шлем *nm*

billiards

billiard ball	билья́рдный шар *nm*
billiards cue	кий *nm*
billiards table	билья́рд *nm*
billiards room	билья́рдная *nf*
carom	карамбо́ль *nm*

other terms

bluff [poker]	блефова́ть *impf, pf*
booby prize	приз проигра́вшему игроку́ *nm*
joker	джо́кер *nm*
lottery ticket	лотере́йный биле́т *nm*
playing card	(игра́льная) ка́рта *nf*
to play cards	игра́ть в ка́рты *impf*
to break the bank	сорва́ть банк *impf*
winning number	вы́игрышный но́мер *nm*

TOYS

glockenspiel	гло́кеншпиль *nm*

kaleidoscope	калейдоскóп *nm*
matryoshka	матрёшка *nf*
music box	музыкáльная шкатýлка *nf*
toy soldier	солдáтик *nm*
yo-yo	йо-йо *nn, indecl*

PERSONS

banker	банкомёт *nm*
billiards player	бильярди́ст *nm*
bridge player	бриджи́ст, -ка *nmf*
card player	картёжник *nm*, картёжница *nf*
croupier	крупьé *nm*
grandmaster	гроссмéйстер *nm*
lotto player	лотóшник *nm*
partner	партнёр, -ша *nmf*

See also **ENTERTAINMENT**, **SPORTS**

TV, VIDEO, AND RADIO

GENERAL TERMS

program (BR programme)	прогрáмма *nf*
programming	программи́рование *nn*
radio	рáдио *nn, indecl*
radio program	радиопостанóвка *nf*
radio station	радиостáнция *nf*
radio/broadcasting studio	радио-стýдия *nf*
television, TV	телеви́дение *nn*, ТВ
television channel	телевизиóнный канáл *nm*
television program	телепрогрáмма *nf*
television station	телестáнция *nf*
television studio	телестýдия *nf*
transmission	трансми́ссия *nf*
video	ви́део *nn, indecl*

ASPECTS OF MEDIA ENTERTAINMENT

kinds of television/radio

black-and-white television	чёрно-бéлое телеви́дение *nn*
cable television	кáбельное телеви́дение *nn*
closed-circuit television	зáмкнутое телеви́дение *nn*
color television	цветнóе телеви́дение *nn*
commercial radio/television	коммéрческое рáдио/телеви́дение *nn*
educational radio/television	учéбное рáдио/телеви́дение *nn*
public radio/television	общéственное рáдио/телеви́дение *nn*
satellite television	спýтниковое телеви́дение *nn*

programs and programming

adaptation (of book, play)	адаптáция *nf*
comedy	комéдия *nf*
documentary (film)	документáльный фильм *nm*
dramatization	драматизáция *nf*
episode	эпизóд *nm*
interview	интервью́ *nn, indecl*
miniseries	минисериáл *nm*
serial	сериáл *nm*
situation comedy [= sitcom]	комеди́йный сериáл *nm*
soap opera	мы́льная óпера *nf*
sports *npl*	спорт *nm*
telecourse	образовáтельная прогрáмма *nf*
telefilm	телефи́льм *nm*
telethon	телемарафóн *nm*

transmission and reception

antenna	антéнна *nf*
channel	канáл *nm*
synchronism	синхрони́зм *nm*
television signal	телевизиóнный сигнáл *nm*

other terms

BBC [= British Broadcasting Corporation]	Би-Би-Си *nn, indecl*
kinescope	кинескóп *nm*
rating	рéйтинг *nm*
telegenic	телегени́чный *aj*
videography	видеогрáфия *nf*

TOOLS AND EQUIPMENT

camera	кáмера *nf*
satellite	сателли́т *nm*
selector	селéктор *nm*
telecamera	телекáмера *nf*

television antenna	телевизио́нная анте́нна *nf*
television camera	телека́мера *nf*, телевизио́нная ка́мера *nf*
television monitor	телемонито́р *nm*
videocamera	видеока́мера *nf*
videocassette	видеокассе́та *nf*
videofilm	видеофи́льм *nm*
videotape	видеоле́нта *nf*

PERSONS

commentator	коммента́тор *nm*
disc jockey, DJ	диск-жоке́й, ди-дже́й *nm*
interviewee	интервьюи́руемый, -мая *nmf*
interviewer	интервьюе́р *nm*
producer	продю́сер *nm*
radio announcer	ди́ктор ра́дио *nm*
talent	тала́нт *nm*

See also **ENTERTAINMENT**, **MOVIES**

MOVIES

GENERAL TERMS

cinema	кино́ *nn, indecl*
cinemascope	синемаско́п *nm*
cinematographic	кинематографи́ческий *aj*
cinematography	кинематогра́фия *nf*
film	фильм, кинофи́льм *nm*
film festival	кинофестива́ль *nm*
Oscar	О́скар *nm*
studio	сту́дия *nf*
version	ве́рсия *nf*

ASPECTS OF FILMMAKING

film categories and genres

art film	худо́жественный фильм *nm*
comedy (film)	коме́дия *nf*, комеди́йный фильм *nm*
documentary (film)	документа́льный фильм *nm*
erotica	эро́тика *nf*
fantasy	фанта́зия *nf*, фэ́нтези *nm, indecl*
horror film	фильм у́жасов *nm*
musical (film)	музыка́льный фильм *nm*
nature film	фи́льм о приро́де *nm, nf*
romance	романти́ческий фильм *nm*
silent film	немо́й фильм *nm*
stereoscopic film	стереоскопи́ческий фильм, стереофи́льм *nm*
western (film)	ве́стерн *nm*

elements

actors	актёры *nmpl*
dialog(ue)	диало́г *nm*
scenario	сцена́рий *nm*
scene	сце́на *nf*
subtitle	субти́тр *nm*

techniques

crowd scene	ма́ссовая сце́на *nf*
effects, sound	звуковы́е/шумовы́е эффе́кты *nmpl*
effects, visual	зри́тельные эффе́кты *nmpl*
montage	монта́ж *nm*
panorama	панора́ма *nf*
panoramic effect	панора́мный эффе́кт *nm*
stroboscopic light	стробоскопи́ческий свет *nm*
synchronism	синхрони́зм *nm*

popular characters

cowboy	ковбо́й *nm*
detective	детекти́в *nm*
gangster	га́нгстер *nm*
sex symbol	секс-си́мвол *nm*

other terms

clip	клип *nm*
filmstrip	диафи́льм *nm*
projection	прое́кция *nf*, проекти́рование *nn*
restoration	реставра́ция *nf*
titled	снабжённый ти́трами *nmpl*
color film	цветно́й фильм *nm*

TOOLS AND EQUIPMENT

camera	ка́мера *nf*
film/movie studio	киносту́дия *nf*

movie camera	кинока́мера *nf*
projection booth/room	проекцио́нная бу́дка/каби́на *nf*
projector	прое́ктор *nm*

PERSONS

documentary filmmaker	документали́ст *nm*
cinematographer	кинематографи́ст *nm*
composer	компози́тор *nm*
critic	кри́тик *nm*
decorator	декора́тор *nm*
film actor	киноактёр *nm*
film actress	киноактри́са *nf*
film critic	кинокри́тик *nm*
montage specialist	монтажёр *nm*
producer	продю́сер *nm*
scenario writer	сценари́ст *nm*
talent scout	открыва́тель тала́нтов *nm, nmpl*

See also **LITERATURE**, **ENTERTAINMENT**, **PHOTOGRAPHY**, **VISUAL ARTS**

PHOTOGRAPHY

GENERAL TERMS

camera	ка́мера *nf*
copy	ко́пия *nf*
lens	ли́нза *nf*
photo	фо́то *nn, indecl*
photograph	фотогра́фия *nf*
photographic	фотографи́ческий *aj*
photography	фотогра́фия *nf*

ASPECTS OF PHOTOGRAPHY

kinds of cameras and processes

camcorder	камко́рдер *nm*
daguerrotype	дагерроти́п *nm*
gamma camera	га́мма *nf*
holography	гологра́фия *nf*
microphotography	микрофотогра́фия *nf*
movie camera	кинока́мера *nf*
photo-offset	фотоофсе́т *nm*
photocopier	копирова́льная маши́на *nf*, копиро́вщик *nm*
photogravure	фотогравю́ра *nf*
photojournalism	фотожурнали́стика *nf*
Polaroid [film, camera]	Поляро́ид *nm*
reprography, reprographics *nplsv*	репрогра́фия *nf*
telephotography	телефотогра́фия *nf*
television camera	телека́мера *nf*, телевизио́нная ка́мера *nf*
videocamera	видеока́мера *nf*

still photographs

daguerrotype [obs]	дагерроти́п *nm*
documentary photograph	фотодокуме́нт *nm*
ferrotype	ферроти́пия *nf*
group photograph	группово́й сни́мок *nm*
hologram	гологра́мма *nf*
montage	монта́ж *nm*
photocopy	фотоко́пия *nf*
photoengraving	фотогравю́ра *nf*
photomontage	фотомонта́ж *nm*
photostat	фотоста́т *nm*
portrait	портре́т *nm*
projection	прое́кция *nf*
transparency	транспара́нт *nm*

taking pictures

aperture	аперту́ра *nf*
center (BR centre)	центри́ровать *impf, pf*
detail	дета́ль *nf*
double exposure	двойна́я экспози́ция *nf*
exposure	экспози́ция *nf*
focal length/distance	фо́кусное расстоя́ние *nn*
focus (*pl* focuses or foci)	фо́кус *nm*
masking	маскиро́вка *nm*
panorama	панора́ма *nf*
pose	по́за *nf*
subject	субъе́кт *nm*

kinds of lenses

crystalline lens	хруста́лик *nm*
objective lens	объекти́в *nm*
telephoto lens	телеобъекти́в *nm*
telescopic lens	телескопи́ческий объекти́в *nm*
wide-angle lens	широкоуго́льная ли́нза *nf*

tools and equipment

exposure meter	экспоно́метр *nm*
filter	фильтр *nm*
light meter	экспоно́метр *nm*

microfilm	микрофи́льм *nm*
panchromatic (film)	панхромати́ческий *aj*
photocopier	фотокопирова́льный аппарат *nm*
photometer	фото́метр *nm*
projector	прое́ктор *nm*
sensitometer	сенситоме́тр *nm*
sensitometry	сенситоме́трия *nf*
slide projector	диапрое́ктор *nm*
stereoscope	стереоско́п *nm*

processing

emulsion	эму́льсия *nf*
fixation, fixing	фикса́ция *nf*
matte	ма́товый *aj*
mount	монти́ровать *impf*
optical effect	опти́ческий эффе́кт *nm*
original	оригина́л *nm*
photo lab	фотолаборато́рия *nf*
positive	позити́в *nm*
retouching	ре́тушь *nf*
thermometer	термо́метр *nm*
tone	тон *nm*

other terms

album	альбо́м *nm*
copy	копи́ровать *impf*, скопи́ровать *pf*
photo (graph) album	фотоальбо́м *nm*
photogenic	фотогени́чный *aj*
Xerox	ксе́рокс *nm*

PERSONS

montager, montage specialist	монтажёр *nm*
photographer	фото́граф *nm*
photojournalist	фотожурнали́ст, -ка *nmf*
retoucher	ретушёр *nm*

See also **VISUAL ARTS**, **MOVIES**

TOURISM

GENERAL TERMS

baggage	бага́ж *nm*
class	класс *nm*
season	сезо́н *nm*
shopping	шо́пинг *nm*
tourism	тури́зм *nm*
transportation	тра́нспорт *nm*

ASPECTS OF TOURISM

kinds of vacations

cruise	круи́з *nm*
excursion	экску́рсия *nf*
expedition	экспеди́ция *nf*
odyssey	одиссе́я *nf*
safari	сафа́ри *nn, indecl*
tour	турне́ *nn, indecl*
visit	визи́т *nm*

lodging

deluxe cabin	каю́та люкс *nf*
guest room	ко́мната для госте́й *nf, nmpl*
hotel	оте́ль *nm*
luxury hotel	гости́ница-люкс *nf*
motel	моте́ль *nm*
pension	пансио́н, пансиона́т *nm*

travel arrangements

charter flight	ча́ртерный рейс *nm*
Intourist	Интури́ст *nm*
passport	па́спорт *nm*
seasonal rate	сезо́нный тари́ф *nm*
tourist office	туристи́ческое бюро́ *nn*
tourist season	тури́стский сезо́н *nm*
tourist/travel agency	туристи́ческое аге́нтство *nn*
visa	ви́за *nf*

shopping

Beryozka [hard currency shop]	«Берёзка» *nf*
credit card	креди́тная ка́рточка *nf*
dollar	до́ллар *nm*
ruble	рубль *nm*
souvenir	сувени́р *nm*
traveler's check	доро́жный/тури́стский чек *nm*

starting, ending, and en route

airport	аэропо́рт *nm*
baggage compartment	бага́жное отделе́ние *nn*
baggage claim	вы́дача багажа́ *nf, nm*
baggage check	бага́жная квита́нция *nf*

baggage car [train]	бага́жный ваго́н *nm*
customs declaration	тамо́женная деклара́ция *nf*
in transit	транзи́том *nm*
pack one's bags, to	пакова́ть чемода́ны *nmpl*
passport control	па́спортный контро́ль *nm*
point of entry/exit	пункт вво́за/вы́воза *nm, nm*
port of call	порт захо́да *nm, nm*
river port	речно́й порт *nm*
seaport	морско́й порт *nm*
station	ста́нция *nf*
way station	попу́тная ста́нция *nf*

other terms

deluxe	люкс *aj, indecl*
first-class	пе́рвый кла́сс *nm*
public toilet	туале́т *nm*
restaurant	рестора́н *nm*
second-class	второ́й кла́сс *nm*
service	се́рвис *nm*

SEEING THE SIGHTS

things to visit

ancient ruins	дре́вние руи́ны *nfpl*
local color	ме́стный колори́т *nm*
national park	национа́льный парк *nm*

famous tourist attractions

Alhambra	Альга́мбра *nf*
Buckingham Palace	Букинге́мский дворе́ц *nm*
Eiffel Tower	Э́йфелева ба́шня *nf*
Empire State Building	Эмпа́йр Стейт Би́лдинг *nm*
Grand Canyon	Большо́й Каньо́н *nm*
Kremlin	Кремль *nm*
Niagara Falls *npl*	Ниага́рский водопа́д *nm*
Sistine Chapel	Сиксти́нская капе́лла *nf*
Taj Mahal	Тадж-Маха́л *nm*
Westminster Abbey	Вестми́нстерское абба́тство *nn*

PERSONS

excursion leader	экскурсово́д *nm*
excursionist	экскурса́нт *nm*
guide	гид *nm*
passenger	пассажи́р, -ка *nmf*
porter [in hotel]	портье́ *nm, indecl*
taxi driver	такси́ст *nm*
tourist	тури́ст, -ка *nmf*

See also **ENTERTAINMENT, THE CITY, AVIATION AND SPACE TRAVEL, BOATS AND SHIPS, LAND TRANSPORTATION**

The Arts

MUSIC ◆ DANCE ◆ THEATER PERFORMANCE ◆ VISUAL ARTS ◆ ARCHITECTURE

MUSIC

GENERAL TERMS

composition	компози́ция *nf*
hit	хит *nm*
music	му́зыка *nf*
musical instrument	музыка́льный инструме́нт *nm*
musical	музыка́льный *aj*
musical technique	музыка́льная те́хника *nf*
musical notation	но́тное письмо́ *nn*
musicality, musicianship	музыка́льность *nf*
musicology	музыкове́дение *nn*
notation	нота́ция *nf*
opera, operatic art	о́пера *nf*, о́перное иску́сство *nn*
opus (*pl* opuses, opera)	о́пус *nm*
piece	пье́са *nf*
practice (BR practise)	пра́ктика *nf*
repertoire	репертуа́р *nm*
style	стиль *nm*
theory	тео́рия *nf*

STYLES AND GENRES

kinds of music

accompaniment	аккомпанеме́нт *nm*
background music	музыка́льный фон *nm*
classical music	класси́ческая му́зыка *nf*
electronic music	электро́нная му́зыка *nf*
instrumental music	инструмента́льная му́зыка *nf*
movie music	му́зыка к кинофи́льму *nf*, *nm*
pop music	поп-му́зыка *nf*
popular music	популя́рная му́зыка *nf*
program music	програ́ммная му́зыка *nf*
vocal music	вока́льная му́зыка *nf*

major classical styles

baroque	баро́кко *nn*, *indecl*
impressionism	импрессиони́зм *nm*
romanticism	романти́зм *nm*

popular styles

Beatlemania	битлома́ния *nf*
blues *npl*	блюз *nm*
boogie-woogie	бу́ги-ву́ги *nn*, *indecl*
calypso	кали́псо *nn*, *indecl*
country & western	ка́нтри *nn*, *indecl*
dance music	танцева́льная му́зыка *nf*
folk music	наро́дная му́зыка *nf*
gospel music	го́спелз *nm*, *indecl*
heavy metal	хэ́ви ме́тал, металли́ческий рок *nm*
jazz	джаз *nm*
punk, punk-rock	панк, панк-рок *nm*
ragtime	регта́йм *nm*, *indecl*
rap music	рэп-му́зыка *nf*
reggae	ре́гги *nm*, *indecl*
rhythm & blues	ритм-и-блюз *nm*
rock, rock music	рок, рок-му́зыка *nf*
rock-'n'-roll	рок-н-ро́лл *nm*

COMPOSITIONS

religious forms

antiphon	антифо́н *nm*
cantata	канта́та *nf*
gospel music	го́спелз *nm*, *indecl*
Gregorian (chant)	григориа́нское песнопе́ние *nn*
hymn	гимн *nm*
mass	ме́сса *nf*
motet	моте́т *nm*
oratorio	орато́рия *nf*
requiem	ре́квием *nm*

historical dance forms

allemande	аллема́нда *nf*
arabesque	арабе́ска *nf*
bourre	бурр́э *nn*, *indecl*
galliard	галья́рда *nf*

gavotte	гаво́т *nm*
gigue	жи́га, джи́га *nf*
minuet	менуэ́т *nm*
passacaglia	пасака́лья *nf*
passe-pied	паспье́ *nn, indecl*
pavan(e)	пава́на *nf*
saraband(e)	сараба́нда *nf*

vocal compositions

aria	а́рия *nf*
ballad	балла́да *nf*
cantilena	кантиле́на *nf*
canzonet(te)	канцо́на *nf*
cavatina	савати́на *nf*
chorale	хора́л *nm*
madrigal	мадрига́л *nm*
national anthem	национа́льный гимн *nm*
popular song	популя́рная пе́сня *nf*
recitative	речитати́в *nm*
refrain	рефре́н *nm*
song cycle	цикл пе́сен *nm, nfpl*
vocalise	вокали́з *nm*

instrumental compositions

barcarol(l)e	баркаро́ла *nf*
canon	кано́н *nm*
capriccio	капри́чч(и)о *nn, indecl*
chaconne	чако́на *nf*
chamber music	ка́мерная му́зыка *nf*
concerto grosso	конче́рто гро́ссо *nn, indecl*
concerto	конце́рт *nm*
divertissement	дивертисме́нт *nm*
etude, étude	этю́д *nm*
fanfare	фанфа́ра *nf*
fantasia	фанта́зия *nf*
fugue	фу́га *nf*
humoresque	юморе́ска *nf*
impromptu	экспро́мт *nm*
interlude	интерлю́дия *nf*
intermezzo (*pl* intermezzos, intermezzi)	интерме́ццо *nn, indecl*
march	марш *nm*
nocturne	ноктю́рн *nm*
organ music	орга́нная му́зыка *nf*
overture	увертю́ра *nf*
partita	партиту́ра *nf*
pastorale	пастора́ль *nf*
prelude	прелю́дия *nf*
raga	ра́га *nf*
rhapsody	рапсо́дия *nf*
romance	рома́н *nm*
rondo	ро́ндо *nn, indecl*
scherzo (*pl* scherzos, scherzi)	ске́рцо *nn, indecl*
serenade	серена́да *nf*
sonata	сона́та *nm*
sonatina	сонати́на *nf*
suite	сюи́та *nf*
symphony	симфо́ния *nf*
tantara, taramtara	там-тарара́м *nm*
theme and variations	те́ма с вариа́циями *nf, nfpl*
toccata	токка́та *nf*
tone poem	симфони́ческая поэ́ма *nf*
improvisation	импровиза́ция *nf*

INSTRUMENTS

sound sources

acoustic(al)	акусти́ческий *aj*
electric	электри́ческий *aj*
electronic	электро́нный *aj*
stereo system	стереосисте́ма *nf*

keyboard

accordion	аккордео́н *nm*
celesta	челе́ста *nf*
clavichord *nsg*	клавико́рды *npl*
concert grand piano	конце́ртный роя́ль *nm*
organ	орга́н *nm*
piano [large]	фортепья́но *nn, indecl*
piano [upright]	пиани́но *nn, indecl*
pianola	пиано́ла *nf*
spinet	спине́т *nm*

string

Aeolian harp	Эо́лова а́рфа *nf*
balalaika	балала́йка *nf*
bandura	банду́ра *nf*
banjo (*pl* banjos, banjoes)	ба́нджо *nn, indecl*
cello	виолонче́ль *nf*
cittern, cithern [obs]	кифа́ра *nf*
contrabass, double bass	контраба́с *nm*
electric guitar	электри́ческая гита́ра *nf*
gamelan [Indonesian]	гамела́н *nm*
guitar	гита́ра *nf*
harp	а́рфа *nf*
koto [Japanese]	ко́то *nn, indecl*
lute [obs]	лю́тня *nf*
lyre [obs]	ли́ра *nf*

psaltery [obs]	псалтерио́н *nm*
samisen [Japanese]	сямисэ́н *nm*
sitar [Indian]	сита́р *nm*
viol, viola	вио́ла *nf*
violoncello	виолонче́ль *nf*
zither	ци́тра *nf*

wind

bass horn	ту́ба-бас *nm*
basset horn	бассетго́рн *nm*
clarinet	кларне́т *nm*
cornet	корне́т *nm*
English horn	англи́йский рожо́к *nm*
flageolet	флажоле́т *nm*
flute	фле́йта *nf*
harmonica	губна́я гармо́ника, гармо́шка *nf*
oboe	гобо́й *nm*
ocarina	окари́на *nf*
panpipes *npl*	свире́ль *nf*
piccolo	(фле́йта) пи́кколо *nn, indecl*
saxophone	саксофо́н *nm*
tenor saxophone	те́нор-саксофо́н *nm*
sousaphone	сузафо́н *nm*
trombone	тромбо́н *nm*
tuba	ту́ба *nf*

percussion

castanets	кастанье́ты *nfpl*
concertina	концерти́но *nn, indecl*
cymbals	цимба́лы *npl*
gamelan	гамела́н *nm*
glockenspiel	гло́кеншпиль *nm*
gong	гонг *nm*
marimba	мари́мба *nf*
tambourine	тамбури́н *nm*
tom-tom, tam-tam	тамта́м *nm*
vibraphone	вибрафо́н *nm*
xylophone	ксилофо́н *nm*

other instruments

carillon	карильо́н *nm*
harmonium	фисгармо́ния *nf*
monochord	моноко́рд *nm*

MUSIC THEORY

basic concepts

atonality	атона́льность *nf*
chord	акко́рд *nm*
harmony	гармо́ния *nf*
interval	интерва́л *nm*
melody	мело́дия *nf*
meter (BR metre)	метр *nm*
note	но́та *nf*
polytonality	политона́льность *nf*
rhythm	ритм *nm*
tempo (*pl* tempos, tempi)	темп *nm*
tonality	тона́льность *nf*
tone	тон *nm*

scales and modes

Aeolian mode	эоли́йский лад *nm*
chromatic	хромати́ческий *aj*
diatonic	диатони́ческий *aj*
dodecaphonic	додекафони́ческий *aj*
major (key)	мажо́рный *aj*
major key	мажо́р *nm*
minor	мино́рный *aj*
minor (key)	мино́р *nm*
pentatonic	пентато́нный *aj*

notes of the diatonic scale

do	до *nn, indecl*
fa (BR fah)	фа *nn, indecl*
la	ля *nf, indecl*
mi	ми *nn, indecl*
re	ре *nn, indecl*
sol	соль *nn, indecl*
ti	си *nn, indecl*
dominant	домина́нта *nf*
subdominant	субдомина́нта *nf*
tonic	то́ника *nf*

intervals

halftone, semitone	полуто́н *nm*
octave	окта́ва *nf*
quint	кви́нта *nf*
second	секу́нда *nf*
sixth	се́кста *nf*

chords

dissonant	диссони́рующий *aj*
subdominant	субдомина́нта *nf*
tetrachord	тетрахо́рд *nm*
triad	триа́да *nf*

textures

homophonic	гомофо́нный *aj*
monophonic	монофони́ческий *aj*
polyphonic	полифони́ческий *aj*

harmonic devices

cadence	каде́нция *nf*

consonance	консона́нс *nm*
disharmony	дисгармо́ния *nf*
dissonance	диссона́нс *nm*
modulation	модуля́ция *nf*
progression	прогре́ссия *nf*

polyphonic devices

counterpoint	контрапу́нкт *nm*
imitation	имита́ция *nf*
parallel motion	паралле́льное движе́ние *nn*

melodic devices

caesura (*pl* caesuras, caesurae)	цезу́ра *nf*
descant	ди́скант *nm*
figure	фигу́ра *nf*
leitmotif, leitmotiv	лейтмоти́в *nm*
monotone, in a	моното́нно *av*
motif	моти́в *nm*
obbligato (*pl* obbligatos, obbligati)	облига́то *nn, indecl*
pause	па́уза *nf*
pedal/organ point	орга́нный пункт *nm*
sequence	секве́нция *nf*
syncopation	синкопа́ция *nf*
theme	те́ма *nf*
transposition	транспози́ция *nf*, транспони́рование *nn*
variation	вариа́ция *nf*

notation

bass clef	басо́вый ключ *nm*
enharmonic	энгармони́ческий *aj*
symbol	си́мвол *nm*
tenor clef	теноро́вый ключ *nm*

parts of compositions

cadenza	каде́нция *nf*
coda	ко́да *nf*
exposition	экспози́ция *nf*
finale	фина́л *nm*
fragment	фрагме́нт *nm*
introduction	интроду́кция *nf*
passage	пасса́ж *nm*
phrase	фра́за *nf*
reprise	репри́за *nf*

other terms

diapason	диапазо́н *nm*
gamut	га́мма *nf*
harmonization	гармониза́ция *nf*
inversion	инве́рсия *nf*
part	па́ртия *nf*
register	реги́стр *nm*
solfeggio	сольфе́джио *nn, indecl*
tessitura	тесситу́ра *nf*
transcription	транскри́пция *nf*
polyphony	полифони́я *nf*
arpeggio	арпе́джио *nn, indecl*
plagal (cadence)	плага́льный *aj*

PERFORMANCE TERMS

dynamics

crescendo	креще́ндо *nn, indecl, av*
diminuendo	диминуэ́ндо *nn, indecl, av*
forte	фо́рте *nn, indecl, av*
fortissimo	форти́ссимо *nn, indecl, av*
pianissimo	пиани́ссимо *nn, indecl, av*
piano	пиа́но *aj, av*
prestissimo	прести́ссимо *nn, indecl, av*
presto	пре́сто *nn, indecl, av*
rallentando	раллента́ндо *av*

tempo

adagio	ада́жио *nn, indecl*
agitato	ажита́то *nn, indecl*
allegretto	аллегре́тто *nn, indecl, av*
allegro	алле́гро *nn, indecl, av*
andante	анда́нте *nn, indecl, av*
larghetto	ларге́тто *nn, indecl, av*
largo	ла́рго *nn, indecl, av*
lento	ле́нто *nn, indecl, av*

execution

bravura	браву́рность *nf*
false note	фальши́вая но́та *nf*
falsetto	фальце́т *nm*
fermata	ферма́та *nf*
intonation	интона́ция *nf*
legato	лега́то *aj, av*
ligature	лигату́ра *nf*
maestoso	маэсто́зо *av*
nuance	нюа́нс *nm*
ostinato	остина́то *av*
pause	па́уза *nf*

pedalling	педализáция *nf*
phrasing	фразеолóгия *nf*
pizzicato	пиццикáто, пиччикáто *nn, indecl, av*
rubato	рубáто *av, nn, indecl*
scherzando	скерцáндо *av*
sforzando	сфорцáндо *av*
spiccato	спиккáто *av*
staccato	стаккáто *av*
subito	сýбито *av*
tutti	тýтти *nn, indecl*
unison	унисóн *nm*
vibrato	вибрáто *nn, indecl*
vivo	вúво *av*

embellishment

glissando	глиссáндо *nn, indecl*
roulade	рулáда *nf*
tremolo	трéмоло *nn, indecl*
trill	трéль *nf*

places and events

concert	концéрт *nm*
concert hall	концéртный зал *nm*
conservatory	консерватóрия *nf*
discothèque	дискотéка *nf*
jam session	джем-сéйшен *nm*
music hall	мю́зик-хóлл *nm*
music school	музыкáльная шкóла *nf*
musicale	музыкáльный вечер *nm*
opera house	óперный теáтр *nm*
pop concert	поп-концéрт *nm*
studio	стýдия *nf*

other performance terms

accompaniment	аккомпанемéнт *nm*
antiphonal	антифóнный *aj*
arrangement	аранжирóвка *nf*
beat (a drum)	бить *impf*
instrumentation	инструментóвка *nf*
interpretation	интерпретáция *nf*
libretto (*pl* librettos, libretti)	либрéтто *nn, indecl*
melodics *npl*	мелóдика *nf*
orchestration	оркестрóвка *nf*
solo	сóло *nn, indecl*
vocalization	вокализáция *nf*

MUSICAL ACOUSTICS

absolute pitch	абсолю́тный слух *nm*
cacophony	какофóния *nf*
echo (*pl* echoes)	э́хо *nn*
harmonic	гармонúческий *aj*
harmonics *npl*	гармóния *nf*
overtone	обертóн *nm*
partial (tone)	парциáльный *aj*
quadraphonic	квадрофонúческий *aj*
resonance	резонáнс *nm*
reverberator	ревербератóр *nm*
stereo	стéрео *nn*
stereophonic	стереофонúческий *aj*
sympathetic (vibrations)	симпатúческий *aj*
temperament	темперáмент *nm*
tone control	тон-контрóль *nm*

PARTS, TOOLS, AND EQUIPMENT

audiocassette	аудиокассéта *nf*
cassette	кассéта *nf*
cassette recorder	кассéтный магнитофóн *nm*
compact disk, CD	компáкт-дúск *nm*
damper	дéмпфер *nm*
gramophone [obs]	граммофóн *nm*
metronome	метронóм *nm*
organ pipe	оргáнная трубá *nf*
pedal	педáль *nf*
phonograph [obs]	фонóграф *nm*
piston	пистóн *nm*
plectrum (*pl* plectrums, plectra)	плектр *nm*
resonator	резонáтор *nm*
sordino	сурдúн(к)а *nf*
synthesizer	синтезáтор *nm*

PERSONS

vocal performers

alto [male]	альт *nm*
baritone	баритóн *nm*
bass, basso	бас *nm*
bass-baritone	бас-баритóн *nm*
cantor (in synagogue)	кáнтор *nm*
choirboy	мáльчик-хорúст *nm*
chorister	хорúст *nm*
chorus girl	хорúстка *nf*
coloratura	колоратýра *nf*
coloratura soprano	колоратýрное сопрáно *nn*
contralto	контрáльто *nn, indecl*
diva	дúва *nf*

lyric soprano	лири́ческое сопра́но *nn*
mezzo-soprano	ме́ццо-сопра́но *nn, indecl*
opera singer	о́перный певе́ц *nm*, о́перная певи́ца *nf*
prima donna	примадо́нна *nf*
soprano	сопра́но *nmf, indecl*
tenor	те́нор *nm*
troubadour [obs]	трубаду́р *nm*
vocalist	вокали́ст *nm*

instrumental performers

accompanist	аккомпаниа́тор *nm*
accordionist	аккордеони́ст, -ка *nmf*
balalaika player	балала́ечник *nm*
bandura player	бандури́ст *nm*
cellist	виолончели́ст, -ка *nmf*
clarinet(t)ist	кларнети́ст *nm*
contrabass player	контрабаси́ст *nm*
cornettist	корнети́ст *nm*
flutist (BR flautist)	флейти́ст *nm*
guitarist, guitar player	гитари́ст, -ка *nmf*
harpist, harp player	арфи́ст, -ка *nmf*
instrumentalist	инструментали́ст *nm*
jazz musician	джази́ст *nm*
mandolin(e) player	мандолини́ст *nm*
minstrel [obs]	менестре́ль *nm*
oboist	гобоист, -ка *nmf*
orchestra member	оркестра́нт *nm*
organist	органи́ст, -ка *nmf*
pianist	пиани́ст, -ка *nmf*
rock musician	рок-музыка́нт *nm*
saxophonist	саксофони́ст *nm*
trombonist	тромбони́ст *nm*
violoncellist	виолончели́ст, -ка *nmf*
xylophonist	ксилофони́ст *nm*

performance groups

choir, chorus	хор *nm*
duet	дуэ́т *nm*
ensemble	анса́мбль *nm*
jazz band	джа́зовый орке́стр *nm*
octet	окте́т *nm*
orchestra	орке́стр *nm*
philharmonic	филармо́ния *nf*
quartet(te)	кварте́т *nm*
quintet(te)	квинте́т *nm*
rock group	рок-гру́ппа *nf*
septet(te)	септе́т *nm*
sextet(te)	сексте́т *nm*
symphony orchestra	симфони́ческий орке́стр *nm*
trio	три́о *nn, indecl*

other persons

choirmaster	хорме́йстер *nm*
composer	компози́тор *nm*
concert performer	концерта́нт *nm*
concertmaster	концертме́йстер *nm*
contrapuntist	контрапункти́ст *nm*
genius	ге́ний *nm*
impressionist	импрессиони́ст *nm*
improvisor	импровиза́тор *nm*
interpreter	интерпрета́тор *nm*
kapellmeister	капельме́йстер *nm*
librettist	либретти́ст *nm*
maestro	маэ́стро *nm, indecl*
musician	музыка́нт *nm*
musicologist	музыкове́д *nm*
protégé(e)	протеже́ *nmf, indecl*
romanticist	рома́нтик *nm*
soloist	соли́ст, -ка *nmf*
symphonist	симфони́ст *nm*
virtuoso (*pl* virtuosos, virtuosi)	виртуо́з *nm*

See also **DANCE** ***(popular dances)***, **THEATER PERFORMANCE** ***(musical productions)***

DANCE

GENERAL TERMS

art of dance, the	танцева́льное иску́сство *nn*
choreography	хореогра́фия *nf*
dancing *nsg*	та́нцы *nmpl*
gesture	жест *nm*
line	ли́ния *nf*
music	му́зыка *nf*
position	пози́ция *nf*
rhythm	ритм *nm*

TYPES OF DANCING

acrobatic	акробати́ческий *aj*
aerobics *npl*	аэро́бика *nf*
ballet	бале́т *nm*
ballroom dancing *nsg*	ба́льные та́нцы *nmpl*
ceremonial	церемониа́льный *aj*
costume ball	костюми́рованный бал *nm*
folk dance	наро́дный та́нец *nm*

masquerade/masked ball	бал-маскара́д *nm*
modern	та́нец моде́рн *nm*
popular	популя́рный *aj*
religious	религио́зный *aj*
ritual	ритуа́л *nm*
theatrical	театра́льный *aj*

POPULAR DANCES

belly dance	та́нец живота́ *nm, nm*
bolero	болеро́ *nn, indecl*
bossa nova	боссано́ва *nf*
break-dancing	бре́йк *nm*
cancan	канка́н *nm*
carioca	карио́ка *nf*
cha-cha(-cha)	ча-ча-ча́ *nn, indecl*
Charleston	ча́рльстон *nm*
czardas	ча́рдаш *nm*
fandango	фанда́нго *nn, indecl*
flamenco	фламе́нко *nn, indecl*
foxtrot	фокстро́т *nm*
galop	гало́п *nm*
habanera	хабане́ра *nf*
hopak	гопа́к *nm*
hora	хо́ра *nf*
hula	ху́ла *nf*
jig	джи́га *nf*
jitterbug	джи́ттербаг *nm*
mazurka	мазу́рка *nf*
polka	по́лька *nf*
polonaise	полоне́з *nm*
quadrille	кадри́ль *nf*
rhumba, rumba	ру́мба *nf*
saber dance	та́нец с са́блями *nm, nfpl*
salsa	са́льса *nf*
saltarello	сальтаре́лло *nn*
samba	са́мба *nf*
schottische	шотла́ндка *nf*
tango	та́нго *nn, indecl*
tarantella	таранте́лла *nf*
trepak	трепа́к *nm*
waltz	вальс *nm*
zarzuela	сарсу́эла *nf*

BALLET TERMS

arabesque	арабе́ска *nf*
ballet company	бале́тная тру́ппа *nf*
balletomania	балетома́ния *nf*
duet	дуэ́т *nm*
entrechat	антраша́ *nm, indecl*
pas de deux	па-де-де́ *nn, indecl*
pirouette	пируэ́т *nm*

PLACES AND EVENTS

ball	бал *nm*
ballroom	ба́льный зал *nm*
dancing school	шко́ла та́нцев, *nmpl*
discothèque	дискоте́ка *nf*
dance hall	танцева́льный зал *nm*

PERSONS

ballerina	балери́на *nf*
ballet dancer	артист(-ка) бале́та *nmf*
ballet master	балетме́йстер *nm*
balletomane	балетома́н *nm*
break dancer	бре́йкер *nm*
choreographer	хорео́граф *nm*
corps de ballet	кордебале́т *nm*
dancer	танцо́р, танцо́вщик *nm*, танцо́вщица *nf*
dancing master	танцме́йстер *nm*
partner	партнёр, -ша *nmf*
prima ballerina	при́ма-балери́на *nf*

See also **ENTERTAINMENT**, **MUSIC** *(compositions)*, **THEATER PERFORMANCE**, **FAMOUS FIGURES OF YESTERDAY AND TODAY** *(artists)*

THEATER PERFORMANCE

GENERAL TERMS

dramatics *nplsv*, dramatic arts *npl*	драмати́ческое иску́сство *nn*
theater arts *nplsv*	театра́льное иску́сство *nn*

ASPECTS OF PERFORMANCE THEATER

types of theater

avant-garde	аванга́рд *nm*
classical	класси́ческий *aj*
comedy	коме́дия *nf*
drama	дра́ма *nf*
experimental	эксперимента́льный *aj*
improvisation	импровиза́ция *nf*
happening	хэ́ппенинг *nm*

kabuki — кабу́ки *nn, indecl*
marionette — марионе́тка *nf*
professional — профессиона́льный *aj*
repertory theater — репертуа́рный теа́тр *nm*
Shakespearean — шекспи́ровский *aj*
theater of the absurd — теа́тр абсу́рда *nm*

musical productions

comic opera — коми́ческая о́пера *nf*
musical — мю́зикл *nm*
musical comedy — музыка́льная коме́дия *nf*
opera — о́пера *nf*
opera bouffe — о́пера-буфф *nf*
operetta — опере́тта, опере́тка *nf*
pastiche — пасти́ччо *nn, indecl*
rock opera — рок-о́пера *nf*

other productions

fairy tale play — фее́рия *nf*
farce — фарс *nm*
melodrama — мелодра́ма *nf*
miracle play — мира́кль *nm*
morality play — моралите́ *nn, indecl*
pantomime — пантоми́ма *nf*
revue — ревю́ *nn, indecl*
sketch — скетч *nm*
tragedy — траге́дия *nf*
vaudeville — водеви́ль *nf*

elements of performance

act — акт *nm*
characterization — характери́стика *nf*
dramatic effect — драмати́зм *nm*
dramatization — драматиза́ция *nf*
effects — эффе́кты *nmpl*
entr'acte — антра́кт *nm*
epilog(ue) — эпило́г *nm*
interpretation — интерпрета́ция *nf*
mise en scène — мизансце́на *nf*
prolog(ue) — проло́г *nm*
repertory — репертуа́р *nm*
role — роль *nf*
scene — сце́на *nf*
scenic effects — сцени́ческие эффе́кты *nmpl*
situation — ситуа́ция *nf*
style — стиль *nm*

tools and equipment

costume — костю́м *nm*
decor, decoration *nsg* — декора́ция *nfpl*
false beard — фальши́вая борода́ *nf*
mask — ма́ска *nf*

places

amphitheater — амфитеа́тр *nm*
balcony — балко́н *nm*
center stage — центр сце́ны *nm, nf*
coulisse — кули́са *nf*
foyer — фойе́ *nn, indecl*
loge — ло́жа *nf*
opera house — о́перный теа́тр *nm*
orchestra [Greek theater] — орхе́стра *nf*
parterre — парте́р *nm*
proscenium — просце́ниум *nm*
theater (BR theatre) — теа́тр *nm*

audiences

applause *nsg* — аплодисме́нты *nmpl*
bravo! — бра́во! *intj*
claque — кла́ка *nf*
electrify — электризова́ть *impf*, наэлектризова́ть *pf*
ovation — ова́ция *nf*
public — пу́блика *nf*

other terms

benefit performance — бенефи́с *nm*
debut — дебю́т *nm*
opera glasses *npl* — о́перный бино́кль *nm*
premiere, première — премье́ра *nf*
tetralogy — тетрало́гия *nf*
theater season — театра́льный сезо́н *nm*
theatrical company — театра́льная тру́ппа *nf*
theatrics *nplsv* — театра́льность *nf*

PERSONS

actor — актёр *nm*
actress — актри́са *nf*
artiste — арти́ст, -ка *nmf*
avant-gardist — авангарди́ст *nm*
character actor — хара́ктерный актёр *nm*
claquer — клакёр *nm*
costumer — костюме́р, -ша *nmf*
decorator — декора́тор *nm*
double — дублёр *nm*
dramatic actor — драмати́ческий актёр *nm*
dramatist — драмату́рг *nm*

dramaturge	драматургия *nf*
impresario	импресарио *nm, indecl*
ingenue, ingénue	инженю *nf, indecl*
interpreter	интерпретатор *nm*
mime	мим *nm*
mimic	мимист *nm*
protagonist	протагонист *nm*
technician	техник *nm*
theater/drama critic	театральный критик *nm*
theatergoer	театрал, -ка *nmf*
tragedian, tragic actor	трагик *nm*
tragedienne	трагическая актриса *nf*

See also **ENTERTAINMENT** *(forms of entertainment)*, **MUSIC**, **LITERATURE** *(forms of drama)*

VISUAL ARTS

GENERAL TERMS

authentic	аутентичный *aj*
figure	фигура *nf*
form	форма *nf*
materials	материалы *nmpl*
plastic arts	пластические искусства *nnpl*
style	стиль *nm*

FORMS OF VISUAL ART

bonsai	бонсай *nm*
calligraphy	каллиграфия *nf*
ceramics *nplsv*	керамика *nf*
cloisonne	клуазоне *nn, indecl*
decor	декор *nm*
decoration *nsg*	декорация *nfpl*
decoration, decorating	декорирование *nn*
decorative art	декоративное искусство *nn*
engraving	гравёрное искусство *nn*
graphic art	графика *nf*
ikebana	икебана *nf*
lacquering	лакировка *nf*
lithography	литография *nf*
modeling, modelling	моделизм *nm*
origami	оригами *nn, indecl*
photography	фотография *nf*
portraiture	портретная живопись *nf*
sculpture	скульптура *nf*
taxidermy	таксидермия *nf*
xylography	ксилография *nf*

CREATING AND DISPLAYING ART

art objects

antique	антик *nm*
aquarelle	акварель *nf*
aquatint	акватинта *nf*
arabesque	арабеска *nf*
bas-relief	барельеф *nm*
bronze [object]	бронза *nf*
bust	бюст *nm*
caricature	карикатура *nf*
caryatid	кариатида *nf*
collage	коллаж *nm*
diorama	диорама *nf*
diptych	диптих *nm*
engraving	гравирование *nn*, гравировка *nf*
figurine	фигурка *nf*
filigree	филигрань *nf*
fresco (*pl* frescos, frescoes)	фреска *nf*
garland	гирлянда *nf*
Gobelin (tapestry)	гобелен *nm*
grotesque	гротеск *nm*
icon, ikon	икона *nf*
illustration	иллюстрация *nf*
kakemono	какемоно *nn*
lacquerware *nsg*	лакированные изделия *nnpl*
lithograph	литография *nf*
mask	маска *nf*
medallion	медальон *nm*
mezzotint	меццо-тинто *nn, indecl*
miniature	миниатюра *nf*
mobile	мобайл *nm*
montage	монтаж *nm*
monument	монумент *nm*
mosaic	мозаика *nf*
obelisk	обелиск *nm*
oleograph	олеография *nf*
ornament	орнамент *nm*
pedestal	пьедестал *nm*
photograph	фотография *nf*
portrait	портрет *nm*
primitive (painting)	примитив *nm*
relief	рельеф *nm*
replica	реплика *nf*
reproduction	репродукция *nf*
restoration	реставрация *nf*
rosette	розетка *nf*
sculpture	скульптура *nf*

self-portrait	автопортре́т *nm*
statue	ста́туя *nf*
statuette	стату́этка *nf*
tattoo	татуиро́вка *nf*
torso	торс *nm*
triptych	три́птих *nm*
urn	у́рна *nf*
vignette	винье́тка *nf*
xylograph	ксилогравю́ра *nf*

design

asymmetry	асимме́трия *nf*
composition	компози́ция *nf*
contour	ко́нтур *nm*
contrast	контра́ст *nm*
dissymmetry	несимметри́чность *nf*
figuration	фигура́ция *nf*
forming	формо́вка *nf*
graffiti	граффи́ти *nnpl, indecl*
illumination	иллюмина́ция *nf*
line	ли́ния *nf*
mannerism	маньери́зм *nm*
maquette	маке́т *nm*
mass	ма́сса *nf*
motif	моти́в *nm*
ornamentation	орнамента́ция *nf*
pastel (painting)	пасте́ль *nf*
pastorale (painting)	пастора́ль *nf*
perspective	перспекти́ва *nf*
pose	по́за *nf*
profile	про́филь *nm*
silhouette	силу́эт *nm*
symmetry	симметри́я *nf*
tonality	тона́льность *nf*
zigzag	зигза́г *nm*

tools, materials, techniques

acrylic	акри́л *nm*
chiascuro	чиаску́ро *nn*
color (BR colour)	ко́лер, коло́р *nm*
coloring (BR colouring)	колори́т *nm*
enamel paint	эма́левые кра́ски *nfpl*
fixative	фиксати́в, фикса́ж *nm*
glaze	глазу́рь *nf*
gouache	гуа́шь *nf*
graphite	графи́т *nm*
gum arabic	гуммиара́бик *nm*
gutta-percha	гуттапе́рча *nf*
lac, lacquer	лак *nm*
latex	ла́текс *nm*
macrame, macramé	макраме́, макрамэ́ *nn, indecl*
mannequin, manikin	манеке́н *nm*
metal	мета́лл *nm*
model	моде́ль *nf*
modeling (BR modelling)	моделирование *nn*
palette	пали́тра *nf*
papier-mâché	папье́-маше́ *nn, indecl*
patina	пати́на *nf*
pigment	пигме́нт *nm*
plastic	пла́стика *nf*
rice paper	ри́совая бума́га *nf*
sfumato	сфума́то *nn*
sgraffito	сграффи́то *nn*
shellac	шелла́к *nm*
siccative	сиккати́в *nm*
spatula	шпа́тель *nm*
tachisme	таши́зм *nm*
talc	тальк *nm*
tempera	те́мпера *nf*
terra-cotta	террако́та *nf*
tessera (*pl* tesserae)	тессе́ра *nf*
turpentine	терпенти́н *nm*

places

atelier	ателье́ *nn, indecl*
gallery	галере́я *nf*
Hermitage	Эрмита́ж *nm*
Prado	Пра́до *nn, indecl*
museum	музе́й *nm*
salon	сало́н *nm*
studio	сту́дия *nf*

COLOR

pigments and dyes

carmine	карми́н *nm*
chrome	хром *nm*
cobalt	ко́бальтовая си́нька *nf*
ocher (BR ochre)	о́хра *nf*
sienna	сие́на *nf*
zinc white *nsg*	ци́нковые бели́ла *pl*

other color names

beige	цвет беж *nm*
canary-yellow	канаре́ечный *aj* (цвет)
chocolate	шокола́дный *aj* (цвет)
coffee	кофе́йный *aj* (цвет)
coral	кора́лловый *aj* (цвет)

cream	кре́мовый *aj* (цвет)
ebony	эбе́новый *aj*
indigo (*pl* indigos, indigoes)	инди́го *nn, indecl*
jacinth	гиаци́нт *nm*
khaki	ха́ки *aj/nn, indecl*
lavender	лава́нда *nf*
lemon	лимо́нный цвет *nm*
olive-green	оли́вковый цвет *nm*
orange	ора́нжевый *aj*
pastel shade	пасте́льный тон *nm*
pistachio	фиста́шковый *aj*
purple	пу́рпур *nm*
rose	ро́зовой *aj*
ruby	руби́новый *aj*
saffron	шафра́нный, шафра́новый *aj*
sepia	се́пия *nf*
terra-cotta	террако́товый цвет *nm*
ultramarine	ультрамари́н *nm*
umber	у́мбра *nf*
vermilion	вермильо́н *nm*
violet	фиоле́товый *aj*

descriptive words

avant-garde	аванга́рдный, авангарди́стский *aj*
cherubic	херуви́мский *aj*
colorful (BR colourful)	колори́тный *aj*
contrasting (colors)	контрасти́рующий *aj*
disc-shaped	ди́сковый *aj*
figured	фигу́рный *aj*
formless	бесфо́рменный *aj*
glazed	покры́тый глазу́рью
grotesque	гроте́скный *aj*
illustrated	иллюстри́рованный *aj*
impressionist(ic)	импрессиони́стский *aj*
lacquered	лакиро́ванный, ла́ковый *aj*
lined	лино́ванный *aj*
matte	ма́товый *aj*
modernistic	модерни́стский *aj*
monochrome	монохро́мный *aj*
naturalistic	натуралисти́ческий *aj*
neutral	нейтра́льный *aj*
opalescent	опа́ловый *aj*
original	оригина́льный *aj*
pastoral	пастора́льный *aj*
plastic	пласти́ческий, пласти́чный *aj*
polychrome	полихро́мия *nf*
postimpressionist(ic)	постимпрессио- ни́стский *aj*
primitive	примити́вный *aj*
realistic	реалисти́ческий *aj*
relief, in	релье́фно *av*
symbolist(ic)	символисти́ческий *aj*
unlined	нелино́ванный *aj*
unrealistic	нереалисти́ческий *aj*
zigzag	зигзагообра́зный *aj*

STYLES AND GENRES

avant-garde	аванга́рд *nm*
baroque	баро́кко *nn, indecl*
cubism	куби́зм *nm*
Dadaism	дадаи́зм *nm*
eclecticism	эклекти́зм *nm*
erotica *npl*	эро́тика *nf*
Fauvism	фови́зм *nm*
Gothic	го́тика *nf*, готи́ческий стиль *nm*
grisaille	гриза́ль *nf*
impressionism	импрессиони́зм *nm*
kitsch	китч *nm*
minimalism	минимали́зм *nm*
modernism	модерни́зм *nm*
naturalism	натурали́зм *nm*
pointillism	пуантили́зм *nm*
Pop art, pop art	поп-арт *nm*
realism	реали́зм *nm*
Renaissance	Ренесса́нс *nm*
rococo	рококо́ *nn, indecl*
surrealism	сюрреали́зм *nm*

PERSONS

animal painter	анимали́ст *nm*
aquarellist	акварели́ст *nm*
avant-gardist	авангарди́ст *nm*
battle-scene painter	батали́ст *nm*
calligrapher	каллигра́ф *nm*
caricaturist	карикатури́ст *nm*
colorist (BR colourist)	колори́ст *nm*
cubist	куби́ст *nm*
Dadaist	дадаи́ст *nm*
engraver	гравёр, гравиро́вщик *nm*

illustrator иллюстра́тор *nm*
impressionist импрессиони́ст *nm*
lithographer лито́граф *nm*
mannerist маньери́ст *nm*
miniaturist миниатюри́ст *nm*
minimalist минимали́ст *nm*
modeler, modeller моде́льщик *nm*
modernist модерни́ст *nm*
naturalist натуралист *nm*
pointillist пуантили́ст *nm*
portrait painter портрети́ст *nm*
post-Impressionist постимпрессиони́ст *nm*
pre-Raphaelite прерафаэли́т *nm*
primitivist примитиви́ст *nm*
realist реали́ст *nm*
reproducer репроду́ктор *nm*
restorer реставра́тор *nm*
sculptor ску́льптор *nm*
stylist стили́ст *nm*
surrealist сюрреали́ст *nm*
symbolist символи́ст *nm*
tachist таши́ст *nm*
taxidermist таксидерми́ст *nm*

See also **ARCHITECTURE**, **FAMOUS FIGURES OF YESTERDAY AND TODAY** *(artists)*

ARCHITECTURE

GENERAL TERMS

architectonics *nplsv* архитекто́ника *nf*
architectural архитекту́рный *aj*
architecture архитекту́ра *nf*
complex ко́мплекс *nm*
construction констру́кция *nf*
model моде́ль *nf*
order о́рдер *nm*
reconstruction реконстру́кция *nf*
restoration реставра́ция *nf*
style стиль *nm*

TYPES OF CONSTRUCTION

dwellings

bungalow бу́нгало *nn, indecl*
chalet шале́ *nn, indecl*
cottage котте́дж *nm*
dacha да́ча *nf*
hacienda гасие́нда *nf*
hut ха́та *nf*
igloo и́глу *nn, indecl*
manor, manor-house мано́р *nm*
residence резиде́нция *nf*
villa ви́лла *nf*
wigwam вигва́м *nm*
yurt ю́рта *nf*

religious

basilica базили́ка *nf*
pagoda па́года *nf*
synagog(ue) синаго́га *nf*

public use

auditorium аудито́рия *nf*
coliseum колизе́й *nm*
concert hall конце́ртный зал *nm*
hotel оте́ль *nm*
motel моте́ль *nm*
museum музе́й *nm*
observatory обсервато́рия *nf*
planetarium (*pl* planetariums, planetaria) планета́рий *nm*
school шко́ла *nf*
stadium (*pl* stadiums, stadia) стадио́н *nm*
theater (BR theatre) теа́тр *nm*

other construction

aqueduct акведу́к *nm*
garage гара́ж *nm*
monument монуме́нт *nm*
obelisk обели́ск *nm*
palisade палиса́д *nm*
pavilion павильо́н *nm*
pyramid пирами́да *nf*
terrace терра́са *nf*
triumphal arch триумфа́льная а́рка *nf*
viaduct виаду́к *nm*

ARCHITECTURAL FEATURES

parts of buildings

alcove алько́в *nm*
belvedere бельведе́р *nm*
chamber ка́мера *nf*
corridor коридо́р *nm*
entresol *nsg* антресо́ли *nfpl*
exterior экстерье́р *nm*
foyer фойе́ *nn, indecl*
hall(way) холл *nm*
interior интерье́р *nm*
lift лифт *nm*

mezzanine	мезони́н *nm*
parterre	парте́р *nm*
toilet	туале́т *nm*
veranda(h)	вера́нда *nf*
vestibule	вестибю́ль *nm*

structural

abacus	аба́ка *nf*
apse, apsis	апси́да *nf*
arcade	арка́да *nf*
arch	а́рка *nf*
architrave	архитра́в *nm*
atrium	а́триум *nm*
balcony	балко́н *nm*
balustrade	балюстра́да *nf*
colonnade	колонна́да *nf*
column	коло́нна *nf*
cupola	ку́пол *nm*
embrasure	амбразу́ра *nf*
entablature	антабleме́нт *nm*
foundation	фунда́мент *nm*
gallery	галере́я *nf*
loggia	ло́джия *nf*
mansard (roof)	манса́рда *nf*
minaret	минаре́т *nm*
monolith	моноли́т *nm*
narthex	на́ртекс *nm*
nave	неф *nm*
patio	па́тио *nn, indecl*
peristyle	перисти́ль *nm*
podium (*pl* podiums, podia)	по́диум, по́дий *nm*
portal	порта́л *nm*
portico (*pl* porticos, porticoes)	по́ртик *nm*
pylon	пило́н *nm*
rotunda	рото́нда *nf*
stoa (*pl* stoas, stoae)	сто́а *nf*
transept	трансе́пт *nm*

decorative

acanthus	ака́нт *nm*
arabesque	арабе́ска *nf*
archivolt	архиво́льт *nm*
capital	капите́ль *nf*
caryatid	кариати́да *nf*
cornice	карни́з *nm*
dentil	денти́кула *nf*
facade	фаса́д *nm*
false front	фальши́вый фаса́д *nm*
fascia	фа́ска *nf*
festoon	фесто́н *nm*
fountain [large]	фонта́н *nm*
fresco (*pl* frescos, frescoes)	фре́ска *nf*
frieze	фриз *nm*
frontispiece	фронтиспи́с *nm*
gargoyle	горгу́лья *nf*
marquee	марки́за *nf*
mosaic	моза́ика *nf*
motif	моти́в *nm*
niche	ни́ша *nf*
palmette	пальме́тта *nf*
paneling (BR panelling)	пане́льная обши́вка *nf*
parapet	парапе́т *nm*
pedestal	пьедеста́л *nm*
pergola	пе́ргола *nf*
pilaster	пиля́стр *nm*
plafond	плафо́н *nm*
plinth	пли́нтус *nm*
relief	релье́ф *nm*
rose window	окно́-розе́тка *nn*
socle	цо́коль *nm*
stela, stele (*pl* stelae)	сте́ла *nf*
tambour	та́мбур *nm*
triglyph	тригли́ф *nm*
tympanum	тимпа́н *nm*
volute	волю́та *nf*

ARCHITECTURAL STYLES

Byzantinesque	византи́йский *aj*
colonial	колониа́льный *aj*
Corinthian order	кори́нфский о́рдер *nm*
Doric order	дори́ческий о́рдер *nm*
Georgian	георгиа́нский *aj*
Gothic	готи́ческий *aj*
Grecian	гре́ческий *aj*
Ionic order	иони́ческий о́рдер *nm*
Moorish	маврита́нский *aj*
Renaissance	Ренесса́нс *nm*
rococo	рококо́ *nn, indecl*
Romanesque	рома́нский *aj*

TERMS IN CONSTRUCTION

breach	брешь *nf*
building block	блок *nm*
building materials	строи́тельные материа́лы *nmpl*
bulldozer	бульдо́зер *nm*
cement	цеме́нт *nm*
cistern	цисте́рна *nf*

crane — кран *nm*
derrick — дéррик *nm*
encrust (with marble) — инкрусти́ровать *impf, pf*
excavator — экскавáтор *nm*
granite — грани́т *nm*
gravel — грáвий *nm*
mastic — масти́ка *nf*
plan — план *nm*
plank — планка *nf*
plastic — плáстик *nm*
specification — спецификáция *nf*
stucco — штукатýрка *nf*
substructure — субструктýра *nf*
terra-cotta — терракóта *nf*
terrazzo — терáццо *nn, indecl*
ventilation — вентиля́ция *nf*

PERSONS

architect — архитéктор *nm*
bulldozer driver — бульдозери́ст *nm*
constructor — констрýктор *nm*
engineer, civil/structural — инженéр-строи́тель *nm*
excavator operator — экскавáторщик *nm*

See also **HISTORY AND ARCHEOLOGY**, **ANCIENT CIVILIZATIONS** *(places and things)*, **THE CITY**

Knowledge, Faith, and the Paranormal

PHILOSOPHY ◆ RELIGION ◆ MAGIC

PHILOSOPHY

GENERAL TERMS

a posteriori — апостерио́ри *av*
a priori — априо́ри *av*
Absolute, the — абсолю́т *nm*
concept, conception — конце́пция *nf*
doctrine — доктри́на *nf*
fate — фата́льность *nf*
idea — иде́я *nf*
ideal — идеа́л *nm*
ideology — идеоло́гия *nf*
materiality — материа́льность *nf*
monad — мона́да *nf*
moral dilemma — мора́льная диле́мма *nf*
morality — мора́ль *nf*
object — объе́кт *nm*
perception — перце́пция *nf*
philosophy — филосо́фия *nf*
principle — при́нцип *nm*
reality — реа́льность *nf*
substance — субста́нция *nf*
thesis (*pl* theses) — те́зис *nm*
universal principle — универса́льный при́нцип *nm*
universality — универса́льность *nf*

SPECIALIZATIONS

major fields

epistemology — эпистемоло́гия *nf*
esthetics (BR aesthetics) *nplsv* — эсте́тика *nf*
ethics *nplsv* — э́тика *nf*
logic — ло́гика *nf*
metaphysics *nplsv* — метафи́зика *nf*

related fields

cosmology — космоло́гия *nf*
etiology — этиоло́гия *nf*
ontology — онтоло́гия *nf*
phenomenology — феноменоло́гия *nf*
semiotics *nplsv* — семио́тика *nf*
teleology — телеоло́гия *nf*

PHILOSOPHIES

ancient and medieval

atomism — атоми́зм *nm*
cynicism — цини́зм *nm*
demiurge — демиу́рг *nm*
entelechy — энтеле́хия *nf*
Epicureanism — эпикуре́йство *nn*
hedonism — гедони́зм *nm*
Logos — ло́гос *nm*
Neo-Platonism — неоплатони́зм *nm*
peripathetic — перипатети́ческий *aj*
Platonism — платони́зм *nm*
skepticism (BR scepticism) — скептици́зм *nm*
Sophism — софи́зм *nm*
Stoicism — стоици́зм *nm*
Gnosticism — гностици́зм *nm*
scholasticism — схола́стика *nf*

other philosophical theories

animalism — анимали́зм *nm*
anthropocentrism — антропоцентри́зм *nm*
conceptualism — концептуали́зм *nm*
determinism — детермини́зм *nm*
dualism — дуали́зм *nm*
empiricism — эмпири́зм *nm*
existentialism — экзистенциали́зм *nm*
fatalism — фатали́зм *nm*
Hegelianism — гегельи́нство *nn*
idealism — идеали́зм *nm*
individualism — индивидуали́зм *nm*
instrumentalism — инструментали́зм *nm*
intellectualism — интеллектуали́зм *nm*
Kantianism — kантиа́нство *nn*
Machiavellianism — макиавелли́зм *nm*
materialism — материали́зм *nm*
mechanism — механи́зм *nm*
mentalism — ментали́зм *nm*

monism	мони́зм *nm*
nativism	нативи́зм *nm*
naturalism	натурали́зм *nm*
Nietzscheanism	ницшеа́нство *nn*
nihilism	нигили́зм *nm*
nominalism	номинали́зм *nm*
obscurantism	обскуранти́зм *nm*
parallelism	параллели́зм *nm*
phenomenalism	феноменали́зм *nm*
positivism	позитиви́зм *nm*
pragmatism	прагмати́зм *nm*
rationalism	рационали́зм *nm*
realism	реали́зм *nm*
relativism	релятиви́зм *nm*
solipsism	солипси́зм *nm*
spiritualism	спиритуали́зм *nm*
subjectivism	субъективи́зм *nm*
transcendentalism	трансцендентали́зм *nm*
utilitarianism	утилитари́зм *nm*
vitalism	витали́зм *nm*
voluntarism	волюнтари́зм *nm*

terms in non-Western philosophies

karma	ка́рма *nf*
kismet	ки́смет *nm*
nirvana	нирва́на *nf*
yin and yang	инь и янь *nf*, *nm*

other terms

noumenon	ноу́мен *nm*
objective reality	объекти́вная реа́льность *nf*
phenomenon (*pl* phenomena)	фено́мен *nm*
postulate	постула́т *nm*
reality, in	в реа́льности *nf*
reductionism	редукциони́зм *nm*

TERMS IN ETHICS

casuistry [ethics]	казуи́стика *nf*
deontology	деонтоло́гия *nf*
ethic	э́тика *nf*
ethical	эти́ческий, эти́чный *aj*
intuitionism	интуитиви́зм *nm*
objectivism	объективи́зм *nm*

TERMS IN LOGIC

counterargument	контраргуме́нт *nm*
deduce	дедуци́ровать *impf*, *pf*
dialectics *nplsv*	диале́ктика *nf*
effect	эффе́кт *nm*
formal logic	форма́льная ло́гика *nf*
paralogism	паралоги́зм *nm*
symbolic logic	символи́ческая ло́гика *nf*
symbolically	символи́чески *av*
symbolization	символиза́ция *nf*
symbology	симво́лика *nf*

general

analytics *nplsv*	анали́тика *nf*
argument	аргуме́нт *nm*
category	катего́рия *nf*
causality	кауза́льность *nf*
method	ме́тод *nm*
modality	мода́льность *nf*
nexus	не́ксус *nm*
quantifier	ква́нтор, квантифика́тор *nm*
rationality	рациональность *nf*
sophistry	софи́стика *nf*
subject	субъе́кт *nm*
symbol	си́мвол *nm*
system	систе́ма *nf*
universal	универса́лия *nf*

operations

abstraction	абстра́кция *nf*
analogy	анало́гия *nf*
antithesis (*pl* antitheses)	антите́за *nf*, антите́зис *nm*
argumentation	аргумента́ция *nf*
deduction	деду́кция *nf*
disjunction	дизъю́нкция *nf*
idealization	идеализа́ция *nf*
induction	инду́кция *nf*
predication	предика́ция *nf*
quantification	квантова́ние *nn*
rationalization	рационализа́ция *nf*
tautology	тавтоло́гия *nf*

statements

antecedent	антеце́дент *nm*
axiom	аксио́ма *nf*
homology	гомоло́гия *nf*
lemma	ле́мма *nf*
paradox	парадо́кс *nf*
predicate	предика́т *nm*
syllogism	силлоги́зм *nm*
truism	трюи́зм *nm*

other terms

base (x on y)	бази́ровать *impf*

cardinal principle	кардинáльный принци́п *nm*
presumption	презýмпция *nf*

PERSONS

Aristotelian	послéдователь, -ница Аристóтеля *nmf*
Cartesian	картезиáнец, послéдователь, -ница Декáрта *nmf*
casuist	казуи́ст *nm*
Confucian	конфуциáнец *nm*
determinist	детермини́ст *nm*
dialectician	диалéктик *nm*
empiricist	эмпи́рик *nm*
Epicurean	эпикурéец *nm*
existentialist	экзистенциали́ст *nm*
fatalist	фатали́ст *nm*
gnostic	гнóстик *nm*
hedonist	гедони́ст *nm*
Hegelian	гегельянец *nm*
Kantian	кантиáнец *nm*
logician	лóгик *nm*
materialist	материали́ст *nm*
mechanist	механи́ст *nm*
metaphysician	метафи́зик *nm*
moralist	морали́ст *nm*
Neo-Platonist	неоплатóник *nm*
Nietzschean	ницшеáнец *nm*
nihilist	нигили́ст *nm*
nominalist	номинали́ст *nm*
obscurantist	обскурáнт *nm*
philosoper	филóсоф *nm*
positivist	позитиви́ст *nm*
pragmatist	прагмáтик *nm*
rationalist	рационали́ст *nm*
realist	реали́ст, -ка *nmf*
reductionist	редукциони́ст *nm*
solipsist	солипси́ст *nm*
sophist	софи́ст *nm*
spiritualist	спиритуали́ст *nm*
Stoic	стóик *nm*
subjectivist	субъективи́ст *nm*
teleologist	телеóлог *nm*
utilitarian	утилитари́ст, -ка *nmf*

See also **FAMOUS FIGURES OF YESTERDAY AND TODAY** *(philosophers and religious figures)*, **RELIGION** *(aspects of religion)*, **POLITICS AND GOVERNMENT** *(policies, movements, and philosophies)*

RELIGION

GENERAL TERMS

congregation	конгрегáция *nf*
credo, creed	крéдо *nn, indecl*
cult	культ *nm*
doctrine	доктри́на *nf*
dogma (*pl* dogmas, dogmata)	дóгма *nf*, дóгмат *nm*
ethics *nplsv*	э́тика *nf*
moral code	морáльный кóдекс *nm*
morality	морáль *nf*
religion	рели́гия *nf*
ritual	ритуáл *nm*
sect	сéкта *nf*
theology	теолóгия *nf*

ASPECTS OF RELIGION

basic forms of religion

animism	аними́зм mn
atheism	атеи́зм *nm*
monotheism	монотеи́зм *nm*
pantheism	пантеи́зм *nm*
polytheism	политеи́зм *nm*

doctrines and beliefs

agnosticism	агностици́зм *nm*
Anabaptism [obs]	анабапти́зм *nm*
apologetics *nplsv*	апологéтика *nf*
cabala	кабалá *nf*
cabalism	кабали́стика *nf*
caste	кáста *nf*
caste system	кáстовая систéма *nf*
celibacy	целибáт *nm*
clericalism	клерикали́зм *nm*
creationism	креациони́зм *nm*
deism	деи́зм *nm*
dharma	дхáрма *nf*
dualism	дуали́зм *nm*
ecumenism	экумени́зм *nm*
fideism	фидеи́зм *nm*
fundamentalism	фундаментали́зм *nm*
hypostasis	ипостáсь *nf*
iconoclasm	иконобóрчество *nn*
immanence	имманéнтность *nf*
limbo	лимб *nm*
Logos	лóгос *nm*
Messianism	мессиáнство *nn*
monasticism	монáшество *nn*
Mosaic law *nsg*	Моисéевы закóны *nmpl*
mysticism	мистици́зм *nm*, ми́стика *nf*

nirvana — нирва́на *nf*
orthodoxy — ортодо́ксия *nf*
Pietism — пиети́зм *nm*
providence — провиде́ние *nn*
schism — схи́зма *nf*
sectarianism — секта́нтство *nn*
secularism — секуляри́зм *nm*
secularization — секуляриза́ция *nf*
spiritism, spiritualism — спирити́зм *nm*
syncretism — синкрети́зм *nm*
theism — теи́зм *nm*
theocracy — теокра́тия *nf*
theosophy — теосо́фия *nf*
transcendence — трансценде́нтность *nf*
universalism — универсали́зм *nm*
zoomorphism — зооморфи́зм *nm*

unusual forms of worship

asceticism — аскети́зм *nm*
fetishism — фетиши́зм *nm*
hero worship — культ геро́я *nm*
idolatry — идолопокло́нство *nn*
necrolatry — некрола́трия *nf*
Satanism — сатани́зм *nm*
shamanism — шама́нство *nn*
totemism — тотеми́зм *nm*
zoolatry — зоолатри́я *nf*

holy places

abbey — абба́тство *nm*
altar — алта́рь *nm*
baptistry — баптисте́рий *nm*
chapel — капе́лла *nf*
lamasery — ламаи́стский монасты́рь *nm*
mission — ми́ссия *nf*
monastery — монасты́рь *nm*
pagoda — па́года *nf*
stupa [Buddhist shrine] — сту́па *nf*
synagog(ue) — синаго́га *nf*

organizations and offices

apostolate — апо́стольство *nn*
consistory — консисто́рия *nf*
deaconate — дья́конство *nn*
eparchy — епа́рхия *nf*
episcopate — епископа́т *nm*
exarchate — экзарха́т *nm*
missionary work — миссионе́рство *nn*
monastic order — мона́шеский о́рден *nm*
papacy, popedom — па́пство *nn*
pastorate — пастора́т *nm*
pontificate — понтифика́т *nm*
prelacy — прела́тство *nn*
primacy — прима́т *nm*
rabbinate — раввина́т *nn*
synod — сино́д *nm*
Vatican — Ватика́н *nm*

scholarship and translation

demonology — демоноло́гия *nf*
eschatology — эсхатоло́гия *nf*
hagiography — агиогра́фия *nf*
martyrology — мартиро́лог *nm*
pneumatology — пневматоло́гия *nf*
seminary — семина́рия *nf*
Sunday school — воскре́сная шко́ла *nf*
yeshiva — еши́ва *nf*

anti-religious expressions

anti-Semitism — антисемити́зм *nm*
anticlericalism — антиклерикали́зм *nm*
antipope — антипа́па *nm*
apostasy — апоста́зия *nf*
popery, papistry — папи́зм *nm*

other terms

audience [with Pope] — аудие́нция *nf*
canon — кано́н *nm*
ecstasy — экста́з *nm*
immorality — амора́льность *nf*
infernal — инферна́льный *aj*
jihad — джиха́д *nm*
Judeo-Christian — иуде́о-христиа́нский *aj*
monastery cell — ке́лья *nf*
paschal — пасха́льный *aj*
prebend — пребе́нда *nf*
sacramental — сакрамента́льный *aj*

NAMES

founders of religions

Abraham — Авраа́м *nm*
Buddha — Бу́дда *nm*
Jesus Christ — Иису́с Христо́с *nm*
Luther — Лю́тер *nm*
Muhammed, Mohammmed — Муха́ммед *nm*
Zarathustra, Zoroaster — Зарату́стра, Зороа́стр *nm*

major world religions

Buddhism — будди́зм *nm*
Christianity — христиа́нство *nn*
Hinduism — индуи́зм *nm*
Islam — исла́м *nm*
Jainism — джайн, джайни́зм *nm*

Judaism	иудаи́зм *nm*
Mohammedanism	магомета́нство *nn*
Shinto(ism)	синтои́зм *nm*
Taoism	даоси́зм *nm*
Zen-Buddhism	дзэн-будди́зм *nm*

other religions and groups

Anglicanism	англика́нство *nn*
Bahaism	бахаи́зм *nm*
Brahminism	брахмани́зм *nm*
Calvinism	кальвини́зм *nm*
Catholicism	католици́зм *nm*, католи́чество *nn*
Druidism	друиди́зм *nm*
Dukhobor sect	духобо́рчество *nn*
Evangelical Church	евангели́ческая це́рковь *nf*
Hasidism	хасиди́зм *nm*
Hizbollah	Хезболла́ *nf*
Jesuitry	иезу́итство *nn*
Jewry	евре́йство *nn*
Lamaism	ламаи́зм *nm*
Lutheranism	лютера́нство *nn*
Methodism	методи́зм *nm*
Mithraism [obs]	митраи́зм *nm*
Mormonism	мормони́зм *nm*
Order of Jesuits	о́рден иезу́итов *nm, nmpl*
Protestantism	протестанти́зм *nn*
Puritanism [obs]	пуритани́зм *nm*, пурита́нство *nn*
Sikhism	сикхи́зм *nm*
Sufism	суфи́зм *nm*
Trappist order	о́рден траппи́стов *nm, nmpl*
Uniat(e)	униа́т *nm*
Zoroastrianism	зороастри́зм *nm*

names of chief deities

Allah	Алла́х *nm*
Elohim	Элохи́м *nm*
Jahveh, Jehovah	Я́хве *nm, indecl*, Иего́ва *nm*
Juggernaut	Джагерна́ут *nm*
Krishna	Кри́шна *nm*
Ormazd, Ormyzd	Орму́зд *nm*
Rama	Ра́ма *nm*
Shiva	Ши́ва *nm*
Vishnu	Ви́шну *nm*
Yahweh, Yahveh	Я́хве *nm, indecl*

holy cities

Bethlehem	Вифлее́м *nm*
Jerusalem	Иерусали́м *nm*
Mecca	Ме́кка *nf*
Rome	Рим *nm*

sacred books

Avesta	Аве́ста *nf*
Bible	Би́блия *nf*
Koran	Кора́н *nm*
Talmud	Талму́д *nm*
Tantra	Та́нтра *nf*
Torah	То́ра *nf*
Vedas, the	Ве́ды *pl*

PRACTICES AND TRADITIONS

holidays and celebrations

Hanukkah	Ха́нука *nf*
Michaelmas	Миха́йлов день *nm*
Purim	Пу́рим *nm*
Ramadan	Рамада́н *nm*
Sabbath [Jewish]	Суббо́та *nf*
Yom Kippur	Йом-Киппу́р *nm*

rites and ceremonies

apotheosis	апофео́з *nm*
baptism	бапти́зм *nm*
bar mitzvah	бар-ми́цва *nf*
canonization	канониза́ция *nf*
catechism	катехи́зис *nm*
ceremonial	церемониа́л *nm*
christening	креще́ние *nn*, крести́ны *npl*
confirmation	конфирма́ция *nf*
Eucharist	евхари́стия *nf*
hajj [pilgrimage to Mecca]	хадж *nm*
indulgence	индульге́нция *nf*
jubilee	юбиле́й *nm*
Mass [Catholic]	ме́сса *nf*
occultism	оккульти́зм *nm*
procession	проце́ссия *nf*
yoga	йо́га *nf*

eating and drinking

dietary laws	диети́ческие зако́ны *nmpl*
kosher	коше́рный *aj*
Seder [Passover feast]	се́дер *nm*
tref foods	трефно́й *aj*
vegetarianism	вегетариа́нство *nn*

objects, charms, symbols

fetish	фети́ш *nm*
Grail [obs]	граа́ль *nf*
iconostasis	иконоста́с *nm*

idol	и́дол *nm*
ikon, icon	ико́на *nf*
menorah	мено́ра *nf*
phallic symbol	фалли́ческий си́мвол *nm*
simony	симони́я *nf*
star of Bethlehem	вифлее́мская звезда́ *nf*
star of David	звезда́ Давидова *nf, nm*
stigma (*pl* stigmas, stigmata)	сти́гма *nf*
taboo, tabu	табу́ *nn, indecl*
talisman	талисма́н *nm*
totem	тоте́м *nm*

clothing and appearance

miter (BR mitre)	ми́тра *nf*
mozzet(t)a	мозе́тта *nf*
phylactery	филакте́рия *nf*
tallith	та́лис *nm*
tephillin	тефилли́н *nm*
tonsure	тонзу́ра *nf*
yarmulka	ермо́лка *nf*

sins and crimes

anathema	ана́фема *nf*
heresy	е́ресь *nf*
profanation	профана́ция *nf*
proscription	проскри́пция *nf*
sanction	са́нкция *nf*

prayers

alleluia!, hallelujah!	аллилу́йя! *nf, indecl, intj*
amen!	ами́нь! *intj*
hosanna	оса́нна *nf, intj*
kaddish	ка́ддиш *nm*
kol nidre	кол ни́дрэ *nm*
liturgy	литурги́я *nf*

other language uses

bull	бу́лла *nf*
encyclical	энцикли́ка *nf*
hymnal	сбо́рник ги́мнов *nm, nmpl*
litany	лита́ния *nf*
psalm	псало́м *nm*
psalmody	псалмо́дия *nf*
psalter	псалты́рь *nf*

Roman Catholic hymns

Agnus Dei	А́гнец Бо́жий *nm*
Ave Maria	А́ве Мари́я
Magnificat	Магнифика́т *nm*
Miserere	Мизере́ре *nn, indecl*
Stabat Mater	Ста́бат Ма́тер
Te Deum	Теде́ум *nm*

religious persecution

anti-Semitism	антисемити́зм *nm*
auto-da-fé	аутодафе́ *nn, indecl*
Diaspora	диа́спора *nf*
ethnic cleansing	этни́ческая чи́стка *nf*
ghetto (*pl* ghettos, ghettoes)	ге́тто *nn, indecl*
holocaust	холоко́ст *nm*
Inquisition	инквизи́ция *nf*
pogrom	погро́м *nm*

PERSONS

members of religious groups

Adventist (Seventh-day)	адвенти́ст, -ка *nmf*
Anabaptist [obs]	анабапти́ст *nm*
Anglican	англика́нец *nm*
Bahaist	бахаи́ст, -ка *nmf*
Baptist	бапти́ст, -ка *nmf*
Benedictine (monk)	бенедикти́нец *nm*
Benedictine (nun)	бенедикти́нка *nf*
Brahma	Бра́хма *nm*
Brahman, Brahmin	брахма́н, брами́н *nm*
Buddhist	будди́ст, -ка *nmf*
Calvinist	кальвини́ст *nm*
Capuchin (friar)	капуци́н *nm*
Carmelite	кармели́т, -ка *nmf*
Catholic	като́лик *nm*, католи́чка *nf*
Christian	христиа́нин *nm*, христиа́нка *nf*
Cistercian	цистерциа́нец *nm*
Copt	копт, -ка *nmf*
Druid, druid [obs]	друи́д, -ка *nmf*
Druse	друз *nm*
Dukhobor [obs]	духобо́р *nm*
Episcopalian	член Епископа́льной церкви *nm, nf*
Franciscan	францизка́нец *nm*
Hindu	инду́с, -ка *nmf*
Huguenot [obs]	гугено́т *nm*
Hussite [obs]	гуси́т *nm*
Jacobite [obs]	якоби́т *nm*
Jehovah's Witness	иегови́ст *nm*
Jesuit	иезуи́т *nm*
Jew	иуде́й, -ка *nmf*
Lutheran	лютера́нин *nm*, лютера́нка *nf*
Mennonite	меннони́т *nm*

Methodist методи́ст *nm*
Mohammedan магомета́нин *nm*, магомета́нка *nf*
Mormon мормо́н, -ка *nmf*
Muslim, Moslem мусульма́н(ин), -ка *nmf*
Orthodox Jew ортодокса́льный евре́й *nm*
Pietist [obs] пиети́ст *nm*
Presbyterian пресвитериа́нин *nm*, пресвитериа́нка *nf*
Protestant протеста́нт *nm*
Puritan [obs] пурита́нин *nm*, пурита́нка *nf*
Quaker ква́кер *nm*, ква́керша *nf*
Rastafarian растафа́ри *nmf*, *indecl*
Roman Catholic като́лик *nm*, католи́чка *nf*
Rosicrucian [obs] розенкре́йцер *nm*
Sephardi сефа́рд *nm*
Sephardim *npl* сефа́рды *nmpl*
Shaker ше́кер *nm*
Shiite, Shiah шии́т *nm*
Sikh сикх *nm*
Sufi суфи́ст *nm*
Sunni, Sunnite сунни́т *nm*
Trappist (monk) член о́рдена траппи́стов *nm*, *nm*, *nmpl*
Unitarian унита́рий *nm*
Zarathustrian после́дователь, -ница Зарату́стры *nmf*
Zen Buddhist дзэн-будди́ст *nm*
Zoroastrian после́дователь, -ница Зороа́стра *nmf*

scholars and religious functionaries

cantor ка́нтор *nm*
choirboy ма́льчик-хори́ст *nm*
cleric кли́рик *nm*
evangelist евангели́ст *nm*
exarch экза́рх *nm*
fundamentalist фундаментали́ст *nm*
guru гу́ру *nm*, *indecl*
hagiographer агио́граф *nm*
inquisitor [obs] инквизи́тор *nm*
missionary миссионе́р, -ка *nmf*
monk мона́х *nm*
muezzin муэдзи́н *nm*
mufti му́фтий *nm*
mujaheddin моджахе́ды *npl*
neophyte неофи́т *nm*
nuncio ну́нций *nm*
padre па́дре *nm*, *indecl*
proselyte прозели́т, -ка *nmf*
psalmist псалми́ст *nm*
seminarian семинари́ст *nm*
shaman шама́н *nm*
spiritist, spiritualist спири́т *nm*
Talmudist талмуди́ст *nm*
theist теист *nm*
theologian тео́лог *nm*
theosophist теосо́ф *nm*
yogi йог *nm*
zaddik ца́дик *nm*

other persons

agnostic агно́стик *nm*
anchorite анахоре́т *nm*
animist аними́ст *nm*
anti-Semite антисеми́т, -ка *nmf*
antichrist анти́христ *nm*
ascetic аске́т *nm*
atheist атеист, -ка *nmf*
deist деист *nm*
dissident диссиде́нт, -ка *nmf*
dogmatist догма́тик *nm*
fetishist фетиши́ст *nm*
giaour гяу́р *nm*
goy гой *nm*
heretic ерети́к *nm*
icon painter иконопи́сец *nm*
iconoclast иконобо́рец *nm*
idolater идолопокло́нник *nm*
monotheist монotéист *nm*
mullah мулла́ *nm*
mystic ми́стик *nm*
pantheist пантеист *nm*
papist [pej] папи́ст *nm*
pilgrim пилигри́м *nm*
polytheist политеист *nm*
religious person религио́зный челове́к *nm*
sectarian секта́нт, -ка *nmf*

See also **TITLES** *(kinds of titles)*, **PHILOSOPHY**, **MAGIC** *(forms of magic)*, **THE BIBLE**, **ANCIENT CIVILIZATIONS**, **VISUAL ARTS**, **MUSIC** *(compositions)*, **CLASSICAL MYTHOLOGY**

MAGIC

GENERAL TERMS

magic ма́гия *nf*
magical маги́ческий *aj*
paranormal паранорма́льный *aj*

pseudoscience	псевдонау́ка *nf*

PRACTICES AND TRADITIONS

pseudosciences

alchemy	алхи́мия *nf*
astrology	астроло́гия *nf*
black magic	чёрная ма́гия *nf*
chiromancy	хирома́нтия *nf*
graphology	графоло́гия *nf*
occult, the	окку́льтные нау́ки *nfpl*
occultism	оккульти́зм *nm*
parapsychology	парапсихоло́гия *nf*
phrenology	френоло́гия *nf*
physiognomy	физиогно́мия *nf*
psychokinesis	психокине́з *nm*
telekinesis	телекине́з *nm*
telepathy	телепа́тия *nf*
teleportation	телепорта́ция *nf*
theosophy	теосо́фия *nf*

entertainment

cards	ка́рты *nmpl*
hypnosis	гипно́з *nm*
illusion	иллю́зия *nf*
levitation	левита́ция *nf*
trick	трюк *nm*

prediction

horoscope	гороско́п *nm*

communication with the dead

metamorphosis (*pl* metamorphoses)	метаморфо́за *nf*
metempsychosis	метемпсихо́з *nm*
necromancy	некрома́нтия *nf*
séance	спирити́ческий сеа́нс *nm*
trance	транс *nm*

imagination

fantasy	фанта́зия *nf*
folklore	фолькло́р *nm*
legend	леге́нда *nf*
mirage	мира́ж *nm*
mysticism	ми́стика *nf*
mythology	мифоло́гия *nf*
phantasmagoria	фантасмаго́рия *nf*
science fiction	нау́чная фанта́стика *nf*

supernatural creatures

angel	а́нгел *nm*
cherub (*pl* cherubs, cherubim)	херуви́м *nm*
demon	де́мон *nm*
devil	дья́вол *nm*
fairy	фе́я *nf*
genie (*pl* genies, genii)	джинн *nm*
jinn, jinni (*pl* jinns, jinn)	джинн *nm*
phantom	фанто́м *nm*
poltergeist	полтерге́йст *nm*
seraph (*pl* seraphs, seraphim)	серафи́м *nm*
vampire	вампи́р *nm*
zombie	зо́мби *nn, indecl*

zodiac signs

Leo	Лев *nm*
Scorpio	Скорпио́н *nm*

other terms

ethereal	эфи́рный *aj*
lycanthropy	ликантро́пия *nf*
materialize *vi*	материализова́ться *impf, pf*
shamanism	шама́нство *nn*
surreal	сюрреалисти́ческий *aj*
taboo, tabu	табу́ *nn, indecl*
unreality	нереа́льность *nf*

TOOLS AND EQUIPMENT

words and actions

abracadabra	абракада́бра *nf*
hocus-pocus	фо́кус-по́кус *nm*
open sesame!	сеза́м, откро́йся!
pass	пас *nm*
ritual	ритуа́л *nm*

objects and symbols

amulet	амуле́т *nm*
crystal ball	маги́ческий криста́лл *nm*
fetish	фети́ш *nm*
pentagram	пентагра́мма *nm*
planchette	планше́тка *nf*
swastika	сва́стика *nf*
talisman	талисма́н *nm*
zodiac	зодиа́к *nm*

substances

aura	а́ура *nf*

ectoplasm	эктопла́зма *nf*
elixir	эликси́р *nm*

PERSONS

astrologer, astrologist	астро́лог *nm*
chiromancer	хирома́нт, -ка *nmf*
fakir	факи́р *nm*
fantasizer	фантазёр *nm*
illusionist	иллюзиони́ст *nm*
medium	ме́диум *nm*
mystic	ми́стик *nm*
mystifier	мистифика́тор *nm*
necromancer	некрома́нт *nm*
parapsychologist	парапсихо́лог *nm*
phrenologist	френо́лог *nm*
physiognomist	физиономи́ст *nm*
shaman	шама́н *nm*
spiritist, spiritualist	спири́т, -ка *nmf*
telepath	телепа́т *nm*

See also **THE BIBLE** ***(supernatural beings)***, **FICTION AND FOLKLORE**, **CLASSICAL MYTHOLOGY**, **RELIGION**

Daily Living

THE CITY ◆ HOME FURNISHINGS ◆ AUTOMOBILES ◆ WORK

THE CITY

GENERAL TERMS

cosmopolitan	космополити́ческий *aj*
megalopolis	мегало́полис *nm*
municipality	муниципалите́т *nm*
planning commission	пла́новая коми́ссия *nf*
port city	порто́вый го́род *nm*
quarter (of the city)	кварта́л *nm*
section	се́кция *nf*
urban transport	городско́й тра́нспорт *nm*
urbanism	урбани́зм *nm*
urbanization	урбаниза́ция *nf*
urbanize	урбанизи́ровать *impf, pf*
urbanology	урбаноло́гия *nf*

ASPECTS OF THE CITY

urban problems

city planning	городско́е плани́рование *nn*
graffiti	граффи́ти *nnpl, indecl*
prostitution	проститу́ция *nf*
race relations	ра́совые отноше́ния *nnpl*
recycling	реци́клинг *nm*
redevelopment plan	план реконстру́кции *nm, nf*
smog	смог *nm*
transportation	тра́нспорт *nm*

sections

Casbah, Kasbah	ка́сба *nf*
center	центр *nm*
Chinatown	кита́йский кварта́л *nm*
commercial	комме́рческий *aj*
ethnic	этни́ческий *aj*
ghetto (*pl* ghettos, ghettoes)	ге́тто *nn, indecl*
industrial	индустриа́льный *aj*
Latin quarter	Лати́нский кварта́л *nm*
periphery	перифери́я *nf*

streets and traffic

alley [broad street]	алле́я *nf*
asphalt	асфа́льт *nm*
boulevard	бульва́р *nm*
esplanade	эспλана́да *nf*
house number	но́мер до́ма *nm, nm*
hydrant	гидра́нт *nm*
neon light	нео́новый свет *nm*
parkway	па́рковая доро́га *nf*
piazza	пья́цца *nf*
tunnel	тунне́ль, тонне́ль *nm*
zebra crossing	пешехо́дный перехо́д «зе́бра» *nm, nf*

business and industry

airport	аэропо́рт *nm*
bazaar	база́р *nm*
casino	казино́ *nn, indecl*
commercial/trade center	комме́рческий центр *nm*
gasworks *npl*	га́зовый заво́д *nm*
hotel	оте́ль *nm*
industrial park	те́хно-парк *nm*
motel	моте́ль *nm*
restaurant	рестора́н *nm*
supermarket	суперма́ркет *nm*

recreation

auditorium	аудито́рия *nf*
club	клуб *nm*
aquarium	аква́риум *nm*
concert hall	конце́ртный зал *nm*
cultural center	культу́рный центр *nm*
gym, gymnasium (*pl* gymnasiums, gymnasia)	гимнасти́ческий зал *nm*
museum	музе́й *nm*
night club	ночно́й клуб *nm*
park	парк *nm*
pavilion	павильо́н *nm*
public library	публи́чная библиоте́ка *nf*
stadium (*pl* stadiums, stadia)	стадио́н *nm*

theater (BR theatre) — теáтр *nm*
zoo, zoological garden/park — зоосáд, зоопáрк, зоологи́ческий парк/сад *nm*

dwellings

bungalow — бýнгало *nn, indecl*
condominium — кондоми́ниум *nm*
hacienda — гасиéнда, асьéнда *nf*
lodge — лóжа *nf*
penthouse — пентхáус *nm*
residence — резидéнция *nf*

beautification

fountain [large] — фонтáн *nm*
illumination — иллюминáция *nf*
monument — монумéнт *nm*
plaza — плáза *nf*
promenade — променад *nm*
square [small] — сквер *nm*

other places

chapel — капéлла *nf*
clinic — кли́ника *nf*
garage — гарáж *nm*
public toilet — туалéт *nm*
registry office — регистратýра *nf*
school — шкóла *nf*
synagog(ue) — синагóга *nf*
university — университéт *nm*
viaduct — виадýк *nm*

public transportation

bus — автóбус *nm*
express (train) — экспрéсс *nm*
Metro — метрó *nm, indecl*
monorail — монорéльс *nm*, монорéльсовая дорóга *nf*
subway station — стáнция метрó *nf*
taxi — такси́ *nn*
tram, tramway — трамвáй *nm*
tramway stop — трамвáйная остановка *nf*
transit — транзи́т *nm*
trolleybus — троллéйбус *nm*

PERSONS

city planner — планови́к *nm*, планирóвщик городóв *nm, nmpl*
cosmopolite — космополи́т, -ка *nmf*
police officer — полицéйский *nmf*
prostitute — проститýтка *nf*
squatter — сквáттер *nm*
taxi driver — такси́ст *nm*
tourist — тури́ст, -ка *nmf*
transport worker — трáнспортник *nm*

See also **ARCHITECTURE**, **AUTOMOBILES**

HOME FURNISHINGS

GENERAL TERMS

color (BR colour) — кóлер, колóр *nm*
combination — комбинáция *nf*
decor, decoration *nsg* — декóр *nm*, декорáции *nfpl*
exterior — экстерьéр *nm*
furniture — фурнитура *nf*
interior — интерьéр *nm*
style — стиль *nm*

FURNITURE

styles

antique — антиквáрный *aj*
Chippendale — чиппендéйл (мéбель)
colonial style — колониáльный стиль *nm*
Empire style — ампи́р *nm*
Regency — эпóха Рéгенства *nf, nn*
Victorian — викториáнский *aj*

materials and appearance

bamboo — бамбýк *nn*
lacquered — лакирóванный, лáковый *aj*
metal — метáлл *nm*
plastic — плáстик *nm*
polished — полирóванный *aj*
rattan — ротáнг *nm*
sectional — секциóнный *aj*
solid — соли́дный *aj*
teak — тик *nm*
vinyl — вини́л *nm*

ITEMS

living room

bureau — бюрó *nn, indecl*
candelabrum (*pl* candelabra) — канделя́бр *nm*
card table — кáрточный стол *nm*
coffee table — кофéйный стол *nm*
console — консóль *nf*
divan — дивáн *nm*

étagère	этажéрка *nf*
ottoman	оттомáнка *nf*
radio set	радиоаппарáт *nm*
sofa	софá *nf*
television set	телеви́зор *nm*

bedroom and bathroom

bidet	бидé *nn, indecl*
chiffonier	шифоньéр *nm*, шифоньéрка *nf*
commode	комóд *nm*
mattress	матрáс, матрáц *nm*
roll of toilet paper	рулóн туалéтной бумáги *nm, nf*
tatami	татáми *nn, indecl*
toilet	туалéт *nm*
water-closet [= WC]	ватерклозéт *nm*

windows and lighting

draperies *npl*	драпри́ *nn, indecl*
drapery, draping	драпирóвка *nf*
electric light	электри́ческий свет *nm*
jalousie	жалюзи́ *nn, indecl*
lamp	лáмпа *nf*
quartz lamp	квáрцевая лáмпа *nf*
triplex (glass)	три́плекс *nm*

floors and walls

doormat	мат *nm*
linoleum	линóлеум *nm*
paneling (BR panelling)	панéльная обши́вка *nf*
parquet floor	паркéтный пол *nm*
parquet (flooring)	паркéт *nm*
Persian carpet	перси́дский ковёр *nm*
portière	портьéра *nf*

outdoors

barbecue	барбекю́ *nn, indecl*
chaise longue	шезлóнг *nm*
hammock	гамáк *nm*
hibachi	хибáти *nnpl*

appliances

air conditioner	кондиционéр *nm*
microwave oven	микроволнóвая пéчь *nf*
refrigerator	рефрижерáтор *nm*
food mixer	ми́ксер *nm*

other terms

air-conditioning	кондициони́рование *nn*
central heating	центрáльное отоплéние *nn*
polish [substance]	политýра *nf*
safe	сейф *nm*

See also **ARCHITECTURE, FOOD AND NUTRITION** *(preparation and consumption)*

AUTOMOBILES

GENERAL TERMS

auto	автó *nn, indecl*
automobile	автомоби́ль *nm*
automobile industry	автомоби́льная промы́шленность *nf*
chauffeur	шофёр *nm*
model	модéль *nf*

ASPECTS OF AUTOMOBILES

models

coupe	купé *nn*
jeep	джип *nm*
pickup (truck)	пикáп *nm*
sedan	седáн *nm*
sports car	спорти́вный автомоби́ль *nm*

parts and equipment

accelerator	акселерáтор *nm*
balloon tire	баллóн *nm*
bumper	бáмпер *nm*
car telephone	автомоби́льный телефóн *nm*
carburetor (BR carburettor)	карбюрáтор *nm*
catalytic converter	каталити́ческий преобразовáтель *nm*
chassis	шáсси *nn, indecl*
cylinder	цили́ндр *nm*
differential	дифференциáл *nm*
filter	фильтр *nm*
gas station	автозапрáвочная стáнция *nf*
hydraulic brake	гидравли́ческий тóрмоз *nm, nm*
ignition system	систéма зажигáния *nf, nn*
motor	мотóр *nm*
pedal	педáль *nf*
radial (tire)	радиáльный *aj*
radiator	радиáтор *nm*

service station — бензозапра́вочная ста́нция *nf*
speedometer — спидо́метр *nm*
starter — ста́ртер, стартёр *nm*
thermostat — термоста́т *nm*

maintenance and repairs

antifreeze — антифри́з *nm*
garage — гара́ж *nm*
gas station — запра́вочная ста́нция *nf*
gas, gasoline — газоли́н *nm*
motor oil — мото́рное ма́сло
odometer — одо́метр *nm*
panel — пане́ль *nf*

driving

automobile accident — автомоби́льная ава́рия *nf*
car park — парк/па́ркинг (для маши́н) *nm, nfpl*
circulate [traffic] — циркули́ровать *impf*
driving school — автошко́ла *nf*
mileage [distance] — расстоя́ние в ми́лях *nn, nfpl*
mileage [efficiency] — пробе́г в ми́лях *nm, nfpl*
neutral (gear) — нейтра́льная ско́рость *nn*
registration — регистра́ция *nf*
regulate traffic — регули́ровать у́личное движе́ние *impf*
signal — сигна́л *nm*
stop — стоп *nm*
transit, in — транзи́том *nm*

See also **THE CITY** *(aspects of the city)*, **LAND TRANSPORTATION**, **TOURISM**

WORK

GENERAL TERMS

career — карье́ра *nf*
ergonomics *nplsv* — эргоно́мика *nf*
profession — профе́ссия *nf*
trade unionism — тред-юниони́зм *nm*

ASPECTS OF EMPLOYMENT

factors affecting work

absenteeism — абсентеи́зм *nm*
competence — компете́нтность *nf*
exploitation — эксплуата́ция *nf*
nepotism — непоти́зм *nm*
practical experience — пра́ктикум *nm*, практи́ческий о́пыт *nm*
professionalism — профессионали́зм *nm*
qualifications *npl* — квалифика́ция *nf*
resume, résumé — резюме́ *nn, indecl*
speciality — специа́льность *nf*
subordination — субордина́ция *nf*
technology — техноло́гия *nf*
vacancy — вака́нсия *nf*

labor relations

contract — контра́кт *nm*
picket line — ли́ния пике́тов *nf, nmpl*
picketing — пикети́рование *nn*
trade union — тред-юнио́н *nm*

income

base period — ба́зисный пери́од *nm*
bonus — бо́нус *nm*
commission (fee) — комиссио́нное вознагражде́ние *nn*
compensation — компенса́ция *nf*
honorarium (*pl* honorariums, honoraria) — гонора́р *nm*
pension — пе́нсия *nf*
pension plan — пенсио́нный план *nm*
real wages — реа́льная за́работная пла́та *nf*
Social Security — социа́льное обеспе́чение *nn*
stipend — стипе́ндия *nf*
wage scale — шкала́ за́работной пла́ты *nf*

places

collective — коллекти́в *nm*
farm — ферма *nf*
office — о́фис *nm*

terms describing workers

accurate — аккура́тный *aj*
qualified — квалифици́рованный *aj*
unprofessional — непрофессиона́льный *aj*
unqualified — неквалифици́рованный *aj*

terms describing work

interesting — интере́сный *aj*
nerve-wracking — не́рвный *aj*

nonprofessional	непрофессиона́льный *aj*
professional	профессиона́льный *aj*
specialized	специа́льный *aj*
stressful	стре́ссовый *aj*
unspecialized	неспециализи́рованный *aj*

other terms

economy [thrift]	эконо́мия *nf*
sinecure	синеку́ра *nf*
tandem, to work in	рабо́тать в танде́ме *nm*
uniform	унифо́рма *nf*

PERSONS

absentee	абсентеи́ст *nm*
assistant	ассисте́нт, -ка *nmf*
boss	босс *nm*
careerist	карьери́ст *nm*
colleague	колле́га *nmf*
electrician	эле́ктрик *nm*
ergonomist	эргономи́ст *nm*
expert	экспе́рт *nm*
factotum	факто́тум *nm*
guild [obs]	ги́льдия *nf*
inspector	инспе́ктор *nm*
pensioner	пенсионе́р, -ка *nmf*
personnel	персона́л *nm*
picket	пике́тчик *nm*
professional	профессиона́л *nm*
seasonal worker	сезо́нный рабо́чий, сезо́нник *nm*
specialist	специали́ст *nm*
strikebreaker	штрейкбре́хер *nm*
textile worker	тексти́льщик *nm*, тексти́льщица *nf*
trade unionist	тред-юниони́ст *nm*

See also **BUSINESS**, **ECONOMICS**, **TECHNOLOGY OVERVIEW**

Keeping the Body Beautiful

CLOTHING AND ACCESSORIES ◆ PERSONAL GROOMING ◆ FOOD AND NUTRITION ◆ BEVERAGES

CLOTHING AND ACCESSORIES

GENERAL TERMS

accessory	аксессуа́р *nm*
chic	шик *nm*
décolletage	декольте́ *nn, indecl*
decoration, decorating	декори́рование *nn*
dishabille, deshabille	дезабилье́ *nn, indecl*
ensemble	анса́мбль *nm*
fashion	фасо́н *nm*
jewelry (BR jewellery)	ювели́рные изде́лия *nnpl*
mode	мо́да *nf*
ornament	орна́мент *nm*
pair	па́ра *nf*

ASPECTS OF CLOTHING

types

ceremonial	церемониа́льный *aj*
elegant	элега́нтный *aj*
ethnic	этни́ческий *aj*
formal	форма́льный *aj*
informal	неформа́льный *aj*
modish	мо́дный *aj*
national	национа́льный *aj*
outmoded	не мо́дный *aj*
religious	религио́зный *aj*
sportswear	спорти́вный *aj*
stylish	сти́льный *aj*
theatrical	театра́льный *aj*
traditional	традицио́нный *aj*

cleaning

detergent	детерге́нт *nm*
washing machine	стира́льная маши́на *nf*

ARTICLES OF CLOTHING

headwear

beret	бере́т *nm*
castor	касто́р *nm*
cowboy hat	ковбо́йка *nf*
fez (*pl* fezzes)	фе́ска *nf*
Panama hat	пана́ма *nf*
sombrero	сомбре́ро *nn, indecl*
toque	ток *nm*
turban	тюрба́н *nm*
yashmak	яшма́к *nm*

footwear

gaiters	ге́тры *nmpl*
galosh	гало́ша, кало́ша *nf*
huarache	гуара́чи *nn*
moccasin	мокаси́н *nm*
sandal	санда́лия, сандале́та *nf*
tennis shoes	те́ннисные ту́фли *nfpl*

undergarments and sleepwear

camisole	камзо́л *nm*
corset	корсе́т *nm*
kimono	кимоно́ *nn, indecl*
negligee, negligé	неглиже́ *nn, indecl*
pajamas (BR pyjamas) *npl*	пижа́ма *nf*
peignoir	пеньюа́р *nm*

outerwear

anorak	анора́к *nm*
Bermuda shorts	шо́рты-берму́ды *npl*
blazer	бле́йзер *nm*
blouse	блу́зка *nf*
caftan, kaftan	кафта́н *nm*
cardigan	кардига́н *nm*
dashiki	даши́ки *nn*
jacket [for women]	жаке́т *nm*
jeans, blue jeans	джи́нсы *nmpl*
mackintosh	макинто́ш *nm*
mantle [cloak]	ма́нтия *nf*
maxi (skirt)	ма́кси *nn, indecl*
midi (skirt)	ми́ди *nn, indecl*
miniskirt	ми́ни-ю́бка *nf*
muu-muu	му́му *nn*
nylons	нейло́новые чулки́ *nmpl*
pair of pants	па́ра брюк *nf, npl*
pair of stockings/gloves	па́ра чу́лок/перча́ток *nf, npl*
parka	па́рка *nf*
poncho	по́нчо *nn, indecl*
pullover	пуло́вер *nm*
sari	са́ри *nf, indecl*

sarong	capóнг *nm*
shorts	шóрты *pl, indecl*
sports jacket	спортúвный жакéт *nm*
sweater	свúтер *nm*

special-purpose garments

ball gown	бáльное плáтье *nn*
bikini	бикúни *nn, indecl*
costume	костю́м *nm*
domino (*pl* dominoes)	доминó *nn, indecl*
leotard	леотáрд *nm*
riding breeches	брúджи *pl*

historical clothing

pantaloons	панталóны *nmpl*
sarafan	сарафáн *nm*
toga	тóга *nf*
tunic	тунúка *nf*

ACCESSORIES AND ORNAMENTS

ascot (tie)	аскóтский гáлстук *nm*
boa	боá *nnpl*
boutonniere	бутоньéрка *nf*
bracelet	браслéт *nm*
brooch	брошь, брóшка *nf*
clip	клúпсы *nmpl*
cockade	кокáрда *nf*
corsage	корсáж *nm*
diadem	диадéма *nf*
epaulet, epaulette	эполéт *nm*, эполéтка *nf*
galoon	галýн *nm*
garland	гирля́нда *nf*
mask	мáска *nf*
mantilla	мантúлья *nf*
monocle	монóкль *nm*
parasol	парасóль *nf*
pompom	помпóн *nm*
scarf (*pl* scarves)	шарф *nm*
shawl	шаль *nm*
stole	стóла *nf*
tiara	тиáра *nf*
veil	вуáль, вуалéтка *nf*

SEWING TERMS

design features

appliqué	апликáция *nf*
border	бордю́р *nm*
dolman (sleeve)	доломáн *nm*
fichu	фишю́ *nn, indecl*
filigree	филигрáнь *nf*
raglan	реглáн *nm*
jabot	жабó *nn, indecl*
pouf(fe)	пуф *nm*
zigzag	зигзáг *nm*

tools and equipment

mannequin, manikin [dummy]	манекéн *nm*
sewing machine	швéйная машúна *nf*
bobbin	бобúна *nf*
stiletto (*pl* stilettos, stilettoes)	стилéт *nm*
Velcro	велкрó *nn, indecl*

measurements

yardage	длинá в я́рдах *nf, nmpl*
yard	ярд *nm*
meter	метр *nm*

other terms

plaid (garment)	плед *nm*
elastic	эластúчный *aj*
natural leather	натурáльная кóжа *nf*
natural fur	натурáльный мех *nm*
nutria (fur)	нýтрия *nf*
sable fur	собóлий/соболúный мех *nm*
tweed (suit)	твúдовый *aj*

PERSONS

costumer	костюмéр, -ша *nmf*
jeweler, jeweller	ювелúр *nm*
mannequin	манекéнщик *nm*, манекéнщица *nf*
model	модéль *nf*
modiste	модúстка *nf*
transvestite	трансвестúт *nm*

See also **TEXTILES** *(aspects of textiles)*, **THE MILITARY ESTABLISHMENT** *(aspects of military life)*, **RELIGION** *(practices and traditions)*, **MINERALS AND MINING** *(names of rocks and minerals)*

PERSONAL GROOMING

GENERAL TERMS

beauty secret	секрет красоты́ *nm, nf*
cosmetics *npl*	космéтика *nf*
cosmetology	космéтика *nf*
personal hygiene	лúчная гигиéна *nf*

toiletries	туале́тные принадле́жности *nfpl*
toilette	туале́т *nm*
treatment	ухо́д *nm*

ASPECTS OF GOOD GROOMING

places

beauty salon	космети́ческий сало́н *nm*
boudoir	будуа́р *nm*
hairdresser's salon	сало́н-парикма́херская *nm*
perfumery	парфюме́рия *nf*
solarium (*pl* solariums, solaria)	соля́рий *nm*

hair care terms

Afro	причёска «а́фро» *nf*
brilliantine	бриллианти́н *nm*
chignon	шиньо́н *nm*
henna	хна *nf*
natural color	натура́льный цвет *nm*
permanent (wave)	пермане́нт *nm*
peroxide	пе́рекись *nf*
pomade	пома́да *nf*

skin care terms

antiperspirant	антиперспира́нт *nm*
balm, balsam	бальза́м *nm*
calamine lotion	калами́нный лосьо́н *nm*
camphorated oil	ка́мфарное ма́сло *nn*
cold cream	кольдкре́м *nm*
cream	крем *nm*
deodorant	дезодора́нт *nm*
electrolysis	электро́лиз *nm*
eucalyptus oil	эвкали́птовое ма́сло *nn*
face powder	пу́дра *nf*
glycerin(e)	глицери́н *nm*
lanolin(e)	ланоли́н *nm*
lotion	лосьо́н *nm*
manicure	маникю́р *nm*
masque	ма́ска *nf*
massage	масса́ж *nm*
palm oil	па́льмовое ма́сло *nn*
pedicure	педикю́р *nm*
shampoo	шампу́нь *nm*
shiatsu (massage)	сиа́цу *nf*
talcum powder	та́льковый порошо́к *nm*
toilet soap	туале́тное мы́ло *nn*

scents

cologne, eau-de-Cologne	одеколо́н *nm*
extract	экстра́кт *nm*
lavender	лава́нда *nf*
rose water	ро́зовая вода́ *nf*
sachet	саше́ *nn, indecl*
toilet water	туале́тная вода́ *nf*

tools and equipment

atomizer	атомиза́тор *nm*
douche	душ *nm*
Jacuzzi	джаку́зи *nn, indecl*
manicure set	маникю́рный набо́р *nm*
pincers *npl*	пинце́т *nm*
sauna	са́уна *nf*
sunlamp	ультрафиоле́товая ла́мпа *nf*
Turkish bath	туре́цкая ба́ня *nf*

other terms

gel	гель *nm*
tattoo	татуиро́вка *nf*
toilet paper	туале́тная бума́га *nf*
toothpaste	зубна́я паста *nf*

PERSONS

cosmetician	космети́чка *nf*
cosmetologist	космето́лог *nm*
manicurist	маникю́рша *nf*
masseur	массажи́ст *nm*
masseuse	массажи́стка *nf*

See also **SPORTS**

FOOD AND NUTRITION

GENERAL TERMS

appetite	аппети́т *nm*
aroma	арома́т *nm*
culinary	кулина́рный *aj*
delicacy	деликате́с *nm*
diet	дие́та *nf*
food product	проду́кт пита́ния *nm, nn*
gastronomy	гастроно́мия *nf*
provisions *npl*	прови́зия *nf*
recipe	реце́пт *nm*

service	сервиз *nm*

ASPECTS OF FOOD CONSUMPTION

places to buy or eat food

automat	автомат *nm*
bistro	бистро *nn, indecl*
cafe, café	кафе *nn, indecl*
cafeteria	кафетерий *nm*
coffee house/shop	кафетерий *nm*
delicatessen	магазин деликатесов *nm, nmpl*
exotic	экзотический *aj*
pizzeria	пиццерия, пиццерия *nf*
restaurant	ресторан *nm*
snack bar	бар *nm*
supermarket	супермаркет *nm*
sushi bar	суши-бар, суси-бар *nm*

tastes, textures, quality, type

appetizing	аппетитный *aj*
aromatic	ароматический, ароматный *aj*
ethnic	этнический *aj*
fruity	фруктовый *aj*
glazed, glacé	глазированный *aj*
lemony	лимонный *aj*
marinated	маринованный *aj*
mentholated	ментоловый *aj*
organic	органический *aj*
piquant	пикантный *aj*
salty	солёный *aj*
sugary	сахарный, сахаристый *aj*
unappetizing	неаппетитный *aj*
vegetarian	вегетарианский *aj*

KINDS OF FOOD

meals

banquet	банкет *nm*
barbecue	барбекю *nn, indecl*
buffet	буфет *nm*
business lunch	бизнес-ланч *nm*
lunch	ланч *nm*
picnic	пикник *nm*

major types

croquette	крокет *nm*
dessert	десерт *nm*
extract	экстракт *nm*
filet, fillet	филе *nn, indecl*
fruit	фрукт *nm*
garnish	гарнир *nm*
pasta, paste	паста *nf*
produce *nsg*	продукты *nmpl*
puree, purée	пюре *nn, indecl*
salad	салат *nm*
sandwich	сандвич *nm*
sauce	соус *nm*
soup	суп *nm*
spice	специя *nf*
syrup	сироп *nm*

soups

bouillon	бульон *nm*
consommé	консоме *nn, indecl*
goulash	гуляш *nm*
ragout	рагу *nn, indecl*
rassolnik	рассольник *nm*

meat and poultry

bacon	бекон *nm*
beef stroganoff	бефстроганов *nm*
beefsteak	бифштекс *nm*
broiler (chicken)	бройлер *nm*
burger	бургер *nm*
cheeseburger	чизбургер *nm*
cutlet [chop]	(отбивная) котлета *nf*
entrecote, entrecôte	антрекот *nm*
escalope	эскалоп *nm*
fricassee	фрикасе *nn, indecl*
goose-flesh	гусятина *nf*
hamburger	гамбургер *nm*
hot dog	хот-дог *nm*
kebab, kebob	кебаб *nm*
liver sausage	ливерная колбаса *nf*
London broil	жаркое по-лондонски *nn*
pastrami	пастрами *nn, indecl*
Peking duck	утка по-пекински *nf*
pepperoni	пепперони *nf, indecl*
roast beef	ростбиф *nm*
rump steak	ромпштекс *nm*
salami	салями *nf, indecl*
salt beef	солонина *nf*
sausage	сосиска *nf*
schnitzel	шницель *nm*
shashlik	шашлык *nm*
shish-kebab	шиш-кебаб *nm*
steak	стейк, бифштекс *nm*

seafood

anchovy	анчоус *nm*
beluga (whale)	белуха *nf*
mackerel	макрель *nf*

oyster	у́стрица *nm*
sardine	сарди́на, сарди́нка *nf*
shad (*pl* shads, shad)	шэд *nm*
tuna	туне́ц *nm*

names of cheeses

Brie	бри *nm*
Cheddar	чёддар *nm*
Edam	эда́мский сыр *nm*
Emmentaler	эмента́льский сыр *nm*
Gorgonzola	горгонзо́ла *nf*
Liederkranz	ли́дерkранц *nm*
Limburger	лимбу́ргский сыр *nm*
Parmesan	пармеза́н *nm*
Roquefort	рокфо́р *nm*

pasta

lasagna, lasagne	лаза́нья *nn*
macaroni	макаро́ны *nfpl*
pilaf	пила́в, плов *nm*
ravioli	равио́ли *nnpl, indecl*
spaghetti	спаге́тти *nn, indecl*
tortellini	тортелли́ни *pl*
vermicelli *npl*	вермише́ль *nf*

bread and cereal

challah	ха́ла *nf*
cracker	кре́кер *nm*
kasha	ка́ша *nf*
matzo, matzoth	маца́ *nf*
polenta	поле́нта *nf*
popcorn	по́пкорн *nm*
rice	рис *nm*
rissotto	рисо́тто *nn, indecl*
toast	тост *nm*
waffle	ва́фля *nf*

vegetables

artichoke	артишо́к *nm*
Bermuda onion	берму́дка *nf*
broccoli	бро́кколи *nn, indecl*
Brussels sprouts *npl*	брюссе́льская капу́ста *nf*
celery	сельдере́й *nm*
cress, watercress	кресс *nm*, кресс-сала́т *nm*
endive	энди́вий *nm*
kohlrabi (*pl* kohlrabies)	кольра́би *nf, indecl*
lima bean	ли́мская фасо́ль *nf*
maize	маи́с *nm*
okra	о́кра *nf*
pearl-barley	перло́вая крупа́ *nf*
radish	реди́с *nm*, реди́ска *nf*
Savoy (cabbage)	саво́йская капу́ста *nf*
soybean	со́я *nf*, со́евый боб *nm*
spinach	шпина́т *nm*
succotash	сакото́ш *nm*
tomato (*pl* tomatoes)	тома́т *nm*
truffle	трю́фель *nm*
turnip	турне́пс *nm*
yam	ямс *nm*
yucca	ю́кка *nf*

fruits

apricot	абрико́с *nm*
avocado pear	авока́до *nn, indecl*
banana	бана́н *nm*
cantaloup(e)	каталу́па *nf*
citron	цитро́н *nm*
citrus	ци́трус *nm*
coconut	коко́с *nm*
coconut	коко́совый оре́х *nm*
Duchess pear	дюше́с *nm*
fig	фи́га *nf*
grapefruit	гре́йпфрут *nm*
guava	гуа́ва *nf*
kiwi	ки́ви *nn, indecl*
kumquat, cumquat	кумква́т *nm*
lemon	лимо́н *nm*
lime	лайм *nm*
mandarin orange	мандари́н *nm*
mango (*pl* mangos, mangoes)	ма́нго *nn, indecl*
mirabelle plum	мирабе́ль *nf*
mousse	мусс *nm*
muscat (grapes)	муска́т *nm*
navel orange	на́вель *nm*
nectarine	нектари́н *nm*
olive	оли́ва, оли́вка *nf*
papaya	папа́йя *nf, indecl*
pippin (apple)	пепи́нка *nf*
pomegranate	грана́т *nm*
rennet (apple)	ране́т *nm*
tamarind	тамари́нд *nm*
tangelo	танжело́ *nn, indecl*
tangerine	танжери́н *nm*

nuts

lichee, litchi	личжи́ *nn, indecl*
pecan	оре́х-пека́н *nm*

desserts and candies

apricot jam	абрико́совый джем *nm*
baba au rhum	ро́мовая ба́ба *nf*
blancmange	бланманже́ *nn, indecl*
cake, (fruit-)	кекс *nm*
caramel	караме́ль, караме́лька *nf*

charlotte	шарло́тка *nf*
chocolate	шокола́д *nm*
chocolate bar	шокола́дка *nf*, шокола́дная пли́тка *nf*
chocolate candy	шокола́дная конфе́та *nf*
coffee cake	кофе́йный торт *nm*
compote	компо́т *nm*
confection	конфе́та *nf*
conserves	консерви́рованные фру́кты *nmpl*
crepe, crêpe	креп *nm*
Danish pastry	пиро́жное по-да́тски *nn*
dragée	драже́ *nn, indecl*
eclair, éclair	экле́р *nm*
fondue	фондю́ *nn*
fruit salad	фрукто́вый сала́т *nm*
fruitcake	фрукто́вый торт *nm*
halva, halvah	халва́ *nf*
jam	джем *nm*
jelly	желе́ *nn, indecl*
jujube	ю́юба *nf*
licorice, liquorice	лакри́ца *nf*
marmalade	мармела́д *nm*
marzipan	марципа́н *nm*
meringue	мере́нга *nf*
napoleon	наполео́н *nm*
nesselrode	нессельро́де *nn*
nougat	нуга́ *nf*
parfait	парфе́ *nn, indecl*
petit four	петифу́р *nm*
praline	прали́не *nn*
profiterole	профитро́ль *nm*
pudding	пу́динг *nm*
refined sugar	рафини́рованный са́хар *nm*
rice pudding	ри́совый пу́динг *nm*
sherbet	щербе́т *nm*
strudel	штру́дель *nm*
sugar	са́хар *nm*
sugar cube	ку́бик са́хара *nm*
tapioca	тапио́ка *nf*
tartlet	тартале́тка *nf*
toffee	то́ффи *nn, indecl*
vol-au-vent [pastry]	волова́н *nm*

sauces, spices, syrups, flavorings

aniseed	ани́совое се́мя *nn*
basil	базили́к *nm*
bechamel (sauce)	бешаме́ль *nf*
capers	ка́персы *nmpl*
cardamom, cardamon	кардамо́н *nm*
cayenne pepper	кайе́нский пе́рец *nm*
chicory	цико́рий *nm*
chili pepper	чили́йский пе́рец *nm*
chutney	ча́тни *nn, indecl*
coriander	кориа́ндр *nm*
curry	кэ́рри *nn, indecl*
fennel	фе́нхель *nm*
iodized salt	йо́дистая соль *nf*
ketchup (BR catsup)	ке́тчуп *nm*
lemon juice	лимо́нный сок *nm*
marjoram	майора́н *nm*
oregano	оре́ган *nm*
paprika	па́прика *nf*
pimento, pimiento	пиме́нт *nm*
remoulade (sauce)	ремула́д *nm*
rosemary	розмари́н *nm*
saffron	шафра́н *nm*
salt	соль *nf*
sesame	сеза́м *nm*
shallot	шало́т *nm*
soy sauce	со́евый со́ус *nm*
thyme	тимья́н, тимиа́н *nm*
tomato paste	тома́тная па́ста *nf*
tomato sauce	тома́тный со́ус *nm*
vanilla	вани́ль *nf*

fats and oils

coconut oil	коко́совое ма́сло *nn*
lard	лярд *nm*
margarine	маргари́н *nm*
mayonnaise	майоне́з *nm*
mineral oil	минера́льное ма́сло *nn*
oleo, oleomargarine	олеомаргари́н *nm*
olive oil	оли́вковое ма́сло *nn*
safflower	сафло́р *nm*
soybean oil	со́евое ма́сло

popular Russian dishes

blini	блины́ *nmpl*
bor(t)sch	борщ *nm*
kulich	кули́ч *nm*
pelmeni	пельме́ни *nmpl*
piroshki	пирожки́ *nmpl*

other ethnic dishes

haggis	ха́ггис *nm*
pizza	пи́цца *nf*
poi	по́и *nn, indecl*
quiche	киш *nm*
rollmops	ро́льмопс *nm*
moussaka	мусса́ка *nn*

paella	паэ́лья *nf*
Wiener schnitzel	шни́цель по-ве́нски *nm*

miscellaneous foods

marinade	марина́д *nm*
molasses	мела́сса *nf*
omelet, omelette	омле́т *nm*
pemican, pemmican	пеммика́н *nm*
pickles	пи́кули *npl*
powdered sugar	са́харная пу́дра *nf*
sago	са́го *nn*
souffle	суфле́ *nn, indecl*
yogurt, yoghurt	йо́гурт *nm*

PROCESSED FOODS

additives

agar-agar, agar	ага́р-ага́р *nm*
coloring	колори́т *nm*
emulsifier	эмульга́тор *nm*
gelatin(e)	желати́н *nm*
glaze	глазиро́вка *nf*
monosodium glutamate [= MSG]	глютамина́т на́трия *nm, nm*
pectin	пекти́н *nm*
saccharin	сахари́н *nm*
stabilizer	стабилиза́тор *nm*

processes

dehydration	дегидрата́ция *nf*
fermentation	фермента́ция *nf*
hydrogenation	гидрогениза́ция *nf*
irradiation	иррадиа́ция *nf*
pasteurization	пастериза́ция *nf*

PREPARATION AND CONSUMPTION

tools and equipment

deodorizer	дезодора́тор *nm*
gas stove	га́зовая плита́ *nf*
ingredient	ингредие́нт *nm*
kerosene stove	кероси́нка *nf*
refrigerator	рефрижера́тор *nm*
spatula	шпа́тель *nm*
teflon frying pan	тефло́новая сковоро́дка *nf*
timer	та́ймер *nm*
toaster	то́стер *nm*
waffle iron	ва́фельница *nf*
macerate	мацери́ровать *impf, pf*

food service

banquet table	банке́тный стол *nm*
dessert spoon	десе́ртная ло́жка *nf*
menu	меню́ *nn, indecl*
portion	по́рция *nf*
salad bowl	сала́тник *nm*, сала́тница *nf*
saltcellar, saltshaker	соло́нка *nf*
sauce boat	со́усник *nm*
sugar bowl	са́харница *nf*
table d'hote	табльдо́т *nm*

religious and historical terms

kosher	коше́рный *aj*
manna	ма́нна *nf*
paschal	пасха́льный *aj*
tref food	треф *nm*

TERMS IN NUTRITION

balanced diet	сбаланси́рованная дие́та *nf*
calorie	кало́рия *nf*
calorific value	калори́йность *nf*
low-calorie	низкокалори́йный *aj*
macrobiotic diet	макробиоти́ческая дие́та *nf*
mineral	минера́л *nm*
protein	протеи́н *nm*
vitamin	витами́н *nm*
vitamin-fortified	витаминизи́рованный *aj*
salt-free diet	бессолева́я дие́та *nf*

PERSONS

chef	шеф-по́вар *nm*
dietitian	дието́лог *nm*
epicure	эпикуре́ец *nm*
gastronome	гастроно́м *nm*
gourmet, gourmand	гурма́н, -ка *nmf*
maître d'hôtel	метрдоте́ль *nm*
restaurateur	рестора́тор *nm*
vegetarian	вегетариа́нец *nm*, вегетариа́нка *nf*

See also **HOME FURNISHINGS** *(items)*, **AGRICULTURE** *(aspects of farming)*, **PLANTS**, **ANIMALS**, **THE HUMAN BODY** *(biochemicals)*, **PHYSICAL DISORDERS** *(names of disorders)*

BEVERAGES

ALCOHOLIC BEVERAGES

kinds of drinks

aperitif	аперити́в *nm*

liqueur	ликёр *nm*
wine	винó *nn*

wines

Bordeaux	бордó *nn, indecl*
Burgundy	бургýндское винó *nn*
Chablis	шабли́ *nn*
champagne	шампáнское *nn*
Chianti	кья́нти *nn, indecl*
claret	кларéт *nm*
Madeira	мадéра *nf*
Malaga	малáга *nf*
Marsala	марсалá *nf*
Medoc	медóк *nm*
Moselle	мозельвéйн *nm*
Port	портвéйн *nm*
Reisling	ри́слинг *nm*
Rhine wine	рéйнское винó *nn*
rosé	рóзовое винó *nn*
sake, saki	сакэ́ *nn, indecl*
Sauterne	сотéрн *nm*
sherry	хéрес *nm*, чéрри *nn, indecl*
Tokay	токáйское винó *nn*
vermouth	вéрмут *nm*
zinfandel	зинфандéль *nm*

liqueurs

anis, anise	ани́с *nm*
anisette	ани́совка *nf*, ани́совый ликёр *nm*
Benedictine	бенедикти́н *nm*
chartreuse	шартрéз *nm*
cognac	конья́к *nm*
curaçao	кюрасó *nn, indecl*
kirsch	киршвáссер *nm*
kummel	кю́ммель *nm*
maraschino	мараски́н *nm*
raki	раки́я *nf*

mixed drinks

cocktail	коктéйль *nm*
gin and tonic	джин с тóником *nm, nm*
martini	марти́ни *nn, indecl*
punch	пунш *nm*

other alcoholic beverages

absinth(e)	абсéнт *nm*
akvavit	аквави́т *nm*
ale	эль *nm*
bourbon	бéрбон, бурбóн *nm*
brandy	брéнди *nn, indecl*
elixir	эликси́р *nm*
gin	джин *nm*
grog	грог *nm*
kvass	квас *nm*
Pilsener (beer)	пльзéньское пи́во *nn*
porter (ale)	пóртер *nm*
rum	ром *nm*
sangria	сангри́я *nf*
schnapps	шнапс *nm*
Scotch (whisky)	скотч *nm*, шотлáндское ви́ски *nn*
slivovitz	слива́нка *nf*
spirits *npl*	спирт *nm*, спиртны́е напи́тки *nfpl*
tequila	теки́ла *nf*
vodka	вóдка *nf*
whiskey, whisky	ви́ски *nn, indecl*
yorsh	ёрш *nm*

drinking practices

toast	тост *nm*
winetasting	дегустáция вин *nf, nnpl*

places

bar	бар *nm*
cocktail party	коктéйль *nm*
tavern	тавéрна *nf*
winery shop/trade	винодéльня *nf*

NON-ALCOHOLIC BEVERAGES

cappuccino	капуччи́но *nn*
cider	сидр *nm*
Coca-Cola, coke	кóка-кóла *nf*
cocoa, cacao	какáо *nn, indecl*
coffee	кóфе *nm, indecl*
distilled water	дистиллирóванная водá *nf*
espresso (coffee)	эспрéссо *nn*
fruit juice	фруктóвый сок *nm*
gogol-mogol	гóголь-мóголь *nm*
hot chocolate	шоколáд *nm*
kefir	кефи́р *nm*
kumiss, koumiss	кумы́с *nm*
lemonade	лимонáд *nm*
mineral water	минерáльная водá *nf*
mocha	мóкко *nn, indecl*
nectar	нектáр *nm*
oolong (tea)	улýнг *nm*
orangeade	оранжáд *nm*
sarsaparilla (tea)	сарсапари́ль *nm*
seltzer (water)	сéльтерская водá *nf*
toddy	тодди *nn, indecl*

tomato juice — тома́тный сок *nm*
tonic (water) — то́ник *nm*
Turkish coffee — ко́фе по-туре́цки *nm*
Vichy (water) — виши́ *nn, indecl*

DESCRIPTIVE TERMS

alcohol-free — безалкого́льный *aj*
alcoholic — алкого́льный *aj*
bouquet (of wine) — буке́т *nm*
decaffeinated — бескофе́йновый *aj*
gassy — газиро́ванный *aj*
homogenized (milk) — гомогенизи́рованный *aj*
nonalcoholic — безалкого́льный *aj*
pasteurized (milk) — пастеризо́ванный *aj*

CONTAINERS AND ACCESSORIES

cocktail shaker — ше́йкер *nm*
coffee cup — кофе́йная ча́шка *nf*
coffee filter — фильтр для ко́фе *nm, nm*
coffee grinder — кофемо́лка *nf*
coffee mill — кофе́йница *nf*
coffee service — кофе́йный серви́з *nm*
coffeemaker — кофева́рка *nf*
coffeepot — кофе́йник *nm*
drinking fountain — фонта́нчик *nm*
erzatz (coffee) — эрза́ц *nm*
extractor — экстра́ктор *nm*
granule (of coffee) — гра́нула *nf*
ice cube — ку́бик льда
percolator — перколя́тор *nm*
samovar — самова́р *nm*
soda water, club soda — со́довая вода́
thermos (bottle) — те́рмос *nm*
wine bottle — ви́нная буты́лка *nf*
wine list — ка́рта вин *nf, nnpl*
wine press — пресс для виногра́да *nm, nm*

PERSONS

alcoholic — алкого́лик *nm*, алкоголи́чка *nf*
barmaid — барме́нша *nf*
barman (*pl* barmen) — ба́рмен *nm*
distiller — дистилля́тор *nm*
wine merchant — виноторго́вец *nm*
winemaker — виноде́л *nm*

See also **FOOD AND NUTRITION**

The Inner Self

ROLES AND RELATIONSHIPS ◆ CHARACTER TRAITS ◆ EMOTIONS AND EXPERIENCES ◆ VALUE JUDGMENTS

ROLES AND RELATIONSHIPS

GENERAL TERMS

role	роль *nf*
active role	акти́вная роль *nf*
passive role	пасси́вная роль *nf*

RELATIONSHIPS

friendly

agent	аге́нт, -ша *nmf*
assistant	ассисте́нт, -ка *nmf*
client	клие́нт *nm*
colleague	колле́га *nmf*
companion	компаньо́н *nm*
fan	фана́т *nm*
guest	гость *nm*
partner	партнёр, -ша *nmf*
patron	патро́н *nm*
protector	проте́ктор *nm*
protégé(e)	протеже́ *nmf, indecl*
sympathizer	симпатизи́рующий, -щая *nmf*
tovarisch	това́рищ *nm*

unfriendly

antagonist	антагони́ст *nm*
censor	це́нзор *nm*
critic	кри́тик *nm*
criticaster	критика́н *nm*
exploiter	эксплуата́тор *nm*
manipulator	манипуля́тор *nm*
opponent	оппоне́нт *nm*
revenge-seeker	реванши́ст *nm*

ROLES

peacemakers

arbiter	арби́тр *nm*
coordinator	координа́тор *nm*
diplomat	диплома́т *nm*
mediator	медиато́р *nm*
pacifist	пацифи́ст *nm*

troublemakers

agitator	агита́тор *nm*
disorganizer	дезорганиза́тор *nm*
intriguer	интрига́н, -ка *nmf*
obstructionist	обструкциони́ст *nm*
panic-monger	паникёр *nm*
protester	протесту́ющий *nm*
renegade	ренега́т *nm*

advisers

group leader	группово́д *nm*
guide	гид *nm*
guru	гу́ру *nm, indecl*
instructor	инстру́ктор *nm*
leader	ли́дер *nm*
mentor	ме́нтор *nm*
trainer	тре́нер *nm*

jokesters

buffoon	буффо́н *nm*
comic, comedian	ко́мик *nm*
humorist (BR humourist)	юмори́ст *nm*
master of ceremonies	церемонийме́йстер *nm*

thinkers

genius	ге́ний *nm*
intellectual	интеллектуа́л *nm*
philosopher	фило́соф *nm*
pragmatist	прагма́тик *nm*
rationalist	рационали́ст *nm*
skeptic (BR sceptic)	ске́птик *nm*
strategist	страте́г *nm*
walking encyclopedia	ходя́чая энциклопе́дия *nf*

doers

adventurist	авантюри́ст *nm*
constructor	конструкто́р *nm*
entrepreneur	антрепренёр *nm*
initiator	инициа́тор *nm*
innovator	нова́тор *nm*
organizer	организа́тор *nm*
pioneer	пионе́р, -ка *nmf*
planner	планови́к *nm*

givers

altruist	альтруи́ст *nm*

donor	до́нор *nm*
good Samaritan	до́брый самаритя́нин *nm*
humanitarian	гумани́ст *nm*
philanthropist	филантро́п *nm*
surrogate	суррога́т *nm*
volunteer	волонтёр *nm*

mavericks

dissident	диссиде́нт, -ка *nmf*
iconoclast	иконобо́рец *nm*
individualist	индивидуали́ст *nm*
nonconformist	нонконформи́ст, -ка *nmf*
revolutionary	революционе́р, -ка *nmf*

advocates

activist	активи́ст *nm*
apologist	апологе́т *nm*
enthusiast	энтузиа́ст *nm*
partisan	партиза́н, -ка *nmf*
propagandist	пропаганди́ст *nm*
zealot	зило́т *nm*

unconventional

bohemian	представи́тель боге́мы, боге́мный челове́к *nm*
eccentric	эксцентри́к *nm*
eclectic	экле́ктик *nm*
fanatic	фана́тик *nm*
original	оригина́л *nm*
unique person	у́никум *nm*

lovers and pleasure-seekers

cosmopolite	космополи́т, -ка *nmf*
Don Juan	донжуа́н *nm*
epicure	эпикуре́ец *nm*
esthete (BR aesthete)	эсте́т *nm*
gourmet	гурма́н *nm*
hedonist	гедони́ст *nm*
romantic	рома́нтик *nm*
sensualist	сенсуали́ст *nm*
sentimentalist	сентимента́льный челове́к *nm*
sybarite	сибари́т *nm*
xenophile	ксенофи́л *nm*

haters

anti-Semite	антисеми́т, -ка *nmf*
misanthrope	мизантро́п *nm*
neo-Nazi	неонаци́ст *nm*
racist (BR racialist)	раси́ст, -ка *nmf*
xenophobe	ксенофо́б *nm*

self-centered

egoist	эгои́ст *nm*
egotist	эготи́ст, -ка *nmf*
exhibitionist	эксгибициони́ст *nm*
megalomaniac	мегаломанья́к *nm*
opportunist	оппортуни́ст *nm*

bullies

bandit	банди́т *nm*
barbarian	ва́рвар *nm*
hooligan	хулига́н *nm*
masochist	мазохи́ст, -ка *nmf*
sadist	сади́ст *nm*
tyrant	тира́н *nm*

narrow-minded

chauvinist	шовини́ст *nm*
doctrinaire	доктринёр *nm*
dogmatist	догма́тик *nm*
extremist	экстреми́ст *nm*
ideologue	идео́лог *nm*
jingo, jingoist	джингои́ст *nm*
Philistine	фили́стер *nm*
provincial	провинциа́л, -ка *nmf*
purist	пури́ст *nm*
radical	радика́л *nm*
reactionary	реакционе́р *nm*

liars

charlatan	шарлата́н, -ка *nmf*
falsifier	фальсифика́тор *nm*
poseur	позёр *nm*
pseudointellectual	псевдоинтеллектуа́л *nm*
pseudoliberal	псевдолибера́л *nm*
sycophant	сикофа́нт *nm*

immoral

decadent	декаде́нт *nm*
degenerate	дегенера́т *nm*
sociopath	социопа́т *nm*

martinets

autocrat	автокра́т *nm*
boss	босс *nm*
demagog(ue)	демаго́г *nm*
despot	де́спот *nm*
dictator	дикта́тор *nm*
tyrant	тира́н *nm*

celebrities

personage	персона́ж *nm*

very important person [= VIP]	ва́жная персо́на *nf*
hero (*pl* heroes)	геро́й *nm*
heroine	герои́ня *nf*
Wunderkind	вундерки́нд *nm*

other persons—good

cavalier	кавале́р *nm*
cultured person	культу́рный человек *nm*
doyen	дуайе́н *nm*
expert	экспе́рт *nm*
gentleman (*pl* gentlemen)	джентльме́н *nm*
idealist	идеали́ст *nm*
lady	ле́ди *nf, indecl*
master	ма́стер *nm*
optimist	оптими́ст, -ка *nmf*
paragon	параго́н *nm*
practical person	пра́ктик *nm*, практи́чный челове́к *nm*
realist	реали́ст *nm*
reformer	реформа́тор *nm*
Utopian	утопи́ст *nm*

other persons—bad

conformist	конформи́ст *nm*
cynic	ци́ник *nm*
dandy	де́нди *nm, indecl*
dilettante	дилета́нт *nm*
hypochondriac	ипохо́ндрик *nm*
imitator	имита́тор *nm*
lackey	лаке́й *nm*
nervous person	не́рвный челове́к *nm*
neurotic	невро́тик *nm*
parasite	парази́т *nm*
pariah	па́рия *nmf*
parvenu	парвеню́ *nm, indecl*
pessimist	пессими́ст, -ка *nmf*
simulator	симуля́нт *nm*
snob	сноб *nm*
doubting Thomas	Фома́ неве́рный *nm*
vulgarizer	вульгариза́тор *nm*

See also **INHABITANTS AND ETHNIC GROUPS** *(special interests and attitudes)*, **PSYCHOLOGY**, **CHARACTER TRAITS**

CHARACTER TRAITS

GENERAL TERMS

character formation	формирова́ние хара́ктера *nn, nm*
character	хара́ктер *nm*
emotion	эмо́ция *nf*
idiosyncrasy	идиосинкрази́я *nf*
individuality	индивидуа́льность *nf*
intellect	интелле́кт *nm*
manner	мане́ра *nf*
morals *npl*	мора́ль *nf*
nature	нату́ра *nf*
reputation, repute	репута́ция *nf*
temperament	темпера́мент *nm*
volition	во́ля *nf*

DESIRABLE QUALITIES

accuracy	аккура́тность *nf*
altruism	альтруи́зм *nm*
ambition	амби́ция *nf*
aplomb	апло́мб *nm*
charisma	хари́зма *nf*
charm	шарм *nm*
congeniality	конгениа́льность *nf*
correctness	корре́ктность *nf*
critical attitude	критици́зм *nm*
delicacy	делика́тность *nf*
diplomacy	дипломати́чность *nf*
discipline	дисциплина *nf*
dynamism	динами́зм *nm*
elegance	элега́нтность *nf*
empathy	эмпа́тия *nf*
enthusiasm	энтузиа́зм *nm*
gallantry	гала́нтность *nf*
genius [talent]	гениа́льность *nf*
gentlemanliness	джентльме́нство *nn*
good manners	хоро́шие мане́ры *nmpl*
good organization	организо́ванность *nf*
heroism	герои́зм *nm*, геро́йство *nn*
humaneness	гума́нность *nf*
humanism	гумани́зм *nm*
idealism	идеали́зм *nm*
initiative	инициати́вность *nf*
introspection	интроспе́кция *nf*
intuition	интуи́ция *nf*
loyalty	лоя́льность *nf*
mastery	мастерство́ *nn*
optimism	оптими́зм *nm*
pathos	па́фос *nm*
philanthropy	филантро́пия *nf*
practicality	практи́чность *nf*
punctuality	пунктуа́льность *nf*
respectability	респекта́бельность *nf*
self-criticism	самокри́тика *nf*
self-discipline	самодисципли́на *nf*
sense of humor	чу́вство ю́мора *nn, nm*

sensualism	сенсуали́зм *nm*
sentimentalism	сентиментали́зм *nm*
seriousness	серьёзность *nf*
spontaneity	спонта́нность *nf*
subjectivity	субъекти́вность *nf*
tact	такт *nm*, такти́чность *nf*
tactfulness	такти́чность *nf*
talent	тала́нт *nm*
virtuosity	виртуо́зность *nf*

UNDESIRABLE QUALITIES

affectation	аффекта́ция *nf*
aggressiveness	агресси́вность *nf*
amorality	амора́льность *nf*
antagonism	антагони́зм *nm*
antipathy	антипа́тия *nf*
apathy	апа́тия *nf*
bad manners	плохи́е мане́ры *nmpl*
bravado	брава́да *nf*
capriciousness	капри́зность *nf*
charlatanism	шарлата́нство *nn*
chauvinism	шовини́зм *nm*
conformism	конформи́зм *nm*
cynicism	цини́чность *nf*
decadence	декаде́нтство *nn*, декаданс *nm*
degeneracy	дегенерати́вность *nf*
despotism	деспоти́зм *nm*
dictatorial attitude	диктато́рство *nn*
disloyalty	нелоя́льность *nf*
doctrinaire attitude	доктринёрство *nn*
dogmatism	догмати́зм *nm*
eccentricity	эксцентри́чность *nf*
egocentrism	эгоцентри́зм *nm*
egoism	эгои́зм *nm*
egotism	эготи́зм *nm*
extravagance	экстрава́гантность *nf*
fanaticism	фанати́зм *nm*
frivolity	фриво́льность *nf*
immorality	амора́льность *nf*
impracticality	непракти́чность *nf*
inaccuracy	неаккура́тность *nf*
incompetence	некомпете́нтность *nf*
indelicacy	неделика́тность *nf*
indifference	индифферéнтность *nf*
ineffectiveness	неэффекти́вность *nf*
inelegance	неэлега́нтность *nf*
lack of control	бесконтро́льность *nf*
lack of discipline	недисциплини́рованность *nf*
lack of ideas	безыде́йность *nf*
lack of initiative	безынициати́вность *nf*
lethargy	летарги́я *nf*
masochism	мазохи́зм *nm*
misanthropy	мизантро́пия *nf*
naivete	наи́вность *nf*
opportunism	оппортуни́зм *nm*
passivity	пасси́вность *nf*
pedantry	педанти́зм *nm*, педанти́чность *nf*
pessimism	пессими́зм *nm*
pomposity	помпе́зность *nf*
pretentiousness	претенцио́зность *nf*
provincialism	провинциа́льность *nf*
quixotry, quixotism	донкихо́тство *nn*
rigorism	ригори́зм *nm*
sadism	сади́зм *nm*
sentimentality	сентимента́льность *nf*
snobbery, snobbishness	сноби́зм *nm*
tactlessness	беста́ктность, нетакти́чность *nf*
tendentiousness	тенденцио́зность *nf*
vulgarity	вульга́рность *nf*

DESCRIPTIVE EXPRESSIONS

nerves of steel	стальны́е не́рвы *nmpl*
salt of the earth	соль земли́ *nf*, *nf*
second nature	втора́я нату́ра *nf*

See also **PSYCHOLOGY**, **EMOTIONS AND EXPERIENCES**

EMOTIONS AND EXPERIENCES

GENERAL TERMS

activity	акти́вность *nf*
emotion	эмо́ция *nf*
fortune	форту́на *nf*
sensualism	сенсуали́зм *nm*
tactile	такти́льный *aj*

FEELINGS

pleasant

comfort	комфо́рт *nm*
ecstacy	экста́з *nm*
euphoria	эйфори́я *nf*
exaltation	экзальта́ция *nf*
nostalgia	ностальги́я *nf*

unpleasant

apathy	апа́тия *nf*

frustration	фрустра́ция *nf*
fury	фу́рия *nf*
melancholy	меланхо́лия *nf*
nervousness	не́рвность, нерво́зность *nf*
panic	па́ника *nf*
revenge	рева́нш *nm*
shock	шок *nm*
trepidation	тре́пет *nm*
Weltschmerz	ве́льтшмерц *nm*

ACTIONS AND EVENTS

beneficial effect

adventure	авантю́ра *nf*
applause *nsg*	аплодисме́нты *nmpl*
approbation, approval	апроба́ция *nf*
caprice	капри́з *nm*
ceremony	церемо́ния *nf*
communication	коммуника́ция *nf*
company	компа́ния *nf*
compliment	компли́мент *nm*
compromise	компроми́сс *nm*
constructive criticism	конструкти́вная кри́тика *nf*
cooperation	коопера́ция *nf*
correction [result]	корре́кция, корректиро́вка *nf*
correction [act]	корректи́рование *nn*
escapade	эскапа́да *nf*
favoritism (BR favouritism)	фаворити́зм *nm*
harmony	гармо́ния *nf*
initiative	инициати́ва *nf*
laurels	ла́вры *nmpl*
popularity	популя́рность *nf*
prestige	прести́ж *nm*
progress	прогре́сс *nm*
recommendation	рекоменда́ция *nf*
rendevous	рандеву́ *nn, indecl*

harmful effect

anomaly	анома́лия *nf*
automobile accident	автомоби́льная ава́рия *nf*
banality	бана́льность *nf*
bedlam	бедла́м *nm*
catastrophe	катастро́фа *nf*
chaos	ха́ос *nm*
collision	колли́зия *nf*
confiscation	конфиска́ция *nf*
conflict	конфли́кт *nm*
confrontation	конфронта́ция *nf*
defamation	диффама́ция *nf*
degeneration	дегенера́ция *nf*
degradation	деграда́ция *nf*
dehumanization	дегуманиза́ция *nf*
demoralization	деморализа́ция *nf*
deprivation	деприва́ция *nf*
dilemma	диле́мма *nf*
discreditation	дискредита́ция *nf*
discrimination	дискримина́ция *nf*
disorganization	дезорганиза́ция *nf*
disorientation	дезориента́ция *nf*
dispute	диспу́т *nm*
domination	домини́рование *nn*
exploitation	эксплуата́ция *nf*
expropriation	экспроприа́ция *nf*
falsification	фальсифика́ция *nf*
familiarity [disrespect]	фамилья́рность *nf*
fiasco (*pl* fiascoes)	фиа́ско *nn, indecl*
furor, furore	фуро́р *nm*
idiocy [stupid behavior]	идио́тство *nn*
intrigue	интрига́нство *nn*
machination	махина́ция *nf*
manipulation	манипуля́ция *nf*
misalliance	мезалья́нс *nm*
misinterpretation	неве́рная интерпрета́ция *nf*
ostracism	острaки́зм *nm*
panic-mongering	паникёрство *nn*
protest	проте́ст *nm*
provocation	провока́ция *nf*
racism (BR racialism)	раси́зм *nm*
routine	рути́на *nf*
scandal	сканда́л *nm*
stigma (*pl* stigmas, stigmata)	сти́гма *nf*
tragedy	траги́чность *nf*
travesty	травести́ *nn, indecl*
tyranny	тирани́я *nn*
ultimatum (*pl* ultimatums, ultimata)	ультима́тум *nm*
unpopularity	непопуля́рность *nf*
vendetta	венде́тта *nf*
vulgarization	вульгариза́ция *nf*

See also **VALUE JUDGMENTS**, **SIZE AND DEGREE**

VALUE JUDGMENTS

UNUSUAL

atypical, untypical	нетипи́чный *aj*
eclectic	эклекти́ческий, эклекти́чный *aj*
esoteric	эзотери́ческий *aj*

idiosyncratic | идиосинкрази́ческий *aj*
individualistic | индивидуалисти́ческий *aj*
original | оригина́льный *aj*
uncharacteristic | не характе́рный *aj*
untraditional | нетрадицио́нный *aj*

FAVORABLE

accurate | аккура́тный *aj*
active | акти́вный *aj*
adventurous | авантю́рный *aj*
altruistic [person] | альтруисти́чный *aj*
altruistic [action] | альтруисти́ческий *aj*
ambitious | амбицио́зный *aj*
attractive | аттракти́вный *aj*
ceremonious | церемо́нный *aj*
charismatic | харизмати́ческий *aj*
classy, high-class | кла́ссный *aj*
comfortable | комфорта́бельный *aj*
communicative | коммуника́бельный *aj*
companionable | компане́йский *aj*
compromising | компроми́ссный *aj*
concrete | конкре́тный *aj*
congenial | конгениа́льный *aj*
constructive | конструкти́вный *aj*
coordinating | координацио́нный *aj*
correct | корре́ктный *aj*
cultured | культу́рный *aj*
detailed | дета́льный *aj*
diplomatic | дипломати́чный *aj*
disciplined | дисциплини́рованный *aj*
dramatic | драмати́чный *aj*
dynamic | динами́чный *aj*
economical | эконо́мный *aj*
ecstatic | экстати́ческий *aj*
effective | эффекти́вный *aj*
elegant | элега́нтный *aj*
empathetic, empathic | эмпати́ческий *aj*
energetic | энерги́чный *aj*
enthusiastic | по́лный энтузиа́зма *aj*
ethical | эти́чный *aj*
euphoric | эйфори́йный *aj*
exalted | экзальти́рованный *aj*
expert | э́кспертный *aj*
gallant | гала́нтный *aj*
gentlemanly | джентльме́нский *aj*
graceful | грацио́зный *aj*
harmonious | гармони́чный *aj*
heroic [person] | геро́йский *aj*
heroic [act] | герои́ческий *aj*
humane | гума́нный *aj*
humanitarian | гуманита́рный *aj*
humorous | юмористи́ческий *aj*
idealistic | идеалисти́чный *aj*
informed | информи́рованный *aj*
intellectual | интеллектуа́льный *aj*
intelligent | интеллиге́нтный *aj*
interesting | интере́сный *aj*
intimate | инти́мный *aj*
intriguing | интригу́ющий *aj*
intuitive | интуити́вный *aj*
liberal | либера́льный *aj*
logical | логи́чный *aj*
loyal | лоя́льный *aj*
methodical | методи́ческий, методи́чный *aj*
moral | мора́льный *aj*
normal | норма́льный *aj*
objective | объекти́вный *aj*
optimistic | оптимисти́ческий, оптимисти́чный *aj*
philanthropic | филантропи́ческий *aj*
philosophical | филосо́фский *aj*
popular | популя́рный *aj*
practical | практи́ческий, практи́чный *aj*
pragmatic | прагмати́ческий *aj*
presentable | презента́бельный *aj*
prestigious | прести́жный *aj*
principled | принципиа́льный *aj*
progressive | прогресси́вный *aj*
rational | рациона́льный *aj*
realistic | реалисти́чный *aj*
relevant | релева́нтный *aj*
respectable | респекта́бельный *aj*
romantic | романти́ческий, романти́чный *aj*
rosy | ро́зовый *aj*
sanguine | сангвини́ческий *aj*
sensual | сенсуали́стский *aj*
sentimental | сентимента́льный *aj*
serious | серьёзный *aj*
simpatico | симпати́чный, симпати́ческий *aj*
solid [reliable] | соли́дный *aj*
spontaneous | спонта́нный *aj*
steely | стально́й *aj*
stimulating | стимули́рующий *aj*
stoical | стои́ческий *aj*
subjective | субъекти́вный *aj*
tactful | такти́чный *aj*
talented | тала́нтливый *aj*

traditional	традицио́нный *aj*
utilitarian	утилита́рный *aj*
well-organized	организо́ванный *aj*

UNFAVORABLE

aggressive	агресси́вный *aj*
amoral, immoral	амора́льный *aj*
anomalous	анома́льный *aj*
antagonistic	антагонисти́ческий *aj*
antipathetic	антипати́чный *aj*
antisocial	антисоциа́льный *aj*
apathetic	апати́чный *aj*
authoritarian	авторита́рный *aj*
banal	бана́льный *aj*
barbaric, barbarous	ва́рварский *aj*
capricious	капри́зный *aj*
catastrophic	катастрофи́ческий *aj*
chaotic	хаоти́ческий *aj*
characterless	бесхара́ктерный *aj*
chauvinistic	шовинисти́ческий *aj*
compromising	компромети́рующий *aj*
conflicting	конфли́ктный *aj*
corrupt	коррумпи́рованный *aj*
critical	крити́чный *aj*
cynical	цини́чный, цини́ческий *aj*
decadent	декаде́нтский *aj*
degenerate	дегенерати́вный *aj*
demoralized	деморализо́ванный *aj*
despotic	деспоти́чный *aj*
diabolic(al)	дья́вольский *aj*
dictatorial	дикта́торский *aj*
disinterested, uninterested	незаинтересо́ванный *aj*
disloyal	нелоя́льный *aj*
disorganized	неорганизо́ванный *aj*
doctrinaire	доктринёрский *aj*
dogmatic	догмати́ческий *aj*
eccentric	эксцентри́чный *aj*
egocentric	эгоцентри́ческий *aj*
egoistic(al)	эгоисти́чный *aj*
egotistical	эгоисти́ческий *aj*
extravagant	экстравага́нтный *aj*
false	фальши́вый *aj*
fanatical	фанати́чный, фанати́ческий *aj*
fragmentary	фрагмента́рный *aj*
frivolous	фриво́льный *aj*
idiotic	идио́тский, идиоти́ческий *aj*
immoral	иммора́льный *aj*
impractical [thing]	непракти́ческий *aj*
impractical [person]	непракти́чный *aj*
impulsive	импульси́вный *aj*
inaccurate	неаккура́тный *aj*
incompetent	некомпете́нтный *aj*
indelicate	неделика́тный *aj*
indifferent	индифференти́ный *aj*
ineffective, ineffectual	неэффекти́вный *aj*
inelegant	неэлега́нтный *aj*
infantile	инфанти́льный *aj*
inhumane	негума́нный, антигума́нный *aj*
irrational	иррациона́льный, нерациона́льный *aj*
irrelevant	нерелева́нтный *aj*
lethargic	летарги́ческий *aj*
mannered	мане́рный *aj*
masochistic	мазохи́стский *aj*
melodramatic	мелодрамати́чный *aj*
misanthropic	мизантропи́ческий, мизантро́пский *aj*
naive	наи́вный *aj*
negative	негати́вный *aj*
nerve-wracking	нерви́рующий *aj*
nervous	не́рвный, нерво́зный *aj*
odious	одио́зный *aj*
opportunistic	оппортунисти́ческий, оппортуни́стский *aj*
over-emotional	сли́шком эмоциона́льный *aj*
overly familiar	фамилья́рный *aj*
parasitic	парази́тный, паразити́ческий *aj*
passive	пасси́вный *aj*
pathetic	патети́ческий *aj*
pedantic	педанти́чный *aj*
pessimistic	пессимисти́ческий *aj*
pompous	помпе́зный *aj*
pretentious	претенцио́зный *aj*
prosaic	прозаи́чный *aj*
provincial	провинциа́льный *aj*
provocative	провокацио́нный *aj*
puritanical	курита́нский *aj*
quixotic	донкихо́тский *aj*
revengeful	реванши́стский *aj*
risqué	риско́ванный *aj*
sadistic	сади́стский *aj*
sarcastic	саркасти́ческий *aj*
sardonic	сардони́ческий *aj*
satanic	сатани́нский *aj*
scandalous	сканда́льный *aj*
snobbish	сноби́стский *aj*

sociopathic — социопати́ческий *aj*
sybaritic — сибари́тский *aj*
tactless — нетакти́чный, беста́ктный *aj*
temperamental — темпера́ментный *aj*
tendentious — тенденцио́зный *aj*
tragic — траги́чный *aj*
trivial — тривиа́льный *aj*
tyrannical — тирани́ческий *aj*
ultraconservative — кра́йне консервати́вный *aj*
unceremonious — бесцеремо́нный *aj*
uncomfortable — некомфорта́бельный *aj*
uncommunicative — некоммуника́бельный *aj*
uncompromising — бескомпроми́ссный *aj*
uncontrolled — неконтроли́руемый, бесконтро́льный *aj*
uncritical — некрити́чный, некрити́ческий *aj*
uncultured — некульту́рный *aj*
undiplomatic — недипломати́чный *aj*
undisciplined — недисциплини́рованный *aj*
undiscriminating — недискримини́рующий *aj*
unemotional — неэмоциона́льный *aj*
unesthetic (BR unaesthetic) — неэстети́чный *aj*
unethical — неэти́чный *aj*
uninteresting — неинтере́сный *aj*
unoriginal — неоригина́льный *aj*
unpopular — непопуля́рный *aj*
unpresentable — непрезента́бельный *aj*
unpretentious — непретенцио́зный *aj*, без прете́нзий
unprincipled — беспринци́пный *aj*
unrealistic — нереалисти́чный *aj*
unromantic — нероманти́ческий, нероманти́чный *aj*
unsentimental — несентимента́льный *aj*
untalented — нетала́нтливый *aj*
vulgar — вульга́рный *aj*

See also **CHARACTER TRAITS**, **SIZE AND DEGREE**

Forms of Address

PERSONAL NAMES ◆ TITLES ◆ FAMOUS FIGURES OF YESTERDAY AND TODAY

PERSONAL NAMES*

GENERAL TERMS

anonymity	анони́мность *nf*
eponym	эпони́м *nm*
family name	фами́лия *nf*
identity	иденти́чность *nf*
incognito	инко́гнито *av*
Joneses, the	Джо́нсы *npl*
Mister X	ми́стер Икс *nm*
onomastics *nplsv*	онома́стика *nf*
patronymic	патрони́м *nm*
pseudonym	псевдони́м *nm*

FEMININE NAMES

Biblical

Deborah (Debby)	Дебо́ра *nf*
Elizabeth (Bess, Betty, Betsy, Liza)	Елизаве́та (Ли́за) *nf*
Esther (Essie)	Эсфи́рь *nf*
Eva, Eve	Е́ва *nf*
Hannah	А́нна *nf*
Josephine (Jo)	Жосе́фа, Жозефи́на *nf*
Judith (Judy)	Юди́фь *nf*
Leah	Ле́я, Ли́я *nf*
Mary (May, Molly)	Мэ́ри, Мари́я *nf*
Miriam	Мириа́м *nf*
Naomi	Ноэ́ми *nf*
Paula	Па́вла *nf*
Rachel	Рахи́ль *nf*
Rebecca (Becky)	Ребе́кка, Реве́кка *nf*
Ruth (Ruthy)	Руфь *nf*
Sarah	Са́рра, Са́ра *nf*

Greek or Latin

Adrienne	Адриа́на *nf*
Agatha	Ага́та *nf*
Agnes	Агне́сса *nf*
Alexandra (Sandy)	Алекса́ндра *nf*
Anastasia (Stacy)	Анаста́сия (На́стя) *nf*
Angela	Анже́ла *nf*
Angelica	Анже́лика *nf*
Angelina	Ангели́на *nf*
Annabelle	Анабе́лла *nf*
Antonia	Анто́ния *nf*
Arabella	Арабе́лла *nf*
Augusta	Авгу́ста *nf*
Augustine	Августи́на *nf*
Aurora	Авро́ра *nf*
Barbara (Babs)	Варва́ра (Ва́ря) *nf*
Beatrice (Bea)	Беатри́са *nf*
Camille, Camilla	Ками́лла *nf*
Catherine (Kate, Katie, Kitty, Cathy)	Екатери́на (Ка́тя) *nf*
Cecelia, Cecily	Сеси́лия, Цеци́лия *nf*
Christine, Christina (Tina)	Кристи́на, Христи́на *nf*
Clara	Кла́ра *nf*
Clarissa	Клари́сса *nf*
Claudia	Кла́вдия *nf*
Clementine	Клементи́на *nf*
Constance (Connie)	Конста́нция *nf*
Cora	Ко́ра *nf*
Cornelia	Корне́лия *nf*
Daphne	Да́фна *nf*
Diana	Диа́на *nf*
Dominica	Домини́ка *nf*
Dora	До́ра *nf*
Doris	До́рис *nf*
Dorothy (Dottie)	Дороте́я, Дорофе́я *nf*
Eleanor	Элеоно́ра *nf*
Ella	Э́лла *nf*
Ellen (Ellie)	Эле́на, Эле́н (Ле́на) *nf*
Emily	Э́ми́лия *nf*
Eugenia	Евге́ния *nf*
Felicia	Фели́ция *nf*
Flora	Фло́ра *nf*
Florence (Flo, Floy)	Флоре́нция *nf*
Georgina	Георги́на *nf*
Gloria	Глорио́за *nf*
Grace (Gracie)	Гра́ция *nf*
Helen, Helena	Еле́на (Ле́на) *nf*
Hilary	Хи́лари *nf*
Hortense	Горте́нзия *nf*
Inez	Ине́сса *nf*
Irene	Ири́на (И́ра) *nf*
Isadora	Исидо́ра *nf*

* Names in parentheses are diminutive forms.

Julia	Ю́лия *nf*
Juliana (Julie)	Юлиа́на *nf*
Juliet	Джулье́тта *nf*
June	Юния *nf*
Justina	Юсти́на *nf*
Laura (Lauretta, Loretta)	Лау́ра *nf*
Lavinia	Лави́ния *nf*
Leona	Лео́ния *nf*
Lila, Leila	Ле́йла *nf*
Lillian	Лилиа́на *nf*
Lily	Ли́лия *nf*
Lucretia	Лукре́ция *nf*
Lucy	Лю́ция *nf*
Lydia	Ли́дия (Ли́да) *nf*
Madeline	Магдали́на *nf*
Mae, May	Ма́я *nf*
Magda	Ма́гда *nf*
Margaret (Marge, Marjorie, Margie, Meg, Greta, Rita)	Маргари́та *nf*
Monica	Мо́ника *nf*
Octavia	Окта́вия *nf*
Odette	Оде́тта *nf*
Olive, Olivia	Оли́вия *nf*
Olympia	Оли́мпия *nf*
Ophelia	Офе́лия *nf*
Patricia (Pat, Patty)	Патри́кия *nf*
Philippa	Фили́ппия *nf*
Priscilla	Приски́лла *nf*
Regina	Реги́на *nf*
Rose, Rosa (Rosie)	Ро́за *nf*
Sibyl, Sybil	Сиби́лла *nf*
Sophia, Sophie	Со́фья (Со́ня) *nf*
Stephanie	Стефа́ния *nf*
Sylvia, Silvia	Си́львия *nf*
Theodora (Theo)	Федо́ра *nf*
Theresa (Terry)	Тере́за *nf*
Ursula	Урсу́ла *nf*
Valentina	Валенти́на (Ва́ля) *nf*
Vera	Ве́ра *nf*
Veronica	Верони́ка *nf*
Victoria (Vicky)	Викто́рия *nf*
Viola (Vi)	Вио́ла *nf*
Violet (Vi)	Виоле́тта *nf*
Vivian	Вивиа́на *nf*

Germanic

Adele	Аде́ль *nf*
Alberta	Альбе́рта *nf*
Alice	Али́са *nf*
Amelia	Ама́лия *nf*
Bertha	Бе́рта *nf*
Bridgit	Бриги́тта *nf*
Caroline	Кароли́на *nf*
Edith (Edie)	Э́дит, Эди́т *nf*
Eloise	Элои́за *nf*
Emma	Э́мма *nf*
Ernestine	Эрнести́на *nf*
Frances (Fran, Fanny)	Франче́ска, Франци́ска *nf*
Frederica	Фридери́ка *nf*
Frieda	Фри́да *nf*
Gertrude (Gert, Trudy)	Гертру́да *nf*
Henrietta (Etta, Hetty)	Генрие́тта *nf*
Hilda	Хи́льда *nf*
Ida	И́да *nf*
Irma	И́рма *nf*
Isold(e)	Изо́льда *nf*
Louise, Louisa	Луи́за *nf*
Matilda (Matty, Tilly)	Мати́льда *nf*
Pauline	Паули́на, Па́ула, Пао́ла *nf*
Roberta (Bobby)	Робе́рта *nf*
Rosalind	Розали́нда *nf*
Virginia (Ginny)	Вирги́ния *nf*
Wilhemina	Вильгельми́на *nf*

Russian

Masha	Ма́ша *nf*
Nadezhda	Наде́жда (На́дя) *nf*
Natasha	Ната́ша *nf*
Olga	О́льга (О́ля, Лёля) *nf*
Svetlana	Светла́на *nf*
Tamara	Тама́ра *nf*
Tatiana	Татья́на (Та́ня) *nf*
Vera	Ве́ра *nf*

French

Bernadette	Бернаде́т *nf*
Celeste, Celestina	Селе́ста *nf*
Charlotte (Lottie)	Шарло́тта *nf*
Lorraine	Лора́н *nf*
Lotta	Ло́та *nf*
Maria, Marie	Мари́я *nf*
Natalie	Ната́лья *nf*
Nicole	Ни́кола *nf*
Rosalie	Роза́лия *nf*
Stella	Сте́лла *nf*
Susan (Sue, Susanna, Susie)	Сюза́нна *nf*
Valerie (Val)	Вале́рия *nf*

English, Irish, Celtic, Welsh

Audrey	О́дри *nf*
Cordelia	Корде́лия *nf*
Evelyn	Эвели́на *nf*

Mildred (Millie)	Ми́лдред *nf*
Muriel	Мю́риель *nf*
Nora	Но́ра *nf*
Winifred (Frieda, Winnie)	Уи́нифред *nf*

Hebrew

Ada	А́да *nf*
Ann, Anne, Anna (Annie, Nancy)	А́нна (А́ня, Аню́та, А́ннушка) *nf*
Dinah	Ди́на *nf*
Edna	Э́дна *nf*
Lilith	Лили́т *nf*

other names

Bella	Бе́лла *nf*
Dolores	Доло́рес *nf*
Elvira	Эльви́ра *nf*
Ethel	Эте́ль *nf*
Greta	Гре́та *nf*
Inga	И́нга *nf*
Isabel, Isabella (Bella)	Изабе́лла *nf*
Janet, Jenny	Жане́та *nf*
Joan, Joanna	Ио́анна *nf*
Larissa	Лари́са *nf*
Lenore, Leonora, Leonore (Nora)	Леоно́ра *nf*
Lola	Ло́лия (Ло́ла) *nf*
Lorna	Ло́рна *nf*
Ludmilla	Людми́ла (Лю́да, Ми́ла) *nf*
Marian	Мариа́на *nf*
Marianne	Мариа́нна, Марья́на *nf*
Marietta	Марие́тта *nf*
Marlene	Марле́на *nf*
Martha	Ма́рта *nf*
Melanie	Мела́ния, Мела́нья *nf*
Nellie, Nelly	Не́лли *nf*
Nina	Ни́на *nf*
Nona	Но́нна *nf*
Roxanne	Рокса́на *nf*
Sabina	Саби́на *nf*

MASCULINE NAMES

Biblical

Aaron	Аро́н *nm*
Abel	А́бель, А́вель *nm*
Abraham (Abe, Abie)	А́брахам, Абра́м, Авраа́м *nm*
Adam	Ада́м *nm*
Amos	Амо́с *nm*
Barnaby	Варна́ва *nm*
Bartholomew (Bart)	Варфоломе́й *nm*
Benjamin (Ben, Benny)	Вениами́н *nm*
Daniel (Dan, Danny)	Дании́л *nm*
David (Dave)	Дави́д, Дэ́вид *nm*
Elijah	Илия́ *nm*
Emmanuel, Imanuel (Manny)	Эммануи́л, Иммануи́л *nm*
Enoch	Ено́х *nm*
Ezekiel (Zeke)	Иезеки́иль *nm*
Ezra	Е́здра *nm*
Gabriel (Gabe)	Гаврии́л *nm*
Gideon	Гидео́н *nm*
Isaac (Ike)	Исаа́к *nm*
Isaiah	Иса́й(я) *nm*
Jacob (Jake)	Иа́ков, Я́ков (Я́ша) *nm*
James (Jimmy)	Джеймс, Я́ков *nm*
Jeremiah	Иереми́я *nm*
Jeremy	Дже́реми *nm*
John (Johnny)	Иоа́нн, Джон, Ива́н *nm*
Jonathan	Ионафа́н *nm*
Joseph (Joe, Joey)	Ио́сиф (О́ся) *nm*
Joshua (Josh)	Джо́шуа, Иешу́а *nm*
Lazarus	Лаза́рь *nm*
Luke	Лука́ *nm*
Mark	Марк *nm*
Matthew (Matt)	Матве́й *nm*
Matthias	Матфе́й *nm*
Michael (Mike, Mickey)	Михаи́л *nm*
Nathan (Nat, Nate)	Ната́н *nm*
Nathaniel	Натаниэ́ль *nm*
Noah	Ной *nm*
Paul	Па́вел (Па́влик, Па́ша) *nm*
Peter (Pete)	Пётр (Пе́тя) *nm*
Raphael	Рафаи́л *nm*
Samuel (Sam)	Самуи́л *nm*
Saul	Сау́л *nm*
Simon (Si, Sy)	Си́мон, Семён (Се́ня) *nm*
Solomon (Sol)	Соломо́н *nm*
Thomas (Tom, Tommy)	Фома́ *nm*
Timothy (Tim)	Тимофе́й *nm*
Tobias (Toby)	Тоба́йес, То́вий *nm*

Greek or Latin

Adrian, Hadrian	Адриа́н *nm*
Alex, Alec	А́лек, Але́ксе́й (Алёша, Лёша) *nm*
Alexander (Al, Aleck, Alex, Sandy)	Алекса́ндр (Са́ша, Шу́ра) *nm*
Alexis	Алексе́й *nm*

Ambrose	Амбро́сий *nm*
Andrew (Andy)	Андре́й (Андрю́ша) *nm*
Anthony (Tony)	Анто́н, Антони́н *nm*
August, Augustus (Augie)	Авгу́ст *nm*
Basil	Васи́лий (Ва́ся) *nm*
Benedict	Бенеди́кт *nm*
Cecil	Сесл *nm*
Christian	Кри́стиан, Христиа́н *nm*
Christopher (Chris, Kit)	Кри́стофер, Христофо́р *nm*
Claudius	Кла́вдий *nm*
Clement (Clem)	Климе́нт, Климе́нтий *nm*
Constantine	Константи́н (Ко́стя) *nm*
Cornelius	Корни́лий *nm*
Cyril	Кири́лл *nm*
Cyrus (Cy)	Са́йрус, Кир *nm*
Dennis (Denny)	Дени́с *nm*
Dominick	Домини́к *nm*
Dorian	Дориа́н *nm*
Emil	Эми́ль *nm*
Eugene (Gene)	Евге́ний (Же́ня) *nm*
Felix	Фе́ликс *nm*
George (Georgie)	Гео́ргий *nm*
Gregory (Greg)	Григо́рий (Гри́ша) *nm*
Horace, Horatio	Гора́ций *nm*
Ignatius	Игна́тий *nm*
Isidor(e) (Izzy)	Исидо́р *nm*
Jerome (Jerry)	Джеро́м *nm*
Jules	Ю́лий *nm*
Julian	Юлиа́н *nm*
Julius	Ю́лиус *nm*
Justin	Юсти́н *nm*
Laurence, Lawrence	Ло́ренс, Лавре́нтий *nm*
Leo	Ле́о *nm*
Leon	Лео́н *nm*
Leonard (Lenny)	Леона́рд *nm*
Lucius	Люциа́н *nm*
Marcus (Mark)	Ма́ркус *nm*
Martin (Marty)	Марти́н *nm*
Maximilian (Max)	Максимилья́н *nm*
Nicholas (Nick, Nicky)	Никола́й (Ко́ля) *nm*
Patrick (Pat, Paddy)	Па́трик, Патри́ций, Патри́кий *nm*
Philip (Phil)	Фили́пп *nm*
Sebastian	Себастья́н *nm*
Silvester, Sylvester	Сильве́стр *nm*
Stephen (Steve)	Степа́н (Стёпа) *nm*
Theodore (Ted, Theo)	Фёдор (Фе́дя) *nm*
Valentine (Val)	Валенти́н *nm*
Victor (Vic)	Ви́ктор *nm*
Vincent (Vince)	Винсе́нт, Вике́нтий *nm*

Germanic

Adolf, Adolph	Адо́льф *nm*
Albert (Al, Bert, Bertie)	Альбе́рт *nm*
Alfred (Alf)	Альфре́д *nm*
Alphonso	Альфо́нс *nm*
Archibald (Archie)	Арчиба́льд *nm*
Arnold (Arnie)	Арнольд *nm*
Aubrey	О́бри *nm*
Bernard (Bernie)	Берна́рд *nm*
Bertram (Bert, Bertie)	Бертра́м *nm*
Carl, Karl	Карл *nm*
Charles (Charlie)	Чарльз *nm*
Conrad	Ко́нрад *nm*
Edgar	Э́дгар, Эдга́р *nm*
Edmund (Ed, Ned)	Э́дмунд, Эдму́нд *nm*
Eric	Э́рик *nm*
Ernest, Ernst (Ernie)	Эрне́ст, Эрнст *nm*
Ferdinand	Фердина́нд *nm*
Francis (Frank, Frankie)	Фра́нсис, Франци́ск *nm*
Frederick (Fred, Freddy)	Фредери́к, Фри́дрих *nm*
Fritz	Фриц *nm*
Gerald (Gerry)	Дже́ральд *nm*
Gerard	Гера́рд *nm*
Gilbert (Gil)	Ги́льберт *nm*
Godfrey	Го́дфри *nm*
Hans	Ганс *nm*
Harold (Harry)	Га́рольд *nm*
Henry (Hal)	Ге́нрих *nm*
Herman	Ге́рман *nm*
Hubert	Хью́берт *nm*
Leopold (Leo)	Леопо́льд *nm*
Lewis, Louis (Lew, Lewie, Lou)	Лью́ис, Людо́вик, Лу́ис *nm*
Ralph	Ральф *nm*
Raymond (Ray)	Раимо́нд *nm*
Reginald (Reggie)	Реджина́льд, Регина́льд *nm*
Richard (Dick, Richy)	Ри́чард *nm*
Robert (Bob, Bobbie, Rob, Robbie)	Ро́берт *nm*
Roderick (Rod, Roddy)	Ро́дерик *nm*
Roger	Ри́джер *nm*
Rudolph (Rudy)	Рудо́льф *nm*
Rupert	Ру́перт *nm*
Sigmund (Ziggy)	Сигизму́нд *nm*
Walter (Walt)	Уо́лтер, Ва́льтер *nm*

William (Bill, Billy, Will, Willy)	Уи́льям, Вилья́м, Вильге́льм *nm*

Russian

Arcadiy	Арка́дий *nm*
Boris	Бори́с (Бо́ря) *nm*
Dmitri	Дми́трий (Ми́тя, Ди́ма) *nm*
Igor	И́горь *nm*
Ilya	Илья́ (Илью́ша) *mn*
Ivan	Ива́н (Ва́ня) *nm*
Mischa	Ми́ша *nm*
Oleg	Оле́г *nm*
Ossip	О́сип (О́ся) *nm*
Serge	Серге́й (Серёжа) *nm*
Stanislav (Stan)	Станисла́в *nm*
Vadim	Вади́м *nm*
Vladimir	Владимир (Воло́дя, Во́ва) *nm*
Wassily	Васи́лий *nm*
Yuri	Ю́рий (Ю́ра) *nm*

French

Algernon	Э́лджернон *nm*
Claud, Claude	Клод *nm*
Guy	Гви́до *nm*
Lionel	Лионе́ль *nm*
Marion	Марио́н *nm*
Maurice (Maury)	Мо́рис, Маври́кий *nm*
Morris (Morry)	Мо́рис *nm*
Noel	Ноэ́ль *nm*
Oliver	О́ливер *nm*
Roland	Ро́ланд *nm*
Ronald (Ron, Ronnie)	Ро́нальд, Рона́льд *nm*

English, Irish, Celtic, Welsh

Donald (Don, Donny)	До́нальд *nm*
Douglas (Doug)	Ду́гласс *nm*
Duncan	Дунка́н *nm*
Edward (Ed, Eddie, Ted)	Эдуа́рд *nm*
Edwin (Ed, Ned)	Э́двин *nm*
Elmer	Э́лмер *nm*
Herbert (Herb, Herbie)	Ге́рберт *nm*
Humphrey	Ха́мфри, Ге́мфри *nm*
Meredith	Мереди́т *nm*
Morgan	Мо́рган *nm*
Oscar	Оска́р *nm*
Oswald (Ossie)	Освальд *nm*

other origins

Alan (Al)	Ала́н *nm*
Allen (Al)	Алла́н *nm*
Arthur (Art, Artie)	Арту́р *nm*
Caspar	Каспа́р *nm*
Clifford (Cliff)	Кли́ффорд *nm*
Elliot	Э́ллиот, Эллио́т *nm*
Howard (Howie)	Го́вард *nm*
Hugh, Hugo	Хью, Хью́го *nm*
Ismael	Измаи́л *nm*
Lucas	Лу́кас *nm*
Manuel (Manny)	Мануе́ль *nm*
Maxim (Max)	Макси́м *nm*
Mortimer (Mort, Mortie)	Мо́ртимер *nm*
Rodney	Родио́н (Ро́дя) *nm*
Ruben	Рубе́н *nm*
Sidney (Sid)	Си́дней *nm*

See also **THE BIBLE**

TITLES

GENERAL TERMS

designation	десигна́ция *nf*
post	пост *nm*
rank	ранг *nm*
title	ти́тул *nm*

KINDS OF TITLES

political and administrative

burgomaster	бургоми́стр *nm*
cacique	каси́к *nm*
chancellor	ка́нцлер *nm*
congressman (*pl* congressmen)	конгрессме́н *nm*
congresswoman (*pl* congresswomen)	же́нщина-конгрессме́н *nf*
consul	ко́нсул *nm*
consul-general	генера́льный ко́нсул *nm*
deputy	депута́т *nm*
emir	эми́р *nm*
emperor	импера́тор *nm*
empress	императри́ца *nf*
First Lady	пе́рвая ле́ди *nf*
Fuhrer [obs]	фю́рер *nm*
governor	губерна́тор *nm*
kadi, cadi	ка́ди *nm, indecl*
khan	хан *nm*
Lord Mayor	лорд-мэ́р *nm*
mayor	мэр *nm*
minister	мини́стр *nm*
minister without portfolio	мини́стр без портфе́ля *nm, nm*
premier	премье́р *nm*
president	президе́нт *nm*

prime minister	премье́р-мини́стр *nm*
regent	ре́гент *nm*
secretary	секрета́рь *nf*
secretary-general	генера́льный секрета́рь *nm*
senator	сена́тор *nm*
sheik(h)	шейх *nm*
Speaker [USA House of Representatives]	спи́кер *nm*
sultan	султа́н *nm*
sultana	султа́нша *nf*
vice-chancellor	вице-ка́нцлер *nm*
vice-consul	вице-ко́нсул *nm*
vice-president	вице-президе́нт *nm*

military

adjutant general	генера́л-адъюта́нт *nm*
admiral	адмира́л *nm*
brigadier general	брига́дный генера́л, бригади́р *nm*
cadet	каде́т *nm*
captain	капита́н *nm*
commodore	коммодо́р *nm*
corporal	капра́л *nm*
field marshal	фельдма́ршал *nm*
first lieutenant	ста́рший лейтена́нт *nm*
general	генера́л *nm*
generalissimo	генерали́ссимус *nm*
lieutenant	лейтена́нт *nm*
lieutenant-general	генера́л-лейтена́нт *nm*
major	майо́р *nm*
major general	генера́л-майо́р *nm*
marshall	ма́ршал *nm*
rear admiral	контр-адмира́л *nm*
second lieutenant	мла́дший лейтена́нт *nm*
sergeant major	ста́рший сержа́нт *nm*
sergeant	сержа́нт *nm*
vice-admiral	вице-адмира́л *nm*

religious

abbess	аббати́са *nf*
abbot	абба́т *nm*
archbishop	архиепи́скоп *nm*
archdeacon	архидиа́кон *nm*
ayatollah	аятолла́ *nm*
cardinal	кардина́л *nm*
chaplain	капелла́н *nm*
Dalai Lama	дала́й-ла́ма *nm*
deacon	дья́кон *nm*
deaconess	диакони́ца *nf*
dervish	де́рвиш *nm*
fakir	факи́р *nm*
hierarch	иера́рхия *nf*
imam	има́м *nm*
lama	ла́ма *nm*
mahatma	маха́тма *nm*
metropolitan	митрополи́т *nm*
Monsignor	монсеньёр *nm*
pastor	па́стор *nm*
pontiff	понти́фик *nm*
Pope	Па́па *nm*
prelate	прела́т *nm*
presbyter	пресви́тер *nm*
primate	прима́с *nm*
prior	прио́р *nm*
prioress	приоресса *nf*
rabbi	равви́н *nm*
vicar	вика́рий *nm*

royalty and nobility

baron	баро́н *nm*
baroness	бароне́сса *nf*
crown prince	кронпри́нц *nm*, короно́ванный принц *nm*
Graf	граф *nm*
lady	ле́ди *nf, indecl*
lord	лорд *nm*
marquis	марки́з *nm*
marquise	марки́за *nf*
milady	миле́ди *nf, indecl*
milord	мило́рд *nm*
peer	пэр *nm*
prince	принц *nm*
prince-consort	принц-консо́рт *nm*
princess	принце́сса *nf*
raja(h)	раджа́ *nm*
rani, ranee	ра́ни *nf, indecl*

historical

ataman	атама́н *nm*
boyar	боя́рин *nm*
boyar's daughter [unmarried]	боя́рышня *nf*
boyar's wife	боя́рыня *nf*
caliph, khalif	кали́ф, хали́ф *nm*
commissar	комисса́р *nm*
czar, tsar	царь *nm*
czarevitch, tsarevitch	царе́вич *nm*
czarevna, tsarevna	царе́вна *nf*
czarina, tsarina	цари́ца *nf*
dauphin	дофи́н *nm*
doge	дож *nm*
Kaiser	ка́йзер *nm*

maharaja(h)	магара́джа, махара́джа *nm*
mandarin	мандари́н *nm*
margrave	маркгра́ф *nm*
mikado	мика́до *nm, indecl*
nabob	набо́б *nm*
Negus	не́гус *nm*
padishah	падиша́х *nm*
pasha	паша́ *nm*
Pharaoh	фарао́н *nm*
satrap	сатра́п *nm*
shah	шах *nm*
shogun	сегу́н *nm*
sire	сир *nm*
suzerain	сюзере́н *nm*
viscount	вико́нт *nm*
viscountess	виконте́сса *nf*
vizier	визи́рь *nm*

professional

doctor	до́ктор *nm*
professor	профе́ссор *nm*

titles of respect

begum	бегу́ма *nf*
bey	бей *nm*
esquire	эсква́йр *nm*
Frau	фрау *nf*
Fraulein	фре́йлин *nf*
Herr	герр *nm*
madam(e)	мада́м *nf, indecl*
mademoiselle	мадемуазе́ль *nf, indecl*
Miss	мисс *nf, indecl*
Mister [= Mr.]	ми́стер *nm*
monsieur	мосье́ *nm, indecl*
Mrs.	ми́ссис *nf*
Ms.	мис *nf*
sahib	са́гиб *nm*
senhor, señor, signore	сеньо́р *nm*
senhora, señora, signora	сеньо́ра *nf*
senhorita, señorita, signorina	сеньори́та *nf*
sir	сэр *nm*

other titles

dame	да́ма *nf*
laureate	лауреа́т *nm*
majordomo	мажордо́м *nm*

DOMAINS

baronet	бароне́т *nm*
barony	баро́нство *nn*
caliphate [obs]	халифа́т *nm*
chancellorship	ка́нцлерство *nn*
commissariat	комиссариа́т *nm*
consulate	ко́нсульство *nn*
czardom, tsardom [obs]	ца́рство *nn*
emirate	эмира́т *nm*
governorship	губерна́торство *nn*
khanate	ха́нство *nn*
patriarchate	патриарха́т *nm*
peerage	пэ́рство *nn*
premiership	премье́рство *nn*
presidency	президе́нство *nn*
regency	ре́генство *nn*
satrapy [obs]	сатра́пия *nf*
secretariat	секретариа́т *nm*
sultanate	султана́т *nm*
suzereignty	сюзерените́т *nm*

See also **RELIGION** *(persons)*, **THE MILITARY ESTABLISHMENT** *(persons)*, **ANCIENT CIVILIZATIONS** *(persons)*

FAMOUS FIGURES OF YESTERDAY AND TODAY

ARTISTS

painters

Botticelli	Боттиче́лли *nm*
Bruegel	Бре́йгель *nm*
Cézanne	Сеза́нн *nm*
Chagall	Шага́л *nm*
da Vinci	да Ви́нчи *nm*
Gauguin	Гоге́н *nm*
Giotto	Джо́тто *nm*
Goya	Го́йя *nm*
Manet	Мане́ *nm*
Matisse	Мати́сс *nm*
Michelangelo	Микела́нджело *nm*
Monet	Моне́ *nm*
Picasso	Пика́ссо *nm*
Raphael	Рафаэ́ль *nm*
Rembrandt	Ре́мбрандт *nm*
Renoir	Ренуа́р *nm*
Rodin	Роде́н *nm*
Rousseau	Руссо́ *nm*
Rubens	Ру́бенс *nm*
van Gogh	ван Гог *nm*

composers and performers

Bach	Бах *nm*
Beethoven	Бетхо́вен *nm*
Bernstein	Бернште́йн *nm*
Bizet	Бизе́ *nm*

Borodin	Бороди́н *nm*
Brahms	Брамс *nm*
Caruso	Кару́зо *nm*
Chaliapin	Шаля́пин *nm*
Chopin	Шопе́н *nm*
Debussy	Дебюсси́ *nm*
Dvořák	Дво́ржак *nm*
Gershwin	Ге́ршвин *nm*
Grieg	Григ *nm*
Handel	Ге́ндель *nm*
Haydn	Гайдн *nm*
Horowitz	Го́ровиц *nm*
Liszt	Лист *nm*
Mendelssohn	Мендельсо́н *nm*
Mozart	Мо́царт *nm*
Oistrakh	Ойстрах *nm*
Paderewski	Падере́вский *nm*
Prokofiev	Проко́фьев *nm*
Puccini	Пучч́ини *nm*
Rachmaninov	Рахма́нинов *nm*
Schumann	Шу́ман *nm*
Shostakovich	Шостако́вич *nm*
Sibelius	Сибе́лиус *nm*
Strauss	Штра́ус *nm*
Stravinsky	Страви́нский *nm*
Tchaikovsky	Чайко́вский *nm*
Toscanini	Тоскани́ни *nm*
Verdi	Ве́рди *nm*
Wagner	Ва́гнер *nm*

Russian ballet dancers

Baryshnikov	Бары́шников *nm*
Markova	Ма́ркова *nf*
Nijinsky	Нижи́нский *nm*
Nureyev	Нури́ев *nm*
Pavlova	Па́влова *nf*

entertainment entrepreneurs

Barnum	Ба́рнум *nm*
Diaghilev	Дя́гилев *nm*
Disney	Диснéй *nm*
Goldwyn	Го́льдвин *nm*
Hurok	Ю́рок *nm*
Stanislavsky	Станисла́вский *nm*
Ziegfield	Зи́гфильд *nm*

WRITERS

Russian

Chekov, Chekhov	Че́хов *nm*
Dostoyevsky	Достое́вский *nm*
Gogol	Го́голь *nm*
Gorki, Gorky	Го́рький *nm*
Mayakovsky	Маяко́вский *nm*
Nabokov	Набо́ков *nm*
Pasternak	Пастерна́к *nm*
Pushkin	Пу́шкин *nm*
Solzhenitsyn	Солжени́цын *nm*
Tolstoy	Толсто́й *nm*
Turgenev	Турге́нев *nm*

American

Dreiser	Дра́йзер *nm*
Emerson	Э́мерсон *nm*
Faulkner	Фо́лкнер *nm*
Hawthorne	Хо́торн *nm*
Hemingway	Хемингуэ́й *nm*
Longfellow	Лонгфе́лло *nm*
Melville	Ме́лвилл *nm*
Poe	По *nm*
Steinbeck	Сте́йнбек *nm*
Thoreau	То́ро *nm*
Twain, Mark	Марк Твен *nm*
Whitman	Уэ́тман *nm*

British

Bacon	Бэ́кон *nm*
Bronte	Бро́нте *nf*
Browning	Бра́унинг *nm*
Burns	Бёрнс *nm*
Byron	Ба́йрон *nm*
Chaucer	Чо́сер *nm*
Dickens	Ди́ккенс *nm*
Dryden	Дра́йден *nm*
Joyce	Джойс *nm*
Keats	Китс *nm*
Kipling	Ки́плинг *nm*
Maugham	Мо́эм, Моэ́м *nm*
Milton	Ми́льтон *nm*
Scott	Скотт *nm*
Shakespeare	Шекспи́р *nm*
Shaw	Шо́у *nm*
Shelley	Ше́лли *nm*
Tennyson	Те́ннисон *nm*
Thackeray	Те́ккерей *nm*
Wordsworth	Во́рдсворт *nm*
Yeats	Йетс *nm*

French

Balzac	Бальза́к *nm*
Flaubert	Флобе́р *nm*
Hugo	Гюго́ *nm*
Moliere, Molière	Молье́р *nm*
Proust	Пруст *nm*
Rabelais	Рабле́ *nm*
Racine	Раси́н *nm*
Stendahl	Стенда́ль *nm*

Voltaire	Вольте́р *nm*
Zola	Золя́ *nm*

other writers

Andersen	А́ндерсен *nm*
Boccaccio	Бокка́ччо *nm*
Cervantes	Серва́нтес *nm*
Dante	Да́нте *nm*
Goethe	Гёте *nm*
Kafka	Ка́фка *nm*
Munchausen, Baron	Ба́рон Мю́нхгаузен *nm*

MILITARY LEADERS

Attila (the Hun)	Атти́ла *nm*
Cid, el	Сид *nm*
Cortez, Cortés	Корте́с *nm*
Eisenhower	Эйзенха́уэр *nm*
Genghis Khan	Чингисха́н *nm*
Joan of Arc	Жа́нна д'Арк *nf*
MacArthur	Мака́ртур *nm*
Napoleon	Наполео́н *nm*
Tamerlane	Тиму́р *nm*
William the Conqueror	Вильге́льм Завоева́тель *nm*
Zhukov	Жу́ков *nm*

PHILOSOPHERS AND RELIGIOUS FIGURES

Confucius	Конфу́ций *nm*
Descartes	Дека́рт *nm*
Diderot	Дидро́ *nm*
Erasmus	Эра́зм *nm*
Hegel	Ге́гель *nm*
King (Martin Luther Jr.)	Кинг *nm*
Lao-tze	Лао-Цзы *nm*
Luther	Лю́тер *nm*
Machiavelli	Макиаве́лли *nm*
Marx	Маркс *nm*
Mother Theresa	Мать Тере́за *nf*
Nietzsche	Ни́цше *nm*
Richelieu	Ришелье́ *nm*
Sartre	Сартр *nm*
Schweitzer	Шве́йцер *nm*
Voltaire	Вольте́р *nm*

SCIENTISTS AND INVENTORS

Burbank	Бе́рбанк *nm*
Copernicus	Копе́рник *nm*
Curie	Кюри́ *nf*
Darwin	Да́рвин *nm*
Edison	Э́дисон *nm*
Einstein	Эйнште́йн *nm*
Freud	Фрейд *nm*
Galileo	Галиле́й *nm*
Gutenberg	Гу́тенберг *nm*
Jung	Юнг *nm*
Linnaeus	Линне́й *nm*
Lobachevski	Лобаче́вский *nm*
Mendeleyev	Менделе́ев *nm*
Newton	Нью́тон *nm*
Pasteur	Пасте́р *nm*
Pavlov	Па́влов *nm*
Sakharov	Са́харов *nm*
Tupolev	Тупо́лев *nm*
Wright	Райт *nm*

POLITICAL LEADERS

Russian/Soviet

Brezhnev	Бре́жнев *nm*
Catherine (the Great)	Екатери́на (Вели́кая) *nf*
Gorbachev	Горбачёв *nm*
Kerensky	Ке́ренский *nm*
Krushchev	Хрущёв *nm*
Lenin	Ле́нин *nm*
Peter (the Great)	Пётр (Вели́кий) *nm*
Putin	Пу́тин *nm*
Stalin	Ста́лин *nm*
Trotsky	Тро́цкий *nm*
Yeltsin	Е́льцин *nm*

American

Adams	А́дамс *nm*
Bush	Буш *nm*
Clinton	Кли́нтон *nm*
Franklin	Фра́нклин *nm*
Hamilton	Га́мильтон *nm*
Jefferson	Дже́фферсон *nm*
Johnson	Джо́нсон *nm*
Kennedy	Ке́ннеди *nm*
Lincoln	Ли́нкольн *nm*
Madison	Ме́дисон *nm*
Marshall	Ма́ршалл *nm*
Nixon	Ни́ксон *nm*
Reagan	Ре́йган *nm*
Roosevelt	Ру́звельт *nm*
Truman	Тру́мэн *nm*
Washington	Ва́шингтон *nm*
Wilson	Ви́льсон *nm*

British

Churchill	Че́рчилль *nm*
Cromwell	Кро́мвель *nm*

Disraeli	Дисраэ́ли *nm*
Thatcher	Тэ́тчер *nm*

French

Clemenceau	Клемансо́ *nm*
de Gaulle	де Голль *nm*
Montesquieu	Монтескьё *nm*
Robespierre	Робеспье́р *nm*
Talleyrand	Талейра́н *nm*

other political leaders

Atatürk	Ататю́рк *nm*
Ben-Gurion	Бен Гурио́н *nm*
Bismarck	Би́смарк *nm*
Bolivar	Боли́вар *nm*
Chiang Kai-shek	Чан Кайши́ *nm*
Franco	Фра́нко *nm*
Gandhi	Га́нди *nm*
Garibaldi	Гариба́льди *nm*
Hammarsköld	Хаммаршельд *nm*
Hitler	Ги́тлер *nm*
Kublai Khan	Хубила́й *nm*
Mao Tse-tung	Ма́о Цзэду́н *nm*
Metternich	Ме́ттерних *nm*
Mussolini	Муссоли́ни *nm*
Sun Yat-sen	Сунь Ятсе́н *nm*
Tito	Ти́то *nm*
Weizmann	Ве́йцман *nm*

EXPLORERS

Columbus	Колумб *nm*
Hillary	Хи́лари *nm*
Magellan	Магелла́н *nm*
Marco Polo	Ма́рко По́ло *nm*
Ponce de Leon	По́нсе де Лео́н *nm*

VERY RICH PERSONS

Carnegie	Ка́рнеги *nm*
Gates	Гейтс *nm*
Murdock	Мэ́рдок *nm*
Onassis	Она́ссис *nm*
Rockefeller	Рокфе́ллер *nm*
Rothschild	Ротши́льд *nm*

OTHER FAMOUS NAMES

Gagarin	Гага́рин *nm*
Houdini	Гуди́ни *nm*
Mata Hari	Ма́та Ха́ри *nf*
Nostradamus	Нострада́мус *nm*
Rasputin	Распу́тин *nm*

See also **RELIGION** *(names)*, **THE BIBLE** *(names in the Old and New Testaments)*, **ANCIENT CIVILIZATION** *(persons)*

Society and Culture

FAMILY ◆ EDUCATION ◆ ORGANIZATIONS AND MEETINGS ◆ SOCIOLOGY ◆ ANTHROPOLOGY

FAMILY

GENERAL TERMS

family, familial — фами́льный *aj*
genealogy — генеало́гия *nf*
institution of marriage — институ́т бра́ка *nm, nm*
lineage — ли́ния *nf*
matriarchy — матриарха́т *nm*
patriarchy — патриа́рхия *nf*, патриарха́т *nm*

ASPECTS OF THE FAMILY

types of families

communal — коммуна́льный *aj*
interracial — межра́совый *aj*
matriarchal — матриарха́льный *aj*
morganatic — морганати́ческий *aj*
nuclear — нуклеа́рный *aj*
patriarchal — патриарха́льный *aj*
traditional — традицио́нный *aj*

family groups

clan — клан *nm*
dynasty — дина́стия *nf*
harem — гаре́м *nm*
seraglio — сера́ль *nm*

marriage practices

endogamy — эндога́мия *nf*
exogamy — экзога́мия *nf*
monogamy — моноѓамия *nf*
polyandry — полиа́ндрия *nf*
polygamy — полига́мия *nf*

parents

biological — биологи́ческий *aj*
maternal — матери́нский *aj*
surrogate — суррога́т *nm*

possible grounds for divorce

adultery — адюльте́р *nm*
alcoholism — алкоголи́зм *nm*
beating — битьё *nn*
bigamy — бига́мия *nf*
extramarital sex — секс вне бра́ка *nm, nm*
impotence — импоте́нция *nf*

other terms

alimony *nsg* — алиме́нты *nmpl*
birth control — контро́ль рожда́емости *nm, nf*
family planning — плани́рование семьи́ *nn, nf*
marriage contract — бра́чный контра́кт *nm*
matricide — матереуби́йство *nn*
pair — па́ра *nf*
parental authority — роди́тельский авторите́т *nm*
register a marriage — регистри́ровать брак *nm*

PERSONS

clansman (*pl* clansmen) — член кла́на *nm*
consort — консо́рт *nm*
cousin — кузе́н *nm*, кузи́на *nf*
governess — гуверна́нтка *nf*
ma, mama, mom, momma — ма́ма *nf*
matriarch — матриа́рх *nm*
matricide [mother-killer] — матереуби́йца *nmf*
matron — матро́на *nf*
mommy, mummy — мама́ша, ма́мочка *nf*
nanny — ня́ня, ня́нька *nf*
pa, papa, pop, poppa — па́па, па́пка, папа́ша *nm*
patriarch — патриа́рх *nm*
polygamist — полигами́ст *nm*
sister — сестра́ *nf*
son — сын *nm*
sonny — сыно́к *nm*
stepsister — сво́дная сестра́ *nf*
stepson — па́сынок *nm*

See also **ANTHROPOLOGY**, **SEX**, **SOCIOLOGY**

EDUCATION

GENERAL TERMS

academe	академи́ческий мир *nm*
academic	академи́ческий *aj*
academic year	академи́ческий год *nm*
academic title	академи́ческое зва́ние *nn*
Alma Mater	а́льма-ма́тер *nf, indecl*
basic knowledge *nsg*	ба́зовые зна́ния *nnpl*
basic (education)	ба́зовый *aj*
calendar	календа́рь *nm*
character formation	формирова́ние хара́ктера *nn, nm*
class	класс *nm*
classroom	кла́ссная ко́мната
consolidation	консолида́ция *nf*
course	курс *nm*
discipline	дисципли́на *nf*
educational system	систе́ма образова́ния *nf, nn*
erudition	эруди́ция *nf*
exam(ination)	экза́мен *nm*
faculty [department]	факульте́т *nm*
instructing, instruction	инструкта́ж *nm*
materials	материа́лы *nmpl*
method	ме́тод *nm*, мето́дика *nf*
methodology	методоло́гия *nf*
program (BR programme)	програ́мма *nf*
school	шко́ла *nf*
specialization	специализа́ция *nf*
study	штуди́ровать *impf*, проштуди́ровать *pf*
test	тест *nm*

SPECIALIZATIONS

didactics *nplsv*	дида́ктика *nf*
heuristics *nplsv*	эври́стика *nf*
methods, methodics *npl*	мето́дика *nf*
pedagogy	педаго́гика *nf*

ASPECTS OF EDUCATION

types of schools

academy	акаде́мия *nf*
alternative school	альтернати́вная шко́ла *nf*
college	колле́дж *nm*
institute	институ́т *nm*
lycée	лице́й *nm*
polytechnic (school)	полите́хникум *nm*
preschool	дошко́льный *aj*
professional	профессиона́льный *aj*
progressive	прогресси́вный *aj*
religious	религио́зный *aj*
school, boarding	шко́ла-интерна́т *nm*
school, high/secondary	сре́дняя шко́ла *nf*
school, junior high	непо́лная сре́дняя шко́ла *nf*
school, night	вече́рняя шко́ла *nf*
school, primary/elementary/grade	нача́льная шко́ла *nf*
school, private	ча́стная шко́ла *nf*
school, trade	профшко́ла *nf*
technical college	те́хникум *nm*
university	университе́т *nm*

major disciplines

history	исто́рия *nf*
humanities	гуманита́рные нау́ки *nfpl*
literature	литерату́ра *nf*
mathematics *nplsv*	матема́тика *nf*
medicine	медици́на *nf*
philosophy	филосо́фия *nf*
physical education	физи́ческое воспита́ние *nn*

courses

course, correspondence	зао́чный курс *nm*
crash/intensive course	ускоренный курс *nm*
lecture course	лекцио́нный курс *nm*
program(m)ed	программи́рованный *aj*
special course	специа́льный курс *nm*
telecourse	телевизио́нный курс обуче́ния *nm, nn*

methods of learning

group study	группові́е заня́тия *nnpl*
program(m)ed learning	програ́ммное обуче́ние *nm*
seminar	семина́р *nm*
Socratic method	сокра́товский ме́тод *nm*

school calendar

semester	семе́стр *nm*
trimester	триме́стр *nm*

degrees and graduation requirements

baccalaureate, Bachelor's degree, B.A.	бакала́врство *nn*, сте́пень бакала́вра *nf, nm*
diploma	дипло́м *nm*
dissertation	диссерта́ция *nf*
Doctor of Philosophy, Ph.D.	до́ктор филосо́фских нау́к *nm, nfpl*
doctor's degree	до́кторская сте́пень *nf*
doctorate	сте́пень до́ктора *nf, nm*
Master of Arts	маги́стр гуманита́рных нау́к *nm, nfpl*
master's degree	маги́стр *nm*
university degree	университе́тская сте́пень *nm*

famous universities

Cambridge	Ке́мбридж *nm*
Harvard	Га́рвард *nm*
Moscow University [= MGU]	Моско́вский Госуда́рственный Университе́т [= МГУ] *nm*
Oxbridge [= Cambridge + Oxford]	О́ксбридж *nm*
Oxford University	Оксфо́рдский университе́т *nm*
Sorbonne	Сорбо́нна *nf*

other terms

financial aid	фина́нсовая по́мощь *nf*
honorarium (*pl* honorariums, honoraria)	гонора́р *nm*
lecture	ле́кция *nf*
lecturing, lectureship	ле́кторство *nn*
lecture *vi*, give a lecture	чита́ть ле́кцию
monitoring	монито́ринг *nm*
object of study	объе́кт изуче́ния *nm, nn*
professorship	профе́ссорство *nn*, профессу́ра *nf*
qualifying exam	квалификацио́нный экза́мен *nm*
registration office	регистрату́ра *nf*
revision	реви́зия *nf*
stipend	стипе́ндия *nf*
student loan	студе́нческий заём *nm*

TOOLS AND MATERIALS

audiovisual	а́удио-визуа́льный *aj*
instructional	инстру́кти́вный *aj*
laboratory	лаборато́рия *nf*
lecture hall	лекцио́нный зал *nm*
transparency	транспара́нт *nm*

PERSONS

academician	акаде́мик *nm*
assistant (lecturer)	ассисте́нт, -ка *nmf*
bachelor	бакала́вр *nm*
diploma-holder	диплома́нт *nm*
dissertation author	диссерта́нт *nm*
docent	доце́нт *nm*
doctor	до́ктор *nm*
doctoral candidate	доктора́нт *nm*
examinee	экзамену́ющийся, экзамену́емый *nm*
examiner	экзамена́тор *nm*
humanist	гумани́ст *nm*
instructor	инстру́ктор *nm*
lecturer [speaker]	ле́ктор *nm*
lycée pupil	лицеи́ст *nm*
mentor	ме́нтор *nm*
methodologist	методо́лог *nm*
methods specialist	методи́ст, -ка *nmf*
monitor	монито́р *nm*
pedagog(ue)	педаго́г *nm*
pedant [pej]	педа́нт, -ка *nmf*
polytechnical student	полите́хник *nm*
preschooler	дошко́льник *nm*, дошко́льница *nf*
proctor	про́ктор *nm*
professor	профе́ссор *nm*
rector	ре́ктор *nm*
registrar	регистра́тор *nm*
schoolboy	шко́льник *nm*
schoolchildren	шко́льники *npl*
student	студе́нт(ка) *nmf*
schoolgirl	шко́льница *nf*
student, engineering	студе́нт(ка)-техно́лог *nmf*
student, medical	студе́нт(ка)-ме́дик *nmf*
student, law	студе́нт(ка)-юри́ст *nmf*

groups

collegium	колле́гия *nf*

professors *npl* [the faculty] — профессу́ра *nf*
student body — студе́нчество *nn*

See also **SOCIOLOGY**, **PSYCHOLOGY**

ORGANIZATIONS AND MEETINGS

GENERAL TERMS

ceremony [event] — церемо́ния *nf*
ceremony [behavior] — церемо́нность *nf*
form — формирова́ть *impf*, сформирова́ть *pf*
group — группа *nf*
hold a meeting — митингова́ть *impf*
meeting — ми́тинг *nm*
organization — организа́ция *nf*
parliamentary — парла́ментский, парламента́рный *aj*
procedure — процеду́ра *nf*

ASPECTS OF ORGANIZATIONS

kinds of organizations

association — ассоциа́ция *nf*
charter — ха́ртия *nf*
club — клуб *nm*
collective — коллекти́в *nm*
commission — коми́ссия *nf*
committee — комите́т *nm*, коми́ссия *nf*
conclave — конкла́в *nm*
consortium — консо́рциум *nm*
coordinating committee — координацио́нный комите́т *nm*
delegation — делега́ция *nf*
lodge — ло́жа *nf*
organizing committee — организацио́нный комите́т *nm*
subcommittee — подкомите́т *nm*, подкоми́ссия *nf*

actions and procedures

debate *nsg* — деба́ты *npl*
declaration — деклара́ция *nf*
discussion — диску́ссия *nf*
memo, memorandum — мемора́ндум *nm*
project — прое́кт *nm*
ratification — ратифика́ция *nf*
regulation — регламента́ция *nf*
resolution — резолю́ция *nf*

names of organizations

Boy Scouts — бойска́уты *nmpl*
Freemasonry — франкмасо́нство *nn*
Girl Scouts — де́вочки-скауты *nfpl*
KKK [= Ku Klux Klan] — ККК [= ку-клукс-кла́н] *nm*
Masonic lodge — масо́нская ло́жа *nf*
Nobel Prize — Но́белевская пре́мия *nf*
Peace Corps — Ко́рпус ми́ра *nm*, *nm*
Rotary Club — Ро́тари-клуб *nm*
Salvation Army — А́рмия спасе́ния *nf*, *nn*

other terms

conference hall — конфере́нц-зал *nm*
disharmony — дисгармо́ния *nf*
group dynamics *npl* — дина́мика гру́ппы *nf*, *nf*
quorum — кво́рум *nm*
solidarity — солида́рность *nf*
sponsoring — спо́нсорский *aj*

KINDS OF MEETINGS

usually small gatherings

camarilla — камари́лья *nf*
clique — кли́ка *nf*
forum (*pl* forums, fora) — фору́м *nm*
literary gathering — литерату́рный ве́чер *nm*
musicale — музыка́льный ве́чер *nm*
soiree — суаре́ *nn*, *indecl*

usually large gatherings

assembly — ассамбле́я *nf*
colloquium — колло́квиум *nm*
conference — конфере́нция *nf*
congress — конгре́сс *nm*
plenum (*pl* plenums, plenae) — пле́нум *nm*
session — се́ссия *nf*
symposium (*pl* symposiums, symposia) — симпо́зиум *nm*

equipment

microphone — микрофо́н *nm*
public-address system — систе́ма звукоусиле́ния *nf*, *nn*

tribune [platform]	трибýна *nf*

PERSONS

members of organizations

Boy Scout	бойскáут *nm*
Freemason	франкмасóн *nm*
Girl Scout	дéвочка-скаут *nf*
Klansman	куклуксклáновец *nm*
mason, Mason	масóн *nm*
Rotarian	ротариáнец *nm*

other persons

delegate	делегáт, -ка *nmf*
guest of honor	почётный гость *nm*, почётная гóстья *nf*
organizer	организáтор *nm*
sponsor	спóнсор *nm*
president	президéнт *nm*
secretary	секретáрь *nm*, секретáрша *nf*
vice-president	вице-президéнт *nm*

See also **POLITICS AND GOVERNMENT**, **USING LANGUAGE**

SOCIOLOGY

GENERAL TERMS

civilization	цивилизáция *nf*
cultural	культýрный *aj*
culture	культýра *nf*
norm	нóрма *nf*
segregation	сегрегáция *nf*
social class	социáльный класс *nm*
social differentiation	социáльная дифференциáция *nf*
social engineering	социáльная инженерíя *nf*
social organization	социáльная организáция *nf*
social sciences	социáльные наýки *nfpl*
social structure	социáльная структýра *nf*
social system	социáльная систéма *nf*
socialization	социализáция *nf*
socialize	социализúровать *impf*, *pf*
sociocultural	социокультýрный *aj*
socioeconomic	социáльно-экономúческий *aj*
sociological	социологúческий *aj*
sociology	социолóгия *nf*
status	стáтус *nm*

SPECIALIZATIONS

criminology	криминолóгия *nf*
demography	демográфия *nf*
ecology	эколóгия *nf*
economics *nplsv*	экономика *nf*
geography	геогрáфия *nf*
gerontology	геронтолóгия *nf*
psychology	психолóгия *nf*
social psychology	социáльная психолóгия *nf*
sociobiology	социобиолóгия *nf*
sociolinguistics *nplsv*	социолингвúстика *nf*
statistics *nplsv*	статúстика *nf*

ASPECTS OF SOCIOLOGY

social groupings

caste	кáста *nf*
clan	клан *nm*
elite, élite	элúта *nf*
enclave	анклáв *nm*
ethnic group	этнúческая грýппа *nf*
immigrants *npl*	иммигрáция *nf*
masses, the	мáссы *nfpl*
national minority	национáльное меньшинствó *nn*
nouveau riche	нуворúш *nm*
public, the general	ширóкая пýблика *nf*
underclass	неимýщий класс *nm*

social problems in American society

desegregation	десегргегáция *nf*
double standard	двойнóй стандáрт *nm*
ethnocentrism	этноцентрúзм *nm*
immigration	иммигрáция *nf*
racial discrimination	рáсовая дискриминáция *nf*
racial integration	расовáя интегрáция *nf*
racial segregation	рáсовая сегрегáция *nf*

factors in social status

age group	возрастнáя грýппа *nf*
culture level	культýрность *nf*
ethnicity	этнúческая принадлéжность *nf*
image, public	úмидж *nm*
prestige	престúж *nm*
privilege	привилéгия *nf*
race	рáса *nf*
reputation, repute	репутáция *nf*

role	роль *nf*
sex	секс *nm*

experimental and restricted societies

commune	коммýна *nf*
nudist colony *nsg*	колóния нудúстов *nf, nmpl*
phalanstery	фаланстéр *nm*
reservation [American Indians]	резервáция *nf*

other terms

antisocial	антисоциáльный *aj*
class distinctions	клáссовые разлúчия *nnpl*
class-conscious	клáссово-сознáтельный *aj*
debut	дебю́т *nm*
declasse, déclassé	деклассúрованный *aj*
mass hysteria	мáссовый психóз *nm*
social Darwinism	социáльный дарвинúзм *nm*
statistics [data]	статистúческие дáнные *npl*
status symbol	сúмвол стáтуса *nm, nm*

LIFESTYLES

bohemianism	богéма *nf*
communal	коммунáльный *aj*
counterculture	контркультýра *nf*
nudism	нудúзм *nm*
subculture	субкультýра *nf*

PERSONS

beatnik [obs]	бúтник *nm*
bohemians *npl*	богéма *nf*
debutante	дебютáнтка *nf*
hippy, hippie [obs]	хúппи *nmf, indecl*
immigrant	иммигрáнт, -ка *nmf*
informant	информáтор *nm*
nudist	нудúст, -ка *nmf*

social scientists

criminologist	криминóлог *nm*
demographer	демóгрáф *nm*
gerontologist	геронтóлог *nm*
social worker	социáльный рабóтник *nm*
sociologist	социóлог *nm*
statistician	статúстик *nm*

See also **THE CITY, ANTHROPOLOGY**

ANTHROPOLOGY

GENERAL TERMS

civilization	цивилизáция *nf*
culture	культýра *nf*
ethos	э́тос *nm*
emigration	миграция *nf*
race	рáса *nf*

SPECIALIZATIONS

anthropology	антропология *nf*
archeology (BR archaeology)	археолóгия *nf*
craniology	краниолóгия *nf*
ethnography	этногрáфия *nf*
ethnology	этнолóгия *nf*
linguistics *nplsv*	лингвúстика *nf*
sociology	социолóгия *nf*

PHYSICAL ANTHROPOLOGY

prehistoric humans

Australopithecus	австралопúтек *nm*
Cro-Magnon Man	кроманьóнец *nm*
hominid	гоминúд *nm*
Homo Erectus	хóмо эрéктус *nm, indecl*
homo sapiens	хóмо сáпиенс *nm, indecl*
Neanderthal man	неандертáлец *nm*
pithecanthropus	питекáнтроп *nm*
troglodyte	троглодúт *nm*

racial types

Anglo-Saxon	англосáкс *nm*
brachycephalous person	брахицефáл *nm*
macrocephalic person	макроцефáл *nm*
metis, mestizo	метúс *nm*
microcephalic person	микроцефáл *nm*
Native American Indians	коренны́е американцы *nmpl*
Negro	негритя́нский *aj*
Negroid	негрóидный *aj*
Nordic	нордúческий *aj*
Pygmy	пигмéй *nm*

CULTURAL ANTHROPOLOGY

kinds of culture

decadent	декадéнтский *aj*

ethnic	этни́ческий *aj*
material	материа́льный *aj*
matriarchal	матриарха́льный *aj*
national	национа́льный *aj*
nomadism	номади́зм *nm*
patriarchal	патриарха́льный *aj*
primitive	примити́вный *aj*
subculture	субкульту́ра *nf*

elements of developed cultures

decorum	деко́рум *nm*
etiquette	этике́т *nm*
institution [custom]	институ́т *nm*
instrument	инструме́нт *nm*
religion	рели́гия *nf*
symbols	си́мволы *nmpl*
technology	техноло́гия *nf*
tradition	тради́ция *nf*

elements of undeveloped cultures

barbarism, barbarity	ва́рварство *nn*
cannibalism	каннибали́зм *nm*
lack of culture	некульту́рность *nf*
primitivism	примитиви́зм *nm*
taboo, tabu	табу́ *nn, indecl*

cultural periods

Bronze Age	Бро́нзовый век *nm*
Mesolithic Age	мезоли́т *nm*
Neolithic Age	неоли́т *nm*
Paleolithic Age	э́поха палеоли́та *nf*

PERSONS

aborigine	абориге́н, -ка *nmf*
barbarian	ва́рвар *nm*
bedouin	бедуи́н, -ка *nmf*
cannibal	канниба́л *nm*
decadent	декаде́нт *nm*
Indian [Native American]	инде́ец *nm*, индиа́нка *nf*
mulatto	мула́т, -ка *nmf*
Negro	негр *nm*, негритя́нка *nf*
nomad	нома́д *nm*
Teuton	тевто́н *nm*

specialists

anthropologist	антропо́лог *nm*
ethnographer	этно́граф *nm*
ethnologist	этно́лог *nm*
sociologist	социо́лог *nm*

See also **LANGUAGES OF THE WORLD, INHABITANTS AND ETHNIC GROUPS, HISTORY AND ARCHEOLOGY**

Affairs of State

LAW ◆ THE MILITARY ESTABLISHMENT ◆ POLITICS AND GOVERNMENT

LAW

GENERAL TERMS

appeal	апелля́ция *nf*
argument	аргуме́нт *nm*
code	ко́декс *nm*
competence	компете́нция *nf*
consultation	консульта́ция *nf*
criminal [illegal]	кримина́льный *aj*
criminal [relating to crime]	криминоге́нный *aj*
criminality	кримина́льность *nf*
document	докуме́нт *nm*
documentation	документа́ция *nf*
domicile	домици́лий *nm*
forum (*pl* forums, fora)	фору́м *nm*
illegal	нелега́льный *aj*
illegal activities *npl*	нелега́льщина *nf*
illegality	нелега́льность *nf*
illegally	нелега́льно *av*
instance	инста́нция *nf*
institution [custom]	институ́т *nm*
jurisdiction	юрисди́кция *nf*
justice	юсти́ция *nf*
law practice	юриди́ческая пра́ктика *nf*
legal	лега́льный *aj*
legality	лега́льность *nf*
legalization	легализа́ция *nf*
legalize	легализи́ровать *impf, pf*
legally	лега́льно *av*
offer	офе́рта *nf*
official	официа́льный *aj*
practice (BR practise)	пра́ктика *nf*
process	проце́сс *nm*
reform	рефо́рма *nf*
regulatory	регули́рующий *aj*
residency	резиде́нция *nf*
status	ста́тус *nm*
tribunal	трибуна́л *nm*

SPECIALIZATIONS

criminalistics *nplsv*	криминали́стика *nf*
criminology	криминоло́гия *nf*
dactyloscopy	дактилоскопи́я *nf*
jurisprudence	юриспруде́нция *nf*
penology	пеноло́гия *nf*

TYPES OF LAW

public law

administrative	администрати́вное *aj* (право)
constitutional	конституцио́нное *aj*
criminal code	уголо́вное *aj*
federal	федера́льный *aj* (закон)
municipal	муниципа́льный *aj* (закон)
political	полити́ческое *aj* (право)
statute	стату́тное *aj* (пра́во)

civil

canon	канони́ческое *aj*
commercial	комме́рческое *aj*
financial	фина́нсовое *aj*
patent	пате́нтное *aj*

historical

Justinian	Юстиниа́н *nm*
Mosaic	Моисе́ев *aj*
Napoleonic code	ко́декс Наполео́на *nm*
Roman	ри́мское *aj* (право)

ASPECTS OF LEGAL PRACTICE

kinds of courts

appellate	апелляцио́нный *aj*
arbitration	арбитра́жный *aj*

rights

freedom of association	свобо́да ассоциа́ций *nf, nfpl*
religion	рели́гия *nf*

law enforcement

arrest	аре́ст *nm*
cordon [police]	кордо́н *nm*

dactylography	дактилогра́фия *nf*
lie detector	дете́ктор лжи *nm, nf*
organized crime	организо́ванная престу́пность *nf*
patrol	патру́ль *nm*
patrol car	полице́йская патру́льная маши́на *nf*
police dog	полице́йская соба́ка *nf*
police station	полице́йский уча́сток *nm*
polygraph	полигра́ф *nm*
telephone tap	прослу́шивание телефо́на *nn, nm*

judicial actions

alimony *nsg*	алиме́нты *nmpl*
annulment [contract]	аннули́рование *nn*
arbitrage, arbitration	арбитра́ж *nm*
cassation	螺ка́ссация *nf*
censorship	цензу́ра *nf*
certification	сертифика́ция *nf*
deportation	депорта́ция *nf*
expropriation	экспроприа́ция *nf*
legitimation	легитима́ция *nf*
moratorium (*pl* moratoriums, moratoria)	морато́рий *nm*
naturalization	натурализа́ция *nf*
nullification	аннули́рование *nn*
partnership	партнёрство *nn*
patenting	патентова́ние *nn*
prolong	пролонги́ровать *impf, pf*
public trial	публи́чный суд *nm*
sanction	са́нкция *nf*
usufruct	узуфру́кт *nm*

documents

act	акт *nm*
cadastre	када́стр *nm*
certificate	сертифика́т *nm*
contract	контра́кт *nm*
copy, certified	заве́ренная ко́пия *nf*
countersigning	контрассигна́ция *nf*
decree	декре́т *nm*
legal title	правово́й ти́тул *nm*
license (BR licence)	лице́нзия *nf*
notification	нотифика́ция *nf*
order	о́рден *nm*
paragraph of a contract	пара́граф контра́кта *nm, nm*
patent	пате́нт *nm*
petition	пети́ция *nf*
publication (of a law)	опубликова́ние *nn*
regulations *npl*	регла́мент *nm*

legal argumentation

constitutionality	конституцио́нность *nf*
motive	моти́в *nm*
prerogative	прерогати́ва *nf*
protest	проте́ст *nm*
unconstitutional	неконституцио́нный, антиконституцио́нный *aj*

evidence

attest	аттестова́ть *impf, pf*
authenticity	аутенти́чность *nf*
dossier	досье́ *nn, indecl*
expert opinion	мне́ние экспе́рта *nn, nm*

other terms

clause	клау́зула *nf*
counteroffer	контрофе́рта *nf*
cumulative	кумуляти́вный *aj*
de jure	де-ю́ре *av*
fictitious	фикти́вный *aj*
intellectual property	интеллектуа́льная со́бственность *nf*
pretension [claim]	прете́нзия *nf*
ratify	ратифици́ровать *impf, pf*
sequestration	секвестра́ция *nf*
statute	стату́т *nm*

CRIMES AND MISDEMEANORS

violent

banditry	банди́тизм *nm*
gangsterism	гангстери́зм *nm*
genocide	геноци́д *nm*
hooliganism	хулига́нство *nn*
physical violence	физи́ческое наси́лие *nn*
terrorism	террори́зм *nm*
vandalism	вандали́зм *nm*

financial

bankruptcy	банкро́тство *nn*

breach of contract	наруше́ние контра́кта *nn*, *nm*
racket [organized crime]	рэ́кет *nm*

sex

pedophilia (BR paedophilia)	педофили́я *nf*
prostitution	проститу́ция *nf*
sex discrimination	сексуа́льная дискримина́ция *nf*

political & military

desertion	дезерти́рство *nn*
espionage	шпиона́ж *nm*
false passport	фальши́вый па́спорт *nm*
sabotage	сабота́ж *nm*

language

pirated copy	пира́тская ко́пия *nf*
plagiarism	плагиа́т *nm*

miscellaneous

conspiracy	конспира́ция *nf*
defamation of character	диффама́ция *nf*
kleptomania	клептома́ния *nf*
lynching	линчева́ние *nn*
piracy	пира́тство *nn*
racial discrimination	ра́совая дискрими-на́ция *nf*
usurpation	узурпа́ция *nf*

legal defenses

alibi	а́либи *nn*, *indecl*
immunity	иммуните́т *nm*
indemnity	индемните́т *nm*
precedent	прецеде́нт *nm*
presumption of innocence	презу́мпция невино́вности *nf*
privilege	привиле́гия *nf*
technicality	техни́ческая дета́ль *nf*

other terms

beneficial	бенефициа́рный *aj*
contraband	контраба́нда *nf*
habeas corpus	Ха́беас Ко́рпус *nm*, *indecl*
incriminating, *aj* incriminatory	инкримини́рующий
obstruction (of justice)	обстру́кция *nf*
recidivism	рецидиви́зм *nm*
verdict	верди́кт *nm*

crime-fighting organizations

FBI [= Federal Bureau of Investigation]	ФБР *nn*, *indecl* [Федера́льное бюро́ рассле́дований]
Interpol	Интерпо́л *nm*
Scotland Yard	Ско́тланд-Ярд *nm*

PUNISHMENT

kinds of punishment

electric chair	электри́ческий стул *nm*
execution	экзеку́ция *nf*
gas chamber	га́зовая ка́мера *nf*
internment	интерни́рование *nn*
penal colony	исправи́тельно-трудова́я коло́ния *nf*
penitentiary	пенитенциа́рный *aj*

famous prisons

Alcatraz	Алькатра́с *nm*
Bastille	Басти́лия *nf*
Lyubyanka	Лубя́нка *nf*
Sing-Sing	Синг-Синг *nm*
Spandau	Шпанда́у *nf*
Tower of London	Та́уэр *nm*

PERSONS

offenders

arrestee	арестант, -ка *nmf*
bandit	банди́т *nm*
conspirator	конспира́тор *nm*
contrabandist	контрабанди́ст, -ка *nmf*
deportee	депорта́нт *nm*
expropriator	экспроприа́тор *nm*
gangster	га́нгстер *nm*
hooligan	хулига́н, -ка *nmf*
kleptomaniac	клептома́н, -ка *nmf*
Mafioso	мафио́зи *nm*, *indecl*
pedophile (BR paedophile)	педофи́л *nm*
pirate	пира́т *nm*

plagiarist	плагиа́тор *nm*
racketeer	рэкети́р, рэкетёр *nm*
recidivist	рецидиви́ст *nm*
saboteur	сабота́жник *nm*
terrorist	террори́ст, -ка *nmf*
usurper	узурпа́тор *nm*
vandal	ванда́л *nm*

law enforcement personnel

arbiter, arbitrator	арби́тр *nm*
barrister [British usage]	барри́стер *nm*
constable	консте́бль *nm*
criminalist	кримина́ли́ст *nm*
criminologist	кримино́лог *nm*
detective	детекти́в *nm*
expert witness	суде́бный экспе́рт *nm*
inspector [police]	инспе́ктор *nm*
jurist	юри́ст *nm*
legal consultant	юриско́нсульт *nm*
legatee	легата́рий *nm*
licentiate	лиценциа́т *nm*
magistrate	магистра́т *nm*
notary, notary public	нота́риус *nm*
ombudsman	о́мбудсман *nm*
patrolman, patrol officer	патру́льный *nm*
penologist	пено́лог *nm*
police commissioner	комисса́р поли́ции *nm*, *nf*
police officer	полице́йский *nmf*
policeman (*pl* policemen)	полисме́н *nm*
policewoman (*pl* policewomen)	же́нщина-полице́йский *nf*
recorder [British usage]	рико́рдер *nm*
sheriff	шери́ф *nm*

other individuals

appellant	апелля́нт *nm*
beneficiary	бенефициа́рий *nm*
countersignatory	контрассигна́нт *nm*
individual	индиви́дуум, индиви́д *nm*
juror	член жюри́ *nm*, *nn*
licensee	лицензиа́т *nm*
patent-holder, patentee	патентооблада́тель *nm*
resident	резиде́нт *nm*
respondent	респонде́нт *nm*
tipster	ти́пстер *nm*
usufructuary	узуфрукта́рий *nm*

groups

band [gang]	ба́нда *nf*
hooligans *npl*	хулиганьё *nm*
jury	жюри́ *nn*, *indecl*
Mafia	ма́фия *nf*
magistrates *npl*	магистрату́ра *nf*
militia	мили́ция *nf*
police (force)	поли́ция *nf*
secret police	секре́тная поли́ция *nf*

See also **BUSINESS** *(legal terms)*, **DEATH** *(aspects of dying)*, **FAMILY** *(aspects of the family)*, **TITLES** *(kinds of titles)*

THE MILITARY ESTABLISHMENT

GENERAL TERMS

base	ба́за *nf*
command [order]	кома́нда *nf*
command [jurisdiction]	кома́ндование *nn*
conflict	конфли́кт *nm*
control	контро́ль *nm*
equip	экипирова́ть *impf*, *pf*
equipping, equipment	экипиро́вка *nf*
fortification	фортифика́ция *nf*
fortunes of war *npl*	вое́нная форту́на *nf*
materiel, matériel	материа́льная часть *nf*
objective	объе́кт *nm*
pacifism	пацифи́зм *nm*
plan	план сраже́ния *nm*
protocol	протоко́л *nm*
rank	ранг *nm*

MILITARY SCIENCE SPECIALIZATIONS

ballistics *nplsv*	балли́стика *nf*
communications	коммуника́ции *nfpl*
counterespionage	контршпиона́ж *nm*
cryptography	криптогра́фия *nf*
echelon	эшело́н *nm*
espionage	шпиона́ж *nm*
military engineering	вое́нно-инжене́рное де́ло *nn*
strategy	страте́гия *nf*
tactics *nplsv*	та́ктика *nf*

ASPECTS OF MILITARY LIFE

groups

alliance	алья́нс *nm*
armada	арма́да *nf*
army	а́рмия *nf*
battalion	батальо́н *nm*
battery	батаре́я *nf*
brigade	брига́да *nf*

cadet corps	кадéтский кóрпус *nm*
cadres	кáдры *nmpl*
column of soldiers	колóнна солдáт *nf, nmpl*
contingent	контингéнт *nm*
corps	кóрпус *nm*
cortege	кортéж *nm*
disarmament commission	комиссия по разоружéнию *nf, nn*
division	дивизия *nf*
escort	эскóрт *nm*
expedition	экспедиция *nf*
fleet	флот *nm*
gendarmerie	жандармéрия *nf*
general staff	генерáльный штаб *nf*
guard, guards	гвáрдия *nf*
High Command	глáвное комáндование *nn*
irregular (forces)	иррегулярный *aj*
irregular/nonregular (army)	нерегулярный *aj*
junta	хýнта *nf*
legion	легиóн *nm*
military mission	воéнная миссия *nf*
military tribunal	воéнный трибунáл *nm*
militia	милиция *nf*
missile battery	ракéтная батарéя *nf*
mobile unit	мобильная грýппа *nf*
National Guard	национáльная гвáрдия *nf*
officer corps	офицéрство *nn*, офицéрский кóрпус *nm*
operational staff	оперативный штаб *nm*
parachute troops *npl*	парашютный десáнт *nm*
partisans *npl*	партизáны *nmpl*
party [reconnaissance]	пáртия *nf*
patrol	патрýль *nm*
rear guard	арьергáрд *nm*
regular army *nsg*	регулярная áрмия *nf*
reserves *npl*	резéрв *nm*
shock brigade	удáрная бригáда *nf*
squadron [cavalry unit]	эскадрóн *nm*
squadron [naval unit]	эскáдра *nf*
squadron [air force unit]	эскадрилья *nf*
vanguard	авангáрд *nm*

places and locations

airbase	авиабáза *nf*
barracks *npl*	барáк *nm*
base hospital	бáзовый гóспиталь *nm*
base camp	бáзовый лáгерь *nm*
bivouac site	бивáчный пункт *nm*
blockhouse	блокгáуз *nm*
campsite	кéмпинг *nm*
command post	комáндный пункт *nm*
commandant's office	комендатýра *nf*
concentration camp	концентрациóнный лáгерь *nm*
control post	контрóльный пост *nm*
defile	дефилé *indecl*
front	фронт *nm*
garrison	гарнизóн *nm*
hospital	гóспиталь *nf*
military/naval academy	воéнная/воéнно-морскáя акадéмия *nf*
military base	воéнная бáза *nf*
minefield	минное пóле *nn*
missile base	ракéтная бáза *nf*
naval base	воéнно-морская бáза *nf*
observation point/post	наблюдáтельный пункт/пост *nm*
officers' mess	офицéрская столóвая *nf*
Pentagon	Пентагóн *nm*
post	пост *nm*
quarters	квартиры *nfpl*
supply base	бáза снабжéния *nf, nn*
theater of operations	теáтр воéнных дéйствий *nm, nnpl*
West Point	Уэ́ст-Пойнт *nm*

fortifications

barricade	баррикáда *nf*
bastion	бастиóн *nm*
bomb shelter	бомбоубéжище *nn*
casemate	каземáт *nm*
citadel	цитадéль *nf*
counterscarp	контрэскáрп *nm*
escarpment	эскáрп *nm*
fort	форт *nm*
lunette	люнéт *nm*
palisade	палисáд *nm*
parapet	парапéт *nm*
redoubt	редýт *nm*
trench	траншéя *nf*

ranks and offices

admiralty	адмиралтéйство *nn*
general's rank	генерáльный чин *nm*
rank of corporal	капрáл *nm*

rank of marshall	ма́ршал *nm*

uniform

chevron	шевро́н *nm*
kepi	ке́пи *nn, indecl*
khaki	ха́ки *aj/nn, indecl*

other terms

desertion	дезерти́рство *nn*
flag	флаг *nm*
flagstaff	флагшто́к *nm*
inspection	инспе́кция *nf*
line of communication	коммуникацио́нная ли́ния *nf*
march	марш *nm*
military secret	вое́нный секре́т *nm*
ration	рацио́н *nm*
salute (with guns)	салю́т *nm*

TACTICS AND COMBAT

kinds of warfare

bacteriological	бактериологи́ческий *aj*
chemical	хими́ческий *aj*
global war	глоба́льный *aj*
intervention	интерве́нция *nf*
military adventure	вое́нная авантю́ра *nf*
preventive	превенти́вный *aj*
psychological	психологи́ческий *aj*
total	тота́льный *aj*

military zones

buffer zone	бу́ферная зо́на *nf*
danger zone	опа́сная зо́на *nf*
demilitarized zone	демилитаризо́ванная зо́на *nf*
front line	ли́ния фро́нта *nf, nm*
no-fly zone	запре́тная возду́шная зо́на *nf*
nuclear-free zone	внея́дерная зо́на *nf*

beginnings of wars

aggressor nation	страна́-агре́ссор *nm*
incident	инциде́нт *nm*
militarization	милитариза́ция *nf*
mobilization	мобилиза́ция *nf*
parade	пара́д *nm*
preventive measures	превенти́вные ме́ры *nfpl*
remilitarization	ремилитариза́ция *nf*
war hysteria	вое́нная истери́я *nf*

during wars

campaign	кампа́ния *nf*
commanding heights	кома́ндные высо́ты *nfpl*
disposition (of troops)	диспози́ция *nf*
escalation	эскала́ция *nf*
firing position	огнева́я пози́ция *nf*
flank	фланг *nm*
foraging	фуражиро́вка *nf*
maneuver (BR manoevre)	манёвр *nm*
maneuvering (BR manoevring)	маневри́рование *nn*
marching	марширо́вка *nf*
military objective	вое́нный объе́кт *nm*
operation	опера́ция *nf*
parachute drop	парашю́тный деса́нт *nm*
position	пози́ция *nf*
reconnaissance	рекогносциро́вка *nf*
strategy	страте́гия *nf*
tactic	та́ктика *nf*
tactical error	такти́ческая оши́бка *nf*
troop formation	формирова́ние *nn*

ends of wars

arms control	контро́ль вооруже́ний *nm, nnpl*
capitulation	капитуля́ция *nf*
deescalation	деэскала́ция *nf*
demilitarization	демилитариза́ция *nf*
demobilization	демобилиза́ция *nf*
mass arrests	ма́ссовые аре́сты *nmpl*
medal	меда́ль *nf*
parade	пара́д *nm*
reparations	репара́ции *nfpl*
triumph	триу́мф *nm*
triumphal procession	триумфа́льное ше́ствие *nn*
trophy [of war]	трофе́й *nm*

offensive actions

aggression	агре́ссия *nf*
amphibious operation	морска́я деса́нтная опера́ция *nf*
attack	ата́ка *nf*
blitzkrieg	блицкри́г *nm*
blockade	блока́да *nf*
bombardment	бомбардиро́вка *nf*
bombing	бомбомета́ние *nn*, бомбёжка *nf*
embargo (*pl* embargoes)	эмба́рго *nn, indecl*
flank attack	фла́нговая ата́ка *nf*
frontal attack	фронта́льная ата́ка *nf*

gas attack	га́зовая ата́ка *nf*
infiltration	инфильтра́ция *nf*
occupation	оккупа́ция *nf*
occupier	оккупа́нт *nm*
raid	рейд *nm*
sabotage	сабота́ж *nm*
spying	шпиона́ж *nm*
storming [assault]	штурм *nm*
terrorism	террори́зм *nm*
terrorist act	террористи́ческий акт *nm*

defensive actions

camouflage	камуфля́ж *nm*
concentration (of troops)	концентра́ция *nf*
counterattack	контрата́ка *nf*
countermaneuver	контр-манёвр *nm*
countermarch	контрма́рш *nm*
counterrevolution	контрреволю́ция *nf*
diversion	диве́рсия *nf*
diversionary	диверсио́нный *aj*
evacuation	эвакуа́ция *nf*
forced march	форси́рованный марш *nm*
minelaying	мини́рование *nn*
siren [warning]	сире́на *nf*

descriptive words

aggressive	агресси́вный *aj*
brave (danger)	брави́ровать *impf*
demilitarized	демилитаризиро́ванный *aj*
frontal	фронта́льный *aj*
heroic	герои́ческий, геро́йский *aj*
heroics *npl*	геро́ика *nm*
maneuverable (BR manoeverable)	манёвренный *aj*
mechanized	механизи́рованный *aj*
mobile (forces)	моби́льный *aj*
motorized	моторизо́ванный *aj*
operational	операти́вный *aj*
preventive	превенти́вный *aj*
strategic	стратеги́ческий *aj*
triumphal	триумфа́льный *aj*
unheroic	негерои́ческий, негерои́чный *aj*

other terms

bivouac	бива́к *nm*
dictates *npl*	дикта́т *nm*
fifth column	пя́тая коло́нна *nf*
firing line, line of fire	ли́ния огня́ *nf*
home front	вну́тренний фронт *nm*
intern	интерни́ровать *impf, pf*
mobility	моби́льность *nf*
paper tiger	бума́жный тигр *nm*
unmask	демаскирова́ть *impf, pf*
Victoria Cross	Крест Викто́рии *nm, nf*

WEAPONS AND EQUIPMENT

general terms

arsenal	арсена́л *nm*
requisition	реквизи́ция *nf*
war machine	вое́нная маши́на
weapons system	систе́ма ору́жия *nf, nn*

kinds of weapons

gas mask	противога́з *nm*, противога́зовая ма́ска *nf*
shrapnel	шрапне́ль *nf*
antiballistic missile	антибаллисти́ческая раке́та *nf*
antitank	противота́нковый *aj*
artillery	артилле́рия *nf*
atomic weapon	а́томное ору́жие *nf*
ballistic missile	баллисти́ческая раке́та *nf*, баллисти́ческий снаря́д *nm*
bazooka	базу́ка *nf*
bomb	бо́мба *nf*
cannonade	канона́да *nf*
chemical weapons *npl*	хими́ческое ору́жие *nn*
heavy/light artillery	тяжёлая/лёгкая артилле́рия *nf*
mine	ми́на *nf*
mine detector	миноиска́тель *nm*
mortar	морти́ра *nf*
poison gas	ядови́тый газ *nm*
tank	танк *nm*
torpedo	торпеди́ровать *impf, pf*

vessels, vehicles, aircraft

amphibious tank	танк-амфи́бия *nm*
bomber	бомбово́з *nm*
dive-bomber	пики́рующий бомбарди́ровщик *nm*
flagship	фла́гманский кора́бль, фла́гман *nm*

medium bomber	средний бомбардиро́вщик *nm*
transport	тра́нспорт *nm*
transport plane	тра́нспортный самолёт *nm*
troop transport	войсково́й тра́нспорт *nm*

HISTORICAL TERMS

cavalry	кавале́рия *nf*
cavalryman (*pl* cavalrymen)	кавалери́ст *nm*
conquistador	конкистадо́р *nm*
cuirass [armor]	кира́са *nf*
cuirassier	кираси́р *nm*
dragoon	драгу́н *nm*
duel	дуэ́ль *nf*
duelist (BR duellist)	дуэля́нт, дуэли́ст *nm*
gladiator	гладиа́тор *nm*
Golden Horde	Золота́я Орда́ *nf*
halberd	алеба́рда *nf*
Hessian	ге́ссенский наёмник *nm*
hussar	гуса́р *nm*
janissary, janizary	яныча́р *nm*
kamikaze (pilot)	камика́дзе *nm, indecl*
Luftwaffe	Лю́фтваффе *nn, indecl*
musket	мушке́т *nm*
musketeer	мушкетёр *nm*
petard	пета́рда *nf*
phalanx	фала́нга *nf*
Red Army	Кра́сная А́рмия *nf*
Red/White Guard	Кра́сная/Бе́лая гва́рдия *nf*
samurai (*pl* samurai)	самура́й *nm*
scalp [Indian trophy]	скальп *nm*
Soviet Army	Сове́тская А́рмия *nf*
stalag [German prisoner-of-war camp]	шта́лаг *nm*
Wehrmacht	Ве́рмахт *nm*

wars and battle sites

Boer War	англо-бу́рская война́ *nf*
Crimean War	Кры́мская Война́ *nf*
Gettysburg	Ге́ттисберг *nm*
Waterloo	Ватерло́о *nn, indecl*

PERSONS

adjutant	адъютант *nm*
aggressor	агре́ссор *nm*
artilleryman (*pl* artillerymen)	артиллери́ст *nm*
ballistics expert	балли́стик *nm*
bombardier	бомбарди́р *nm*
bomber [plane, person]	бомбардиро́вщик *nm*
carabineer	карабинёр *nm*
collaborator [bad]	коллаборациони́ст *nm*
commandant	коменда́нт *nm*
commander	команди́р *nm*
commanding officer	кома́ндующий *nm*
counterrevolutionary	контрреволюционе́р *nm*
deserter	дезерти́р *nm*
evacuee	эвакуи́рованный *nm*, эвакуи́рованная *nf*
forager	фуражи́р *nm*
frontline soldier	фронтови́к *nm*
gendarme	жанда́рм *nm*
grenadier	гренаде́р *nm*
guardsman	гварде́ец *nm*
hero (*pl* heroes)	геро́й *nm*
internee	интерни́рованный *nm*
legionnaire	легионе́р *nm*
marauder	мародёр *nm*
militarist	милитари́ст *nm*
militiaman (*pl* militiamen)	милиционе́р *nm*
naval officer	офице́р фло́та *nm*
noncommissioned officer	у́нтер-офице́р *nm*
officer	офице́р *nm*
officer of the day	дежу́рный офице́р *nm*
orderly	ордина́рец *nm*
pacifist	пацифи́ст, -ка *nmf*
partisan	партиза́н, -ка *nmf*
personnel	персона́л *nm*
petty officer	у́нтер-офице́р *nm*
quartermaster	квартирме́йстер *nm*
renegade	ренега́т *nm*
reserve officer	офице́р запа́са *nm, nm*
reservist	резерви́ст *nm*
saboteur	сабота́жник *nm*
sapper	сапёр *nm*
sniper	сна́йпер *nm*
soldier	солда́т *nm*
spy	шпио́н *nm*
strategist	страте́г *nm*
tactician	та́ктик *nm*
tankman, tank soldier	танки́ст *nm*
terrorist	террори́ст, -ка *nmf*
veteran	ветера́н *nm*

See also **TITLES** ***(kinds of titles)***, **HISTORY AND ARCHEOLOGY**, **ANCIENT CIVILIZATIONS**

POLITICS AND GOVERNMENT

GENERAL TERMS

constitution	конститу́ция *nf*
control	контро́ль *nm*
diplomacy	диплома́тия *nf*
emigration	эмигра́ция *nf*
geopolitics *nplsv*	геополи́тика *nf*
government apparatus	госуда́рственный аппара́т *nm*
ideology	идеоло́гия *nf*
interests	интере́сы *nmpl*
masses, the	ма́ссы *nfpl*
national character	национа́льный хара́ктер *nm*
nationality	национа́льность *nf*
official	официа́льный *aj*
organ	о́рга́н *nm*
party	па́ртия *nf*
patriotism	патриоти́зм *nm*
political arena	полити́ческая аре́на *nf*
political crisis	полити́ческий кри́зис *nm*
political science	политоло́гия *nf*
political system	полити́ческая систе́ма *nf*
politics *nplsv* [good]	поли́тика *nf*
politics *nplsv* [bad]	политика́нство *nn*
psephology	псефоло́гия *nf*
reform	рефо́рма *nf*
regime	режи́м *nm*
ruling class	пра́вящий класс *nm*
secrecy	секре́тность *nf*
sovereignty	суверените́т *nm*
system	систе́ма *nf*
veto (*pl* vetoes)	ве́то *nn, indecl*
vote	во́тум *nm*

ORGANIZATION

form of government

anarchy	ана́рхия *nf*
autonomy	автоно́мия *nf*
coalition	коали́ция *nf*
democracy	демокра́тия *nf*
duumvirate	дуумвира́т *nm*
federation	федера́ция *nf*
feudalism [obs]	феодали́зм *nm*
mandate	манда́т *nm*
matriarchy	матриарха́т *nm*
monarchy	мона́рхия *nf*
monarchy, absolute	абсолю́тная мона́рхия *nf*
monarchy, constitutional	конституцио́нная мона́рхия *nf*
multinational	многонациона́льный *aj*
multiparty	многопарти́йный *aj*
parliamentary system	парламентари́зм *nm*
patriarchy	патриа́рхия *nf*
peonage [obs]	пеона́ж *nm*
planned economy	пла́новая эконо́мика *nf*
pluralistic	плюралисти́ческий *aj*
quadrumvirate	квадрумвира́т *nm*
republic	респу́блика *nf*
socialist system	социалисти́ческая систе́ма *nf*
tetrarchy	тетрархи́я *nf*
triumvirate	триумвира́т *nm*

scope of government

autonomous	автоно́мный *aj*
de facto	де-фа́кто *av*
federal	федера́льный, федерати́вный *aj*
global	глоба́льный *aj*
national	национа́льный *aj*
provincial	провинциа́льный *aj*

ruling group

aristocracy	аристокра́тия *nf*
autocracy	автокра́тия *nf*
bureaucracy	бюрократи́зм *nm*
dynasty	дина́стия *nf*
gerontocracy	геронтокра́тия *nf*
oligarchy	олига́рхия *nf*
plutocracy	плутокра́тия *nf*
technocracy	технокра́тия *nf*
theocracy	теокра́тия *nf*

political entities

autonomous republic/region	автоно́мная респу́блика/о́бласть *nf*
bloc	блок *nm*
canton	канто́н *nm*
colony	коло́ния *nf*
confederacy, confederation	конфедера́ция *nf*
domain [obs]	доме́н *nm*
dominion	доминио́н *nm*
empire	импе́рия *nf*
federation	федера́ция *nf*
guberniya [obs]	губе́рния *nf*

mandated territory	подманда́тная террито́рия *nf*
nation	на́ция *nf*
prefecture	префекту́ра *nf*
protectorate	протектора́т *nm*
province	прови́нция *nf*
regency	ре́гентство *nn*
Reich	рейх *nm*
reservation (for Indians)	резерва́ция *nf*
state	штат *nm*
territory	террито́рия *nf*
zemstvo [obs]	зе́мство *nn*

FUNCTIONING

governmental concerns

administration	администра́ция *nf*
amnesty	амни́стия *nf*
annexation	анне́ксия *nf*, аннекси́рование *nn*
assimilation [of immigrants]	ассимиля́ция *nf*
centralization	централиза́ция *nf*
colonization	колониза́ция *nf*
confiscation	конфиска́ция *nf*
corrective action	корректи́рование *nn*
crisis situation	кри́зисная ситуа́ция *nf*
expatriation	экспатриа́ция *nf*
federal budget	федера́льный бюдже́т *nm*
immigration	иммигра́ция *nf*
impeachment	импи́чмент *nm*
investiture	инвеститу́ра *nf*
justice [institutions]	юсти́ция *nf*
legislative act	законода́тельный акт *nm*
official inquiry	официа́льный запро́с *nm*
regulation, regulating	регули́рование *nn*
sanction	са́нкция *nf*

legislative, administrative, and regulatory bodies

bureau (*pl* bureaux or bureaus)	бюро́ *nn*, *indecl*
cabinet	кабине́т *nm*
department	департа́мент *nm*
junta	ху́нта *nf*
ministry	министе́рство *nn*
parliament	парла́мент *nm*
presidium (BR praesidium)	прези́диум *nm*
secret service	секре́тная слу́жба
senate	сена́т *nm*

official announcements

communiqué	коммюнике́ *nn*, *indecl*
declaration	деклара́ция *nf*
manifesto (*pl* manifestos, manifestoes)	манифе́ст *nm*
memorandum (*pl* memorandums, memoranda)	мемора́ндум *nm*
note	но́та *nf*
official communication	официа́льное сообще́ние *nn*
order	о́рден *nm*
proclamation	проклама́ция *nf*
propaganda	пропага́нда *nf*
regulation	регламента́ция *nf*
resolution	резолю́ция *nf*
ukase	ука́з *nm*
ultimatum (*pl* ultimatums, ultimata)	ультима́тум *nm*

international relations

accreditation (of ambassador)	аккредитова́ние *nn*
alliance	алья́нс *nm*
buffer state	бу́ферное госуда́рство *nn*
confrontation	конфронта́ция *nf*
consensus	консе́нсус *nm*
convention	конве́нция *nf*
démarche	дема́рш *nm*
diplomacy	диплома́тия *nf*
diplomatic immunity	дипломати́ческий иммуните́т *nm*
embargo (*pl* embargoes)	эмба́рго *nn*
expansion	экспа́нсия *nf*
extraterritoriality	экстратерриториа́льность *nf*
goodwill mission	ми́ссия до́брой во́ли *nf*, *nf*
intervention	интерве́нция *nf*
line of communication	коммуникацио́нная ли́ния *nf*
mission	ми́ссия *nf*
neutrality	нейтралите́т *nm*
normalization	нормализа́ция *nf*
official visit	официа́льный визи́т *nm*

pact	пакт *nm*
post	пост *nm*
protocol	протоко́л *nm*
ratification	ратифика́ция *nf*
round of talks	ра́унд перегово́ров *nm, nmpl*
sphere of influence	сфе́ра влия́ния *nf, nn*
territorial waters	территориа́льные во́ды *nfpl*

immigration and emigration

naturalization	натурализа́ция *nf*
passport	па́спорт *nm*
repatriation	репатриа́ция *nf*
residency	резиде́нция *nf*
visa	ви́за *nf*

influences on government

lobby	ло́бби *nn, indecl*
mass meeting	ма́ссовый ми́тинг, массо́вка *nf*
mass demonstration	ма́ссовая демонстра́ция *nf*
pamphlet	памфле́т *nm*
plebiscite	плебисци́т *nm*
political scandal	полити́ческий сканда́л *nm*
pressure group	инициати́вная гру́ппа *nf*
referendum (*pl* referendums, referenda)	рефере́ндум *nm*
vote of confidence	во́тум дове́рия *nm, nn*

opposition to government

agitation	агита́ция *nf*
demonstration	демонстра́ция *nf*
denunciation	денонса́ция *nf*
espionage	шпиона́ж *nm*
protest march	марш проте́ста *nm, nm*
provocation	провока́ция *nf*
public protest	публи́чный проте́ст *nm*
putsch	путч *nm*
revolution	револю́ция *nf*
sabotage	савота́ж *nm*
terror	терро́р *nm*

ceremonies and events

coronation	корона́ция *nf*
crowning	коронова́ние *nn*
inauguration	инаугура́ция *nf*
meeting	ми́тинг *nm*
national holiday	национа́льный пра́здник *nm*
session	се́ссия *nf*

symbols

coronet [small], crown [large]	коро́на *nf*
emblem	эмбле́ма *nf*
flag	флаг *nm*
Internationale	«Интернациона́л» *nm*
Marseillaise	«Марселье́за» *nf*
regalia	рега́лии *nfpl*
scepter (BR sceptre)	ски́петр *nm*
standard [flag]	штанда́рт *nm*
swastika	сва́стика *nf*
throne room	тро́нный зал *nm*
throne	трон *nm*

political parties and elections

absolute majority	абсолю́тное большинство́ *nn*
ballot (voting)	баллотиро́вка *nf*
campaign	кампа́ния *nf*
candidacy	кандидату́ра *nf*
electoral college	колле́гия вы́борщиков *nf, nmpl*
faction	фра́кция *nf*
governing party	пра́вящая па́ртия *nf*
opposition party	оппозицио́нная па́ртия *nf*
party conference	партконфере́нция *nf*
party line	парти́йная ли́ния *nf*
party loyalty	парти́йная лоя́льность *nf*
party membership	парти́йность *nf*
party platform	парти́йная платфо́рма *nf*
party politics *nplsv*	парти́йная поли́тика *nf*
political arena	полити́ческая аре́на *nf*
political climate	полити́ческий кли́мат *nm*
presidential elections	президе́нтские вы́боры *nmpl*
rally	ра́лли *nn, indecl*
strategy	страте́гия *nf*
united front	еди́ный фронт *nm*

places

10 Downing Street	10 Да́унинг-стрит *nm*
Capitol (building)	Капито́лий *nm*

chancellery	канцеля́рия *nf*
consulate	ко́нсульство *nn*
Kremlin	Кремль *nm*
Oval Office	Ова́льный кабине́т *nm* (в Бе́лом до́ме)

terms describing bad government

absolutism	абсолюти́зм *nm*
authoritarian	авторита́рный *aj*
corruption [graft]	корру́пция *nf*
despotism	деспоти́зм *nm*
destabilization	дестабилиза́ция *nf*
dictatorship	диктату́ра *nf*
disinformation	дезинформа́ция *nf*
police state	полице́йское госуда́рство *nn*
proliferation	пролифера́ция *nf*
repression	репре́ссия *nf*
terrorism	террори́зм *nm*
tyranny	тирани́я *nf*

other pejorative terms

anti-American	антиамерика́нский *aj*
anti-colonial	антиколониа́льный *aj*
anti-Communist	антикоммунисти́ческий *aj*
anti-fascist	антифаши́стский *aj*
banana republic	бана́новая респу́блика *nf*
demagogy, demagoguery	демаго́гия *nf*
despotic	деспоти́ческий *aj*
dogma (*pl* dogmas, dogmata)	до́гма *nf*
elitism	элити́зм *nm*
ethnic cleansing	этни́ческая чи́стка *nf*
extremism	экстреми́зм *nm*
fractional, factional	фракцио́нный *aj*
jingoism	джингои́зм *nm*
obstructive	обструкцио́нный *aj*
provocative	провокацио́нный *aj*
radical	радика́льный *aj*
reactionary	реакцио́нный *aj*
repressive	репресси́вный *aj*
smear tactics *npl*	та́ктика очерне́ния *nf*, *nn*
tyrannical	тирани́ческий *aj*
ultraconservative	кра́йне консервати́вный *aj*
un-American	антиамерика́нский *aj*
undemocratic	недемократи́ческий, антидемократи́ческий *aj*
unpatriotic	непатриоти́ческий *aj*

POLICIES, MOVEMENTS, AND PHILOSOPHIES

anarchism	анархи́зм *nm*
apartheid [obs]	апартеи́д *nm*
authoritarianism	авторитари́зм *nm*
centralism	централи́зм *nm*
centralization	централиза́ция *nf*
centrism	центри́зм *nm*
collectivism	коллективи́зм *nm*
colonialism	колониали́зм *nm*
communism	коммуни́зм *nm*
conservatism	консервати́зм *nm*
constitutionalism	конституционали́зм *nm*
decentralization	децентрализа́ция *nf*
decolonization	деколониза́ция *nf*
democratization	демократиза́ция *nf*
denationalization	денационализа́ция *nf*
denazification	денацифика́ция *nf*
domino theory	тео́рия домино́ *nf*
egalitarianism	эгалитари́зм *nm*
emancipation	эмансипа́ция *nf*
expansionism	экспансиони́зм *nm*
fascism, Fascism	фаши́зм *nm*
federalism	федерали́зм *nm*
feminism	фемини́зм *nm*
Fourierism	фурьери́зм *nm*
Gandhism	ганди́зм *nm*
hegemony	гегемо́ния *nf*
Hitlerism [obs]	гитлери́зм *nm*
imperialism	империали́зм *nm*
internationalism	интернационали́зм *nm*
internationalization	интернационализа́ция *nf*
isolationism	изоляциони́зм *nm*
Jacobinism [obs]	якоби́нство *nn*
liberalism	либерали́зм *nm*
liberalization	либерализа́ция *nf*
Maoism [obs]	маои́зм *nm*
Marxism	маркси́зм *nm*
materialism	материали́зм *nm*
mercantilism	меркантили́зм *nm*
militarism	милитари́зм *nm*
monarchism	монархи́зм *nm*
nationalism	национали́зм *nm*
Nazi(i)sm	наци́зм *nm*
neo-Fascism	неофаши́зм *nm*
neo-Nazism	неонаци́зм *nm*
neocolonialism	неоколониали́зм *nm*

nihilism	нигили́зм *nm*
obstructionism	обструкциони́зм *nm*
pacifism	пацифи́зм *nm*
Pan-Americanism	панамерикани́зм *nm*
passive resistance	пасси́вное сопротивле́ние *nn*
paternalism	патернали́зм *nm*
peace initiative	ми́рная инициати́ва *nf*
pluralism	плюрали́зм *nm*
populism	попули́зм *nm*
populist	попули́стский *aj*
privatization	приватиза́ция *nf*
prohibitionism [US, obs]	прогибициони́зм *nm*
protectionism	протекциони́зм *nm*
radicalism	радикали́зм *nm*
reform movement	реформи́стское движе́ние *nn*
reformism	реформи́зм *nm*
regionalism	регионали́зм *nm*
republicanism	республикани́зм *nm*
revanchism	реванши́зм *nm*
revisionism	ревизиони́зм *nm*
royalism	роялі́зм *nm*
separatism	сепарати́зм *nm*
socialism	социали́зм *nm*
totalitarianism	тоталитари́зм *nm*

POLITICS AND GOVERNMENT IN ACTION

major political parties

Communist Party	коммунисти́ческая па́ртия *nf*
Democratic Party	демократи́ческая па́ртия *nf*
Falange [obs]	Фала́нга *nf*
Kuomintang	гоминда́н *nm*
Labour Party	лейбори́стская па́ртия *nf*
Nicaraguan Contras	ко́нтрас *npl, indecl*
Republican Party	Республика́нская Па́ртия *nf*
Sinn Fein	па́ртия Шинфе́йн *nf*
Social-Democratic Party	Социа́л-Демократи́ческая Па́ртия *nf*
Zionism	сиони́зм *nm*

legislative bodies

Chamber of Deputies	Пала́та депута́тов *nf, nmpl*
Congress	Конгре́сс *nm*
Cortes *nsg*	Корте́сы *npl*
Duma	Ду́ма *nf*
General Assembly [United Nations]	Генера́льная Ассамбле́я *nf*
House of Lords	Пала́та ло́рдов *nf, nmpl*
House of Commons	Пала́та о́бщин *nf, nfpl*
Knesset(h)	Кне́ссет *nm*
Reichstag [obs]	Рейхста́г *nm*
United Nations Organization	Организа́ция Объединённых На́ций *nf, nfpl*

other governmental organizations

CIA [= Central Intelligence Agency]	ЦРУ *nn* [= Центра́льное разве́дывательное управле́ние]
Federal Reserve Board	Федера́льное резе́рвное правле́ние *nn*
Federal Trade Commission	Федера́льная торго́вая коми́ссия *nf*
Gestapo [obs]	геста́по *nn, indecl*
GPU [obs]	ГПУ *nm, indecl*
KGB [obs]	КГБ *nm, indecl*
NKVD [obs]	НКВД *nm, indecl*
Politburo [obs]	Политбюро́ *nn, indecl*
UNESCO [= United Nations Educational, Scientific & Cultural Organization]	ЮНЕСКО *nf* [= Организа́ция Объединённых На́ций по вопро́сам образова́ния, нау́ки и культу́ры]
UNICEF [= United Nations Children's Fund]	ЮНИСЕФ *nm* [= Де́тский фонд ООН]
USIA [= United States Information Agency]	ЮСИА *nf*

ALLIANCES AND AGREEMENTS

Arab League	Лига ара́бских стран *nf, nfpl*
Atlantic Charter	Атланти́ческая Ха́ртия *nf*
Entente	Анта́нта *nf*
GATT	ГАТТ *nn*
League of Nations [obs]	Ли́га на́ций *nf, nfpl*
NATO	НАТО *nn, indecl*
OPEC	ОПЕК *nm, indecl*
SEATO	СЕАТО *nn, indecl*
Treaty of Versailles	Верса́льский догово́р *nm*

Warsaw Pact	Варша́вский догово́р *nm*

terms associated with the United States

Bill of Rights	Билль о Права́х *nm, nnpl*
impeachment	импи́чмент *nm*
lynching	линчева́ние *nn*
Manhattan Project	Манха́ттанский прое́кт *nm*
Mason–Dixon line	ли́ния Ме́йсона–Ди́ксона *nf*
McCarthyism [obs]	маккарти́зм *nm*
preamble to the Constitution	преа́мбула конститу́ции *nf, nf*
the Clinton administration	администра́ция Кли́нтона *nf*
Watergate	Уотерге́йт *nm*

terms associated with the Soviet Union and Communism

artel	арте́ль *nf*
Bolshevism	большеви́зм *nm*
Central Committee	Центра́льный Комите́т *nm*
Comintern [1914–43]	Коминте́рн *nm*
cult of personality	культ ли́чности *nm, nf*
dictatorship of the proletariat	диктату́ра пролета-риа́та *nf, nm*
five-year plan	пятиле́тний план *nm*
glasnost	гла́сность *nf*
ideological struggle	иде́йная борьба́ *nf*
Komsomol	комсомо́л *nm*
Kremlinology	кремлиноло́гия *nf*
kulaks *npl*	кула́чество *nn*
Marxism-Leninism	маркси́зм-ленини́зм *nm*
Menshevism [obs]	меньшеви́зм *nm*
New Economic Policy [= NEP, 1922–27] *nf*	но́вая экономи́ческая поли́тика (= нэп)
October Revolution	Октя́брьская револю́ция *nf*
Order of Lenin	О́рден Ле́нина *nm*
perestroika	перестро́йка *nf*
Pioneers *npl*	пионе́рия *nf*
proletarian revolution	пролета́рская револю́ция *nf*
Russification	русифика́ция *nf*
Soviet	сове́т *nm*
Stalinism	сталини́зм *nm*
subbotnik [Saturday volunteer work]	суббо́тник *nm*
Supreme Soviet	Верхо́вный Сове́т *nm*
Trotskyism	троцки́зм *nm*

PERSONS

scholars

constitutionalist	конституционали́ст *nm*
Kremlinologist	кремлино́лог *nm*
political scientist	полито́лог *nm*
psephologist	псефо́лог *nm*
Sovietologist	советолог *nm*

members and followers

Bolshevik [USSR, obs]	большеви́к *nm*, большеви́чка *nf*
Confederate [US, obs]	конфедера́т *nm*
Decembrist [obs]	декабри́ст *nm*
Democrat	демокра́т, -ка *nmf*
Falangist [obs]	фаланги́ст *nm*
Fascist, fascist	фаши́ст, -ка *nmf*
Hitlerite [obs]	ги́тлеровец *nm*
Jacobin [obs]	якоби́нец *nm*
Komsomol [USSR, obs]	комсомо́лец *nm*, комсомо́лка *nf*
Laborite (BR Labourite)	лейбори́ст, -ка *nmf*
Leninist [USSR, obs]	ле́нинец *nm*
Marxist	маркси́ст, -ка *nmf*
McCarthyite [US, obs]	маккарти́ст *nm*
Menshevik [USSR, obs]	меньшеви́к *nm*, меньшеви́чка *nf*
Nazi	наци́ст, -ка *nmf*
NEPman [USSR, obs]	нэ́пман *nm*, нэ́пманша *nf*
Republican	республика́нец *nm*
Social Democrat	социа́л-демокра́т *nm*
Stalinist [USSR, obs]	сталини́ст, -ка *nmf*
Tory [obs]	то́ри *nmf, indecl*
Trotskyist, Trotskyite [USSR, obs]	троцки́ст, -ка *nmf*
Victorian [obs]	викториа́нец *nm*
Zionist	сиони́ст, -ка *nmf*

government employees

administrator	администра́тор *nm*
attache, attaché	атташе́ *nm, indecl*
bureaucrat	бюрокра́т, -ка *nmf*
delegate	делега́т, -ка *nmf*
deputy	депута́т, -ка *nmf*
diplomat	диплома́т *nm*
diplomatic courier	дипломати́ческий курье́р *nm*

double agent	двойно́й аге́нт *nm*
emissary	эмисса́р *nm*
functionary	функционе́р *nm*
Gestapo agent [obs]	геста́повец *nm*
member of parliament	парламента́рий *nm*
official	официа́льное лицо́ *nn*
page	паж *nm*
parliamentarian	парламента́рий *nm*
prefect	префе́кт *nm*
press attache	пресс-атташе́ *nm, indecl*
propagandist	пропаганди́ст, -ка *nmf*
secret agent	секре́тный аге́нт *nm*
spy	шпио́н, -ка *nmf*
technocrat	технокра́т *nm*

advocates

absolutist	абсолюти́ст *nm*
anarchist	анархи́ст, -ка *nmf*
anti-fascist	антифаши́ст, -ка *nmf*
anti-Soviet	антисове́тчик *nm*, антисове́тчица *nf*
centrist	центри́ст *nm*
colonialist	колониза́тор *nm*
communist	коммуни́ст, -ка *nmf*
conservative	консерва́тор *nm*
extremist	экстреми́ст, -ка *nmf*
federalist	федерали́ст *nm*
feminist	феми́нистка *nf*
imperialist	империали́ст *nm*
internationalist	интернационали́ст *nm*
interventionist	интерве́нт *nm*
isolationist	изоляциони́ст *nm*
liberal	либерал *nm*
loyalist	лояли́ст, -ка *nmf*
militarist	милитари́ст, -ка *nmf*
monarchist	монархи́ст, -ка *nmf*
nationalist	национали́ст, -ка *nmf*
neo-fascist	неофаши́ст, -ка *nmf*
neo-Nazi	неонаци́ст, -ка *nmf*
pacifist	пацифи́ст, -ка *nmf*
progressive	прогресси́вный челове́к *nm*
prohibitionist [US, obs]	прогибициони́ст *nm*
proletarian	пролета́рий *nm*
provincial	провинциа́л, -ка *nmf*
radical	радика́л *nm*
reactionary	реакционе́р *nm*
reformist	реформи́ст, -ка *nmf*
revanchist	реванши́ст, -ка *nmf*
revisionist	ревизиони́ст, -ка *nmf*
royalist	рояли́ст, -ка *nmf*
separatist	сепарати́ст, -ка *nmf*
socialist	социали́ст, -ка *nmf*
suffragette [US, obs]	суфражи́стка *nf*

anti-government

agitator	агита́тор *nm*
demonstrator	демонстра́нт, -ка *nmf*
dissident	диссиде́нт, -ка *nmf*
insurgent	инсурге́нт *nm*
obstructionist	обструкциони́ст *nm*
opponent	оппоне́нт *nm*
opposition, member of the	оппозиционе́р *nm* оппозиционерша *nf*
provocateur	провока́тор *nm*
revolutionary, revolutionist	революционе́р, -ка *nmf*
saboteur	сабота́жник *nm*, сабота́жница *nf*

other persons

activist	активи́ст, -ка *nmf*
aristocrat	аристокра́т, -ка *nmf*
candidate	кандида́т, -ка *nmf*
colonist	колони́ст, -ка *nmf*
colonizer	колониза́тор *nm*
demagog(ue)	демаго́г *nm*
despot	де́спот *nm*
dictator	дикта́тор *nm*
emancipator	эмансипа́тор *nm*
emigrant, emigre, émigré	эмигра́нт, -ка *nmf*
expatriate	экспатри́ант *nm*
immigrant	иммигра́нт, -ка *nmf*
jingo, jingoist	джингои́ст *nm*
leader	ли́дер *nm*
lobbyist	лобби́ст *nm*
monarch	мона́рх *nm*
oligarch	олига́рх *nm*
pamphleteer	памфлети́ст *nm*
party member	парти́ец, парти́йный *nm*

patriot	патрио́т, -ка *nmf*
persona non grata	персо́на нон гра́та *nf, indecl*
plutocrat	плутокра́т *nm*
politician	поли́тик *nm*
politician [pej]	политика́н *nm*
pretender (to the throne)	претенде́нт, -ка *nmf*
professional politician	профессиона́льный поли́тик *nm*
quisling [traitor]	кви́слинг *nm*
repatriate	репатриа́нт *nm*
resident	резиде́нт *nm*
tyrant	тира́н *nm*
very important person, VIP	ва́жная персо́на *nf*

groups

delegation	делега́ция *nf*
deputation	депута́ция *nf*
diplomatic corps	дипломати́ческий ко́рпус *nm*
emigrants *npl*	эмигра́ция *nf*, эмигра́нты *pl*

See also **TITLES** *(kinds of titles)*, **FAMOUS FIGURES OF YESTERDAY AND TODAY** *(political leaders)*, **ANCIENT CIVILIZATIONS** *(persons)*

Buying and Selling

ECONOMICS ♦ BUSINESS ♦ MONEY AND FINANCE

ECONOMICS

GENERAL TERMS

arbitrage	арбитра́ж *nm*
balance	бала́нс *nm*
banking system	ба́нковская систе́ма *nf*
capital	капита́л *nm*
capital and labor	труд и капита́л *nm*
collectivity	коллекти́вность *nf*
commercialization	коммерциализа́ция *nf*
concern	конце́рн *nm*
control	контро́ль *nm*
conversion [monetary]	конве́рсия, конверта́ция *nf*
credit	креди́т *nm*
crisis (*pl* crises)	кри́зис *nm*
economic [of the economy]	экономи́ческий *aj*
economic system	экономи́ческая систе́ма *nf*
economically [of economy]	экономи́чески *av*
economy [system]	эконо́мика *nf*
ECU, ecu	экю́ *nm, indecl*
financial	фина́нсовый *aj*
gross national product	валово́й национа́льный проду́кт *nm*
index	и́ндекс *nm*
indexing, indexation	индекса́ция *nf*
industry	инду́стрия *nf*
infrastructure	инфраструкту́ра *nf*
mass production	ма́ссовая проду́кция *nf*
model	моде́ль *nf*
modeling (BR modelling)	моделúрование *nn*
monetaristic	монетари́стский *aj*
monometallic	монометалли́ческий *aj*
normative, norm	нормати́в *nm*
petrodollars	петродо́ллары *nmpl*
price control	контро́ль над це́нами *nm, nfpl*
price index	и́ндекс цен *nm, nfpl*
product	проду́кт *nm*
production	проду́кция *nf*
productivity	продукти́вность *nf*
protective tariff	протекциони́стский тари́ф *nm*
quota	кво́та *nf*
regulate	регламенти́ровать *impf, pf*
rent	ре́нта *nf*
sanction	са́нкция *nf*
sector [public/private]	се́ктор *nm*
Social Security	социа́льное обеспе́чение *nn*
tariff	тари́ф *nm*
trust	трест *nm*
wage scale	шкала́ за́работной пла́ты *nf*

SPECIALIZATIONS

econometrics *nplsv*	экономе́трия *nf*
macroeconomics *nplsv*	макроэконо́мика *nf*
microeconomics *nplsv*	микроэконо́мика *nf*
political economics *nplsv*	политэконо́мия *nf*

ASPECTS OF ECONOMICS

classes

aristocracy	аристокра́тия *nf*
bourgeoisie	буржуази́я *nf*
intelligentsia	интеллиге́нция *nf*
lower class	ни́зший класс *nm*
lumpenproletariat	люмпенпролетариа́т *nm*
middle class	сре́дний класс *nm*
nobility	нобилите́т *nm*
proletariat	пролетариа́т *nm*
upper class	вы́сший класс *nm*
working class	рабо́чий класс *nm*

systems and theories

autarchy	авта́ркия *nf*
capitalism	капитали́зм *nm*
classlessness	бескла́ссовость *nf*
collectivism	коллективи́зм *nm*
fascism, Fascism	фаши́зм *nm*
feudalism [obs]	феодали́зм *nm*

industrialism — индустриали́зм *nm*
mercantilism — меркантили́зм *nm*
monetarism — монетари́зм *nm*
nationalization — национализа́ция *nf*
privatization — приватиза́ция *nf*
protectionism — протекциони́зм *nm*
socialism — социали́зм *nm*
syndicalism — синдикали́зм *nm*
vassalage — васса́льная зави́симость *nf*

kinds of economies

capitalistic — капиталисти́ческий *aj*
centralized — централизи́рованный *aj*
controlled — контроли́руемый *aj*
cooperative — кооперати́вный *aj*
European Economic Community — Европе́йское Экономи́ческое Соо́бщество *nn*
industrialized — индустриализи́рованный *aj*
international — интернациона́льный *aj*
planned — пла́новый *aj*

economic conditions

blockade — блока́да *nf*
boom — бум *nm*
boycott — бойко́т *nm*
chronic unemployment — хрони́ческая безрабо́тица *nf*
controlled inflation — контроли́руемая инфля́ция *nf*
crash — крах *nm*
deflation — дефля́ция *nf*
depression — депре́ссия *nf*
destabilization — дестабилиза́ция *nf*
economic crisis — кри́зис эконо́мики *nm, nf*
economic sanctions — экономи́ческие са́нкции *nfpl*
energy crisis — энергети́ческий кри́зис *nm*
gallop [inflation] — галопи́ровать *impf*
hyperinflation — гиперинфля́ция *nf*
inflation — инфля́ция *nf*
inflationary spiral — спира́ль инфля́ции *nf, nf*
instability — нестаби́льность *nf*
reflation — рефля́ция *nf*
stability — стаби́льность *nf*
stagnation — стагна́ция *nf*
tariff barrier — тари́фный барье́р *nm*
unbalanced — несбаланси́рованный *aj*

other terms

balanced budget — сбаланси́рованный бюдже́т *nm*
barter — ба́ртер *nm*
capitalization — капитализа́ция *nf*
cooperative — кооперати́в *nm*
monometallism — монометалли́зм *nm*
Parkinson's law — зако́н Паркинсо́на *nm, nm*
progressive tax — прогресси́вное обложе́ние нало́гом *nn, nm*
protective tariff — протекцио́нный тари́ф *nm*
import/export quota — и́мпортная/э́кспортная кво́та *nf*

PERSONS

individuals

bourgeois — буржуа́ *nm, indecl*
economist — экономи́ст *nm*
entrepreneur — антрепренёр *nm*
manager — ме́неджер *nm*
monetarist — монетари́ст *nm*
monopolist — монополи́ст *nm*
proletarian — пролета́рий *nm*
protectionist — протекциони́ст *nm*

groups

brain trust — мозгово́й трест *nm*
consortium — консо́рциум *nm*
management — ме́неджмент *nm*
petit bourgeois [obs] — мелкобуржуа́зный *aj*

See also **BUSINESS, POLITICS AND GOVERNMENT** *(organization)*

BUSINESS

GENERAL TERMS

business — би́знес *nm*
commerce — комме́рция *nf*
credit — креди́т *nm*
export-import — э́кспортно-и́мпортный *aj*
financing — финанси́рование *nn*
fiscal year — фиска́льный год *nm*
holding — хо́лдинг *nm*
inventory — инвента́рь *nm*

leasing	ли́зинг *nm*
management	ме́неджмент *nm*
mass production	ма́ссовая проду́кция *nf*
office	о́фис *nm*
operation	опера́ция *nf*
order number	номер заказа *nm, nm*
packaging	пакети́рование *nn*
product	проду́кт *nm*
production	проду́кция *nf*
shopping	шо́пинг *nm*
transportation	тра́нспорт *nm*

BUSINESSES

ownership and organization

cartel	карте́ль *nm*
charter	ча́ртер *nm*
company	компа́ния *nf*
conglomerate	конгломера́т *nm*
cooperative	коопера́ция *nf*
corporation	корпора́ция *nf*
firm	фи́рма *nf*
franchise	франши́за *nf*
monopoly	монопо́лия *nf*
mortgage company	ипоте́чная компа́ния *nf*
multinational	многонациона́льный *aj*
offshore	офшо́рный *aj*
parent company	матери́нская компа́ния *nf*
partnership	партнёрство *nn*
private company	ча́стная компа́ния *nf*
sporting goods	спорти́вные това́ры *nmpl*
syndicate	синдика́т *nm*
trading company	торго́вая компа́ния *nf*

type of product or service

agency	аге́нтство *nn*
agrobusiness	агроби́знес *nm*
banking	ба́нковское де́ло *nn*
bottlers *npl*	бо́ттлерс *nm*
cabotage	кабота́ж *nm*
clearing	кли́ринг *nm*
container ship	контейнерово́з *nm*
exporting	экспорти́рование *nn*
fabrication	фабрика́ция *nf*
franchising	франча́йзинг *nm*
holding company	хо́лдинг-компа́ния *nf*
importing	импорти́рование *nn*
insurance company	страхова́я компа́ния *nf*
leasing company	ли́зинговая компа́ния *nf*
offshore company	офшо́рная компа́ния *nf*
shipping company	судохо́дная компа́ния *nf*
sugar refinery	са́харный заво́д *nm*
sugar refining	сахароваре́ние *nn*
textile industry	тексти́льная промы́шленность *nf*
transit	транзи́т *nm*
transport company	транспо́ртная компа́ния *nf*

operations and management

business cycle	произво́дственный цикл *nm*
business lunch	би́знес-ланч *nm*
dotted line	пункти́рная ли́ния *nf*
inventory making	инвентариза́ция *nf*
know-how	но́у-ха́у *nn, indecl*
market position	пози́ция на ры́нке *nf, nm*
marketing organization	организа́ция ма́ркетинга *nf, nm*
material incentive	материа́льная заинтересо́ванность *nf*
net (profit)	не́тто *aj, indecl*
office equipment	о́фисная оргте́хника *nf*
point of entry/exit	пункт ввоза/вы́воза *nm, nm*
production plan	произво́дственный план *nm*
production line	пото́чная ли́ния *nf*
trade deficit	торго́вый дефици́т *nm*
trade organization	торго́вая организа́ция *nm*
venture capital	ве́нчурный капита́л *nm*

other terms

boycott	бойко́т *nm*
moratorium (*pl* moratoriums, moratoria)	морато́рий *nm*
potential	потенциа́л *nm*
productive	продукти́вный *aj*
rent	арендова́ть *impf*
section (of store)	се́кция *nf*

solid [well-established] соли́дный *aj*

RETAIL MARKETING

places

antiquary [antique shop/store] антиква́рный магази́н *nm*
bazaar база́р *nm*
Beryozka [hard currency shop] «Берёзка» *nf*
boutique бути́к *nm*
commercial center комме́рческий центр *nm*
concession конце́ссия *nf*
hotel оте́ль *nm*
jewelry store ювели́рный магази́н *nm*
kiosk кио́ск *nm*
motel моте́ль *nm*
perfume shop парфюме́рный магази́н *nm*
perfumery парфюме́рия *nf*
restaurant рестора́н *nm*
shopping center торго́вый центр *nm*
supermarket суперма́ркет *nm*
wine shop ви́нный магази́н *nm*

advertising

announcement ано́нс *nm*
brochure брошю́ра *nf*
campaign кампа́ния *nf*
catalog(ue) катало́г *nm*
demonstrate демонстри́ровать *impf*, продемонстри́ровать *pf*
exposition экспози́ция *nf*
line of products ли́ния проду́ктов *nf*, *nmpl*
logo логоти́п *nm*
Madison Avenue Ме́дисон-авеню́ *nn*
market analysis ана́лиз ры́нка *nm*
market research марке́тинговые иссле́дования *nnpl*
marketing марке́тинг *nm*
offer офе́рта *nf*
placard плака́т *nm*
presentation презента́ция *nf*
prospectus проспе́кт *nm*
public offer публи́чная офе́рта *nf*
slogan сло́ган *nm*
strategy страте́гия *nf*
trademark торго́вая/фабри́чная ма́рка *nf*

selling

assortment ассортиме́нт *nm*
auction аукцио́н *nm*
bar code бар-ко́д *nm*, штрихово́й код *nm*
cash register ка́ссовый аппара́т *nm*
concrete proposal конкре́тное предложе́ние *nn*
consignment консигна́ция *nf*
coupon купо́н *nm*
credit card креди́тная ка́рточка *nf*
customer profile про́филь покупа́теля *nm*, *nm*
discount диско́нт *nf*
duty-free zone беспо́шлинная зо́на *nf*
exclusive эксклюзи́вный *aj*
fixed price фикс *nm*
free port по́рто-фра́нко *nn*, *indecl*
liquidation ликвида́ция *nf*
lump sum лу́мпсум *nm*
nominal price номина́л *nm*, номина́льная цена́ *nf*
option опцио́н *nm*
potential market потенциа́льный ры́нок *nm*
price fixing фикса́ция цен *nf*
profit margin ма́ржа при́быльности *nf*, *nf*
season, seasonal сезо́нный *aj*

products

container конте́йнер *nm*
defect [in product] дефе́кт *nm*
defective (product) дефе́ктный *aj*
economical [efficient] экономи́чный *aj*
end product коне́чный проду́кт *nm*
export, exportation э́кспорт *nm*
free-trade zone зо́на свобо́дной торго́вли *nf*, *nf*
imitation [fake] имита́ция *nf*
import, importation и́мпорт *nm*
marked маркиро́ванный *aj*
marking (of goods) маркиро́вка *nm*
order number но́мер зака́за *nm*
quality control контро́ль ка́чества *nm*, *nn*

serial number	сери́йный но́мер *nm*
substandard	нестанда́ртный това́р *nm*
tare	та́ра *nf*
tare weight	вес та́ры *nm*
uneconomical	неэкономи́чный, неэконо́мный *aj*
unmarked	немаркиро́ванный *aj*

packaging and containers

bottle	буты́лка *nf*
bottle, large	буты́ль *nf*
canister	кани́стра *nf*
carton	карто́нка *nf*
cellophane	целлофа́н *nm*
fiberboard	фи́бровый карто́н *nm*
flacon	флако́н *nm*
flask	фля́жка *nf*
hermetically sealed	гермети́чески закры́тый/ закупо́ренный *aj*
packet, package	паке́т *nm*
phial	фи́ал *nm*
tube	тю́бик *nm*

LEGAL TERMS

condition	конди́ция *nf*
contract	контра́кт *nm*
embargo (*pl* embargoes)	эмба́рго *nn*
guarantee	гара́нтия *nf*
guaranteed	гаранти́рованный *aj*
import duty	импо́ртная по́шлина *nf*
import/export license	лице́нзия на ввоз/ вы́воз това́ра *nf*, *nm*, *nm*
import quota	импо́ртная кво́та *nf*
incorporation	инкорпора́ция *nf*
license (BR licence)	лице́нзия *nf*
licensing	лицензи́рование *nn*
patent	пате́нт *nm*
registered trademark	зарегистри́рованный това́рный знак *nm*
tariff barrier	тари́фный барье́р *nm*
trademark	маркирова́ть *impf*, *pf*
warehouse warrant	варра́нт *nm*
directive	директи́ва *nf*
directorship	дире́кторство *nn*
diversification	диверсифика́ция *nf*
dumping	де́мпинг *nm*

OFFICE EQUIPMENT

dictaphone [obs]	диктофо́н *nm*
fax	факс *nm*
pallet	палле́т *nm*
photocopier	фотокопирова́льный аппарат *nm*
portfolio	портфе́ль *nm*
stapler	сте́плер *nm*
telephone	телефо́н *nm*

PERSONS

individuals

agent	аге́нт *nm*
antique dealer	антиква́р *nm*
auctioneer	аукциони́ст *nm*
businessman (*pl* businessmen)	бизнесме́н *nm*
cashier	касси́р, -ша *nmf*
client	клие́нт, -ка *nmf*
concessionaire	концессионе́р *nm*
consignee	консигна́тор *nm*
consignor	консигна́нт *nm*
consultant	консульта́нт *nm*
contractor	контраге́нт *nm*
dealer	ди́лер *nm*
demonstrator	демонстра́тор *nm*
director	дире́ктор *nm*
discounter	дисконтер *nm*
distributor	дистрибью́тор *nm*
entrepreneur	антрепренёр *nm*
exporter	экспортёр *nm*
fabricator	фабрика́нт *nm*
importer	импортёр *nm*
licensee	лицензиа́т *nm*
licensor	лицензиа́р *nm*
manager	ме́неджер *nm*
partner	партнёр, -ша *nmf*
raider	ре́йдер *nm*
renter	аренда́тор *nm*
secretary	секрета́рь *nm*, секрета́рша *nf*
stenographer	стено́граф *nm*, стенографи́стка *nf*
tycoon	тайку́н *nm*

groups

board of directors	директора́т *nm*, дире́кция *nf*

clientele	клиенту́ра *nf*
consortium	консо́рциум *nm*
management	ме́неджмент *nm*
personnel	персона́л *nm*

See also **ECONOMICS, FOOD AND NUTRITION** *(aspects of food consumption)*, **LAW**

MONEY AND FINANCE

GENERAL TERMS

amortization	амортиза́ция *nf*
bank	банк *nm*
budget	бюдже́т *nm*
consolidate *vt(i)*	консолиди́ровать(ся) *impf, pf*
credit	креди́т *nm*
finances *npl*	фина́нсы *nmpl*
financial center	фина́нсовый центр *nm*
financing	финанси́рование *nn*
fund	фонд *nm*
monetary	моне́тный *aj*
numismatics *nplsv*	нумизма́тика *nf*
reserve fund	резе́рвный фонд *nm*
reserves	резе́рвы *nmpl*
resources	ресу́рсы *nmpl*
sum	су́мма *nf*
transaction	транса́кция *nf*

FINANCIAL CONDITION

having/making money

accumulation	аккумуля́ция *nf*
advance (payment)	ава́нс *nm*
annuity	аннуите́т *nm*
certificate of deposit	депози́тный сертифика́т *nm*
compensation	компенса́ция *nf*
coupon	купо́н *nm*
dividend	дивиде́нд *nm*
honorarium (*pl* honariums, honoraria)	гонора́р *nm*
investment income	дохо́д с инвести́ций *nm, nfpl*
pension	пе́нсия *nf*
reserve fund	резе́рвный фонд *nm*
social security/welfare	социа́льное обеспече́ние *nn*
stipend	стипе́ндия *nf*
student loan	студе́нческий заём *nm*
subsidy	субси́дия *nf*
voucher	ва́учер *nm*

not having/losing money

bankrupt	обанкро́тившийся *aj*
bankrupt, to become/go	обанкро́титься *pf*
bankruptcy	банкро́тство *nn*
debit balance	дебето́вый оста́ток
debit	де́бет *nm*, дебетова́ние *nn*
deficit	дефици́т *nm*
pauperism	паупери́зм *nm*
pauperization	паупериза́ция *nf*

ASPECTS OF MONEY AND FINANCE

banking

acceptance	акце́пт *nm*
balance (bookkeeping)	бала́нс *nm*
bank	ба́нковый, ба́нковский *aj*
bank deposit	депози́т *nm*
banker	банки́рский *aj*
banking operation	ба́нковская опера́ция *nf*
banking system	банко́вская систе́ма *nf*
banknote	банкно́т *nm*
blank check	бла́нковый чек *nm*
certificate (of deposit)	сертифика́т *nm*
check (BR cheque)	чек *nm*
clearing bank	кли́ринг-банк *nm*
commercial bank	комме́рческий банк *nm*
credit balance	кре́дитовый бала́нс *nm*
credit limit	креди́тный лими́т *nm*
credit risk	креди́тный риск *nm*
creditworthy	кредитоспосо́бный *aj*
creditworthiness	кредитоспосо́бность *nf*
depositary, depository	депозита́рий *nm*
endorse	индосси́ровать *impf, pf*
endorsement	индоссаме́нт *nm*
import-export bank	э̀кспортно-и́мпортный банк *nm*
investment bank	инвестицио́нный банк *nm*
national bank	национа́льный банк *nm*
on-call (account)	онко́ль *nm*

overdraft	овердра́фт *nm*
percent	проце́нт *nm*
prolong (credit)	пролонги́ровать *impf, pf*
refinance	рефинанси́ровать *impf, pf*
refinancing	рефинанси́рование *nn*

stock market

adventurism	авантю́ра *nf*, авантюри́зм *nm*
brokerage	брокера́ж *nm*, бро́керское аге́нство *nn*
broker's	бро́керский *aj*
broker's commission	бро́керская коми́ссия *nf*
brokerage house	бро́керский дом *nm*
cash order	ка́ссовый о́рдер *nm*
consolidated fund	консолиди́рованный фонд *nm*
debenture	дебенту́ра *nf*
Dow-Jones average/index	и́ндекс До́у-Джо́нса *nm*
futures	фьючерсы *npl*
investment [activity]	инвести́рование *nn*
investment [amount]	инвести́ция *nf*
limit [on price]	лими́т *nm*
liquid assets	ликви́дные акти́вы *nmpl*
liquidation	ликвида́ция *nf*
liquidity	ликви́дность *nf*
listing	ли́стинг *nm*
lot	лот *nm*
parity	парите́т *nm*
point	пункт *nm*
pool	пул *nm*
quotation	квотиро́вка *nm*, квоти́рование *nn*
quote	коти́ровать *impf, pf*
quoted at, to be	коти́роваться *impf*
realization	реализа́ция *nf*
realize (profits)	реализо́вывать *impf*, реализова́ть *pf*
reinvestment	реинвести́рование *nn*
risk factor	фа́ктор ри́ска *nm*, *nm*
risk	риск *nm*
settlement	сэ́тлмент *nm*
speculation	спекуля́ция *nf*
trust fund	тра́стовый фонд *nm*
unrealized (profits)	нереализо́ванный *aj*
Wall Street	Уолл-стрит *nm*

insurance terms

policy	по́лис *nm*
premium	пре́мия *nf*

taxes

audit	ауди́т *nm*
declaration	деклара́ция *nf*
declare income, to	деклари́ровать дохо́д *nm*
progressive tax	прогресси́вный нало́г *nm*

other terms

assignation	ассигнова́ние *nn*
falsification	фальсифика́ция *nf*
falsify (accounts)	фальсифици́ровать *impf, pf*
finance	фина́нси́ровать *impf, pf*
financial interests	фина́нсовые интере́сы *nmpl*
guaranty	гара́нтия *nf*
manipulation	манипуля́ция *nf*

MONETARY UNITS

widely used world currencies

dollar	до́ллар *nm*
drachma (*pl* drachmas, drachmae)	дра́хма *nf*
ECU, ecu	экю́ *nn, indecl*
franc	франк *nm*
guilder	гу́льден *nm*
krona (*pl* kronor)	кро́на *nf*
krone (*pl* kroner)	кро́на *nf*
lira (*pl* lire, liras)	ли́ра *nf*
mark	ма́рка *nf*
peseta	песе́та *nf*
peso	пе́со *nn, indecl*
pound sterling	фунт сте́рлингов *nm, nmpl*
real	реа́л *nm*
ruble, rouble	рубль *nm*
schilling	ши́ллинг *nm*
sterling	сте́рлинг *nm*
yen (*pl* yen)	ие́на *nf*
yuan (*pl* yuan)	юа́нь *nm*
zloty (*pl* zlotys, zloty)	зло́тый *nm*

other monitory units

afghani [Afghanistan]	афга́ни *nn*

baht [Indonesia]	бахт *nm*
balboa [Panama]	бальбо́а *nf*
birr [Ethiopia]	быр *nm*
boliviano [Bolivia]	боливиано *nn*
cedi [Ghana]	седи *nn*
colon [El Salvador]	коло́н *nm*
cordoba [Nicaragua]	ко́рдоба *nf*
dalasi [Gambia]	даласи́ *nn*
dinar [Iran]	дина́р *nm*
dirham [Morocco]	ди́рхам *nm*
dong [Viet Nam]	донг *nm*
escudo [Portugal]	эску́до *nn, indecl*
forint [Hungary]	фо́ринт *nm*
gourde [Haiti]	гурд *nm*
grivna [Ukraine]	гри́вна *nf*
guarani [Peru]	гварани́ *nn*
kina [Papua New Guinea]	ки́на *nf*
kip [Laos]	кип *nm*
koruna [Czech Republic, Slovakia]	кро́на *nf*
kwacha [Zambia, Malawi]	ква́ча *nf*
kwanza [Angola]	ква́нза *nf*
kyat [Myanmar]	кьят *nm*
lat [Latvia]	лат *nm*
lek [Albania]	лек *nm*
lempira [Honduras]	лемпи́ра *nf*
leone [Sierra Leone]	лео́не *nm*
leu [Moldavia, Rumania]	лей *nm*
lev [Bulgaria]	лев *nm*
lilangeni [Swaziland]	лиланге́ни *nn*
litas [Lithuania]	лит *nm*
loti (*pl* maloti) [Lesotho]	ло́ти *nn*
manat [Azerbaidjan, Turkmenistan]	мана́т *nm*
metical [Mozambique]	метика́ль *nm*
naira [Nigeria]	на́йра *nf*
ngultrum [Bhutan]	нгултру́м *nm*
ouguiya [Mauritania]	уги́я *nf*
pa'anga [Tonga]	паа́нга *nf*
pataca [Macao]	пата́ка *nf*
pula [Botswana]	пу́ла *nf*
quetzal [Guatemala]	кетса́ль *nn*
rand [South Africa]	ранд *nm*
rial, riyal [Iran, Yemen, Saudi Arabia]	риа́л, рия́л *nm*
riel [Cambodia]	рие́ль *nm*
ringgit [Malaysia]	ринги́т *nm*
rupee [India, Pakistan, Sri Lanka]	ру́пия *nf*
rupiah [Indonesia]	ру́пия *nf*
sol [Peru]	сол *nm*
som [Kirghizia]	сом *nm*
sucre [Ecuador]	су́кре *nn*
sum [Uzbekistan]	сум *nm*
taka [Bangladesh]	та́ка *nf*
tala [Western Samoa]	та́ла *nf*
tenga [Kazakhstan]	те́ньга *nf*
tolar [Slovenia]	тола́р *nm*
tugrik [Mongolia]	ту́грик *nm*
won [Korea]	во́на *nf*
zaire [Zaire]	зайр *nm*

historical and obsolete monetary terms

baksheesh	бакши́ш *nm*
crown	кро́на *nf*
doubloon	дубло́н *nm*
ducat	дука́т *nm*
farthing	фа́ртинг *nm*
florin	флори́н *nm*
guinea	гине́я *nf*
napoleon	наполеондо́р *nm*
sovereign	соверéн *nm*
teston	тесто́н *nm*

coins and smaller denominations

cent	цент *nm*
centavo	сента́во *nn*
centime	санти́м *nm*
groschen	грош *nm*
kopeck, copeck	копе́йка *nf*
lepton	ле́пта *nf*
pence *npl*	пенс *nm*
penny	пе́нни *nn, indecl*
pfennig	пфе́нниг *nm*
piaster (BR piastre)	пиа́стр *nm*
sen	сен *nm*
shekel	ше́кель *nm*
shilling	ши́ллинг *nm*
thaler	та́лер *nm*

terms referring to coins

bimetallism	биметалли́зм *nm*
false	фальши́вый *aj*
legend	леге́нда *nf*
reverse (of coin)	ре́верс *nm*

terms referring to currency

circulation	циркуля́ция *nf*
conversion	конве́рсия, конверта́ция *nf*
convertible	конверти́руемый *aj*
denomination	деномина́ция *nf*
devaluation	девальва́ция *nf*
emission	эми́ссия *nf*

Eurodollar	евродóллар *nm*
inconvertible, nonconvertible	неконверти́руемый *aj*
petrodollar	нефтедóллар *nm*
reform	рефóрма *nf*
revaluation	ревальвáция *nf*
stabilization	стабилизáция *nf*
stable (currency)	стаби́льный *nf*
standard	стандáрт *nm*

PERSONS

actuary	актуáрий *nm*
adventurist	авантюри́ст, -ка *nmf*
auditor	ауди́тор *nm*
bank clerk	бáнковский слýжащий *nm*, бáнковская слýжащая *nf*
banker	банки́р *nm*
bankrupt person	банкрóт *nm*
broker	брóкер *nm*
comptroller	контролёр *nm*
creditor	кредитóр *nm*
debtor	дебитóр *nm*
depositor	депози́тор *nm*
falsifier	фалсификáтор *nm*
financier	финанси́ст *nm*
guarantor	гарáнт *nm*
investor	инвéстор *nm*
liquidator	ликвидáтор *nm*
magnate	магнáт *nm*
manipulator	манипуля́тор *nm*
millionaire	миллионéр *nm*
millionairess	миллионéрша *nf*
multimillionaire	мультимиллионéр *nm*
numismatist	нумизмáт *nm*
pauper	пáупер *nm*
speculator	спекуля́нт, -ка *nmf*
stockbroker	биржевóй брóкер *nm*

See also **BUSINESS, PLACE NAMES II: POLITICAL ENTITIES**

Transportation

AVIATION AND SPACE TRAVEL ◆ BOATS AND SHIPS ◆ LAND TRANSPORTATION

AVIATION AND SPACE TRAVEL

FIELDS OF SPECIALIZATION

aeronautics *nplsv*	аэрона́втика *nf*
aerostatics *nplsv*	аэроста́тика *nf*
aviation	авиа́ция *nf*
navigation (science)	навига́ция *nf*
telemetry	телеметри́я *nf*

ASPECTS OF AIR TRAVEL

places

aerodrome, airdrome	аэродро́м *nm*
airport	аэропо́рт *nm*
hangar	анга́р *nm*
terminal	термина́л *nm*

types of aircraft

aeroplane [obs]	аэропла́н *nm*
aerostat	аэроста́т *nm*
air-taxi	возду́шное такси́ *nn*
airbus	аэробу́с *nm*
biplane	бипла́н *nm*
dirigible	дирижа́бль *nm*
liner	ла́йнер *nm*
monocoque	моноко́к *nm*
monoplane	монопла́н *nm*
ornithopter	орнитопте́р *nm*
transport, military	тра́нспорт *nm*
triplane	трипла́н *nm*
zeppelin	цеппели́н *nm*

parts and equipment

aileron	элеро́н *nm*
cabin	каби́на *nf*
fuselage	фюзеля́ж *nm*
nose	нос *nm*
oxygen mask	кислоро́дная ма́ска *nf*
panel	пане́ль *nf*
propellor	пропе́ллер *nm*
rotor	ро́тор *nm*
stabilizer	стабилиза́тор *nm*
vertical stabilizer	вертика́льный стабилиза́тор *nm*

instruments

altimeter	альтиме́тр *nm*
goniometer (BR goniometre)	гоно́метр *nm*
gyroscope	гироско́п *nm*
metal detector	металлоиска́тель *nm*
parachute	парашю́т *nm*
telemeter	телеме́тр *nm*

flying and navigation

air corridor	возду́шный коридо́р *nm*
automatic pilot, autopilot	автопило́т *nm*
chart	ка́рта *nf*
control tower	контро́льно-диспе́тчерский пункт *nm*
deviation (of compass)	девиа́ция *nf*
horizon	горизо́нт *nm*
manifest	маниф́ест *nm*
piloting	пилота́ж *nm*
pilotless	беспило́тный *aj*
training flight	трениро́вочный полёт *nm*

communications

radar	рада́р *nm*
radar control	рада́рный контро́ль *nm*
radio	ра́дио *nn, indecl*
teleran	телера́н *nm*

TERMS IN SPACE TRAVEL

capsule	ка́псула *nf*
catapult	катапу́льта *nf*
command module	кома́ндный отсе́к корабля́ *nm*
ion engine	ио́нный раке́тный двига́тель *nm*

Mach (number) — мах *nm*, число Ма́ха *nn*
NASA — НАСА *nf*
nose cone — носово́й ко́нус *nm*
orbit — орби́та *nf*
orbital — орбита́льный *aj*
retrorocket — ретрораке́та *nf*
rocket launch site — ракетодро́м *nm*
rocket — раке́та *nf*
rocket (-powered) — раке́тный *aj*
satellite — сателли́т *nm*
sound barrier — звуково́й барье́р *nm*
space station — косми́ческая ста́нция *nf*
sputnik — спу́тник *nm*
suborbital — суборбита́льный *aj*
unidentified flying object [= UFO] — неопо́знанный лета́ющий объе́кт *nm*

PERSONS

ace — ас *nm*
aeronaut — аэрона́вт *nm*
astronaut — астрона́вт *nm*
aviator — авиа́тор *nm*
co-pilot — второ́й пило́т *nm*
cosmonaut — космона́вт *nm*
navigator — навигато́р *nm*
passenger — пассажи́р, -ка *nmf*
pilot — пило́т *nm*
steward — стю́ард *nm*
stewardess — стюарде́сса *nf*
ufologist [UFO] — уфо́лог *nm*

See also **TOURISM**, **ASTRONOMY**, **THE MILITARY ESTABLISHMENT**, **METEOROLOGY**

BOATS AND SHIPS

GENERAL TERMS

board — борт *nm*
board, (to be) on — на бо́рту
board, (to go) on — на борт
boarding — аборда́ж *nm*
boat — бот *nm*
cruise — круи́з *nm*
cruising [military] — кре́йсерство *nn*
cruising [tourism] — круи́зинг *nm*
navigation science — навига́ция *nf*
ocean-going — океа́нский *aj*
onboard, aboard — бортово́й *aj*
regatta — рега́та *nf*
tonnage — тонна́ж *nm*

WATER VESSELS

sailboats

brig — бриг *nm*
brigantine — бриганти́на *nf*
caique — ка́ик *nm*
caravel — карavéлла *nf*
catamaran — катамара́н *nm*
clipper — кли́пер *nm*
cutter — ка́тер *nm*
felucca — фелю́га *nf*
junk — джо́нка *nf*
ketch — кеч *nm*
lugger — лю́гер *nm*
schooner — шху́на *nf*
sloop — шлюп *nm*, шлю́пка *nf*
trimaran — тримара́н *nm*
yawl — ял *nm*

military ships

convoy — конво́й *nm*
corsair — корса́р *nm*
corvette — корве́т *nm*
cruiser — кре́йсер *nm*
frigate — фрега́т *nm*
galleon [obs] — гале́он *nm*
minelayer — минёр *nm*, минный загради́тель *nm*
minesweeper — ми́нный тра́льщик *nm*
monitor [obs] — монито́р *nm*
torpedo boat — торпе́дный ка́тер *nm*
troop transport — войсково́й тра́нспорт *nm*

other craft

aquaplane — аквапла́н *nm*
barge — ба́ржа *nf*
bathysphere — батисфе́ра *nf*
canoe — кано́э *nn*, *indecl*
container ship — контейнерово́з *nm*
gondola — гондо́ла *nf*
hydroplane — гидросамолёт *nm*
kayak — кая́к *nm*
lighter — ли́хтер *nm*
liner — ла́йнер *nm*
motorboat — мотобо́т *nm*, мото́рная ло́дка *nf*
ocean liner — океа́нский ла́йнер *nm*
oil tanker — нефтяно́й та́нкер, нефтета́нкер *nm*
outrigger — а́утригер *nm*

passenger ship	пассажи́рское су́дно *nn*
pirate ship	пира́тский кора́бль *nm*
pirogue, piragua	пиро́га *nf*
refrigerator ship	рефрижера́торное су́дно *nn*
sampan	сампа́н *nm*
skiff	ски́ф *nm*
tanker	та́нкер *nm*
tramp steamer	трамп *nm*
trawler	тра́улер *nm*
umiak	умиа́к *nm*
whaleboat, whaler	вельбо́т *nm*
yacht	я́хта *nf*

groups of ships

armada	арма́да *nf*
flotilla	флоти́лия *nf*
squadron	эска́дра *nf*

parts and equipment

anchor	я́корь *nm*
ballast	балла́ст *nm*
beam	бимс *nm*
bowline	бу́линь *nm*
brace	брас *nm*
bunker	бу́нкер *nm*
buoy	буй *nm*
caisson	кессо́н *nm*
capstan	кабеста́н *nm*
flag	флаг *nm*
galley	гале́ра *nf*
keel	киль *nm*
line	линь *nm*
marline	марли́нь *nm*
martingale	мартинга́л *nm*
mast	ма́чта *nf*
outboard motor	подвесно́й мото́р *nm*
quarterdeck	квартерде́к *nm*
reef [sail]	риф *nm*
reef knot	ри́фовый у́зел *nm*
saloon	сало́н *nm*
spinnaker	спи́накер *nm*
stabilizer	стабилиза́тор *nm*
topsail	то́псель *nm*
trawl	трал *nm*
trysail	три́сель *nm*

NAVIGATION

tools, instruments, equipment

compass	ко́мпас *nm*
goniometer (BR goniometre)	гоно́метр *nm*
gyrocompass	гироко́мпас *nm*
gyroscope	гироско́п *nm*
hydrophone	гидрофо́н *nm*
hydroscope	гидроско́п *nm*
navigational chart	навигацио́нная ка́рта *nf*
periscope	периско́п *nm*
radar	рада́р *nm*
radiocompass	радиоко́мпас *nm*
sextant	секста́нт *nm*

plotting

compass needle	ко́мпасная стре́лка *nf*
course	курс *nm*
course correction	корректиро́вка ку́рса *nf*, *nm*
deviation (of compass)	девиа́ция *nf*
drift	дрейф *nm*
east	ост *nm*
position	пози́ция *nf*

measurements and directions

cruising speed	кре́йсерская ско́рость *nf*
nautical mile	морска́я ми́ля *nf*
north	норд *nm*
north-north-east	норд-норд-ост *av*
north-north-west	норд-норд-вест *av*
northeast, north by east, northeaster(ly) wind	норд-вест *nm*
northwest, north by west, northwester(ly) wind	норд-ост *nm*
waterline	ватерли́ния *nf*
west by southwest	вест-зюйд-вест *av*
west, westwind	вест *nm*
west by northwest	вест-норд-вест *av*
westerlies	ве́сты *npl*
westerly	весто́вый *aj*
westward, westwardly	вестово́й *aj*, *av*

starting and ending

anchorage	я́корная стоянка *nf*
dock, dockyard	док *nm*
haven [harbor]	га́вань *nf*
marina	мари́на *nf*
port	порт *nm*
sluice (gate)	шлюз *nm*

other terms

Bermuda Triangle	Берму́дский треуго́льник *nm*
canal	кана́л *nm*

pontoon	понтóн *nm*
pontoon bridge	понтóнный мост *nm*
trawling	трáление *nn*
trimming (of sails)	тримминг *nm*

MARITIME TRADE TERMS

cabotage	каботáж *nm*
lay days *npl*	лейдейс *nm*
manifest	манифéст *nm*
quarantine	карантúн *nm*
shipping line	судохóдная лúния *nf*

PERSONS

aquanaut	акванáвт *nm*
canoeist	каноэúст *nm*
captain	капитáн *nm*
docker, dockworker	дóкер *nm*
gondolier	гондольéр *nm*
navigator	навигатóр *nm*
passenger	пассажúр, -ка *nmf*
pirate	пирáт *nm*
ship's cook	кок *nm*
signalman, signaller	сигнáльщик *nm*
skipper	шкúпер *nm*
stevedor	стивидóр *nm*
steward	стю́ард *nm*
stewardess	стюардéсса *nf*
yachtsman (*pl* yachtsmen)	яхтсмéн *nm*
yachtswoman (*pl* yachtswomen)	яхтсмéнка *nf*

See also **LAW**, **METEOROLOGY** *(aspects of meteorology)*, **SPORTS** *(common sports)*

LAND TRANSPORTATION

GENERAL TERMS

bus line	автóбусная лúния *nf*
bus station	автóбусная стáнция *nf*
depot	депó *nn, indecl*
means of transportation	трáнспортное срéдство *nn*
public transport	общéственный трáнспорт *nm*
rail transport	железндорóжный трáнспорт *nm*
railway line	лúния желéзной дорóги *nf*
station	стáнция *nf*
streetcar line	трамвáйная лúния *nf*
terminal	терминáл *nm*
train platform	платфóрма *nf*
train station	железнодорóжная стáнция *nf*
tramline	трамвáйная лúния *nf*

MEANS OF TRANSPORTATION

motor-driven

automobile	автомобúль *nm*
bus	автóбус *nm*
electric train	электропóезд *nm*
escalator	эскалáтор *nm*
express (train)	экспрéсс *nm*
funicular (railway)	фуникулёр *nm*
lift	лифт *nm*
limousine	лимузúн *nm*
Metro	метрó *nm, indecl*
monorail	монорéльс *nm*, монорéльсовая дорóга *nf*
motorcycle	мотоцúкл *nm*
passenger train	пассажúрский пóезд *nm*
taxi	таксú *nn, indecl*
taxicab	тахомотóр *nm*
telpher [overhead cable]	тéльфер *nm*
tramway	трамвáй *nm*
trolleybus	троллéйбус *nm*

human-driven

bobsled, bobsledding	бóбслей *nm*
go-cart	карт *nm*
monocycle	моноцúкл *nm*
moped	мопéд *nm*
palanquin [obs]	паланкúн *nm*
rickshaw, jinricksha	рúкша *nf*
tandem	тáндéм *nm*
toboggan	тобóгган *nm*
velocipede [obs]	велосипéд *nm*

animal-driven

cabriolet	кабриолéт *nm*
caravan	каравáн *nm*
caravansery	каравáн-сарáй *nm*
droshky *nsg*	дрóжки *npl*
landau	ландó *nn, indecl*
troika	трóйка *nf*

other terms

artery	артéрия *nf*
blocking [on railway]	блокúрование *nn*
passenger car [on train]	пассажúрский вагóн *nm*
rails *npl*	рельс *nm*

railway track	ре́льсовый путь *nm*
season ticket	сезо́нный биле́т *nm*
semaphore	семафо́р *nm*
taximeter	тахо́метр *nm*
tender	те́ндер *nm*
trans-Siberian railway	транссиби́рская магистра́ль *nf*
tunnel	тонне́ль, тунне́ль *nm*
wheelbase	колёсная ба́за *nf*

PERSONS

chauffeur	шофёр *nm*
conductor	конду́ктор, -ша *nmf*
dispatcher	диспе́тчер *nm*
lift operator	лифтёр, -ша *nmf*
motorcyclist	мотоцикли́ст, -ка *nmf*
muleteer	пого́нщик му́лов *nm, nmpl*
passenger	пассажи́р, -ка *nmf*
taxi driver	такси́ст *nm*
tram worker	трамва́йщик *nm*

See also **AUTOMOBILES**, **THE CITY** *(aspects of the city)*, **TOURISM**

Living Things Great and Small

PLANTS ◆ ANIMALS ◆ BIOLOGY

PLANTS

GENERAL TERMS

aroma	аромáт *nm*
botany	ботáника *nf*
cultivation	культиви́рование *nn*
exotic	экзоти́ческий *aj*
flora (*pl* floras, florae)	флóра *nf*
hybrid	гибри́дный *aj*
ornamental	орнаментáльный *aj*

botany specializations

algeology	альголóгия *nf*
dendrology	дендролóгия *nf*
flora, study of	флори́стика *nf*
hydroponics *nplsv*	гидропóника *nf*
paleobotany (BR palaeobotany)	палеоботáника *nf*

NAMES OF PLANTS

trees and shrubs

acacia	акáция *nf*
acanthus	акáнт *nm*
balsa	бáльза *nf*
banyan	банья́н *nm*
baobab	баобáб *nm*
barberry	барбари́с *nm*
bergamot	бергамóт *nm*
betel (palm)	бéтель *nm*
bougainvillaea	бугенви́ллия *nf*
cacao (tree)	дéрево какáо *nn*
camellia	камéлия *nf*
cassia	кáссия *nf*
catalpa	катáльпа *nf*
cedar	кедр *nm*
cedar of Lebanon	ливáнский кедр *nm*
coca	кóка *nf*
coco palm	кокóсовая пáльма *nf*
coco, coconut palm	кокóс *nm*
cryptomeria	криптомери́я *nf*
cypress	кипари́с *nm*
ebony (tree)	эбéновое дéрево *nn*
elm	ильм *nm*
eucalyptus	эвкали́пт *nm*
ficus (*pl* ficus)	фи́кус *nm*
ginkgo (*pl* ginkgoes)	ги́нкго *nn*, *indecl*
gum	гу́мми *nn*, *indecl*
jacaranda	джакарáнда *nf*
jasmine	жасми́н *nm*
laurel	лавр *nm*
lemon (tree)	лимóнное дéрево *nn*
magnolia	магнóлия *nf*
mangrove (tree)	мáнгровое дéрево *nn*
mastic (tree)	масти́ковое дéрево *nn*
mimosa	мимóза *nf*
musk rose	му́скусная рóза *nf*
myrtle	мирт *nm*
oleander	олеáндр *nm*
olive tree	оли́ва *nf*, оли́вковое дéрево *nn*
palm	пáльма *nf*
palmetto	пальмéтто *nn*
Palmyra (palm)	пáльма пальми́рская *nf*
pistachio	фистáшка *nf*
quassia	кáссия *nf*
rhododendron	рододéндрон *nm*
rosebush	рóзовый куст *nm*
rosewood (tree)	рóзовое дéрево *nn*
sago (palm)	сáго *nn*, *indecl*, сáговая пáльма *nf*
sandalwood	сандáл *nm*, сандáловое дéрево *nn*
sandarac (tree)	сандарáковое дéрево *nn*
sassafras	сассафрáс *nm*
sequoia	секвóйя *nf*
sumac(h)	сумáх *nm*
sycamore	сикомóр *nm*
tamarisk	тамари́ск *nm*
teak	тик *nm*
tearose	чáйная рóза *nf*
tulip tree	тюльпáновое дéрево *nn*
tung tree	тунг *nm*, ту́нговое дéрево *nn*

house and garden plants

African violet	африкáнская фиáлка *nf*
anemone	анемóн *nm*

aspidistra — аспиди́стра *nf*
aster — а́стра *nf*
begonia — бего́ния *nf*
belladonna — белладо́нна *nf*
cattleya (orchid) — каттле́я *nf*
chrysanthemum — хризанте́ма *nf*
cineraria — цинера́рия *nf*
crocus — кро́кус *nm*
cyclamen — цикламе́н *nm*
delphinium — дельфи́ниум *nm*
dracaena — драко́нник *nm*
freesia — фре́зия *nf*
fuchsia — фу́ксия *nf*
gardenia — гарде́ния *nf*
geranium — гера́нь *nf*
gladiolus (*pl* gladioluses, gladioli) — гладио́лус *nm*
gloxinia — глокси́ния *nf*
heliotrope — гелиотро́п *nm*
hibiscus (*pl* hibiscus) — гиби́скус *nm*
hyacinth — гиаци́нт *nm*
iris — и́рис *nm*
jonquil — жонки́лия *nf*
lily — ли́лия *nf*
lobelia (*pl* lobelias, lobelia) — лобе́лия *nf*
lupin — люпи́н *nm*
marguerite (daisy) — маргари́тка *nf*
narcissus (*pl* narcissuses, narcissi) — нарци́сс *nm*
nasturtium — насту́рция *nf*
orchid — орхиде́я *nf*
pelargonium — пеларго́ния *nf*
peony — пио́н *nm*
petunia — пету́ния *nf*
philodendron — филоде́ндрон *nm*
phlox (*pl* phloxes, phlox) — флокс *nm*
portulaca — портула́к *nm*
primula — при́мула *nf*
pyrethrum — пире́трум *nm*
rose — ро́за *nf*
tiger lily — тигро́вая ли́лия *nf*
tuberose — туберо́за *nf*
tulip — тюльпа́н *nm*
valerian — валерья́на, валериа́на *nf*
verbena — вербе́на *nf*
zinnia — ци́нния *nf*

wild flowers

aconite — акони́т *nm*
clover — кле́вер *nm*
cockle — ку́коль *nm*
edelweiss — эдельве́йс *nm*

herbs

anise — ани́с *nm*
arnica — а́рника *nf*
ginseng — женьше́нь *nf*
indigo (*pl* indigos, indigoes) — инди́го *nn, indecl*
lavender — лава́нда *nf*

aquatic plants

chlorella (algae) — хлоре́лла *nf*
diatom — диато́мея *nf*
hydrophyte — гидрофи́т *nm*
kelp — келп *nm*
lotus — ло́тос *nm*
papyrus — папи́рус *nm*
sargasso (algae) — сарга́сса *nf*
water lily — водяна́я ли́лия *nf*

succulents

agave — ага́ва *nf*
aloe — ало́э *nn, indecl*
cactus (*pl* cactuses, cacti) — ка́ктус *nm*

grasses

bamboo — бамбу́к *nn*
Bermuda grass — берму́дская трава́ *nf*
esparto — эспа́рто *nn, indecl*
pampas grass — трава́ пампа́сная *nf*
sorghum — со́рго *nn, indecl*

other plants

arum — а́рум *nm*
asphodel — асфоде́ль *nm*
cardoon — ка́рда *nf*
colocynth (vine) — колокви́нт *nm*
grapevine — виногра́д *nm*
hyssop — иссо́п *nm*
liana (vine) — лиа́на *nf*
mandrake — мандраго́ра *nf*
moss — мох *nm*
myrrh — ми́рра *nf*
nard, spikenard — нард *nm*
rattan — рота́нг *nm*
veronica — верони́ка *nf*

PLANT PARTS AND ANATOMY

abaxial (leaf) — абаксиа́льный *aj*
bud — буто́н *nm*

crown (of tree)	кро́на *nf*
fiber (BR fibre)	фи́бра *nf*
latex	ла́текс *nm*
mycelium [part of fungus]	мице́лий *nm*
nectar	некта́р *nm*
pore	по́ра *nf*
pulp	пу́льпа *nf*
rhizome	ризо́ма *nf*
stela, stele (*pl* stelae)	стэ́ла *nf*
testa (*pl* testae)	те́ста *nm*
tubercle	тубе́ркул *nm*

tissues and fibers

lignin	ли́гнин *nm*
parenchyma	паренхи́ма *nf*
phloem	флоэ́ма *nf*
xylem	ксиле́ма *nf*

GROWING OF PLANTS

groupings

herbarium (*pl* herbariums, herbaria)	герба́рий *nm*
laurel grove	ла́вровая ро́ща *nf*
rose garden	роза́рий *nm*
terrarium	терра́рий, терра́риум *nm*

display

bonsai	бонса́й *nm*
bouquet	буке́т *nm*
espalier	шпале́ра *nf*
garland	гирля́нда *nf*
ikebana	икеба́на *nf*
jardiniere, jardinière	жардинье́рка *nf*
trellis	трелья́ж *nm*
vase	ва́за *nf*

stages and processes

cambium	ка́мбий *nm*
chlorophyll	хлорофи́лл *nm*
osmosis	о́смос *nm*
photosynthesis	фотоси́нтез *nm*
transplantation	транспланта́ция *nf*
vegetation	вегета́ция *nf*

pests and disease control

algaecide	альтици́д *nm*
chlorosis	хлоро́з *nm*
defoliant	дефолиа́нт *nm*
herbicide	гербици́д *nm*
insecticide	инсектици́д *nm*
parasite	парази́т *nm*
phylloxera	филлоксе́ра *nf*

PERSONS

botanist	бота́ник *nm*
flora specialist	флори́ст *nm*
naturalist	натурали́ст *nm*

See also **BIOLOGY**, **AGRICULTURE**, **FOOD AND NUTRITION** *(kinds of food)*, **TEXTILES** *(aspects of textiles)*

ANIMALS

GENERAL TERMS

amphibian (*pl* amphibia)	амфи́бия *nf*
anthropoid	антропо́ид *nm*
colony	коло́ния *nf*
dinosaur	диноза́вр *nm*
exotic	экзоти́ческий *aj*
fauna (*pl* faunas, faunae)	фа́уна *nf*
hermaphrodite	гермафроди́т *nm*
mollusc, mollusk	моллю́ск *nm*
parasite	парази́т *nm*
primate	прима́т *nm*
protozoa	протозо́а *pl, indecl*
reptile	репти́лия *nf*
zoology	зооло́гия *nf*

ZOOLOGY SPECIALIZATIONS

conchology	конхи(ли)оло́гия *nf*
entomology	энтомоло́гия *nf*
helminthology	гельминтоло́гия *nf*
ichthyology	ихтеоло́гия *nf*
ornithology	орнитоло́гия *nf*
primatology	приматоло́гия *nf*
taxidermy	таксиде́рмия *nf*
veterinary medicine	ветерина́рия *nf*
zoography	зоогеогра́фия *nf*

MAMMALS

primates

baboon	бабуи́н *nm*
capuchin	капуци́н *nm*
chimpanzee	шимпанзе́ *nn, indecl*
gibbon	гибо́н *nm*
gorilla	гори́лла *nf*
lemur	лему́р *nm*

macaque	макáка *nf*
mandrill	мандри́л *nm*
orangutan(g)	орангутáнг *nm*
Rhesus monkey	рéзус *nm*

felines

cat, tomcat	кот *nm*
cougar	когуáр *nm*
jaguar	ягуáр *nm*
leopard	леопáрд *nm*
ocelot	оцелóт *nm*
panther	пантéра *nf*
puma	пýма *nf*
tiger cub	тигрёнок *nm*
tiger	тигр *nm*
tigress	тигри́ца *nf*

canines

Airedale	эрдельтерьéр *nm*
basset hound	бáс(с)ет *nm*
beagle	бигль *nm*
borzoi	борзáя *nf*
boxer	боксёр *nm*
bull terrier	бультерьéр *nm*
bulldog	бульдóг *nm*
chihuahua	чихуáхуа *nf, indecl*
cocker spaniel	кóкер-спаниéль *nm*
collie	кóлли *nm, indecl*
coyote	койóт *nm*
dalmatian	далмáтский дог *nm*
dingo (*pl* dingoes)	ди́нго *nmf, indecl*
fox terrier	фокстерьéр *nm*
Great Dane	дáтский дог *nm*
griffon	грифóн *nm*
jackal	шакáл *nm*
labrador	лабрадóр *nm*
mastiff	масти́фф *nm*
Newfoundland dog	ньюфáундленд *nm*
Pekin(g)ese	пекинéс *nm*
pinscher	пи́нчер *nm*
pit bull	пит-бýль *nm*
pointer	пойнтер *nm*
poodle	пýдель *nm*
Russian wolfhound	рýсская борзáя *nf*
Siberian husky	сиби́рская лáйка *nf*
Skye terrier	скáйтерьер *nm*
terrier	терьéр *nm*

equines

Arabian horse	арáбская лóшадь *nf*
hunter	гýнтер *nm*
mule	мул *nm*
mustang	мýстанг *nm*
onager	онáгр *nm*
percheron	першерóн *nm*
pony	пóни *nm, indecl*
zebra (*pl* zebras, zebra)	зéбра *nf*

marsupials

kangaroo (*pl* kangaroos, kangaroo)	кенгурý *nm, indecl*
koala	коáла *nf*
opossum	опóссум *nm*
wallaby	кенгурý-валлáби *nm, indecl*
wombat	вомбáт *nm*

ruminants

alpaca	альпакá *nmf, indecl*
antelope (*pl* antelopes, antelope)	антилóпа *nf*
Bactrian camel	бактриáн *nm*
bison (*pl* bison)	бизóн *nm*
buffalo (*pl* buffalo, buffalos, buffaloes)	бýйвол *nm*, буйволи́ца *nf*
caribou (*pl* caribou)	кари́бу *nm, indecl*
cheviot	шевиóт *nm*
dromedary	дромадéр *nm*
gazelle	газéль *nf*
giraffe (*pl* giraffes, giraffe)	жирáф *nm*, жирáфа *nf*
gnu (*pl* gnus, gnu)	гну *nm, indecl*
Jersey cow	джерсéйская корóва *nf*
karakul, caracul	карáкуль *nm*
llama (*pl* llamas, llama)	лáма *nf*
merino	меринóс *nm*
moufflon	муфлóн *nm*
musk ox (*pl* oxen)	мускýсный бык *nm*
okapi (*pl* okapis, okapi)	окáпи *nn, indecl*
peccary	пéкари *nm, indecl*
vicuna (*pl* vicunas, vicuna)	викýнья *nf*
yak (*pl* yaks, yak)	як *nm*
zebu (*pl* zebus, zebu)	зéбу *nm, indecl*

rodents

chinchilla	шинши́лла *nf*
gopher	гóфер *nm*
lemming	лéмминг *nm*
mongoose	мангýста *nf*

pachyderms

hippopotamus (*pl* hippopotamuses, hippopotami)	гиппопотáм *nm*

rhinoceros (*pl* rhinoceroses, rhinoceri)	носорóг *nm*

other mammals

armadillo	армади́лл *nm*
beluga (whale)	белу́га *nf*
cachalot (whale)	кашалóт *nm*
dolphin	дельфи́н *nm*
echidna	ехи́дна *nf*
genet	генéтта *nf*
grizzly (bear)	гри́зли *nm, indecl*
hyena	гиéна *nf*
narwal, narhwal (whale)	нарвáл *nm*
panda	пáнда *nf*
polar bear	поля́рный медвéдь *nm*
sable	сóболь *nm*
tapir	тапи́р *nm*
vampire bat	вампи́р *nm*

BIRDS

flying

canary	канарéйка *nf*
cardinal	кардинáл *nm*
cockatoo	какаду́ *nn, indecl*
condor	кóндор *nm*
cuckoo	куку́шка *nf*
frigate bird	фрегáт *nm*
kookaburra	кокабу́рра *nf*
marabou	марабу́ *nm, indecl*
myna, mina(h)	ми́на *nf*
pheasant	фазáн *nm*
tanager	танáгра *nf*
toucan	тукáн *nm*

flightless and aquatic

albatross	альбатрóс *nm*
cassowary	казуáр *nm*
egret-plume	эгрéт *nm*
emu	э́му *nm, indecl*
flamingo (*pl* flamingos, flamingoes)	флами́нго *nm, indecl*
goose	гусь *nm*, гусы́ня *nf*
gosling	гусёнок *nm*
ibis (*pl* ibises, ibis)	и́бис *nm*
kiwi bird	ки́ви, ки́ви-ки́ви *nf, indecl*
leghorn	леггóрн *nm*
pelican	пеликáн *nm*
penguin	пингви́н *nm*

INSECTS AND WORMS

anopheles (mosquito)	анóфелес *nm*
cicada	цикáда *nf*
cochineal	кошени́ль *nf*
ephemerid (*pl* ephemeridae)	эфемери́да *nf*
mosquito	моски́т *nm*
nematode	нематóда *nf*
phylloxera	филлоксéра *nf*
Spanish fly	шпáнская му́ха *nf*
tachina fly	му́ха-тахи́на *nf*
tarantula	тарáнтул *nm*
tegmen	тéгмен *nm*
termite	терми́т *nm*
trichina (*pl* trichinae)	трихи́на *nf*
tsetse (fly)	(му́ха) цецé *nf, indecl*

FISH AND MARINE LIFE

fish

barracuda	баррaку́да *nf*
carp	карп *nm*
dugong	дюгóнь *nm*
hake	хек *nm*
mackerel	макрéль *nf*
moray (eel)	мурéна *nf*
piranha	пирáнья *nf*
tarpon	тарпóн *nm*
tuna	тунéц *nm*
turbot	тюрбó *nn, indecl*

marine animals

amoeba, ameba	амёба *nf*
crab	краб *nm*
hydra (*pl* hydras, hydrae)	ги́дра *nf*
krill (*pl* krill)	криль *nm*
nautilus (*pl* nautiluses, nautili)	наути́лус *nm*
nekton	нектóн *nm*
oyster	у́стрица *nm*
paramecium (*pl* paramecia)	парамéция *nf*
pluteus	плу́теус *nm*
polyp	поли́п *nm*

anemone, sea	морско́й анемо́н nm

REPTILES

snakes

anaconda	анако́нда nf
asp	а́спид nm
boa	боа́ nm, indecl
cobra	ко́бра nf
mamba	ма́мба nf
moccasin	мокаси́новая змея́ nf
python	пито́н nm

other reptiles

alligator	аллига́тор nm
cayman, caiman	кайма́н nm
chameleon	хамелео́н nm
crocodile	крокоди́л nm
gecko (*pl* geckos, geckoes)	гекко́н nm
iguana	игуа́на nf

EXTINCT ANIMALS

brontosaurus	бронтоза́вр nm
diplodocus	диплодо́к nm
ichthyosaurus	ихтиоза́вр nm
mammoth	ма́монт nm
mastodon	мастодо́нт nm
plesiosaurus	плезиоза́вр nm
pterodactyl	птерода́ктиль nm
stegosaurus	стегоза́вр nm

TERMS RELATING TO ANIMALS

specialized animal anatomy

cloaca	клоа́ка nf
croup	круп nm
plume	плюма́ж nm
pulp	пу́льпа nf
telson	тельсо́н nm
tergum	терги́т nm
thorax (*pl* thoraxes, thoraces)	то́ракс nm
vibrissa	вибри́сса nf

reproduction

cocoon	ко́кон nm
imago (*pl* imagos, imagoes, imagines)	има́го nn
medusa	меду́за nf
pheronome	феро́мон nm

dogs and horses

caracole	карако́ль nm
curvet	курбе́т nm
gallop	гало́п nm
groom	грум nm
lasso (*pl* lassos, lassoes)	лассо́ nn, indecl
livery	ливре́я nf
manege, manège	мане́ж nm
martingale	мартинга́л nm
saddle	седло́ nn

places

aquarium	аква́риум nm
dolphinarium	дельфина́рий nm
rodeo	роде́о nn, indecl
vivarium (*pl* vivaria)	вива́рий nm
zoo, zoological garden/park	зооса́д, зоопа́рк, зоологи́ческий парк/сад nm

other terms

animal magnetism	зоомагнети́зм nm
anthrax	антра́кс nm
epizootic	эпизооти́ческий aj
leonine	леони́нский aj
migratory	миграцио́нный /мигри́рующий aj
pasture	па́стбище nn
territoriality	территориа́льность nm
vivisection	вивисе́кция nf
zoophilia [sexual love for animals]	зоофили́я nf

PERSONS

entomologist	энтомоло́г nm
jockey	жоке́й nm
ornithologist	орнито́лог nm
taxidermist	таксидерми́ст nm
trapper	тра́ппер nm
veterinarian	ветерина́р nm
vivisectionist	вивисе́ктор nm
zoographer	зоогео́граф nm
zoologist	зоо́лог nm

See also **AGRICULTURE** *(aspects of farming)*, **FOOD AND NUTRITION** *(kinds of food)*, **CLASSICAL MYTHOLOGY**, **THE BIBLE** *(other biblical vocabulary)*, **FICTION AND FOLKLORE** *(famous characters)*

BIOLOGY

GENERAL TERMS

aberrant	аберра́нтный *aj*
activate	активи́ровать *impf, pf*
activation	актива́ция, активиза́ция *nf*
bio-	био- *pref*
biological research station	биоста́нция *nf*
biological	биологи́ческий *aj*
biology	биоло́гия *nf*
bioresources	биоресу́рсы *npl*
biorhythm	биори́тм *nm*
biosphere	биосфе́ра *nf*
biotype	биоти́п *nm*
characteristic	характе́рная черта́ *nf*
circadian	цирка́дный *aj*
class	класс *nm*
classification	классифика́ция *nf*
colony	коло́ния *nf*
culture	культу́ра *nf*
cycle	цикл *nm*
differentiation	дифференци́рование *nn*
genesis	гене́зис *nm*
instinct	инсти́нкт *nm*
latency	лате́нтность *nf*
microorganism	микрооргани́зм *nm*
molecule	моле́кула *nf*
ontogenesis	онтогене́з *nm*
ontogeny	онтоге́ния *nf*
organic world	органи́ческий мир *nm*
organism	органи́зм *nm*
organogenesis	органогене́з *nm*
phylum	фи́лом *nm*
phyto-	фи́то- *pref*
phytotron	фототро́н *nm*
population	популя́ция *nf*
protoplasm	протопла́зма *nf*
specialized organ	специа́льный о́рган *nm*
stimulus (*pl* stimuli)	сти́мул *nm*
subculture	субкульту́ра *nf*
subtype	подти́п *nm*

BRANCHES OF BIOLOGY

major fields

bacteriology	бактериоло́гия *nf*
biophysics *nplsv*	биофи́зика *nf*
biotechnology	биотехноло́гия *nf*
botany	бота́ника *nf*
cryobiology	криобиоло́гия *nf*
cytology	цитоло́гия *nf*
ecology	эколо́гия *nf*
embryology	эмбриоло́гия *nf*
entomology	энтомоло́гия *nf*
evolution	эволю́ция *nf*
exobiology	экзобиоло́гия *nf*
genetics *nplsv*	гене́тика *nf*
histology	гистоло́гия *nf*
hybridization	гибридиза́ция *nf*
ichthyology	ихтиоло́гия *nf*
immunology	иммуноло́гия *nf*
microbiology	микробиоло́гия *nf*
molecular	молекуля́рный *aj*
morphology	морфоло́гия *nf*
mycology	миколо́гия *nf*
neurobiology	нейробиоло́гия *nf*
ornithology	орнитоло́гия *nf*
paleontology (BR palaeontology)	палеонтоло́гия *nf*
physiology	физиоло́гия *nf*
psychobiology	психобиоло́гия *nf*
radiobiology	радиобиоло́гия *nf*
sociobiology	социобиоло́гия *nf*
systematics *nplsv*	система́тика *nf*
taxonomy	таксоно́мия *nf*
virology	вирусоло́гия *nf*
xerophily	ксерофи́лия *nf*
zoology	зооло́гия *nf*

related fields

agrobiology	агробиоло́гия *nf*
anatomy	анато́мия *nf*
anthropology	антрополо́гия *nf*
biochemistry	биохи́мия *nf*
bioengineering	биоинжене́рия *nf*
bionics *nplsv*	био́ника *nf*
eugenics *nplsv*	евге́ника *nf*
geomicrobiology	геомикробиоло́гия *nf*
macrobiotics *nplsv*	макробио́тика *nf*
oology	ооло́гия *nf*
organography	органогра́фия *nf*
parasitology	паразитоло́гия *nf*
phenology	феноло́гия *nf*
phytogenesis	фитогене́з *nm*
phytogeography	фитогеогра́фия *nf*
phytography	фитографи́я *nf*
phytopathology	фитопатоло́гия *nf*
sociobiology	социобиоло́гия *nf*
somatology	соматоло́гия *nf*

teratology	тератология *nf*
organology	органология *nf*

ASPECTS OF BIOLOGY

theories

anthropogenesis	антропогенéз *nm*
Darwinism	дарвинúзм *nm*
evolution	эволюциóнное учéние *nn*
Malthusianism	мальтузиáнство *nn*
Mendelian theory	мéнделеевское учéние *nn*
monogenesis	моногенéзис *nm*
monogenism	моногенúзм *nm*
orthogenesis	ортогенéз *nm*
telegony	телегóния *nf*
teleonomy	телеонóмия *nf*
vitalism	виталúзм *nm*

major biotypes

ecotype	экотúп *nm*
genotype	генотúп *nm*
monotype	монотúп *nm*
phenotype	фенотúп *nm*

life forms

bacteria	бактéрии *nfpl*
epiphyte	эпифúт *nm*
hermaphrodite	гермафродúт *nm*
hybrid	гибрúд *nm*
infusoria	инфузóрия *nf*
lanceolate	ланцетовúдный *aj*
lichen	лишáй, лишáйник *nm*
microbe	микрóб *nm*
moss	мох *nm*
mutagen	мутагéн *nm*
oophyte	оофúт *nm*
parasite	паразúт *nm*
polymorph	полимóрф *nm*
pteridophyte	птеридофúт *nm*
virus	вúрус *nm*
xerophyte	ксерофúт *nm*
zoophyte	зоофúт *nm*

biological processes

acclimation, acclimatization	акклиматизáция *nf*
anabiosis	анабиóз *nm*
gamogenesis	гамогенéз *nm*
incrustation	инкрустáция *nf*
involution	инволюция *nf*
isomorphism	изоморфúзм *nm*
meiosis	мейóзис *nm*
metamorphosis (*pl* metamorphoses)	метаморфóза *nf*
mimesis	миметúзм *nm*
mimicry	мимикрúя *nf*
mutagenesis	мутагенéз *nm*
mutation	мутáция *nf*
necrobiosis	некробиóз *nm*
ovulation	овулúция *nf*
palingenesis	палингенéз *nm*
parasitism	паразитúзм *nm*
photosynthesis	фотосúнтез *nm*
phototaxis	фототáксис *nm*
phototropism	фототропúзм *nm*
phylogenesis, phylogeny	филогенéз *nm*
plasmolysis	плазмолúз *nm*
regeneration	регенерáция *nf*
reversion	ревéрсия *nf*
stereotaxis	стереотáксис *nm*
symbiosis (*pl* symbioses)	симбиóз *nm*
taxis	тáксис *nm*

reproduction

– plants –

endosperm	эндоспéрм *nm*
microspore	микроспóра *nf*
oospore	ооспóра *nf*
spore	спóра *nf*
teleutospore	телевтоспóра *nf*
zoospore	зооспóра *nf*
zygospore	зигоспóра *nf*

– animals –

gamete	гамéта *nf*
gonad	гонáда *nf*
mating season	брáчный сезóн
oogenesis	оогенéз *nm*
parthenogenesis	партеногенéз *nm*
sperm	сперма *nf*
spermatogenesis	сперматогенéз *nm*
spermatozoid	сперматозóид *nm*
syngamy	сингáмия *nf*
syngenesis	сингенéз *nm*

other terms

analogous	аналогúчный *aj*
autochtonous	автохтóнный *aj*
autogenous	автогéнный *aj*
biocide	биоцúд *nm*
epidermis	эпидéрмис *nm*
generative	генератúвный *aj*
heterogeneous	гетерогéнный *aj*

homolog(ue)	гомóлог *nm*
immunity	иммунитéт *nm*
impulse	и́мпульс *nm*
incubation	инкубáция *nf*
pigmentation	пигментáция *nf*
proliferation	пролиферáция *nf*
spontaneous	спонтáнный *aj*
undifferentiated	недифференци́рованный *aj*
vegetative	вегетациóнный *aj*
xenobiotic	ксенобиóтик *nm*

TERMS IN EMBRYOLOGY

ectoderm	эктодéрма *nf*
embryo	эмбриóн *nm*
rudiment	рудимéнт *nm*
rudimentary organ	рудимéнтарный óрган *nm*
spermatozoon (*pl* spermatozoa)	сперматозóид *nm*
teratogen	тератогéн *nm*
zygote	зигóта *nf*

TERMS IN GENETICS

albinism	альбини́зм *nm*
albino	альбинóс, -ка *nmf*
atavism	атави́зм *nm*
chimera	химéра *nf*
chromosome	хромосóма *nf*
clone	клон *nm*
defective gene	дефéктный ген *nm*
dominant (gene)	доминáнта *nf*
dyad	диáда *nf*
gene	ген *nm*
genetic code	генети́ческий код *nm*
genetic engineering	гéнная инженéрия *nf*
maternal	матери́нский *aj*, по мáтери *nf*
mutant	мутáнт *nm*
nannoplankton	наннопланктóн *nm*
plasmagene	плазмогéн *nm*
plasmid	плазми́да *nf*
recessive gene	рецесси́вный ген *nm*
repressible gene	репресси́руемый ген *nm*
repressor, represser gene	ген-репрéссор *nm*
ribonucleic acid [= RNA]	рибонуклеи́новая кислотá
synapsis (*pl* synapses)	си́напсис *nm*
tetrad	тетрáда *nf*
X chromosome	X-хромосóма *nf*

TERMS IN CYTOLOGY

cell structure	структýра клéтки *nf*, *nf*
cytoplasm	цитоплáзма *nf*
ectoplasm	эктоплáзма *nf*
endoplasm	эндоплáзма
haploid	гаплóид *nm*
hypertrophy	гипертрофи́я *nf*
lacuna (*pl* lacunae)	лакýна *nf*
membrane	мембрáна *nf*
mitosis	митóз *nm*
phagocyte	фагоци́т *nm*
phytoplankton	фитопланктóн *nm*
plankton	планктóн *nm*
ribosome	рибосóма *nf*
somatoplasm	соматоплáзма *nf*
telophase	телофáза *nf*
vacuole	вакуóль *nf*
zooplankton	зоопланктóн *nm*

TERMS IN ECOLOGY

ecosystem	экосистéма *nf*
niche	ни́ша *nf*
quadrat	квадрáт *nm*

TERMS IN BIOCHEMISTRY

antigen	антигéн *nm*
enzyme	энзи́м *nm*
histamine	гистами́н *nm*
hormone	гормóн *nm*
hydrolysis	гидрóлиз *nm*
lecithin	лецити́н *nm*
lipid(e)	липи́д *nm*
neurotransmitter	нейротрансми́ттер *nm*
peptide	пепти́д *nm*
protein	протеи́н *nm*
vitamin	витами́н *nm*

PERSONS

bacteriologist	бактериóлог *nm*
biochemist	биохи́мик *nm*
biologist	биóлог *nm*
Darwinist	дарвини́ст *nm*
ecologist	экóлог *nm*
embryologist	эмбриóлог *nm*
evolutionist	эволюциони́ст *nm*

geneticist	гене́тик *nm*
histologist	гисто́лог *nm*
ichthyologist	ихтио́лог *nm*
Malthusian	мальтузиа́нец *nm*
microbiologist	микробио́лог *nm*
mycologist	мико́лог *nm*
neurobiologist	нейробио́лог *nm*
paleontologist (BR palaeontologist)	палеонто́лог *nm*
taxonomist	таксономи́ст *nm*

See also **PLANTS *(general terms)*, THE HUMAN BODY, MEDICAL PRACTICE, PHYSICAL DISORDERS, CHEMISTRY**

Medical Matters

THE HUMAN BODY ◆ MEDICAL PRACTICE ◆ PHYSICAL DISORDERS ◆ PSYCHOLOGY ◆ SEX ◆ DRUGS ◆ DEATH

THE HUMAN BODY

GENERAL TERMS

anatomy	анатóмия *nf*
circulate [blood]	циркули́ровать *impf*
constitution	конститу́ция *nf*
figure	фигу́ра *nf*
motor	motóрный *aj*
organ	óрган *nm*
physiological	физиологи́ческий *aj*
pigment	пигмéнт *nm*
portal	портáл *nm*
psychomotor	психомотóрный *aj*
pulse	пульс *nm*
secretion	секрéция *nf*
somatic	сомати́ческий *aj*
system	систéма *nf*
tone	тóнус *nm*
tract	тракт *nm*
vasomotor	вазомотóрный *aj*

STRUCTURE

systems

central nervous system	центрáльная нéрвная систéма *nf*
digestive system	пищевари́тельная систéма *nf*
endocrine sysem	эндокри́нная систéма *nf*
excretory system	экскретóрная систéма *nf*
immune system	имму́нная систéма *nf*
lymphatic system	лимфати́ческая систéма *nf*
respiratory system	респиратóрная систéма *nf*
skeletal system	скелéтная систéма *nf*

components

artery	артéрия *nf*
canal	канáл *nm*
circulatory organs	óрганы кровообра-щéния *nnpl*
digestive tract	пищевари́тельный тракт *nm*
muscle	му́скул *nm*
musculature	мускулату́ра *nf*
nerve	нерв *nm*
organs of hearing	óрганы слу́ха *nmpl*
organs of speech	óрганы рéчи *nmpl*
sensory organs	óрганы чувств *nmpl*
sex organs	половы́е óрганы *nmpl*

major sections

cerebro-spinal	цереброспинáльный *aj*
dorsal	дорсáльный *aj*
perineal	перинеáльный *aj*
thoracic	торакáльный *aj*

NAMES OF BODY PARTS

bones and joints

patella (*pl* patellas, patellae)	патéлла *nf*
phalanx (*pl* phalanxes, phalanges)	фалáнга пáльца *nf, nm*
skeleton	скелéт *nm*
spinal column	спиннóй хребéт *nm*
trapezium	трапéция *nf*
trapezoid	трапезóид *nm*

muscles

biceps	би́цепс *nm*
deltoid muscle	дельтови́дная мы́шца *nf*
diaphragm	диафрáгма *nf*
sphincter	сфи́нктер *nm*

glands

endocrine glands	эндокри́нные жéлезы *nfpl*
lymph nodes	лимфати́ческие узлы́ *nmpl*
pancreas	пáнкреас *nm*
parietal lobe	паритáльная дóля *nf*

blood and blood vessels

aorta	аóрта *nf*
capillary	капилля́р *nm*
corpuscle	корпу́скула *nf*
erythrocyte	эритроци́т *nm*

gamma globulin — га́мма-глобули́н *nm*
hem-, haem- — гем- *pref*
hemoglobin (BR haemoglobin) — гемоглоби́н *nm*
leukocyte — лейкоци́т *nm*
lymphocyte — лимфоци́т *nm*
osteoblast — остеобла́ст *nm*
plasma — пла́зма *nf*
vein — ве́на *nf*

tissues

adenoids — адено́иды *nmpl*
collagen — коллаге́н *nm*
macrophage — макрофа́г *nm*
membrane — мембра́на *nf*
parenchyma — паренхи́ма *nf*

eyes and ears

crystalline lens — хруста́лик *nm*
pair of eyes — па́ра глаз *nf, nmpl*
retina (*pl* retinas, retinae) — рети́на *nf*
sclera — скле́ра *nf*
Eustachian tube — евста́хиева труба́ *nf*

digestive tract

appendix — аппе́ндикс *nm*
duodenal — дуодена́льный *aj*
gastric — гастри́ческий *aj*
pylorus — пило́рус *nm*

organs of reproduction

clitoris — кли́тор *nm*
Fallopian tube — фалло́пиева труба́ *nf*
genitalia — генита́лии *nfpl*
penis (*pl* penises, peni) — пе́нис *nm*
phallus (*pl* phalluses, phalli) — фа́ллос *nm*
placenta (*pl* placentas, placentae) — плаце́нта *nf*
prostate — проста́та *nf*
vulva (*pl* vulvas, vulvae) — ву́льва *nf*

head and brain

Adam's apple — ада́мово я́блоко *nn*
cerebral — церебра́льный *aj*
cheek — щека́ *nf*
dentin(e) — денти́н *nm*
follicle — фолли́кул *nm*
hairline — ли́ния воло́с *nf*
hypothalamus — гипота́ламус *nm*
laryngeal — ларинга́льный *aj*
lock (of hair) — ло́кон *nm*
mandibula — манди́була *nf*
nose — нос *nm*
sagittal — сагита́льный *aj*
scalp — скальп *nm*
sinus — си́нус *nm*

skin

cutis — ку́тис *nm*
epidermis — эпиде́рмис *nm*
epithelium (*pl* epitheliums, epithelia) — эпите́лий *nm*
squamous — сквамо́зный *aj*

heart and lung

bronchi(a), bronchial tubes — бро́нхи *nmpl*
coronary — корона́рный *aj*
diastole — диа́стола *nf*
myocardium — миока́рд *nm*
pericardium (*pl* pericardia) — перика́рд *nm*
pleura (*pl* pleurae) — пле́вра *nf*
systole — си́стола *nf*
trachea (*pl* tracheas, tracheae) — трахе́я *nf*

nerves

dendrite — дендри́т *nm*
erogenous — эроге́нный *aj*
ganglion (*pl* ganglions, ganglia) — га́нглий *nm*
nerve cell — не́рвная кле́тка *nf*
nerve center — не́рвный центр *nm*
nerve ending — не́рвное оконча́ние *nn*
nerve fiber — не́рвное волокно́ *nn*
neuroglia — нейроглия́ *nf*
neuron — нейро́н *nm*
optic nerve — опти́ческий нерв *nm*
parasympathetic — парасимпати́ческий *aj*
spinal cord — спинно́й мозг *nm*
sympathetic nerve — симпати́чный нерв *nm*
synaps — си́напс *nm*

other terms

anus (*pl* anuses, ani) — а́нус *nm*, ана́льное отве́рстие *nn*
cuticle — кути́кула *nf*
meniscus (*pl* meniscuses, menisci) — мени́ск *nm*
thorax (*pl* thoraxes, thoraces) — то́ракс *nf*

urethra (*pl* urethras, urethrae) — уре́тра *nf*

PHYSIOLOGY

physical body types

ectomorphic — эктомо́рфный *aj*
endomorphic — эндомо́рфный *aj*

functions and states

accommodation (of eye) — аккомода́ция *nf*
beat (of heart) *vi* — би́ться *impf*
circulation — циркуля́ция *nf*
climacteric — кли́макс, климакте́рий *nm*
coordination — координа́ция *nf*
erection — эре́кция *nf*
excretion — экскре́ция *nf*
inhalation — ингаля́ция *nf*
lactation — лакта́ция *nf*
menarch — мена́рхе *nn*, *indecl*
menstruation — менструа́ция *nf*
metabolism — метаболи́зм *nm*
nervous impulse — не́рвный и́мпульс *nm*
orgasm — orга́зм *nm*
peristalsis — периста́льтика *nf*
pulsation — пульса́ция *nf*
stimulation — стимули́рование *nn*

movements and body positions

gesticulation — жестикуля́ция *nf*
grimace — грима́са *nf*
motor reflex — мото́рный рефле́кс *nm*
reflex — рефле́кс *nm*
reflex reaction — рефлекто́рная реа́кция *nf*

fluids, secretions, and products

excrement *nsg*, excreta *npl* — экскреме́нты *nmpl*
feces (BR faeces) — фека́лии *nfpl*
semen — се́мя *nf*
sperm — сперма *nf*
spinal fluid — спинномозгова́я жи́дкость *nf*
stool [feces] — стул *nm*

BIOCHEMICALS

classification

enzyme — энзи́м *nm*
hormone — гормо́н *nm*
protein — протеи́н *nm*
vitamin — витами́н *nm*

hormones

adrenalin — адренали́н *nm*
aldosterone — альдостеро́н *nm*
estrogen (BR oestrogen) — эстроге́н *nm*
insulin — инсули́н *nm*
lipotropen — липотропи́н *nm*
progesterone — прогестеро́н *nm*
prolactin — пролакти́н *nm*
prostaglandin — простагланди́н *nm*
serotonin — серотони́н *nm*
somatostatin — соматостати́н *nm*
somatotropin — соматотропи́н *nm*
steroid — стеро́ид *nm*
testosterone — тестостеро́н *nm*

enzymes

amylase — амила́за *nf*
histaminase — гистамина́за *nf*
lipase — липа́за *nf*
pancreatin — панкреати́н *nm*
papain — папаин *nm*
pectase — пекта́за *nf*
pepsin — пепси́н *nm*
peptic — пепти́ческий *aj*
peroxidaze — пероксида́за *nf*
plasmin — плазми́н *nm*
polymerase — полимера́за *nf*
protease — протеа́за *nf*
ribonuclease — рибонуклеа́за *nf*
trypsin — трипси́н *nm*
urokinase — урокина́за *nf*
zymase — зима́за *nf*
zymogen — зимоге́н *nm*

proteins and vitamins

albumen — альбуми́н *nm*
fibrin — фибри́н *nm*
fibrinogen — фибриноге́н *nm*
keratin — керати́н *nm*
peptone — пепто́н *nm*
prolamine — пролами́н *nm*
properdin — проперди́н *nm*
retinol — ретино́л *nm*
riboflavin [= Vitamin B] — рибофлави́н *nm*

sugars

dextrose — декстро́за *nf*
fructose — фрукто́за *nf*
glucose — глюко́за *nf*
glycogen — гликоге́н *nm*

lactose	лакто́за *nf*
maltose	мальто́за *nf*
sucrose	сахаро́за *nf*

other common biochemicals

casein	казеи́н *nm*
cholesterol	холестери́н *nm*
lecithin	лецити́н *nm*
pectin	пекти́н *nm*

DESCRIPTIVE TERMS

blond(e)	блонди́н, -ка *nmf*
bronzed	бро́нзовый *aj*
brunet(te)	брюне́т, -ка *nmf*
dissymmetrical	несимметри́чный *aj*
energetically	энерги́чно *av*
mien	ми́на *nf*
muscular [muscle-bound]	мускули́стый *aj*
muscular [relating to muscles]	му́скульный *aj*
normal height	норма́льный рост *nm*
physical strength	физи́ческая си́ла *nf*
profile	про́филь *nm*
Roman nose	ри́мский нос *nm*
rosy-cheeked	розовощёкий *aj*

See also **ANTHROPOLOGY**, **BIOLOGY**, **CHEMISTRY**, **MEDICAL PRACTICE**, **DRUGS**

MEDICAL PRACTICE

GENERAL TERMS

antidote	антидо́т *nm*
asymptomatic	бессимпто́мный *aj*
auto-immune	аутоимму́нный *aj*
caduceus	кадуце́й *nm*
chronic illness	хрони́ческая боле́знь *nf*
clinical	клини́ческий *aj*
consult (with)	консульти́роваться *impf*, проконсульти́роваться *pf*
consultation	консульта́ция *nf*
correction	корре́кция *nf*
course of treatment	курс лече́ния *nm*, *nn*
crisis (*pl* crises)	кри́зис *nm*
critical	крити́ческий *aj*
diagnose	диагности́ровать *impf*, *pf*
diagnosis (*pl* diagnoses)	диа́гноз *nm*
doctor [title]	до́ктор *nm*
dose	до́за *nf*
group practice	гру́ппа враче́й *nf*, *nmpl*
Hippocratic oath	кля́тва Гиппокра́та *nf*
hygiene	гигие́на *nf*
immunity	иммуните́т *nm*
instrument	инструме́нт *nm*
license (BR licence)	лице́нзия *nf*
medicine	медици́на *nf*
operation	опера́ция *nf*
pathogenesis	патогене́з *nm*
placebo (*pl* placebos, placeboes)	плаце́бо *nn*, *indecl*
practice (BR practise)	практикова́ть *impf*
procedure	процеду́ра *nf*
prognosis (*pl* prognoses)	прогно́з *nm*
prophylaxis	профила́ктика *nf*
serious illness	серьёзная боле́знь *nf*
specialty	специа́льность *nf*
symptom	симпто́м *nm*
test	тест *nm*
therapy	терапи́я *nf*
toxin	токси́н *nm*

medical facilities

ambulatory clinic	амбулато́рия *nf*
clinic	кли́ника *nf*
dispensary	диспансе́р *nm*
hospital [military]	го́спиталь *nf*
isolation ward	изоля́тор *nm*
laboratory	лаборато́рия *nf*
leprosarium, leper colony	лепрозо́рий *nm*
operating room	операцио́нная *nf*
polyclinic	поликли́ника *nf*
sanatorium (*pl* sanatoriums, sanatoria)	санато́рий *nm*
solarium (*pl* solaria)	соля́рий *nm*
speech clinic	логопеди́ческая кли́ника *nf*

common medical prefixes

osteo-	остео- *pref*
oto-	ото- *pref*
patho-	пато- *pref*
pneumono-	пневмо- *pref*
psycho-	психо- *pref*

BRANCHES OF MEDICINE

major fields

aeromedicine	авиацио́нная медици́на *nf*

allergy	аллерги́я *nf*
cardiology	кардиоло́гия *nf*
dermatology	дерматоло́гия *nf*
endocrinology	эндокриноло́гия *nf*
epidemiology	эпидемоло́гия *nf*
gastroenterology	гастроэнтероло́гия *nf*
geriatrics *nplsv*	гериатри́я *nf*
gynecology (BR gynaecology)	гинеколо́гия *nf*
hematology (BR haemotology)	гематоло́гия *nf*
laryngology	ларинголо́гия *nf*
neurology	невроло́гия *nf*
odontology	одонтоло́гия *nf*
oncology	онколо́гия *nf*
ophthalmology	офтальмоло́гия *nf*
orthopedics (BR orthopaedics) *nplsv*	ортопе́дия *nf*
pathology	патоло́гия *nf*
pediatrics (BR paediatrics) *nplsv*	педиатри́я *nf*
proctology	проктоло́гия *nf*
psychiatry	психиатри́я *nf*
space medicine	косми́ческая медици́на *nf*
therapeutics *nplsv*	терапе́втика *nf*
urology	уроло́гия *nf*
veterinary medicine	ветерина́рия *nf*

subspecialties

cosmetic surgery	космети́ческая хирурги́я, косметоло́гия *nf*
diagnostics *nplsv*	диагно́стика *nf*
etiology (BR aetiology)	этиоло́гия *nf*
immunology	иммуноло́гия *nf*
microsurgery	микрохирурги́я *nf*
myology	миоло́гия *nf*
neuropathology	невропатало́гия *nf*
neurophysiology	нейрофизиоло́гия *nf*
neurosurgery	нейрохирурги́я *nf*
optics *nplsv*	о́птика *nf*
otology	отоло́гия *nf*
pharmacology	фармаколо́гия *nf*
plastic surgery	пласти́ческая хирурги́я *nf*
radiology	радиоло́гия *nf*
rhinology	риноло́гия *nf*
sports medicine	спорти́вная медици́на *nf*
stomatology	стоматоло́гия *nf*
toxicology	токсиколо́гия *nf*
traumatology	травматоло́гия *nf*
venereology	венероло́гия *nf*
virology	вирусоло́гия *nf*

related fields

alternative medicine	альтернати́вная медици́на *nf*
anatomy	анато́мия *nf*
bacteriology	бактериоло́гия *nf*
craniometry	кранеометри́я *nf*
dietetics *nplsv*	диете́тика *nf*
electroencephalography	электроэнцефало-гра́фия *nf*
kymography	кимогра́фия *nf*
naturopathy	натуропа́тия *nf*
occupational therapy	трудотерапи́я *nm*
optometry	оптометри́я *nf*
osteology	остеоло́гия *nf*
osteopathy	остеопа́тия *nf*
pharmacy	фармаце́втика *nf*
radiography	радиогра́фия *nf*
reflexology	рефлексоло́гия *nf*
serology	сероло́гия *nf*

DIAGNOSIS

symptoms and conditions

amnesia	амнези́я *nf*
analgesia	аналгези́я *nf*
asphyxia	асфи́ксия *nf*
ataxia	атакси́я *nf*
atrophy	атрофи́я *nf*
autointoxication	автоинтоксика́ция *nf*
blockage	блокиро́вка *nf*
catalepsy	катале́псия *nf*
coma	ко́ма *nf*
comatose	комато́зный *aj*
convulsion	конву́льсия *nf*
diabetic	диабети́ческий *aj*
diastolic	диастоли́ческий *aj*
dyspepsia	диспепси́я *nf*
ectopia	эктопи́я *nf*
exudation	экссуда́т *nm*
fibrillation	фибрилля́ция *nf*
hypothermia	гипотерми́я *nf*
hysteria	истери́я *nf*
immune (to)	имму́нный (к) *aj*
inoperable	неопера́бельный *aj*
lethargy	летарги́я *nf*
lumbago	люмба́го *nn, indecl*
macrocephaly	макроцефа́лия *nf*
microcephaly	микроцефа́лия *nf*
necrotic (tissue)	некроти́ческий *aj*

neuralgia — невралги́я *nf*
palpable — пальпиру́емый *aj*
paralysis — парали́ч *nm*
paroxysm — пароксй́зм *nm*
phlegm — флє́гма *nf*
precancerous — преканцеро́зный *aj*
prolapse — прола́пс *nm*
prostration — простра́ция *nf*
pulse — пульс *nm*
Rhesus factor — ре́зус-фа́ктор *nm*
rhinitis — рини́т *nm*
shock — шок *nm*
spasm — спазм *nm*, спа́зма *nf*
spastic — спасти́ческий *aj*
stasis — ста́сис *nm*
state of shock — шо́ковое состоя́ние *nn*
stress — стресс *nm*
toxemia (BR toxaemia) — токсеми́я *nf*
vaccination — вакцина́ция *nf*

diagnostic fields

fluorography — флюорогра́фия *nf*
laparascopy — лапараскопи́я *nf*
reflexology — рефлексоло́гия *nf*
roentgenography — рентгеногра́фия *nf*
symptomatology — симптоматоло́гия *nf*
tomography — томогра́фия *nf*

devices

kymograph — кимо́граф *nm*
laparoscope — лапароско́п *nm*
laryngoscope — ларингоско́п *nm*
microscope — микроско́п *nm*
microtome — микрото́м *nm*
ophthalmoscope — офтальмоско́п *nm*
sphygmomanometer — сфигмо́метр *nm*
sterilizer — стерилиза́тор *nm*
thermometer — термо́метр *nm*
tonsillectomy — тонзиллэктоми́я *nf*
tracheotomy — трахеотоми́я *nf*
urethroscope — уретроско́п *nm*

charts and pictures

cardiogram — кардиогра́мма *nf*
cardiograph — кардио́граф *nm*
echocardiogram — эхокардиогра́мма *nf*
electrocardiogram — электрокардиогра́мма *nf*
electrocardiograph — электрокардиогра́ф *nm*
electroencephalogram — электроэнцефалогра́мма *nf*
encephalogram — энцефалогра́мма *nf*
roentgenogram — рентгеногра́мма *nf*
stethoscope — стетоско́п *nm*
temperature chart — температу́рный гра́фик *nm*

diagnostic techniques and procedures

auscultation — аускульта́ция *nf*
autopsy — аутопси́я, ауто́псия *nf*
bacterial culture — культу́ра *nf*
biopsy — биопси́я *nf*
case history — исто́рия боле́зни *nf*, *nf*
liposome — липосо́ма *nf*
palpation — пальпа́ция *nf*
percussion — перку́ссия *nf*
resonance — резона́нс *nm*
ultrasound — ультразву́к *nm*
urinalysis — ана́лиз мочи́ *nm*, *nf*
X-rays — икс-лучи́ *nmpl*

TREATMENT

prevention

immunity — иммуните́т *nm*
immunization — иммуниза́ция *nf*
inoculation — инокуля́ция *nf*
prophylactic — профилакти́ческое сре́дство *nn*
Salk vaccine — вакци́на Солка *nf*
sanitary conditions *npl* — санита́рное состоя́ние *nn*
sanitation — санитари́я *nf*
vaccine — вакци́на *nf*

medications

antibiotic — антибио́тик *nm*
antidepressant — антидепресса́нт *nm*
antitoxin — антитокси́н *nm*
fungicide — фунгици́д *nm*
oral (medicine) — ора́льный *aj*
palliative — паллиати́в *nm*
percutaneous — перкута́нный *aj*
placebo effect — эффе́кт плаце́бо *nm*, *nn*
tranquilizer — транквилиза́тор *nm*

other treatments

acupressure — акупрессу́ра *nf*
acupuncture — акупункту́ра *nf*
allopathy — аллопа́тия *nf*
aromatherapy — ароматерапи́я *nf*
balneology — бальнеоло́гия *nf*
chemotherapy — химиотерапи́я *nf*
climatotherapy — климатотерапи́я *nf*

compress	компре́сс *nm*
decompression	декомпре́ссия *nf*
defibrillation	дефибрилля́ция *nf*
dialysis (*pl* dialyses)	диа́лиз *nm*
diathermy	диатерми́я *nf*
diet	дие́та *nf*
electrosurgery	электрохирурги́я *nf*
electrotherapy	электротерапи́я *nf*
euthanasia	эйтана́зия *nf*
galvanism	гальвани́зм *nm*, гальваниза́ция *nf*
gamma rays	га́мма-лучи́ *nmpl*
homeopathy (BR homoeopathy)	гомеопа́тия *nf*
hormone replacement therapy	гормона́льная терапи́я *nf*
hospitalization	госпитализа́ция *nf*
hydrotherapy	гидротерапи́я *nf*
hypnosis (*pl* hypnoses)	гипно́з *nm*
hypnotherapy	гипнотерапи́я *nf*
hysterectomy	гистерэктоми́я *nf*
immobilization (of arm, leg)	иммобилиза́ция *nf*
immunotherapy	иммунотерапи́я *nf*
implantation	имплanта́ция *nf*
inhalation	ингаля́ция *nf*
injection	инъе́кция *nf*
intensive care	интенси́вная терапи́я *nf*
isolation	изоля́ция *nf*
laser surgery	ла́зерная хирурги́я *nf*
lobotomy	лоботоми́я *nf*
localization	локализа́ция *nf*
massage	масса́ж *nm*
mastectomy	мастэктоми́я *nf*
medication *nsg*	медикаме́нты *nmpl*
neurectomy	нейрэктоми́я *nf*
neurotomy	нейротоми́я *nf*
organotherapy	органотерапи́я *nf*
ovarectomy	овариотоми́я *nf*
phlebotomy	флеботоми́я *nf*
plaster	пла́стырь *nf*
pneum(on)ectomy	пневм(он)эктоми́я *nf*
prostatectomy	простатектоми́я *nf*
puncture	пу́нкция *nf*
quarantine	каранти́н *nm*
radiation therapy	радиотерапи́я *nf*
radiotherapy	радиотерапи́я *nf*
regimen	режи́м *nm*
rehabilitation	реабилита́ция *nf*
rhinoplasty	ринопла́стика *nf*
sex therapy	сексотерапи́я *nf*
shock therapy	шо́ковая терапи́я, шокотерапи́я *nf*
stimulation	стимули́рование *nn*
surgery	хирурги́я *nf*
surgical operation	хирурги́ческая опера́ция *nf*
trepanation	трепана́ция *nf*

tools and devices

aspirator	аспира́тор *nm*
atomizer	атомиза́тор *nm*
bandage	банда́ж *nm*
catheter	кате́тер *nm*
decompression chamber	декомпрессио́нная ка́мера *nf*
drainage (tube)	дрена́ж *nm*
inhaler	ингаля́тор *nm*
laryngophone	ларингофо́н *nm*
oxygen mask	кислоро́дная ма́ска *nf*
oxygenator	оксигена́тор *nm*
prosthesis (*pl* prostheses)	проте́з *nf*
radiology unit	радиологи́ческая устано́вка *nf*
respirator	респира́тор *nm*
scalpel	ска́льпель *nm*
scanner	ска́нер *nm*
tampon	тампо́н *nm*
tourniquet	турнике́т *nm*
trephine	трепа́н *nm*

TERMS IN SELECTED SPECIALIZED FIELDS

gynecology and obstetrics

abortion	або́рт *nm*
amniotic (fluid)	амниоти́ческий *aj*
Cesarean section	ке́сарево сече́ние *nn*
contraception	контраце́пция *nf*
contraceptive	контраце́птив *nm*
ectopic (pregnancy)	эктопи́ческий *aj*
incubator	инкуба́тор *nm*
maternity	матери́нство *nn*
pessary	песса́рий *nm*
placenta (*pl* placentas, placentae)	плаце́нта *nf*
progesterone	прогестеро́н *nm*
sterilization	стерилиза́ция *nf*

oncology

carcinoma	карцино́ма *nf*
metastasis (*pl* metastases)	метаста́з *nm*
remission	реми́ссия *nf*
roentgen	рентге́н *nm*

sarcoma (*pl* sarcomas, sarcomata)	саркóма *nf*

ophthalmology

bifocal	бифокáльный *aj*
bifocals	бифокáльные очкú *nnpl*
contact lens	контáктная лúнза *nf*
diopter	диоптрúя *nf*
dioptrics *nplsv*	диóптрика *nf*
ocular	окуля́р *nm*
ophthalmia	офтальмúя *nf*
optometric	оптометрúческий *aj*
peripheral vision	периферúческое зрение *nn*

dentistry

caries	кáриез *nm*
crown	корóнка *nf*
curette	кюрéтка *nf*
dentin(e)	дентúн *nm*
enamel	эмáль *nf*
extraction	экстрáкция *nf*
gingivitis	гингивúт *nm*
gutta-percha	гуттапéрча *nf*
implant	имплáнт *nm*
mobility	мобúльность *nf*
orthodontics *nplsv*	ортодонтúя *nf*
periodontal disease	парадонтóз *nm*
polish	полировáть *impf*, отполировáть *pf*
prosthesis (*pl* prostheses)	протéз *nf*
pyorrhea (BR pyorhoea)	пиорéя *nf*
restoration	реставрáция *nf*
toothpaste	зубнáя пáста

TERMS IN SURGERY

anesthesia (BR anaesthesia)	анестезúя *nf*
anesthetic (BR anaesthetic)	анестéтик *nm*
anesthetize (BR anaesthetize)	анестезúровать, наркотизировать *impf*
blood group	грýппа крóви *nf*, *nf*
granulation	грануля́ция *nf*
heroic measures	героúческие мéры *nfpl*
implant	имплáнт *nm*
inoperable	неоперáбельный *aj*
life-support system	систéма жизнеобеспечéния *nf*, *nn*
ligature	лигатýра *nf*
operable	оперáбельный *aj*
operate *vi*	оперúровать *impf*, *pf*
premedication	премедикáция *nf*
surgical instrument	хирургúческий инструмéнт *nm*

types of anesthesia

antiseptic	антисéптик *nm*
asepsis	асéптика *nf*
aseptic	асептúческий *aj*
chloroform	хлорофóрм *nm*
ether	эфúр *nm*
laughing gas	веселя́щий газ *nm*

surgical techniques and procedures

amputation	ампутáция *nf*
appendectomy	аппендэктомúя *nf*
gastrectomy	гастрэктомúя *nf*
laparotomy	лапаротомúя *nf*
laryngotomy	ларинготомúя *nf*
laser	лáзер *nm*
lipectomy	липэктомúя *nf*
liposome	липосóма *nf*
liposuction	липосáкция *nf*
photocoagulation	фотокоагуля́ция *nf*
resection	резéкция *nf*
vasectomy	вазэктомúя *nf*
venipuncture	венопýнкция *nf*

tools and equipment

ampule, ampoule	áмпула *nf*
catgut	кетгýт *nm*
collodion	коллóдий *nm*
disinfectant	дезинфектáнт *nm*
lancet [= scalpel]	ланцéт *nm*
mask	мáска *nf*
operating table	операционный стол *nm*
trocar	троакáр *nm*

PERSONS

health professionals

allopath	аллопáт *nm*
anatomist	анáтом *nm*
anesthesiologist (BR anaesthesiologist)	анестезиóлог *nm*
anesthetist (BR anaesthetist)	анестезиóлог *nm*
balneologist	бальнеóлог *nm*
cardiologist	кардиóлог *nm*
chiropractor	хиропрáктик *nm*
clinician	клиницúст *nm*

consultant, medical	врач-консульта́нт *nm*
cosmetic surgeon	(врач-)космето́лог *nm*
dental technician	зубно́й те́хник *nm*
dentist	данти́ст *nm*
dermatologist	дермато́лог *nm*
diagnostician	диагно́ст *nm*
dietitian	дието́лог *nm*
endocrinologist	эндокрино́лог *nm*
epidemiologist	эпидемео́лог *nm*
epileptic	эпиле́птик *nm*
gastroenterologist	гастроентеро́лог *nm*
geriatrician	гериатро́лог *nm*
gynecologist (BR gynaecologist)	гинеко́лог *nm*
hematologist (BR haematologist)	гемато́лог *nm*
homeopath (BR homoeopath)	гомеопа́т *nm*
hypnotist	гипнотизёр *nm*
immunologist	иммуно́лог *nm*
intern	инте́рн *nm*
lab(oratory) technician	лабора́нт, -ка *nmf*
medic	ме́дик *nm*
medical student	студе́нт(ка)-ме́дик *nmf*
myologist	мио́лог *nm*
narcotics expert	нарко́лог *nm*
naturopath	натуропа́т *nm*
neurologist	невро́лог, невропато́лог *nm*
neuropathologist	невропато́лог *nm*
neurosurgeon	нейрохиру́рг *nm*
oculist	окули́ст *nm*
odontologist	одонто́лог *nm*
oncologist	онко́лог *nm*
ophthalmologist	офтальмо́лог *nm*
optician, optometrist	о́птик *nm*
optometrist	о́птик *nm*
orthopedist (BR orthopaedist)	ортопе́д *nm*
osteologist	остео́лог *nm*
osteopath	остеопа́т *nm*
otolaringologist	отоларинго́лог *nm*
paramedic	параме́дик *nm*
pathologist	пато́лог *nm*
pediatrician (BR paediatrician)	педиа́тр *nm*
pharmacist	фармаце́вт *nm*
pharmacologist	фармако́лог *nm*
proctologist	прокто́лог *nm*
prosthetist	протези́ст *nm*
psychiatrist	психиа́тр *nm*
radiographer	радио́граф *nm*
radiologist	радио́лог *nm*
roentgenographer	рентгено́лог *nm*
specialist	специали́ст *nm*
stomatologist	стомато́лог *nm*
surgeon	хиру́рг *nm*
technician	те́хник *nm*
therapist	терапе́вт *nm*
toxicologist	токсико́лог *nm*
urologist	уро́лог *nm*
venereal disease specialist	венеро́лог *nm*
veterinarian	ветерина́р *nm*

other persons

blood donor	до́нор крови *nm, nf*
organ donor	до́нор о́ргана *nm, nm*
patient	пацие́нт, -ка *nmf*

See also **ANCIENT CIVILIZATIONS** *(persons)*, **BIOLOGY**, **PHYSICAL DISORDERS**

PHYSICAL DISORDERS

GENERAL TERMS

collapse	collaпс
dysfunction	дисфу́нкция *nf*
epidemic	эпиде́мия *nf*
incubation period	инкубацио́нный перио́д *nm*
infection	инфе́кция *nf*
physical disability	физи́ческий недоста́ток *nm*
risk group	гру́ппа ри́ска *nf, nm*
syndrome	синдро́м *nm*

TYPES OF ILLNESS

etiology

bacterial	бактериа́льный *aj*
carcinogenic	канцероге́нный *aj*
dietary, dietetic	диети́ческий *aj*
genetic	генети́ческий *aj*
geriatric	гериатри́ческий *aj*
hormonal	гормо́нный *aj*
immunological	иммунологи́ческий *aj*
infectious	инфекцио́нный *aj*
nervous	не́рвный *aj*
neurasthenic	неврастени́ческий *aj*
neurotoxic	нейротокси́ческий *aj*
oncological	онкологи́ческий *aj*
organic	органи́ческий *aj*
parasitic	паразита́рный, паразити́ческий *aj*
pediatric (BR paediatric)	педиатри́ческий *aj*

psychosomatic — психосоматический *aj*
respiratory — респираторный *aj*

descriptive terms

defective — дефективный *aj*
delicate — деликатный *aj*
endemic — эндемический *aj*
hyperactive — гиперактивный *aj*
mongoloid [obs] — монголоидный *aj*
pandemic — пандемический *aj*
progressive — прогрессирующий *aj*
virulent — вирулентный *aj*

CAUSES OF ILLNESS

infectious diseases

bacillus (*pl* bacilli) — бацилла *nf*
bacteria — бактерии *nfpl*
carcinogen — канцероген *nm*
coccus (*pl* cocci) — кокк *nm*
gonococcus (*pl* gonococci) — гонококк *nm*
micrococcus (*pl* micrococci) — микрококк *nm*
microorganism — микроорганизм *nm*
pneumococcus (*pl* pneumococci) — пневмококк *nm*
proteus — протеус *nm*
protozoa — протозоа *npl, indecl*
retrovirus — ретровирус *nm*
sepsis — сепсис *nm*
staphylococcus (*pl* staphylococci) — стафилококк *nm*
streptococcus (*pl* streptococci) — стрептококк *nm*
tubercle — туберкул *nm*
typhoid, typhus — тиф *nm*
virus — вирус *nm*

other causes

allergen — аллерген *nm*
dislocation — дислокация *nf*
parasite — паразит *nm*
toxin — токсин *nm*

NAMES OF DISORDERS

lungs

emphysema — эмфизема *nf*
pneumonia — пневмония *nf*
siderosis — сидероз *nm*
silicosis — силикоз *nm*
tuberculosis — туберкулёз *nm*

infection, contagious

abscess — абсцесс *nm*
anthrax — антракс *nm*
bubonic plague — бубонная чума *nf*
cholera — холера *nf*
diphtheria — дифтерия *nf*
grippe — грипп *nm*
herpes — герпес *nm*
influenza, flu — инфлюэнца *nf*
malaria — малярия *nf*
mononucleosis — мононуклеоз *nm*
paratyphoid fever — паратиф *nm*
scarlet fever — скарлатина *nf*
typhoid fever — тифозная лихорадка *nf*
venereal disease — венерическая болезнь *nf*

inflammatory

appendicitis — аппендицит *nm*
arthritis — артрит *nm*
bronchitis — бронхит *nm*
colitis — колит *nm*
cystitis — цистит *nm*
encephalitis — энцефалит *nm*
enteritis — энтерит *nm*
hepatitis — гепатит *nm*
laryngitis — ларингит *nm*
meningitis — менингит *nm*
myelitis — миелит, миэлит *nm*
nephritis — нефрит *nm*
neuritis — неврит *nm*
osteitis — остит *nm*
osteoarthritis — остеоартрит *nm*
osteomyelitis — остеомиэлит *nm*
pancreatitis — панкреатит *nm*
parotitis [= mumps] — паротит *nm*
peritonitis — перитонит *nm*
pharyngitis — фарингит *nm*
phlebitis — флебит *nm*
pneumonitis — пневмонит *nm*
sinusitis — синусит *nm*
thrombophlebitis — тромбофлебит *nm*
tonsillitis — тонзиллит *nm*
tracheitis — трахеит *nm*
urethritis — уретрит *nm*

digestive

anorexia — анорексия *nf*
avitaminosis — авитаминоз *nm*
bulimia — булимия *nf*
colic *nsg* — колики *npl*, колика *nf*

dysentery	дизентери́я *nf*
gastritis	гастри́т *nm*
gastroenteritis	гастроэнтери́т *nm*
hemorrhoids (BR haemorrhoids) *npl*	геморро́й *nm*
ileitis	илеи́т *nm*
marasmus	мара́зм *nm*
trichinosis	трихинеллёз *nm*

heart

angina	анги́на *nf*
arrhythmia	аритми́я *nf*
coronary thrombosis	корона́рный тромбо́з, коронаротромбо́з *nm*
endocarditis	эндокарди́т *nm*
infarct, infarction	инфа́ркт *nm*
myocardial infarction	инфа́ркт миока́рда *nm, nm*
myocarditis	миокарди́т *nm*
pericarditis	перикарди́т *nm*
rheumatic fever	суста́вный ревмати́зм *nm*
tachycardia	тахикарди́я *nf*
thrombosis	тромбо́з *nm*

skin

cancroid	канкро́ид *nm*
carbuncle	карбу́нкул *nm*
contusion	конту́зия *nf*
cyst	киста́ *nf*
dermatitis	дермати́т *nm*
eczema	экзе́ма *nf*
lesion	ле́зия *nf*
papule [= pimple]	па́пула *nf*
psoriasis	псориа́з *nm*
roseola	розео́ла *nf*
xerosis	ксеро́з *nm*

blood

anemia (BR anaemia)	анеми́я *nf*
angioma	ангио́ма *nf*
anoxia	аноkси́я *nf*
chlorosis	хлоро́з *nm*
cyanosis	циано́з *nm*
diabetes	диабе́т *nm*
hemophilia (BR haemophilia)	гемофили́я *nf*
hyperglycemia (BR hyperglycaemia)	гипергликеми́я *nf*
hypertension	гиперте́нзия *nf*
hypoglycemia	гипогликеми́я *nf*
ischemia (BR ischaemia)	ишеми́я *nf*
leucoma	лейко́ма *nf*
leukemia (BR leukaemia)	лейкеми́я *nf*
septicemia (BR septicaemia)	септицеми́я *nf*
stigma (*pl* stigmas, stagmata)	сти́гма *nf*
telangiectasis	телеангиэкта́зия *nf*

muscles

ataxia	атакси́я *nf*
muscular dystrophy	му́скульная дистрофи́я *nf*
paralysis (*pl* paralyses)	парали́ч *nm*
paraplegia	параплеги́я *nf*
tetany	тета́ния *nf*

brain

Alzheimer's disease	боле́знь Альцге́ймера *nf, nm*
apoplexy	апопле́ксия *nf*
cerebral palsy	церебра́льный парали́ч *nm*
epilepsy	эпиле́псия *nf*
hemiplegia [= stroke]	гемиплеги́я *nf*
insult	инсу́льт *nm*
migraine	мигре́нь *nf*
Parkinson's disease	боле́знь Паркинсо́на *nf, nm*

poisoning

autointoxication	автоинтоксика́ция *nf*
botulism	ботули́зм *nm*
ergotism	эрготи́зм *nm*
intoxication	интоксика́ция *nf*
nicotine poisoning, nicotinism	никотини́зм *nm*
ptomaine	птомаи́н *nm*
radioactive poison(ing)	радиоакти́вный яд *nm*
salmonella	сальмоне́лла *nf*

language

aphasia	афа́зия *nf*
dyslexia	дисле́ксия *nf*
echolalia	эхола́лия *nf*
speech defect	дефе́кт ре́чи *nm, nf*

eyes

ametropia	аметро́пия *nf*
astigmatism	астигмати́зм *nm*
cataract	катара́кта *nf*
conjunctivitis	коньюнктиви́т *nm*

daltonism [= color-blindedness]	дальтони́зм *nm*
glaucoma	глауко́ма *nf*
myopia	миопи́я *nf*
nystagmus	ниста́гм *nm*
presbyopia	пресбиопи́я *nf*
scotoma	ското́ма *nf*
strabismus	страби́зм *nm*
trachoma	трахо́ма *nf*

diseases associated with animals

bilharziasis	бильгарцио́з *nm*
ornithosis	орнито́з *nm*
psittacosis	пситтако́з *nm*

other disorders

Addison's disease	Аддисо́нова боле́знь
alcoholism	алкоголи́зм *nm*
arteriosclerosis	артериосклеро́з *nm*
beriberi	бе́ри-бе́ри *nf, indecl*
brucellosis [= undulant fever]	бруцеллёз *nm*
carcinoma	карцино́ма *nf*
catarrh	ката́р *nm*
chancre	шанкр *nm*
chancroid	мя́гкий шанкр *nm*
chorea	хоре́я *nf*
cirrhosis	цирро́з *nm*
cretinism	кретини́зм *nm*
croup	круп *nm*
dengue (fever)	де́нге *nn, indecl*
Down's syndrome	боле́знь Да́уна *nf, nm*
embolism	эмболи́я *nf*
embolus (*pl* emboli)	эмбо́л *nm*
fibroma, fibroid	фибро́ма *nf*
fistula	фи́стула *nf*
furuncle	фуру́нкул *nm*
furunculosis	фурункулёз *nm*
gangrene	гангре́на *nf*
hydrocephaly	гидроцефа́лия *nf*
hyperplasia	гиперпла́зия *nf*
hyperthyroidism	гиптирео́з *nm*
hypertrophy	гипертрофи́я *nf*
hyperventilation	гипервентиля́ция *nf*
hypervitaminosis	гипервитамино́з *nm*
hypoplasia	гипопла́зия *nf*
hypothermia	гипоте́рмия *nf*
hypoxia	гипокси́я *nf*
impotence	импоте́нция *nf*
Legionnaires' disease	боле́знь легионе́ров *nf, nmpl*
leprosy	ле́пра *nf*
lipoma [benign fat tumor]	липо́ма *nf*
mongolism [= Down's syndrome]	монголи́зм *nm*
morphine addiction	морфини́зм *nm*
multiple sclerosis	рассе́янный склеро́з *nm*
mycosis	мико́з *nm*
myoma	мио́ма *nf*
narcolepsy	нарколе́псия *nf*
narcosis (*pl* narcoses)	нарко́з *nm*
necrosis (*pl* necroses)	некро́з *nm*
neoplasia	неопла́зия *nf*
neoplasm	неопла́зма *nf*
nephrosis (*pl* neproses)	нефро́з *nm*
nervous tic	не́рвный тик *nm*
neuralgia	невралги́я *nf*
neurasthenia	неврасте́ния *nf*
neuroma (*pl* neuromas, neuromata)	невро́ма *nf*
neuropathy	невропа́тия *nf*
osteoporosis	остеопоро́з *nf*
paresis (*pl* pareses)	паре́з *nm*
parkinsonism	паркинсони́зм *nm*
paroxysm	парокси́зм *nm*
pediculosis	педикулёз *nm*
pellagra	пелла́гра *nf*
perforated ulcer	перфорати́вная я́зва желу́дка *nf, nm*
pleurisy	плеври́т *nm*
pneumothorax	пневмото́ракс *nm*
polio, poliomyelitis	полиомели́т *nm*
polyp	поли́п *nm*
progeria	проге́рия *nf*
prostration	простра́ция *nf*
psychosis (*pl* psychoses)	психо́з *nm*
ptosis	птоз *nm*
puria	пиури́я *nf*
rheumatism	ревмати́зм *nm*
rheumatoid arthritis	ревмати́ческий артри́т *nm*
rickets, rachitis	рахи́т *nm*
sclerosis (*pl* scleroses)	склеро́з *nm*
slipped disk	смеще́ние межпозво-но́чного ди́ска *nn, nm*
somnambulism	сомнамбули́зм *nm*
St. Vitus' dance [obs] [= chorea]	пля́ска свя́того Ви́тта *nf, nm*
syphilis	си́филис *nm*
tenesmus	тене́зм *nm*

teratoma (*pl* teratomas, teratomata)	терато́ма *nf*
tetanus	те́танус *nm*
trauma (*pl* traumas, tramata)	тра́вма *nf*
trench foot	транше́йная стопа́ *nf*
uremia (BR uraemia)	уреми́я *nf*
varicose veins *npl*	варико́зное расшире́ние *nn*

PERSONS

allergic person	алле́ргик *nm*
amnesiac	страда́ющий/страда́ющая амнези́ей *nmf*
asthmatic	астма́тик *nm*
chronic alcoholic	хрони́ческий алкого́лик *nm*, хрони́ческая алкоголи́чка *nf*
cretin	крети́н *nm*
diabetic	диабе́тик *nm*
dyslexic	дисле́ктик *nm*
hemophiliac (BR haemophiliac)	гемофи́лик *nm*
hypochondriac	ипохо́ндрик *nm*
impotent man	импоте́нт *nm*
invalid	инвали́д *nm*
neurasthenic	неврасте́ник *nm*
paralytic	парали́тик *nm*
paraplegic	больно́й/больна́я параплеги́ей *nmf*
rheumatic	ревма́тик *nm*
rickets/rachitis sufferer	рахи́т *nm*
somnambulist	страда́ющий/страда́ющая сомнамбули́змом *nmf*
syphilitic	сифили́тик *nm*
venereal patient	венери́ческий больно́й *nm*, венери́ческая больна́я *nf*

See also **MEDICAL PRACTICE** *(branches of medicine)*, **PSYCHOLOGY** *(mental and emotional disorders)*, **SEX** *(medical aspects)*

PSYCHOLOGY

GENERAL TERMS

abnormality	ненорма́льность *nf*
affect	аффе́кт *nm*
alter ego	а́льтер э́го *nm*, *indecl*
complex	ко́мплекс *nm*
dysfunction, disfunction	дисфу́нкция *nf*
dysfunctional	дисфункциона́льный *aj*
emotion	эмо́ция *nf*
impulse	и́мпульс *nm*
instinct	инсти́нкт *nm*
latent	лате́нтный *aj*
mania	ма́ния *nf*
mentality	менталите́т *nm*, мента́льность *nf*
neurosis (*pl* neuroses)	невро́з *nm*
normal	норма́льный *aj*
normalcy, normality	норма́льность *nf*
phobia	фо́бия *nf*
psyche	пси́хика *nf*
psychiatric	психиатри́ческий *aj*
psychic disorder	психи́ческий сдвиг *nm*
psycho-	психо- *pref*
psychodynamics *nplsv*	психодина́мика *nf*
psychogenesis	психогене́з *nm*
psychology	психоло́гия *nf*
psychoneurosis (*pl* psychoneuroses)	психонервóз *nm*
psychosis (*pl* psychoses)	психо́з *nm*
role	роль *nf*
stimulus (*pl* stimuli)	сти́мул *nm*
temperament	темпера́мент *nm*

FIELDS OF SPECIALIZATION

branches

abnormal	ненорма́льный *aj*
experimental	эксперимента́льный *aj*
social	социа́льный *aj*

schools of psychology

behaviorism	бихевиори́зм *nm*
Freudism	фрейди́зм *nm*
Gestalt	гешта́льт-психоло́гия *nf*
humanistic	гуманисти́ческий *aj*
Jungian	юнгиа́нский *aj*
structuralism	структурали́зм *nm*

related fields

mnemonics *nplsv*	мнемо́ника *nf*
parapsychology	парапсихоло́гия *nf*
psychoanalysis	психоана́лиз *nm*
psychobiology	психовиоло́гия *nf*
psycholinguistics *nplsv*	психолингви́стика *nf*

psychometrics *nplsv*	психометри́я *nf*
psychopathology	психопатало́гия *nf*
psychopathy	психопа́тия *nf*
psychotherapy	психотерапи́я *nf*
sexology	сексоло́гия *nf*

ASPECTS OF PSYCHOLOGY

thought processes

apperception	апперце́пция *nf*
concentration	концентра́ция *nf*
concept, conception	конце́пция *nf*
integration	интегри́рование *nn*
introspection	интроспе́кция *nf*
intuition	инту́иция *nf*
meditation	медита́ция *nf*
reflection	рефле́ксия *nf*

psychological mechanisms

association	ассоциа́ция *nf*
compensation	компенса́ция *nf*
empathy	эмпа́тия *nf*
frustration	фрустра́ция *nf*
motivation	мотива́ция *nf*
projection	проекти́рование *nn*
reaction	реа́кция *nf*
stimulation	стимуля́ция *nf*
synesthesia	синесте́зия *nf*
telepathy	телепа́тия *nf*

other terms

associative	ассоциати́вный *aj*
center of attention	центр внима́ния *nm, nn*
dominate	домини́ровать *impf*
extrasensory perception [= ESP]	экстрасе́нсорное восприя́тие *nn*
motivational research	иссле́дование мотива́ций *nn, nfpl*
paranormal	паранорма́льный *aj*
pathological	патологи́ческий *aj*
proxemic	проксеми́ческий *aj*
psychedelic, psychodelic	психедели́ческий *aj*
psychosomatic	психосомати́ческий *aj*
real world, the	реа́льный мир *nm*
schema	схе́ма *nf*

MENTAL AND EMOTIONAL DISORDERS

phobias

agoraphobia	агорафо́бия *nf*
claustrophobia	клаустрофо́бия *nf*
necrophobia	некрофо́бия *nf*
pyrophobia	пирофо́бия *nf*
xenophobia	ксенофо́бия *nf*
zoophobia	зоофо́бия *nf*

manias

erotomania	эротома́ния *nf*
kleptomania	клептома́ния *nf*
megalomania	мегалома́ния *nf*
monomania	монома́ния *nf*
nymphomania	нимфома́ния *nf*
persecution mania	ма́ния пресле́дования *nf, nn*
pyromania	пирома́ния *nf*

complexes

inferiority complex	ко́мплекс неполноце́нности *nm, nf*
Oedipus complex	Эди́пов ко́мплекс *nm*

other mental conditions

amnesia	амнези́я *nf*
autism	ауи́зм *nm*
coprophilia	копрофи́лия *nf*
depression	депре́ссия *nf*
egocentricity	эгоцентри́чность *nf*
escapism	эскапи́зм *nm*
euphoria	эйфори́я *nf*
exhibitionism	эксгибициони́зм *nm*
fetishism	фетиши́зм *nm*
hallucination	галлюцина́ция *nf*
hypochondria	ипохо́ндрия *nf*
hysterics *npl*	исте́рика *nf*
idée fixe	иде́я фикс *nf*
idiocy	идиоти́зм *nm*
infantilism	инфантили́зм *nm*
mania	ма́ния *nf*
manic-depressive	маниакально-депресси́вный *aj*
melancholia	меланхо́лия *nf*
narcissism	нарцисси́зм *nm*
necrophilia	некрофи́лия *nf*
negativism	негативи́зм *nm*
nerves	не́рвы *nmpl*
nervousnous	нерво́зность *nf*
neurasthenic	неврастени́ческий *aj*
panic	па́ника *nf*
paramnesia	парамне́зия *nf*
paranoia	парано́йя *nf*
pederasty (BR paederasty)	педера́стия *nf*
regression	регре́сс *nm*
schizoid	шизо́идный *aj*
schizophrenia	шизофрени́я *nf*

stress — стресс *nm*
trance — транс *nm*
trauma (*pl* traumas, traumata) — тра́вма *nf*
xenophilia — ксенофили́я *nf*

forms of psychotherapy

catharsis — като́рсис *nm*
group therapy — группова́я терапи́я *nf*
hypnotism — гипноти́зм *nm*
modification — модифика́ция *nf*
psychodrama — психодра́ма *nf*
self-help group — гру́ппа самопо́мощи *nf, nf*
transcendental meditation — трансцендента́льная медита́ция *nf*

terms in psychoanalysis

ego — э́го *nn, indecl*
Eros — Э́рос *nm*
Freudian — фрейди́стский *aj*
Freudian slip — огово́рка по Фре́йду *nf, nm*
libido — ли́бидо *nn, indecl*
repression — репре́ссия *nf*

PERSONS

professionals

psychoanalyst — психоанали́тик *nm*
psychologist — психоло́г *nm*
psychotherapist — психотерапе́вт *nm*
telepath — телепа́т *nm*

other persons

analyst — анали́тик *nm*
erotomaniac — эротома́н *nm*
exhibitionist — эксгибициони́ст *nm*
extrovert — экстрове́рт *nm*
Freudian — фрейди́ст *nm*
hypnotic subject — гипно́тик *nm*
hypnotist — гипнотизёр *nm*
hysteric, hysterical person — исте́рик *nm*, истери́чка *nf*
idiot — идио́т, -ка *nmf*
informant — информа́тор *nm*
introvert — интрове́рт *nm*
kleptomaniac — клептома́н, -ка *nmf*
maniac — маньи́к *nm*
melancholic (person) — меланхо́лик *nm*
monomaniac — монома́н *nm*
negativist — негативи́ст *nm*
neurasthenic — неврасте́ник *nm*
neuropath [obs] — невропа́т *nm*
neurotic — невро́тик *nm*
nymphomaniac — нимфома́нка *nf*
paranoiac — парано́ик *nm*
parapsychologist — парапсихо́лог *nm*
pederast (BR paederast) — педера́ст *nm*
psychoneurotic — психоневро́тик *nm*
psychopath — психопа́т, -ка *nmf*
pyromaniac — пирома́н *nm*
schizoid — шизо́ид *nm*
schizophrenic — шизофре́ник *nm*, шизофрени́чка *nf*

See also **MEDICAL PRACTICE *(treatment)*, SCIENCE AND THE SCIENCES, EDUCATION, EMOTIONS AND EXPERIENCES**

SEX

GENERAL TERMS

condom — кондо́м *nm*
ecstasy — экста́з *nm*
erotica — эро́тика *nf*
libido — ли́бидо *nn, indecl*
orientation — ориента́ция *nf*
potency — поте́нция *nf*
romance — рома́н *nm*
safe sex — безопа́сный секс *nm*
sex act — сексуа́льный акт *nm*
sex appeal — сексуа́льная привлека́тельность *nf*
sex life — сексуа́льная жизнь *nf*
sex object — сексуа́льный объе́кт *nm*
sexiness — сексуа́льность *nf*
sexology — сексоло́гия *nf*
sexual — сексуа́льный *aj*
sexual orientation — сексуа́льная ориента́ция *nf*
sexuality — сексуа́льность *nf*
sexually — сексуа́льно *av*
venereal disease — венери́ческая боле́знь *nf*

SEXUAL PRACTICES

sexual orientation

bisexualism — бисексуали́зм *nm*
heterosexuality — гетеросексуа́льность *nf*
homosexuality — гомосексуали́зм *nm*
lesbianism — лесби́йская любо́вь *nf*
lesbianism, Lesbianism — лесбиа́нство *nn*

platonic love	платони́ческая любо́вь *nf*

aids to sex

birth-control pill	противозача́точная пилю́ля *nf*
fetish	фети́ш *nm*
flirting, flirtation	флирт *nm*
intimacy	инти́мность *nf*
Kamasutra	«Камасу́тра» *nf*
phallic symbol	фалли́ческий си́мвол *nm*
porno film	порнофи́льм *nm*
porno magazine	порножурна́л *nm*
pornography	порногра́фия *nf*
striptease	стрипти́з *nm*
Viagra	Виа́гра *nf*

physiology

coitus interruptus	ко́итус прерыва́емый *nm*
coitus	ко́итус *nm*
ejaculation	эякуля́ция *nf*
erection	эре́кция *nf*
orgasm	орга́зм *nm*
sex organ	полово́й о́рган *nm*

places

bordello	борде́ль *nm*
harem	гаре́м *nm*
lonely-hearts club	клуб одино́ких серде́ц *nm, nnpl*
porno shop	порномагази́н *nm*
sex shop	секс-шоп *nm*

abnormal practices

exhibitionism	эксгибициони́зм *nm*
masochism	мазохи́зм *nm*
onanism	онани́зм *nm*
pederasty (BR paederasty)	педера́стия *nf*
pedophilia (BR paedophilia)	педофили́я *nf*
sadism	сади́зм *nm*
sadomasochism	са́до-мазохи́зм *nm*
voyeurism	вуайери́зм *nm*
zoophilia	зоофили́я *nf*

other terms

adultery	адюльте́р *nm*
amour [love affair]	аму́р *nm*
castration	кастра́ция *nf*
concubinage [obs]	конкубина́т *nm*
coquetry	коке́тство *nn*
masturbation	мастурба́ция *nf*
orgy	о́ргия *nf*
prostitution	проститу́ция *nf*

MEDICAL ASPECTS

sexual dysfunction

eroticism	эроти́зм *nm*, эроти́чность *nf*
erotomania	эротома́ния *nf*
frigidity	фриги́дность *nf*
impotence	импоте́нция *nf*
necrophilia	некрофили́я *nf*
nymphomania	нимфома́ния *nf*
satyriasis	сатириа́зис *nm*

venereal diseases

chancroid	мя́гкий шанкр *nm*
gonorrhea (BR gonorrhoea)	гоноре́я *nf*
herpes	ге́рпес *nm*
syphilis	си́филис *nm*

DESCRIPTION

describing women

coquettish	коке́тливая *aj*
frigid	фриги́дная *aj*
lesbian, Lesbian	лесбия́нка *nf*

describing men

Don Juan	донжуа́н *nm*
impotent	импоте́нт *nm*
male chauvinism	мужско́й шовини́зм *nm*
virile	вири́льный *aj*

other descriptive terms

amorous	аму́рный *aj*
asexual	асексуа́льный *aj*
bisexual	бисексуа́льный *aj*
ecstatic	экстати́ческий *aj*
erogenous	эроге́нный *aj*
erotic	эроти́ческий, эроти́чный *aj*
heterosexual	гетеросексуа́льный *aj*
homosexual	гомосексуа́льный *aj*
intimate	инти́мный *aj*
risqué	риско́ванный *aj*
romantic	романти́ческий, романти́чный *aj*
sadistic	сади́стский *aj*

sexy	сексуа́льный *aj*
transsexual	транссексуа́льный *aj*
undersexed	сексуа́льно холо́дный *aj*

PERSONS

ancient love gods

Aphrodite	Афроди́та *nf*
Cupid	Купидо́н *nm*
Eros	Э́рос *nm*
Venus	Вене́ра *nf*

real persons

bisexual	бисексуа́л(ист), -ка *nmf*
castrate, castrated man	кастра́т *nm*
cocotte	коко́тка *nf*
companion [paid female]	компаньо́нка *nf*
coquette	коке́тка *nf*
courtesan	куртиза́нка *nf*
erotomaniac	эротома́н *nm*
eunuch [obs]	е́внух *nm*
exhibitionist	эксгибициони́ст *nm*
gigolo	жи́голо *nm*, *indecl*
heterosexual	гетеросексуа́л, -ка *nmf*
homosexual	гомосексуали́ст, -ка *nmf*
impotent man	импоте́нт *nm*
lesbian, Lesbian	лесбия́нка *nf*
madam(e)	мада́м *nf*, *indecl*
nymphet	нимфе́тка *nf*
nymphomaniac	нимфома́нка *nf*
odalisque [obs]	одали́ска *nf*
pair of lovers	влюблённая па́ра *nf*
pederast (BR paederast)	педера́ст *nm*
pedophile (BR paedophile)	педофи́л *nm*
prostitute	проститу́тка *nf*
sadist	сади́ст, -ка *nmf*
sex symbol	секс-си́мвол *nm*
sex maniac	сексуа́льный манья́к *nm*
sexologist	сексо́лог *nm*
sexpot	секс-бо́мба *nf*
transsexual	транссексуал *nm*
transvestite	трансвести́т *nm*
vamp	вамп *nf*, *indecl*
voyeur	вуайери́ст *nm*

See also **FAMILY** *(aspects of the family)*, **PHYSICAL DISORDERS** *(names of disorders)*

DRUGS

GENERAL TERMS

antidote	антидо́т *nm*
disinfection	дезинфе́кция *nf*
dosage	дозиро́вка *nf*
effect	эффе́кт *nm*
effectiveness	эффекти́вность *nf*
mixture	миксту́ра *nf*
narcotize	наркот(из)и́ровать *impf*, *pf*
overdose	сли́шком больша́я до́за *nf*
patent medicine	патенто́ванное лека́рство *nn*
pharmacology	фармаколо́гия *nf*
pharmacopeia (BR pharmacopoeia)	фармакопе́я *nf*
pharmacy [science]	фармаце́втика *nf*
potency	поте́нтность *nf*
preparation	препара́т *nm*
psychopharmacology	психофармаколо́гия *nf*
react	реаги́ровать *impf*, отреаги́ровать *pf*
reaction	реа́кция *nf*
synergism	синерги́зм *nm*
synergy	синерги́я *nf*
synthetic	синтети́ческий *aj*
toxic	токси́чный, токси́ческий *aj*
toxicity	токси́чность *nf*

CLASSES OF DRUGS

antibiotic	антибиоти́ческий *aj*
antidepressant	антидепресса́нт *nm*
antihistamine	антигистами́н *nm*
antipyrin	антипири́н *nm*
disinfectant	дезинфекта́нт *nm*
germicide	гермици́д *nm*
hormones	гормо́ны *nmpl*
narcotic	нарко́тик *nm*
salts	со́ли *nfpl*
steroid	стеро́ид *nm*
stimulant	стимуля́тор *nm*
sulfa drug	сульфанилами́дный препара́т *nm*
vaccine	вакци́на *nf*

MEDICINES

antibiotics

aureomycin	ауреомици́н *nm*

calomel	ка́ломель *nf*
iodine	йод *nm*
penicillin	пеницилли́н *nm*
streptomycin	стрептомици́н *nm*
sulfonamide (BR sulfphonamide)	сульфами́д *nm*
terramycin	террамици́н *nm*
tetracycline	тетрацикли́н *nm*

cardiovascular drugs

digitalis	дигита́лис *nm*
morphine	мо́рфий *nm*
nitroglycerin(e)	нитроглицери́н *nm*

analgesics

aspirin	аспири́н *nm*
codeine	кодеи́н *nm*
menthol	менто́л *nm*
novocain(e)	новокаи́н *nm*

stimulants

adrenalin	адренали́н *nm*
benzedrine	бензедри́н *nm*
elixir	эликси́р *nm*
nicotine	никоти́н *nm*
tonic	то́ник *nm*

antianxiety drugs

barbiturate	барбитура́т *nm*
bromide	броми́д *nm*
neuroleptic	нейроле́птик *nm*

poisons

aconite	акони́т *nm*
curare	кура́ре *nn, indecl*
strychnine	стрихни́н *nm*
tetanic	тетани́ческий *aj*
vanillin	ванили́н *nm*

other common medicines

aloe	ало́э *nn, indecl*
atropine	атропи́н *nm*
belladonna	белладо́нна *nf*
camphor	ка́мфара *nf*
castor oil	касто́ровое ма́сло *nn*
cortisone	кортизо́н *nm*
cough mixture	миксту́ра от ка́шля *nf, nm*
cough syrup	сиро́п от ка́шля *nm, nm*
creosote	креозо́т *nm*
insulin	инсули́н *nm*
iodoform	йодофо́рм *nm*
lanolin(e)	ланоли́н *nm*
milk of magnesia	молочко́ магне́зии *nn, nf*
nose drops	ка́пли для но́са *nfpl, nm*
peroxide	пе́рекись *nf*
quinine	хини́н *nm*
smelling salts	нюхательные соли *nfpl*
thalidomide	талидоми́д *nm*
Vaseline	вазели́н *nm*
zinc ointment	ци́нковая мазь *nf*

FORMS AND ADMINISTRATION

capsule	ка́псула *nf*
inhalant, inhaler	ингаля́тор *nm*
injection	инъе́кция *nf*
pastille	пастила́, пасти́лка *nf*
phial	фиа́л *nm*
pill	пилюля *nf*
tablet	табле́тка *nf*

TERMS IN DRUG ABUSE

types of drugs

amphetamine	амфетами́н *nm*
depressant	депресса́нт *nm*
hallucinogen	галлюциноге́н *nm*
opiate	опиа́т *nm*

commonly abused drugs

cocaine	кокаи́н *nm*
crack	крэк *nm*
hashish	гаши́ш *nm*
heroin	герои́н *nm*
LSD	ЛСД *nm*
marijuana, marihuana	марихуа́на *nf*
mescaline	мескали́н *nm*
opium	о́пиум, о́пий *nm*

possible effects of drug abuse

euphoria	эйфори́я *nf*
hallucination	галлюцина́ция *nf*
lethal dose	лета́льная до́за *nf*
panic	па́ника *nf*
psychosis (*pl* psychoses)	психо́з *nm*

smoking

cigar smoke	сига́рный дым *nm*

cigar	сигáра *nf*
cigar case	портсигáр *nm*
cigarette	сигарéта *nf*
filter	фильтр *nm*
Havana cigar	гавáнская сигáра *nf*
opium den	кури́льня óпиума *nf, nm*
passive smoking	пасси́вное курéние *nn*
tobacco	табáк *nm*

MEASUREMENTS

milligram (BR milligramme)	миллигрáмм *nm*
scruple	скрýпул *nm*
tincture	тинктýра *nf*

PERSONS

chronic alcoholic	хрони́ческий алкогóлик *nm*, хрони́ческая алкоголи́чка *nf*
cocaine addict	кокаини́ст, -ка *nmf*
heroin addict	герои́нщик *nm*
marijuana smoker	кури́льщик/кури́льщица марихуáны *nmf*
morphine addict	морфини́ст, -ка *nmf*
pharmacist	фармацéвт *nm*
pharmacologist	фармакóлог *nm*

See also **PERSONAL GROOMING**, **BEVERAGES**

DEATH

GENERAL TERMS

agony	агóния *nf*
fatal	фатáльный *aj*
funeral procession	похорóнная процéссия *nf*
lethal	летáльный *aj*
necro-	некро- *pref*
tragic death	траги́ческая ги́бель *nf*

CAUSES OF DEATH BY KILLING

individual

electric chair	электри́ческий стул *nm*
euthanasia	эйтанáзия *nf*
execution	экзекýция *nf*
hara-kiri	харакúри *nn, indecl*
lethal dose	летáльная/смертéльная дóза *nf*
lynching	линчевáние *nn*
matricide	матереуби́йство *nn*
scalp [Indian trophy]	скальпи́ровать *impf, pf*

mass

bubonic plague	бубóнная чумá *nf*
cannibalism	каннибали́зм *nm*
cataclysm	катаkли́зм *nm*
catastrophe	катастрóфа *nf*
epidemic	эпидéмия *nf*
gas chamber	гáзовая кáмера *nf*
genocide	геноци́д *nm*
holocaust	холокóст *nm*
pandemic disease	пандеми́я *nf*
pogrom	погрóм *nm*

instruments

garrote, garotte	гаррóта *nf*
guillotine	гильоти́на *nf*
pistol	пистолéт *nm*
poison gas	ядови́тый газ *nm*

ASPECTS OF DYING

medical, legal, religious, psychological

autopsy	аутопси́я, аутóпсия *nf*
cremation	кремáция *nf*
embalming	бальзамирóвка *nf*, бальзами́рование *nn*
eschatology	эсхатолóгия *nf*
exhumation	эксгумáция *nf*
metempsychosis	метемпсихóз *nm*
necrolatry	некролáтрия *nf*
necromancy	некромáнтия *nf*
necrophilia	некрофи́лия *nf*
necrophobia	некрофóбия *nf*

places and things

columbarium [niche in crematorium]	колумбáрий *nm*
crematorium (*pl* crematoriums, crematoria)	крематóрий *nm*
crypt	кри́пта *nf*

mausoleum (*pl* mausoleums, mausolea)	мавзоле́й *nm*
morgue	морг *nm*

historical terms

catacomb	катако́мба *nf*
catafalque	катафа́лк *nm*
cenotaph	кенота́ф *nm*
necropolis	некро́поль *nm*
Pantheon	пантео́н *nm*
sarcophagus (*pl* sarcophaguses, sarcophagi)	саркофа́г *nm*

art, music, dress, language

crape, mourning	тра́урный креп *nm*
death mask	посме́ртная ма́ска *nf*
elegy	эле́гия *nf*
epitaph	эпита́фия *nf*
memorial	мемориа́л *nm*
necrology	некроло́г *nm*
requiem	ре́квием *nm*
stela, stele (*pl* stelas, stelae)	стэ́ла *nf*

PERSONS

killers

cannibal	канниба́л *nm*
matricide, mother-killer	матереуби́йца *nmf*
pogrom instigator	погро́мщик *nm*

other persons

embalmer	бальзиро́вщик *nm*
necromancer	некрома́нт *nm*
necrophile	некрофи́л *nm*
spiritualist	спири́т *nm*

See also **DRUGS** *(medicines)*, **AGRICULTURE** *(aspects of farming)*, **LAW** *(crimes and misdemeanors)*, **RELIGION** *(practices and traditions)*

Understanding Our Universe

SCIENCE AND THE SCIENCES ◆ MATHEMATICS ◆ PHYSICS ◆ CHEMISTRY ◆ ASTRONOMY ◆ GEOLOGY ◆ METEOROLOGY

SCIENCE AND THE SCIENCES

GENERAL TERMS

Academy of Sciences	Акаде́мия нау́к *nf, nfpl*
behavioral sciences *nplsv*	бихевиори́стика *nf*
biological sciences	биологи́ческие нау́ки *nfpl*
nomenclature	номенклату́ра *nf*
physical sciences	физи́ческие нау́ки *nfpl*
popularization	популяриза́ция *nf*
pseudoscience	псевдонау́ка *nf*
research center	нау́чно-иссле́довательский центр *nm*
scientific terminology	нау́чная терминоло́гия *nf*

MAJOR SCIENTIFIC FIELDS

abstract sciences

logic	ло́гика *nf*
mathematics *nplsv*	матема́тика *nf*
metaphysics *nplsv*	метафи́зика *nf*

physical sciences

astronomy	астроно́мия *nf*
chemistry	хи́мия *nf*
geology	геоло́гия *nf*
meteorology	метеороло́гия *nf*
physics *nplsv*	фи́зика *nf*
physiology	физиоло́гия *nf*

biological sciences

anatomy	анато́мия *nf*
biochemistry	биохи́мия *nf*
biology	биоло́гия *nf*
botany	бота́ника *nf*
medicine	медици́на *nf*
paleontology (BR palaeontology)	палеонтоло́гия *nf*
psychology	психоло́гия *nf*
zoology	зооло́гия *nf*

social sciences

anthropology	антрополо́гия *nf*
economics *nplsv*	эконо́мика *nf*
history	исто́рия *nf*
linguistics *nplsv*	лингви́стика *nf*
political science	политоло́гия *nf*
sociology	социоло́гия *nf*

technical and applied sciences

automation	автома́тика *nf*
bionics *nplsv*	био́ника *nf*
engineering science	инжене́рная нау́ка *nf*
information science	информа́тика *nf*
metrology	метроло́гия *nf*
micography	микрогра́фия *nf*
radiology	радиоло́гия *nf*
systematics *nplsv*	системáтика *nf*
typology	типоло́гия *nf*

TERMS IN SCIENTIFIC RESEARCH

classification	классифика́ция *nf*
control group	контро́льная гру́ппа *nf*
formula (*pl* formulas, formulae)	фо́рмула *nf*
hypothesis (*pl* hypotheses)	гипо́теза *nf*
hypothetical	гипотети́ческий *aj*
method	ме́тод *nm*
methodology	методоло́гия *nf*
microstructure	микрострукту́ра *nf*
model	моде́ль *nf*
notation	нота́ция *nf*
principle	при́нцип *nm*
result	результа́т *nm*
system	систе́ма *nf*
theory	тео́рия *nf*
type	тип *nm*

TOOLS AND EQUIPMENT

Bunsen burner	бу́нзеновская горе́лка *nf*, горе́лка Бу́нзена *nf, nm*
electron microscope	электро́нный микроско́п *nm*

laboratory — лаборато́рный *aj*

PERSONS

analyst — анали́тик *nm*
experimenter — эксперимента́тор *nm*
genius — ге́ний *nm*
popularizer — популяриза́тор *nm*
theoretician — теоре́тик *nm*

See also **PHILOSOPHY** *(terms in logic)*, **FAMOUS FIGURES OF YESTERDAY AND TODAY** *(scientists and inventors)*

MATHEMATICS

GENERAL TERMS

algorithm — алгори́тм *nm*
analysis — ана́лиз *nm*
axiom — аксио́ма *nf*
calculate — калькули́ровать *impf, pf*
chaos — ха́ос *nm*
characteristic — характери́стика *nf*
element — элеме́нт *nm*
equivalence — эквивале́нтность *nf*
function — фу́нкция *nf*
gradient — градие́нт *nm*
higher mathematics — вы́сшая матема́тика *nf*
homogenous — гомоге́нный *aj*
isomorphism — изоморфи́зм *nm*
lemma — ле́мма *nf*
line — лине́йка *nf*
linearity — лине́йность *nf*
logarithm — логари́фм *nm*
mathematics *nplsv* — матема́тика *nf*
mathematician — матема́тик *nm*
matrix (*pl* matrices) — ма́трица *nf*
modulus (*pl* moduli) — мо́дуль *nf*
notation — нота́ция *nf*
number — но́мер *nm*
operand — опера́нд *nm*
operation — опера́ция *nf*
parameter — пара́метр *nm*
percent — проце́нт *nm*
postulate — постула́т *nm*
principle — при́нцип *nm*
progression — прогре́ссия *nf*
proportion — пропо́рция *nf*
radical — радика́л *nm*
subgroup — подгру́ппа *nf*
tensor — те́нзор *nm*
theorem — теоре́ма *nf*
theory — тео́рия *nf*
vector — ве́ктор *nm*

mathematical prefixes

deci- — де́ци- *pref*
hecto- — ге́кто- *pref*
milli- — ми́лли- *pref*

theories

Monte Carlo method — ме́тод Монте-Ка́рло *nm*
Pythagorean theorem — теоре́ма Пифаго́ра *nf*
set theory — тео́рия мно́жеств *nf, nnpl*
theory of games — тео́рия игр *nf, nfpl*

tables

logarithmic table — табли́ца логари́фмов *nf, nmpl*
multiplication table — табли́ца умноже́ния *nf, nn*
trigonometric table — тригонометри́ческая та́блица *nf*

BRANCHES

pure mathematics

algebra — а́лгебра *nf*
arithmetic — арифме́тика *nf*
geometry — геоме́трия *nf*
logic — ло́гика *nf*
topology — тополо́гия *nf*
trigonometry — тригономе́трия *nf*

applied mathematics

econometrics *nplsv* — экономе́трия *nf*
geodesy — геоде́зия *nf*
statistics *nplsv* — стати́стика *nf*

BASIC CONCEPTS

systems

binary — бина́рный *aj*
metric — метри́ческий *aj*
scale — шкала́ *nf*

numerals

Arabic — ара́бский *aj*
Roman — ри́мский *aj*

numbers and quantities

abstract — абстра́ктный *aj*
antilogarithm — антилогари́фм *nm*
complex number — ко́мплексное число́ *nn*

constant	конста́нта *nf*
continuum	конти́нуум *nm*
coordinate, co-ordinate	координа́тный, координацио́нный *aj*
decimal	децима́льный *aj*
dichotomy	дихотоми́я *nf*
index (*pl* indexes, indices)	и́ндекс *nm*
integral	интегра́л *nm*
irrational number	иррациона́льное число́ *nn*
rational number	рациона́льное число́ *nn*
recursive number	рекурси́вное число́ *nn*
triad	триа́да *nf*

fractions

equivalent	эквивале́нт *nm*
mantissa	манти́сса *nf*
numerator	нумера́тор *nm*
term	те́рмин *nm*

operations and processes

calculation	калькуля́ция *nf*
derivation	дерива́ция *nf*
duplication	дубли́рование *nn*
integrate	интегри́ровать *impf, pf*
inversion	инве́рсия *nf*
permutation	пермута́ция *nf*
transform	трансфо́рм *nm*
transposition	транспози́ция, транспониро́вка *nf*

TERMS IN ALGEBRA

abscissa (*pl* abcsisas or abscisae)	абсци́сса *nf*
binomial	бино́м *nm*
Boolean expression	бу́лево выраже́ние *nn*
Boolean algebra	бу́лева а́лгебра *nf*
coefficient	коэффицие́нт *nm*
coordinate, co-ordinate	координа́та *nf*
exponent	экспоне́нт *nm*
exponential	экспоненциа́льный *aj*
formula (*pl* formulas, formulae)	фо́рмула *nf*
linear algebra	лине́йная а́лгебра *nf*
monomial	моно́м *nm*
ordinate	ордина́та *nf*
polynomial	полино́м *nm*
quadratic (equation)	квадра́тный *aj*
trinomial	трино́м *nm*
X	икс *nm*

TERMS IN ARITHMETIC

arithmetic problem	арифмети́ческая зада́ча *nf*
cube [third power]	куб *nm*
cube root	куби́ческий ко́рень *nm*
factor	фа́ктор *nm*
minus	ми́нус *nm, prep*
minus sign	знак ми́нус *nm*
plus sign	знак плюс *nm*
plus or minus	плюс-ми́нус *prep*
sum	су́мма *nf*

TERMS IN CALCULUS

calculus of variations	вариацио́нное исчисле́ние *nn*
differential calculus	дифференциа́льное исчисле́ние *nn*
differential	дифференциа́льный *aj*
differential	дифференциа́л *nm*
differentiation	дифференциа́ция *nf*
integral	интегра́льный *aj*
integral calculus	интегра́льное исчисле́ние *nn*
integration	интегра́ция *nf*

TERMS IN TRIGONOMETRY

cosecant	косе́канс *nm*
cosine	ко́синус *nm*
cotangent	кота́нгенс *nm*
sine	си́нус *nm*
sine wave	синусоида́льная волна́ *nf*
trigonometric	тригонометри́ческий *aj*
trigonometric function	тригонометри́ческая фу́нкция *nf*

TERMS IN STATISTICS

chance	шанс *nm*
correlation	корреля́ция *nf*
extrapolate	экстраполи́ровать *impf, pf*
extrapolation	экстраполя́ция *nf*
gauss (curve)	га́усс *nm*
histogram	гистогра́мма *nf*
interpolation	интерполя́ция *nf*
median (number)	медиа́на *nf*

one chance in ten	оди́н шанс из десяти́ *nm*
projection	прое́кция *nf*
quartile	кварти́ль *nm*
standard deviation	станда́ртная девиа́ция *nf*
statistic	стати́стик *nm*
statistical	статисти́ческий *aj*
statistician	стати́стик *nm*
statistics	статисти́ческие да́нные *nnpl*
trend	тренд *nm*

TERMS IN GEOMETRY

branches

analytic(al)	аналити́ческий *aj*
Cartesian	картезиа́нский *aj*
elliptical	эллипти́ческий *aj*
Euclidean	евкли́дов *aj*
hyperbolic	гиперболи́ческий *aj*
non-Euclidian	неэвкли́дов *aj*
plane geometry	планиме́трия *nf*
solid geometry	стереоме́трия *nf*
stereography	стереогра́фия *nf*

general terms

congruence	конгруэ́нтность *nf*
convergence	конверге́нция *nf*
coordinates	координа́ты *nfpl*
diagram	диагра́мма *nf*
directrix	директри́са *nf*
equivalent	эквивале́нтный *aj*
figure	фигу́ра *nf*
focus (*pl* focuses, foci)	фо́кус *nm*
generate	генери́ровать *impf, pf*
horizontal	горизонта́ль *nf*
hypothesis (*pl* hypotheses)	гипо́теза *nf*
line	ли́ния *nf*
median (line)	медиа́на *nf*
minute	мину́та *nf*
pi	число «пи» *nn*
planar	плана́рный *aj*
polar (coordinates)	поля́рный *aj*
second [angle measurement]	секу́нда *nf*
symmetry	симметри́я *nf*
vertical	вертика́льный *aj*

geometric figures

– lines –

asymptote	асимпто́та *nf*
curvilinear	криволине́йный *aj*
diagonal	диагона́ль *nf*
paraboloid	параболо́ид *nm*
parallel	паралле́льный *aj*
pentagram	пентагра́мма *nm*
perpendicular	перпендикуля́р *nm*
perpendicular	перпендикуля́рный *aj*

– plane –

cycloid	цикло́ида *nf*
ellipse	э́ллипс *nm*
ellipsoid	элипсо́ид *nm*
epicycle	эпици́кл *nm*
oval	ова́л *nm*
parabola	пара́бола *nf*
polygon	полиго́н *nm*
spiral	спира́ль *nf*
toroid	торо́ид *nm*
trihedron	триэ́др *nm*
trochoid	трохо́ида *nf*

– solid (regular polyhedra) –

decahedron	дека́эдр *nm*
dodecahedron	додека́эдр *nm*
hexahedron	декса́эдр *nm*
octahedron	окта́эдр *nm*
tetrahedron	тетра́эдр *nm*

– other 3-dimensional figures –

cone	ко́нус *nm*
cube	куб *nm*
cylinder	цили́ндр *nm*
parallelepiped	параллелепи́пед *nm*
polyhedron	полиэ́др *nm*
prism	при́зма *nf*
pyramid	пирами́да *nf*
sphere	сфе́ра *nf*
spheroid	сферо́ид *nm*

– parts of figures –

bisector	биссектри́са *nf*
center (BR centre)	центр *nm*
chord	хо́рда *nf*
conic section	кони́ческое сече́ние *nn*
diameter	диа́метр *nm*
hypotenuse	гипотену́за *nf*
parallel	паралле́ль *nf*
perimeter	пери́метр *nm*
quadrant (of circle)	квадра́нт *nm*
radius (*pl* radiuses, radii)	ра́диус *nm*
secant	се́канс *nm*
sector	се́ктор *nm*

segment	сегмéнт *nm*
sextant	секстáнт *nm*
tangent	тáнгенс *nm*
transversal	трансверсáльный *aj*

– angles and triangles –

dihedral	дигедрáльный *aj*
vertical	вертикáль *nf*

– kinds of quadrilaterals –

parallelogram	параллелогрáмм *nm*
rhombus (*pl* rhombuses, rhombi)	ромб *nm*
trapezoid	трапезóид *nm*

– description –

concentric	концéнтрический *aj*
cone-shaped, conical	конусообрáзный *aj*
congruent	конгруэ́нтный *aj*
conic(al)	кони́ческий *aj*
cubiform	кубови́дный *aj*
cylindrical	цили́ндровый, цилиндри́ческий *aj*
diagonally	по диагонáли *nf*
diametric(al)	диаметрáльный *aj*
diametrically	диаметрáльно *av*
eccentric	эксцентри́ческий *aj*
eccentricity	эксцентри́чность *nf*
geometric(al)	геометри́ческий *aj*
horizontal	горизонтáльный *aj*
linear	линéйный *aj*
normal	нормáль *nf*
oval	овáльный *aj*
parabolic	параболи́ческий *aj*
parallel	параллéльный *aj*
perpendicular	перпендикуля́рный *aj*
polygonic	полигони́ческий *aj*
pyramidal	пирамидáльный *aj*
rhombic	ромби́ческий *aj*
rhomboid	ромбóид *nm*
sigmoid [S-shaped]	сигмови́дный *aj*
spherical	сфери́ческий *aj*
spheroidal	сфероидáльный *aj*
spiral	спирáльный *aj*
symmetrical	симметри́ческий, симметри́чный *aj*
tangential	тангенциáльный *aj*
tetragonal	тетрагонáльный *aj*
triadic	триади́ческий *aj*

TOOLS

calculator	калькуля́тор *nm*
computer	компью́тер *nm*
graph	грáфик *nm*
nomograph	номогрáмма *nf*
planimeter	планимéтр *nm*
pocket calculator	кармáнный калькуля́тор *nm*
table	табли́ца *nf*

See also **COUNTING AND ARRANGEMENT, MEASUREMENTS, ASTRONOMY, GEOGRAPHY**

PHYSICS

GENERAL TERMS

activity	акти́вность *nf*
atom	áтом *nm*
center of gravity	центр тя́жести *nm, nf*
component	компонéнт *nm*
constant	констáнта *nf*
critical	крити́ческий *aj*
electric(al)	электри́ческий *aj*
electron	электрóн *nm*
energy	энéргия *nf*
ether [obs]	эфи́р *nm*
gas	газ *nm*
gravitation	гравитáция *nf*
impulse	и́мпульс *nm*
ion	иóн *nm*
magnetic	магни́тный *aj*
magnetism	магнети́зм *nm*
mass	мáсса *nf*
matter	матéрия *nf*
metal	метáлл *nm*
molecule	молéкула *nf*
photoelectric	фотоэлектри́ческий *aj*
physical property	физи́ческое свóйство *nn*
physicist	фи́зик *nm*
pole	пóлюс *nm*
quantum number	квáнтовое числó *nn*
radiation	радиáция *nf*
radioactive	радиоакти́вный *aj*
radioactivity	радиоакти́вность *nf*
reaction	реáкция *nf*
space-time continuum	прострáнственно-временнóй конти́нуум *nm*
spectral/spectrum analysis	спектрáльный анáлиз *nm*
spectrography	спектрогрáфия *nf*
stability	стаби́льность *nf*
temperature	температýра *nf*

transformation	трансформáция *nf*

SOURCES OF ENERGY

atomic energy	áтомная энéргия *nf*
electrical energy	электроэнéргия *nf*
kinetic energy	кинети́ческая энéргия *nf*

theories and effects

chaos theory	теóрия хаóса *nf, nm*
Doppler effect	эффéкт Дóпплера *nm, nm*
Hall effect	эффéкт Хóлла *nm, nm*
quantum theory	квáнтовая теóрия *nf, nm*
theory of relativity	теóрия относи́тельности *nf, nf*
tunnel effect	туннéльный эффéкт *nm*
Tyndall effect	эффéкт Ти́ндаля *nm, nm*
Zeeman effect	эффéкт Зи́мана *nm, nm*

BRANCHES OF PHYSICS

major fields

acoustics *nplsv*	акýстика *nf*
atomic	áтомный *aj*
biophysics *nplsv*	биофи́зика *nf*
cryogenics *nplsv*	криогéника *nf*
electromagnetism	электромагнети́зм *nm*
geophysics *nplsv*	геофи́зика *nf*
mathematical	математи́ческий *aj*
mechanics *nplsv*	механика *nf*
molecular	молекуля́рный *aj*
nuclear physics *nplsv*	я́дерная фи́зика *nf*
optics *nplsv*	óптика *nf*
plasma	плáзма *nf*
quantum physics *nplsv*	квáнтовая фи́зика *nf*
solid-state physics *nplsv*	фи́зика твёрдых тел *nf, nmpl*
theoretical physics *nplsv*	теорети́ческая фи́зика *nf*
thermodynamics *nplsv*	термодинáмика *nf*

subfields

astronomy	астронóмия *nf*
astrophysics *nplsv*	астрофи́зика *nf*
cosmology	космолóгия *nf*
crystal	хрустáль *nm*
crystallography	кристаллогрáфия *nf*
electricity	электри́чество *nn*
electrodynamics *nplsv*	электродинáмика *nf*
electronics *nplsv*	электрóника *nf*
electrostatics *nplsv*	электростáтика *nf*
energetics *nplsv*	энергéтика *nf*
hydrodynamics *nplsv*	гидродинáмика *nf*
hydromechanics *nplsv*	гидромехáника *nf*
hydrostatics *nplsv*	гидростáтика *nf*
kinematics *nplsv*	кинемáтика *nf*
kinetics *nplsv*	кинéтика *nf*
micrography	микрогрáфия *nf*
microscopy	микроскопи́я *nf*
pneumatics, *nplsv*	пневмáтика *nf*
quantum mechanics *nplsv*	квáнтовая мехáника *nf*
radiography	радиогрáфия *nf*
rheology	реолóгия *nf*
spectroscopy	спектроскопи́я *nf*
stereoscopy	стереоскопи́я *nf*
thermionics *nplsv*	термиóника *nf*

TERMS IN MECHANICS

subfields

aerodynamics *nplsv*	аэродинáмика *nf*
ballistics *nplsv*	балли́стика *nf*
dynamics *nplsv*	динáмика *nf*
hydraulics *nplsv*	гидрáвлика *nf*
statics *nplsv*	стáтика *nf*

other terms

decompression	декомпрéссия *nf*
dynamic	динами́ческий *aj*
gradient	градиéнт *nm*
inertia	инéрция *nf*
kinematic	кинемати́ческий *aj*
kinetic	кинети́ческий *aj*
metacenter	метацéнтр *nm*
moment	момéнт *nm*
Newtonian	ньютóнов *aj*
osmosis	óсмос *nm*
pneumatic	пневмати́ческий *aj*
position	пози́ция *nf*
resultant (force)	результáнт *nm*
static	стати́ческий, стати́чный *aj*
traction	трáкция *nf*
trajectory	траектóрия *nf*
vacuum	вáкуум *nm*
viscosity	вя́зкость *nf*

TERMS IN THERMODYNAMICS

convection	конвéкция *nf*

critical temperature — крити́ческая температу́ра *nf*
entropy — энтропи́я *nf*
isotherm — изоте́рма *nf*
isothermal — изотерми́ческий *aj*
thermodynamic — термодинами́ческий *aj*
dispersion — диспе́рсия *nf*

TERMS IN WAVE PHYSICS

acoustics

acoustic — акусти́ческий *aj*
echo (*pl* echoes) — э́хо *nn*
harmonics *npl* — гармо́ния *nf*
resonance — резона́нс *nm*
reverberate — ревербери́ровать *impf, pf*
reverberation — ревербера́ция *nf*

optics

abberration — аберра́ция *nf*
binocular — бинокуля́рный *aj*
cathode rays — като́дные лучи́ *nfpl*
catoptric — катоптри́ческий *aj*
diffraction — дифра́кция *nf*
diffusion — диффу́зия *nf*
fluorescence — флюоресце́нция *nf*
fluorescent — флюоресци́рующий *aj*
focal — фо́кусный, фока́льный *aj*
focus (*pl* focuses, foci) — фо́кус *nm*
laser — ла́зер *nm*
luminescence — люминесце́нция *nf*
luminescent — люминесце́нтный *aj*
optic axis — опти́ческая ось *nf*
optic(al) — опти́ческий *aj*
optical illusion — опти́ческая иллю́зия *nf*
parallax — паралла́кс *nm*
photon — фото́н *nm*
polarization — поляриза́ция *nf*
prism — при́зма *nf*
prismatic — призмати́ческий *aj*
reflector — рефле́ктор *nm*
refraction — рефра́кция *nf*
refractor — рефра́ктор *nm*
spectral — спектра́льный *aj*
spectrogram — спектрогра́мма *nf*
spectrum (*pl* spectrums, spectra) — спектр *nm*
stereoscope — стереоско́п *nm*
stereoscopic — стереоскопи́ческий *aj*
ultraviolet — ультрафиоле́товый *aj*
ultraviolet rays — ультрафиоле́товые лучи *nmpl*

terms in common

absorption — абсо́рбция *nf*
amplitude — амплиту́да *nf*
intensity — интенси́вность *nf*
interference — интерфере́нция *nf*
optoacoustic — оптоакусти́ческий *aj*
phase — фа́за *nf*
vibration — вибра́ция *nf*
vibration, vibratory — вибрацио́нный *aj*

TERMS IN ELECTROMAGNETISM

depolarization — деполяриза́ция *nf*
dielectric — диэле́ктрик *nm*
electric field — электри́ческое поле *nn*
electrodynamic — электродинами́ческий *aj*
electromagnetic — электромагни́тный, магнито-электри́ческий *aj*
ferromagnetic — ферромагни́тный *aj*
inductance — индукти́вность *nf*
magnet — магни́т *nm*
magnetic field — магни́тное по́ле *nn*
magnetization (state) — намагни́ченность *nf*
magnetization (process) — намагни́чивание *nn*
magnetize — намагни́чивать *impf*, намагни́тить *pf*
oscillation — осцилля́ция *nf*
polarity — поля́рность *nf*
radio wave — радиовол́на *nf*

TERMS IN NUCLEAR PHYSICS

alpha rays — а́льфа-лучи́ *nmpl*
alpha particle — а́льфа-части́ца *nf*
beta rays — бе́та-лучи́ *nfpl*
beta particle — бе́та-части́ца *nf*
critical mass — крити́ческая ма́сса *nf*
delta rays — де́льта лучи́ *nmpl*
disintegration — дезинтегра́ция *nf*
elementary particle — элемента́рная части́ца *nf*
emission (light, heat) — эми́ссия *nf*
ionization — иониза́ция *nf*
isomer — изоме́р *nm*
neutron — нейтро́н *nm*
Planck's constant — конста́нта Пла́нка *nf, nm*
proton — прото́н *nm*
quantum (*pl* quanta) — квант *nm*

radioactive isotope	радиоакти́вный изото́п *nm*
radioactive fallout *nsg*	радиоакти́вные оса́дки *nmpl*
radioactive series *nsg*	радиоакти́вный ряд *nm*
radioactive waste *nsg*	радиоакти́вные отхо́ды *nmpl*
radioactive contamination	радиоакти́вное заражение *nn*
subatomic	суба́томный *aj*
thermal	терми́ческий *aj*
thermonuclear	термоя́дерный *aj*
tritium	три́тий *nm*
triton	трито́н *nm*

TERMS IN PARTICLE PHYSICS

elementary	элемента́рный *aj*
gamma-rays	га́мма-лучи́ *nmpl*
meson	мезо́н *nm*
neutrino	нейтри́но *nn, indecl*
omega	оме́га *nf*
positron	позитро́н *nm*
psi	пси *nn*
quark [particle]	кварк *nm*
tachyon [particle]	тахио́н *nm*
tardyon [particle]	тардио́н *nm*
upsilon	ипсило́н *nm*

TOOLS AND EQUIPMENT

atomic reactor	а́томный реа́ктор *nm*
cyclotron	циклотро́н *nm*
decompressor	декомпре́ссор *nm*
detector (radio)	дете́ктор *nm*
electromagnet	электромагни́т *nm*
electroscope	электроско́п *nm*
filter	фильтр *nm*
heliograph	гелио́граф *nm*
hygrograph	гигро́граф *nm*
Leyden jar	ле́йденская ба́нка *nf*
locator (of sounds)	лока́тор *nm*
microscope	микроско́п *nm*
nuclear reactor	я́дерный реа́ктор *nm*
objective lens	объе́кт *nm*
oscillator	осцилля́тор *nm*
oscillograph	осцилло́граф *nm*
oscilloscope	осциллоско́п *nm*
reactor	реа́ктор *nm*
scintillation scanner	сцинтиллоско́п *nm*
scintillator	сцинтилля́тор *nm*
siphon	сифо́н *nm*
spectrograph	спектро́граф *nm*
spectroscope	спектроско́п *nm*
synchrocyclotron	синхроциклотро́н *nm*
synchroton	синхротро́н *nm*
thermoelement	термоэлеме́нт *nm*
thermoscope	термо́скоп *nm*
tokamak [Russian reactor]	токама́к *nm*

See also **SCIENCE AND THE SCIENCES, CHEMISTRY, MEASUREMENTS** ***(units of measurement, measuring tools)***, **ELECTRICITY AND ELECTRONICS, TECHNOLOGY OVERVIEW**

CHEMISTRY

GENERAL TERMS

activate	активи́ровать *impf, pf*
active	акти́вный *aj*
atomic weight	а́томный вес *nm*
by-product	побо́чный проду́кт *nm*
catalyst	катализа́тор *nm*
chemical	химика́т *nm*
chemical element	хими́ческий элеме́нт *nm*
chemical process	хими́ческий проце́сс *nm*
chemical product	хими́ческий проду́кт *nm*
chemical reaction	хими́ческая реа́кция *nf*
chemicals	химика́лии, химика́ты *nnpl*
chemist	хи́мик *nm*
equivalence	эквивале́нтность *nf*
formula (*pl* formulas, formulae)	фо́рмула *nf*
fraction	фра́кция *nf*
group	группа *nf*
halogen	галоге́н *nm*
homolog(ue)	гомо́лог *nm*
macromolecule	макромоле́кула *nf*
mass	ма́сса *nf*
metal	мета́лл *nm*
mineral	минера́л *nm*
molecular structure	молекуля́рная структу́ра *nf*
nonmetal, metalloid	немета́лл *nm*
orbit	орби́та *nf*
organic	органи́ческий *aj*
periodic table	периоди́ческая табли́ца, табли́ца Менделе́ева *nf, nm*
periodicity	периоди́чность *nf*
preparation	препара́т *nm*

product	продукт *nm*
radioelement	радиоэлемент *nm*
reaction, chain	цепная реакция *nf*
reaction	реакция *nf*
reagent	реагент *nm*
reducing agent	редуктор *nm*
series	ряд *nm*
symbol	символ *nm*
synthetic	синтетический *aj*
trace element	микроэлемент *nm*
valence, valency	валентность *nf*

BRANCHES

major fields

analytic(al)	аналитический *aj*
inorganic	неорганический *aj*
organic	органический *aj*
physical	физический *aj*

interdisciplinary fields

biochemistry	биохимия *nf*
electrochemistry	электрохимия *nf*
geochemistry	геохимия *nf*
photochemistry	фотохимия *nf*
piezochemistry	пьезохимия *nf*
radiochemistry	радиохимия *nf*
thermochemistry	термохимия *nf*

other specializations

metallurgy	металлургия *nf*
microchemistry	микрохимия *nf*
stereochemistry	стереохимия *nf*

BASIC CONCEPTS

components

atom	атом *nm*
electron	электрон *nm*
element	элемент *nm*
ion	ион *nm*
molecule	молекула *nf*
neutron	нейтрон *nm*
proton	протон *nm*
proton	протонный *aj*

composition

dyad	диада *nf*
radiocarbon	радиоактивный углерод *nm*
tetrad	тетрада *nf*

forms of matter

crystal	кристалл *nm*
gas	газ *nm*
gelatinous	желатиновый *aj*
liquid	ликвидный *aj*
radioactive isotope	радиоактивный изотоп *nm*

kinds of substances

aerosol	аэрозоль *nm*
concentrate	концентрат *nm*
derivative	дериват *nm*
isotope	изотоп *nm*
plastics *npl*	пластика *nf*
polymer	полимер *nm*
polymorph	полиморф *nm*
radioisotope	радиоизотоп *nm*
stereoisomer	стереоизомер *nm*
sublimate	сублимат *nm*

properties

amorphous	аморфный *aj*
coagulant	коагулянт *nm*
compactness	компактность *nf*
concentrated	концентрированный *aj*
condensate	конденсат *nm*
consistency	консистенция *nf*
corrosive	коррозийный *aj*
distilled	дистиллированный *aj*
elasticity	эластичность *nf*
ethereal	эфирный *aj*
hermetic	герметический *aj*
inert	инертный *aj*
isomer	изомер *nm*
isomorphism	изоморфизм *nm*
linear	линейный *aj*
monoatomic	моноатомный, одноатомный *aj*
paramagnetism	парамагнетизм *nm*
phosphorescence	фосфоресценция *nf*
plasticity	пластичность *nf*
polyatomic	многоатомный *aj*
polymorphism	полиморфизм *nm*
radioactive	радиоактивный *aj*
salinity	солёность *nf*
stability	стабильность *nf*
thermoplastic	термопластический *aj*
univalent	одновалентный *aj*

CHEMICAL ELEMENTS

gases

argon [Ar]	аргон *nm*
helium [He]	гелий *nm*

krypton [Kr] — криптóн *nm*
neon [Ne] — неóн *nm*
radon [Rn] — радóн *nm*
xenon [Xe] — ксенóн *nm*

radioactive metals

berkelium [Bk] — беркéлий *nm*
californium [Cf] — калифóрний *nm*
curium [Cm] — кю́рий *nm*
einsteinium [Es] — эйнштéйний *nm*
fermium [Fm] — фéрмий *nm*
francium [Fr] — фрáнций *nm*
lawrencium [Lr] — лоурéнсий *nm*
nobelium [No] — нобéлий *nm*
plutonium [Pu] — плутóний *nm*
polonium [Po] — полóний *nm*
promethium [Pm] — промéтий *nm*
protactinium [Pa] — протакти́ний *nm*
radium [Ra] — рáдий *nm*
technetium [Te] — технéций *nm*
thorium [Th] — тóрий *nm*
uranium [U] — урáн *nm*

rare-earth metals

cerium [Ce] — цéрий *nm*
dysprosium [Dy] — диспрóзий *nm*
erbium [Er] — э́рбий *nm*
europium [Eu] — еврóпий *nm*
gadolinium [Gd] — гадоли́ний *nm*
holmium [Ho] — гóльмий *nm*
lanthanum [La] — лантáн *nm*
neodymium [Nd] — ниоди́мий *nm*
praseodymium [Pr] — празеоди́мий *nm*
samarium [Sm] — самáрий *nm*
scandium [Sc] — скáндий *nm*
terbium [Tb] — тéрбий *nm*
thulium [Tm] — ту́лий *nm*
ytterbium [Yb] — иттéрбий *nm*
yttrium [Y] — и́ттрий *nm*

other metals

aluminum [Al] (BR aluminium) — алюми́ний *nm*
bismuth [Bi] — ви́смут *nm*
cadmium [Cd] — кáдмий *nm*
calcium [Ca] — кáльций *nm*
cesium, caesium [Cs] — цéзий *nm*
chromium [Cr] — хром *nm*
cobalt [Co] — кóбальт *nm*
gallium [Ga] — гáллий *nm*
germanium [Ge] — гермáний *nm*
hafnium [Hf] — гáфний *nm*
indium [In] — и́ндий *nm*
iridium [Ir] — ири́дий *nm*
lithium [Li] — ли́тий *nm*
lutetium [Lu] — лютéций *nm*
magnesium [Mg] — мáгний *nm*
manganese [Mn] — мáрганец *nm*
mendelevium [Md] — менделéвий *nm*
molybdenum [Mo] — молибдéн *nm*
neptunium [Np] — непту́ний *nm*
nickel [Ni] — ни́кель *nm*
niobium [Nb] — ниóбий *nm*
osmium [Os] — óсмий *nm*
palladium [Pd] — паллáдий *nm*
platinum [Pt] — плáтина *nf*
rhenium [Re] — рéний *nm*
rhodium [Rh] — рóдий *nm*
rubidium [Rb] — руби́дий *nm*
ruthenium [Ru] — рутéний *nm*
strontium [Sr] — стрóнций *nm*
thallium [Tl] — тáллий *nm*
titanium [Ti] — титáн *nm*
vanadium [V] — ванáдий *nm*
wolfram [= tungsten] [W] — вольфрáм *nm*
zinc [Zn] — цинк *nm*
zirconium [Zr] — цирконий *nm*

halogens

bromine [Br] — бром *nm*
chlorine [Cl] — хлор *nm*
haloid — галóид *nm*
iodine [I] — йод *nm*

other elements

barium [Ba] — бáрий *nn*
beryllium [Be] — бери́ллий *nm*
boron [B] — бóр *nm*
deuterium [D] — дейтéрий *nm*
hahnium [Ha] — гáний *nm*
phosphorus [P] — фóсфор *nm*
rutherfordium [Rf] — рузерфóрдий *nm*
selenium [Se] — селéн *nm*
tantalum [Ta] — тантáл *nm*
tellurium [Te] — теллу́р *nm*

CHEMICAL COMPOUNDS

types of compounds and mixtures

aldehyde — альдеги́д *nm*
antifreeze — антифри́з *nm*
aromatic — аромáтный *aj*
carbide — карби́д *nm*
carbonate — карбонáт *nm*
chloride — хлори́д *nm*
colloid — коллóид *nm*
electrolyte — электроли́т *nm*

emulsion	эму́льсия *nf*
essence [extract]	эссе́нция *nf*
hydrate	гидра́т *nm*
hydroxide	гидроо́кись *nf*
ketone	ке́тон *nm*
nitrate	нитра́т *nm*
petrochemical	нефтехими́ческий *aj*
phosphate	фосфа́т *nm*
ptomaine	птомаи́н *nm*
radical	радика́л *nm*
salt	соль *nf*
soda	со́да *nf*
sulfate (BR sulphate)	сульфа́т *nm*
sulfide (BR sulphide)	сульфи́д *nm*
suspension	суспе́нзия *nf*
tincture	тинкту́ра *nf*

common compounds

acetone	ацето́н *nm*
alcohol	алкого́ль *nm*
anhydride	ангидри́д *nm*
aniline	анили́н *nm*
benzine	бензи́н *nm*
calcium carbide	карби́д ка́льция *nm*, *nm*
calcium chloride	хло́ристый ка́льций *nm*
chloroform	хлорофо́рм *nm*
dextrose	декстро́за *nf*
dioxin	диокси́н *nm*
ethanol	этано́л *nm*
ether	эфи́р *nm*
ethylene	этиле́н *nm*
glucose	глюко́за *nf*
glycogen	гликоге́н *nm*
indigo (*pl* indigos, indigoes)	инди́го *nn*, *indecl*
maltose	мальто́за *nf*
menthol	менто́л *nm*
methanol	метано́л *nm*
methyl	мети́л *nm*
naphthalene	нафтали́н *nm*
naphthol	нафто́л *nm*
nicotine	никоти́н *nm*
octane	окта́н *nm*
olein	олеи́н *nm*
paraffin	парафи́н *nm*
pentane	пента́н *nm*
phenol	фено́л *nm*
phenolphthalein	фенолфталеи́н *nm*
phosgene	фосге́н *nm*
potash	пота́ш *nm*
propane (gas)	пропа́н *nm*
retinol [= Vitamin A]	ретино́л *nm*
saccharine	са́харный *aj*
stearin	стеари́н *nm*
tannin	тани́н *nm*
toluene	толуо́л *nm*
urethane	урета́н *nm*

acids

ascorbic	аскорби́новая *aj*
boric	бо́рная *aj*
carbolic	карбо́ловая *aj*
chloric	хло́рная *aj*
chromic acid	хро́мовая *aj*
cyanic acid	циа́новая *aj*
gallic acid	га́лловая *aj*
nicotinic acid	никоти́новая *aj*
oleic acid	олеи́новая *aj*
pectic acid	пекти́новая *aj*
pelargonic acid	пеларгони́ческая *aj*
phosphoric	фо́сфорная *aj*
phthelic acid	фта́левая *aj*
picric	пикри́новая *aj*
salicylic	салици́ловая *aj*
tannic	тани́нная *aj*
xanthic	кса́нтовая *aj*

bases

alkaloid	алкало́ид *nm*
caustic	каусти́ческий *aj*
picoline	пиколи́н *nm*

salts

bisulphate	бисульфа́т *nm*
bromide	броми́д *nm*
citrate	цитра́т *nm*
cyanide	циани́д *nm*
hydride	гидри́д *nm*
iodide	йод *nm*
perchlorate	перхлора́т *nm*
permanganate	пермангана́т *nm*
picrate	пикра́т *nm*
salicylate	салици́л *nm*
silicate	силика́т *nm*
sulfite (BR sulphite)	сульфи́т *nm*
sulfonamide (BR sulphonamide)	сульфами́д *nm*
superphosphate	суперфосфа́т *nm*
tannate	танна́т *nm*
tantalate	тантала́т *nm*
tartrate	тартра́т *nm*
tellurite	теллури́т *nm*

gases

acetylene	ацетиле́н *nm*
ammonia	аммиа́к *nm*

carbon monoxide	монокси́д углеро́да *nm*, *nm*
cyanogen	циа́н *nm*
ethane	эта́н *nm*
formaldehyde	формальдеги́д *nm*
methane	мета́н *nm*
niton [= radon]	нито́н *nm*
ozone	озо́н *nm*

alkaloids

caffein(e)	кофеи́н *nm*
cocaine	кокаи́н *nm*
mescaline	мескали́н *nm*
morphine	мо́рфий *nm*
quinine	хини́н *nm*
strychnine	стрихни́н *nm*

saccharides

dextrin(e)	декстри́н *nm*
fructose	фрукто́за *nf*
lactose	лакто́за *nf*
polysaccharide	полисахари́д *nm*

oxides

peroxide	пе́рекись *nf*
zinc oxide	о́кись ци́нка *nf*, *nm*

radicals

ammonium	аммо́ний *nm*
butyl	бути́л *nm*
butylene	бутиле́н *nm*
ethyl	эти́л *nm*
methylene	метиле́н *nm*
uranyl	урани́л *nm*

isotopes

radiothorium	радиото́рий *nm*
thoron	торо́н *nm*

synthetics

acetate	ацета́т *nm*
acrylic	акри́л *nm*
bakelite	бакели́т *nm*
cellophane	целлофа́н *nm*
celluloid	целлуло́ид *nm*
linoleum	лино́леум *nm*
mylar	майла́р *nm*
neoprene	неопре́н *nm*
nylon	нейло́н *nm*
phthalein	фталеи́н *nm*
plasticene, plasticine	пластили́н *nm*
polyester	полиэфи́р *nm*
polyethylene	полиэтиле́н *nm*
polystyrene	полистиро́л *nm*
polyvinylchloride, PVC	поливинилхлори́д *nm*
rhodamine	родами́н *nm*
silicone	силокса́н *nm*
vinyl	вини́л *nm*

other common compounds

ammonium chloride	хло́ристый аммо́ний *nm*
benzoin	бензои́н *nm*
butane	бута́н *nm*
denatured alcohol	денатура́т *nm*
distillate	дистилля́т *nm*
ethyl alcohol	эти́ловый спирт *nm*
ferment	ферме́нт *nm*
filtrate	фильтра́т *nm*
glycerin(e)	глицери́н *nm*
hydrogen chloride	хло́ристый водоро́д *nm*
magnesia	магне́зия *nf*
methyl alcohol	мети́ловый спирт *nm*
potassium bromide	бро́мистый ка́лий *nm*
potassium cyanide	циа́нистый ка́лий *nm*
potassium iodide	йо́дистий ка́лий *nm*
sodium chloride	хло́ристый на́трий *nm*
vinyl chloride	хло́ристый вини́л *nm*

PROCESSES, REACTIONS, TESTS

absorption	абсо́рбция *nf*
activation	актива́ция *nf*, активиза́ция *nf*
adsorption	адсо́рбция *nf*
analysis (*pl* analyses)	ана́лиз *nm*
calcination	кальцина́ция *nf*
carbonization	карбониза́ция *nf*
catalysis	ката́лиз *nm*
chlorination	хлори́рование *nn*
coagulation	коагуля́ция *nf*
concentration	концентра́ция *nf*
condensation	конденса́ция *nf*
corrosion	корро́зия *nf*
cracking	кре́кинг *nm*
crystallization	кристаллиза́ция *nf*
distillation	дистилля́ция *nf*
electrolysis	электро́лиз *nm*
electrosynthesis	электроси́нтез *nm*
emanation	эмана́ция *nf*
extraction	экстра́кция *nf*
fermentation	фермента́ция *nf*
filtration	фильтра́ция *nf*
galvanization	гальваниза́ция *nf*
gasification	газифика́ция *nf*

homogenization	гомогениза́ция *nf*
hydrolysis	гидро́лиз *nm*
inversion	инве́рсия *nf*
ion exchange	ио́нный обме́н *nm*
ionization	иониза́ция *nf*
irreversible process	необрати́мый проце́сс *nm*
neutralization	нейтрализа́ция *nf*
nitration	нитрова́ние *nn*
nitrification	нитрифика́ция *nf*
ozonization	озони́рование *nn*
pasteurization	пастериза́ция *nf*
photolysis	фотоли́з *nm*
polymerization	полимериза́ция *nf*
radioactivity	радиоакти́вность *nf*
radiolysis	радиоли́з *nm*
reduction	реду́кция *nf*
sublimation	сублима́ция *nf*
synthesis (*pl* syntheses)	си́нтез *nm*
synthesize	синтези́ровать *impf, pf*
titration	титрова́ние *nn*
vulcanization	вулканиза́ция *nf*

TOOLS

buret(te)	бюре́тка *nf*
colorimeter	колори́метр *nm*
filter	фильтр *nm*
filter paper	фильтрова́льная бума́га *nf*
indicator	индика́тор *nm*
ionizer	ионизи́рующая устано́вка *nf*
litmus	ла́кмус *nm*
litmus paper	ла́кмусовая бума́га *nf*
neutralizer	нейтрализа́тор *nm*
ozonizer	озона́тор *nm*
pestle	пест, пе́стик *nm*
Petri dish	чашка Пе́три *nf*
pipet(te)	пипе́тка *nf*
retort	рето́рта *nf*

USES AND PRODUCTS

aniline dyes	анили́новые кра́ски *nfpl*
chlorinated water	хлори́рованная вода́ *nf*
defoliant	дефолиа́нт *nm*
fungicide	фунгици́д *nm*
herbicide	гербици́д *nm*
hydrogen peroxide	пе́рекись водоро́да *nf, nm*
insecticide	дезинсе́кция *nf*, инсектици́д *nm*
lysol	лизо́л *nm*
monosodium glutamate	глютамина́т на́трия *nm, nm*
paraffin oil	парафи́новое ма́сло *nn*
petrochemical	нефтехими́ческий проду́кт *nm*
silica gel	силикаге́ль *nm*
turpentine	терпенти́н *nm*

commercial names

Carborundum	карбору́нд *nm*
Dacron	дакро́н *nm*
Freon	фрео́н *nm*
Plexiglas	плексигла́с *nm*
Teflon	тефло́н *nm*

HISTORICAL TERMS

alchemy	алхи́мия *nf*
elixir	эликси́р *nm*
phlogiston	флогисто́н *nm*
ylem	иле́м *nm*

See also **SCIENCE AND THE SCIENCES**, **FOOD AND NUTRITION**, **THE HUMAN BODY** *(biochemicals)*, **METALLURGY**, **DRUGS**, **MEASUREMENTS**

ASTRONOMY

GENERAL TERMS

astral	астра́льный *aj*
astronomer	астроно́м *nm*
astronomy	астроно́мия *nf*
cosmic	косми́ческий *aj*
cosmos	ко́смос *nm*
cycle	цикл *nm*
distance	диста́нция *nf*
ether [obs]	эфи́р *nm*
gravitation	гравита́ция *nf*
interplanetary space	межплане́тное простра́нство *nn*
lunar	лу́нный *aj*
macrocosm	макроко́см *nm*
microcosm	микроко́см *nm*
observatory	обсервато́рия *nf*
orbit	орби́та *nf*
parallax	паралла́кс *nm*
period	пери́од *nm*
planetarium (*pl* planetariums, planetaria)	планета́рий *nm*
solar disk	со́лнечный диск *nm*

solar system	со́лнечная систе́ма *nf*
telescope	телеско́п *nm*
ufologist	уфо́лог *nm*
zodiac	зодиа́к *nm*

SPECIALIZATIONS

astronautics *nplsv*	астрона́втика *nf*
astrophysics *nplsv*	астрофи́зика *nf*
cosmogony	космого́ния *nf*
cosmography	космогра́фия *nf*
cosmology	космоло́гия *nf*
radioastronomy	радиоастроно́мия *nf*
selenology	селеноло́гия *nf*
telemetry	телеметри́я *nf*
telescopy	телескопи́я *nf*
ufology	уфоло́гия *nf*

DESCRIPTION & CLASSIFICATION

theories and models

Big-Bang theory	тео́рия большо́го взры́ва *nf*, *nm*
Copernican system	систе́ма Копе́рника *nf*, *nm*
Ptolemaic system	Птоломе́ева систе́ма *nf*

heavenly bodies

asteroid	астеро́ид *nm*
comet	коме́та *nf*
constellation	констелля́ция *nf*
galaxy	гала́ктика *nf*
meteor	метео́р *nm*
meteoroid, meteorite	метеори́т *nm*
planet	плане́та *nf*
pulsar	пульса́р *nm*
quasar	кваза́р *nm*
radio galaxy	радиогала́ктика *nf*
satellite	сателли́т *nm*

types of stars

binary	бина́рный *aj*
meridian	меридиа́н *nm*
neutron star	нейтро́нная звезда́ *nf*
nova (*pl* novas, novae)	но́вая звезда́ *nf*

movement, configuration, distance, position

aberration	аберра́ция *nf*
aphelion	афе́лий *nm*
apogee	апоге́й *nm*
apse, apsis (*pl* apsides)	апси́да *nf*
culmination	кульмина́ция *nf*
eccentric	эксцентри́ческий *aj*
ecliptic	эклиптика *nf*
epicycle	эпици́кл *nm*
heliocentric	гелеоцентри́ческий *aj*
interplanetary	межплане́тный *aj*
nadir	нади́р *nm*
parallax	паралла́кс *nm*
periapsis (*pl* periapsides)	периапси́да *nf*
perigee	периге́й *nm*
perihelion	периге́лий *nm*
perturbation	пертурба́ция *nf*
quadrature	квадрату́ра *nf*
syzygy	сизи́гий *nm*
tropic	тро́пик *nm*
zenith	зени́т *nm*

visual phenomena

aureole	орео́л *nm*
corona	коро́на *nf*
halo	гало́ *nn*
lunar eclipse	лу́нное затме́ние *nn*
parhelion	парге́лий *nm*
phase	фа́за *nf*
photosphere	фотосфе́ра *nf*
refraction	рефра́кция *nf*
Saturn's rings	ко́льца Сату́рна *nnpl*, *nm*
terminator (line)	термина́тор *nm*

other terms

heliocentrism	гелиоцентри́зм *nm*
lunar surface	лу́нная пове́рхность *nf*
lunar year	лу́нный год *nm*
magnetic storm	магни́тная бу́ря *nf*

NAMES

planets

Jupiter	Юпи́тер *nm*
Mars	Марс *nm*
Mercury	Мерку́рий *nm*
Neptune	Непту́н *nm*
Pluto	Плуто́н *nm*
Saturn	Сату́рн *nm*
Uranus	Ура́н *nm*
Venus	Вене́ра *nf*

stars

Alcyone	Альцио́на *nf*
Aldebaron	Альдебара́н *nm*
Alpha Centauri	а́льфа Цента́вра *nm*
Antares	Анта́рес *nm*
Arcturus	Аркту́р *nm*
Castor	Ка́стор *nm*

Polaris, Pole Star	Поля́рная звезда́ *nf*
Pollux	По́ллюкс *nm*
Procyon	Процио́н *nm*
Rigel	Ри́гель *nm*
Sirius	Си́риус *nm*
Vega	Ве́га *nf*

constellations

Cassiopeia	Кассиопе́я *nf*
Cepheus	Цефе́й *nm*
Draco, Dragon	Драко́н *nm*
Hydrus	Ги́дра *nf*
Lyra	Ли́ра *nf*
Octans	Окта́нт *nm*
Orion	Орио́н *nm*
Pavo	Павли́н *nm*
Pegasus	Пега́с *nm*
Perseus	Персе́й *nm*
Phoenix	Фе́никс *nm*
Pleiades	Плея́ды *npl*
Scorpio	Скорпио́н *nm*

asteroids, moons, satellites, meteors, comets

Ariel [Uranus]	Арие́ль *nm*
Callisto [Jupiter]	Калли́сто *nn*
Ceres [asteroid]	Царе́ра *nf*
Ganymede [Jupiter]	Ганиме́д *nm*
Halley's comet	коме́та Галле́я *nf, nm*
Hyperion [Saturn]	Гиперио́н *nm*
Io [Jupiter]	И́о *nf*
Leonids, Leonides [meteor showers]	Леони́ды *npl*
Perseids [meteor showers]	Персеиды *npl*
Phobos [Mars]	Фо́бос *nm*
Phoebe [Saturn]	Фе́ба *nf*
Titan [Saturn]	Тита́н *nm*
Triton [Neptune]	Трито́н *nm*

TOOLS

kinds of telescopes

radiotelescope	радиотелеско́п *nm*
reflecting telescope	телеско́п-рефле́ктор, зерка́льный телеско́п *nm*
refractor telescope	рефра́ктор *nm*

other tools

astrolabe	астроля́бия *nf*
astronomical chart	ка́рта звёздного не́ба *nf, nn*
azimuth	а́зимут *nm*
ephemerid (chart)	эфемери́да *nf*
planisphere	планисфе́ра *nf*
spectrometer	спектро́метр *nm*
spectroscope	спектроско́п *nm*
spectrum (*pl* spectrums, spectra)	спектр *nm*
telespectroscope	телеспектроско́п *nm*
tellurion	теллу́рий *nm*

See also **SCIENCE AND THE SCIENCES**, **AVIATION AND SPACE TRAVEL**, **MEASUREMENTS**, **FAMOUS FIGURES OF YESTERDAY AND TODAY** *(scientists and inventors)*

GEOLOGY

GENERAL TERMS

epoch	эпо́ха *nf*
era	э́ра *nf*
formation	форма́ция *nf*
paleo-, palaeo-	па́лео- *pref*
period	пери́од *nm*
rock structure	структу́ра скал *nf, nfpl*
substrate, substratum (*pl* substratums, substrata)	субстра́т *nm*
volcano (*pl* volcanos, volcanoes)	вулка́н *nm*

SPECIALIZATIONS

geophysics *nplsv*	геофи́зика *nf*
orography	орографи́я *nf*
orology	droло́гия *nf*
paleontology (BR palaeontology)	палеонтоло́гия *nf*
petrography	петрогра́фия *nf*
petrology	петроло́гия *nf*
physiography	физиогра́фия *nf*
seismography	сейсмогра́фия *nf*
seismology	сейсмоло́гия *nf*
speleology	спелеоло́гия *nf*
structural geology	структу́рная геоло́гия *nf*
tectonics *nplsv*	текто́ника *nf*
topography	топогра́фия *nf*
volcanology, vulcanology	вулканоло́гия *nf*

HISTORICAL DIVISIONS

Cambrian	кембри́йский
Cenozoic	кайнозо́йский *aj*

Devonian	дево́н *nm*, дево́нский пери́од *nm*
Eocene	эоце́н *nm*
Holocene	голо́цен *nm*
Jurassic	ю́рский *aj*
Mesozoic	мезозо́йский *aj*
Miocene	миоце́новый *aj*
Neolithic	неоли́т *nm*
Neozoic	неозо́йский *aj*
Oligocene	оли́гоцен *nm*
Ordovician	ордови́кский *aj*
Paleocene	палеоце́н *nm*
Paleolithic (BR Palaeolithic)	палеолити́ческий *aj*
Paleozoic (BR Palaeozoic)	палеозо́йский *aj*
Permian	пе́рмский *aj*
Pleistocene	плейстоце́н *nm*
Pliocene	плиоце́н *nm*
pre-Cambrian	доке́мбрий, докембри́йский *aj*
Proterozoic	протерозо́й(ский) *aj*
Silurian	силури́йский *aj*
Triassic	триа́совый *aj*

DESCRIPTION

geological formations

canyon	каньо́н *nm*
continental shelf	шельф *nm*
deformity	деформа́ция *nf*
geyser	ге́йзер *nm*
glacier	гле́тчер *nm*
stalactite	сталакти́т *nm*
stalagmite	сталагми́т *nm*
syncline	синклина́ль *nf*

deposits

alluvium	аллю́вий *nm*
loess	лёсс *nm*
moraine	море́на *nf*

other descriptive terms

agglomerate	агломера́т *nm*
conglomerate	конгломера́т *nm*
detritis	детри́т *nm*
eluvium	эло́вий *nm*
geothermal	геотерма́льный, геотерми́ческий *aj*
gneiss	гнейс *nm*
karst	карст *nm*
metamorphic	метаморфи́ческий *aj*
oolite	ооли́т *nm*
perlite	перли́т *nm*
petrification	петрифика́ция *nf*
Plutonic	плутони́ческий *aj*
pluvial	плювиа́льный *aj*
porous	по́ристый *aj*
porphyroid	порфиро́ид *nm*
seismic	сейсми́ческий *aj*
stratified	стратифици́рованный *aj*
tachylite	тахили́т *nm*
tectonic	тектони́ческий *aj*
tektite, tectite	текти́т *nm*
tufa	ту́ф *nm*
volcanic	вулкани́ческий *aj*
xenolith	ксеноли́т *nm*

EARTHQUAKES AND VOLCANOES

crater	кра́тер *nm*
epicenter (BR epicentre)	эпице́нтр *nm*
lava	ла́ва *nf*
magma	ма́гма *nf*
magnitude	магниту́да *nf*
Richter scale	шка́ла Ри́хтера *nf*, *nm*
seismograph	сейсмо́граф *nm*
seismological	сейсмологи́ческий *aj*
seismometer	сейсмо́метр *nm*
tephra	те́фра *nf*

GEOLOGICAL PROCESSES

agglomeration	агломера́ция *nf*
crystallization	кристаллиза́ция *nf*
deflation	дефля́ция *nf*
deformation	деформа́ция *nf*
diluvium	дилю́вий *nm*
disintegration	дезинтегра́ция *nf*
erosion	эро́зия *nf*
metamorphism	метаморфи́зм *nm*
mineralization	минерализа́ция *nf*
orogenesis, orogeny	орогене́з *nm*
paragenesis	параге́незис *nm*
pneumatolysis	пневматоли́з *nm*
stratification	стратифика́ция *nf*
volcanism, vulcanism	вулкани́зм *nm*

PERSONS

geologist	гео́лог *nm*
paleontologist (palaeontologist)	палеонто́лог *nm*
petrographer	петро́граф *nm*

petrologist — петро́лог *nm*
seismologist — сейсмо́лог *nm*
speleologist — спелео́лог *nm*
volcanologist, vulcanologist — вулкано́лог *nm*

See also **GEOGRAPHY**, **MINERALS AND MINING**

METEOROLOGY

GENERAL TERMS

atmospheric pressure — атмосфе́рное давле́ние *nn*
chart — ка́рта *nf*
circulate (air) — циркули́ровать *impf*
circulation — циркуля́ция *nf*
climate — кли́мат *nm*
climatic conditions — климати́ческие усло́вия *nnpl*
cold front — холо́дный фронт *nm*
front — фронт *nm*
greenhouse effect — парнико́вый/тепли́чный эффе́кт *nm*
meteorological station — метеорологи́ческая ста́нция, метеоста́нция *nf*
meteorologist — метеоро́лог *nm*
ozone — озо́н *nm*
prognostication — прогнози́рование *nn*
temperature — температу́ра *nf*
zone — зо́на *nf*

FIELDS OF SPECIALIZATION

climatography — климатогра́фия *nf*
climatology — климатоло́гия *nf*
meteorology — метеороло́гия *nf*
nephology — нефоло́гия *nf*
phenology — фенологи́я *nf*
pluviometry — плювиометри́я *nf*

ASPECTS OF METEOROLOGY

climates

Arctic — аркти́ческий *aj*
continental — континента́льный *aj*
global — глоба́льный *aj*
tropical — тропи́ческий *aj*

air zones

atmosphere — атмосфе́ра *nf*
hydrosphere — гидросфе́ра *nf*
ionosphere — ионосфе́ра *nf*
mesosphere — мезосфе́ра *nf*
ozonosphere — озоносфе́ра *nf*
stratosphere — стратосфе́ра *nf*
thermosphere — термосфе́ра *nf*
troposphere — тропосфе́ра *nf*

storms

cyclone — цикло́н *nm*
hurricane — урага́н *nm*
monsoon — муссо́н *nm*
squall — шквал *nm*
tornado (*pl* tornados, tornadoes) — торна́до *nn*, *indecl*
typhoon — тайфу́н *nm*

winds

anticyclone — антицикло́н *nm*
breeze — бриз *nm*
kamsin, khamsin — хамси́н *nm*
mistral — мистра́ль *nm*
simoom — саму́м *nm*
sirocco — сиро́кко *nm*, *indecl*
zephyr — зефи́р *nm*

other weather terms

boreal — боре́альный *aj*
depression — депре́ссия *nf*
normal temperature — норма́льная температу́ра *nf*
ozone hole — озо́новая дыра́ *nm*
ozone layer — озо́новый слой *nm*
squally — шква́льный *aj*
stormy — штормово́й *aj*

AIR QUALITY TERMS

inversion — инве́рсия *nf*
miasma *nsg* (*pl* miasmas, miasmata) — миа́змы *nfpl*
smog — смог *nm*

TOOLS, EQUIPMENT, MEASUREMENTS

anemometer — анемо́метр *nm*
aneroid barometer — баро́метр-анеро́ид *nm*
barograph — баро́граф *nm*
barometer — баро́метр *nm*
Beaufort scale — шка́ла Бофо́рта *nf*, *nm*
hygrometer — гигро́метр *nm*
isobar — изоба́ра *nf*
isotherm — изоте́рма *nf*
millibar — миллиба́р *nm*

nephoscope	нефоско́п *nm*
pluviometer	плювио́метр *nm*
radiosonde	радиозо́нд *nm*
thermometer	термо́метр *nm*
weather station	метеоста́нция *nf*
weather chart	синопти́ческая ка́рта *nf*

See also **GEOGRAPHY**, **AVIATION AND SPACE TRAVEL**, **BOATS AND SHIPS**, **MEASUREMENTS**

Putting Science to Work

TECHNOLOGY OVERVIEW ◆ AGRICULTURE ◆ COMMUNICATIONS ◆ COMPUTERS ◆ ELECTRICITY AND ELECTRONICS ◆ FUELS ◆ METALLURGY ◆ MINERALS AND MINING ◆ PRINTING ◆ TEXTILES ◆ WEAPONS

TECHNOLOGY OVERVIEW

GENERAL TERMS

automated	автоматизи́рованный *aj*
automatic	автомати́ческий *aj*
automation	автоматиза́ция *nf*
by-product	побо́чный проду́кт
design [industrial]	диза́йн *nm*
economically [efficiently]	эконо́мно *av*
engineer	инжене́р *nm*
engineering	инжене́рное де́ло *nn*
function	функциони́ровать *impf*
hi-tech	высокосло́жная техноло́гия *nf*
industrial park	те́хно-парк *nm*
industrialization	индустриализа́ция *nf*
industry	инду́стрия *nf*
innovation	нова́торство *nn*, нова́ция *nf*
instructions for use	инстру́кции по́льзования *nfpl*, *nn*
instrument	инструме́нт *nm*
instruments *npl*	инструмента́рий *nm*
know-how	но́у-ха́у *nn*, *indecl*
machine	маши́на *nf*
machine-made *aj*	маши́нной вы́работки
machinery *nsg*	маши́ны *nfpl*
mechanism	механи́зм *nm*
mechanize	механизи́ровать *impf*, *pf*
model	моде́ль *nf*
modernization	модерниза́ция *nf*
motor	мото́р *nm*
operation	опера́ция *nf*
patent	пате́нт *nm*
polytechnic (school)	полите́хникум *nm*
process	проце́сс *nm*
progress	прогре́сс *nm*
project	прое́кт *nm*
prototype	прототи́п *nm*
revolutionize	революционизи́ровать *impf*, *pf*
safety factor	фа́ктор безопа́сности *nm*
specification	специфика́ция *nf*
system	систе́ма *nf*
technical term	техни́ческий те́рмин *nm*
technical terminology	техни́ческая терминоло́гия *nf*
technique	те́хника *nf*
technology	техноло́гия *nf*
turbo-	ту́рбо- *pref*
working model	де́йствующая моде́ль *nf*

ASPECTS OF TECHNOLOGY

new technologies

alternative sources of energy	альтернати́вные исто́чники *nmpl*
bioengineering	биоинжене́рия *nf*
biotechnology	биотехноло́гия *nf*
computerization	компьютериза́ция *nf*
electrotechnology	электротехноло́гия *nf*
machine translation	маши́нный перево́д *nm*
microelectronics *nplsv*	микроэлектро́ника *nf*
plastics *npl*	пла́стика *nf*
radiography	радиогра́фия *nf*
recycling	рециркуля́ция *nf*
robotics *nplsv*	робототе́хника *nf*
rocketry	раке́тная те́хника *nf*
telecommunications	телекоммуника́ции *nfpl*

engineering fields

consulting	конса́лтинг *nm*, консульти́рование *nn*
electrical engineering	электроте́хника *nf*

hydraulic engineering	гидроте́хника *nf*
sanitary engineering	санте́хника *nf*
structural	структу́рный *aj*

inventions

adding machine	счётная маши́на *nf*
air-conditioning	кондициони́рование *nn*
audiocassette	аудиокассе́та *nf*
automaton (*pl* automata)	автома́т *nm*
bulldozer	бульдо́зер *nm*
cassette recorder	кассе́тный магнитофо́н *nm*
cassette	кассе́та *nf*
central heating	центра́льное отопле́ние *nn*
combination (of a safe)	ко́довая комбина́ция *nf*
compass	ко́мпас *nm*
computer	компью́тер *nm*
photocopier	копиро́вщик *nm*
cotton gin	джин *nm*
crane	кран *nm*
derrick	де́ррик *nm*
diesel (engine, motor)	ди́зель *nm*
drill (hand-)	дрель *nf*
dynamo	дина́мо *nn, indecl*
electric light	электри́ческий свет *nm*
electric motor	электромото́р *nm*
electronic device	электро́нная аппарату́ра *nf*
escalator	эскала́тор *nm*
fax machine	факсими́льный аппара́т *nm*
filter pump	фильтрова́льный насо́с *nm*
hydraulic press	гидравли́ческий пресс *nm*
knitting machine	вяза́льная маши́на *nf*
laser	ла́зер *nm*
linotype [obs]	линоти́п *nm*
locomotive	локомоти́в *nm*
magnetic tape	магни́тная ле́нта *nf*
magneto [machine]	магне́то *nn, indecl*
microphone	микрофо́н *nm*
microscope	микроско́п *nm*
mimeograph [obs]	мимео́граф *nm*
optical fiber	опти́ческое волокно́ *nn*
pantograph [machine]	панто́граф *nm*
photocopier, copy machine	копирова́льная маши́на *nf*
pistol	пистоле́т *nm*
pneumatic brake [on a train]	пневмати́ческий тормо́з *nm*
pneumatic drill	пневмати́ческое сверло́ *nn*, пневмати́ческая дрель *nf*
polishing machine	полирова́льная маши́на *nf*
press [machine]	пресс *nm*
pulsometer [vacuum pump]	пульсо́метр *nm*
punching press	штампо́вочный пресс *nm*
radar	рада́р *nm*
radio	ра́дио *nn, indecl*
revolver	револьве́р *nm*
robot	ро́бот *nm*
sewing machine	шве́йная маши́на *nf*
stethoscope	стетоско́п *nm*
telegraph	телегра́ф *nm*
telephone	телефо́н *nm*
television	телеви́дение *nn*
tractor	тра́ктор *nm*
transistor	транзи́стор *nm*
turbine, turbo	турби́на *nf*
vacuum pump	ва́куум-насо́с *nm*
washing machine	стира́льная маши́на *nf*

TECHNICAL TERMS

tools, parts, equipment

abrasive	абрази́в *nm*, абрази́вный материа́л *nm*
anchor	а́нкер *nm*
apparatus	аппарату́ра *nf*
armature [fittings]	армату́ра *nf*
balance (beam)	баланси́р *nm*
balance wheel	бала́нс (часо́в) *nm*
block [pulley]	блок *nm*
boiler	бо́йлер *nm*
bolt	болт *nm*
calender [machine with rollers]	кала́ндр *nm*
centrifuge	центрифу́га *nf*
circular saw	циркуля́рная пила́ *nf*
circulating pump	циркуляцио́нный насо́с *nm*
compressor	компре́ссор *nm*
condenser	конденса́тор *nm*
converter	конве́ртор *nm*
conveyor	конве́йер *nm*
conveyor belt	конве́йерная ле́нта *nf*
cylinder head	кры́шка цили́ндра *nf*

damper	дéмпфер *nm*
drilling platform	нефтянáя платфóрма *nf*
fixing solution	фиксáтор *nm*
generator	генерáтор *nm*
grader, grading machine	грéйдер *nm*
hectograph	гектóграф *nm*
indicator	индикáтор *nm*
indicator light	световóй индикáтор *nm*
lubricator, lubricating machine	лубрикáтор *nm*
muffle(r)	мýфель *nm*
multiplier	мультипликáтор *nm*
nipple	ни́ппель *nm*
perforator	перфорáтор *nm*
plunger	плýнжер *nm*
polisher	полирóвщик *nm*
pulverizer	пульверизáтор *nm*
pump	пóмпа *nf*
register	реги́стр *nm*
regulator	регуля́тор *nm*
resistor	рези́стор *nm*
roller bearing	рóликовый подши́пник *nm*
roller [wheel]	рóлик *nm*
rotor	рóтор *nm*
selector	селéктор *nm*
servomechanism	сервомехани́зм *nm*
siphon	сифóн *nm*
sorter [machine]	сортирóвочная маши́на *nf*
stamper	штéмпель, штамп *nm*
stator	стáтор *nm*
stoker	стóкер *nm*
stopper	штóпор *nm*
synchronizer	синхронизáтор *nm*
tabulator [typewriter]	табуля́тор *nm*
thermometer	термóметр *nm*
thermoregulator	терморегуля́тор *nm*
thermostat	термостáт *nm*
traverse (beam)	трáверс *nm*
trolley	троллéй *nm*
tubing	тю́бинг *nm*
turbogenerator	турбогенерáтор *nm*
universal joint	универсáльный шарни́р *nm*

other terms

absorption	абсóрбция *nf*
Bessemer process	бессемеровáние *nn*
compensate *vt(i)*	компенси́ровать *impf, pf*
compensation	компенсáция *nf*
compression	компрéссия *nf*
copying	копи́рование *nn*, копирóвка *nf*
crack	креки́ровать *impf, pf*
drag [dredge]	драги́ровать *impf, pf*
gum, to stick with	гумми́ровать *impf, pf*
mercerization	мерсеризáция *nf*
model	модели́ровать *impf, pf*
modification	модификáция *nf*
modular [unit]	мóдульный *aj*
mount	монти́ровать *impf*
one-cylinder (motor)	одноцили́ндровый *aj*
perforation	перфорáция *nf*
phase	фáзный, фáзовый *aj*
projected capacity	проéктная мóщность *nf*
pulverization	пульверизáция *nf*
rationalization	рационализáция *nf*
resonance	резонáнс *nm*
reverberation	реверберáция *nf*
reversing	ревéрсия *nf*
satinize [paper]	сатини́ровать *impf*
specifics *npl*	специ́фика *nf*
stimulator	стимуля́тор *nm*
strobe	строб *nm*
synchronism	синхрони́зм *nm*
synchronization	синхронизáция *nf*
synchronize *vt(i)* [sound, movement]	синхронизи́ровать(ся) *impf, pf*
tamping	тампонáж *nm*
telodynamic	телединами́ческий *aj*
tempered	темпери́рованный *aj*
uneconomical	неэкономи́чный, неэконóмный *aj*
vibration	вибрáция *nf*
zinc-plate	цинковáть *impf*

PERSONS

engineers

chemical engineer	инженéр-хи́мик *nm*
consulting engineer	инженéр-консультáнт *nm*
electrical engineer	инженéр-элéктрик, электротéхник *nm*
mechanical engineer	инженéр-механик *nm*
mining engineer	гóрный инженéр *nm*

other persons

bulldozer driver	бульдозери́ст *nm*
crane operator	крановщи́к *nm*, крановщи́ца *nf*
electrician	элéктрик *nm*

hydraulic engineer	гидротéхник *nm*
innovator	новáтор *nm*
industrial designer	дизáйнер *nm*
instrument-maker	инструментáльщик *nm*
machine operator	оперáтор *nm*
machinist	машини́ст *nm*
mechanic	механик *nm*
mechanization expert	механизáтор *nm*
modeler (BR modeller)	модели́ст, -ка *nmf*, модéльщик *nm*
motor mechanic	моторúст *nm*
polytechnical student	политéхник *nm*
presser, press operator	прессовщи́к *nm*
technician	тéхник *nm*
technologist	технолóг *nm*

See also **MEASUREMENTS**, **SCIENCE**, **ELECTRICITY AND ELECTRONICS**, **COMPUTERS**

AGRICULTURE

GENERAL TERMS

agricultural product	сельскохозя́йственный продýкт *nm*
cultivation (of plants)	культиви́рование *nn*
cultivation (of soil)	культивáция *nf*
electrification	электризáция *nf*
farm	фéрма *nf*
hybrid	гибри́д *nm*
land reform	земéльная реформа *nf*
mechanization	механизáция *nf*
melioration	мелиорáция *nf*
pesticide	пестици́д *nm*
produce	продýкция *nf*
selection	селéкция *nf*

SPECIALIZATIONS

agrobiology	агробиолóгия *nf*
agrobusiness	агроби́знес *nm*
agronomy	агронóмия *nf*
hydroponics *nplsv*	гидропóника *nf*
pedology	педолóгия *nf*
pomology	помолóгия *nf*

ASPECTS OF FARMING

organization and ownership

collective	коллекти́в *nm*
collective farm	коллекти́вное хозя́йство *nn*
experimental station	óпытная стáнция
kibbutz (*pl* kibbutzim)	ки(б)бýц *nm*
kolkhoz	колхóз *nm*
sovkhoz	совхóз *nm*

land units

acre	акр *nm*
acreage	плóщадь в áкрах *nf*, *nmpl*
hectare	гектáр *nm*
land parcel	парцéлла *nf*

farming method

monoculture	монокультýра *nf*
rotation	ротáция *nf*
terracing	терраси́рование *nn*

soils and soil conservation

cultivation (of soil)	культивáция *nf*
drainage	дренáж *nm*
erosion	эрóзия *nf*
loess	лёсс *nm*

types of farms

dairy farm	молóчная фéрма *nf*
fish farm	рыбовóдческая фéрма *nf*
olive grove	оли́вковая рóща *nf*
oyster bed	ýстричный садóк *nm*
plantation	плантáция *nf*
poultry farm	птицефéрма *nf*
ranch	рáнчо *nn, indecl*
rice field/paddy	ри́совое пóле *nn*
rice-growing	рисовóдство *nn*
sugar plantation	сáхарная плантáция *nf*
sugar refinery	сáхарный завóд *nm*
tobacco farming	табаковóдство *nn*
vineyard	виногрáдник *nm*
wine-making	винодéлие *nn*
winegrowing	виногрáдарство *nn*

major crops

copal (resin)	копáл *nm*
copra	кóпра *nf*
fiber	фи́бра *nf*
fruit	фрýкт *nm*
raffia	рáффия *nf*
rape seed	рапс *nm*
rice	рис *nm*
sesame	сезáм *nm*
sorghum	сóрго *nn, indecl*
soy, soya	сóя *nf*
sugar beet	сáхарная свёкла *nf*
sugar cane	сáхарный тростни́к *nm*
taro (root)	тáро *nn, indecl*

tobacco	таба́к *nm*

care of animals

farmyard	двор фе́рмы *nm*
forage	фура́ж *nm*
pasture	па́стбище *nn*

pests and pesticides

DDT	ДДТ *nm*
fruit fly	фрукто́вая му́шка *nf*
fungicide	фунгици́д *nm*
herbicide	гербици́д *nm*
insecticide	дезинсе́кция *nf*, инсектици́д *nm*
parasite	парази́т *nm*

plant cultivation

agrochemical	агрохимика́т *nm*
chemical fertilizer	хими́ческое удобре́ние *nn*
compost	компо́ст *nm*
compost pit	компо́стная я́ма *nf*
guano	гуа́но *nn, indecl*
humus	гу́мус *nm*
nitrify	нитрифици́ровать *impf, pf*
organic fertilizer	органи́ческое удобре́ние *nn*
potash	пота́ш *nm*
scarify	скарифици́ровать *impf, pf*

TOOLS AND EQUIPMENT

artesian well	артезиа́нский коло́дец *nm*
combine	комба́йн *nm*
cultivator	культива́тор *nm*
drainage pipe	дрена́жная труба́ *nf*
elevator, grain	элева́тор *nm*
farmhouse	фе́рмерский дом *nm*
machete	маче́те *nn*
separator	сепара́тор *nm*
silo	си́лосная ба́шня
tractor	тра́ктор *nm*

PERSONS

agronomist	агроно́м *nm*
combine operator	комба́йнер *nm*
cowboy	ковбо́й *nm*
farmer	фе́рмер *nm*
farmhand	рабо́тник фе́рмы *nm, nf*
gaucho	га́учо *nm, indecl*
kibbutznik	кибу́цник *nm*
kolkhoznik	колхо́зник *nm*, колхо́зница *nf*
melioration specialist	мелиора́тор *nm*
planter	планта́тор *nm*
pomologist	помо́лог *nm*
ranchero	ранче́ро *nm*
silage	си́лос *nm*
tobacco farmer	табаково́д *nm*
tobacco worker	таба́чник *nm*, таба́чница *nf*
tractor driver	трактори́ст *nm*
wine-grower	виноде́л *nm*

See also **PLANTS**, **FOOD AND NUTRITION**

COMMUNICATIONS

GENERAL TERMS

address	а́дрес *nm*
communication	коммуника́ция *nf*
contact	конта́кт *nm*
inform	информи́ровать *impf*, проинформи́ровать *pf*
information	информа́ция *nf*
Internet	Интерне́т *nm*
licence (BR license)	лице́нзия *nf*
line of communication	коммуникацио́нная ли́ния *nf*
misinform	непра́вильно инфор-ми́ровать, дезинформи́ровать *impf, pf*
misinformation	непра́вильная информа́ция, дезинформа́ция *nf*
radar	рада́р *nm*
radio	ра́дио *nn, indecl*
radio station	радиоста́нция *nf*
selection	селе́кция *nf*
signal	сигна́л *nm*
transmission	трансми́ссия *nf*
uninformed	неинформи́рованный *aj*
well-informed	хорошо́ информи́ро-ванный *aj*

SPECIALIZATIONS

codification	кодифика́ция *nf*
cryptanalysis	криптана́лиз *nm*
cryptography	криптогра́фия *nf*

radio engineering	радиоте́хника *nf*
radiotelegraphy	радиотелеграфи́я *nf*
radiotelephony	радиотелефони́я *nf*
signalling, signalization	сигнализа́ция *nf*
telecommunications	телекоммуника́ции *nfpl*
teleconferencing	телеконференцсвя́зь *nf*
telegraphy	телеграфи́я *nf*
telephony	телефони́я *nf*

FORMS OF COMMUNICATION

cablegram	каблогра́мма *nf*
correspondence	корреспонде́нция *nf*
cryptogram	криптогра́мма *nf*
distress signal	сигна́л бе́дствия *nm, nn*
E-mail, electronic mail	электро́нная по́чта *nf*
fax	факс *nm*
Morse code (alphabet)	а́збука Мо́рзе *nf, nm,* код Мо́рзе *nm, nm,* морзя́нка *nf*
pager	пе́йджер *nm*
personal contacts	ли́чные конта́кты *nmpl*
radio communication	радиосвя́зь *nf*
radiogram	радиогра́мма *nf*
radio linkup	радиоперекли́чка *nf*
radiotelegraph	радиотелегра́ф *nm*
radiotelephone	радиотелефо́н *nm*
radio transmission	радиопереда́ча *nf*
satellite	сателли́т *nm*
semaphore	семафо́р *nm*
teleconference	телеконфере́нция *nf*
telegram	телегра́мма *nf*
telepathy	телепа́тия *nf*
telephone	телефо́н *nm*
telex	те́лекс *nm*
Telstar	Телстар *nm*
videotelephone, videophone	видеотелефо́н *nm*
yodel	йо́дль *nm*

RELATED TERMS

mail

box number	но́мер абоне́нтского я́щика *nm, nm*
frank (a letter)	франки́ровать *impf,* зафранки́ровать *pf*
franking machine	франкорова́льная маши́на *nf*
postscript, P.S.	постскри́птум *nm*
sender's address	а́дрес отправи́теля *nm*

telephone

area code [city]	код го́рода *nm, nm*
cordless telephone	беспроводно́й телефо́н *nm*
pay/public telephone	телефо́н-автома́т *nm*
push-button telephone	кно́почный телефо́н *nm*
telephone answering machine	телефо́нный отве́тчик *nm*
telephone booth	телефо́нная бу́дка *nf*
telephone call	телефо́нный звоно́к *nm*
telephone conversation	телефо́нный разгово́р *nm*
telephone exchange	телефо́нная ста́нция *nf,* телефо́нный узёл *nm*
telephone number	но́мер телефо́на *nm, nm*
telephone receiver	телефо́нная тру́бка *nf*
telephone service	телефо́нная связь *nf*
telephone tap	прослу́шивание телефо́на *nm, nm*

SECRET MESSAGES

cipher [code]	шифр *nm*
cipher, encipher	шифрова́ть *impf,* зашифрова́ть, *pf*
code	код *nm*
code, encode	коди́ровать *impf, pf,* закоди́ровать *pf*
code name	ко́довое назва́ние *nn*
code symbol	ко́довый знак *nm*
coding, encoding	коди́рование *nn*
confidential	конфиденциа́льный *aj*
confidentiality	конфиденциа́льность *nf*
confidentially	конфиденциа́льно *av*
decipher	дешифрова́ть *impf, pf*
decipherment	дешифро́вка *nf*
decode	декоди́ровать *impf, pf*
decoding	декоди́рование *nn*

tools and equipment

coaxial cable	коаксиа́льный ка́бель *nm*
decoder	деко́дер *nm*
fax machine	факсими́льный аппара́т *nm*
optical fiber	опти́ческое волокно́ *nn*

radio transmitter	радиопередáтчик *nm*
telegraph pole	телегрáфный столб *nm*
teletype, teletypewriter	телетáйп *nm*

RADIO COMMUNICATIONS

components and tools

antenna	антéнна *nf*
detector (radio)	детéктор *nm*
goniometer	гониóметр *nm*
heterodyne	гетероди́нный *aj*
microphone	микрофóн *nm*
modulator	модуля́тор *nm*
oscillator	осцилля́тор *nm*
radio beacon	радиомая́к *nm*
radio receiver	радиоприёмник *nm*
radio transmitter	радиопередáтчик *nm*
radiolocator	радиолокáтор *nm*
selector	селéктор *nm*
tone control	тон-контрóль *nm*
transformer	трансформáтор *nm*
transistor	транзи́стор *nm*
transmitter	трансми́ттер *nm*

other terms

atmospherics	атмосфéрные помéхи *nfpl*
echo (*pl* echoes)	э́хо *nn*
modulation	модуля́ция *nf*
radiolocation	радиолокáция *nf*
scan [radar]	скани́ровать *impf*
static	стáтика *nf*
superheterodyne	супергетероди́н *nm*

PERSONS

addressee	адресáт *nm*
coder	кодирóвщик *nm*
Morse code signaller	морзи́ст *nm*
novice	новичóк *nm*
operator	оперáтор *nm*
radio ham	радиолюби́тель *nm*, радиолюби́тельница *nf*
radio mechanic	радиотéхник *nm*
radio operator	ради́ст, -ка *nmf*
signalman	сигнáльщик *nm*
technician	тéхник *nm*
telegraph operator	телеграфи́ст, -ка *nmf*
yodeller	йóдлер *nm*

See also **COMPUTERS**, **LINGUISTIC SCIENCE**, **ENTERTAINMENT**, **USING LANGUAGE**

COMPUTERS

GENERAL TERMS

specializations

cybernetics *nplsv*	кибернéтика *nf*
information science	информáтика *nf*
robotics *nplsv*	рóбототéхника *nf*
systems analysis	систéмный анáлиз *nm*

other general terms

analog(ue)	анáлог *nm*
binary	бинáрный *aj*
computer	компью́тер *nm*
computer literacy	компью́терная грáмотность *nf*
computer programming	программи́рование *nn*
computerized	компью́терный *aj*
data-processing center	информациóнно-вычисли́тельный центр *nm*
disk, diskette	диск *nm*, дискéта *nf*
documentation	документáция *nf*
electronic data processing	электрóнная обрабóтка информáции *nf*, *nf*
hard copy	печáтная кóпия *nf*
hardware	хардвер *nm*
human factor	человéческий фáктор *nm*
interface	интерфéйс *nm*
Internet	Интернéт *nm*
local network	локальная сеть *nf*
multimedia	мультимéдия *nf*
optimize	оптимизи́ровать *impf*, *pf*
portability	портати́вность *nf*
printer	при́нтер *nm*
program (BR programme)	прогрáмма *nf*
robot	рóбот *nm*
software	сóфтвер *nm*
virtuality	виртуáльность *nf*

TYPES OF COMPUTERS

home computer	домáшный компью́тер *nm*
IBM-compatible computer	ИБМ-совмести́мый компью́тер *nm*
laptop computer	портати́вный компью́тер *nm*
microcomputer	микрокомпью́тер *nm*

minicomputer	миникомпьютер *nm*
notebook computer	компьютер-блокнот, ноутбук *nm*
personal computer, PC	персональный компьютер, ПК *nm*
portable computer	портативный компьютер *nm*
supercomputer	супер-компьютер *nm*

HARDWARE TERMS

acoustic coupler	акустический соединитель *nm*
adapter, adaptor	адаптер *nm*
cartridge (of printer)	картридж *nm*
chip	чип *nm*
compact disk, CD	компакт-диск *nm*
computer peripheral	периферийное устройство *nn*
configuration	конфигурация *nf*
CPU [= central processing unit]	ЦП [= центральный процессор] *nm*
cursor	курсор *nm*
decoder	декодер *nm*
disk drive	дисковод *nm*
diskette	дискета *nf*
display	дисплей *nm*
DOS [= disk operating system]	ДОС [= дисковая операционная система] *nf*
dot-matrix printer	матричный принтер *nm*
fax	факс *nm*
floppy disk	гибкий диск *nm*
function key	функциональная клавиша *nf*
hard disk	жёсткий диск *nm*
integrated circuit	интегральная схема *nf*
joystick	джойстик *nm*
laser printer	лазерный принтер *nm*
magnetic disk	магнитный диск *nm*
microchip	микрочип *nm*
microphone	микрофон *nm*
microprocessor	микропроцессор *nm*
MIDI system	стандарт МИДИ *nm*
miniaturization	миниатюризация *nf*
modem	модем *nm*
monitor	монитор *nm*
on-screen graphics	экранная графика *nf*
peripheral	периферия *nf*, периферийное устройство *nn*
peripherals *npl*	периферия *nf*
pixel	пиксель *nm*
plotter	плоттер *nm*
port	порт *nm*
processor	процессор *nm*
scanner	сканер *nm*
scanning	сканирующий *aj*
sound card	звуковая карта *nf*
systems disk	системный диск *nm*
terminal	терминал *nm*

SOFTWARE TERMS

programming languages

ALGOL	АЛГОЛ *nm*
assembly language	язык ассемблера *nm*
BASIC	Бейсик *nm*
COBOL	КОБОЛ *nm*
FORTRAN	ФОРТРАН *nn*
PASCAL	Паскаль *nm*

other terms

application program	прикладная программа *nf*
archive file	архивный файл *nm*
assembler	ассемблер *nm*
bit-mapped	битовый *aj*
block	блокировать *impf, pf*
buffer	буфер *nm*
buffering	буферизация *nf*
character code	код символа *nm, nm*
codification	кодификация *nf*
codify	кодировать *impf, pf*
coding, encoding	кодирование *nn*, кодировка *nf*
command	команда *nf*
compile	компилировать *impf, pf*
computer diagnostics *npl*	компьютерная диагностика *nf*
database	база данных *nf*
data bank	банк данных *nm*
decode	декодировать *impf, pf*
decoding	декодирование *nn*
file	файл *nm*
format	формат *nm*
initialize	инициализировать *impf, pf*
interactive	интерактивный *aj*
interpreter	программа-интерпретатор *nm*
machine code	машинный код *nm*
machine language	машинный язык *nm*
machine-readable	машиночитаемый *aj*
menu	меню *nn, indecl*

menu-driven	управляемый с помощью меню́ *nf, nn, indecl*, меню-управля́емый *aj*
module	мо́дуль *nf*
parameter	пара́метр *nm*
procedure	процеду́ра *nf*
program (BR programme)	программи́ровать *impf*, запрограмми́ровать *pf*
program(m)ing	программи́рование *nn*
program(m)ing language	язы́к программи́рования *nm, nn*
real-time *aj*	реальное время *nn*, реальный масштаб времени *nm, nn*
reformat	переформати́ровать *impf, pf*
register	реги́стр *nm*
simulation	симуля́ция *nf*
software package	паке́т програ́мм *nm, nfpl*
sort	сорт *nm*
sort	сортирова́ть *impf, pf*
sorting [action]	сортиро́вка *nf*
subprogram	подпрогра́мма *nf*
syntax error	синтакси́ческая оши́бка *nf*
tabulation	табули́рование *nn*
test	тести́ровать *impf, pf*
test	тест *nm*
text editor	текстово́й реда́ктор *nm*
unformatted	бесформа́тный, неформати́рованный *aj*
version	ве́рсия *nf*
virus	ви́рус *nm*
word processor	текстово́й проце́ссор *nm*

INTERNET TERMS

address	а́дрес *nm*
browser	бро́узер *nm*
electronic mail, E-mail	электро́нная по́чта *nf*
on-line	онла́йновый *aj*
provider	прова́йдер *nm*
rating	ре́йтинг *nm*
server	се́рвер *nm*
site	сайт *nm*
spam	спэм *nm*
surfing	сёрфинг *nm*
virtual reality	виртуа́льная реа́льность *nf*
visit	визи́т *nm*

COMPUTER UNITS AND MEASUREMENTS

baud	бод *nm*
bit	бит *nm*
byte	байт *nm*
gigabyte	гигаба́йт *nm*
kilobit [1024 bits]	килоби́т *nm*
megabyte	мегаба́йт *nm*
terabit [trillion bits]	тераби́т *nm*

PERSONS

cyberneticist	киберне́тик *nm*
encoder	кодировщик *nm*
hacker	ха́кер *nm*
program(m)er	программи́ст *nm*
systems analyst	систе́мный анали́тик *nm*

See also **ELECTRICITY AND ELECTRONICS, COMMUNICATIONS, MEASUREMENTS**

ELECTRICITY AND ELECTRONICS

GENERAL TERMS

amplitude	амплиту́да *nf*
electric current	электри́ческий ток *nm*
electrical impulse	электри́ческий и́мпульс *nm*
electricity	электри́чество *nn*
electro-	электро- *pref*
electrolytic	электролити́ческий *aj*
electronic-	электро́нно- *pref*
generation	генера́ция *nf*, генери́рование *nn*
parallel, in	паралле́льно *av*
photoelectric	фотоэлектри́ческий *aj*
polar	поля́рный *aj*
power line	ли́ния электропереда́чи *nf, nf*
resonance	резона́нс *nm*
substation	подста́нция *nf*

ASPECTS OF ELECTRICITY

sources

accumulator [battery]	аккумуля́тор *nm*
battery	батаре́я *nf*

crystal	кристалл *nm*
dynamo	дина́мо *nn, indecl*
electrolyte	электроли́т *nm*
flashlight battery	батаре́йка *nf*
galvanism	гальвани́зм *nm*
generator	генера́тор *nm*
hydroelectric power station	гидроэлектроста́нция *nf*
power station	электроста́нция *nf*
quartz	кварц *nm*
static electricity	стати́ческое электри́чество *nn*
storage battery	аккумуля́торная батаре́я *nf*
voltaic (cell)	во́льтов *aj*

kinds of circuits

cycle	цикл *nm*
integrated	интегра́льный *aj*
parallel	паралле́льный *aj*

conduction

anode	анод *nm*
cathode	като́д *nm*
contact (touching)	конта́кт *nm*
electrode	электро́д *nm*
impulse	и́мпульс *nm*
inductance	индукти́вность *nf*
multipolar	многопо́люсный *aj*
neutral	нейтра́льный *aj*
oscillation	осцилля́ция *nf*
peak load	пик нагру́зки *nm, nf*
polarization	поляриза́ция *nf*
pole	по́люс *nm*
potential	потенциа́л *nm*
reactance	реакти́вность *nf*
unipolar	однопо́люсный *aj*

effects

electrolysis	электро́лиз *nm*
magnetism	магнети́зм *nm*

control

commutation	коммута́ция *nf*
condenser	конденса́тор *nm*
impedance	импеда́нс *nm*
multipolar switch	многопо́люсный выключа́тель *nm*
relay	реле́ *nn, indecl*
relay station	радиореле́йная ста́нция *nf*
rheostat	реоста́т *nm*
shunt	шунт *nm*
solenoid	солено́ид *nm*
transformer	трансформа́тор *nm*

tools and parts

adapter, adaptor	ада́птер *nm*
cable	ка́бель *nm*
commutator	коммута́тор *nm*
induction coil	индукцио́нная кату́шка *nf*
inductor	инду́ктор *nm*
line	ли́ния *nf*
magneto	магне́то *nn, indecl*
oscillator	осцилля́тор *nm*
oscillograph	осцилло́граф *nm*
regulator	регуля́тор *nm*
resistor	рези́стор *nm*
vibrator	вибра́тор *nm*

ASPECTS OF ELECTRONICS

specializations

avionics *nplsv*	авиацио́нная электро́ника *nf*
bioelectronics *nplsv*	биоэлектро́ника *nf*
microelectronics *nplsv*	микроэлектро́ника *nf*
optoelectronics *nplsv*	оптоэлектро́ника *nf*
radio electronics *nplsv*	радиоэлектро́ника *nf*
thermionics *nplsv*	термио́ника *nf*

functioning

bleep	блип *nm*
echo (*pl* echoes)	э́хо *nn*
ion	ио́н *nm*
microcircuit	микросхе́ма *nf*
signal	сигна́л *nm*

tools and parts

diode	дио́д *nm*
magnetron	магнетро́н *nm*
maser	ма́зер *nm*
pentode	пенто́д *nm*
servomechanism	сервомехани́зм *nm*
stroboscope	стробоско́п *nm*
synchronizer	синхрониза́тор *nm*
tetrode	тетро́д *nm*
transistor	транзи́стор *nm*
triode	трио́д *nm*
vacuum [tube]	ва́куум *nm*

useful applications

audio	а́удио *nn*
computer	компью́тер *nm*
diathermy	диатерми́я *nf*
electrocardiograph	электрокардиогра́ф *nm*

electroencephalograph	электроэнцефалогра́ф *nm*
electron microscope	электро́нный микроско́п *nm*
electronic device	электро́нная аппарату́ра *nf*
fax	факс *nm*
Geiger counter	счётчик Ге́йгера *nm*, *nm*
laser	ла́зер *nm*
microscope	микроско́п *nm*
radar	рада́р *nm*
radio	ра́дио *nn, indecl*
spectrograph	спектро́граф *nm*
stroboscopic light	стробоскопи́ческий свет *nm*
telephone	телефо́н *nm*
television	телеви́дение *nn*
vocoder [speech synthesizer]	воко́дер *nm*
parity	парите́т *nm*
radiofrequency	радиочастота́ *nf*

See also **AGRICULTURE** *(aspects of farming)*, **COMMUNICATIONS** *(radio communications)*, **MEASUREMENTS** *(units of measurement, measuring tools)*, **PHYSICS** *(terms in electromagnetism)*

FUELS

GENERAL TERMS

carburetor (BR carburettor)	карбюра́тор *nm*
catalytic converter	каталити́ческий нейтрализа́тор *nm*
energy crisis	энергети́ческий кри́зис *nm*
gas pipeline/main/pipe	газопрово́д *nm*
gas	газ *nm*
gas	га́зовый *aj*
gas burner	га́зовая горе́лка *nf*
gas meter	га́зовый счётчик *nm*
high-octane	высокоокта́новый *aj*
octane	окта́н *nm*
octane rating	окта́новое число́ *nn*
petrology	петроло́гия *nf*
supertanker	суперта́нкер *nm*

KINDS OF FUELS

solid fuels

anthracite	антраци́т *nm*
bitumen	би́тум *nm*
briquette	брике́т *nm*
coke	кокс *nm*
lignite	лигни́т *nm*

liquid fuels

benzene, benzol	бензо́л *nm*
diesel fuel	ди́зельное то́пливо *nn*
gas, gasoline	газоли́н *nm*
kerosene	кероси́н *nm*
toluene	толуо́л *nm*

gas fuels

acetylene	ацетиле́н *nm*
butane	бута́н *nm*
cyanogen	циа́н *nm*
ethane	эта́н *nm*
ethylene	этиле́н *nm*
methane	мета́н *nm*
methanol	метано́л *nm*
natural gas	приро́дный газ *nm*

chemical fuels

lithium	ли́тий *nm*
magnesium	ма́гний *nm*
titanium	тита́н *nm*

atomic fuels

plutonium	плуто́ний *nm*
thorium	то́рий *nm*
uranium	ура́н *nm*

PROCESSES

coke oven	ко́ксовая печь *nf*
cracking	кре́кинг *nm*
gasify (coal)	газифици́ровать *impf, pf*

See also **CHEMISTRY**, **TECHNOLOGY OVERVIEW**

METALLURGY

GENERAL TERMS

ferro-	фе́рро- *pref*
metal	мета́лл *nm*
metal goods	металли́ческие изде́лия *nnpl*
metal-working industry	металлопромы́шленность *nf*
metalwork	металлообрабо́тка *nf*

steel industry	сталелите́йная промы́шленность *nf*

SPECIALIZATIONS

cryology	криоло́гия *nf*
metallography	металлогра́фия *nf*

ASPECTS OF METALLURGY

types of metal

cast metal	металли́ческая отли́вка *nf*
heavy metal	тяжёлый мета́лл *nm*
metalloid	металло́ид *nm*
pig metal	металли́ческая болва́нка *nf*
precious metal	благоро́дный мета́лл *nm*
scrap metal	металлоло́м *nm*
sheet metal	листово́й мета́лл *nm*

alloys and metallic substances

amalgam	амальга́ма *nf*
chrome	хром *nm*
cryolite	криоли́т *nm*
duralumin	дюралюми́ний *nm*
flux	флюс *nm*
martensite	мартенси́т *nm*
permalloy	пермалло́й *nm*
pewter	пью́тер *nm*
steel	сталь *nf*

processes

corrosion	корро́зия *nf*
electrolysis	электро́лиз *nm*
galvanize	гальванизи́ровать *impf, pf*

plating

chrome plating	хроми́рование *nn*, хромиро́вка *nf*
chrome-plated	хроми́рованный *aj*
nickel-plate, nickel-plating	никелиро́вка *nf*
nickel-plate	никелирова́ть *impf, pf*, отникелирова́ть *pf*
nickel-plated	никелиро́ванный *aj*

other terms

metal fatigue	уста́лость мета́лла *nf, nm*
metallurgical factory	металлурги́ческий заво́д *nm*
patina	пати́на *nf*
slag	шлак *nm*

TOOLS AND EQUIPMENT

metal detector	металлоиска́тель *nm*
stamp	штамп *nm*
stamper	ште́мпель, штамп *nm*

PERSONS

metallurgist	металлу́рг *nm*
metalworker	металли́ст *nm*
steelworker	сталелите́йщик *nm*

See also **CHEMISTRY** *(chemical elements)*, **TECHNOLOGY OVERVIEW**

MINERALS AND MINING

GENERAL TERMS

carat, karat	кара́т *nm*
crystal	хруста́ль *nm*
crystallization	кристаллиза́ция *nf*
exploitation	эксплуата́ция *nf*
mineral	минера́л *nm*
salt mine	соляна́я ша́хта *nf*

SPECIALIZATIONS

crystallography	кристаллогра́фия *nf*
geology	геоло́гия *nf*
minerology	минерало́гия *nf*
petrology	петроло́гия *nf*

ASPECTS OF MINERALS

classification

apatite	апати́т *nm*
dendrite	дендри́т *nm*
ophite	офи́т *nm*
taconite	такони́т *nm*

identification

opalescence	опалесце́нция *nf*
porosity	по́ристость *nf*

descriptive terms

crystal	хруста́льный *aj*
crystalline	кристальный *aj*

crystallographic	кристаллографи́ческий *aj*
isomorphous	изомо́рфный *aj*
metallic	металли́ческий *aj*
mineral	минера́льный *aj*
opalescent, opaline	опа́ловый *aj*
polymorphous	полимо́рфный *aj*

NAMES OF ROCKS AND MINERALS

igneous, metamorphic, and sedimentary rocks

basalt	база́льт *nm*
bituminous	битумино́зный *aj*
gneiss	гнейс *nm*
granite	грани́т *nm*
obsidian	обсидиа́н *nm*
porphyry	порфи́р *nm*
quartzite	кварци́т *nm*

ores

bauxite	бокси́т *nm*
beryl	бери́лл *nm*
chromite	хроми́т *nm*
cinnabar	ки́новарь *nf*
corundum	кору́нд *nm*
galena	галени́т *nm*
wolframite	вольфрами́т *nm*

gemstones and other jewelry materials

agate	ага́т *nm*
amethyst	амети́ст *nm*
aquamarine	аквамари́н *nm*
brilliant [diamond]	бриллиа́нт *nm*
carbuncle	карбу́нкул *nm*
chalcedony	халцедо́н *nm*
coral	кора́лл *nm*
lapis lazuli	ля́пис-лазу́рь *nf*
mother-of-pearl	перламу́тр *nm*
nephrite	нефри́т *nm*
onyx	о́никс *nm*
opal	опа́л *nm*
peridot	перидо́т *nm*
platinum	пла́тина *nf*
ruby	руби́н *nm*
sapphire	сапфи́р *nm*
sardonyx	сардо́никс *nm*
solitaire	солите́р *nm*
topaz	топа́з *nm*
tourmaline	турмали́н *nm*
zircon	цирко́н *nm*

other common minerals

alabaster	алеба́стр *nm*
asbestos	асбе́ст *nm*
asphalt	асфа́льт *nm*
barite	бари́т *nm*
bitumen	би́тум *nm*
calcite	кальци́т *nm*
dolomite	доломи́т *nm*
fluorite	флюри́т *nm*
graphite	графи́т *nm*
gypsum	гипс *nm*
jacinth [obs]	гиаци́нт *nm*
kaolin(e)	каоли́н *nm*
lignite	лигни́т *nm*
magnetite	магнети́т *nm*
malachite	малахи́т *nm*
ocher (BR ochre)	о́хра *nf*
perlite	перли́т *nm*
pyrite	пири́т *nm*
quartz	кварц *nm*
rock crystal	го́рный хруста́ль
talc(um)	тальк *nm*
zinc blende	ци́нковая обма́нка *nf*

TERMS IN MINING

Davy lamp [obs]	ла́мпа Дэ́ви *nf*
seismograph	сейсмо́граф *nm*
ventilator	вентиля́тор *nm*
flotation	флота́ция *nf*
paramorphism	параморфи́зм *nm*
ventilation shaft	вентиляцио́нная ша́хта *nf*

PERSONS

crystallographer	кристалло́граф *nm*
minerologist	минеро́лог *nm*
mining engineer	го́рный инжене́р *nm*

See also **CHEMISTRY**, **GEOLOGY**

PRINTING

GENERAL TERMS

format	форма́т *nm*
graphic	гра́фика *nf*
line	ли́ния *nf*
printed matter *nsg*	печа́тные материа́лы *nm*
symbol	си́мвол *nm*
typography	типогра́фское иску́сство *nn*
Xerography	ксерогра́фия *nf*

Xerox	ксéрокс *nm*

ASPECTS OF PRINTING

printing processes

electrotype	электроти́пия *nf*
engraving	гравю́ра *nf*
offset	офсéт *nm*
photo-offset	фотоофсéт *nm*
photoengraving, photogravure	фотогравю́ра *nf*

printing presses

cylinder	цили́ндр *nm*
lithograph	литогрáфия *nf*
rotary press	ротациóнная маши́на *nf*

characters and type sizes

elite, élite	эли́та *nf*
point	пункт *nm*
script	шрифт *nm*

printing books and magazines

centerfold (BR centrefold)	центрáльная вклáдка *nf*
pagination	пагинáция *nf*
quarto	ин-квáрто *nn, indecl*
signature	сигнатýра *nf*

other terms

center (BR centre)	центри́ровать *impf, pf*
lettered	ли́терный *aj*
logogram	логогрáмма *nf*
logotype	логоти́п *nm*
typographical error	типогрáфская оши́бка *nf*
Xerox copy	ксерокóпия *nf*
Xeroxing	ксерокопировáние *nn*

TOOLS AND EQUIPMENT

case [for storing type]	кáсса *nf*
linotype	линоти́п *nm*
matrix (*pl* matrices)	мáтрица *nf*
monotype	моноти́п *nm*
polygraph [obs]	полигрáф *nm*
stereotype	стереоти́п *nm*
teleprinter	телепри́нтер *nm*
teletype	телетáйп *nm*

PERSONS

lithographer	литóграф *nm*
typographer	типóграф *nm*

See also **BOOKS AND LIBRARIES**, **JOURNALISM**

TEXTILES

GENERAL TERMS

material	матéрия *nf*
roll (of fabric)	рулóн *nm*
sanforization	санфоризáция *nf*
staple (fiber)	штáпель *nm*
synthetic fabric	синтети́ческая ткань *nf*
textile factory	тексти́льная фáбрика *nf*
textiles *npl*	тексти́ль *nm*
texture	текстýра *nf*

ASPECTS OF TEXTILES

types of fibers

chemical fiber	хими́ческое волокнó *nn*
staple fiber	штáпельное волокнó *nn*
synthetic fiber	синтети́ческое волокнó *nn*

natural fibers

angora (wool)	ангóрская шерсть *nf*
batting	вати́н *nm*
jute	джут *nm*
kapok	капóк *nm*
raffia	рáффия *nf*
ramie	волокнó рáми *nn*
sisal	сизáль *nm*

artificial fibers

acetate	ацетáт *nm*
acrylic	акри́л *nm*
fiberglass (BR fibreglass)	фибергла́с *nm*
lurex	лю́рекс *nm*
nylon	нейлóн *nm*
polyester	полиэфи́р *nm*
spandex	спáндекс *nm*
viscose	вискóза *nf*

clothing and decorative fabrics

barathea	баратéя *nf*
batik	бати́к *nm*
batiste	бати́ст *nm*
cashmere	кашеми́р *nm*
chenille	синéль *nf*
cheviot	шевиóт *nm*

chiffon — шифóн *nm*
crepe de Chine — крепдеши́н *nm*
cretonne — кретóн *nm*
crinoline — криноли́н *nm*
damask — дамáск *nm*
denim — дéним *nm*
faille — фай *nm*
felt — фетр *nm*
flannel — фланéль *nf*
flannelette — фланелéт *nm*
foulard — фуля́р *nm*
gabardine, gaberdine — габарди́н *nm*
gauze — газ *nm*
jersey — джерси́ *nn, indecl*
khaki — хáки *aj/nn, indecl*
lamé — ламé *nn, indecl*
lasting — лáстик *nm*
marquisette — маркизéт *nm*
merino (wool) — мериносовая шерсть *nf*
mohair — мохéр *nm*
moire, moiré — муáр *nm*
moleskin — молески́н *nm*
muslin — мусли́н *nm*
organdie, organdy — органди́ *nf, indecl*
paisley — пéйсли *nn*
percale — перкáль *nm/nf*
piqué — пикé *nn, indecl*
plush — плюш *nm*
poplin — попли́н *nm*
prunella — прюнéлла *nf*
rep — репс *nm*
sateen — сати́н *nm*
satinet(te) — сатинéт *nm*
serge — сáржа *nf*
surah — сю́ра *nf*
taffeta — тафтá *nf*
tapa cloth — тáпа *nm*
tricot — трикó *nn, indecl*
tulle — тюль *nm*
tweed — тви́д *nm*
velour — велю́р *nm*
velvet — вельвéт *nm*
velveteen — вельвети́н *nm*
voile — вуáль *nf*
waffle cloth — вáфельная ткань *nf*

laces

Brussels lace — брюссéльские кружевá *nnpl*
Chantilly lace — крýжева шантильи́ *nnpl*
guipure — гипю́р *nm*
macramé — макрамé *nn*
picot — пикó *nn, indecl*

paper

crepe paper — крепи́рованная бумáга *nf*
manila paper — мани́льская бумáга *nf*

See also **CLOTHING AND ACCESSORIES**

WEAPONS

GENERAL TERMS

automatic weapon — автомати́ческое орýжие *nn*
bomb — бóмба *nf*
detonation — детонáция *nf*
pistol shot — пистолéтный вы́стрел *nm*
poison gas — ядови́тый газ *nm*
ricochet — рикошéт *nm*
semiautomatic (firearm) — полуавтомати́ческий *aj*
trajectory — траектóрия *nf*

TYPES OF WEAPONS

explosive

antitank grenade — противотáнковая гранáта *nf*
cordite — корди́т *nm*
dynamite — динами́т *nm*
gelignite — гелигни́т *nm*
grenade — гранáта *nf*
hand grenade — ручнáя гранáта *nf*
mine — ми́на *nf*
Molotov cocktail — коктéйль Мóлотова *nm, nm*
nitroglycerin(e) — нитроглицери́н *nm*
tetryl — тетри́л *nm*
trinitrotoluene [= TNT] — тринитротолуóл *nm*

crushing and piercing

Colt (pistol) — кольт *nm*
garrote, garotte — гаррóта *nf*
guillotine [obs] — гильоти́на *nf*
harpoon — гарпýн *nm*
knout — кнут *nm*
machete — мачéте *nn, indecl*
musket — мушкéт *nm*
pike — пи́ка *nf*
pistol — пистолéт *nm*
rapier — рапи́ра *nf*

revolver	револьве́р *nm*
Sten gun	пулемёт Сте́на *nm, nm*
stiletto (*pl* stiletto, stilettoes)	стиле́т *nm*
tomahawk	томага́вк *nm*
torpedo (*pl* torpedoes)	торпе́да *nf*
Winchester (rifle)	винче́стер *nm*
yataghan [Turkish sword]	ятага́н *nm*

bombs

atom(ic) bomb, A-bomb	а́томная бо́мба *nf*
cluster bomb	кассе́тная бо́мба *nf*
demolition bomb	фуга́сная бо́мба *nf*
H-bomb, hydrogen bomb	водоро́дная бо́мба *nf*
incendiary bomb	зажига́тельная бо́мба *nf*
neutron bomb	нейтро́нная бо́мба *nf*
plastic bomb	пла́стиковая бо́мба *nf*
smart bomb	самонаводя́щаяся бо́мба *nf*
time bomb	бо́мба заме́дленого де́йствия *nf, nn*

poison gas

cyanogen	циа́н *nm*
mustard gas	горчи́чный газ *nm*
napalm	напа́лм *nm*
nerve gas	не́рвный газ *nm*
tear gas	слезоточи́вый газ *nm*

other weapons

antitank	противота́нковый *aj*
ballistic missile	баллисти́ческая раке́та *nf*, баллисти́ческий снаря́д *nm*
bazooka	базу́ка *nf*
boomerang	бумера́нг *nm*
carbine	караби́н *nm*
defoliant	дефолиа́нт *nm*
Mace	газ мейс *nm*

PARTS AND EQUIPMENT

catapult	катапу́льта *nf*
detonator	детона́тор *nm*
grenade launcher	гранатомёт *nm*
harpoon gun	гарпу́нная пу́шка *nf*
magazine (of a firearm)	магази́н *nm*
tracer bullet	трасси́рующая пу́ля *nf*

PERSONS

dynamiter	динами́тчик *nm*
harpoonist	гарпу́нщик *nm*

See also **THE MILITARY ESTABLISHMENT** *(weapons and equipment)*, **DRUGS** *(medicines)*

Quantification

MEASUREMENTS ◆ TIME ◆ SIZE AND DEGREE ◆ COUNTING AND ARRANGEMENT

MEASUREMENTS

GENERAL TERMS

calibration — калибро́вка *nf*
conversion table — табли́ца преобразова́ния *nf, nn*
graduation — градуиро́вка *nf*
isometric — изометри́ческий *aj*
scale — шка́ла *nf*

ASPECTS OF MEASUREMENT

specializations

calorimetry — калориме́трия *nf*
chronometry — хронометра́ж *nm*
hydrometry — гидроме́трия *nf*
micrometry — микроме́трия *nf*
photometry — фотоме́трия *nf*
pyrometry — пирометри́я *nf*
radiometry — радиометри́я *nf*
stereometry — стереоме́трия *nf*
tachometry — тахометри́я *nf*
telemetry — телеметри́я *nf*
thermometry — термоме́трия *nf*

kinds of measures

cubic — куби́ческий *aj*
linear — лине́йный *aj*

scales

Celsius — шкала́ Це́льсия *nf*
Fahrenheit — шкала́ Фаренге́йта *nf*
Kelvin scale — шкала́ Ке́львина *nf*

things measured

acreage — пло́щадь в а́крах *nf, nmpl*
caliber (BR calibre) — кали́бр *nm*
cubic capacity — куби́ческий объём *nm*
cubic content — кубату́ра *nf*
distance — диста́нция *nf*
distance in kilometers — километра́ж *nm*
intensity — интенси́вность *nf*
liter capacity — литра́ж *nm*
mass — ма́сса *nf*
mileage — расстоя́ние/пробе́г в ми́лях *nn/nm, nmpl*
net weight — вес не́тто *nm*
temperature — температу́ра *nf*
tonnage — тонна́ж *nm*
voltage — вольта́ж *nm*

UNITS OF MEASUREMENT

length and distance

archin — арши́н *nm*
centimeter (BR -metre) — сантиме́тр *nm*
decameter (BR -metre) — декаме́тр *nm*
decimeter (BR -metre) — дециме́тр *nm*
fermi — фе́рми *nn*
foot — фут *nm*
hectometer (BR -metre) — гектоме́тр *nm*
kilometer (BR -metre) — киломе́тр *nm*
meter (BR metre) — метр *nm*
metric area/length — метра́ж *nm*
micromillimeter (BR -metre) — микромиллиме́тр *nm*
micron — микро́н *nm*
mil — мил *nm*
mile — ми́ля *nf*
millimeter (BR -metre) — миллиме́тр *nm*
parsec — парсе́к *nm*
statute mile [5280 ft.] — стату́тная ми́ля [1609.3 m]
yard — ярд *nm*

electricity

ampere — ампе́р *nm*
coulomb — куло́н *nm*
farad — фара́да *nf*
gauss — га́усс *nm*
gigawatt — гигава́тт *nm*
kilovolt — килово́льт *nm*
kilowatt [= kW] — килова́тт *nm* [= кВт]
kilowatt-hour — килова́тт-час *nm*
megawatt — мегава́тт *nm*
megohm — мегао́м *nm*
microfarad — микрофара́да *nf*
microvolt — микрово́льт *nm*
milliampere — миллиампе́р *nm*

millivolt	милливо́льт *nm*
ohm	ом *nm*
volt	вольт *nm*
watt	ватт *nm*
watt-hour	ватт-час *nm*

volume

barrel	ба́ррель *nm*
bushel	бу́шель *nm*
centiliter (BR -litre)	сантили́тр *nm*
cubic meter/centimeter (BR -metre)	кубоме́тр *nm*
decaliter (BR -litre)	декали́тр *nm*
deciliter (BR -litre)	децили́тр *nm*
gallon	галло́н *nm*
hectoliter (BR -litre)	гектоли́тр *nm*
kiloliter (BR -litre)	килоли́тр *nm*
liter (BR litre)	литр *nm*
milliliter (BR -litre)	миллили́тр *nm*
pint	пи́нта *nf*
quart	ква́рта *nf*
wagonload	ваго́н *nm*

weight

centigram (BR -gramme)	сантигра́мм *nm*
centner	це́нтнер *nm*
decagram (BR -gramme)	декагра́мм *nm*
decigram (BR -gramme)	децигра́мм *nm*
grain	гран *nm*
gram (BR gramme)	грамм *nm*
gram-atom	грамм-а́том *nm*
gram-molecule	грамм-моле́кула *nf*
hectogram	гектогра́мма *nf*
kilo	кило́ *nn, indecl*
kilogram (BR -gramme)	килогра́мм *nm*
kiloton	килото́нна *nf*
megaton	мегато́нна *nf*
metric ton	метри́ческая то́нна *nf*
milligram (BR -gramme)	миллигра́мм *nm*
mole	моль *nf*
ounce	у́нция *nf*
quintal	квинта́л *nm*
scruple	скру́пул *nm*
ton	то́нна *nf*
troy	тро́йский вес *nm*

force

dyne	ди́на *nf*
erg	эрг *nm*
joule	джо́уль *nm*
kilojoule	килоджо́уль *nm*
newton	ньюто́н *nm*

light and sound

angstrom	ангстрём *nm*
candela	канде́ла *nf*
decibel	децибе́л *nm*
lumen	лю́мен *nm*
lux	люкс *nm*

pressure

bar	бар *nm*
millibar	миллиба́р *nm*
torr	торр *nm*

radiation

curie	кюри́ *nn, indecl*
rad	рад *nm*
roentgen	рентге́н *nm*

other units

carat	кара́т *nm*
diopter	диоптри́я *nf*
hertz (*pl* hertz) [= Hz]	герц *nm* [= Гц]
kilocycle [obs]	килоци́кл *nm*
kilohertz (*pl* kilohertz) [= kHz]	килоге́рц *nm*
megahertz (*pl* megahertz) [= mHz]	мегаге́рц *nm*
oersted [magnetism]	эрсте́д *nm*
tesla [magnetic density]	те́сла *nf*
therm [heat]	терм *nm*
titer (BR titre) [chemical concentration]	титр *nm*

MEASURING TOOLS

altimeter	альтиме́тр *nm*
ammeter	амме́тр, амперме́тр *nm*
anemoter	анемо́метр *nm*
barometer	баро́метр *nm*
bathometer	бато́метр *nm*
calorimeter	калори́метр *nm*
chronometer	хроно́метр *nm*
clinometer	клино́метр *nm*
craniometer	кранио́метр *nm*
dynamometer	динамо́метр *nm*
electrometer	электро́метр *nm*
galvanometer	гальвано́метр *nm*
gasometer	газо́метр *nm*

Geiger counter	счётчик Гейгера *nm*
goniometer	гонио́метр *nm*
gyroscope	гироско́п *nm*
hydrometer	гидро́метр *nm*
hygrometer	гигро́метр *nm*
hygroscope	гигроско́п *nm*
interferometer	интерферо́метр *nm*
light meter	экспоно́метр *nm*
magnetometer	магнето́метр *nm*
manometer	мано́метр *nm*
meter ruler/measure (BR metre)	метр *nm*
micrometer	микрометр *nm*
odometer	одо́метр *nm*
ohmmeter	омме́тр *nm*
pedometer	педо́метр *nm*
photometer	фото́метр *nm*
piezometer	пьезо́метр *nm*
planimeter	планиме́тр *nm*
pluviometer	плювио́метр *nm*
potentiometer	потенцио́метр *nm*
pyrometer	пиро́метр *nm*
radiocompass	радиоко́мпас *nm*
radiometer	радио́метр *nm*
rheometer	рео́метр *nm*
rheostat	реоста́т *nm*
sclerometer	склеро́метр *nm*
seismometer	сейсмо́метр *nm*
sensitometer	сенситоме́тр *nm*
sextant	секста́нт *nm*
spectrometer	спектро́метр *nm*
spectrophotometer	спектрофото́метр *nm*
speedometer	спидо́метр *nm*
spherometer	сферо́метр *nm*
sphygmomanometer	сфигмо́метр *nm*
tachometer	тахо́метр *nm*
tachymeter	тахео́метр *nm*
taximeter	таксо́метер *nm*
telemeter	телеме́тр *nm*
tensiometer	тенсио́метр *nm*
tetrameter	тетра́метр *nm*
thermometer	термо́метр *nm*
thermostat	термоста́т *nm*
variometer	варио́метр *nm*
vernier	вернье́р *nm*
viscosimeter	вискози́метр *nm*
voltmeter	вольтме́тр *nm*
volumeter	волю́метр *nm*
wattmeter	ваттме́тр *nm*

See also **TIME** *(time units)*, **ASTRONOMY**, **GEOGRAPHY**, **MATHEMATICS**, **COMPUTERS**, **PHYSICS**, **CHEMISTRY**

TIME

GENERAL TERMS

calendar month/year	календа́рный ме́сяц/год *nm*
calendar	календа́рь *nm*
chronometry	хронометра́ж *nm*
date	да́та *nf*
date	дати́ровать *impf, pf*
dated	дати́рованный *aj*
dating	датиро́вка *nf*
International Date Line	ли́ния переме́ны дат *nf, nf, nfpl*
standard time	станда́ртное вре́мя *nn, nn*
time factor	фа́ктор вре́мени *nm, nn*
time scale	шка́ла вре́мени *nf, nn*
time zone	временна́я зо́на *nf*
undated	недати́рованный *aj*

ASPECTS OF TIME

kinds of time

biological	биологи́ческий *aj*
chronological	хронологи́ческий *aj*
circadian	цирка́дный *aj*
geological	геологи́ческий *aj*
historical	истори́ческий *aj*
linguistic	лингвисти́ческий *aj*
lunar	лу́нный *aj*
sidereal	сидери́ческий *aj*

clocks

clepsydra	клепси́дра *nf*
clock radio *nsg*	ра́диочасы́ *nmpl*
cuckoo clock	часы́ с куку́шкой *nmpl, nf*
gnomon	гно́мон *nm*
quartz	ква́рцевый *aj*
ticktock	тик-та́к *nm*

calendars

Gregorian calendar	григориа́нский календа́рь *nm*
Julian calendar	юлиа́нский календа́рь *nm*

recurrent events

jubilee	юбиле́й *nm*
May Day	Первома́й *nm*, Пе́рвое Ма́я *nn*

Sabbath [Jewish] — суббо́та *nf*

recording and preserving

almanac — альмана́х *nm*
annals — анна́лы *nmpl*
archives *npl* — архи́в *nm*
chronology — хроноло́гия *nf*
time capsule — мемориа́льная ка́псула *nf*

MONTHS OF THE YEAR

January — янва́рь *nm*
February — февра́ль *nm*
March — март *nm*
April — апре́ль *nm*
May — май *nm*
June — ию́нь *nm*
July — ию́ль *nm*
August — а́вгуст *nm*
September — сентя́брь *nm*
October — октя́брь *nm*
November — ноя́брь *nm*
December — дека́брь *nm*

TIME UNITS

exact

decade — дека́да *nf*
microsecond — микросеку́нда *nf*
millisecond — миллисеку́нда *nf*
minute, half a — полмину́ты *nf*
minute — мину́та *nf*
moment — моме́нт *nm*
quarter (of a year) — кварта́л *nm*
second — секу́нда *nf*

inexact

epoch — эпо́ха *nf*
era — э́ра *nf*
interval — интерва́л *nm*
moratorium (*pl* moratoriums, moratoria) — морато́рий *nm*
period — пери́од *nm*
season — сезо́н *nm*
weekend — уике́нд, уик-э́нд *nm*

TOOLS AND PARTS

chronograph — хроно́граф *nm*
minute hand — мину́тная стре́лка *nf*
second hand — секу́ндная стре́лка *nf*
timer — та́ймер *nm*

TIME ASSOCIATIONS

duration and speed

momentary — момента́льный *aj*
period, short/long — коро́ткий/дли́тельный пери́од *nm*
permanent — перманé́нтный *aj*
prolongation — пролонга́ция *nf*
tempo (*pl* tempos or tempi) — темп *nm*

frequency

at regular intervals — с регуля́рными интерва́лами *nmpl*
cyclic(al) — цикли́чный, цикли́ческий *aj*
episodic — эпизоди́ческий *aj*
fixed — фикси́ровать *impf, pf*, зафикси́ровать *pf*
irregular — нерегуля́рный *aj*
periodically — периоди́чески *av*
quarterly — кварта́льный *aj*
regular — регуля́рный *aj*
sporadic — споради́ческий *aj*

relational

advance, in — ава́нсом *av*
anachronism — анахрони́зм *nm*
antiquarian — антиква́рий *nm*
archaic — архаи́ческий *aj*, архаи́чный *aj*
Greenwich — Гри́нвич *nm*
incunabula — инкуна́булы *nfpl*
isochronous — изохро́нный *aj*
moment, in a — момента́льно *av*
peak hours — часы́ пик *nmpl, nm*
peak period — пи́ковый пери́од *nm*
retrospective — ретроспекти́ва *nf*
synchronous — синхро́нный *aj*
traditional — традицио́нный *aj*

manner

critical moment — крити́ческий моме́нт *nm*
epochal, epoch-making — эпоха́льный *aj*
planned — плани́рованный *aj*
punctual — пунктуа́льный *aj*
unplanned — незаплани́рованный *aj*

See also **HISTORY AND ARCHEOLOGY**, **ANCIENT CIVILIZATIONS**

SIZE AND DEGREE

GENERAL TERMS

complexity — ко́мплексность *nf*
criterion (*pl* criteria) — крите́рий *nm*
gradation — града́ция *nf*
norm — норма *nf*
scale — шкала́ *nf*
standard — станда́рт *nm*

RATINGS

things rated

activity — акти́вность *nf*
adequacy — адеква́тность *nf*
complexity — ко́мплексность *nf*
intensity — интенси́вность *nf*
rank — ранг *nm*

average

adequate — адеква́тный *aj*
general — генеральный *aj*
model — моде́льный *aj*
neutral — нейтра́льный *aj*
normal — норма́льный *aj*
ordinary — ордина́рный *aj*
proportional, proportionate — пропорциона́льный *aj*
regular — регуля́рный *aj*
standard — станда́ртный *aj*
typical — типи́чный *aj*
universal — универса́льный *aj*

nonaverage

abnormal — ненорма́льный *aj*
atypical — атипи́ческий *aj*
disproportion — диспропо́рция *nf*
disproportionate — непропорциона́льный *aj*
inaccurate — неаккура́тный *aj*
nonstandard — нестанда́ртный *aj*
specialized — специализиро́ванный *aj*
unique — уника́льный *aj*

above the norm

astronomical — астрономи́ческий *aj*
colossal — колосса́льный *aj*
dominant, dominating — домини́рующий *aj*
dramatic — драмати́чный *aj*
en masse — в массе *av*
excess — эксце́сс *nm*
extensive — экстенси́вный *aj*
extraordinary — экстраордина́рный *aj*
extravagant — экстравага́нтный *aj*
gigantic — гига́нтский *aj*
grandiose — грандио́зный *aj*
imposing — импоза́нтный *aj*
intense — интенси́вный *aj*
intensive — интенси́вный *aj*
macro- — ма́кро- *pref*
macroscopic — макроскопи́ческий *aj*
massive — масси́вный *aj*
mega- — ме́га- *pref*
monumental — монумента́льный *aj*
phenomenal — феномена́льный *aj*
priority — приорите́т *nm*
radical — радика́льный *aj*
serious — серьёзный *aj*
super- — су́пер- *pref*
Titanic — титани́ческий *aj*
ultra- — ультра- *pref*

below the norm

inadequate — неадеква́тный *aj*
marginal — маргина́льный *aj*
micro- — ми́кро- *pref*
microscopic — микроскопи́чный, микроскопи́ческий *aj*
mini- — ми́ни- *pref*
miniature — миниатю́рный *aj*
second-class — второкла́ссный *aj*
sub- — суб- *pref*
summary [brief] — сумма́рный *aj*
trivial — тривиа́льный *aj*

ends of the scale

absolute — абсолю́тный *aj*
critical — крити́ческий *aj*
first-class — первокла́ссный *aj*
fundamental — фундамента́льный *aj*
maxi- — ма́кси- *pref*
maximum, maximal — максима́льный *aj*
minimal — минима́льный *aj*
optimal, optimum — оптима́льный *aj*
peak — пи́ковый *aj*
quantum leap — ква́нтовый скачо́к *nm*
total — тота́льный *aj*

REPRESENTATIONS

accumulation — аккумуля́ция *nf*
colossus — коло́сс *nm*
giant — гига́нт *nm*
grandeur — грандио́зность *nf*
intensification — интенсифика́ция *nf*

mass character	ма́ссовость *nf*
maximum (*pl* maximums, maxima)	ма́ксимум *nm*
miniature	миниатю́ра *nf*
minimum (*pl* minimums, minima)	ми́нимум *nm*
optimum	о́птимум *nm*
quintessence	квинтэссе́нция *nf*

See also **VALUE JUDGMENTS, USING LANGUAGE**

COUNTING AND ARRANGEMENT

GENERAL TERMS

classified	классифици́рованный *aj*
classify	классифици́ровать *impf, pf*
group	группа *nf*
grouping [action]	группирова́ние *nn*
grouping [unit]	группиро́вка *nf*
organization	организа́ция *nf*

COUNTING

exact quantities

billion	биллио́н *nm*
dozen	дю́жина *nf*
gross	грос *nm*
half a million	полмиллио́на *nm*
million	миллио́н *nm*
nil	нуль, ноль *nm*
octillion	октильо́н *nm*
quadrillion	квадрильо́н *nm*
three	(число́) три *nn*
trillion	триллио́н *nm*

inexact quantities

astronomical sum	астрономи́ческая су́мма *nf*
baker's dozen	чёртова дю́жина
horde	орда́ *nf*
myriad *nsg*	мириа́ды *npl*

copies

copy	ко́пия *nf*
duplicate	дублика́т *nm*
facsimile	факси́миле *nn, indecl*

other terms

millionth	миллио́нный *aj*
numeration, numbering	нумера́ция *nf*
Roman numeral	ри́мская ци́фра *nf*

ARRANGEMENT

things to be organized

details	дета́ли *nfpl*
facts	факты *nmpl*
points	пункты *nmpl*
specifics *npl*	специ́фика *nf*
statistics *npl*	статисти́ческие да́нные *nnpl*

types of organization

card-index	картоте́ка *nf*
catalog	катало́г *nm*
conglomeration	конгломера́ция *nf*
diagram	диагра́мма *nf*
graph	гра́фика *nf*
hierarchy	иера́рхия *nf*
index	и́ндекс *nm*
paired	па́рный *aj*
scheme	схе́ма *nf*
series (*pl* series)	се́рия *nf*
structure	структу́ра *nf*
subsystem	подсисте́ма *nf*
system	систе́ма *nf*
table	табли́ца *nf*

basic sorting orders

alphabetical	алфави́тный *aj*
chronological	хронологи́ческий *aj*
serial	сери́йный *aj*

groupings

assortment	ассортиме́нт *nm*, ассорти́ *nn, indecl*
category	катего́рия *nf*
class	кла́ссный *aj*
classification	классифика́ция *nf*
collection	колле́кция *nf*
combination	комбина́ция *nf*
compilation	компиля́ция *nf*
consolidation	консолида́ция *nf*
module	мо́дуль *nf*
subclass	подкла́сс *nm*
subgroup	подгру́ппа *nf*
type	тип *nm*

boundaries

demarcation	демарка́ция *nf*
line of demarcation	демаркацио́нная ли́ния *nf*

marginal	маргина́льный *aj*
periphery	перифери́я *nf*

other terms

central	центра́льный *aj*
component	компоне́нт *nm*
constitute	конституи́ровать *impf, pf*
correspond	корреспонди́ровать *impf*
fragment	фрагме́нт *nm*
individualization	индивидуализа́ция *nf*
massing	масси́рование *nn*
portion	по́рция *nf*
separable	сепара́бельный *aj*
separate	сепара́тный *aj*
variation, varying	варьи́рование *nn*

PERSONS

classifier	классифика́тор *nm*
compiler	компиля́тор *nm*
sorter	сортиро́вщик *nm*

See also **MATHEMATICS** *(basic concepts)*, **MUSIC** *(persons)*

All About Language

LINGUISTIC SCIENCE ◆ PHONOLOGY ◆ GRAMMAR ◆ WRITING ◆ USING LANGUAGE ◆ LANGUAGES OF THE WORLD

LINGUISTIC SCIENCE

GENERAL TERMS

analysis	ана́лиз *nm*
dialect	диале́кт *nm*
grammar	грамма́тика *nf*
grammatical	граммати́ческий *aj*
language barrier	языково́й барье́р *nm*
lexicon [words]	ле́ксика *nf*
linguistic	лингвисти́ческий *aj*
linguistics *nplsv*	лингви́стика *nf*
metalanguage	метаязы́к *nm*
model	моде́ль *nf*
onomatopoeia	ономатопе́я *nf*
Prague School	Пра́жский лингвисти́ческий кружо́к *nm*
signal	сигна́л *nm*
symbol	си́мвол *nm*
system	систе́ма *nf*
theory	тео́рия *nf*

BRANCHES OF LINGUISTICS

approaches

anthropological	антропологи́ческий *aj*
diachronic	диахрони́ческий *aj*
historical	истори́ческий *aj*
mathematical	математи́ческий *aj*
synchronic	синхро́нный *aj*
theoretical	теорети́ческий *aj*
traditional	традицио́нный *aj*

major fields

morphology	морфоло́гия *nf*
phonology	фоноло́гия *nf*
semantics *nplsv*	сема́нтика *nf*
syntax	си́нтаксис *nm*

subfields

metalinguistics *nplsv*	металингви́стика *nf*
neurolinguistics *nplsv*	нейролингви́стика *nf*
sociolinguistics *nplsv*	социолингви́стика *nf*

related specializations

bilingualism	билингви́зм *nm*
cryptography	криптогра́фия *nf*
dialectology	диалектоло́гия *nf*
epigraphy	эпигра́фика *nf*
etymology	этимоло́гия *nf*
glottochronology	глоттохроноло́гия *nf*
graphology	графоло́гия *nf*
kinesics *nplsv*	кине́сика *nf*
language universals	языковы́е универса́лы *nmpl*
lexicography	лексикогра́фия *nf*
lexicology	лексиколо́гия *nf*
lexicostatistics *nplsv*	лексикостати́стика *nf*
machine translation	маши́нный перево́д *nm*
metrics *nplsv*	ме́трика *nf*
Mongolian studies	монголове́дение *nn*
paleography	палеогра́фия *nf*
papyrology	папироло́гия *nf*
paralinguistics *nplsv*	паралингви́стика *nf*
philology	филоло́гия *nf*
phonetics *nplsv*	фоне́тика *nf*
psycholinguistics *nplsv*	психолингви́стика *nf*
Romance philology	романи́стика *nf*
Russian philology	руси́стика *nf*
semasiology	семасиоло́гия *nf*
semiotics *nplsv*	семио́тика *nf*
stylistics *nplsv*	стили́стика *nf*
syntactics *nplsv*	синта́ктика *nf*

ASPECTS OF LINGUISTICS

grammatical models

normative	нормати́вный *aj*
structural	стру́ктурный *aj*
tagmemic	тагме́мный *aj*

basic linguistic units

grapheme	графе́ма *nf*
lexeme	лексе́ма *nf*
morpheme	морфе́ма *nf*
phoneme	фоне́ма *nf*
semanteme	семанте́ма *nf*
sememe	семе́ма *nf*
syntagma (*pl* syntagmas, syntagmata)	синта́гма *nf*

tagmeme	тагме́ма *nm*
taxeme	таксе́ма *nf*

formative processes

affixation	аффикса́ция *nf*
agglutination	агглютина́ция *nf*
calque	калька *nf*
collocation	коллока́ция *nf*
derivation	дерива́ция *nf*
inflection (BR inflexion)	фле́ксия *nf*
reduplication	редуплика́ция *nf*
syncretism	синкрети́зм *nm*
transformation	трансформа́ция *nf*

language typology

agglutinative	агглютинати́вный *aj*
analytical	аналити́ческий *aj*
inflected	флекти́вный *aj*
polysynthetic	полисинтети́ческий *aj*
synthetic	синтети́ческий *aj*
tone	тон *nm*

communication signals

acoustic	акусти́ческий *aj*
gesture	жест *nm*
semaphore	семафо́р *nm*
tactile, tactual	такти́льный *aj*
visual	визуа́льный *aj*

other terms

consonantism	консонанти́зм *nm*
critical age (of acquisition)	крити́ческий во́зраст *nm*
derivative	дерива́т *nm*
doublet	дубле́т *nm*
polysemy	полисеми́я *nf*
recursive	рекурси́вный *aj*
vocalism	вокали́зм *nm*

PERSONS

linguists

dialectician	диале́ктик *nm*
etymologist	этимо́лог *nm*
grammarian	грамма́тик *nm*
graphologist	графо́лог *nm*
Latinist	латини́ст *nm*
lexicographer	лексикогра́ф *nm*
linguist	лингви́ст *nm*
paleographer (BR palaeographer)	палео́граф *nm*
philologist	фило́лог *nm*
phonetician	фоне́тик *nm*
structuralist	структурали́ст *nm*

other persons

bilingual	били́нгв, билингви́ст *nm*
informant	информа́тор *nm*
polyglot	полигло́т *nm*
purist	пури́ст *nm*

See also **DICTIONARIES**, **PHYSICAL DISORDERS** *(names of disorders–language)*

PHONOLOGY

GENERAL TERMS

accentuation	акцентуа́ция *nf*
allophone	аллофо́н *nm*
articulation	артикуля́ция *nf*
consonantism	консонанти́зм *nm*
euphony	эвфони́я *nf*
homonym	омо́ним *nm*
homophone	омофо́н *nm*
intonation	интона́ция *nf*
phoneme	фоне́ма *nf*
phonemic	фонемати́ческий *aj*
phonetic	фонети́ческий *aj*
phonetics *nplsv*	фоне́тика *nf*
phonological	фонологи́ческий *aj*
phonology	фоноло́гия *nf*
prosodic	просоди́ческий *aj*
prosody	просо́дия *nf*
symbol	си́мвол *nm*
tone	тон *nm*
transcribe	транскриби́ровать *impf, pf*
transcription	транскри́пция *nf*
variant	вариа́нт *nm*
vocalism	вокали́зм *nm*

SPECIALIZATIONS

acoustic phonetics *nplsv*	акусти́ческая фоне́тика *nf*
articulatory phonetics *nplsv*	артикуляцио́нная фоне́тика *nf*
dialectology	диалектоло́гия *nf*
experimental phonetics *nplsv*	эксперимента́льная фоне́тика *nf*
homonymy	омони́мия *nf*
homophony	гомофони́я *nf*

study of homonyms — омонимика *nf*
orthoepy — орфоэпия *nf*

ASPECTS OF PHONOLOGY

kinds of consonants

aspirate, aspirated consonant — аспират *nm*
bilabial — билабиальный *aj*
cacuminal — какуминальный *aj*
fricative — фрикативный *aj*
implosive — имплозивный *aj*
labial — лабиальный *aj*
labiodental — лабиодентальный *aj*
nasal — назальный *aj*
palatal — палатальный *aj*
retroflex — ретрофлексивный *aj*
uvular — увулярный *aj*
velar — велярный *aj*
vibrant — вибрирующий *aj*

kinds of vowels

accented — акцентированный *aj*
cardinal — кардинальный *aj*
diphthong — дифтонг *nm*
epenthetic — эпентетический *aj*
monophthong — монофтонг *nm*
reduced — редуцированный *aj*
triphthong — трифтонг *nm*

phonetic processes

alliteration — аллитерация *nf*
assimilation — ассимиляция *nf*
dissimilation — диссимиляция *nf*
elision — элизия *nf*
epenthesis (*pl* epentheses) — эпентеза *nf*
haplology — гаплология *nf*
labialization — лабиализация *nf*
metathesis — метатеза *nf*
nasalization — назализация *nf*
palatalization — палатализация *nf*
rhotacism — ротацизм *nf*
syncope — синкопа *nf*
velarization — веляризация *nf*

other terms

caesura — цезура *nf*
foreign accent — иностранный акцент *nm*
formant — форманта *nf*
monotone (speech) — монотонная речь *nf*
phonetic transcription — фонетическая транскрипция *nf*
syllabic — силлабический *aj*
yod [= name of sound (j)] — йот *nm*

PERSONS

dialectologist — диалектолог *nm*
phonetician — фонетист *nm*
phonologist — фонолог *nm*

See also **LITERATURE** *(forms of poetry)*, **USING LANGUAGE**

GRAMMAR

GENERAL TERMS

ablaut — аблаут *nm*
attribute — атрибут *nm*
class — класс *nm*
combinatory, combining — комбинаторный *aj*
construction — конструкция *nf*
form — форма *nf*
formative — форматив *nm*
function — функция *nf*
grammar — грамматика *nf*
grammar exercise — грамматическое упражнение *nn*
grammatical sentence — грамматическое предложение *nn*
grammatical system — грамматическая система языка *nf*, *nm*
grammatically correct/incorrect — грамматически правильный /неправильный *aj*
morphology — морфология *nf*
paradigm — парадигма *nf*
phraseology — фразеология *nf*
structure — структура *nf*
syntax — синтаксис *nm*

ASPECTS OF GRAMMAR

word and sentence formatives

affix — аффикс *nm*
allomorph — алломорфема *nf*
article — артикль *nm*
enclitic — энклитика *nf*
flexion — флексия *nf*
morpheme — морфема *nf*

phrase фра́за *nf*
prefix пре́фикс *nm*
suffix су́ффикс *nm*
variant вариа́нт *nm*

grammatical processes

hypotaxis гипота́ксис *nm*
inflection фле́кция *nf*
inversion инве́рсия *nf*
prefixation префикса́ция *nf*
suffixation суффикса́ция *nf*

NOUNS

classification

abstract noun абстра́ктное (и́мя) существи́тельное *nn*
concrete noun конкре́тное (и́мя) существи́тельное *nn*

cases

ablative аблати́в *nm*
ablative absolute аблати́в абсолю́тный *nm*
dative case да́тельный паде́ж *nm*
instrumental case инструмента́льный паде́ж *nm*
objective case объе́ктный паде́ж *nm*

VERBS

classification

aorist ао́рист *nm*
causative каузати́вный *aj*
gerund геру́ндий *nm*
infinitive инфинити́в *nm*
modal (verb) мода́льный *aj*

tenses

historical (present) истори́ческий *aj*
imperfect имперфе́кт *nm*
perfect перфе́кт *nm*
pluperfect плюсквамперфе́кт *nm*
preterit(e) прете́рит *nm*

aspect and mood

indicative индикати́в *nm*
iterative итерати́вный *aj*
optative оптати́вный *aj*
optative (mood) оптати́в *nm*
passive (form) пасси́вная фо́рма *nf*
passive (voice) пасси́в *nm*

PHRASES, CLAUSES, AND SENTENCES

grammatical граммати́ческий *aj*
ungrammatical негра́мотный, безгра́мотный *aj*
absolute construction абсолю́тная констру́кция *nf*
anacoluthon анаколу́ф *nm*
apodosis апо́дозис *nm*
declaratory, declarative деклarати́вный *aj*
ellipsis (*pl* ellipses) э́ллипсис *nm*
emphatic эмфати́ческий *aj*
imperative императи́в *nm*
parataxis парата́ксис *nm*
passive construction пасси́вная констру́кция *nf*
periphrastic перифрасти́ческий *aj*
phrasing фразиро́вка *nf*
predicate предика́т *nm*
suppletive супплети́вный *aj*

OTHER TERMS

definite/indefinite article определённый /неопределённый арти́кль *nm*
gerundive герунди́в *nm*
productive suffix продукти́вный су́ффикс *nm*

See also **DICTIONARIES**, **LINGUISTIC SCIENCE**

WRITING

GENERAL TERMS

alphabet алфави́т *nm*
diacritic, diacritical mark диакрити́ческий знак *nm*
orthography орфогра́фия *nf*
punctuation пунктуа́ция *nf*

SPECIALIZATIONS

calligraphy каллигра́фия *nf*
cryptanalysis криптана́лиз *nm*
cryptography криптогра́фия *nf*
decipherment дешифро́вка *nf*
encipherment шифро́вка *nf*

epigraphy	эпигра́фика *nf*
graphology	графоло́гия *nf*
paleography	палеогра́фия *nf*
philology	филоло́гия *nf*
stenography	стеногра́фия *nf*
tachygraphy	тахогра́фия *nf*

ASPECTS OF WRITTEN LANGUAGE

forms

abbreviation	аббревиату́ра *nf*
contraction	контракту́ра *nf*
initials	инициа́лы *nmpl*
monogram	моногра́мма *nf*
paragraph	пара́граф *nm*
text	текст *nm*

writing systems

alphabetic	алфави́тный *aj*
hieroglyphic	иероглифи́ческий *aj*
ideography	идеогра́фия *nf*
logography	логогра́фия *nf*
pictography	пиктогра́фия *nf*
stenography	стеногра́фия *nf*
stenotype	стеноти́пия *nf*
syllabic	силлаби́ческий *aj*

UNITS

character

cipher	шифр *nm*
cryptograph, cryptogram	криптогра́мма *nf*
digraph	диграф́ *nm*
grapheme	графе́ма *nf*
hieroglyph	иеро́глиф *nm*
icon, ikon	ико́на *nf*
ideogram, ideograph	идеогра́мма *nf*
logogram, logograph	логогра́мма *nf*
phonogram	фоногра́мма *nf*
pictogram, pictograph	пиктогра́мма *nf*
stenotype	стенотипи́ческий знак *nm*
symbol	си́мвол *nm*

diacritics, graphic accents, and punctuation

acute accent	аку́т *nm*
aphaeresis	афе́резис *nm*
apostrophe	апостро́ф *nm*
cedilla	седи́ль *nm*
circumflex	циркумфле́кс *nm*
ligature	лигату́ра *nf*
tilde	ти́льда *nf*
umlaut	умля́ут, умлау́т *nm*

alphabets and script

Braille	шрифт Бра́йля *nm, nm*
cursive (script)	курси́в *nm*
Cyrillic	кири́ллица *nf*
Glagolitic	глаго́лица *nf*
Gothic (script)	готи́ческий шрифт *nm*
Greek	гре́ческий *aj*
Phoenician	финики́йский *aj*
phonetic	фонети́ческий *aj*
Roman	ри́мский *aj*
runic	руни́ческий *aj*
Semitic	семи́тский, семити́ческий *aj*

historical terms

digamma	дига́мма *nf*
hieratic script	иерати́ческое письмо́ *nn*
hieroglyphics *npl*	иерогли́фика *nf*
palimpsest	палимпсе́ст *nm*
Rosetta stone	Розе́ттский ка́мень *nm*
rune	ру́на *nf*

tools and writing implements

blank [to fill in]	бланк *nm*
goose-quill (pen)	гуси́ное перо́ *nn*
reservoir [for ink]	резервуа́р *nm*
stenotype machine	стеноти́п *nm*
writing tablet	табли́чка *nf*

other terms

homograph	омо́граф *nm*
Latinization	латиниза́ция *nf*
palindrome	палиндро́м *nm*
Romanization	романиза́ция *nf*
spelling reform	рефо́рма правописа́ния *nf, nn*
syllabism	силлаби́зм *nm*
transliteration	транслитера́ция *nf*
zed [= British letter Z]	зет *nm*

THE GREEK ALPHABET

alpha	а́льфа *nf*
beta	бе́та *nf*
gamma	га́мма *nf*
delta	де́льта *nf*
epsilon	эпсило́н *nm*
zeta	дзе́та *nf*
eta	э́та *nf*

theta	тéта *nf*
iota	иóта, йóта *nf*
kappa	кáппа *nf*
lambda	лáмбда, ля́мбда *nm*
mu	мю *nn, indecl*
nu	ню *nn, indecl*
xi	кси *nm*
omicron	омикрóн *nm*
pi	пи *nn, indecl*
rho	ро *nn*
sigma	си́гма *nf*
tau	тáу *nm*
upsilon	ипсилóн *nm*
phi	фи *nn, indecl*
chi	хи *nm*
psi	пси *nn*
omega	омéга *nf*

PERSONS

calligrapher	каллигрáф *nm*
copyist	копирóвщик *nm*, копирóвщица *nf*
cryptographer	криптóграф *nm*
graphologist	графóлог *nm*
paleographer (BR palaeographer)	палеóграф *nm*
philologist	филóлог *nm*
stenographer	стенóграф *nm*, стенографи́стка *nf*

See also **LITERATURE**, **JOURNALISM**, **COMMUNICATIONS** *(secret messages)*

USING LANGUAGE

GENERAL TERMS

active vocabulary	акти́вный словáрь *nm*
basic vocabulary	бáзовая лéксика *nf*
context	контéкст *nm*
oratory, study of	орáторское искýсство *nn*
passive vocabulary	пасси́вный словáрь *nm*
phrasing	фразеолóгия *nf*
verbal [spoken]	вербáльный *aj*

LANGUAGE FUNCTIONS

good purpose

annotation, annotating	аннoти́рование *nn*
announcement	анóнс *nm*
comment, commentary	комментáрий *nm*
communication	коммуникáция *nf*
compliment	комплимéнт *nm*
consultation	консультáция *nf*
correspondence	корреспондéнция *nf*
declaration	декларáция *nf*
discussion	дискýссия *nf*
formulation	формулирóвка *nf*
identification	идентификáция *nf*
information	информáция *nf*
interpretation	интерпретáция *nf*
iteration	итерáция *nf*
letter of recommendation	рекомендáтельное письмó *nm*
notification	нотификáция *nf*
panegyric	панеги́рик *nm*
poetic, to wax	поэтизи́ровать *impf*
practical advice	практи́ческий совéт *nm*
proclamation	проклямáция *nf*
recommendation	рекомендáция *nf*
report	рáпорт *nm*
socialization	социализáция *nf*
specification	спецификáция *nf*
summarize	сумми́ровать *impf, pf*
toast	тост *nm*
verbalization	вербализáция *nf*

bad purpose

argument	аргумéнт *nm*
diatribe	диатри́ба *nf*
dispute, disputation	ди́спут *nm*
fabrication [lie]	фабрикáция *nf*
falsification [lie]	фальсификáция *nf*
fiction [lie]	фи́кция *nf*
insinuation	инсинуáция *nf*
invective	инвекти́ва *nf*
misinformation	дезинформáция *nf*
profanation	профанáция *nf*
tirade	тирáда *nf*

SPECIFIC FORMS

written

annotation	аннотáция *nf*
anonymous letter	анони́мное письмó, анони́мка *nf*
apologia	аполóгия *nf*
autograph	автóграф *nm*
circular (letter)	циркуля́р *nm*
communiqu(e)	коммюникé *nn, indecl*
conspectus	конспéкт *nm*
document	докумéнт *nm*
epigraph	эпи́граф *nm*
excursus	э́кскурс *nm*

gloss	гло́сса *nf*
list of questions	опро́сный лист *nm*
marginalia, marginal notes	маргина́лии *npl*
memo, memorandum	мемора́ндум *nm*
postscript, P.S.	постскри́птум *nm*
preamble	преа́мбула *nf*
resume, résumé	резюме́ *nn, indecl*

spoken

debate *nsg*	деба́ты *npl*
declamation	деклами́рование *nn*
dialog(ue)	диало́г *nm*
dictation	дикто́вка *nf*
dictation	дикта́нт *nm*
interpolation	интерполя́ция *nf*
lecture	ле́кция *nf*
monolog(ue)	моноло́г *nm*
parry (a question)	пари́ровать *impf, pf*
public address	публи́чное выступле́ние *nn*
salaam	селя́м *nm*
telephone conversation	телефо́нный разгово́р *nm*

other usages

academic question	академи́ческий вопрос *nm*
acronym	акро́ним *nm*
anecdote	анекдо́т *nm*
aphorism	афори́зм *nm*
archaism	архаи́зм *nm*
Biblical expression	библеи́зм *nm*
cliché	клише́ *nn, indecl*
delicate question/subject	делика́тный вопро́с *nm*
euphemism	эвфеми́зм *nm*
formula	формулиро́вка *nf*
idiomatic expression	идиомати́ческое выраже́ние *nn*
laconism	лакони́зм *nm*
magic word	маги́ческое сло́во *nn*
main points	основны́е пу́нкты *nmpl*
metaphor	мета́фор *nm*
neologism	неологи́зм *nm*
prolegomena	пролего́мены *pl*
propaganda	пропага́нда *nf*
protest	проте́ст *nm*
rhetorical question	ритори́ческий вопро́с *nm*

restricted language usage

argot	арго́ *nn, indecl*
jargon	жарго́н *nm*
nomenclature	номенклату́ра *nf*
officialese	официа́льная терминоло́гия *nm*
slang	слэнг *nm*
specialized terms/terminology	специа́льные те́рмины *nmpl*

undesirable language usage

barbarism	варвари́зм *nm*
catachresis	катахре́за *nf*
Freudian slip	огово́рка по Фре́йду *nf, nm*
hyperbole	гипе́рбола *nf*
hypercorrection	гиперкорре́кция *nf*
indelicacy	неделика́тность *nf*
lapse	ля́псус *nm*
pleonasm	плеона́зм *nm*
sarcastic	саркасти́ческий *aj*
solecism	солеци́зм *nm*
vulgarism	вульгари́зм *nm*

DESCRIBING LANGUAGE USERS

indicators

emphasis (*pl* emphases)	эмфа́за *nf*
figuratively speaking	фигура́льно выража́ясь *impf*
foreign accent	иностра́нный акце́нт *nm*
gesture	жест *nm*
pause	па́уза *nf*
tone of voice	тон ре́чи *nm, nf*

style of speaking/writing

formal	форма́льный *aj*
humorous	юмористи́ческий *aj*
informal	неформа́льный *aj*
ironic, to be	иронизи́ровать *impf*
laconic	лакони́чный, лакони́ческий *aj*
monotonous	моното́нный *aj*
sardonic	сардони́ческий *aj*
sententious	сентенцио́зный *aj*
telegraphic style	телегра́фный стиль *nm*
tendentious	тенденцио́зный *aj*

TERMS IN SEMANTICS AND RHETORIC

antithesis (*pl* antitheses)	антите́за *nf*, антите́зис *nm*
antonym	анто́ним *nm*
apostrophe	апостро́ф *nm*

argumentation	аргумента́ция *nf*
connotation	коннота́ция *nf*
diction	ди́кция *nf*
figure of speech	ритори́ческая фигу́ра, фигу́ра ре́чи *nf, nf*
oxymoron	оксю́морон *nm*
paraphrase	парафра́за *nf*
periphrasis (*pl* periphrases)	перифра́з *nm*
polemic, polemics *npl*	поле́мика *nf*
prolepsis	проле́псис *nm*
syllogism	силлоги́зм *nm*
synecdoche	сине́кдоха *nf*
synonym	сино́ним *nm*
synonymy	синони́мия, синони́мика *nf*

PERSONS

apologist	апологе́т *nm*
correspondent	корреспонде́нт, -ка *nmf*
declaimer	деклама́тор *nm*
lecturer	ле́ктор *nm*
orator	ора́тор *nm*
panegyrist	панегири́ст *nm*
phrase-monger	фразёр *nm*
polemicist	полеми́ст *nm*
purist	пури́ст *nm*
rhetorician	ри́тор *nm*

See also **DICTIONARIES** *(dictionary information)*, **LITERATURE** *(aspects of literature)*, **GAMES AND TOYS** *(names of games)*

LANGUAGES OF THE WORLD

KINDS OF LANGUAGES

classical language	класси́ческий язы́к *nm*
lingua franca (*pl* linguae francae)	ли́нгва фра́нка *nf*
literary language	литерату́рный язы́к *nm*
national language	национа́льный язы́к *nm*
official language	официа́льный язы́к *nm*

LANGUAGE FAMILIES

major groups

Afro-Asiatic	а́фро-азиа́тский *aj*
Dravidian	драви́дский *aj*
Indo-European	индоевропе́йский *aj*
Malayo-Polynesian	мала́йо-полинези́йский *aj*
Sino-Tibetan	сино-тибе́тский *aj*
Uralic-Altaic	ура́ло-алта́йский *aj*

other groups

Altaic	алта́йский *aj*
Aryan	ари́йский *aj*
Austro-Asiatic	а́встро-азиа́тский *aj*
Caucasian	кавка́зский *aj*
Cymric	ки́мрский *aj*
Finno-Ugric	фи́нно-уго́рский *aj*
Indo-Germanic	индогерма́нский *aj*
Nilotic	нило́тский *aj*
Semitic	семи́тский *aj*
Teutonic	тевто́нский *aj*
Turkic	тю́ркский *aj*

branches of Indo-European

Albanian	алба́нский *aj*
Armenian	армя́нский *aj*
Baltic	ба́лтский *aj*
Celtic	ке́льтский *aj*
Germanic	герма́нский *aj*
Greek	гре́ческий *aj*
Indo-Iranian	индоира́нский *aj*
Romance	рома́нский *aj*
Slavic	славя́нский *aj*

language specializations

Germanic studies	германи́стика *nf*
Hispanic studies	испани́стика *nf*
Mongolian studies	монголове́дение *nn*
Sinology	синоло́гия *nf*
Slavic studies	слави́стика *nf*

LANGUAGE NAMES

major world languages

Arabic	ара́бский язы́к *nm*
Bengali	бенга́льский язы́к *nm*
English	англи́йский язы́к *nm*
French	францу́зский язы́к *nm*
Hindi	хи́нди *nm, indecl*
Indonesian	индонези́йский язы́к *nm*
Japanese	япо́нский язы́к *nm*
Korean	коре́йский язы́к *nm*
Portuguese	португа́льский язы́к *nm*
Punjabi	язы́к пенджа́би *nm*
Russian	ру́сский язы́к *nm*
Spanish	испа́нский язы́к *nm*

Tamil	тами́льский язы́к *nm*
Urdu	у́рду *nm, indecl*

other European languages and dialects

Basque	ба́скский язы́к *nm*
Breton	брето́нский язы́к *nm*
Bulgarian	болга́рский язы́к *nm*
Byelorussian	белору́сский язы́к *nm*
Castilian	касти́льский язы́к *nm*
Catalan	катало́нский язы́к *nm*
Czech	че́шский язы́к *nm*
Danish	да́тский язы́к *nm*
Estonian	эсто́нский язы́к *nm*
Finnish	фи́нский язы́к *nm*
Flemish	флама́ндский язы́к *nm*
Frisian	фризский язы́к *nm*
Gaelic	гэ́льский язы́к *nm*
Greek, ancient	гре́ческий язы́к *nm*
Greek, modern	новогре́ческий язы́к *nm*
Hungarian	венге́рский язы́к *nm*
Icelandic	исла́ндский язы́к *nm*
Irish	ирла́ндский язы́к *nm*
Italian	италья́нский язы́к *nm*
Lappish	лопа́рский язы́к *nm*
Latvian/Lettish	латы́шский язы́к *nm*
Lithuanian	лито́вский язы́к *nm*
Maltese	мальти́йский язы́к *nm*
Norwegian	норве́жский язы́к *nm*
Polish	по́льский язы́к *nm*
Provençal	провансальский язы́к *nm*
Romanian	румы́нский язы́к *nm*
Serbo-Croatian	се́рбско-хорва́тский язы́к *nm*
Slovak, Slovakian	слова́цкий язы́к *nm*
Slovene, Slovenian	слове́нский язы́к *nm*
Swedish	шве́дский язы́к *nm*
Turkish	туре́цкий язы́к *nm*
Ukrainian	украи́нский язы́к *nm*
Welsh	у́эльский язы́к *nm*
Yiddish	и́диш *nm*

other Asian languages and dialects

Azerbaijani	азербайджа́нский язы́к *nm*
Burmese	бирма́нский язы́к *nm*
Cambodian	камбоджи́йский язы́к *nm*
Cantonese	канто́нский диале́кт *nm*
Farsi	язы́к фарси́ *nm*
Hawaiian	гава́йский язы́к *nm*
Hebrew, modern	иври́т *nm*
Hindustani	хиндуста́ни *nm, indecl*
Javanese	ява́нский язы́к *nm*
Kashmiri	кашми́рский язы́к *nm*
Kurdish	ку́рдский язы́к *nm*
Laotian	лао́сский язы́к *nm*
Malay	мала́йский язы́к *nm*
Manchu	маньчжу́рский язы́к *nm*
Mandarin	мандари́нский диале́кт *nm*
Maori	маори́йский язы́к *nm*
Mongolian	монго́льский язы́к *nm*
Nepali	непа́льский язы́к *nm*
Ossetic	осети́нский язы́к *nm*
Pashto, Pashtu	язы́к пушту́ *nm*
Persian	перси́дский язы́к *nm*
Samoan	самоа́нский язы́к *nm*
Siamese	сиа́мский язы́к *nm*
Sin(g)halese	синга́льский язы́к *nm*
Tagalog	тага́льский язы́к *nm*
Telugu	язы́к телу́гу *nm*
Thai	та́йский язы́к *nm*
Tibetan	тибе́тский язы́к *nm*
Uzbek	узбе́кский язы́к *nm*
Vietnamese	вьетна́мский язы́к *nm*

American Indian languages

Aymara	язы́к айма́ра *nm*
Eskimo	эскимо́сский язы́к *nm*
Guarani	язы́к гуара́ни *nm*
Navajo	язы́к нава́хо *nm*
Quechua	язы́к ке́чуа *nm*

African languages

Afrikaans	африка́анс *nm*
Amharic	амха́рский язы́к *nm*
Bantu	ба́нту *nm, indecl*
Berber	бербе́рский язы́к *nm*
Coptic	ко́птский язы́к *nm*
Hausa	язы́к ха́уса *nm*
Malagasy	малагаси́йский язы́к *nm*
Somali	язы́к сомали́ *nm*
Swahili	суахи́ли *nn, indecl*
Yoruba	язы́к йору́ба *nm*
Zulu	зулу́сский язы́к *nm*

minority languages of the former Soviet Union

Bashkir	башки́рский язы́к *nm*
Buryat	буря́тский язы́к *nm*
Kalmuk	калмы́кский язы́к *nm*

Karakalpak	каракалпа́кский язы́к *nm*
Kazakh	каза́хский язы́к *nm*
Kirghiz	кирги́зский язы́к *nm*
Nenets	не́нецкий язы́к *nm*
Tatar	тата́рский язы́к *nm*
Yakut	яку́тский язы́к *nm*

historical languages

Akkadian	акка́дский язы́к *nm*
Anglo-Saxon	англосаксо́нский язы́к *nm*
Aramaic	араме́йский язык *nm*
Assyrian	ассири́йский язы́к *nm*
Babylonian	вавило́нский язы́к *nm*
Cornish	корнуо́ллский язы́к *nm*
Etruscan	этру́сский язы́к *nm*
Gothic	го́тский язы́к *nm*
Greek, ancient/classical	древнегре́ческий язы́к *nm*
Hamitic	хами́тский язы́к *nm*
Hebrew, ancient	древнеевре́йский язы́к *nm*
Hittite	хе́ттский язы́к *nm*
Japhetic	яфети́ческий *aj*
Latin	лати́нский язы́к, латы́нь *nf*
Manx	мэ́нский язы́к *nm*
Mayan	язы́к ма́йя *nm*
Old English	древнеангли́йский язы́к *nm*
Old Russian	древнеру́сский/староpу́сский язы́к *nm*
Pali	па́ли *nn*
Pehlev, Pahlavi	пехлеви́ *nn, indecl*
Phoenician	финики́йский язы́к *nm*
Phrygian	фриги́йский язы́к *nm*
Prakrit languages	пракри́ты *npl*
Sanskrit	санскри́т *nm*
Sumerian	шуме́рский язы́к *nm*
Tocharian, Tokharian	тоха́рский *aj*
Vedic	веди́йский *aj*
Vulgar Latin	вульга́рная латы́нь *nf*

mixed and artificial languages

Basic English	бе́йсик и́нглиш *nm*
Braille	шрифт Бра́йля *nm*
Creole	крео́льский язы́к *nm*
Esperanto	эспера́нто *nn*
Franglais	фра́нко-англи́йский язы́к *nm*
Japlish	япо́но-англи́йский язы́к *nm*
macaronism	макарони́зм *nm*
pidgin English	пи́джин-и́нглиш *nm*
Spanglish	испа́но-англи́йский язы́к *nm*
Volapuk	воляпю́к *nm*

other terms

English, in	по-англи́йски *av*
English-speaking	англоязы́чный *aj*
Russian, in	по-ру́сски *av*
Russian-speaking	русскоязы́чный *aj*

BORROWINGS AND COINAGES

Americanism	американи́зм *nm*
Anglicism	англици́зм *nm*
Biblical expression	библеи́зм *nm*
Gallicism	галлици́зм *nm*
Hebraism	гебраи́зм *nm*
Latinism	латини́зм *nm*
Slavism, Slavicism	славяни́зм *nm*

LANGUAGE SCHOLARS

Arabist	араби́ст *nm*
Germanist	германи́ст *nm*
Hebraist	гебраи́ст *nm*
Hispanist	испани́ст *nm*
Sanskritist	санскрито́лог *nm*
Sinologist	сино́лог *nm*

See also **ANTHROPOLOGY, PLACE NAMES II: POLITICAL ENTITIES, INHABITANTS AND ETHNIC GROUPS**

Our Planet and Its Peoples

GEOGRAPHY ◆ PLACE NAMES I: PHYSICAL ENTITIES ◆ PLACE NAMES II: POLITICAL ENTITIES ◆ INHABITANTS AND ETHNIC GROUPS

GEOGRAPHY

GENERAL TERMS

major branches

biological geography	биологи́ческая геогра́фия *nf*
economic geography	экономи́ческая геогра́фия *nf*
physical geography	физи́ческая геогра́фия *nf*
political geography	полити́ческая геогра́фия *nf*

other general terms

climate	кли́мат *nm*
distance	диста́нция *nf*
geographic(al)	географи́ческий *aj*
geography	геогра́фия *nf*
global	глоба́льный *aj*
globally	глоба́льно *av*
isometric	изометри́ческий *aj*
line	ли́ния *nf*
orient (oneself)	ориенти́ровать(ся) *impf*, сориенти́ровать(ся) *pf*
orientation	ориента́ция, ориентиро́вка *nf*, ориенти́рование *nn*
pole	по́люс *nm*
region	регио́н, райо́н *nm*
resource	ресу́рс *nm*
zone	зо́на *nf*

SPECIALIZATIONS

biological geography

biogeography	биогеографи́я *nf*
ecology	эколо́гия *nf*
geomicrobiology	геомикробиоло́гия *nf*
oceanography	океаногра́фия *nf*
phytogeography	фитогеогра́фия *nf*
zoography	зоогеогра́фия *nf*

physical geography

climatography	климатогра́фия *nf*
climatology	климатоло́гия *nf*
geodesy	геоде́зия *nf*
hydrography	гидрографи́я *nf*
hydrology	гидроло́гия *nf*
oceanology	океаноло́гия *nf*
orography	орографи́я *nf*
physiography	физиогра́фия *nf*

allied fields

cartography	картогра́фия *nf*
geomorphology	геоморфоло́гия *nf*
geopolitics *nplsv*	геополи́тика *nf*
limnology	лимноло́гия *nf*
meteorology	метеороло́гия *nf*
photogrammetry	фотограмметри́я *nf*
topography	топогра́фия *nf*
toponymy	топони́мия *nf*

ASPECTS OF GEOGRAPHY

physical formations

archipelago	архипела́г *nm*
atoll	ато́лл *nm*
bank [of a river]	ба́нка *nf*
basin [lowland]	бассе́йн *nm*
canyon	каньо́н *nm*
cascade	каска́д *nm*
cataract	катара́кт *nm*
coastline, shoreline	берегова́я ли́ния *nf*
continent	контине́нт *nm*
coral reef	кора́лловый риф *nm*
delta	дельта *nf*
dune	дю́на *nf*
estuary	эстуа́рий *nm*
fiord, fjord	фьорд, фио́рд *nm*
grotto (*pl* grottos, grottoes)	грот *nm*
iceberg	а́йсберг *nm*
jungle *nsg*	джу́нгли *npl*
lagoon	лагу́на *nf*
massif [mountain mass]	(го́рный) масси́в *nm*
oasis (*pl* oases)	оа́зис *nm*
ocean	океа́н *nm*
pack-ice	пак *nm*

peak	пик *nm*
plateau (*pl* plateaus, plateaux)	плато́ *nn, indecl*
point	пункт *nm*
prairie	пре́рия *nf*
reef	риф *nm*
saltwater lake	солёное о́зеро *nn*
sand dune	(песча́ная) дю́на *nf*
sierra	сье́рра *nf*
tropic	тро́пик *nm*
volcano (*pl* volcanos, volcanoes)	вулка́н *nm*
wadi, wady	ва́ди *nn, indecl*

regions and zones

arctic	аркти́ческий *aj*
equatorial	экваториа́льный *aj*
hydrosphere	гидросфе́ра *nf*
oceanic	океа́нский, океани́ческий *aj*
pampas	пампа́сы *pl*
pelagic	пелаги́ческий *aj*
polar	поля́рный *aj*
savanna(h)	сава́нна *nf*
steppe	степь *nf*
subtropics	субтро́пики *nfpl*
taiga	тайга́ *nf*
transoceanic	трансокеа́нский *aj*
tropics *npl*	тро́пики *npl*
tundra	ту́ндра *nf*

directions and locations

antipodes	антипо́ды *nmpl*
intercontinental	межконтинента́льный *aj*
magnetic pole	магни́тный по́люс *nm*
polar circle	поля́рный круг *nm*
Pole, North	Се́верный по́люс *nm*
Pole, South	Ю́жный по́люс *nm*
subcontinent	субконтине́нт *nm*

climates

continental	континента́льный *aj*
microclimate	микрокли́мат *nm*
subantarctic	субантаркти́ческий *aj*
subartic	субарти́ческий *aj*
subtropical	субтропи́ческий *aj*
tropical	тропи́ческий *aj*

other terms

enclave	анкла́в *nm*
geocentric	геоцентри́ческий *aj*
geomagnetic	геомагни́тный *aj*
geophysical year	геофизи́ческий год *nm*
greenhouse effect	парнико́вый/тепли́чный эффе́кт *nm*
natural resources	приро́дные ресу́рсы *nmpl*
regionalism	регионали́зм *nm*
time zone	временна́я зо́на *nf*
topographical survey	топографи́ческая съёмка *nf*

CARTOGRAPHY

kinds of maps

contour map	ко́нтурная ка́рта *nf*
physical map	физи́ческая ка́рта *nf*
political map	полити́ческая ка́рта *nf*
projection	прое́кция *nf*
provincial map	провинциа́льная ка́рта *nf*
relief map	релье́фная ка́рта *nf*
sinusoidal map	синусоида́льная ка́рта *nf*
territorial map	территориа́льная ка́рта *nf*
thematic map	темати́ческая ка́рта *nf*
transit map	транзи́тная ка́рта *nf*

forms of maps

atlas	а́тлас *nm*
globe	гло́бус *nm*
planisphere	планисфе́ра *nf*

imaginary lines

equator	эква́тор *nm*
horizon	горизо́нт *nm*
International Date Line	ли́ния переме́ны дат *nf, nf, nfpl*
meridian	меридиа́н *nm*
parallel	паралле́ль *nf*
prime meridian	нулево́й меридиа́н *nm*
Tropic of Cancer	тро́пик Ра́ка *nm, nm*
Tropic of Capricorn	тро́пик Козеро́га *nm, nm*

other terms

hachure	гашю́ра *nf*
isobath	изоба́та *nf*
isogloss	изогло́сса *nf*
isotherm	изоте́рма *nf*

Mercator projection	меркаторская проекция *nf*
triangulation	триангуляция *nf*

TOOLS

clinometer	клинометр *nm*
hydrograph	гидрограф *nm*
pantograph	пантограф *nm*
theodolite	теодолит *nm*

PERSONS

cartographer	картограф *nm*
geographer	географ *nm*
hydrographer	гидрограф *nm*
hydrologist	гидролог *nm*
ocean explorer	океанавт *nm*
oceanographer	океанограф *nm*
polar explorer	полярник *nm*
topographer	топограф *nm*
zoographer	зоогеограф *nm*

See also **BOATS AND SHIPS** *(navigation)*, **GEOLOGY**, **METEOROLOGY**, **FAMOUS FIGURES OF YESTERDAY AND TODAY** *(explorers)*

PLACE NAMES I: PHYSICAL ENTITIES

GEOGRAPHICAL REGIONS

America, the Americas	Америка *nf*
Antarctic, the	Антарктика *nf*
Arctic, the	Арктика *nf*
Australasia	Австралия и Океания *nf*
Balkans, the	Балканы *nmpl*
Baltic (region)	Прибалтика *nf*
Central America	Центральная Америка *nf*
Central Asia	Центральная Азия *nf*
East Indies *npl*	Ост-Индия *nf*
Eurasia	Евразия *nf*
Indo-China	Индокитай *nm*
Latin America	Латинская Америка *nf*
Levant, the	Левант *nm*
North Atlantic	североатлантический *aj*
Oceania	Океания *nf*
Polynesia	Полинезия *nf*
Scandinavia	Скандинавия *nf*
Southeast Asia	Юго-восточная Азия *nf*
Spanish America	Испанская Америка
Trans-Caucasia	Закавказье *nn*
West Indies *npl*	Вест-Индия *nf*

CONTINENTS

Africa	Африка *nf*
Antarctica	Антарктида *nf*
Asia	Азия *nf*
Australia	Австралия *nf*
Europe	Европа *nf*
North America	Северная Америка *nf*
South America	Южная Америка *nf*

PENINSULAS

Arabia, Arabian Peninsula	Аравия *nf*, Аравийский полуостров *nm*
Asia Minor	Малая Азия *nf*
Balkan Peninsula	Балканский полуостров *nm*
Crimea	Крым *nm*
Iberia	Иберия *nf*
Jutland	Ютландский полуостров *nm*
Kamchatka	Камчатка *nf*
Labrador	Лабрадор *nf*
Malay Peninsula	полуостров Малайя *nf*
Sinai	Синай *nm*
Yucatan	Юкатан *nm*

ISLANDS AND OTHER WATER FORMATIONS

Antigua	Антигуа *nf*
Aruba	Аруба *nf*
Bali	Бали *nmpl*
Barbados	Барбадос *nm*
Basse-Terre	Бас-тер *nm*
Borneo	Борнео *nn, indecl*
Bornholm	Борнхольм *nm*
Capri	Капри *nm*
Celebes	Целебес *nm*
Corfu	Корфу *nm, indecl*
Corsica	Корсика *nf*
Crete	Крит *nm*
Cuba	Куба *nf*
Curaçao	Кюрасо *nm*
Cyprus	Кипр *nm*
Elba	Эльба *nf*
Gotland	Готланд *nm*
Great Barrier Reef	Большой Барьерный риф *nm*

Greenland	Гренла́ндия *nf*
Grenada	Грена́да *nf*
Guadalcanal	Гвадалкана́л *nm*
Guadeloupe	Гваделу́па *nf*
Guam	Гуа́м *nm*
Guernsey	Ге́рнси *nm, indecl*
Hispaniola	Испаньо́ла *nf*
Honshu	Хо́нсю *nn, indecl*
Ireland	Ирла́ндия *nf*
Isle of Wight	о́стров Уайт *nm*
Isle of Man	о́стров Мэн *nm*
Iwo Jima	Иводзи́ма *nf*
Jamaica	Яма́йка *nf*
Java	Я́ва *nf*
Jersey	Дже́рси *nm, indecl*
Leyte	Ле́йте *nm*
Long Island	Лонг-А́йленд *nm*
Luzon	Лусо́н *nm*
Madagascar	Мадагаска́р *nm*
Madeira	Маде́йра *nf*
Majorca	Мальо́рка, Майо́рка *nf*
Malta	Ма́льта *nf*
Martinique	Мартини́ка *nf*
Mauritius	Маври́кий *nm*
Midway	о́стров Ми́дуэй *nm*
Mindanao	Минданао *nn*
Minorca	Мино́рка *nf*
New Guinea	Но́вая Гвине́я *nf*
Newfoundland	Ньюфа́ундленд *nm*
Okinawa	Окина́ва *nf*
Puerto Rico	Пуэ́рто Ри́ко *nn, indecl*
Rhodes	Ро́дос *nm*
Sakhalin	Сахали́н *nm*
Sardinia	Сарди́ния *nf*
Sicily	Сици́лия *nf*
Singapore	Сингапу́р *nm*
Sulawesi	Сулаве́си *nm, indecl*
Sumatra	Сума́тра *nf*
Tahiti	Таити *nm, indecl*
Taiwan	Тайва́нь *nm*
Tasmania	Тасма́ния *nf*
Tenerife	Тенери́фе *nm, indecl*
Tobago	Тоба́го *nm*
Trinidad	Тринида́д *nm*
Vancouver	Ванку́вер *nm*
Zanzibar	Занзиба́р *nm*

ISLAND GROUPS AND ARCHIPELAGOS

Admiralty Islands	острова́ Адмиралте́йства *nmpl*
Aleutian Islands	Алеу́тские острова́ *nmpl*
Andaman Islands	Андама́нские острова́ *nmpl*
Antilles (Islands), the	Анти́льские острова́ *nmpl*
Azores (Islands), the	Азо́рские острова́ *nmpl*
Bahamas, the	Бага́мские острова́ *nmpl*
Bahrain Islands	острова́ Бахре́йн *nmpl, indecl*
Balearic Islands	Балеа́рские острова́ *nmpl*
Bermuda (Islands), the Bermudas	Берму́дские острова́ *nmpl*
British Isles	Брита́нские острова́ *nmpl*
Canary Islands	Кана́рские острова́ *nmpl*
Caroline Islands	Кароли́нские острова́ *nmpl*
Dodecanese Islands	Додекане́зские острова́ *nmpl*
Falkland (Islands), the Falklands	Фолкле́ндские острова́ *nmpl*
Faro(s), Faero(s)	Фаре́рские острова́ *nmpl*
Fiji (Islands)	Фи́джи *nn, indecl*
Galapagos Islands	острова́ Галапаго́с *nmpl*
Grenadines	Гренадёрские острова́ *nmpl*
Hawaiian Islands	Гава́йские острова́ *nmpl*
Hebrides (Islands), the	Гебри́дские острова́ *nmpl*
Isles of Scilly	острова́ Си́ли *nmpl*
Kuril(e) Islands	Кури́льские острова́ *nmpl*
Lofoten Islands	Лофоте́нские острова́ *nmpl*
Malay Archipelago	Мала́уский архипела́г *nm*
Maldive Islands, the Maldives	Мальди́вские острова́ *nmpl*
Mariana Islands, the Marianas	Мариа́нские острова́ *nmpl*
Marquesas Islands	Марки́зские острова́ *nmpl*
Marshall Islands	Марша́лловы острова́ *nmpl*
Melanesia	Мелане́зия *nf*
Micronesia	Микроне́зия *nf*

Molucca Islands, the Moluccas	Молу́ккские острова́ *nmpl*
Novaya Zemlya	Но́вая Земля́ *nf*
Orkney Islands, the Orkeys	Оркне́йские острова́ *nmpl*
Pescadores	Пескадо́рские острова́ *nmpl*
Philippines, the Phillipine Islands	Филиппи́ны, Филиппи́нские острова́ *nmpl*
Polynesia	Полине́зия *nf*
Ryukyu Islands	острова́ Рюкю́ *nmpl*
Samoa	Само́а *nf*
Seychelles	Сейше́льские острова́ *nmpl*
Shetland Islands	Шетла́ндские острова́ *nmpl*
Solomon Islands	Соломо́новы острова́ *nmpl*
Spitsbergen	Шпицбе́рген *nm*
Virgin Islands	Вирги́нские острова́ *nmpl*
West Indies *npl*	Вест-Йндия *nf*

OCEANS

Antartic Ocean	Антаркти́ческий океа́н *nm*
Arctic Ocean	Се́верный Ледови́тый океа́н *nm*
Atlantic (Ocean), the	Атланти́ческий океа́н *nm*
Indian Ocean	Инди́йский океа́н *nm*
Pacific (Ocean), the	Ти́хий океа́н *nm*

SEAS

Adriatic (Sea), the	Адриа́тика *nf*, Адриати́ческое мо́ре *nn*
Aegean (Sea), the	Эге́йское мо́ре *nn*
Arabian Sea, the	Арави́йское мо́ре *nn*
Aral Sea	Ара́льское мо́ре *nn*
Baltic (Sea), the	Балти́йское мо́ре *nn*
Barents Sea	Ба́ренцево мо́ре *nn*
Bellingshausen Sea	мо́ре Беллингсга́узена *nn*
Bering Sea	Бе́рингово мо́ре *nn*
Caribbean (Sea), the	Кари́бское мо́ре *nn*
Caspian (Sea), the	Каспи́йское мо́ре *nn*
Chukchi Sea	Чуко́тское мо́ре *nn*
Coral Sea	Кора́лловое мо́ре *nn*
Ionian Sea	Иони́ческое мо́ре *nn*
Irish Sea	Ирла́ндское мо́ре *nn*
Kara Sea	Ка́рское Море *nn*
Laptev Sea	мо́ре Ла́птевых *nn*
Sea of Azov	Азо́вское мо́ре *nn*
Sea of Okhotsk	Охо́тское мо́ре *nn*
Sea of Galilee	Галиле́йское мо́ре *nn*
Sea of Japan	Япо́нское мо́ре *nn*
Tyrrhenian Sea	Тирре́нское мо́ре *nn*

LAKES

Lake Constance	Конста́нцкое о́зеро *nn*
Lake Baikal	Байка́л *nm*
Lake Chad	о́зеро Чад *nn*
Lake Erie	о́зеро Э́ри *nn*
Lake Geneva	Жене́вское о́зеро *nn*
Lake Huron	о́зеро Гуро́н *nn*
Lake Ladoga	Ла́дожское о́зеро *nn*
Lake Michigan	о́зеро Мичига́н *nn*
Lake Onega	Оне́жское о́зеро *nn*
Lake Ontario	о́зеро Онта́рио *nn*
Lake Tanganyika	о́зеро Танганьи́ка *nn*
Lake Titicaca	о́зеро Титика́ка *nn*
Lake Victoria	о́зеро Викто́рия *nn*

RIVERS

Amazon	Амазо́нка *nf*
Amu Darya	Аму́-Дарья́ *nf*
Amur	Аму́р *nm*
Angara	Ангара́ *nf*
Arno	А́рно *nn*
Brahmaputra	Брахмапу́тра *nf*
Columbia	река́ Колу́мбия *nf*
Congo	Ко́нго *nn*
Danube	Дуна́й *nm*
Delaware	Де́лавэр *nm*
Dnieper	Днепр *nm*
Dniester	Днестр *nm*
Don	Дон *nm*
Elbe	Э́льба *nf*
Euphrates	Евфра́т *nm*
Ganges	Ганг *nm*
Huang He	Хуанхэ́ *nn*
Hudson	Гудзо́н *nm*
Indus	Инд *nm*
Irtysh	Иртьи́ш *nm*
Jordan	Иорда́н *nm*
Kama	Ка́ма *nf*
Lena	Ле́на *nf*
Loire	Луа́ра *nf*
Mackenzie	Маке́нзи *nn*, *indecl*

Marne	Ма́рна *nf*
Mekong	Еко́нг *nm*
Mississippi	(река́) Миссиси́пи *nf, indecl*
Missouri	(река́) Миссу́ри *nf, indecl*
Moselle	Мо́зель *nm*
Neva	Нева́ *nf*
Niger	Ни́гер *nm*
Nile	Нил *nm*
Ob	О́бь *nf*
Oder	О́дер *nm*
Ohio	Ога́йо *nn*
Oka	Ока́ *nf*
Orinoco	Орино́ко *nn*
Parana	Парана́ *nf*
Po	По *nn*
Potomac	Потома́к *nm*
Rhine	Рейн *nm*
Rhone	Ро́на *nf*
Rio Grande	Ри́о-Гра́нде *nf, indecl*
Ruhr	Рур *nm*
Saar	Саа́р *nm*
Saskatchewan	река́ Саска́чеван *nf*
Seine	Се́на *nf*
Somme	Со́мма *nf*
St. Lawrence	река́ Св. Лавре́нтия *nf*
Susquehanna	Саскуеха́нна *nf*
Syr Darya	Сыр-Дарья́ *nf*
Thames	Те́мза *nf*
Tiber	Тибр *nm*
Tigris	Тигр *nm*
Trent	Трент *nm*
Tweed	Твид *nm*
Vistula	Ви́сла *nf*
Volga	Во́лга *nf*
Volta	Во́льта *nf*
Yangtze	Янцзы́ *nf, indecl*
Yenisei	Енисе́й *nm*
Yukon	Ю́кон *nm*
Zambezi	Замбе́зи *nn, indecl*
Tagus	Тахо́ *nf, indecl*

GULFS

Gulf of Bothnia	Ботни́ческий зали́в *nm*
Gulf of Aqaba	Ака́бский зали́в *nm*
Gulf of Aden	А́денский зали́в *nm*
Gulf of Carpenteria	зали́в Карпента́рия *nm*
Gulf of Finland	Фи́нский зали́в *nm*
Gulf Stream	Гольфстри́м *nm*
Gulf of Mexico	Мексика́нский зали́в *nm*
Gulf of Oman	Ома́нский зали́в *nm*
Gulf of Tonkin	Тонки́нский зали́в *nm*
Persian Gulf	Перси́дский зали́в *nm*

STRAITS AND CHANNELS

Bab el Mandeb	Баб-ель-Мандебский проли́в *nm*
Bass Strait	Ба́ссов проли́в *nm*
Bering Strait	Бе́рингов проли́в *nm*
Bosp(h)orus	Босфо́р *nm*
Dardanelles	Дардане́ллы *nfpl*
Hellespont [obs]	Геллеспо́нт *nm*
Hudson Strait	Гудзо́нов проли́в *nm*
Strait of Hormuz	Орму́зский проли́в *nm*
Strait of Dover, the	Ду́врский проли́в *nm*
Strait of Magellan	Магелла́нов проли́в *nm*
Straits of Gibraltar *npl*	Гибралта́рский проли́в *nm*
Torres Strait	Торре́сов проли́в *nm*

BAYS, CAPES, WATERFALLS

Baffin Bay	Баффи́нов зали́в *nm*
Bay of Biscay	Биска́йский зали́в *nm*
Bay of Bengal	Бенга́льсий зали́в *nm*
Cape Cod	мыс Кейп-Ко́д *nm*
Cape Trafalgar	мыс Трафальга́р *nm*
Cape Canaveral	мыс Кана́верал *nm*
Cape Horn	мыс Горн *nm*
Hudson Bay	Гудзо́нов зали́в *nm*
Niagara Falls	Ниага́рские водопа́ды *nmpl*
Victoria Falls	водопа́д Викто́рия *nm*

MOUNTAINS

Ararat	Арара́т *nm*
Elbrus	Эльбру́с *nm*
Kilimanjaro	Килиманджа́ро *nn*
Matterhorn	Ма́ттерхорн *nm*
McKinley	Мак-Кинли *nf, indecl*
Mont Blanc	Монбла́н *nm*
Mount Etna /Aetna	Э́тна *nf*
Mount Whitney	Уи́тни *nf, indecl*
Mount Everest	Эвере́ст *nm*
Mount Sinai	Сина́й *nm*
Mount Fuji, Fujiyama	Фудзия́ма *nf*
Mount Vesuvius	Везу́вий *nm*
Parnassus	Парна́с *nm*

Pike's Peak	Пайкс-Пик *nm*
Ranier	Рейни́р *nm*

MOUNTAIN RANGES

Adirondack Mountains, the Adirondacks	го́ры Адиро́ндак *nfpl*
Allegheny Mountains, Alleghenies	Аллега́нские го́ры *nfpl*
Alps, the	А́льпы *nmpl*
Altai/Altay Mountains, Altai	Алта́й *nm*
Andes, the Andes Mountains	А́нды *nmpl*
Apennines, the	Апенни́ны *nmpl*
Appalachian Mountains, the Appalachians	Аппала́чские го́ры *nfpl*, Аппала́чи *npl*
Atlas Mountains	Атла́сские го́ры *nfpl*
Carpathian Mountains, the Carpathians	Карпа́тские го́ры, Карпа́ты *npl*
Catskill Mountains, the Catskills	го́ры Ка́тскилл *nfpl*
Caucasus Mountains, the	Кавка́з *nm*
Dolomites, the	Доломи́товые А́льпы *nfpl*
Himalayas, the	Гимала́и, Гимала́йские го́ры *nfpl*
Pamir Mountains	Пами́р *nm*
Pyrenees, the	Пирене́и *nfpl*
Tian Shan	Тянь-Шань *nm*
Urals, the	Ура́л *nm*, Ура́льские го́ры *nfpl*
Vosges	Воге́зы *nmpl*

DESERTS

Arabian Desert, the	Арави́йская пусты́ня *nf*
Atacama	Атака́ма *nf*
Gobi	Го́би *nf, indecl*
Kalahari	пусты́ня Калаха́ри *nf*
Nubian Desert	Нуби́йская пусты́ня *nf*
Sahara	Саха́ра *nf*

VOLCANOES

Hekla	Э́кла *nf*
Krakatoa	Краката́у *nf*
Mauna Loa	Мау́на-Ло́а *nf*
Mount Etna/Aetna	Э́тна *nf*
Mount Fuji	Фудзия́ма *nf, indecl*
Popocatepetl	Попокатепе́тль *nm*
Vesuvius	Везу́вий *nm*

CANALS AND DAMS

Aswan Dam	Асуа́н *nm*
Bratsk	Братск *nm*
Kiel Canal	Ки́льский кана́л *nm*
Panama Canal	Пана́мский кана́л *nm*
Suez Canal	Суэ́цкий кана́л *nm*

See also **PLACE NAMES II: POLITICAL ENTITIES, INHABITANTS AND ETHNIC GROUPS**

PLACE NAMES II: POLITICAL ENTITIES

COUNTRIES

regional groups

Benelux	Бенилю́кс *nm*
Caucasus	Кавка́з *nm*
Guiana	Гвиа́на *nf*

names of independent states

Afghanistan	Афганиста́н *nm*
Albania	Алба́ния *nf*
Algeria	Алжи́р *nm*
Andorra	Андо́рра *nf*
Angola	Анго́ла *nf*
Argentina	Аргенти́на *nf*
Armenia	Арме́ния *nf*
Australia	Австра́лия *nf*
Austria	А́встрия *nf*
Azerbaijan	Азербайджа́н *nm*
Bahrain	Бахре́йн *nm*
Bangladesh	Бангладе́ш *nm*
Barbados	Барба́дос *nm*
Belarus	Белару́сь *nf*
Belgium	Бе́льгия *nf*
Belize	Бели́з *nm*
Belorussia, Byelorussia	Белору́ссия *nf*
Benin	Бени́н *nm*
Bhutan	Бута́н *nm*
Bolivia	Боли́вия *nf*
Bosnia-Herzogovina	Бо́сния-Герцегови́на *nf*
Botswana	Ботсва́на *nf*
Brazil	Брази́лия *nf*
Brunei	Бруне́й *nm*
Bulgaria	Болга́рия *nf*
Burundi	Буру́нди *nn, indecl*
Cambodia	Камбо́джа *nf*
Cameroon	Камеру́н *nm*
Canada	Кана́да *nf*

Chad	Чад *nm*
Chile	Чи́ли *nn, indecl*
Colombia	Колу́мбия *nf*
Congo	Ко́нго *nn, indecl*
Costa Rica	Ко́ста-Ри́ка *nf*
Croatia	Хорва́тия *nf*
Cuba	Ку́ба *nf*
Czech Republic	Че́шская Респу́блика, Че́хия *nf*
Denmark	Да́ния *nf*
Djibouti	Джибу́ти *nn, indecl*
Dominican Republic	Доминика́нская Респу́блика *nf*
Ecuador	Эквадо́р *nm*
Egypt	Еги́пет *nm*
El Salvador	Сальвадо́р *nm*
England	А́нглия *nf*
Eritrea	Эритре́я *nf*
Estonia	Эсто́ния *nf*
Ethiopia	Эфио́пия *nf*
Federal Republic of Germany	Федерати́вная Респу́блика Герма́ния *nf*
Fiji	Фи́джи *nn, indecl*
Finland	Финля́ндия *nf*
France	Фра́нция *nf*
Gabon	Габо́н *nm*
Gambia	Га́мбия *nf*
Germany	Герма́ния *nf*
Ghana	Га́на *nf*
Great Britain	Великобрита́ния *nf*
Greece	Гре́ция *nf*
Grenada	Грена́да *nf*
Guatemala	Гватема́ла *nf*
Guinea	Гвине́я *nf*
Guyana	Гайа́на *nf*
Haiti	Гаи́ти *nm*
Holland [= The Netherlands]	Голла́ндия *nm*
Honduras	Гондура́с *nm*
Hungary	Венгрия *nf*
Iceland	Исла́ндия *nf*
India	И́ндия *nf*
Indonesia	Индоне́зия *nf*
Iran	Ира́н *nm*
Iraq	Ира́к *nm*
Ireland	Ирла́ндия *nf*
Israel	Изра́иль *nm*
Italy	Ита́лия *nf*
Ivory Coast	Кот д'Ивуа́р, Бе́рег Слоно́вой Ко́сти *nm*
Jamaica	Яма́йка *nf*
Japan	Япо́ния *nf*
Jordan	Иорда́ния *nf*
Kampuchea	Кампучи́я *nf*
Kazakhstan	Казахста́н *nm*
Kenya	Ке́ния *nm*
Kirghizia	Кирги́зия *nf*
Kuwait	Куве́йт *nm*
Kyrgystan	Кирги́зия, Кыргызста́н *nm*
Laos	Лао́с *nm*
Latvia	Ла́твия *nf*
Lebanon	Лива́н *nm*
Lesotho	Лесо́то *nn*
Liberia	Либе́рия *nf*
Libya	Ли́вия *nf*
Liechtenstein	Лихтеншт́ейн *nm*
Lithuania	Литва́ *nf*
Luxemb(o)urg	Люксембу́рг *nm*
Macedonia	Македо́ния *nf*
Madagascar	Мадагаска́р *nm*
Malawi	Мала́ви *nn, indecl*
Malaysia	Мала́йзия *nf*
Mali	Ма́ли *nn, indecl*
Malta	Ма́льта *nf*
Mauritania	Маврита́ния *nf*
Mauritius	Маври́кий *nm*
Mexico	Ме́ксика *nf*
Moldova	Молда́вия, Молдо́ва *nf*
Monaco	Мона́ко *nn, indecl*
Mongolia	Монго́лия *nf*
Morocco	Маро́кко *nn, indecl*
Mozambique	Мозамби́к *nm*
Muscat and Oman	Ома́н и Маска́т *nmpl*
Myanmar	Мья́нма *nf*
Namibia	Нами́бия *nf*
Nepal	Непа́л *nm*
Netherlands	Нидерла́нды *nmpl*
New Zealand	Но́вая Зела́ндия *nf*
Nicaragua	Никара́гуа *nf*
Niger	Ни́гер *nm*
Nigeria	Ниге́рия *nf*
North Korea	Се́верная Коре́я *nf*
Norway	Норве́гия *nf*
Oman	Ома́н *nm*
Pakistan	Пакиста́н *nm*
Panama	Пана́ма *nf*
Papua New Guinea	Па́пуа-Но́вая Гвине́я *nf*
Paraguay	Парагва́й *nm*
Peru	Перу́ *nf, indecl*
Philippines	Филиппи́ны *nmpl*
Poland	По́льша *nf*
Portugal	Португа́лия *nf*
Qatar	Ката́р *nm*
Romania, Roumania	Румы́ния *nf*

Russia	Росси́я *nf*, Русь *nf* [poetic]
Russian Federation	Росси́йская Федера́ция *nm*
Rwanda	Руа́нда *nm*
San Marino	Сан-Мари́но *nn*
Saudi Arabia	Сау́довская Ара́вия *nf*
Senegal	Сенега́л *nm*
Serbia	Се́рбия *nf*
Seychelles	Сейше́льские острова́ *nmpl*
Sierra Leone	Сье́рра-Лео́не *nf, indecl*
Singapore	Сингапу́р *nm*
Slovakia	Слова́кия *nf*
Slovenia	Слове́ния *nf*
Somalia	Сомали́ *nn, indecl*
South Korea	Ю́жная Коре́я *nf*
South Africa	Ю́жная А́фрика *nf*
Spain	Испа́ния *nf*
Sri Lanka	Шри Ла́нка *nf*
Sudan, the	Суда́н *nm*
Surinam(e)	Сурина́м *nm*
Swaziland	Сва́зиленд *nm*
Sweden	Шве́ция *nf*
Switzerland	Швейца́рия *nf*
Syria	Си́рия *nf*
Taiwan	Тайва́нь *nm*
Tajikistan, Tadzhikistan	Таджикиста́н *nm*
Tanzania	Танза́ния *nf*
Thailand	Таила́нд *nm*
Togo	Того *nn*
Trinidad and Tobago	Тринида́д и Toба́го *nmpl*
Tunisia	Туни́с *nm*
Turkey	Ту́рция *nf*
Turkmenistan, Turkmenia	Туркмения, Туркмениста́н *nm*
Uganda	Уга́нда *nf*
Ukraine	Украина *nf*
United States	Соединённые Шта́ты *nmpl*
Uruguay	Уругва́й *nm*
Uzbekistan	Узбекиста́н *nm*
Vatican City State	Ватика́н *nm*
Venezuela	Венесуэ́ла *nf*
Vietnam	Вьетна́м *nm*
Yemen	Йе́мен *nm*
Yugoslavia, Jugoslavia	Югосла́вия *nf*
Zaire	Заир *nm*
Zambia	За́мбия *nf*
Zimbabwe	Зимба́бве *nn, indecl*

parts of countries

Alsace	Эльза́с *nm*
Anatolia	Анато́лия *nf*
Andalucia	Андалуси́я *nf*
Aragon	Араго́н *nm*
Arcadia	Арка́дия *nf*
Assam	Асса́м *nm*
Avon	Э́вон *nm*
Bavaria	Бава́рия *nf*
Bengal	Бенга́лия *nf*
Berkshire	Бе́ркшир *nm*
Bessarabia	Бессара́бия *nf*
Bible Belt	Библе́йский По́яс *nm*
Birobidzhan	Биробиджа́н *nm*
Bohemia	Боге́мия *nf*
Brittany	Брета́нь *nf*
Burgandy	Бургу́ндия *nf*
Castile	Касти́лия *nf*
Catalonia	Катало́ния *nf*
Chechnya	Чечня́ *nf*
Cheshire	Че́шир *nm*
Cork	Корк *nm*
Cornwall	Ко́рнуолл *nm*
Crimea	Крым *nm*
Dalmatia	Далма́ция, Далма́тия *nf*
Devon(shire)	Де́вон, Девонши́р *nm*
Donegal	До́негал *nm*
Donets Basin	Донба́сс *nm*, Доне́цкий бассе́йн *nm*
Essex	Э́ссекс *nm*
Flanders	Фла́ндрия *nf*
Galicia	Гали́ция *nf*
Galilee	Галиле́я *nf*
Gascony	Гаско́нь *nf*
Gaza Strip	се́ктор Га́за *nm*
Hindustan	Индоста́н *nm*
Hunan	Хуна́нь *nm*
Kashmir	Кашми́р *nm*
Kent	Кент *nm*
Kerry	Ке́рри *nm*
Klondike	Кло́ндайк *nm*
Kurdistan	Курдиста́н *nm*
Labrador	Лабрадо́р *nm*
Lankashire	Ла́нкашир *nm*
Lapland	Лапла́ндия *nf*
Lombardy	Ломба́рдия *nf*
Macao	Мака́о *nn*
Manchuria	Маньчжу́рия *nf*
Manitoba	Манито́ба *nf*
Moldavia	Молда́вия *nf*
Moravia	Мора́вия *nf*
New England	Но́вая А́нглия
Normandy	Норма́ндия *nf*
Northern Ireland	Се́верная Ирла́ндия *nf*

Palestine	Палести́на *nf*
Patagonia	Патаго́ния *nf*
Provence	Прова́нс *nm*
Prussia	Пру́ссия *nf*
Punjab	Пенжа́б *nm*
Quebec	Квебе́к *nm*
Queensland	Кви́нсленд *nm*
Riviera	Ривье́ра *nf*
Ruhr	Рур *nm*, Ру́рская о́бласть *nf*
Saar	Саа́р *nm*, Саа́рская о́бласть *nf*
Saskatchewan	Саска́чеван *nm*
Savoy	Саво́йя *nf*
Saxony	Саксо́ния *nf*
Schleswig-Holstein	Шле́звиг-Го́льштейн *nm*
Scotland	Шотла́ндия *nf*
Siberia	Сиби́рь *nf*
Silesia	Силе́зия *nf*
Somaliland	Сомали́ *nn, indecl*
Somerset	Со́мерсет *nm*
Sudetenland	Суде́тская о́бласть *nf*
Suffolk	Су́ффолк *nm*
Surrey	Су́ррей *nm*
Sussex	Су́ссекс *nm*
Tanganyika	Танганьи́ка *nf*
Tibet	Тибе́т *nm*
Tirol, Tyrol	Тиро́ль *nm*
Tonkin	То́нкин *nm*
Transvaal	Трансва́аль *nm*
Transylvania	Трансильва́ния *nf*
Tuscany	Токса́на *nf*
Ulster	О́льстер *nm*
Umbria	У́мбрия *nf*
Volga region	Пово́лжье *nn*
Wales	Уэ́льс *nm*
Westphalia	Вестфа́лия *nf*
York(shire)	Йо́рк (шир) *nm*

CITIES

capital cities

Abu-Dhabi [United Arab Emirates]	Абу́-Да́би *nn, indecl*
Accra [Ghana]	А́ккра *nf*
Addis Ababa [Ethiopia]	Адди́с-Абе́ба *nf*
Aden [Yemen]	А́ден *nm*
Aleppo [Syria]	Але́ппо *nn*
Algiers [Algeria]	Алжи́р *nm*
Alma-Ata [Kazakhstan]	Алма́-ата́ *nf*
Amman [Jordan]	Амма́н *nm*
Ankara [Turkey]	Анкара́ *nm*
Ashkhabad [Turkmenistan]	Ашхаба́д *nm*
Asmara [Eritrea]	Асма́ра *nf*
Asuncion [Paraguay]	Асунсьо́н *nm*
Athens [Greece]	Афи́ны *pl*
Bag(h)dad [Iraq]	Багда́д *nm*
Baku [Azerbaijan]	Баку́ *nm, indecl*
Bangkok [Thailand]	Бангко́к *nm*
Beijing [China]	Бейцзи́н *nm*
Beirut [Lebanon]	Бейру́т *nm*
Belfast [Northern Ireland]	Бе́лфаст *nm*
Belgrade [Yugoslavia]	Белгра́д *nm*
Berlin [Germany]	Берли́н *nm*
Bern(e) [Switzerland]	Берн *nm*
Bogota [Colombia]	Бого́та *nf*
Bratislava [Slovakia]	Братисла́ва *nf*
Brasilia [Brazil]	Брази́лия *nf*
Brazzaville [Congo]	Браззави́ль *nm*
Bridgetown [Barbados]	Бри́джтаун *nm*
Brussels [Belgium]	Брюссе́ль *nm*
Bucharest [Romania]	Бухаре́ст *nm*
Budapest [Hungary]	Будапе́шт *nm*
Buenos Aires [Argentina]	Буэ́нос-А́йрес *nm*
Bujumbura [Burundi]	Бужумбу́ра *nf*
Cairo [Egypt]	Каи́р *nm*
Canberra [Australia]	Канбе́рра *nf*
Caracas [Venezuela]	Кара́кас *nm*
Cardiff [Wales]	Ка́рдифф *nm*
Colombo [Sri Lanka]	Коло́мбо *nm, indecl*
Conakry [Guinea]	Конакри́ *nm, indecl*
Copenhagen [Denmark]	Копенга́ген *nm*
Dacca, Dhaka [Bangladesh]	Да́кка, Да́ка *nf*
Dakar [Senegal]	Дака́р *nm*
Damascus [Syria]	Дама́ск *nm*
Dar es Salaam [Tanzania]	Дар-эс-Сала́м *nm*
Delhi [India]	Де́ли *nm, indecl*
Doha [Qatar]	До́ха *nf*
Dublin [Ireland]	Ду́блин *nm*
Dushambe [Tadjikistan]	Душанбе́ *nm*
Edinburgh [Scotland]	Э́динбург *nm*
Entebbe [former capital of Uganda]	Энте́ббе *nm*
Freetown [Sierra Leone]	Фрита́ун *nm*
Geneva [Switzerland]	Жене́ва *nf*
Georgetown [Guyana]	Джорджта́ун *nm*
Hague, The [Netherlands]	Гаа́га *nf*
Hanoi [Viet Nam]	Хано́й *nm*

Harare [Zimbabwe]	Хара́ре *nn*
Havana [Cuba]	Гава́на *nf*
Helsinki [Finland]	Хе́льсинки *nm, indecl*
Islamabad [Pakistan]	Исламаба́д *nm*
Jakarta [Indonesia]	Джака́рта *nf*
Jerusalem [Israel]	Иерусали́м *nm*
Kabul [Afghanistan]	Кабу́л *nm*
Kampala [Uganda]	Кампа́ла *nf*
Katmandu [Nepal]	Катманду́ *nf, indecl*
Khartoum [Sudan]	Харту́м *nm*
Kiev [Ukraine]	Ки́ев *nm*
Kigali [Rwanda]	Кига́ли *nn*
Kingston [Jamaica]	Ки́нгстон *nm*
Kinshasa [Zaire]	Кинша́са *nf*
Kishinev [Moldava]	Кишинёв *nm*
Kuala Lumpur [Malaysia]	Куа́ла-Лумпу́р *nm*
La Paz [Bolivia]	Ла-Па́с *nm*
Lagos [Nigeria]	Ла́гос *nm*
Lhasa [Tibet]	Лха́са *nf*
Libreville [Gabon]	Либреви́ль *nm*
Lilongwe [Malawi]	Лило́нгве *nn*
Lima [Peru]	Ли́ма *nf*
Lisbon [Portugal]	Лиссабо́н *nm*
Ljubljana [Slovenia]	Любля́на *nf*
Lome [Togo]	Ломе́ *nn*
London [England]	Ло́ндон *nm*
Luanda [Angola]	Луа́нда *nf*
Lusaka [Zambia]	Луса́ка *nf*
Luxemb(o)urg City [Luxemburg]	Люксембу́рг *nm*
Madrid [Spain]	Мадри́д *nm*
Managua [Nicaragua]	Мана́гуа *nf*
Manama [Bahrain]	Мана́ма *nf*
Manila [Philippines]	Мани́ла *nf*
Maputo [Mozambique]	Мапу́ту *nn*
Maseru [Lesoto]	Ма́серу *nn*
Mbabane [Swaziland]	Мбаба́не *nn*
Mexico City [Mexico]	Ме́хико *nm, indecl*
Minsk [Byelorussia]	Минск *nm*
Mogadishu [Somalia]	Могади́шо *nm*
Monaco [Monaco]	Мона́ко *nn, indecl*
Monrovia [Liberia]	Монро́вия *nf*
Monte Carlo [Monaco]	Монте-Ка́рло *nm, indecl*
Montevideo [Uruguay]	Монтевиде́о *nn, indecl*
Moscow [Russian Federation]	Москва́ *nf*
Muscat [Oman]	Муска́т *nm*
Nairobi [Kenya]	Найро́би *nn, indecl*
Nassau [Bahamas]	Насса́у *nn*
Nicosia [Cyprus]	Нико́сия *nf*
Oslo [Norway]	О́сло *nm, indecl*
Ottawa [Canada]	Отта́ва *nf*
Panama City [Panama]	Пана́ма *nf*
Paris [France]	Пари́ж *nm*
Phnom Penh [Cambodia]	Пномпе́нь *nm*
Port Louis [Mauritus]	Порт-Луи́ *nm*
Port Moresby [Papua New Guinea]	Порт-Мо́рсби *nm*
Port-au-Prince [Haiti]	Порт-о-Пре́нс *nm*
Port-of-Spain [Trinidad & Tobago]	Порт-оф-Спе́йн *nm*
Porto-Novo [Benin]	По́рто-Но́во *nn*
Prague [Czech Republic]	Пра́га *nm*
Pretoria [South Africa]	Прето́рия *nf*
Pyongyang [North Korea]	Пхенья́н *nm*
Quito [Ecuador]	Ки́то *nn*
Rabat [Morocco]	Раба́т *nm*
Rangoon [Myanmar]	Рангу́н *nm*
Reykjavik [Iceland]	Рейкья́вик *nm*
Riga [Latvia]	Ри́га *nf*
Riyadh [Saudi Arabia]	Эр-Рия́д *nm*
Rome [Italy]	Рим *nm*
San Jose [Costa Rica]	Сан-Хосе́ *nm*
San Salvador [El Salvador]	Сан-Сальвадо́р *nm*
Sana(a) [Yemen]	Сана́ *nf*
Santiago [Chile]	Сантья́го *nn*
Santo Domingo [Dominican Republic]	Са́нто-Доми́нго *nn*
Sarajevo [Bosnia-Herzegovina]	Сара́ево *nn*
Seoul [South Korea]	Сеу́л *nm*
Skopje [Macedonia]	Ско́пье *nn*
Singapore [Singapore]	Сингапу́р *nm*
Sofia [Bulgaria]	Софи́я *nf*
Stockholm [Sweden]	Стокго́льм *nm*
Suva [Fiji]	Су́ва *nf*
Taipei [Taiwan]	Тайбе́й *nm*
Tallin(n) [Estonia]	Та́ллин *nm*
Tashkent [Uzbekistan]	Ташке́нт *nm*
Tbilisi [Georgia]	Тбили́си *nm, indecl*
Tegucigalpa [Honduras]	Тегусига́льпа *nf*
Teheran, Tehran [Iran]	Тегера́н *nm*
Tirana [Albania]	Тира́на *nf*
Tokyo [Japan]	То́кио *nm, indecl*
Tripoli [Libya]	Три́поли *nn, indecl*
Tunis [Tunisia]	Туни́с *nm*
Ulan Bator [Mongolia]	Ула́н-Ба́тор *nm*
Vaduz [Liechtenstein]	Ваду́ц *nm*
Valletta [Malta]	Валле́тта *nf*
Vienna [Austria]	Ве́на *nf*
Vientianne [Laos]	Вьентья́н *nm*

Vilnius [Lithuania]	Ви́льнюс *nm*
Warsaw [Poland]	Варша́ва *nf*
Washington [USA]	Вашингто́н *nm*
Wellington [New Zealand]	Ве́ллингтон *nm*
Windhoek [Namibia]	Ви́ндхук *nm*
Yaounde [Cameroon]	Яунде́ *nn*
Yerevan [Armenia]	Ерева́н *nm*
Zagreb [Croatia]	За́греб *nm*

cities in Russia

Archangel, Arkhangelsk	Арха́нгельск *nm*
Astrakhan	А́страхань *nm*
Bratsk	Братск *nm*
Chelyabinsk	Челя́бинск *nm*
Irkutsk	Ирку́тск *nm*
Kaliningrad	Калинингра́д *nm*
Kazan	Каза́нь *nf*
Kharkov	Ха́рьков *nm*
Moscow	Москва *nf*
Moscow area, the greater	Подмоско́вье *nn*
Murmansk	Му́рманск *nm*
Nizhny Novgorod	Ни́жний Но́вгород *nm*
Novosibirsk	Новосиби́рск *nm*
Orenburg	Оренбу́рг *nm*
Ryazan	Ряза́нь *nf*
Samara	Сама́ра *nf*
St. Petersburg	Санкт-Петербу́рг *nm*
Tver	Тверь *nf*
Ulyanovsk	Улья́новск *nm*
Vladivostok	Владивосто́к *nm*
Volgograd	Волгоград *nm*
Yekaterinburg, Ekaterinburg	Екатеринбу́рг *nm*

cities in the USA

Albany	О́лбани *nm*
Anchorage	А́нкоридж *nm*
Annapolis	Анна́полис *nm*
Arlington	А́рлингтон *nm*
Atlanta	Атла́нта *nf*
Atlantic City	Атла́нтик-Си́ти *nm*
Austin	О́стин *nm*
Baltimore	Ба́лтимор *nm*
Birmingham	Би́рмингем *nm*
Boston	Бо́стон *nm*
Bridgeport	Бри́джпорт *nm*
Buffalo	Бу́ффало *nm, indecl*
Cambridge	Ке́мбридж *nm*
Charleston	Чарлсто́н *nm*
Chicago	Чика́го *nm, indecl*
Cincinnatti	Цинцинна́ти *nm, indecl*
Cleveland	Кли́вленд *nm*
Dallas	Да́ллас *nm*
Denver	Де́нвер *nm*
Des Moines	Де-Мо́йн *nm*
Detroit	Детро́йт *nm*
Fairbanks	Фэ́рбенкс *nm*
Fort Worth	Форт-Уэ́рт *nm*
Gettysburg	Ге́ттисберг *nm*
Hollywood	Голливу́д *nm*
Honolulu	Гонолу́лу *nm, indecl*
Houston	Хьюстон *nm*
Indianapolis	Индиана́полис *nm*
Jacksonville	Джэ́ксонвилл *nm*
Jersey City	Дже́рси-Си́ти *nm, indecl*
Kansas City	Канза́с-Си́ти *nm, indecl*
Lancaster	Ланка́стер *nm*
Little Rock	Ли́тл-Рок *nm*
Los Angeles	Лос-А́нджелес *nm*
Louisville	Лу́исвилл *nm*
Memphis	Ме́мфис *nm*
Miami	Майа́ми *nm, indecl*
Milwaukee	Милуо́ки *nm, indecl*
Minneapolis	Миннеа́полис *nm*
Mobile	Моби́л *nm*
Nashville	На́швилл *nm*
New Orleans	Но́вый Орлеа́н *nm*
New York (City)	Нью-Йо́рк *nm*
Newark	Нью́арк *nm*
Nome	Ном *nm*
Norfolk	Но́рфолк *nm*
Oakland	О́кленд *nm*
Omaha	Ома́ха *nf*
Pearl Harbor	Пирл-Ха́рбор *nm*
Philadelphia	Филаде́льфия *nf*
Phoenix	Фе́никс *nm*
Pittsburgh	Пи́тсбург *nm*
Portland	По́ртленд *nm*
Providence	Про́виденс *nm*
Raleigh	Ро́ли *nm, indecl*
Reno	Ри́но *nm, indecl*
Richmond	Ри́чмонд *nm*
Rochester	Ро́честер *nm*
Salt Lake City	Со́лт-Лейк-Си́ти *nm, indecl*
San Antonio	Сан-Анто́нио *nm, indecl*
San Diego	Сан-Дие́го *nm, indecl*
San Francisco	Сан-Франци́ско *nm, indecl*
San Juan	Сан-Хуа́н *nm*
Seattle	Сиэ́тл *nm*
St. Louis	Сент-Лу́ис *nm*

St. Paul	Сент-По́л *nm*
Syracuse	Сираку́зы *nfpl*
Toledo	Толе́до *nm, indecl*
Tulsa	Та́лса *nf*
West Point	Вест-Пойнт *nm*
Wilmington	Уи́лмингтон *nm*

other world cities

Abadan [Iran]	Абада́н *nm*
Aberdeen [Scotland]	Аберди́н *nm*
Acapulco [Mexico]	Акапу́лько *nm, indecl*
Adelaide [Australia]	Аделаи́да *nf*
Alexandria [Egypt]	Александри́я *nf*
Amsterdam [Netherlands]	Амстерда́м *nm*
Antwerp [Belgium]	Антве́рпен *nm*
Arles [France]	Арль *nm*
Auckland [New Zealand]	О́кленд *nm*
Avignon [France]	Авиньо́н *nm*
Bandung [Indonesia]	Банду́нг *nm*
Bangalore [India]	Бангалу́р *nm*
Barcelona [Spain]	Барсело́на *nf*
Basel [Switzerland]	Ба́зель *nm*
Basra [Iraq]	Ба́сра *nf*
Bath [England]	Бат *nm*
Batumi [Georgia]	Бату́ми *nm*
Bergen [Norway]	Бе́рген *nm*
Bethlehem [Israel]	Вифлее́м *nm*
Bilbao [Spain]	Бильба́о *nm*
Birmingham [England]	Би́рмингем *nm*
Blackpool [England]	Блэ́кпул *nm*
Bombay [India]	Бомбе́й *nm*
Bonn [Germany]	Бонн *nm*
Bordeaux [France]	Бордо́ *nn*
Bournemouth [England]	Бо́рнмут *nm*
Bremen [Germany]	Бре́мен *nm*
Bremerhaven [Germany]	Бре́мерхафен *nm*
Brighton [England]	Бра́йтон *nm*
Brisbane [Australia]	Бри́сбен *nm*
Bristol [England]	Бри́столь *nm*
Bruges [Belgium]	Брю́гге *nm*
Bukhara [Uzbekistan]	Бухара́ *nf*
Cadiz [Spain]	Ка́дис *nm*
Calais [France]	Кале́ *nm*
Calcutta [India]	Кальку́тта *nf*
Calgary [Canada]	Ка́лгари *nm, indecl*
Cambridge [England]	Ке́мбридж *nm*
Cannes [France]	Ка́нны *npl*
Canterbury [England]	Ке́нтербери *nm, indecl*
Canton [China]	Канто́н *nm*
Capetown [South Africa]	Ке́йптаун *nm*
Casablanca [Morocco]	Касабла́нка *nf*
Cologne [Germany]	Кёльн *nm*
Constantsa [Romania]	Конста́нца *nf*
Coventry [England]	Ко́вентри *nm*
Crakow [Poland]	Кра́ков *nm*
Danzig [= Gdansk] [Poland]	Да́нциг *nm*
Dover [England]	Дувр *nm*
Dresden [Germany]	Дре́зден *nm*
Dubai [United Arab Emirates]	Дуба́й *nm*
Dubrovnik [Croatia]	Дубро́вник *nm*
Dundee [Scotland]	Да́нди *nm, indecl*
Dunkirk [France]	Дюнке́рк *nm*
Düsseldorf [Germany]	Дю́ссельдорф *nm*
Edmonton [Canada]	Э́дмонтон *nm*
Fez [Morocco]	Фес *nm*
Florence [Italy]	Флоре́нция *nf*
Frankfurt [Germany]	Фра́нкфурт *nm*
Gaza [Israel]	Га́за *nf*
Gdansk [Poland]	Гданьск *nm*
Genoa [Italy]	Ге́нуя *nf*
Ghent [Belgium]	Гент *nm*
Gibraltar [Great Britain]	Гибралта́р *nm*
Glasgow [Scotland]	Гла́зго *nn*
Greenwich [England]	Гри́нвич *nm*
Guadalajara [Mexico]	Гвадалаха́ра *nf*
Haifa [Israel]	Ха́йфа *nf*
Halifax [Canada]	Галифа́кс *nm*
Hamburg [Germany]	Га́мбург *nm*
Hanover [Germany]	Ганно́вер *nm*
Harbin [China]	Харби́н *nm*
Heidelberg [Germany]	Ге́йдельберг *nm*
Hiroshima [Japan]	Хироси́ма *nf*
Ho Chi Minh City [Viet Nam]	Хошими́н *nm*
Hong Kong [China]	Гонко́нг *nm*
Hyderabad [India]	Хайдараба́д *nm*
Istanbul [Turkey]	Стамбу́л *nm*
Izmir [Turkey]	Изми́р *nm*
Jaffa [Israel]	Я́ффа *nf*
Jaipur [India]	Джайпу́р *nm*
Jericho [Jordan]	Иерихо́н *nm*
Jidda [Saudi Arabia]	Джи́дда *nf*
Jogjakarta [Indonesia]	Джака́рта *nf*
Johannesburg [South Africa]	Йоха́ннесбург *nm*
Karachi [Pakistan]	Кара́чи *nm, indecl*
Kaunas [Lithuania]	Ка́унас *nm*
Kobe [Japan]	Ко́бе *nm*
Kyoto [Japan]	Кио́то *nn*

La Plata [Argentina]	Ла-Пла́та *nf*
Lahore [Pakistan]	Лахо́р *nm*
Lausanne [Switzerland]	Лоза́нна *nf*
Le Havre [France]	Гавр *nm*
Leeds [England]	Лидс *nm*
Leicester [England]	Ле́стер *nm*
Leipzig [Germany]	Ле́йпциг *nm*
Liege [Belgium]	Льеж *nm*
Liverpool [England]	Ливерпу́ль *nm*
Lucerne [Switzerland]	Люце́рн *nm*
Lvov [Ukraine]	Львов *nm*
Lyon(s) [France]	Лио́н *nm*
Malaga [Spain]	Ма́лага *nf*
Manchester [England]	Манче́стер *nm*
Marrakech [Morocco]	Маррakéш *nm*
Marseilles [France]	Марсе́ль *nm*
Mecca [Saudi Arabia]	Ме́кка *nf*
Medina [Saudi Arabia]	Меди́на *nf*
Melbourne [Australia]	Ме́льбурн *nm*
Milan [Italy]	Мила́н *nm*
Mombasa [Kenya]	Момба́са *nf*
Montreal [Canada]	Монреа́ль *nm*
Munich [Germany]	Мю́нхен *nm*
Nagasaki [Japan]	Нагаса́ки *nm, indecl*
Naples [Italy]	Неа́поль *nm*
Nazareth [Israel]	Назаре́т *nm*
New Delhi [India]	Де́ли *nm*
Newcastle [England]	Нью́касл *nm*
Nice [France]	Ни́цца *nf*
Northampton [England]	Нортге́мптон *nm*
Nuremberg [Germany]	Ню́рнберг *nm*
Odessa [Ukraine]	Оде́сса *nf*
Osaka [Japan]	О́сака *nf*
Ostend [Belgium]	Осте́нде *nm, indecl*
Oxford [England]	О́ксфорд *nm*
Palermo [Italy]	Пале́рмо *nf*
Perth [Scotland]	Перт *nm*
Piraeus [Greece]	Пире́й *nm*
Ploeşti [Romania]	Плое́шти *nn*
Plymouth [England]	Пли́мут *nm*
Port Said [Egypt]	Порт-Са́йд *nm*
Portsmouth [England]	По́ртсмут *nm*
Quebec [Canada]	Квебе́к *nm*
Rawalpindi [Pakistan]	Равалпи́нди *nn*
Reading [England]	Ре́динг *nm*
Recife [Brazil]	Реци́фе *nn*
Regina [Canada]	Ридж́айна *nf*
Reims [France]	Реймс *nm*
Rio de Janeiro [Brazil]	Ри́о-де-Жане́йро *nf, indecl*
Rotterdam [Netherlands]	Ро́ттердам *nm*
Salonika [Greece]	Салони́ки *nmpl*
Samarkand [Uzbekistan]	Самарка́нд *nm*
São Paulo [Brazil]	Сан-Па́улу *nn*
Sevastopol [Ukraine]	Севасто́поль *nm*
Seville [Spain]	Севи́лья *nf*
Shanghai [China]	Шанха́й *nm*
Sheffield [England]	Ше́ффилд *nm*
Simla [India]	Си́мла *nf*
Southampton [England]	Са́утгемптон *nm*
Strasbourg [France]	Стра́сбург *nm*
Stratford-on-Avon [England]	Стра́тфорд-на-Э́йвоне *nm*
Stuttgart [Germany]	Шту́тгарт *nm*
Suez [Egypt]	Суэ́ц *nm*
Sydney [Australia]	Сидне́й *nm*
Tabriz [Iran]	Тебри́з *nm*
Tangier [Morocco]	Танже́р *nm*
Tel Aviv [Israel]	Тель-Ави́в *nm*
Toledo [Spain]	Толе́до *nn*
Tombouctou [Mali]	Тимбукту́ *nm*
Toronto [Canada]	Торо́нто *nm*
Trieste [Italy]	Трие́ст *nm*
Turin [Italy]	Тури́н *nm*
Valencia [Spain]	Вале́нсия *nf*
Valparaiso [Chile]	(го́род) Вальпара́йсо *nm*
Vancouver [Canada]	Ванку́вер *nm*
Venice [Italy]	Вене́ция *nf*
Versailles [France]	Верса́ль *nm*
Vichy [France]	(го́род) Виши́ *nm*
Victoria [Australia, Canada]	Викто́рия *nf*
Windsor [England]	Ви́ндзор *nm*
Winnipeg [Canada]	Ви́ннипег *nm*
Worcester [England]	Ву́стер *nm*
Wroclaw [Poland]	Вро́цлав *nm*
Yalta [Ukraine]	Я́лта *nf*
Yokohama [Japan]	Иокога́ма *nf*
York [England]	Йорк *nm*
Zurich [Switzerland]	Цю́рих *nm*

FAMOUS STREETS AND SECTIONS OF CITIES

– New York –

Brighton Beach	Бра́йтон Би́ч *nm*
Broadway	Бродве́й *nm*
Bronx	Бронкс *nm*
Brooklyn	Бру́клин *nm*
Coney Island	Ко́ни-А́йленд *nm*
Manhattan	Манха́ттан *nm*
Queens	Квинс *nm*
Wall Street	Уолл Стрит *nm*

West Side	Уест-Сайд *nm*

– London –

Covent Garden	Ко́вент Га́рден *nm*
Petticoat Lane	Пе́ттикоут-лейн *nm*
Soho	Со́хо *nn*
Whitehall	Уа́йтхолл *nm*
West End	Уест-Э́нд *nm*
Westminster	Ве́стминстер *nm*

– Paris –

Champs Elysees	Елисе́йские поля́ *nnpl*
Montmartre	Монма́ртр *nm*

STATES IN THE U.S.

Alabama	Алаба́ма *nf*
Alaska	Аля́ска *nf*
Arizona	Аризо́на *nf*
Arkansas	Арканза́с *nm*
California	Калифо́рния *nf*
Colorado	Колора́до *nn, indecl*
Connecticut	Конне́ктикут *nm*
Delaware	Де́лавэр *nm*
District of Columbia	о́круг Колу́мбия *nm*
Florida	Флори́да *nf*
Georgia	Джо́рджия *nf*
Hawaii	Гава́йи *nm, indecl*
Idaho	(штат) Айда́хо *nm*
Illinois	Иллино́йс *nm*
Indiana	Индиа́на *nf*
Iowa	Айо́ва *nf*
Kansas	Канза́с *nm*
Kentucky	(штат) Кенту́кки *nm*
Louisiana	Луизиа́на *nf*
Maine	Мэн *nm*
Maryland	Мэ́риленд *nm*
Massachusetts	Массачу́сетс *nm*
Michigan	Мичига́н *nm*
Minnesota	Минесо́та *nm*
Mississippi	(штат) Миссиси́пи *nm*
Missouri	(штат) Миссу́ри *nm*
Montana	Монта́на *nf*
Nebraska	Небра́ска *nf*
Nevada	Нева́да *nf*
New York (State)	Нью-Йо́рк *nm*
New Jersey	(штат) Нью-Дже́рси *nm*
New Hampshire	Нью-Хэ́мпшир *nm*
New Mexico	(штат) Нью-Ме́ксико *nm*
North Carolina	Се́верная Кароли́на *nf*
North Dakota	Се́верная Дако́та *nf*
Ohio	(штат) Ога́йо *nm*
Oklahoma	Оклахо́ма *nf*
Oregon	Орего́н *nm*
Pennsylvania	Пенсильва́ния *nf*
Rhode Island	Род-Айленд *nm*
South Carolina	Ю́жная Кароли́на *nf*
South Dakota	Ю́жная Дако́та *nf*
Tennessee	(штат) Те́ннесси *nm*
Texas	Теха́с *nm*
Utah	Ю́та *nf*
Vermont	Вермо́нт *nm*
Virginia	Вирджи́ния *nf*
Washington	Вашингто́н *nm*
West Virginia	За́падная Вирджи́ния *nf*
Wisconsin	Висконси́н *nm*
Wyoming	Вайо́минг *nm*

REPUBLICS OF THE RUSSIAN FEDERATION

Adygeya	Адыге́я *nf*
Altay	Алта́й *nm*
Bashkortostan	Башкортоста́н *nm*
Buryatia	Буря́тия *nf*
Chechen	Чечня́, Чече́нская Респу́блика *nf*
Chuvash	Чува́шская Респу́блика *nf*
Dag(h)estan	Дагеста́н *nm*
Gorno-Altay	Го́рный Алта́й *nm*
Ingush	Ингу́шская Республика *nf*
Kabardino-Balkar	Кабарди́но-Балка́рская Респу́блика *nf*
Kalmykia	Калмы́кия *nf*
Karachay-Cherkess	Карача́ево-Черке́сская Респу́блика *nf*
Karelia	Каре́лия *nf*
Khakassia	Хака́сия *nf*
Komi	(респу́блика) Ко́ми *nf*
Mari El	Ма́рий Эл *nm*
Mordovia	Мордо́вия *nf*
North Ossetia	Се́верная Осе́тия *nf*
Tatarstan	Татарста́н *nm*
Tuva	Ту́ва *nf*
Udmurt	Удму́ртская Респу́блика *nf*
Yakutia	Яку́тия *nf*

CANADIAN PROVINCES

Alberta	Альбе́рта *nf*

British Columbia	Брита́нская Колу́мбия *nf*
Manitoba	Манито́ба *nf*
New Brunswick	Нью-Бра́нсуик *nm*
Newfoundland	Ньюфаундле́нд *nm*
Nova Scotia	Но́вая Шотла́ндия *nf*
Ontario	Онта́рио *nn*
Prince Edward Island	о́стров При́нца Э́дуарда *nm*
Quebec	Квебе́к *nm*
Saskatchewan	Саска́чеван *nm*

OBSOLETE NAMES AND NAME CHANGES

Abyssinia → Ethiopia	Абисси́ния *nf*
Basle → Basel	Ба́зель *nm*
Batavia → Jakarta	Бата́вия *nf*
Burma → Myanmar	Би́рма *nf*
Caledonia → Scotland	Каледо́ния *nf*
Cashmere → Kashmir	Кашми́р *nm*
Ceylon → Sri Lanka	Цейло́н *nm*
Chungking → Chongqing	Чунци́н *nm*
Congo → Zaire	Ко́нго *nf*
Constantinople → Istanbul	Константино́поль *nm*
Czechoslovakia → Czech Republic, Slovakia	Чехослова́кия *nf*
East Indies → Malay Archipelago	О́ст-Индия *nf*
Eire → Ireland	Э́йре *nn, indecl*
Formosa → Taiwan	Формо́за *nf*
Gorki, Gorky → Nizhny Novgorod	Го́рький *nm*
Kampuchea → Cambodia	Кампучи́я *nf*
Kuibyshev → Samara	Ку́йбышев *nm*
Leningrad → St. Petersburg	Ленингра́д *nm*
Leopoldville → Kinshasa	Леопольдви́ль *nm*
Madras → Tamil Nadu	Мадра́с *nm*
Malagasy → Madagascar	Малагаси́йская респу́блика *nf*
Muscovy → Russia	Моско́вия *nf*
Nanking → Nanjing	Нанки́н *nm*
Nyasaland → Malawi	Нья́саленд *nm*
Peking → Beijing	Пеки́н *nm*
Persia → Iran	Пе́рсия *nf*
Quezon City → Manila	Ке́сон-Си́ти *nm*
Rhodesia → Zambia, Zimbabwe	Роде́зия *nf*
Saigon → Ho Chi Minh City	Сайго́н *nm*
Siam → Thailand	Сиа́м *nm*
Sinkiang → Xinjiang	Синцзя́н *nm*
Soviet Union → Russian Federation, etc.	Сове́тский Сою́з *nm*
Stalingrad → Volgograd	Сталингра́д *nm*
Timbuktu → Tombouctou	Тимбукту́ *nf*
Transjordan → Jordan	Трансиорда́ния *nf*

See also **INHABITANTS AND ETHNIC GROUPS, LANGUAGES OF THE WORLD**

INHABITANTS AND ETHNIC GROUPS

GLOBAL AREAS AND CONTINENTS

African	африка́нец *nm*, африка́нка *nf*
Afro-Asian	а́фро-азиа́т, -ка *nmf*
Anglo-American	англо-америка́нец *nm*, а́нгло-америка́нка *nf*
Asian	азиа́т, -ка *nmf*
Caucasian	кавка́зец *nm*, кавка́зка *nf*
Eurasian	еврази́ец *nm*, еврази́йка *nf*
European	европе́ец *nm*, европе́йка *nf*
Iberian	ибе́р, ибери́ец *nm*
Latino, Latin-American	латиноамерика́нец *nm*, латино-америка́нка *nf*
Levantine	леванти́нец *nm*, леванти́нка *nf*
Macedonian	македо́нец *nm*, македо́нка *nf*
Melanesian	меланези́ец *nm*, меланези́йка *nf*
North American	североамерика́нец *nm*, североамерика́нка *nf*
Polynesian	полинези́ец *nm*, полинези́йка *nf*
Scandinavian	скандина́в, -ка *nmf*

South American	южноамерика́нец *nm*, южноамерика́нка *nf*
West Indian	жи́тель(ница) Вест-И́ндии *nmf*

ISLANDS AND ISLAND COUNTRIES

Aleut	алеу́т, -ка *nmf*
Barbadian	барбадо́сец *nm*, барбадо́ска *nf*
Corsican	корсика́нец *nm*, корсика́нка *nf*
Cretan	критя́нин *nm*, критя́нка *nf*
Croat	хорва́т, -ка *nmf*
Cuban	куби́нец *nm*, куби́нка *nf*
Cypriot	киприо́т, -ка *nmf*
Dominican	доминика́нец *nm*, доминика́нка *nf*
Fijian	фиджи́ец *nm*, фиджи́йка *nf*
Greenlander	гренла́ндец *nm*, гренла́ндка *nf*
Guyanese (*pl* Guyanese)	гайа́нец *nm*, гайа́нка *nf*
Haitian	гаитя́нин *nm*, гаитя́нка *nf*
Hawaiian	гава́ец *nm*, гава́йка *nf*
Icelander	исла́ндец *nm*, исла́ндка *nf*
Jamaican	яма́ец *nm*, яма́йка *nf*
Japanese (*pl* Japanese)	япо́нец *nm*, япо́нка *nf*
Javanese (*pl* Javanese)	ява́нец *nm*, ява́нка *nf*
Malagasy	малагаси́ец *nm*, малагаси́йка *nf*
Maltese (*pl* Maltese)	мальти́ец *nm*, мальти́йка *nf*
Papuan	папуа́с, -ка *nmf*
Phillipine, Filipino	филиппи́нец *nm*, филиппи́нка *nf*
Puerto Rican	пуэрторика́нец *nm*, пуэрторика́нка *nf*
Samoan	самоа́нец *nm*, самоа́нка *nf*
Sardinian	сарди́нец *nm*, жи́тельница Сарди́нии *nf*, *nf*
Sicilian	сицили́ец, -ка *nmf*
Sin(g)halese (*pl* Sin(g)halese)	синга́лец *nm*, синга́л, -ка *nmf*
Sri Lankan	ланкие́ц *nm*, жи́тельница Шри-Ла́нки *nf*, *nf*
Sumatrian	жи́тель(ница) Сума́тры *nmf*
Tahitian	таитя́нин *nm*, таитя́нка *nmf*
Tasmanian	тасма́нец *nm*, тасма́нка *nf*
Tunisian	туни́сец *nm*, туни́ска *nf*
Zanzibari	занзиба́рец *nm*
Zulu	зулу́с, -ка *nmf*

OTHER COUNTRIES

Afghan	афга́нец *nm*, афга́нка *nf*
Albanian	алба́нец *nm*, алба́нка *nf*
Algerian	алжи́рец *nm*, алжи́рка *nf*
American	америка́нец *nm*, америка́нка *nf*
Angolan	анго́лец *nm*, анго́лка *nf*
Argentine, Argentinian	аргенти́нец *nm*, аргенти́нка *nf*
Armenian	армяни́н *nm*, армя́нка *nf*
Australian	австрали́ец *nm*, австрали́йка *nf*
Austrian	австри́ец *nm*, австри́йка *nf*
Azerbaijani	азербайджа́нец *nm*, азербайджа́нка *nf*
Bangladeshi	бангладе́шец *nm*, бангладе́шка *nf*
Belarussian, Byelorrusian	белору́с *nm* белоруска *nf*
Belgian	бельги́ец *nm*, бельги́йка *nf*
Bolivian	боливи́ец *nm*, боливи́йка *nf*
Brazilian	брази́лец *nm*, бразилья́нка *nf*
British (people), the	брита́нцы *nmpl*
Britisher	брита́нец *nm*, брита́нка *nf*
Bulgar, Bulgarian	болга́рин *nm*, болга́рка *nf*
Cambodian	камбоджи́ец *nm*, камбоджи́йца *nf*

Canadian	кана́дец *nm*, кана́дка *nf*
Chilean	чили́ец *nm*, чили́йка *nf*
Chinese	кита́ец *nm*, китая́нка *nf*
Colombian	колумби́ец *nm*, колумби́йка *nf*
Congolese (*pl* Congolese)	конголе́зец *nm*, конголе́зка *nf*
Costa Rican	костарика́нец *nm*, костарика́нка *nf*
Czech	чех *nm*, че́шка *nf*
Dane	датча́нин *nm*, датча́нка *nf*
Ecuadorean	эквадо́рец *nm*, эквадо́рка *nf*
Egyptian	египтя́нин *nm*, египтя́нка *nf*
English (people), the	англича́не *nmpl*
Englishman (*pl* Englishmen)	англича́нин *nm*
Englishwoman (*pl* Englishwomen)	англича́нка *nf*
Estonian	эсто́нец *nm*, эсто́нка *nf*
Ethiopian	эфио́п, -ка *nmf*
Finn	финн *nm*, финка *nf*
French, the (people)	францу́зы *nmpl*
Frenchman (*pl* Frenchmen)	францу́з *nm*
Frenchwoman (*pl* Frenchwomen)	францу́женка *nf*
Ghanaian	га́нец *nm*, га́нца *nf*
Greek	грек *nm*, греча́нка *nf*
Guatemalan	гватема́лец *nm*, гватема́лца *nf*
Guinean	гвине́ец *nm*, гвине́йка *nf*
Honduran	гондура́сец *nm*, гондура́ска *nf*
Hungarian	венгр, венге́рец *nm*, венге́рка *nf*
Indian (Asian)	инди́ец *nm*, индиа́нка *nf*
Indonesian	индонези́ец *nm*, индонези́йка *nf*
Iranian	ира́нец *nm*, ира́нка *nf*
Iraqi	ира́кец *nm*, ира́чка *nf*
Irish (people), the	ирла́ндцы *nmpl*
Irishman (*pl* Irishmen)	ирла́ндец *nm*
Irishwoman (*pl* Irishwomen)	ирла́ндка *nf*
Israeli	израильтя́нин *nm*, израильтя́нка *nf*
Italian	италья́нец *nm*, италья́нка *nf*
Japanese (*pl* Japanese)	япо́нец *nm*, япо́нка *nf*
Jordanian	иорда́нец *nm*, иорда́нка *nf*
Kazakh	каза́к *nm*, каза́чка *nf*
Kenyan	кени́ец *nm*, кени́йка *nf*
Kirghiz	кирги́з, -ка *nmf*
Korean	коре́ец *nm*, корея́нка *nf*
Kuwaiti	куве́йтец *nm*, куве́йтка *nf*
Lao, Laotian	лао́сец *nm*, лао́ска *nf*
Latvian, Lett	латы́ш, -ка *nmf*
Lebanese (*pl* Lebanese)	лива́нец *nm*, лива́нка *nf*
Liberian	либери́ец *nm*, либери́йка *nf*
Libyan	ливи́ец *nm*, ливи́йка *nf*
Lithuanian	лито́вец *nm*, лито́вка *nf*
Luxemb(o)urger	люксембу́ржец *nm*, люксембу́рженка *nf*
Malay, Malaysian	мала́ец *nm*, мала́йка *nf*
Malian	мали́ец *nm*, мали́йка *nf*
Mauritanian	маврита́нец *nm*, маврита́нка *nf*
Mexican	мексика́нец *nm*, мексика́нка *nf*
Mongol, Mongolian	монго́л, -ка *nmf*
Moroccan	марокка́нец *nm*, марокка́нка *nf*
Namibian	намиби́ец *nm*, намиби́йка *nf*
Nepalese, Nepali (*pl* Nepalese)	непа́лец *nm*, непа́лца *nf*
Netherlander	нидерла́ндец *nm*, нидерла́ндка *nf*
New Zealander	новозела́ндец *nm*, новозела́ндка *nf*
Nicaraguan	никарагуа́нец *nm*, никарагуа́нка *nf*
Nigerian	нигери́ец *nm*, нигери́йка *nf*
Norwegian	норве́жец *nm*, норве́жка *nf*

Pakistani	пакиста́нец *nm*, пакиста́нка *nf*
Panamanian	жи́тель(ница) Пана́мы *nmf*
Paraguayan	парагва́ец *nm*, парагва́йка *nf*
Peruvian	перуа́нец *nm*, перуа́нка *nf*
Pole	поля́к *nm*, по́лька *nf*
Portuguese (*pl* Portuguese)	португа́лец *nm*, португа́лка *nf*
Romanian	румы́н, -ка *nmf*
Russian [country]	ру́сский *nm*, ру́сская *nf*
Russian [federation]	россия́нин *nm*, россия́нка *nf*
Salvadoran	сальвадо́рец *nm*, сальвадо́рка *nf*
Saudi, Saudi-Arabian	сау́довец *nm*, сау́довка *nf*
Scotch (people), the	шотла́ндцы *nmpl*
Senegalese (*pl* Senegalese)	сенега́лец *nm*, сенегалка *nf*
Serb	серб, -ка *nmf*
Somali, Somalian	сомали́ец *nm*, сомали́йка *nf*
South African	южноафрика́нец *nm*, южноафри́канка *nf*
Spaniard	испа́нец *nm*, испа́нка *nf*
Spanish (people), the	испа́нцы *nmpl*
Sudanese (*pl* Sudanese)	суда́нец *nm*, суда́нка *nf*
Swede	швед, -ка *nmf*
Swiss	швейца́рец *nm*, швейца́рка *nf*
Swiss (people), the	швейца́рцы *nmpl*
Syrian	сири́ец *nm*, сири́йка *nf*
Tajik	таджи́к *nm*, таджи́чка *nf*
Tanzanian	танзани́ец *nm*, танзани́йка *nf*
Thai	таила́ндец *nm*, таила́ндка *nf*
Tibetan	тибе́тец *nm*, тибе́тка *nf*
Togolese	тоголе́зец *nm*, тоголе́зка *nf*
Turk	ту́рок *nm*, турча́нка *nf*
Ugandan	уга́ндец *nm*, уга́ндка *nf*
Ukranian	украи́нец *nm*, украи́нка *nf*
Uruguayan	уругва́ец *nm*, уругва́йка *nf*
Uzbek	узбе́к *nm*, узбе́чка *nf*
Venezuelan	венесу́элец *nm*, венесу́элка *nf*
Vietnamese (*pl* Vietnamese)	вьетна́мец *nm*, вьетна́мка *nf*
Yemeni, Yemenite	йе́менец *nm*, йе́менка *nf*
Zairian	заи́рец *nm*, заи́рка *nf*
Zambian	замби́ец *nm*, замби́йка *nf*
Zimbabwean	зимбабви́ец *nm*, зимбабви́йка *nf*

REGIONS WITHIN COUNTRIES

Alaskan	аля́скинец *nm*, аля́скинка *nf*
Alsatian	эльза́сец *nm*, эльза́ска *nf*
Andalucian	андалу́зец *nm*, андалу́зка *nf*
Basque	баск *nm*, баско́нка *nf*
Bavarian	бава́рец *nm*, бава́рка *nf*
Bengali	бенга́лец *nm*, бенга́лка *nf*
Bohemian	боге́мец *nm*, боге́мка *nf*
Breton	брето́нец *nm*, брето́нка *nf*
Californian	калифорни́ец *nm*, калифорни́йка *nf*
Catalan	катало́нец *nm*, катало́нка *nf*
Crimean	крымча́нин *nm*, крымча́нка *nf*
French-Canadian	кана́дец-француз *nm*, кана́дка-францу́женка *nf*
Gascon	гаско́нец *nm*, гаско́нка *nf*
Karelian	каре́л *nm*, каре́лка *nf*
Kashmiri	кашми́рец *nm*, кашми́рка *nf*
Laplander, Lapp	лапла́ндец *nm*, лапла́ндка *nf*
Manchu (*pl* Manchus or Manchu)	маньчжу́р *nm*, маньчжу́рка *nf*

Moldavian	молдава́нин *nm*, молдава́нка *nf*
Norman	норма́ндец *nm*, норма́ндка *nf*
Osset, Ossetian	осети́н *nm*, осети́нка *nf*
Palestinian	палести́нец *nm*, палести́нка *nf*
Provençal	провансálец *nm*, провансálка *nf*
Prussian	прусса́к *nm*, прусса́чка *nf*
Punjabi, Panjabi	пенджа́бец *nm*, пенджа́бка *nf*
Savoyard	савойя́р, -ка *nmf*
Scotsman (*pl* Scotsmen)	шотла́ндец *nm*
Scotswoman (*pl* Scotswomen)	шотла́ндка *nf*
Siberian	сибиря́к *nm*, сибиря́чка *nf*
Slovak, Slovakian	слова́к *nm*, слова́чка *nf*
Slovene, Slovenian	слове́нец *nm*, слове́нка *nf*
Turkmen	туркме́н, -ка *nmf*
Tyrolean, Tirolean	тиро́лец *nm*, тиро́лька *nf*
Uighur	уйгу́р, -ка *nmf*
Volga region inhabitant	волжа́нин, волга́рь *nm*, волжа́нка *nf*
Walloon	валло́нец *nm*, валло́нка *nf*
Welshman (*pl* Welshmen)	уэ́льсец *nm*
Welshwoman (*pl* Welshwomen)	уроже́нка Уэ́льса *nf*, *nm*
Westphalian	вестфа́лец *nm*, вестфа́лка *nf*
Yakut	яку́т, -ка *nmf*
Yankee	я́нки *nm*, *indecl*

CITIES

Athenian	афи́нянин *nm*, афи́нянка *nf*
Berliner	берли́нец *nm*, берли́нка *nf*
Cantonese	канто́нец *nm*, канто́нка *nf*
Dubliner	ду́блинец *nm*, ду́блинка *nf*
Florentine	флоренти́нец *nm*, флоренти́нка *nf*
Genoese, Genovese (*pl* Genoese)	генуэ́зец *nm*, генуэ́зка *nf*
Glaswegian	жи́тель(ница) Гла́зго *nmf*
Kievan	киевля́нин *nm*, киевля́нка *nf*
Londoner	ло́ндонец *nm*, ло́ндонка *nf*
Muscovite	москви́ч, -ка *nmf*
Neapolitan	неаполита́нец *nm*, неаполита́нка *nf*
Odessan	одесси́т, -ка *nmf*
Oxfordian	оксфо́рдец *nm*, оксфо́рдка *nf*
Parisian	парижа́нин *nm*, парижа́нка *nf*
Parisienne	парижа́нка *nf*
Singaporean	сингапу́рец *nm*, сингапу́рка *nf*
St. Petersburger	(санкт-)петербу́ржец *nm*, (санкт-)петербу́ржа́нка *nf*
Venetian	венециа́нец *nm*, венецианка *nf*
Viennese	ве́нец *nm*, ве́нка *nf*
Washingtonian	жи́тель(ница) Вашингто́на *nmf*

ETHNIC MINORITIES

American Indian tribes

Apache	апа́чи *nmf*, *indecl*
Arapaho	ара́пахо *nmf*, *indecl*
Cayuga	каю́га *nmf*, *indecl*
Cherokee	черокéз(ец) *nm*, черокéзка *nf*
Cheyenne	чейе́н *nmf*
Choctaw	чо́кто *nmf*, *indecl*
Comanche	кома́нчи *nmf*, *indecl*
Guarani	гуара́ни *nmf*, *indecl*
Hopi	хо́пи *nmf*, *indecl*
Huron	гуро́н *nm*
Iroquois	ироке́з *nm*
Mohawk	мо́хаук *nm*
Mohican	могика́нин *nm*
Navajo, Navaho	на́вахо *nmf*, *indecl*
Pima	пи́ма *nmf*, *indecl*
Quechua	ке́чуа *nmf*, *indecl*
Seneca	се́нека *nmf*, *indecl*
Shawnee	шо́ни *nmf*, *indecl*
Shoshone	шошо́н *nm*
Sioux	сиу́ *nmf*
Ute	ю́т *nm*
Yuma	ю́ма *nf*, *indecl*

peoples in the Russian Federation

Bashkir	башки́р, -ка *nmf*
Buryat	буря́т, -ка *nmf*
Chuckchi	чу́кча *nmf*
Chuvash	чу́ваш, -ка *nmf*
Daghestani	дагеста́нец *nm*, дагеста́нка *nf*
Kalmyk, Kalmuck	калмы́к *nm*, калмы́чка *nf*
Karakalpak	каракалпа́к *nm*, каракалпа́чка *nf*
Mari	мари́ец *nm*, мари́йка *nf*
Nenets	не́нец *nm*, не́нка *nf*
Samoyed [obs]	самое́д, -ка *nmf*
Tarta, Tatar	тата́рин *nm*, тата́рка *nf*
Tatars, the	тата́ры *nfpl*

other ethnic groups

Afrikaner	африка́нер *nm*
Afro-American	америка́нский негр *nm*
Ainu	айн *nmf*
Arab	ара́б, -ка *nmf*
Berber	бербе́р, -ка *nmf*
Chicano, Chicana	чика́но *nm*, чика́на *nf*
Creole	крео́л, -ка *nmf*
Eskimo	эскимо́с, -ка *nmf*
Fleming	флама́ндец *nm*, флама́ндка *nf*
Flemish, the (people)	флама́ндцы *npl*
Hottentot	готтенто́т, -ка *nmf*
Khmer	кхмер *nm*
Kurd	курд, -ка *nmf*
Magyar	мадья́р, -ка *nmf*
Maori	ма́ори *nmf, indecl*
Neorican	неорика́нец *nm*, неорика́нка *nf*
sabra	са́бра *nmf*
nisei (*pl* nisei or neiseis)	нисе́и *nmpl*
Sin(g)halese (*pl* Sing(g)halese)	синга́лец *nm*, синга́лка *nf*
Slav	славяни́н *nm*, славя́нка *nf*
Slavs, the Slavic people	славя́не *nmpl*
Tamil	тами́л, -ка *nmf*
Telugu	телу́гу *nmf*

OBSOLETE DESIGNATIONS

Abyssinian	абисси́нец *nm*, абисси́нка *nf*
Boer	бур *nm*
Burmese (*pl* Burmese)	бирма́нец *nm*, бирма́нка *nf*
Ceylonese (*pl* Ceylonese)	цейло́нец *nm*, цейло́нка *nf*
Cheremis	череми́с *nm*
Hollander	голла́ндец *nm*
Kampuchean	кампучи́ец *nm*, кампучи́йка *nf*
Leningrader	ленингра́дец *nm*, ленингра́дка *nf*
Persian	перс *nm*, персия́нка *nf*
Rhodesian	родези́ец *nm*, родези́йка *nf*
Saxon	саксо́нец *nm*, саксо́нка *nf*
Siamese (*pl* Siamese)	сиа́мец *nm*, сиа́мка *nf*
Yugoslav(ian)	югосла́в, -ка *nmf*

SPECIAL INTERESTS AND ATTITUDES

scholars

Africanist	африкани́ст *nm*
Egyptologist	египто́лог *nm*
Orientalist	ориентали́ст *nm*
Sinologist	сино́лог *nm*
Slavicist, Slavist	слави́ст *nm*

love-hate relationships

Anglophile	англофи́л *nm*
Anglophobe	англофо́б *nm*
Anglophobia	англофо́бство *nm*, англофо́бия *nf*
Francophile	франкофи́л *nm*
Francophobe	франкофо́б *nm*
Francophobia	франкофо́бия *nf*
Germanophile	германофи́л *nm*
Germanophobe	германофо́б *nm*
Germanophobia	германофо́бия *nf*
Russophile	русофи́л *nm*
Russophobe	русофо́б *nm*
Russophobia	русофо́бия *nf*

other terms

Africanism	африкани́зм *nm*
Africanization	африканиза́ция *nf*
Americanization	американиза́ция *nf*
Americanize	американизи́ровать *impf, pf*
Europeanization	европеиза́ция *nf*

Europeanize	европеизи́ровать *impf, pf*
Orientalism	ориентали́зм *nm*
Panhellenism	панэллини́зм *nm*
Russification	русифика́ция *nf*
Russify	русифици́ровать *impf, pf*

See also **ANTHROPOLOGY**, **PLACE NAMES I: PHYSICAL ENTITIES**, **HISTORY AND ARCHEOLOGY** *(specializations)*, **LANGUAGES OF THE WORLD**

Times Long Past

HISTORY AND ARCHEOLOGY ◆ THE BIBLE ◆ CLASSICAL MYTHOLOGY ◆ ANCIENT CIVILIZATIONS

HISTORY AND ARCHEOLOGY

GENERAL TERMS

Archaic	архаи́ческий *aj*, архаи́чный *aj*
archeology (BR archaeology)	археоло́гия *nf*
chronology	хроноло́гия *nf*
civilization	цивилиза́ция *nf*
date	да́та *nf*
epoch	эпо́ха *nf*
era	э́ра *nf*
fact	факт *nm*
historic(al)	истори́ческий *aj*
historically	истори́чески *av*
historicity	истори́чность *nf*
period	пери́од *nm*
prehistory	доисто́рия *nf*
radiocarbon dating	датиро́вка радиоугле-ро́дным ме́тодом *nf*, *nm*

SPECIALIZATIONS

kinds of history

cultural	культу́рный *aj*
diplomatic	дипломати́ческий *aj*
economic	экономи́ческий *aj*
intellectual	интеллектуа́льный *aj*
political	полити́ческий *aj*
social	социа́льный *aj*

allied fields

anthropology	антрополо́гия *nf*
archeology	археоло́гия *nf*
demography	демогра́фия *nf*
glottochronology	глоттохроноло́гия *nf*
historiography	историогра́фия *nf*
linguistics *nplsv*	лингви́стика *nf*
numismatics *nplsv*	нумизма́тика *nf*
paleobotany (BR palaebotany)	палеобота́ника *nf*
paleography (BR palaeography)	палеогра́фия *nf*
philology	филоло́гия *nf*
technography	техногра́фия *nf*

area studies

Assyriology	ассириоло́гия *nf*
Egyptology	египтоло́гия *nf*
Oriental studies	ориентали́стика *nf*
Sinology	синоло́гия *nf*

ASPECTS OF HISTORY

time divisions

antiquity	анти́чность *nf*
classical	класси́ческий *aj*
colonial	колониа́льный *aj*
feudal	феода́льный *aj*
prehistoric	доистори́ческий *aj*

fact sources

ancient ruins	дре́вние руи́ны *nfpl*
annals	анна́лы *nmpl*
autobiography	автобиогра́фия *nf*
Bible	Би́блия *nf*
biography	биогра́фия *nf*
correspondence	корреспонде́нция *nf*
document	докуме́нт *nm*
folklore	фолькло́р *nm*
genealogy	генеало́гия *nf*
legend	леге́нда *nf*
memoirs	мемуа́ры *nmpl*
myth	миф *nm*
publication	публика́ция *nf*
registry (office)	регистрату́ра *nf*

recording, preservation, and remembrance

antique	анти́к *nm*
archives *npl*	архи́в *nm*
film	фильм *nm*
memorial	мемориа́л *nm*
monument	монуме́нт *nm*
museum	музе́й *nm*
relic	рели́кт *nm*, рели́квия *nf*
restoration	реставра́ция *nf*

retrospective	ретроспекти́ва *nf*
Smithsonian (Museum)	Смитсо́ниан *nm*

prehistoric artifacts

cartouche	карту́ш *nm*
cromlech	кро́млех *nm*
dolmen	дольме́н *nm*
eolith	эоли́т *nm*
heraldry	гера́льдика *nf*
megalith	мегали́т *nm*
menhir	менги́р *nm*
paleolith (BR palaeolith)	палеоли́т *nm*
petroglyph	петро́глиф *nm*

HISTORICAL FACTS

periods

Atomic Age	а́томный век *nm*
Byzantine	византи́йский *aj*
Edwardian	эдвардиа́нский *aj*
Elizabethan	елизаве́тинский *aj*
Greco-Roman	гре́ко-ри́мский *aj*
Hellenic, Hellenistic	э́ллинский, эллинисти́ческий *aj*
Jazz Age	век джа́за *nm*, *nm*
Machine Age	век маши́н *nm*, *nfpl*
Mycenaen	мике́нский *aj*
Napoleonic	наполео́новский *aj*
Soviet Era	сове́тская эпо́ха *nf*
Victorian	викториа́нский *aj*

empires

Austria-Hungary	А́встро-Ве́нгрия *nf*
Byzantine Empire	Византи́я *nf*
Ottoman Empire	Оттома́нская импе́рия *nf*
Roman Empire	Ри́мская импе́рия *nf*

events

Counter-Reformation	контрреформа́ция *nf*
Inquisition	инквизи́ция *nf*
Reformation	Реформа́ция *nf*
Renaissance	Ренесса́нс *nm*
Restoration	Реставра́ция *nf*

European dynasties

Hapsburg	Га́бсбург *nm*
Plantagenet	Планта́генет *nm*
Romanov	Рома́нов *nm*
Tudor	Тюдо́р *nm*
Windsor	Уи́ндсор, Ви́ндзор *nm*

extinct groups

Angles	а́нглы *nmpl*
Aryan	ари́ец *nm*
Aztec	ацте́к *nm*
Byzantine	византи́ец *nm*
Celt	кельт *nm*
Corinthian	кори́нфянин *nm*
Cossack	каза́к *nm*, каза́чка *nf*
Frank	франк *nm*
Golden Horde	Золота́я Орда́ *nf*
Goth	гот *nm*
Hellene	э́ллин *nm*
Hun	гунн *nm*
Hussite	гуси́т *nm*
Inca	и́нка *nmf*
Junker	ю́нкер *nm*
Jute	ют *nm*
Norman	норма́нн *nm*
Osman	осма́н *nm*
Ostrogoth	остго́т *nm*
Ottoman	оттома́н *nm*
Saracen	сараци́н *nm*
Saxon	сакс *nm*
Viking	ви́кинг *nm*
Visigoth	вестго́т *nm*

PERSONS

historians

antiquarian	антиква́рий *nm*
antiquary, antique dealer	антиква́р *nm*
archeologist (BR archaeologist)	археолог *nm*
archivist	архива́риус *nm*
chronologer	хроно́лог *nm*
Egyptologist	египто́лог *nm*
Hellenist	эллини́ст *nm*
historian	исто́рик *nm*
historiographer	историо́граф *nm*
medievalist	медиеви́ст *nm*
numismatist	нумизма́т *nm*
paleographer (BR palaeographer)	палео́граф *nm*

other persons of the past

boyars *npl*	боя́рство *nn*
burgher	бю́ргер *nm*

coolie	ку́ли *nm, indecl*
feudal lord	феода́л *nm*
herald	геро́льд *nm*
hussar	гуса́р *nm*
infanta	инфа́нта *nf*
infante	инфа́нт *nm*
kulak	кула́к *nm*
moujik, muzhik	мужи́к *nm*
paladin	палади́н *nm*
peon	пео́н *nm*
pioneer	пионе́р, -ка *nmf*
pirate	пира́т *nm*
seneschal	сенеша́ль *nm*
vassal	васса́л *nm*
yeoman	йо́мен *nm*

See also **POLITICS AND GOVERNMENT**, **ANTHROPOLOGY**, **ANIMALS** *(extinct animals)*, **ANCIENT CIVILIZATIONS**, **TITLES** *(kinds of titles)*, **THE MILITARY ESTABLISHMENT** *(historical terms)*, **FAMOUS FIGURES OF YESTERDAY AND TODAY**, and terms marked "[obs]" or "historical" in other topics

THE BIBLE

GENERAL TERMS

apostle	апо́стол *nm*
devil	дья́вол *nm*
epistle	эпи́стола *nf*
Mosaic law	Моисе́евы зако́ны *nmpl*
original text	оригина́льный текст *nm*
patriarch	патриа́рх *nm*
psalm	псало́м *nm*
seraph (*pl* seraphim)	серафи́м *nm*
synagog(ue)	синаго́га *nf*
Vulgate	Вульга́та *nf*

NAMES IN THE OLD TESTAMENT

prophets

Amos	Амо́с *nm*
Balaam	Валаа́м *nm*
Elijah	Илия́, Илья́ *nm*
Elisha	Елисе́й *nm*
Ezekiel	Иезеки́иль *nm*
Ezra	Е́зра, Е́здра *nm*
Hosea	Оси́я *nm*
Isaiah	Иса́йя *nm*
Jeremiah	Иереми́я *nm*
Micah	Михе́й *nm*
Nahum	Нау́м *nm*
Zachariah, Zechariah	Заха́рия *nm*

other books

Daniel	Дании́л *nm*
Ecclesiastes	Екклесиа́ст *nm*
Esther	Эсфи́рь *nf*
Exodus	Исхо́д *nm*
Job	Ио́в *nm*
Jonah	Ио́на *nm*
Leviticus	Леви́т *nm*
Psalms	Пса́лмы *npl*
Ruth	Руфь *nf*
Samuel	Самуи́л *nm*

patriarchs

Abraham	Авраа́м *nm*
Isaac	Исаа́к *nm*
Jacob	Иа́ков *nm*

matriarchs

Leah	Ли́я *nf*
Rachel	Рахи́ль *nf*
Rebecca	Реве́кка *nf*
Sarah	Са́рра *nf*

other women

Bathsheba	Вирса́вия *nf*
Deborah	Де́вора *nf*
Delilah	Дали́да *nf*
Eve	Е́ва *nf*
Jezebel	Иезаве́ль *nf*
Judith	Иу́дифь *nf*
Naomi	Ноеми́нь *nf*

kings

Ahab	Аха́в *nm*
Balshazzar	Валтаса́р *nm*
David	Дави́д *nm*
Jeroboam	Иерово́ам *nm*
Josiah	Иоси́я *nm*
Pharaoh	фарао́н *nm*
Saul	Сау́л *nm*
Solomon	Соломо́н *nm*

other men

Aaron	Аро́н, Ааро́н *nm*
Abel	А́вель *nm*
Absalom	Авессало́м *nm*
Adam	Ада́м *nm*
Benjamin	Вениами́н *nm*
Cain	Ка́ин *nm*
Emmanuel, Immanuel	Иммануи́л *nm*
Enoch	Ено́х *nm*
Esau	Иса́в *nm*

Gideon	Гидеóн *nm*
Goliath	Голиáф *nm*
Ham	Хам *nm*
Hezekiah	Езекúя *nm*
Ishmael	Исмаúл *nm*
Japheth	Иáфет *nm*
Jonathan	Ионафáн *nm*
Joseph	Иóсиф *nm*
Joshua	Иешýа *nm*
Judah	Иýда *nm*
Lot	Лот *nm*
Methuselah	Мафусаúл *nm*
Moses	Моисéй *nm*
Nathan	Натáн *nm*
Nehemiah	Неемúя *nm*
Nimrod	Нúмрод *nm*
Noah	Ной *nm*
Samson	Самсóн *nm*
Seth	Сет *nm*
Shem	Сим *nm*
Uriah	Урúя *nm*
Jehoshaphat	Иосафáт *nm*

peoples and tribes

Hamites	хамúт *nm*
Hebrew	еврéй *nm*
Hittites	хéтты *npl*
Israelites	израильтяне *nmpl*
Levite	левúт *nm*
Maccabees	Маккавéи *npl*
Philistines	филистúмляне *nmpl*
Samaritans	самаритяне *npl*

NAMES IN THE NEW TESTAMENT

Gospels

John	Иоáнн *nm*
Luke	Лукá *nm*
Mark	Марк *nm*
Matthew	Матфéй *nm*

Epistles and other books

Apocrypha	апóкрифы *nmpl*
Colossians	колоссяне *nmpl*
Ephesians	ефéсяне *nmpl*
Galatians	галáты *nmpl*
Hebrews	еврéи *nmpl*
Jude	Иýда *nm*
Philemon	Филемóн *nm*
Romans	рúмляне *nmpl*

disciples

Andrew	Андрéй *nm*
Bartholomew	Варфоломéй *nm*
John	Иоáнн *nm*
Judas Iscariat	Иýда Искáриот *nm*
Matthew	Матфéй *nm*
Matthias	Матфúй *nm*
Philip	Филúпп *nm*
Simon	Сúмон *nm*
Thaddeus	Фаддéй *nm*
Thomas	Фомá *nm*

the three Magi

Balthasar	Валтасáр *nm*
Gaspar	Гаспáр *nm*
Melchor	Мельхиóр *nm*

other men and women

Ananias	Ананúя *nm*
Barabbas	Варáвва *nm*
Ephraim	Ефраúм *nm*
Gamaliel	Гамалиúл *nm*
Herod	Йрод *nm*
Herodias	Иродиáда *nf*
Jesus	Исýс *nm*
Lazarus	Лазáрь *nm*
Mary Magdalene	Марúя Магдалúна *nf*
Mary	Марúя *nf*
Nathanael	Нафанаúл *nm*
Paul	Пáвел *nm*
Pontius Pilot	Пóнтий Пилáт *nm*
Salome	Саломéя *nf*
Stephen	Стефáн *nm*
Titus	Тит *nm*
Zebedee	Зеведéй *nm*

members of sects and groups

Amalekite	амалекитянин *nm*
Canaanites	хананéи *npl*
Edomite	эдомитянин *nm*
Ephesian	ефесянин *nm*
Essene	ессéй *nm*
Magi	мáги *npl*
Nazarene	назарéй *nm*
Pharisee	фарисéй *nm*
Sadducee	саддукéй *nm*
Sanhedrin	Синедриóн *nm*
Semite	семúт *nm*
Zealots	зилóты *nmpl*

SUPERNATURAL BEINGS

gods and angels

Adonai	Адонáй *nm*
Apollyon	Аполлиóн *nm*

Christ	Христос *nm*
Gabriel	Гаврии́л *nm*
Jehovah	Иегова́ *nm*
Mammon	мамо́на *nf*
Messiah	месси́я *nm*
Michael	Михаи́л *nm*
Raphael	Рафаи́л *nm*
Yahweh, Yahveh	Я́хве *nm, indecl*

names for the devil

Beelzebub	Вельзеву́л *nm*
Belial	Велиа́р *nm*
Lucifer	Люцифе́р *nm*
Satan	Сатана́ *nm*

PLACES

Abaddon	Авaддо́н *nm*
Armageddon	Армагеддо́н *nm*
Canaan	Ханаа́н *nm*
Damascus	Дама́ск *nm*
Eden	Эде́м *nm*
Egypt	Еги́пет *nm*
Galilee	Галиле́я *nf*
Garden of Eden	сад Эде́мский *nm*
Gehenna	Гее́нна *nf*
Gethsemane	Гефсима́ния *nf*
Golgotha	Голго́фа *nf*
Gomorrah	Гомо́рра *nf*
Jericho	Иерихо́н *nm*
Jerusalem	Иерусали́м *nm*
Judea	Иуде́я *nf*
Nazareth	Назаре́т *nm*
Nineveh	Нине́вия *nf*
Palestine	Палести́на *nf*
Salem	Са́лим *nm*
Samaria	Самари́я *nf*
Sinai	Сина́й *nm*
Sodom	Содо́м *nm*
Tarsus	Та́рс *nm*
Ur	Ур *nm*
Zion	Сио́н *nm*

OTHER BIBLICAL VOCABULARY

events

Apocalypse	Апока́липсис *nm*
Decalogue	Декало́г *nm*

creatures

behemoth	бегемо́т *nm*
cherub	херуви́м *nm*
leviathan	левиафа́н *nm*
scorpion	скорпио́н *nm*

things

Cain, the mark of	ка́инова печа́ть *nf*
Jacob's ladder	ле́стница Иа́кова *nf, nm*
manna	ма́нна небе́сная *nf*
myrrh	ми́рра *nf*
Noah's ark	Но́ев ковче́г *nm*
Solomon's seal	Соломо́нова печа́ть *nf*
Tower of Babel	вавило́нская ба́шня *nf*

See also **RELIGION, ANCIENT CIVILIZATIONS, FICTION AND FOLKLORE**

CLASSICAL MYTHOLOGY

GENERAL TERMS

anthropomorphism	антропоморфи́зм *nm*
empyrean	эмпире́й *nm*
Furies	фу́рии *nfpl*
Grace	гра́ция *nf*
Graces, the three	три гра́ции *nfpl*
legend	леге́нда *nf*
Muse	му́за *nf*
myth-making	мифотво́рчество *nn*
mythic(al)	мифи́ческий *aj*
mythology	миф *nm*
oracle	ора́кул *nm*
personification	персонифика́ция *nf*
theogony	теого́ния *nf*

GREEK MYTHOLOGY

gods

Aeolus	Эо́л *nm*
Alpheus	Алфе́й *nm*
Apollo	Аполло́н *nm*
Ares	А́рес, Аре́й *nm*
Asclepius	Аскле́пий *nm*
Boreas	Боре́й *nm*
Chaos	Ха́ос *nm*
Comus	Ком, Ко́мус *nm*
Dionysius	Диони́с *nm*
Eos	Э́ос *nm*
Eros	Э́рос *nm*
Helios	Ге́лиос *nm*
Hephaestus	Гефе́ст *nm*
Hermes	Герме́с *nm*
Hymen	Гимене́й *nm*
Hypnos	Ги́пнос *nm*
Momus	Мо́мус, Мом *nm*
Morpheus	Морфе́й *nm*
Olympian	олимпи́ец *nm*
Pan	Пан *nm*
Phoebus	Феб *nm*

Pluto	Плутóн *nm*
Poseidon	Посéйдон *nm*
Priapus	Приáп *nm*
Proteus	Протéй *nm*
Thanatos	Танатóс *nm*
Triton	Тритóн *nm*
Uranus	Урáн *nm*
Zephyrus	Зéфир *nm*
Zeus	Зевс *nm*

goddesses

Aphrodite	Афродúта *nf*
Artemis	Артемúда *nf*
Astr(a)ea	Астрéя *nf*
Ata	Áте, Áта *nf*
Athena	Афúна *nf*
Demeter	Демéтра *nf*
Gaea, Gaia	Гéя *nf*
Hebe	Гéба *nf*
Hecate	Гекáта *nf*
Hera	Гéра *nf*
Hestia	Гéстия *nf*
Horae, Hours	Гóры, Óры *nfpl*
Iris	Ирúда *nf*
Nemesis	Немезúда *nf*
Nike	Нúка *nf*
Nox, Nyx	Нокс *nf*
Phoebe	Фéба *nf*
Selene	Селéна *nf*

muses

Calliope	Каллиóпа *nf*
Clio	Клúо *nf, indecl*
Erato	Эрáто *nf, indecl*
Euterpe	Эвтéрпа *nf*
Melpomene	Мельпомéна *nf*
Poly(h)ymnia	Полигúмния *nf*
Terpsichore	Терпсúхора *nf*
Thalia	Тáлия *nf*
Urania	Урáния *nf*

graces

Aglaia	Аглáя *nf*
Euphrosyne	Евфросúна *nf*
Thalia	Тáлия *nf*

nymphs

Arethusa	Аретýза *nf*
Callisto	Каллúсто *nf, indecl*
Daphne	Дáфна *nf*
Hesperides	Гесперúды *pl*
Oceanid (*pl* Oceanides)	Океанúда *nf*

Furies and Fates

Alecto	Алéкто *nf, indecl*
Atropos	Атрóпос *nf*
Clotho	Клóто *nf, indecl*
Megaera	Мегéра *nf*
Tisiphone	Тисифóна *nf*

Titans

Atlas	Áтлас *nm*
Cronus, Cronos	Крóнос *nm*
Hyperion	Гипериóн *nm*
Oceanus	Океáн *nm*
Prometheus	Прометéй *nm*

Homeric characters

Achilles	Ахиллéс *nm*
Agamemnon	Агамéмнон *nm*
Ajax	Аякс *nm*
Calypso	Калúпсо *nf*
Circe	Цирцéя, Кúрка *nf*
Electra	Элéктра *nf*
Hector	Гéктор *nm*
Hecuba	Гéкуба *nf*
Helen of Troy	Елéна Прекрáсная (Троянская) *nf*
Menelaus	Менелáй *nm*
Mentor	Мéнтор *nm*
Nausicae	Навсикáя, Невзикáя *nf*
Nestor	Нéстор *nm*
Odysseus	Одиссéй *nm*
Orestes	Орéст *nm*
Paris	Парúс *nm*
Penelope	Пенелóпа *nf*
Priam	Прúам *nm*
Stentor	Стентóр *nm*
Jason	Я́сон *nm*

other Greek characters–female

Alcestis	Алцéста *nf*
Alcmene	Алкмена *nf*
Alcyone	Альциóна *nf*
Amazon	амазóнка *nf*
Andromeda	Андромéда *nf*
Antigone	Антигóна *nf*
Arachne	Арáхна *nf*
Ariadne	Ариáдна *nf*
Atalanta	Аталáнта *nf*
Cassandra	Кассáндра *nf*
Cassiopeia	Кассиопéя *nf*
Chloe	Хлóя *nf*
Danaides	данайды *nfpl*
Europa	Еврóпа *nf*
Eurydice	Эвридúка *nf*
Galatea	Галатéя *nf*

Harmonia	Гармо́ния *nf*
Hyades	Гиа́ды *nfpl*
Hypermnestra	Гипермне́стра *nf*
Io	И́о *nf*
Iphigenia	Ифиге́ния *nf*
Jocasta	Иока́ста *nf*
Leda	Ле́да *nf*
Medea	Меде́я *nf*
Nereid (*pl* Nereides)	Нереи́да *nf*
Niobe	Нио́ба, Ниобе́я *nf*
Pandora	Пандо́ра *nf*
Persephone	Персефо́на *nf*
Phaedra	Фе́дра *nf*
Philomela	Филоме́ла *nf*
Pleiades	Плея́ды *npl*
Rhea	Ре́я *nf*
Semele	Семе́ла *nf*

other Greek characters–male

Adonis	Адони́с *nm*
Aegeus	Эге́й *nm*
Amphion	Амфио́н *nm*
Argonaut	аргона́вт *nm*
Atreus	Атре́й *nm*
Cadmus	Кадм *nm*
Castor and Pollux	Касто́р и По́ллукс *nm*
Cepheus	Цефе́й *nm*
Charon	Харо́н *nm*
Daedalus	Деда́л *nm*
Damon and Pythias	Дамо́н и Пи́фий *nm*
Echo	Э́хо *nn*
Endymion	Эндимио́н *nm*
Eteocles	Этео́кл *nm*
Ganymede	Ганиме́д *nm*
Hercules	Геркуле́с *nm*
Hermaphroditus	Гермафроди́т *nm*
Hyacinthus	Гиаци́нт *nm*
Icarus	Ика́р *nm*
Memnon	Ме́мнон *nm*
Midas	Ми́дас *nm*
Minos	Ми́нос *nm*
Narcissus	Нарки́сс, Нарци́сс *nm*
Nereus	Нере́й *nm*
Oedipus	Эди́п *nm*
Orion	Орио́н *nm*
Orpheus	Орфе́й *nm*
Perseus	Персе́й *nm*
Phaeton	Фаэто́н *nm*
Pygmalion	Пигмалио́н *nm*
Rhadamanthus	Радама́нт *nm*
Sisyphus	Си́зиф *nm*
Tantalus	Танта́л *nm*
Theseus	Тесе́й *nm*
Cynthia	Ци́нтия *nf*
Daphnis	Да́фна *nm*
Damocles	Да́мокл *nm*

places

Acheron	Ахеро́н *nm*
Atlantis	Атланти́да *nf*
Augean Stables	А́вгиевы коню́шни *nfpl*
Castalia	Каста́лия *nf*
Cocytus	Коци́т, Коки́т *nm*
Elysian fields	Эли́зиум *nm*
Erebus	Эре́б *nm*
Hades	Гаде́с *nm*
Helicon	Гелико́н *nm*
Lethe	Ле́та *nf*
Mt. Olympus	Оли́мп *nm*
Parnassus	Парна́с *nm*
Phlegethon	Флегето́н *nm*
Styx	Стикс *nm*
Thebes	Фи́вы *npl*
Troy	Тро́я *nf*

monsters and other creatures

Amalth(a)ea	Амалте́я *nf*
Antaeus	Анте́й *nm*
Argus	А́ргус *nm*
basilisk	васили́ск *nm*
Calydonian boar	калидо́нский вепрь *nm*
centaur	кента́вр *nm*
Cerberus	Це́рбер, Ке́рбер *nm*
Charybdis	Хари́бда *nf*
Chimera	Химе́ра *nf*
Cyclops	Цикло́п, Кикло́п *nm*
dryad	дриа́да *nf*
faun	фавн *nm*
Gorgon	Горго́на *nf*
griffin, gryphon	грифо́н *nm*
hamadryad	гамадри́л *nm*
Harpy	га́рпия *nf*
Hydra	Ги́дра *nf*
Medusa	Меду́за *nf*
Minotaur	Минота́вр *nm*
naiad	ная́да *nf*
nymph	ни́мфа *nf*
Pegasus	Пега́с *nm*
phoenix, phenix	фе́никс *nm*
Polyphemus	Полифе́м *nm*
Python	Пифо́н *nm*
satyr	сати́р *nm*
Scylla	Сци́лла *nf*
siren	сире́на *nf*
Sphinx	сфинкс *nm*

sylph, sylphide	сильф *nm*, сильфи́да *nf*
Silenus	Силе́н *nm*

things

Achilles' heel	ахилле́сова пята́ *nf*
aegis	эги́да *nf*
ambrosia	амбро́зия *nf*
caduceus	кадуце́й, кадуке́й *nm*
labyrinth	лабири́нт *nm*
lotus	ло́тос *nm*
nectar	некта́р *nm*
nimbus	нимб *nm*

ROMAN MYTHOLOGY

gods

Aesculapius	Эскула́п *nm*
Apollo	Аполло́н *nm*
Bacchus	Ба́хус, Вакх *nm*
Cupid	Купидо́н *nm*
Janus	Я́нус *nm*
Jupiter	Юпи́тер *nm*
Mars	Марс *nm*
Mercury	Мерку́рий *nm*
Neptune	Нептýн *nm*
Penates	пена́ты *nmpl*
Pluto	Плуто́н *nm*
Saturn	Сату́рн *nm*
Silvanus	Сильва́н *nm*
Tellus	Те́ллус *nm*
Vertumnus	Верту́мн *nm*
Vulcan	Вулка́н *nm*

goddesses

Aurora	Авро́ра *nf*
Bellona	Белло́на *nf*
Ceres	Церe̗ра *nf*
Concordia	Конко́рдия *nf*
Diana	Диа́на *nf*
Flora	Фло́ра *nf*
Fortuna	Форту́на *nf*
Juno	Юно́на *nf*
Luna	Луна́ *nf*
Minerva	Мине́рва *nf*
Parcae	Па́рки *nfpl*
Pomona	Помо́на *nf*
Venus	Вене́ра *nf*
Vesta	Ве́ста *nf*

other Roman characters

Dido	Дидо́на *nf*
Proserpina	Прозе́рпина *nf*
Psyche	Психе́я *nf*
Remus	Рем *nm*
Rhea Silvia	Ре́я Си́львия *nf*
Romulus	Ро́мул *nm*
Ulysses	Ули́сс *nm*

EGYPTIAN MYTHOLOGY

Amon, Ammon	Амо́н *nm*
Anubis	Ану́бис *nm*
Apis	А́пис *nm*
Horus	Гор *nm*
Isis	Иси́да, Изи́да *nf*
Osiris	Оси́рис, Ози́рис *nm*
Ra, Re	Ра *nm*
Serapis	Сера́псис *nm*
Sphinx	сфинкс *nm*

NORSE AND GERMANIC MYTHOLOGY

Alberich	А́льберих *nm*
Asgard	Асга́рд *nm*
Edda	Э́дда *nf*
Frey	Фрей *nm*
Freya	Фре́я *nf*
Hel	Хел *nf*
Loki	Ло́ки *nm*
Norn	Но́рна *nf*
Odin	О́дин *nm*
Siegfried	Зи́гфрид *nm*
Thor	Тор *nm*
Valhalla, Walhalla	Валлга́лла *nf*
Valkyrie, Walkyrie	вальки́рия *nf*
Wotan	Вота́н *nm*

OTHER ANCIENT DEITIES

Ashur, Asur	А́шшур *nm*
Astarte	Аста́рта *nf*
Baal	Баа́л, Ваа́л *nm*
Cybele	Кибе́ла *nf*
Dagon	Да́гон *nm*
Gilgamesh	Ги́льгамеш *nm*
Ishtar	И́штар *nf*
Kama	Ка́ма *nm*
Mithras	Ми́тра *nm*
Molech	Мо́лох *nm*
Semiramis	Семирами́да *nf*
Zarathustra	Зарату́штра, Зарату́стра, Зороа́стр *nm*

See also **ANCIENT CIVILIZATIONS**, **ANIMALS**, **THE BIBLE**, **FICTION AND FOLKLORE**

ANCIENT CIVILIZATIONS

PERSONS

writers and artists

Aeschylus — Эсхи́л *nm*
Aesop — Эзо́п *nm*
Aristophanes — Аристофа́н *nm*
Euripides — Еврипи́д *nm*
Homer — Гоме́р *nm*
Horace — Гора́ций *nm*
Ovid — Ови́дий *nm*
Pindar — Пинда́р *nm*
Plutarch — Плута́рх *nm*
Praxiteles — Пракси́тель *nm*
Sappho — Сафо́, Сапфо́ *nf, indecl*
Sophocles — Софо́кл *nm*
Virgil — Верги́лий *nm*

philosophers

Aristotle — Аристо́тель *nm*
Cicero — Цицеро́н *nm*
Democritus — Демокри́т *nm*
Diogenes — Дио́ген *nm*
Lucretius — Лукре́ций *nm*
Plato — Плато́н *nm*
Socrates — Сокра́т *nm*

historians

Cato — Като́н *nm*
Herodotus — Геродо́т *nm*
Josephus — Ио́сиф (Фла́вий) *nm*
Tacitus — Таци́т *nm*
Thucydides — Фукиди́д *nm*

scientists and physicians

Archimedes — Архиме́д *nm*
Euclid — Эвкли́д *nm*
Galen — Га́лен *nm*
Hipparchus — Гиппа́рх *nm*
Hippocrates — Гиппо́крат *nm*
Ptolemy — Птолеме́й *nm*
Pythagoras — Пифаго́р *nm*

statesmen and generals

Demosthenes — Демосфе́н *nm*
Draco — Драко́н(т) *nm*
Hannibal — Ганниба́л *nm*
Pericles — Пери́кл *nm*
Seneca — Се́нека *nm*
Solon — Соло́н *nm*
Xenophon — Ксенофо́нт *nm*

rulers

Augustus — А́вгуст *nm*
Caesar — Це́зарь *nm*
Caligula — Кали́гула *nm*
Cleopatra — Клеопа́тра *nf*
Constantine — Константи́н *nm*
Croesus — Крёз *nm*
Darius — Да́рий *nm*
Hammurabi — Хаммура́пи *nm*
Herod — И́род *nm*
Justinian — Юстиниа́н *nm*
Nebuchadnezzar — Навуходоно́сор *nm*
Nero — Неро́н *nm*
Ramses — Рамзе́с *nm*
Semiramis — Семирами́да *nf*
Titus — Тит *nm*
Vespasian — Веспасиа́н *nm*
Xerxes — Ксеркс *nm*

other famous persons

Nefertiti — Неферти́ти *nf*
Pythia — Пи́фия *nf*
Spartacus — Спарта́к *nm*
Xanthippe — Ксанти́ппа *nf*

professions and social classes

augur — авгу́р *nm*
centurion — центурио́н *nm*
cohort — кого́рта *nf*
consul — ко́нсул *nm*
duumvir — дуумви́р *nm*
gladiator — гладиа́тор *nm*
helot — ило́т *nm*
hetaera, hetaira — гете́ра *nf*
legate — лега́т *nm*
oracle — ора́кул *nm*
patrician — патри́ций *nm*
plebeian — плебе́й *nm*
plebs *npl* — плебс *nm*
Praetorian (Guard) — преториа́нский *aj*
prefect — префе́кт *nm*
proconsul — проко́нсул *nm*
procurator — прокуро́р *nm*
quaestor — квесто́р *nm*
sibyl — сиви́лла *nf*
sophist — софи́ст *nm*
tetrarch — тетра́рх *nm*
tribune — трибу́н *nm*
triumvir — триумви́р *nm*
vestal virgin — веста́лка *nf*

national and religious groups

Assyrian — асси́риец *nm*, асси́рийка *nf*
Babilonian — вавило́нянин *nm*, вавило́нянка *nf*

Carthaginian	карфаге́нянин *nm*, карфаге́нянка *nf*
Druid, druid	друи́д *nm*
Egyptian	египтя́нин *nm*, египтя́нка *nf*
Etruscan	этру́ск *nm*
Gaul	галл *nm*
Greek	грек *nm*, греча́нка *nf*
Ionian	ио́ниец *nm*
Israelite	израильтя́нин *nm*, израильтя́нка *nf*
Judean	иуде́йский *aj*
Jute	ют *nm*
Minoan	мино́йский *aj*
Nubian	нуби́ец *nm*
Phoenician	финики́ец, финики́янин *nm*, финики́янка *nf*
Phrygian	фриги́ец *nm*
Pict	пикт *nm*
Roman	ри́млянин *nm*, ри́млянка *nf*
Sabine	саби́нянин *nm*, саби́нянка *nf*
Saxon	сакс, саксо́нец *nm*
Scythian	скиф *nmf*
Spartan	спарта́нец *nm*, спарта́нка *nf*
Sumer	шуме́р *nm*
Sumerian	шуме́р *nmf*
Trojan	троя́нец *nm*, троя́нка *nf*
Vandal	ванда́л *nm*

PLACES AND THINGS

geographical names

Anglia	А́нглия *nf*
Appian Way	А́ппиева доро́га *nf*
Arcadia	Арка́дия *nf*
Assyria	Асси́рия *nf*
Athens	Афи́ны *npl*
Attica	А́ттика *nf*
Babylon	Вавило́н *nm*
Babylonia	Вавило́ния *nf*
Bethlehem	Вифлее́м *nm*
Byzantium [city]	Виза́нтий *nm*
Carthage	Карфаге́н *nm*
Corinth	Кори́нф *nf*
Delphi	Де́льфы *npl*
Egypt	Еги́пет *nm*
Ephesus	Эфе́с *nm*
Gaul	Га́ллия *nf*
Greece	Гре́ция *nf*
Herculaneum	Геркула́нум *nm*
Ionia	Ио́ния *nf*
Jerusalem	Иерусали́м *nm*
Judea	Иуде́я *nf*
Marathon	Марафо́н *nm*
Mesopotamia	Месопота́мия *nf*
Nicaea	Нике́я *nf*
Olympia	Оли́мпия *nf*
Parnassus, Mt.	Парна́с *nm*
Phoenicia	Финики́я *nf*
Phrygia	Фриги́я *nf*
Pompeii	Помпе́и *nm*
Rhodes	Ро́дос *nm*
Rome	Рим *nm*
Rubicon	Рубико́н *nm*
Scythia	Ски́фия *nf*
Sparta	Спа́рта *nf*
Syracuse *nsg*	Сираку́зы *npl*
Thebes	Фи́вы *npl*
Thermopylae	Фермопи́лы *npl*
Troy	Тро́я *nf*
Vesuvius	Везу́вий *nm*

structures

Acropolis	Акро́поль *nm*
agora	агора́ *nf*
Colosseum	Колизе́й *nm*
Colossus	Коло́сс *nm*
Forum	Фо́рум *nm*
hippodrome	ипподро́м *nm*
Lyceum	Лице́й, Лике́й *nm*
odeum	одео́н *nm*
palestra	пале́стра *nf*
Palladium	Палла́дий *nm*
Pantheon	Пантео́н *nm*
Parthenon	Парфено́н *nm*
pyramid	пирами́да *nf*
Sphinx	Сфинкс *nm*
ziggurat, zikkurat	зиккура́т *nm*

objects

amphora	а́мфора *nf*
cartouche	карту́ш *nm*
curia	ку́рия *nf*
denarius	дена́рий *nm*
laurel wreath	лавро́вый вено́к *nm*
papyrus	папи́рус *nm*
parchment	перга́мен(т) *nm*
quadriga	квадри́га *nf*
Rosetta stone	Розе́ттский ка́мень *nm*
sarcophagus	саркофа́г *nm*

scarab	скарабе́й *nm*
talent	тала́нт *nm*
trireme	триpе́ма *nf*
uraeus	уре́й *nm*

EVENTS

festivals, rites and celebrations, dates

Bacchanalia	вакхана́лия *nf*
calends	кале́нды *npl*
Eleusinian	элевси́нский *aj*
hecatomb	гекато́мба *nf*
Ides	и́ды *npl*
kalends, calends	кале́нды *npl*
Lupercalia	луперка́лии *npl*
Olympiad	олимпиа́да *nf*
ordeal	орда́лия *nf*
Saturnalia	сатурна́лии *npl*

wars

Peloponnesian Wars	Пелопонне́сские во́йны *nfpl*
Punic Wars	Пуни́ческие во́йны *nfpl*
Trojan War	Троя́нская война́ *nf*

EXPRESSIONS

Draconian measure	драко́новская ме́ра *nf*
Gordian knot	Го́рдиев у́зел *nm*
Pandora's box	я́щик Пандо́ры *nm, nf*
Pyrrhic victory	Пи́ррова побе́да *nf*
sword of Damocles	дамо́клов меч *nm*
Trojan horse	троя́нский конь *nm*

LITERATURE AND MUSIC

dithyramb	дифира́мб *nm*
Iliad	«Илиа́да» *nf*
Odyssey	«Одиссе́я» *nf*
Philippic	фили́ппика *nf*
Sapphic verse	сапфи́ческая строфа́ *nf*

See also **THE BIBLE**, **HISTORY AND ARCHEOLOGY**, **CLASSICAL MYTHOLOGY**, **LANGUAGES OF THE WORLD**, **WRITING** *(aspects of written language)*

Supplementary Vocabulary

abort	де́лать/сде́лать або́рт *impf, pf, nm*
absolutely	абсолю́тно *av*
absorb	абсорби́ровать *impf, pf*
abstract	абстраги́ровать *impf, pf*
Abyssinian [obs]	абисси́нский *aj*
accentuate	акценти́ровать *impf, pf*
accept	акцептова́ть *impf, pf*
acclimate, acclimatize *vt(i)*	акклиматизи́роват(ся) *impf, pf*
accompany	аккомпани́ровать *impf*
accredit (as ambassador)	аккредитова́ть *impf, pf*
accredited	аккредито́ванный *aj*
accumulate	аккумули́ровать *impf, pf*
accurately	аккура́тно *av*
acetylene	ацетиле́новый *aj*
acrobatic	акробати́ческий *aj*
acrylic	акри́ловый *aj*
activate	активизи́ровать *impf, pf*
actively	акти́вно *av*
actor's	актёрский *aj*
address	а́дресный *aj*
address	адресова́ть *impf, pf*
adequately	адеква́тно *av*
adjectival	адъекти́вный *aj*
administrate *vi*	администри́ровать *impf*
administrative	администрати́вный *aj*
admiral's	адмира́льский *aj*
advance (money)	аванси́ровать *impf, pf*
adventure	авантю́рный *aj*
adverbial	адвербиа́льный *aj*
aerodynamic	аэродинами́ческий *aj*
aeronautic(al)	аэронавигацио́нный *aj*
Afghan	афга́нский *aj*
African	африка́нский *aj*
Africanize	африканизи́ровать *impf, pf*
Afro-American	а́фро-америка́нский *aj*
Afro-Asian	а́фро-азиа́тский *aj*
agate	ага́товый *aj*
agent	аге́нтский *aj*

agglutinate	агглютини́ровать *impf, pf*
agnostic	агности́ческий *aj*
agronomic	агрономи́ческий *aj*
Ainu	а́йнский *aj*
air-condition, to	кондициони́ровать *impf*
air-conditioned	кондициони́рованный *aj*
alabaster	алеба́стровый *aj*
Alaskan	аля́скский *aj*
Albanian	алба́нский *aj*
albuminous	альбуми́нный *aj*
alcove	алько́вный *aj*
Aleutian	алеу́тский *aj*
algebraic	алгебраи́ческий *aj*
Algerian	алжи́рский *aj*
allegorical	аллегори́ческий *aj*
allergic	аллерги́ческий *aj*
alliterative	аллитери́рующий *aj*
allopathic	аллопати́ческий *aj*
allophonic	аллофони́ческий *aj*
alluvial	аллювиа́льный *aj*
Alpine	альпи́йский *aj*
Alsatian	эльза́сский *aj*
Altaic	алта́йский *aj*
alto	альто́вый *aj*
aluminum (BR aluminium)	алюми́ниевый *aj*
amalgamate	амальгами́ровать(ся) *impf, pf*
Amazonian	амазо́нский *aj*
ambulant, ambulatory	амбулато́рный *aj*
American	америка́нский *aj*
Americanize	американизи́ровать *impf, pf*
Amharic	амха́рский *aj*
ammonia	аммиа́чный *aj*
amnesty	амністи́ровать *impf, pf*
amortize	амортизи́ровать *impf, pf*
amputate	ампути́ровать *impf, pf*
anachronistic	анахрони́ческий *aj*
anal	ана́льный *aj*
analogical, analogous	аналоги́чный *aj*

analytic(al)	аналити́ческий *aj*
analyze (BR analyse)	анализи́ровать *impf*, проанализи́ровать *pf*
anarchic(al), anarchistic	анархи́ческий *aj*
anatomical	анатоми́ческий *aj*
anatomize	анатоми́ровать *impf*, *pf*
Andalucian	андалу́зский *aj*
Andean	анди́йский *aj*
anemic (BR anaemic)	анеми́чный *aj*
angelic	а́нгельский *aj*
Anglican	англика́нский *aj*
Anglicize	англизи́ровать *impf*, *pf*
Anglo-American	англо-америка́нский *aj*
Anglo-Saxon	англосаксо́нский *aj*
Angolan	анго́льский *aj*
aniline	анили́новый *aj*
animistic	анимисти́ческий *aj*
annex	аннекси́ровать *impf*, *pf*
annotate	анноти́ровать *impf*, проаннoти́ровать *pf*
annul, nullify	аннули́ровать *impf*, *pf*
anonymous	анони́мный *aj*
Antarctic	антаркти́ческий *aj*
anthropocentric	антропоцентри́ческий *aj*
anthropogenic	антропоге́нный *aj*
anthropoid	антропо́идный *aj*
anthropological	антропологи́ческий *aj*
anthropomorphic	антропоморфи́ческий *aj*
anti-Semitic	антисеми́тский *aj*
anti-Soviet	антисове́тский *aj*
antichristian	антихристиа́нский *aj*
anticlerical	антиклерика́льный *aj*
antiquarian	антиква́рный *aj*
antique	анти́чный *aj*
antireligious	антирелигио́зный *aj*
antiseptic	антисепти́ческий *aj*
antithetical	антитети́ческий *aj*
aorist(ic)	аористи́ческий *aj*
apatite	апати́товый *aj*
aphoristic	афористи́ческий *aj*
apocalyptic	апокалипти́ческий *aj*
apocryphal	апокрифи́ческий *aj*
apolitical	аполити́чный *aj*
apoplectic	апоплекти́ческий *aj*
apostolic	апо́стольский *aj*
apparatus	аппара́тный *aj*
appeal	апелли́ровать *impf*, *pf*
appellate	апелляцио́нный *aj*
applaud	аплоди́ровать *impf*
approve	апроби́ровать *impf*, *pf*
apricot	абрико́совый *aj*
April	апре́льский *aj*
aquamarine	аквамари́новый *aj*
Arab, Arabic	ара́бский *aj*
Arabian	арави́йский *aj*
arbitrary, arbitration	арбитра́жный *aj*
Arcadian	арка́дский *aj*
archeological (BR archaeological)	археологи́ческий *aj*
architectonic	архитектони́ческий *aj*
archival	архи́вный *aj*
Arctic	аркти́ческий *aj*
Argentinian	аргенти́нский *aj*
argue	аргументи́ровать *impf*, *pf*
aristocratic	аристократи́ческий, аристи́чный *aj*
Aristotelian	аристо́телев(ский) *aj*
arithmetical	арифмети́ческий *aj*
Armenian	армя́нский *aj*
army	арме́йский *aj*
aromatic	арома́ти́ческий, аромати́чный, арома́тный *aj*
arrange	аранжи́ровать *impf*, *pf*
arrest, under	под аре́стом
arrest	арестова́ть *impf*, *pf*
arterial	артериа́льный *aj*
arthritic	артри́тный *aj*
artillery	артиллери́йский *aj*
Aryan	ари́йский *aj*
asbestos	асбе́стовый *aj*
ascetic	аскети́ческий *aj*
Asian, Asiatic	азиа́тский *aj*
asphalt	асфальти́ровать *impf*, *pf*
asphalt, asphalted	асфа́льтовый *aj*
assimilate *vt(i)*	ассимили́ровать(ся) *impf*, *pf*
assist	ассисти́ровать *impf*, *pf*
associate *vt(i)*	ассоции́ровать(ся) *impf*, *pf*
associated	ассоции́рованный *aj*
assorted	сортиро́ванный *aj*
Assyrian	ассири́йский *aj*
asthmatic	астмати́ческий *aj*
astigmatic	астигмати́ческий *aj*
astrological	астрологи́ческий *aj*
astronomical	астрономи́ческий *aj*
astrophysical	астрофизи́ческий *aj*
asymmetrical	асимметри́ческий, асимметри́чный *aj*

atavistic	атависти́ческий *aj*
atheistic	атеисти́ческий *aj*
Athenian	афи́нский *aj*
Atlantic	атланти́ческий *aj*
atmospheric	атмосфе́рный *aj*
atonal	атона́льный *aj*
atonic	атони́ческий *aj*
atrophied	атрофи́рованный *aj*
atrophy	атрофи́роваться *impf*, *pf*
attack	атакова́ть *impf*, *pf*
Attic	атти́ческий *aj*
attributive	атрибути́вный *aj*
August	а́вгустовский *aj*
Australasian	австра́ло-азиа́тский *aj*
Australian	австрали́йский *aj*
Austrian	австри́йский *aj*
Austro-Hungarian	а́встро-венге́рский *aj*
author's	а́вторский *aj*
authoritative	авторите́тный *aj*
autistic	аутисти́ческий *aj*
autobiographical	автобиографи́ческий *aj*
autocratic	автократи́ческий *aj*
automate	автоматизи́ровать *impf*, *pf*
automatically	автомати́чески *av*
automobile	автомоби́льный *aj*
avant-gardism	авангарди́зм *nm*
aviation	авиацио́нный *aj*
axiomatic	аксиомати́чный *aj*
Azerbaijani	азербайджа́нский *aj*
Babylonian	вавило́нский *aj*
Bacchic	вакхи́ческий *aj*
bacon	беко́нный *aj*
bacterial	бактериа́льный *aj*
bactericidal	бактерици́дный *aj*
bacteriological	бактериологи́ческий *aj*
baggage	бага́жный *aj*
Baghdad, Bagdad	багда́дский *aj*
Baku	баки́нский *aj*
balance	бала́нсовый *aj*
balance [bookkeeping]	баланси́ровать *impf* сбаланси́ровать *pf*
balanced	сбаланси́рованный *aj*
Balkan	балка́нский *aj*
ballast	балла́стный *aj*
ballet	бале́тный *aj*
ballistic	баллисти́ческий *aj*
balneological	бальнеологи́ческий *aj*
balsamic	бальзами́ческий *aj*
Baltic (region)	Прибалти́йский *aj*
Baltic	балти́йский *aj*
bamboo	бамбу́ковый *aj*

banana	бана́новый *aj*
bandit	банди́тский *aj*
Bangladeshi	бангладе́шский *aj*
banquet	банке́тный *aj*
Baptist	бапти́стский
Barbadian	барбадо́сский *aj*
barbaric, barbarous	ва́рварский *aj*
baritone	барито́нный *aj*
barometric	барометри́ческий *aj*
baronial	баро́нский *aj*
baroque	баро́чный *aj*
barricade	баррикади́ровать *impf*, забаррикади́ровать *pf*
barricaded	баррика́дный *aj*
barter	ба́ртерный *aj*
basalt	база́льтный *aj*
based on, to be	бази́роваться *impf*
Bashkir	башки́рский *aj*
basketball	баскетбо́льный *aj*
Basque	ба́скский *aj*
bass	баси́стый, басо́вый *aj*
basso	ба́сенный *aj*
batik	бати́ковый *aj*
batiste	бати́стовый *aj*
battalion	батальо́нный *aj*
battery-operated	батаре́йный *aj*
bauxite	бокси́товый *aj*
Bavarian	бава́рский *aj*
bedouin	бедуи́нский *aj*
beige	беж *aj*, *indecl* , бе́жевый *aj*
Beirut	бейру́тский *aj*
Belarussian, Byelorrussian	белору́сский *aj*
Belgian	бельги́йский *aj*
belletristic	беллетристи́ческий, беллетри́стский *aj*
Benedictine	бенедикти́нский *aj*
Bengali	бенга́льский *aj*
Berber	бербе́рский *aj*
Berlin	берли́нский *aj*
Bernese	бе́рнский *aj*
biblical	библе́йский *aj*
bibliographic(al)	библиографи́ческий *aj*
billards	билья́рдный *aj*
bimetallic	биметалли́ческий *aj*
biochemical	биохими́ческий *aj*
biographical	биографи́ческий *aj*
biological	биологи́ческий *aj*
biomedical	биомедици́нский
bionic	биони́ческий *aj*
biophysical	биофизи́ческий *aj*
bituminous	битумино́зный *aj*

block	блоки́ровать *impf, pf*
block	бло́чный *aj*
blockade	блоки́ровать *impf, pf*
bluff	блефова́ть *impf, pf*
boarding	аборда́жный *aj*
Bohemian [place]	боге́мский *aj*
Bohemian [lifestyle]	боге́мный, боге́мствующий *aj*
Bolivian	боливи́йский *aj*
Bolshevist	большеви́стский *aj*
bomb	бо́мбовый *aj*
bomb	бомби́ть *impf*, разбомби́ть *pf*
bombard	бомбардирова́ть *impf*
bombing	бомбардиро́вочный *aj*
Bosnian	босни́йский *aj*
bottle, bottled	буты́лочный *aj*
boudoir	будуа́рный *aj*
boulevard	бульва́рный *aj*
bourgeois	буржуа́зный *aj*
box	бокси́ровать *impf*
boyar	боя́рский *aj*
boycott	бойкоти́ровать *impf*
brachycephaly	брахицефа́лия
bravura	браву́рный *aj*
Brazilian	брази́льский *aj*
Breton	брето́нский *aj*
brigade	брига́дный *aj*
British	брита́нский *aj*
bromide	бро́мистый *aj*
bromine	бро́мовый *aj*
bronchial	бронхиа́льный *aj*
Brussels	брю́ссельский *aj*
bubonic	бубо́нный *aj*
Buddhist(ic)	будди́йский, будди́стский *aj*
budgetary	бюдже́тный *aj*
buffer	бу́ферный *aj*
buffet	буфе́тный *aj*
Bulgarian	болга́рский *aj*
bunker	бункерова́ть *impf, pf*
bureaucratic	бюрократи́ческий *aj*
Burgundian	бургу́ндский *aj*
Burmese	бирма́нский *aj*
Buryat	буря́тский *aj*
bus	авто́бусный *aj*
cabalistic	каб(б)алисти́ческий *aj*
cabinet	кабине́тный *aj*
cable	ка́бельный *aj*
cacophonous	какофони́ческий *aj*
cadastral	када́стровый *aj*
caisson	кессо́ный *aj*
calcine *vt(i)*	кальцини́ровать(ся) *impf, pf*
calcium	ка́льциевый *aj*
calendar	календа́рный *aj*
calibrate	калиброва́ть *impf*
California	калифорни́йский *aj*
calligraphic	каллиграфи́ческий *aj*
calorific	калори́йный *aj*
calque	кальки́ровать *impf, pf*
Calvinist(ic)	кальвини́стский
Cambodian	камбоджи́йский *aj*
Cambridge	кембри́джский *aj*
camouflage	камуфли́ровать *impf, pf*
camphor	ка́мфарный *aj*
Canadian	кана́дский *aj*
cancerogenic	канцероге́нный *aj*
candidate's	кандида́тский *aj*
cannibalistic	канниба́льский *aj*
canonical	канони́ческий *aj*
canonize	канонизи́ровать, канонизова́ть *impf, pf*
Canterbury	ке́нтерберийский *aj*
cantonal	кантона́льный *aj*
Cantonese	канто́нский *aj*
capillary	капилля́рный *aj*
capital	капита́льный *aj*
capitalist(ic)	капиталисти́ческий *aj*
capitalize	капитализи́ровать *impf, pf*
capitol	капитоли́йский *aj*
capitulate	капитули́ровать *impf, pf*
capricious, to be	капри́зничать *impf*
captain's	капита́нский *aj*
caramel	караме́льный *aj*
carbonize	карбонизова́ть *impf, pf*
cardinal	кардина́льский *aj*
career, careerist	карьери́стский *aj*
caricatured	карикату́рный *aj*
carious	карио́зный *aj*
Carmelite	кармели́тский *aj*
carmine	карми́нный *aj*
carnival	карнава́льный *aj*
carousel	карусе́льный *aj*
Cartesian	картезиа́нский
Carthaginian	карфаге́нский *aj*
cartographic	картографи́ческий *aj*
casein	казе́иновый *aj*
cash	ка́ссовый *aj*
cashmere	кашеми́ровый *aj*
caste	ка́стовый *aj*
Castilian	касти́льский *aj*
castrate	кастри́ровать *impf, pf*
casuistic	казуисти́ческий *aj*

Catalan	катало́нский *aj*
cataleptic	каталепти́ческий *aj*
catalog(ue)	каталогизи́ровать *impf, pf*
catalog(ue)	катало́жный *aj*
catalogued	каталогизи́рованный *aj*
catalytic	каталити́ческий *aj*
catapult *vt(i)*	катапульти́ровать(ся) *impf, pf*
catastrophic	катастрофи́ческий *aj*
categorically	категори́чески *av*
Catholic	католи́ческий *aj*
Caucasian	кавка́зский *aj*
causal	кауза́льный *aj*
cavalryman's	кавалери́йский *aj*
cedar	кедро́вый *aj*
cellophane	целлофа́новый *aj*
cement	цементи́ровать *impf, pf*
cement	цеме́нтный *aj*
cemented	цементи́рованный *aj*
censor	цензурова́ть *impf*
censorial	це́нзорский, цензу́рный *aj*
centralize	централизова́ть *impf, pf*
centralized	централизо́ванный *aj*
centrifugal	центробе́жный *aj*
centrist	центри́стский *aj*
ceramic	керами́ческий *aj*
ceremonial	церемониа́льный *aj*
ceremonious	церемо́нный *aj*
ceremony, to stand on	церемо́ниться *impf*
Cesarean (BR Caesarean)	ке́сарев, це́зарев *aj*
Ceylonese	цейло́нский *aj*
Chaldean	халде́йский *aj*
chamber	ка́мерный *aj*
chaotic	хаоти́ческий *aj*
Chaplinesque	чаплино́вский *aj*
characteristic	характе́рный *aj*
characterize	характеризова́ть, охарактеризова́ть *impf, pf*
characterless	бесхара́ктерный *aj*
charter	ча́ртерный *aj*
check	че́ковый *aj*
chef	ше́фский *aj*
Chekhovian	че́ховский *aj*
Cherokee	чероке́зский *aj*
cherubic	херуви́мский *aj*
cheviot	шевио́товый *aj*
chic	шика́рный *aj*
chiffon	шифо́новый *aj*
Chilean	чили́йский *aj*
chimerical	химери́ческий *aj*
chlorinate	хлори́ровать *impf, pf*
chloroform	хлороформи́ровать *impf, pf*
chlorotic	хло́рный *aj*
chlorous	хло́ристый *aj*
chocolate	шокола́дный *aj*
choleric	холери́ческий *aj*
choral	хорово́й *aj*
choreographic	хореографи́ческий *aj*
Christ-like	христоподо́бный *aj*
Christian	христиа́нский *aj*
Christianize	христианизова́ть *impf, pf*
chrome, chromic	хро́мовый *aj*
chronic	хрони́ческий *aj*
chronical	хроника́льный *aj*
Chuvash	чува́шский *aj*
cigar	сига́рный *aj*
cigarette	сигаре́тный *aj*
cipher, encipher	шифрова́ть *impf*, зашифрова́ть, *pf*
circulated	циркуля́рный *aj*
circulating	циркуляцио́нный *aj*
circus	цирково́й *aj*
Cistercian	цистерциа́нский *aj*
citation, citing	цити́рование *nn*
cite [quote]	цити́ровать *impf*, процити́ровать *pf*
citrus	ци́трусовый *aj*
civilize	цивилизова́ть, цивилизи́ровать *impf, pf*
civilized	цивилизо́ванный *aj*
class	классифици́ровать *impf, pf*
class	кла́ссовый, кла́ссный *aj*
classic, classical	класси́ческий *aj*
classless	бескла́ссовый *aj*
classy [informal]	кла́ссный *aj*
claustrophobic	клаустрофо́бный *aj*
clearing	кли́ринговый *aj*
clerical	клерика́льный *aj*
climacteric	климактери́ческий *aj*
climatic	климати́ческий *aj*
clone	клони́ровать *impf, pf*
clover	кле́верный *aj*
clownish, clown's	кло́унский *aj*
co-opt	кооптиро́вать *impf, pf*
coagulate *vt(i)*	коагули́ровать(ся) *impf, pf*

coalition	коалицио́нный *aj*
cobalt	ко́бальтовый *aj*
cocoa	кака́овый *aj*
coconut	коко́совый *aj*
code	ко́довый *aj*
codify	кодифици́ровать *impf, pf*
coffee	кофе́йный *aj*
cognac	коньячный *aj*
coke	ко́ксовый, коксова́льный *aj*
coke	коксова́ть *impf*
collaborationist	коллаборациони́стский *aj*
collect [hobby]	коллекциони́ровать *impf*
collectable [hobby]	коллекцио́нный *aj*
collective	коллекти́вный *aj*
collectivize	коллективизи́ровать *impf, pf*
collegial	коллегиа́льный *aj*
collegiate	колле́жский *aj*
colloidal	колоида́льный, колло́идный *aj*
Colombian	колумби́йский *aj*
colonial	колониа́льный *aj*
colonialist	колониалисти́ческий *aj*
colonize	колонизи́ровать *impf, pf*
coloratura	колорату́рный *aj*
columned	коло́нный *aj*
combination	комбинацио́нный *aj*
combinatory	комбинато́рный *aj*
combine	комбини́ровать *impf,* скомбини́ровать *pf*
combined	комбини́рованный *aj*
comedic	комеди́йный *aj*
comic(al)	коми́чный, коми́ческий *aj*
Comintern	коминте́рновский *aj*
command	кома́ндовать *impf*
command	кома́ндный *aj*
commander's	команди́рский *aj*
comment	комменти́ровать *impf, pf,* прокомменти́ровать *pf*
commercial	комме́рческий *aj*
commissar	комисса́рский *aj*
commission	комиссио́нный *aj*
communist	коммунисти́ческий *aj*
communization	коммуниза́ция *nf*
communize	коммунизовать *impf, pf*
compact	компа́ктный *aj*
companionable	компане́йский *aj*
compass	ко́мпасный *aj*
compensate *vt(i)*	компенси́ровать *impf, pf*
compensatory	компенсацио́нный *aj*
competent (person)	компете́нтный *aj*
compile	компили́ровать *impf, pf*
composition(al)	композицио́нный *aj*
compressor	компре́ссорный *aj*
compromise (someone) *vt*	компромети́ровать *impf,* скомпромети́ровать *pf*
compromise	компроми́ссный *aj*
computer	компью́терный *aj*
concentrate *vt(i)*	концентри́ровать(ся) *impf,* сконцентри́ровать(ся) *pf*
concentrated	концентри́рованный *aj*
concentric	концентри́ческий *aj*
conceptual	концептуа́льный *aj*
concert	конце́ртный *aj*
concertize	концерти́ровать *impf*
concession	концессио́ный *aj*
concrete [real]	конкре́тный *aj*
concretely	конкре́тно *av*
concretize	конкретизи́ровать *impf, pf*
condense *vt(i)*	конденси́ровать(ся) *impf, pf*
conditional	кондицио́нный *aj*
conductor's	конду́кторский *aj*
confederate	конфедерати́вный *aj*
confidential	конфиденциа́льный *aj*
confirm	конфирмова́ть *impf, pf*
confiscate	конфискова́ть *impf, pf*
conflict (with) *vi*	конфликтова́ть *impf*
conflict	конфли́ктный *aj*
conformist	конформи́стский *aj*
Confucian	конфуциа́нский *aj*
confuse [embarrass]	конфу́зить *impf,* сконфу́зить *pf*
conglomerate	конгломера́тный *aj*
Congolese	конголе́зский *aj*
conservative (views)	консерва́торский *aj*
conservative (person)	консервати́вный *aj*
conservatory	консервато́рский *aj*

conserve	консерви́ровать *impf*, законсерви́ровать *pf*
consolidate *vt(i)*	консолиди́ровать(ся) *impf, pf*
conspiratorial	конспира́торский *aj*
constitute	конституи́ровать *impf, pf*
construct	конструи́ровать *impf*, сконструи́ровать *pf*
consular	ко́нсульский *aj*
contact	конта́ктный *aj*
container	конте́йнерный *aj*
contour	ко́нтурный *aj*
contraband	контраба́ндный *aj*
contraceptive	контрацепти́вный *aj*
contract	контрактова́ть *impf*, законтрактова́ть *pf*
contrapuntal	контрапу́нктный, контрапункти́ческий *aj*
contrast	контрасти́ровать *impf*
contrasting	контра́стный *aj*
control	контроли́ровать *impf*, проконтроли́ровать *pf*
conventional	конвенциона́льный *aj*
conversion	конверсио́нный *aj*
convert (money)	конверти́ровать *impf, pf*
convoy	конвои́ровать *impf*
convulsive	конвульси́вный *aj*
cooperate, co-operate	коопери́роваться *impf, pf*
cooperative society	кооперати́вное о́бщество
coordinate, co-ordinate	координи́ровать *impf, pf*
coordinating, co-ordinating	координацио́нный *aj*
copra	копро́вый *aj*
Coptic	ко́птский *aj*
copying	копирова́льный *aj*
copying	копи́рование *nn*, копиро́вка *nf*
coriander	кориа́ндровый *aj*
Corinthian	кори́нфский *aj*
Cornish	корнуо́ллский, корни́йский *aj*
coronation	коронацио́нный *aj*
coronet	коро́на *nf*
corporal's	капра́льский *aj*
corporate	корпорати́вный *aj*
correct	корректи́ровать *impf*, прокорректи́ровать *pf*
correction	корректу́рный *aj*
correlate	коррели́ровать *impf*
correlate	корреля́т *nm*
correlative	корреляти́вный *aj*
corridor	коридо́рный *aj*
corrosive	коррози́йный *aj*
Corsican	корсика́нский *aj*
cosmetic	космети́ческий *aj*
cosmopolitanism	космополити́зм *nm*
Cossack [obs]	каза́цкий *aj*
Cossaks, the [obs]	каза́чество *nn*
Costa Rican	костарика́нский *aj*
costume, to dress in	костюми́роваться *impf, pf*
costumed	костюмиро́ванный *aj*
counter-revolutionary	контрреволюцио́нный *aj*
counterattack	контратакова́ть *impf, pf*
cowboy	ковбо́йский *aj*
creature	креату́ра *nf*
credit	аккредити́вный *aj*
credit	кредитова́ть *impf, pf*
credit	креди́тный *aj*
creditor's	кредито́рский *aj*
cremate	креми́ровать *impf, pf*
crematorium	кремацио́нный *aj*
crepe	кре́повый *aj*
Cretan	кри́тский *aj*
cretonne	крето́нный *aj*
Crimean	кры́мский *aj*
crisis	кри́зисный *aj*
critically	крити́чески *av*
criticize	критикова́ть *impf*
Cro-Magnon	кроманьо́нский *aj*
Croatian	хорва́тский *aj*
crocodile	крокоди́ловый *aj*
crown	короновать *impf, pf*
crown	коро́нный *aj*
cruise	кре́йси́ровать *impf*
cruiser, cruising	кре́йсерский *aj*
cryptographic	криптографи́ческий *aj*
crystallize *vt(i)*	кристаллизова́ть(ся) *impf, pf*
Cuban	куби́нский *aj*
cubic	куби́ческий *aj*
cuckoo	кукова́ть *impf*
culmination	кульминацио́нный *aj*
cultivable	культиви́руемый *aj*
cultivate	культиви́ровать *impf*

curiosity [rare thing]	курьёз *nm*, курьёзность *nf*
cursive	курси́вный *aj*
cutter	ка́терный *aj*
cybernetic	кибернети́ческий *aj*
cyclonic	циклони́ческий *aj*
cypress	кипари́совый *aj*
Cypriot	ки́прский *aj*
cytological	цитологи́ческий
czarist, tsarist	ца́рский *aj*
Czech	че́шский *aj*
Czechoslovak [obs]	чехослова́цкий *aj*
dactylic	дактили́ческий *aj*
Daghestan	дагеста́нский *aj*
daguerrotype	дагерроти́пный *aj*
Dalmatian	далма́тский *aj*
dance	танцева́ть *impf*, протанцева́ть, станцева́ть *pf*
Danish	да́тский *aj*
debate	дебати́ровать *impf*
debit	дебетова́ть *impf, pf*
debut	дебю́тный *aj*
debut, to make one's	дебюти́ровать *impf, pf*
decalcification	декальцина́ция *nf*
decalcify	декальцини́ровать *impf, pf*
December	дека́брьский *aj*
decentralize	децентрализова́ть *impf, pf*
decipher	дешифри́ровать *impf, pf*
declaim	деклами́ровать *impf*
declamatory	декламацио́нный *aj*
declare	деклари́ровать *impf, pf*
décolleté	декольти́рованный *aj*
decorate	декори́ровать *impf, pf*
decorative	декорати́вный *aj*
decree	декрети́ровать *impf, pf*
deductive	дедукти́вный *aj*
deficit	дефици́тный *aj*
deflationary	дефляцио́нный *aj*
defoliation	дефолиа́ция *nf*
deform	деформи́ровать *impf, pf*
deformed	деформи́рованный *aj*
degenerate	дегенери́ровать *impf, pf*
dehumanize	дегуманизи́ровать *impf, pf*
deist(ic)	деисти́ческий *aj*
delegate	делега́тский *aj*
delegate	делеги́ровать *impf, pf*
Delphic	делфи́йский *aj*
deltoid, delta-shaped	дельтови́дный *aj*
demagogic	демагоги́ческий *aj*
demilitarize	демилитаризова́ть *impf, pf*
demobilization	демобилизацио́нный *aj*
demobilize *vt(i)*	демобилизова́ть(ся)
democratic	демократи́ческий, демократи́чный *aj*
democratize	демократизи́ровать *impf, pf*
demographic	демографи́ческий *aj*
demonic, demoniac(al)	демони́ческий *aj*
demonstrate	демонстри́ровать *impf, pf*, продемонстри́ровать *pf*
demonstrative	демонстрати́вный *aj*
demoralize	деморализова́ть *impf, pf*
denationalize	денационализи́ровать *impf, pf*
denaturalization	денатурализа́ция *nf*
denaturalize	денатурализова́ть *impf, pf*
denature	денатури́ровать *impf, pf*
denazify	денацифици́ровать *impf, pf*
denounce	денонси́ровать *impf, pf*
deodorization	дезодора́ция *nf*
deodorize	дезодори́ровать *impf, pf*
depolarize	деполяризова́ть *impf, pf*
deport	депорти́ровать *impf, pf*
deposit	депози́тный *aj*
deposit	депони́ровать *impf, pf*
depression, depressive	депресси́вный *aj*
deputies'	депута́тский *aj*
desegregate	десегреги́ровать *impf, pf*
desert *vi*	дезерти́ровать *impf, pf*
dessert	десе́ртный *aj*
destabilize	дестабилизи́ровать *impf, pf*
detail, in	дета́льно *av*
detail	детализи́ровать *impf, pf*
detailing	детализа́ция *nf*
detective	детекти́вный *aj*
deterministic	детерминисти́ческий, детермини́стский *aj*
detonate	детони́ровать *impf*

devaluate, devalue	девальви́ровать *impf, pf*
devilish	дья́вольский *aj*
diacritical	диакрити́ческий *aj*
diagnostic	диагности́ческий *aj*
diagonal	диагона́льный *aj*
dialectal	диалекта́льный *aj*
dialectical	диалекти́ческий *aj*
dialog(ue)	диало́говый *aj*
dialog(ue)	диалоги́ческий *aj*
diathermic	диатерми́ческий *aj*
dictate (a letter)	диктова́ть *impf,* продиктова́ть, *pf*
dictatorial	диктато́рский *aj*
didactic	дидакти́ческий *aj*
diesel	ди́зельный *aj*
dietary	диети́ческий *aj*
differentiate	дифференци́ровать *impf, pf*
differentiated	дифференци́рованный *aj*
dilettante	дилета́нтский *aj*
diluvial	дилювиа́льный *aj*
diphtheria, diphtherial	дифтери́йный *aj*
diphthongal	дифтонга́льный, дифтонги́ческий *aj*
diploma	дипло́мный *aj*
directive	директи́вный *aj*
directorial, director's	дире́кторский *aj*
disciplinary	дисциплина́рный *aj*
discipline	дисциплини́ровать *impf, pf*
discotèque	дискоте́чный *aj*
discount	дисконти́ровать *impf, pf*
discount	диско́нтный *aj*
discredit	дискредити́ровать *impf, pf*
discriminate (against)	дискримини́ровать *impf, pf*
discriminatory	дискриминацио́нный *aj*
discuss	дискути́ровать *impf, pf*
discussion	дискуссио́нный *aj*
disinfect	дезинфици́ровать *impf, pf*
disinfectant	дезинфици́руюший *aj*
disinform	дезинформи́ровать *impf, pf*
disorganization	неорганизо́ванность *nf*
disorganize	дезорганизова́ть *impf, pf*
disorient	дезориенти́ровать *impf, pf*
disproportionately	непропорциона́льно *av*
disqualify	дисквалифици́ровать *impf, pf*
dissimilate	диссимили́ровать(ся) *impf, pf*
dissonant, to be	диссони́ровать *impf*
distance oneself, to	дистанци́роваться *impf*
distance, at a	дистанцио́нный *aj*
distil(l)	дистилли́ровать *impf, pf*
dithyrambic	дифирамби́ческий *aj*
divisional	дивизио́нный *aj*
doctoral, doctor's	до́кторский *aj*
document	документи́ровать *impf, pf*
dollar	до́лларовый *aj*
dominant	домина́нтовый *aj*
dominate	домини́ровать *impf*
Dominican	доминика́нский *aj*
donor	до́норский *aj*
dose	дози́ровать *impf, pf*
double [role]	дубли́ровать [роль] *impf, pf*
drain	дрени́ровать *impf, pf*
drainage	дрена́жный *aj*
dramatically	драмати́чески *av*
dramatize	драматизи́ровать *impf, pf*
drape (with something)	драпирова́ть *impf,* задрапирова́ть *pf*
drift	дрейфова́ть *impf*
drifting	дрейфу́ющий *aj*
Druidic	друиди́ческий *aj*
dualistic	дуалисти́ческий *aj*
Dublin	ду́блинский *aj*
duplicate	дублика́тный *aj*
duplicate	дубли́ровать *impf*
dynastic	династи́ческий *aj*
dysentery, dysenteric	дизентери́йный *aj*
dyspeptic	страда́ющий диспепси́ей *nf*
ecological	экологи́ческий *aj*
economize	эконо́мить *impf,* сэконо́мить *pf*
Ecuadorean	эквадо́рский *aj*
Edinburgh	эдинбу́ргский *aj*
effective [done for effect]	эффе́ктный *aj*
effectively	эффекти́вно *av*
egalitarian	эгалита́рный *aj*

Egyptian — еги́петский *aj*
electrify (a railroad) — электрифици́ровать *impf, pf*
electrochemical — электрохими́ческий *aj*
electrolytic — электролити́ческий *aj*
electrostatic — электростати́ческий *aj*
elegaic — элеги́ческий *aj*
elegantly — элега́нтно *av*
elite, élite, elitist — элита́рный *aj*
Elysian — елисе́йский *aj*
emancipate — эмансипи́ровать *impf, pf*
emancipated — эмансипи́рованный *aj*
embalm — бальзами́ровать *impf,* набальзами́ровать *pf*
embalmed — набальза́мированный *aj*
emblematic — эмблемати́ческий *aj*
embryonic — эмбриона́льный *aj*
emigrant — эмигра́нтский *aj*
emigrate — эмигри́ровать *impf, pf*
emigration — эмиграцио́нный *aj*
emission — эмиссио́нный *aj*
emit (paper money) — эмитти́ровать *impf, pf*
emitter — эмите́нт, емитте́р *nm*
emotional — эмоциона́льный *aj*
emotionally — эмоциона́льно *av*
empirical — эмпири́ческий, эмпири́чный *aj*
enamel — эмалирова́ть *impf*
encipher — шифрова́ть *impf,* зашифрова́ть *pf*
enclitic — энклити́ческий *aj*
encyclopedic (BR encyclopaedic) — энциклопеди́ческий *aj*
endocrine — эндокри́нный *aj*
endogamous — эндога́мый *aj*
engineering — инжене́рный *aj*
English — англи́йский *aj*
engrave — гравирова́ть *impf,* выгравирова́ть *pf*
engraver's, engraving — гравирова́льный *aj*
entomological — энтомологи́ческий
eolithic — эоли́товый, эолити́ческий *aj*
eparchial — епархиа́льный *aj*
ephemeral — эфеме́рный *aj*
epicurean — эпикуре́йсксий *aj*
epidemic — эпидеми́ческий *aj*
epidermal — эпидерми́ческий *aj*
epigrammatic — эпиграммати́ческий *aj*
epileptic — эпилепти́ческий *aj*
episcopal — епи́скопский *aj*

Episcopalian — епископа́льный *aj*
epistemological — эпистемологи́ческий *aj*
eponymous — эпони́мный *aj*
equip — экипирова́ть *impf, pf*
equivalent — эквивале́нтный *aj*
ergonomic — эргономи́ческий *aj*
erode — эроди́ровать *impf*
erosive — эрози́вный *aj*
erudite — эруди́рованный *aj*
escapist — эскапи́стский *aj*
eschatological — эсхатологи́ческий *aj*
escort — эскорти́ровать *impf, pf*
Eskimo — эскимо́сский *aj*
especially — специально *av*
espionage — шпио́нский *aj*
Estonian — эсто́нский *aj*
Ethiopian — эфио́пский *aj*
ethnocentric — этноцентри́ческий *aj*
ethnographic — этнографи́ческий *aj*
ethnological — этнологи́ческий *aj*
ethyl — этило́вый *aj*
Etruscan — этру́сский *aj*
eucalyptus — эвкали́птовый *aj*
Eucharistic — евхаристи́ческий *aj*
eugenic — евгени́ческий *aj*
euphemistic — эвфемисти́ческий *aj*
euphonious — эвфони́ческий *aj*
Eurasian — еврази́йский *aj*
European — европе́йский *aj*
Europeanize — европеизи́ровать *impf, pf*
evacuate — эваку́ировать *impf, pf*
evacuation — эвакуацио́нный *aj*
evangelical — евангели́ческий *aj*
evolutionary — эволюцио́нный *aj*
evolve — эволюциони́ровать *impf*
examination — экзаменацио́нный *aj*
examine — экзаменова́ть *impf,* проэкзаменова́ть *pf*
excursionary — экскурсио́нный *aj*
exhume — эксгуми́ровать *impf, pf*
existential(ist) — экзистенциа́льный *aj*
exogamous — экзога́мный *aj*
expansionary, expansionist — экспансионисти́ческий *aj*
expansive — экспанси́вный *aj*
expatriate — экспатрии́ровать *impf, pf*
expeditionary — экспедицио́нный *aj*
experiment — эксперименти́ровать *impf*
expert — э́кспертный *aj*

conserve	консерви́ровать *impf*, законсерви́ровать *pf*
consolidate *vt(i)*	консолиди́ровать(ся) *impf, pf*
conspiratorial	конспира́торский *aj*
constitute	конституи́ровать *impf, pf*
construct	конструи́ровать *impf*, сконструи́ровать *pf*
consular	ко́нсульский *aj*
contact	конта́ктный *aj*
container	конте́йнерный *aj*
contour	ко́нтурный *aj*
contraband	контраба́ндный *aj*
contraceptive	контрацепти́вный *aj*
contract	контрактова́ть *impf*, законтрактова́ть *pf*
contrapuntal	контрапу́нктный, контрапункти́ческий *aj*
contrast	контрасти́ровать *impf*
contrasting	контра́стный *aj*
control	контроли́ровать *impf*, проконтроли́ровать *pf*
conventional	конвенциона́льный *aj*
conversion	конверсио́нный *aj*
convert (money)	конверти́ровать *impf, pf*
convoy	конвои́ровать *impf*
convulsive	конвульси́вный *aj*
cooperate, co-operate	коопери́роваться *impf, pf*
cooperative society	кооперати́вное о́бщество
coordinate, co-ordinate	координи́ровать *impf, pf*
coordinating, co-ordinating	координацио́нный *aj*
copra	копро́вый *aj*
Coptic	ко́птский *aj*
copying	копирова́льный *aj*
copying	копи́рование *nn*, копиро́вка *nf*
coriander	кориа́ндровый *aj*
Corinthian	кори́нфский *aj*
Cornish	корнуо́ллский, корни́йский *aj*
coronation	коронацио́нный *aj*
coronet	коро́на *nf*
corporal's	капра́льский *aj*
corporate	корпорати́вный *aj*

correct	корректи́ровать *impf*, прокорректи́ровать *pf*
correction	корректу́рный *aj*
correlate	коррели́ровать *impf*
correlate	корреля́т *nm*
correlative	корреляти́вный *aj*
corridor	коридо́рный *aj*
corrosive	коррози́йный *aj*
Corsican	корсика́нский *aj*
cosmetic	космети́ческий *aj*
cosmopolitanism	космополити́зм *nm*
Cossack [obs]	каза́цкий *aj*
Cossaks, the [obs]	каза́чество *nn*
Costa Rican	костарика́нский *aj*
costume, to dress in	костюми́роваться *impf, pf*
costumed	костюмиро́ванный *aj*
counter-revolutionary	контрреволюцио́нный *aj*
counterattack	контратакова́ть *impf, pf*
cowboy	ковбо́йский *aj*
creature	креату́ра *nf*
credit	аккредити́вный *aj*
credit	кредитова́ть *impf, pf*
credit	креди́тный *aj*
creditor's	кредито́рский *aj*
cremate	креми́ровать *impf, pf*
crematorium	кремацио́нный *aj*
crepe	кре́повый *aj*
Cretan	кри́тский *aj*
cretonne	крето́нный *aj*
Crimean	кры́мский *aj*
crisis	кри́зисный *aj*
critically	крити́чески *av*
criticize	критикова́ть *impf*
Cro-Magnon	кроманьо́нский *aj*
Croatian	хорва́тский *aj*
crocodile	крокоди́ловый *aj*
crown	короновать *impf, pf*
crown	коро́нный *aj*
cruise	кре́йси́ровать *impf*
cruiser, cruising	кре́йсерский *aj*
cryptographic	криптографи́ческий *aj*
crystallize *vt(i)*	кристаллизова́ть(ся) *impf, pf*
Cuban	куби́нский *aj*
cubic	куби́ческий *aj*
cuckoo	кукова́ть *impf*
culmination	кульминацио́нный *aj*
cultivable	культиви́руемый *aj*
cultivate	культиви́ровать *impf*

curiosity [rare thing]	курьёз *nm*, курьёзность *nf*
cursive	курси́вный *aj*
cutter	ка́терный *aj*
cybernetic	кибернети́ческий *aj*
cyclonic	циклони́ческий *aj*
cypress	кипари́совый *aj*
Cypriot	ки́прский *aj*
cytological	цитологи́ческий
czarist, tsarist	ца́рский *aj*
Czech	че́шский *aj*
Czechoslovak [obs]	чехослова́цкий *aj*
dactylic	дактили́ческий *aj*
Daghestan	дагеста́нский *aj*
daguerrotype	дагерроти́пный *aj*
Dalmatian	далма́тский *aj*
dance	танцева́ть *impf*, протанцева́ть, станцева́ть *pf*
Danish	да́тский *aj*
debate	дебати́ровать *impf*
debit	дебетова́ть *impf*, *pf*
debut	дебю́тный *aj*
debut, to make one's	дебюти́ровать *impf*, *pf*
decalcification	декальцина́ция *nf*
decalcify	декальцини́ровать *impf*, *pf*
December	дека́брьский *aj*
decentralize	децентрализова́ть *impf*, *pf*
decipher	дешифри́ровать *impf*, *pf*
declaim	деклами́ровать *impf*
declamatory	декламацио́нный *aj*
declare	деклари́ровать *impf*, *pf*
décolleté	декольти́рованный *aj*
decorate	декори́ровать *impf*, *pf*
decorative	декорати́вный *aj*
decree	декрети́ровать *impf*, *pf*
deductive	дедукти́вный *aj*
deficit	дефици́тный *aj*
deflationary	дефляцио́нный *aj*
defoliation	дефолиа́ция *nf*
deform	деформи́ровать *impf*, *pf*
deformed	деформи́рованный *aj*
degenerate	дегенери́ровать *impf*, *pf*
dehumanize	дегуманизи́ровать *impf*, *pf*
deist(ic)	деисти́ческий *aj*
delegate	делега́тский *aj*
delegate	делеги́ровать *impf*, *pf*
Delphic	делфи́йский *aj*
deltoid, delta-shaped	дельтови́дный *aj*
demagogic	демагоги́ческий *aj*
demilitarize	демилитаризова́ть *impf*, *pf*
demobilization	демобилизацио́нный *aj*
demobilize *vt(i)*	демобилизова́ть(ся)
democratic	демократи́ческий, демократи́чный *aj*
democratize	демократизи́ровать *impf*, *pf*
demographic	демографи́ческий *aj*
demonic, demoniac(al)	демони́ческий *aj*
demonstrate	демонстри́ровать *impf*, *pf*, продемонстри́ровать *pf*
demonstrative	демонстрати́вный *aj*
demoralize	деморализова́ть *impf*, *pf*
denationalize	денационализи́ровать *impf*, *pf*
denaturalization	денатурализа́ция *nf*
denaturalize	денатурализова́ть *impf*, *pf*
denature	денатури́ровать *impf*, *pf*
denazify	денацифици́ровать *impf*, *pf*
denounce	денонси́ровать *impf*, *pf*
deodorization	дезодора́ция *nf*
deodorize	дезодори́ровать *impf*, *pf*
depolarize	деполяризова́ть *impf*, *pf*
deport	депорти́ровать *impf*, *pf*
deposit	депози́тный *aj*
deposit	депони́ровать *impf*, *pf*
depression, depressive	депресси́вный *aj*
deputies'	депута́тский *aj*
desegregate	десегреги́ровать *impf*, *pf*
desert *vi*	дезерти́ровать *impf*, *pf*
dessert	десе́ртный *aj*
destabilize	дестабилизи́ровать *impf*, *pf*
detail, in	дета́льно *av*
detail	детализи́ровать *impf*, *pf*
detailing	детализа́ция *nf*
detective	детекти́вный *aj*
deterministic	детерминисти́ческий, детермини́стский *aj*
detonate	детони́ровать *impf*

conserve	консерви́ровать *impf*, законсерви́ровать *pf*
consolidate *vt(i)*	консолиди́ровать(ся) *impf, pf*
conspiratorial	конспира́торский *aj*
constitute	конституи́ровать *impf, pf*
construct	конструи́ровать *impf*, сконструи́ровать *pf*
consular	ко́нсульский *aj*
contact	конта́ктный *aj*
container	конте́йнерный *aj*
contour	ко́нтурный *aj*
contraband	контраба́ндный *aj*
contraceptive	контрацепти́вный *aj*
contract	контрактова́ть *impf*, законтрактова́ть *pf*
contrapuntal	контрапу́нктный, контрапункти́ческий *aj*
contrast	контрасти́ровать *impf*
contrasting	контра́стный *aj*
control	контроли́ровать *impf*, проконтроли́ровать *pf*
conventional	конвенциона́льный *aj*
conversion	конверсио́нный *aj*
convert (money)	конверти́ровать *impf*, *pf*
convoy	конвои́ровать *impf*
convulsive	конвульси́вный *aj*
cooperate, co-operate	коопери́роваться *impf*, *pf*
cooperative society	кооперати́вное о́бщество
coordinate, co-ordinate	координи́ровать *impf*, *pf*
coordinating, co-ordinating	координацио́нный *aj*
copra	копро́вый *aj*
Coptic	ко́птский *aj*
copying	копирова́льный *aj*
copying	копи́рование *nn*, копиро́вка *nf*
coriander	кориа́ндровый *aj*
Corinthian	кори́нфский *aj*
Cornish	корнуо́ллский, корни́йский *aj*
coronation	коронацио́нный *aj*
coronet	коро́на *nf*
corporal's	капра́льский *aj*
corporate	корпорати́вный *aj*
correct	корректи́ровать *impf*, прокорректи́ровать *pf*
correction	корректу́рный *aj*
correlate	коррели́ровать *impf*
correlate	корреля́т *nm*
correlative	корреляти́вный *aj*
corridor	коридо́рный *aj*
corrosive	коррози́йный *aj*
Corsican	корсика́нский *aj*
cosmetic	космети́ческий *aj*
cosmopolitanism	космополити́зм *nm*
Cossack [obs]	каза́цкий *aj*
Cossaks, the [obs]	каза́чество *nn*
Costa Rican	костарика́нский *aj*
costume, to dress in	костюми́роваться *impf, pf*
costumed	костюмиро́ванный *aj*
counter-revolutionary	контрреволюцио́нный *aj*
counterattack	контратакова́ть *impf*, *pf*
cowboy	ковбо́йский *aj*
creature	креату́ра *nf*
credit	аккредити́вный *aj*
credit	кредитова́ть *impf, pf*
credit	креди́тный *aj*
creditor's	кредито́рский *aj*
cremate	креми́ровать *impf, pf*
crematorium	кремацио́нный *aj*
crepe	кре́повый *aj*
Cretan	кри́тский *aj*
cretonne	крето́нный *aj*
Crimean	кры́мский *aj*
crisis	кри́зисный *aj*
critically	крити́чески *av*
criticize	критикова́ть *impf*
Cro-Magnon	кроманьо́нский *aj*
Croatian	хорва́тский *aj*
crocodile	крокоди́ловый *aj*
crown	короновать *impf, pf*
crown	коро́нный *aj*
cruise	кре́йси́ровать *impf*
cruiser, cruising	кре́йсерский *aj*
cryptographic	криптографи́ческий *aj*
crystallize *vt(i)*	кристаллизова́ть(ся) *impf, pf*
Cuban	куби́нский *aj*
cubic	куби́ческий *aj*
cuckoo	кукова́ть *impf*
culmination	кульминацио́нный *aj*
cultivable	культиви́руемый *aj*
cultivate	культиви́ровать *impf*

curiosity [rare thing]	курьёз *nm*, курьёзность *nf*
cursive	курси́вный *aj*
cutter	ка́терный *aj*
cybernetic	кибернети́ческий *aj*
cyclonic	циклони́ческий *aj*
cypress	кипари́совый *aj*
Cypriot	ки́прский *aj*
cytological	цитологи́ческий
czarist, tsarist	ца́рский *aj*
Czech	че́шский *aj*
Czechoslovak [obs]	чехослова́цкий *aj*
dactylic	дактили́ческий *aj*
Daghestan	дагеста́нский *aj*
daguerrotype	дагерроти́пный *aj*
Dalmatian	далма́тский *aj*
dance	танцева́ть *impf*, протанцева́ть, станцева́ть *pf*
Danish	да́тский *aj*
debate	дебати́ровать *impf*
debit	дебетова́ть *impf, pf*
debut	дебю́тный *aj*
debut, to make one's	дебюти́ровать *impf, pf*
decalcification	декальцина́ция *nf*
decalcify	декальцини́ровать *impf, pf*
December	дека́брьский *aj*
decentralize	децентрализова́ть *impf, pf*
decipher	дешифри́ровать *impf, pf*
declaim	деклами́ровать *impf*
declamatory	декламацио́нный *aj*
declare	деклари́ровать *impf, pf*
décolleté	декольти́рованный *aj*
decorate	декори́ровать *impf, pf*
decorative	декорати́вный *aj*
decree	декрети́ровать *impf, pf*
deductive	дедукти́вный *aj*
deficit	дефици́тный *aj*
deflationary	дефляцио́нный *aj*
defoliation	дефолиа́ция *nf*
deform	деформи́ровать *impf, pf*
deformed	деформи́рованный *aj*
degenerate	дегенери́ровать *impf, pf*
dehumanize	дегуманизи́ровать *impf, pf*
deist(ic)	деисти́ческий *aj*
delegate	делега́тский *aj*
delegate	делеги́ровать *impf, pf*
Delphic	делфи́йский *aj*
deltoid, delta-shaped	дельтови́дный *aj*
demagogic	демагоги́ческий *aj*
demilitarize	демилитаризова́ть *impf, pf*
demobilization	демобилизацио́нный *aj*
demobilize *vt(i)*	демобилизова́ть(ся)
democratic	демократи́ческий, демократи́чный *aj*
democratize	демократизи́ровать *impf, pf*
demographic	демографи́ческий *aj*
demonic, demoniac(al)	демони́ческий *aj*
demonstrate	демонстри́ровать *impf, pf*, продемонстри́ровать *pf*
demonstrative	демонстрати́вный *aj*
demoralize	деморализова́ть *impf, pf*
denationalize	денационализи́ровать *impf, pf*
denaturalization	денатурализа́ция *nf*
denaturalize	денатурализова́ть *impf, pf*
denature	денатури́ровать *impf, pf*
denazify	денацифици́ровать *impf, pf*
denounce	денонси́ровать *impf, pf*
deodorization	дезодора́ция *nf*
deodorize	дезодори́ровать *impf, pf*
depolarize	деполяризова́ть *impf, pf*
deport	депорти́ровать *impf, pf*
deposit	депози́тный *aj*
deposit	депони́ровать *impf, pf*
depression, depressive	депресси́вный *aj*
deputies'	депута́тский *aj*
desegregate	десегреги́ровать *impf, pf*
desert *vi*	дезерти́ровать *impf, pf*
dessert	десе́ртный *aj*
destabilize	дестабилизи́ровать *impf, pf*
detail, in	дета́льно *av*
detail	детализи́ровать *impf, pf*
detailing	детализа́ция *nf*
detective	детекти́вный *aj*
deterministic	детерминисти́ческий, детермини́стский *aj*
detonate	детони́ровать *impf*

conserve	консерви́ровать *impf*, законсерви́ровать *pf*
consolidate *vt(i)*	консолиди́ровать(ся) *impf*, *pf*
conspiratorial	конспира́торский *aj*
constitute	конституи́ровать *impf*, *pf*
construct	конструи́ровать *impf*, сконструи́ровать *pf*
consular	ко́нсульский *aj*
contact	конта́ктный *aj*
container	конте́йнерный *aj*
contour	ко́нтурный *aj*
contraband	контраба́ндный *aj*
contraceptive	контрацепти́вный *aj*
contract	контрактова́ть *impf*, законтрактова́ть *pf*
contrapuntal	контрапу́нктный, контрапункти́ческий *aj*
contrast	контрасти́ровать *impf*
contrasting	контра́стный *aj*
control	контроли́ровать *impf*, проконтроли́ровать *pf*
conventional	конвенциона́льный *aj*
conversion	конверсио́нный *aj*
convert (money)	конверти́ровать *impf*, *pf*
convoy	конвои́ровать *impf*
convulsive	конвульси́вный *aj*
cooperate, co-operate	коопери́роваться *impf*, *pf*
cooperative society	кооперати́вное о́бщество
coordinate, co-ordinate	координи́ровать *impf*, *pf*
coordinating, co-ordinating	координацио́нный *aj*
copra	копро́вый *aj*
Coptic	ко́птский *aj*
copying	копирова́льный *aj*
copying	копи́рование *nn*, копиро́вка *nf*
coriander	кориа́ндровый *aj*
Corinthian	кори́нфский *aj*
Cornish	корнуо́ллский, корни́йский *aj*
coronation	коронацио́нный *aj*
coronet	коро́на *nf*
corporal's	капра́льский *aj*
corporate	корпорати́вный *aj*
correct	корректи́ровать *impf*, прокорректи́ровать *pf*
correction	корректу́рный *aj*
correlate	коррели́ровать *impf*
correlate	корреля́т *nm*
correlative	корреляти́вный *aj*
corridor	коридо́рный *aj*
corrosive	коррози́йный *aj*
Corsican	корсика́нский *aj*
cosmetic	космети́ческий *aj*
cosmopolitanism	космополити́зм *nm*
Cossack [obs]	каза́цкий *aj*
Cossaks, the [obs]	каза́чество *nn*
Costa Rican	костарика́нский *aj*
costume, to dress in	костюми́роваться *impf*, *pf*
costumed	костюмиро́ванный *aj*
counter-revolutionary	контрреволюцио́нный *aj*
counterattack	контратакова́ть *impf*, *pf*
cowboy	ковбо́йский *aj*
creature	креату́ра *nf*
credit	аккредити́вный *aj*
credit	кредитова́ть *impf*, *pf*
credit	креди́тный *aj*
creditor's	кредито́рский *aj*
cremate	креми́ровать *impf*, *pf*
crematorium	кремацио́нный *aj*
crepe	кре́повый *aj*
Cretan	кри́тский *aj*
cretonne	крето́нный *aj*
Crimean	кры́мский *aj*
crisis	кри́зисный *aj*
critically	крити́чески *av*
criticize	критикова́ть *impf*
Cro-Magnon	кроманьо́нский *aj*
Croatian	хорва́тский *aj*
crocodile	крокоди́ловый *aj*
crown	короновать *impf*, *pf*
crown	коро́нный *aj*
cruise	кре́йси́ровать *impf*
cruiser, cruising	кре́йсерский *aj*
cryptographic	криптографи́ческий *aj*
crystallize *vt(i)*	кристаллизова́ть(ся) *impf*, *pf*
Cuban	куби́нский *aj*
cubic	куби́ческий *aj*
cuckoo	кукова́ть *impf*
culmination	кульминацио́нный *aj*
cultivable	культиви́руемый *aj*
cultivate	культиви́ровать *impf*

curiosity [rare thing]	курьёз *nm* , курьёзность *nf*
cursive	курси́вный *aj*
cutter	ка́терный *aj*
cybernetic	кибернети́ческий *aj*
cyclonic	циклони́ческий *aj*
cypress	кипари́совый *aj*
Cypriot	ки́прский *aj*
cytological	цитологи́ческий
czarist, tsarist	ца́рский *aj*
Czech	че́шский *aj*
Czechoslovak [obs]	чехослова́цкий *aj*
dactylic	дактили́ческий *aj*
Daghestan	дагеста́нский *aj*
daguerrotype	дагерроти́пный *aj*
Dalmatian	далма́тский *aj*
dance	танцева́ть *impf*, протанцева́ть, станцева́ть *pf*
Danish	да́тский *aj*
debate	дебати́ровать *impf*
debit	дебетова́ть *impf*, *pf*
debut	дебю́тный *aj*
debut, to make one's	дебюти́ровать *impf*, *pf*
decalcification	декальцина́ция *nf*
decalcify	декальцини́ровать *impf*, *pf*
December	дека́брьский *aj*
decentralize	децентрализова́ть *impf*, *pf*
decipher	дешифри́ровать *impf*, *pf*
declaim	деклами́ровать *impf*
declamatory	декламацио́нный *aj*
declare	деклари́ровать *impf*, *pf*
décolleté	декольти́рованный *aj*
decorate	декори́ровать *impf*, *pf*
decorative	декорати́вный *aj*
decree	декрети́ровать *impf*, *pf*
deductive	дедукти́вный *aj*
deficit	дефици́тный *aj*
deflationary	дефляцио́нный *aj*
defoliation	дефолиа́ция *nf*
deform	деформи́ровать *impf*, *pf*
deformed	деформи́рованный *aj*
degenerate	дегенери́ровать *impf*, *pf*
dehumanize	дегуманизи́ровать *impf*, *pf*
deist(ic)	деисти́ческий *aj*
delegate	делега́тский *aj*
delegate	делеги́ровать *impf*, *pf*
Delphic	делфи́йский *aj*
deltoid, delta-shaped	дельтови́дный *aj*
demagogic	демагоги́ческий *aj*
demilitarize	демилитаризова́ть *impf*, *pf*
demobilization	демобилизацио́нный *aj*
demobilize *vt(i)*	демобилизова́ть(ся)
democratic	демократи́ческий, демократи́чный *aj*
democratize	демократизи́ровать *impf*, *pf*
demographic	демографи́ческий *aj*
demonic, demoniac(al)	демони́ческий *aj*
demonstrate	демонстри́ровать *impf*, *pf*, продемонстри́ровать *pf*
demonstrative	демонстрати́вный *aj*
demoralize	деморализова́ть *impf*, *pf*
denationalize	денационализи́ровать *impf*, *pf*
denaturalization	денатурализа́ция *nf*
denaturalize	денатурализова́ть *impf*, *pf*
denature	денатури́ровать *impf*, *pf*
denazify	денацифици́ровать *impf*, *pf*
denounce	денонси́ровать *impf*, *pf*
deodorization	дезодора́ция *nf*
deodorize	дезодори́ровать *impf*, *pf*
depolarize	деполяризова́ть *impf*, *pf*
deport	депорти́ровать *impf*, *pf*
deposit	депози́тный *aj*
deposit	депони́ровать *impf*, *pf*
depression, depressive	депресси́вный *aj*
deputies'	депута́тский *aj*
desegregate	десегреги́ровать *impf*, *pf*
desert *vi*	дезерти́ровать *impf*, *pf*
dessert	десе́ртный *aj*
destabilize	дестабилизи́ровать *impf*, *pf*
detail, in	дета́льно *av*
detail	детализи́ровать *impf*, *pf*
detailing	детализа́ция *nf*
detective	детекти́вный *aj*
deterministic	детерминисти́ческий, детермини́стский *aj*
detonate	детони́ровать *impf*

devaluate, devalue	девальви́ровать *impf, pf*
devilish	дья́вольский *aj*
diacritical	диакрити́ческий *aj*
diagnostic	диагности́ческий *aj*
diagonal	диагона́льный *aj*
dialectal	диалекта́льный *aj*
dialectical	диалекти́ческий *aj*
dialog(ue)	диало́говый *aj*
dialog(ue)	диалоги́ческий *aj*
diathermic	диатерми́ческий *aj*
dictate (a letter)	диктова́ть *impf,* продиктова́ть, *pf*
dictatorial	диктато́рский *aj*
didactic	дидакти́ческий *aj*
diesel	ди́зельный *aj*
dietary	диети́ческий *aj*
differentiate	дифференци́ровать *impf, pf*
differentiated	дифференци́рованный *aj*
dilettante	дилета́нтский *aj*
diluvial	дилювиа́льный *aj*
diphtheria, diphtherial	дифтери́йный *aj*
diphthongal	дифтонга́льный, дифтонги́ческий *aj*
diploma	дипло́мный *aj*
directive	директи́вный *aj*
directorial, director's	дире́кторский *aj*
disciplinary	дисциплина́рный *aj*
discipline	дисциплини́ровать *impf, pf*
discotèque	дискоте́чный *aj*
discount	дисконти́ровать *impf, pf*
discount	диско́нтный *aj*
discredit	дискредити́ровать *impf, pf*
discriminate (against)	дискримини́ровать *impf, pf*
discriminatory	дискриминацио́нный *aj*
discuss	дискути́ровать *impf, pf*
discussion	дискуссио́нный *aj*
disinfect	дезинфици́ровать *impf, pf*
disinfectant	дезинфици́руюший *aj*
disinform	дезинформи́ровать *impf, pf*
disorganization	неорганизо́ванность *nf*
disorganize	дезорганизова́ть *impf, pf*
disorient	дезориенти́ровать *impf, pf*
disproportionately	непропорциона́льно *av*
disqualify	дисквалифици́ровать *impf, pf*
dissimilate	диссимили́ровать(ся) *impf, pf*
dissonant, to be	диссони́ровать *impf*
distance oneself, to	дистанци́роваться *impf*
distance, at a	дистанцио́нный *aj*
distil(l)	дистилли́ровать *impf, pf*
dithyrambic	дифирамби́ческий *aj*
divisional	дивизио́нный *aj*
doctoral, doctor's	до́кторский *aj*
document	документи́ровать *impf, pf*
dollar	до́лларовый *aj*
dominant	домина́нтовый *aj*
dominate	домини́ровать *impf*
Dominican	доминика́нский *aj*
donor	до́норский *aj*
dose	дози́ровать *impf, pf*
double [role]	дубли́ровать [роль] *impf, pf*
drain	дрени́ровать *impf, pf*
drainage	дрена́жный *aj*
dramatically	драмати́чески *av*
dramatize	драматизи́ровать *impf, pf*
drape (with something)	драпирова́ть *impf,* задрапирова́ть *pf*
drift	дрейфова́ть *impf*
drifting	дрейфу́ющий *aj*
Druidic	друиди́ческий *aj*
dualistic	дуалисти́ческий *aj*
Dublin	ду́блинский *aj*
duplicate	дублика́тный *aj*
duplicate	дубли́ровать *impf*
dynastic	династи́ческий *aj*
dysentery, dysenteric	дизентери́йный *aj*
dyspeptic	страда́ющий диспепси́ей *nf*
ecological	экологи́ческий *aj*
economize	эконо́мить *impf,* сэконо́мить *pf*
Ecuadorean	эквадо́рский *aj*
Edinburgh	эдинбу́ргский *aj*
effective [done for effect]	эффе́ктный *aj*
effectively	эффекти́вно *av*
egalitarian	эгалита́рный *aj*

Egyptian	еги́петский *aj*
electrify (a railroad)	электрифици́ровать *impf, pf*
electrochemical	электрохими́ческий *aj*
electrolytic	электролити́ческий *aj*
electrostatic	электростати́ческий *aj*
elegaic	элеги́ческий *aj*
elegantly	элега́нтно *av*
elite, élite, elitist	элита́рный *aj*
Elysian	елисе́йский *aj*
emancipate	эмансипи́ровать *impf, pf*
emancipated	эмансипи́рованный *aj*
embalm	бальзами́ровать *impf*, набальзами́ровать *pf*
embalmed	набальза́мированный *aj*
emblematic	эмблемати́ческий *aj*
embryonic	эмбриона́льный *aj*
emigrant	эмигра́нтский *aj*
emigrate	эмигри́ровать *impf, pf*
emigration	эмиграцио́нный *aj*
emission	эмиссио́нный *aj*
emit (paper money)	эмитти́ровать *impf, pf*
emitter	эмите́нт, емитте́р *nm*
emotional	эмоциона́льный *aj*
emotionally	эмоциона́льно *av*
empirical	эмпири́ческий, эмпири́чный *aj*
enamel	эмалирова́ть *impf*
encipher	шифрова́ть *impf*, зашифрова́ть *pf*
enclitic	энклити́ческий *aj*
encyclopedic (BR encyclopaedic)	энциклопеди́ческий *aj*
endocrine	эндокри́нный *aj*
endogamous	эндога́мый *aj*
engineering	инжене́рный *aj*
English	англи́йский *aj*
engrave	гравирова́ть *impf*, выгравирова́ть *pf*
engraver's, engraving	гравирова́льный *aj*
entomological	энтомологи́ческий
eolithic	эоли́товый, эолити́ческий *aj*
eparchial	епархиа́льный *aj*
ephemeral	эфеме́рный *aj*
epicurean	эпикуре́йсксий *aj*
epidemic	эпидеми́ческий *aj*
epidermal	эпидерми́ческий *aj*
epigrammatic	эпиграммати́ческий *aj*
epileptic	эпилепти́ческий *aj*
episcopal	епи́скопский *aj*
Episcopalian	епископа́льный *aj*
epistemological	эпистемологи́ческий *aj*
eponymous	эпони́мный *aj*
equip	экипирова́ть *impf, pf*
equivalent	эквивале́нтный *aj*
ergonomic	эргономи́ческий *aj*
erode	эроди́ровать *impf*
erosive	эрози́вный *aj*
erudite	эруди́рованный *aj*
escapist	эскапи́стский *aj*
eschatological	эсхатологи́ческий *aj*
escort	эскорти́ровать *impf, pf*
Eskimo	эскимо́сский *aj*
especially	специально *av*
espionage	шпио́нский *aj*
Estonian	эсто́нский *aj*
Ethiopian	эфио́пский *aj*
ethnocentric	этноцентри́ческий *aj*
ethnographic	этнографи́ческий *aj*
ethnological	этнологи́ческий *aj*
ethyl	этило́вый *aj*
Etruscan	этру́сский *aj*
eucalyptus	эвкали́птовый *aj*
Eucharistic	евхаристи́ческий *aj*
eugenic	евгени́ческий *aj*
euphemistic	эвфемисти́ческий *aj*
euphonious	эвфони́ческий *aj*
Eurasian	еврази́йский *aj*
European	европе́йский *aj*
Europeanize	европеизи́ровать *impf, pf*
evacuate	эвакуи́ровать *impf, pf*
evacuation	эвакуацио́нный *aj*
evangelical	евангели́ческий *aj*
evolutionary	эволюцио́нный *aj*
evolve	эволюциони́ровать *impf*
examination	экзаменацио́нный *aj*
examine	экзаменова́ть *impf*, проэкзаменова́ть *pf*
excursionary	экскурсио́нный *aj*
exhume	эксгуми́ровать *impf, pf*
existential(ist)	экзистенциа́льный *aj*
exogamous	экзога́мный *aj*
expansionary, expansionist	экспансионисти́ческий *aj*
expansive	экспанси́вный *aj*
expatriate	экспатрии́ровать *impf, pf*
expeditionary	экспедицио́нный *aj*
experiment	эксперименти́ровать *impf*
expert	э́кспертный *aj*

exploit (a person)	эксплуати́ровать *impf*
export, exported	э́кспортный *aj*
export	экспорти́ровать *impf, pf*
exportable	экспорти́руемый *aj*
expose	экспони́ровать *impf*
expropriate (property)	экспроприи́ровать *impf, pf*
extraterritorial	экстратерриториа́льный *aj*
extremist	экстреми́стский *aj*
fabricate	фабрикова́ть *impf*, сфабрикова́ть *pf*
fantasize	фантази́ровать *impf*
fantastic	фантасти́ческий, фантасти́чный *aj*
farm, farming	фе́рмовый *aj*
fascist, Fascist	фаши́стский *aj*
fatalistic	фаталисти́ческий, фаталисти́чный *aj*
fatally	фата́льно *av*
fax	перед(ав)а́ть по фа́ксу
February	февра́льский *aj*
fecal (BR faecal)	фека́льный *aj*
feint	сде́лать финт, финти́ть *impf, pf*
felt	фе́тровый *aj*
feminist	фемини́стский, феминисти́ческий *aj*
ferment	ферменти́ровать *impf*
festival	фестива́льный *aj*
fiber	фи́бровый *aj*
fig	фи́говый *aj*
figure	фигу́рный *aj*
figure	фигури́ровать *impf*
Fijian	фиджи́йский *aj*
filigree	филигра́нный *aj*
filter	фильтрова́ть *impf*, профильтрова́ть *pf*
final	фина́льный *aj*
finish	финиши́ровать *impf, pf*
Finnish	финля́ндский, фи́нский *aj*
firm	фи́рменный *aj*
fix	фикси́ровать *impf, pf*, зафикси́ровать *pf*
flank	фланки́ровать *impf, pf*
flanking	фланго́вый *aj*
flannel	фланельный, флане́левый *aj*
Flemish	флама́ндский *aj*
flirt	флиртова́ть *impf*
Florentine	флоренти́йский *aj*
fluoresce	флюоресци́ровать *impf*
flutist	фле́йтовый *aj*
focal	фо́кусный *aj*
focus	фокуси́ровать *impf*, сфокуси́ровать *pf*
forage	фура́жный *aj*
forage	фуражи́ровать *impf*
formalize	оформля́ть *impf*, офо́рмить *pf*
format	формати́ровать *impf, pf*
formative	формиру́ющий *aj*
formatted	форма́тный *aj*
formulate	формули́ровать *impf*, сформули́ровать *pf*
fractional	фракцио́нный *aj*
Franciscan	франциска́нский *aj*
Frankish	фра́нкский *aj*
French	францу́зский *aj*
French-Canadian	фра́нко-кана́дский *aj*
friction	фрикцио́нный *aj*
frontline	фронтово́й *aj*
fruit	фрукто́вый *aj*
funded	фунди́рованный *aj*
futuristic	футуристи́ческий *aj*
gabardine, gaberdine	габарди́новый *aj*
Gaelic	гэ́льский *aj*
galactic	галакти́ческий *aj*
Galician [Spain]	галиси́йский *aj*
Galician [Eastern Europe]	галицийский *aj*
Galilean	галиле́йский *aj*
Gallic	галльский *aj*
galvanic	гальвани́ческий *aj*
Gandhian	ганди́стский *aj*
gangrenous	гангрено́зный *aj*
garnish	гарни́ровать *impf, pf*
garrison	гарнизо́нный *aj*
gas, gaseous	га́зовый, газообра́зный *aj*
Gascon	гаско́нский *aj*
gastronomic	гастрономи́ческий *aj*
gauze	га́зовый *aj*
gelatinous	желати́новый *aj*
genealogical	генеалоги́ческий *aj*
general's	генера́льский *aj*
generator	генера́торный *aj*
Genevan	жене́вский *aj*
genius	гениа́льный *aj*
genocidal	геноци́дный *aj*
Genoese, Genovese	генуэ́зский *aj*
gentlemen's	джентльме́нский *aj*

geodesic, geodetic	геодези́ческий *aj*
geophysical	геофизи́ческий *aj*
geopolitical	геополити́ческий *aj*
German	герма́нский *aj*
Gestapo	геста́повский *aj*
gesticulate	жестикули́рова́ть *impf*
Ghanaian	га́нский *aj*
gladiator, gladiatorial	гладиа́торский *aj*
Glaswegian	гла́зговский *aj*
glaze	глазурова́ть *impf, pf*
gnostic	гности́ческий *aj*
gnotobiotic	гнотобиологи́ческий *aj*
graceful	грацио́зный *aj*
gracefully	грацио́зно *av*
graduate	градуи́ровать *impf*, проградуи́ровать *pf*
graduated	градуи́рованный *aj*
granite	грани́тный *aj*
granulate	гранули́ровать *impf, pf*
graphic(al)	графи́ческий *aj*
graphite	графи́тный, графи́товый *aj*
gravelly	грави́йный *aj*
gravitational	гравитацио́нный *aj*
Greek	гре́ческий *aj*
Greenland	гренла́ндский *aj*
Gregorian	грегориа́нский, григориа́нский *aj*
grenadier's	гренаде́рский *aj*
grimace	грима́сничать *impf*
grimacer	грима́сник *nm*
grotesqueness	гроте́скность *nf*
group	группирова́ть(ся) *impf*, сгруппирова́ть(ся) *pf*
group	группово́й *aj*
guarantee	гаранти́йный *aj*
guarantee	гаранти́ровать *impf, pf*
Guatemalan	гватема́льский *aj*
gubernatorial	губерна́торский *aj*
Guernsey	гернсе́йский *aj*
guest, guests'	гостево́й *aj*
guild [obs]	гильде́йский *aj*
guillotine [obs]	гильотини́ровать *impf, pf*
Guinean	гвине́йский *aj*
gutta-percha	гуттапе́рчевый *aj*
Guyanese	гайа́нский *aj*
gymnastic	гимнасти́ческий *aj*
gynecological (BR gynaecological)	гинекологи́ческий *aj*
gypsum, gypseous	ги́псовый *aj*
gyroscopic	гироскопи́ческий *aj*
Haitian	гаитя́нский *aj*
hallucinate	галлюцини́ровать *impf*
hallucinatory	галлюцинато́рный *aj*
hallucinogenic	галлюциноге́нный *aj*
Hanoi	хано́йский *aj*
harmonize	гармонизи́ровать, гармони́ровать *impf*
harpoon	гарпу́нить *impf*
Hasidic	хаси́дский *aj*
Hawaiian	гава́йский *aj*
hedonistic	гедонисти́ческий *aj*
Hegelian	гегелья́нский
Helsinki	хе́льсинский *aj*
hemorrhoidal (BR haemorrhoidal)	геморроида́льный *aj*
heraldic	геральди́ческий *aj*
Herculean	геркуле́сов *aj*
heretical	ерети́ческий *aj*
hermaphroditism	гермафродити́зм *nm*
hermetically	гермети́чески *av*
hermetically seal, to	герметизи́ровать *impf, pf*, загерметизи́ровать *pf*
heroically	герои́чески *av*
heuristic	эвристи́ческий *aj*
hierarchical	иерархи́ческий *aj*
Himalayan	гимала́йский *aj*
Hindu	инду́сский *aj*
Hispanic	испа́нский *aj*
histological	гистологи́ческий *aj*
Hitlerian, Hitlerite	гитлеровский *aj*
hockey	хокке́йный *aj*
homeopathic (BR homoeopathic)	гомеопати́ческий *aj*
Homeric	гоме́рийский, гоме́ровский *aj*
homogenize	гомогенизи́ровать *impf*
homographic	омографи́ческий *aj*
homologous	гомологи́ческий *aj*
homonymous	омоними́ческий *aj*
Honduran	гондура́сский *aj*
hooligan	хулига́нский *aj*
hooligan, to act like a	хулига́нить *impf*, нахулига́нить *pf*
Horatian	гора́циев *aj*
horizontally	горизонта́льно *av*
hormonal	гормона́льный *aj*
hospital	госпита́льный *aj*
hospitalize	госпитализи́ровать *impf, pf*

hotel	оте́льный *aj*
Hottentot	готтенто́тский *aj*
Huguenot [obs]	гугено́тский *aj*
humanely	гума́нно *av*
Hungarian	венге́рский *aj*
hurricane	урага́нный *aj*
hybridize	гибридизи́ровать *impf*
hydrate	гидрати́ровать *impf*
hydraulic	гидравли́ческий *aj*
hydroelectric	гидроэлектри́ческий *aj*
hydrographic	гидрографи́ческий *aj*
hydrological	гидрологи́ческий *aj*
hydrolytic	гидро́лизный *aj*
hygienic	гигиени́ческий, гигени́чный *aj*
hygroscopic	гигроскопи́ческий *aj*
hyperbolic	гиперболи́ческий *aj*
hypertrophied	гипертрофи́рованный *aj*
hypnotic	гипноти́ческий *aj*
hypnotize	гипнотизи́ровать *impf*, загипнотизи́ровать *pf*
hypothesize	стро́ить гипо́тезу
hysterical	истери́ческий *aj*
iambic	ямби́ческий *aj*
Iberian	ибери́йский *aj*
Icelandic	исла́ндский *aj*
ichthyological	ихтиологи́ческий *aj*
icon, ikon	ико́нный *aj*
iconoclastic	иконобо́рческий *aj*
idea	иде́йный *aj*
ideal	идеа́льный *aj*
idealize	идеализи́ровать *impf*, *pf*
identify (oneself)	идентифици́ровать(ся) *impf*, *pf*
ideographic(al)	идеографи́ческий *aj*
ideological	идеологи́ческий, иде́йный *aj*
idolatrous	идолопокло́ннический *aj*
idyllic	идилли́ческий *aj*
ignore	игнори́ровать *impf*, *pf*, проигнори́ровать *pf*
illogical	нелоги́чный *aj*
illogicality	нелоги́чность *nf*
illogically	нелоги́чно *av*
illuminate	иллюмини́ровать *impf*, *pf*
illusory	иллюзо́рный *aj*
illustrate	иллюстри́ровать *impf*, *pf*, проиллюстри́ровать *pf*
illustrative	иллюстрати́вный *aj*
imitate	имити́ровать *impf*
immanent	имма не́нтный *aj*
immigrate	иммигри́ровать *impf*, *pf*
immigration	иммиграцио́нный *aj*
immobilize	иммобилизова́ть *pf*
immunize	иммунизи́ровать *impf*, *pf*
imperial [of an emperor]	импера́торский *aj*
imperial [of an empire]	импе́рский *aj*
imperialist(ic)	империалисти́ческий *aj*
implant	импланти́ровать *impf*, *pf*
impolitic	неполити́чный *aj*
import, imported	и́мпортный *aj*
import	импорти́ровать *impf*, *pf*
impromptu	экспро́мтом *av*
improvisational	импровиза́торский
improvise	импровизи́ровать *impf*
improvised	импровизи́рованный *aj*
Incan	инкский *aj*
incorporate	инкорпори́ровать *impf*, *pf*
incriminate	инкримини́ровать *impf*, *pf*
incubator	инкуба́торный *aj*
indelicate	неделика́тный *aj*
index	индекси́ровать *impf*
Indian [Native American]	инде́йский *aj*
Indian [Asian]	инди́йский *aj*
indicated	индикато́рный *aj*
individualize	индивидуализи́ровать *impf*, *pf*
Indo-Chinese	индокита́йский *aj*
Indonesian	индонези́йский *aj*
induction	индукцио́нный *aj*
inductive	индукти́вный *aj*
industrial	индустриа́льный *aj*
industrialize	индустриализи́ровать *impf*, *pf*
inertial	инерцио́нный *aj*
inertness	ине́ртность *nf*
infecting	инфици́рование *nn*

infiltrate	инфильтрова́ть *impf*
inflationary	инфля́цио́нный *aj*
inhalant	ингаляцио́нный *aj*
inharmonious	негармони́чный *aj*
initiating, with initiative	инициати́вный *aj*
inject	инъекти́ровать *impf, pf*
innovative	нова́торский *aj*
inoculate	инокули́ровать *impf, pf*
inquisitorial	инквизи́торский *aj*
inspect	инспекти́ровать *impf, pf*
inspection	инспекцио́нный *aj*
inspector's	инспекто́рский *aj*
instinctive	инстинкти́вный *aj*
instinctively	инстинкти́вно *av*
instruct	инструкти́ровать *impf*
instructor's	инстру́кторский *aj*
instrumental	инструмента́льный *aj*
integrate (races)	интегри́ровать *impf, pf*
intensify	интенсифици́ровать *impf, pf*
interested (in), be	интересова́ться *impf*
internationalist(ic)	интернационали́ст-ский *aj*
internationalize	интернационали-зи́ровать *impf, pf*
interpolate	интерполи́ровать *impf, pf*
interpret	интерпрети́ровать *impf, pf*
interview	интервьюи́ровать *impf*, проинтер-вьюи́ровать *pf*
intimately	инти́мно *av*
intone	интони́ровать *impf*
intrigue	интригова́ть *impf*, заинтригова́ть *pf*
introspective	интроспекти́вный *aj*
invalid's	инвали́дный *aj*
inventory	инвента́рный *aj*
inventory	инвентаризи́ровать *impf, pf*
invest	инвести́ровать *impf, pf*
investment	инвестицио́нный *aj*
iodine, iodic	йо́дистый *aj*
ion, ionic	ио́нный *aj*
Ionian	иони́йский *aj*
Ionic	иони́ческий *aj*
ionize	ионизи́ровать *impf*
ionospheric	ионосфе́рный *aj*
Iranian	ира́нский *aj*

Iraqi	ира́кский *aj*
Irish	ирла́ндский *aj*
ironic (person)	ирони́чный *aj*
ironic(al)	ирони́ческий *aj*
ironically	ирони́чно *av*
irregularity	нерегуля́рность *nf*
Islamic	ислами́стский *aj*
isolate	изоли́ровать *impf, pf*
isolated	изоли́рованный *aj*
isolationist(ic)	изоляциони́стский *aj*
isomeric	изоме́рный *aj*
Israeli	изра́ильский *aj*
Italian	италья́нский *aj*
Jamaican	яма́йский *aj*
January	янва́рский *aj*
Japanese	япо́нский *aj*
jargon	жарго́нный *aj*
jasmine	жасми́нный, жасми́новый *aj*
Javanese	ява́нский *aj*
jazz, jazzy	джа́зовый *aj*
jeans	джи́нсовый *aj*
jersey	джерсо́вый *aj*
Jesuit(ic)	иезуи́тский *aj*
jockey's	жоке́йский *aj*
Jordanian	иорда́нский *aj*
journalistic	журнали́стский *aj*
jubilee	юбиле́йный *aj*
Judaic	иуде́йский *aj*
juggle	жонгли́ровать *impf*
July	ию́льский *aj*
June	ию́ньский *aj*
juridical	юриди́ческий *aj*
jute	джу́товый *aj*
kaleidoscopic	калейдоскопи́ческий *aj*
Kalmyk, Kalmuck	калмы́цкий *aj*
Kampuchean [obs]	кампучи́йский *aj*
Kantian	кантиа́нский *aj*
Karakalpak	каракалпа́кский *aj*
Karelian	каре́льский *aj*
karst	ка́рстовый *aj*
Kashmiri	кашми́рский *aj*
Kazakh	каза́хский *aj*
Kenyan	кени́йский *aj*
kerosene	кероси́новый *aj*
Khmer	кхме́рский *aj*
Kievan	ки́евский *aj*
kilogram, of one	килограммо́вый *aj*
kilometric	километро́вый *aj*
Kirghiz	кирги́зский *aj*
knock out	нокаути́ровать *impf, pf*
kolkhoz	колхо́зный *aj*
Komsomol	комсомо́льский *aj*

Korean	коре́йский *aj*
Kremlin	кремлёвский *aj*
Kurdish	курдский *aj*
Kuwaiti	куве́йтский *aj*
labialize	лабиализова́ть *impf, pf*
Laborite (BR, Labourite)	лейбори́стский *aj*
laconically	лакони́чно *av*
lacquer	лакирова́ть *impf,* отлакирова́ть *pf*
lamp	ла́мповый *aj*
lancet	ланце́тный *aj*
Laotian	лао́сский *aj*
Lappish	лапла́ндский *aj*
laser	ла́зерный *aj*
Latin	лати́нский *aj*
Latin-American	латиноамерика́нский *aj*
Latinize	латинизи́ровать *impf, pf*
Latvian, Lettish	латы́шский *aj*
lavender	лава́ндовый *aj*
leasing	ли́зинговый *aj*
Lebanese	лива́нский *aj*
lecturing	ле́кторский *aj*
legislative	легислату́рный *aj*
lemon	лимо́нный *aj*
Leningrad	ленингра́дский *aj*
Leninist	ле́нинский *aj*
leprous	лепро́зный *aj*
Levantine	леванти́йский *aj*
lexically	лекси́ческий *aj*
liberalize	либерализова́ть *impf, pf*
liberally	либера́льно *av*
Liberian	либери́йский *aj*
Libyan	ливи́йский *aj*
licensing	лицензио́нный *aj*
licorice, liquorice	лакри́чный *aj*
Lilliputian	лилипу́тский *aj*
limit	лимити́ровать *impf, pf*
line [draw lines]	линова́ть *impf,* налинова́ть *pf*
liquidate	ликвиди́ровать *impf, pf*
liter, litre	литро́вый *aj*
lithograph	литографи́ровать *impf, pf*
lithographic	литогра́фский *aj*
Lithuanian	лито́вский *aj*
liturgical	литурги́ческий *aj*
lobby	лобби́ровать *impf, pf*
lobbying	лобби́рование *nn*
localize	локализова́ть *impf, pf*

logarithmic	логарифми́ческий *aj*
logic, lack of	нелоги́чность *nf*
logically	логи́чно *av*
Lombard	ломбарди́йский, ломба́рдский *aj*
London	ло́ндонский *aj*
loyally	лоя́льно *av*
lute	лю́тный *aj*
Lutheran	лютера́нский
Luxemb(o)urg	люксембу́ргский *aj*
lycée	лице́йский *aj*
lymph	ли́мфа *nf*
lymphatic	лимфати́ческий *aj*
lynch	линчева́ть *impf, pf*
macaronic [style]	макарони́ческий *aj*
Macedonian	македо́нский *aj*
maceration	мацера́ция *nf*
machine	маши́нный *aj*
macrocephalic	макроцефа́льный *aj*
Madrid	мадри́дский *aj*
Mafia	мафио́зный *aj*
magazine	магази́нный *aj*
magnesium	ма́гниевый *aj*
Magyar	мадья́рский *aj*
maize	маи́совый *aj*
malachite	малахи́товый *aj*
Malagasy	малагаси́йский *aj*
malarial	маляри́йный *aj*
Malay(an)	мала́йский *aj*
Malian	мали́йский *aj*
Maltese	мальти́йский *aj*
Malthusian	мальтузиа́нский *aj*
Manchurian	маньчжу́рский *aj*
mandarin	мандари́нский, мандари́нный, мандари́новый *aj*
mandate	манда́тный *aj*
mandibular	мандибуля́рный *aj*
maneuver (BR manoevre)	маневри́ровать *impf,* сманеври́ровать *pf*
maneuverability (BR manoeverability)	манёвренность *nf*
manganese	ма́рганцевый *aj*
mango	ма́нговый *aj*
maniacal, manic	маниака́льный *aj*
manicure	маникю́рный *aj*
Manila	мани́льский *aj*
manipulate	манипули́ровать *impf*
manometric	манометри́ческий *aj*
manorial	манориа́льный *aj*
Maoist	маои́стский *aj*
Maori	маори́йский *aj*
marathon	марафо́нский *aj*

maraud	мародёрствовать *impf, pf*
marauding	мародёрский *aj*
March	ма́ртовский *aj*
march	марши́ровать *impf, pf*
marching	ма́ршевый, марширо́вочный *aj*
margarine	маргари́новый *aj*
Mari	мари́йский *aj*
marinate	маринова́ть *impf*, замаринова́ть *pf*
marionette	марионе́точный *aj*
marshall	ма́ршальский *aj*
Martian	марсиа́нский *aj*
Marxist, Marxian	маркси́стский *aj*
Marxist-Leninist	маркси́стско-ле́нинский *aj*
mask	маскирова́ть *impf*, замаскирова́ть *pf*
masked	замаскиро́ванный *aj*
Masonic	масо́нский *aj*
masquerade	маскара́дный *aj*
mass	ма́ссовой *aj*
massage	масси́ровать *impf, pf*
massed	масси́рованный *aj*
master's	маги́стерский *aj*
mastic	масти́ковый *aj*
masturbate	мастурби́ровать *impf, pf*
materialist	материалисти́ческий *aj*
materialistic	материалисти́чный *aj*
materially	материа́льно *av*
Mauritanian	маврита́нский *aj*
May	ма́йский *aj*
mechanistic	механи́ческий *aj*
medical	медици́нский *aj*
meditate	медити́ровать *impf*
meeting	митинго́вый *aj*
melancholic	меланхоли́ческий *aj*
melancholy	меланхоли́чный *aj*
Melanesian	меланези́йский *aj*
meliorative	мелиорати́вный *aj*
melodic	мелоди́ческий *aj*
melodious	мелоди́чный *aj*
melodiousness	мелоди́чность *nf*
melodramatic	мелодрамати́ческий *aj*
memorial	мемориа́льный *aj*
Menshevist [obs]	меньшеви́стский *aj*
menstrual	менструа́льный *aj*
menstruate	менструи́ровать *impf*
mercerized	мерсеризо́ванный *aj*
meridian, meridianal	меридиона́льный *aj*
merino	мерино́совый *aj*
Mesolithic	мезолити́ческий *aj*
Messianic	мессиа́нский *aj*
metal(l)ization	металлиза́ция *nf*
metal(l)ize	металлизи́ровать *impf, pf*
metalliferous	металлоно́сный *aj*
metallurgical	металлурги́ческий *aj*
metaphoric(al)	метафори́ческий *aj*
metaphysical	метафизи́ческий *aj*
meteoric	метео́рный *aj*
meteorological	метеорологи́ческий *aj*
methodological	методологи́ческий *aj*
metrological	метрологи́ческий *aj*
metropolitan [of church]	митрополи́чий *aj*
Mexican	мексика́нский *aj*
microcephalic	микроцефали́ческий *aj*
migrate	мигри́ровать *impf*
militaristic	милитаристи́ческий *aj*
militarize	милитаризи́ровать *impf, pf*
militia	милице́йский *aj*
Miltonian	мильтоно́вский *aj*
mimic	мими́ческий *aj*
mine	мини́ровать *impf*, замини́ровать *pf*
mineralogical	минералоги́ческий *aj*
miniaturize	миниатюризова́ть *impf, pf*
ministerial	министе́рский *aj*
minute	мину́тный *aj*
misinform	непра́вильно информи́ровать, дезинфици́ровать *impf, pf*
missionary	миссионе́рский *aj*
mnemonic	мнемони́ческий *aj*
mobilization	мобилизацио́нный *aj*
mobilize *vt(i)*	мобилизова́ть(ся) *impf, pf*
model	модели́ровать *impf, pf*
modern	моде́рный, моде́рновый *aj*
modernize	модернизова́ть, модернизи́ровать *impf, pf*
modify	модифици́ровать *impf, pf*
modulate	модули́ровать *impf*
mohair	мохе́ровый *aj*
Mohammedan	магомета́нский *aj*
moire, moiré	муа́ровый *aj*
Moldavian	молда́вский *aj*

molybdic	молибде́новый *aj*
monarch's	мона́рший *aj*
monarchical, monarchist(ic)	монархи́ческий *aj*
monasterial	монасты́рский *aj*
monastic	мона́шеский *aj*
Monegasque	мона́кский *aj*
Mongol, Mongolian	монго́льский *aj*
monistic	монисти́ческий *aj*
monochromatic	монохромати́ческий *aj*
monogamous	монога́мный *aj*
monographic	моногра́фи́ческий *aj*
monolithic character	моноли́тность *nf*
monolithic	моноли́тный *aj*
monopolistic	монополисти́ческий *aj*
monopolization	монополиза́ция *nf*
monopolize	монополизи́ровать *impf, pf*
monopoly	монопо́льный *aj*
monorail	моноре́льсовый *aj*
monotheistic	монотеисти́ческий *aj*
monotone, in a	моното́нно *av*
monotype	моноти́пный
montage	монта́жный *aj*
moraine	море́нный *aj*
moralize	морализи́ровать *impf*
morally	мора́льно *av*
Morcan	майо́рский *aj*
Mordvinian	мордо́вский *aj*
Mormon	мормо́нский *aj*
Moroccan	марокка́нский *aj*
morphological	морфологи́ческий *aj*
Mosaic [of Moses]	Моисе́ев *aj*
mosaic	моза́ичный *aj*
Moscow	моско́вский *aj*
Moscow, near	подмоско́вный *aj*
Moslem, Muslim	мусульма́нский *aj*
mosquito	моски́тный *aj*
motivate	мотиви́ровать *impf*
motor	мото́рный *aj*
motorcycle	мотоцикле́тный *aj*
motorization	моториза́ция *nf*
motorize	моторизова́ть *impf*
mount	монти́ровать *impf*
Mozambican	мозамби́кский *aj*
municipalize	муниципализи́ровать *impf*
muscat (grapes)	муска́тный *aj*
Muscovy	моско́вский *aj*
museum	музе́йный *aj*
muslin	мусли́новый *aj*
mutant	мута́нтный *aj*
mutate	мути́ровать *impf, pf*
mutative	мутацио́нный *aj*
myopic	миопи́ческий *aj*
myrtle	ми́ртовый *aj*
mystic(al)	мисти́ческий *aj*
mystification	мистифика́ция *nf*
mystify	мистифици́ровать *impf, pf*
mythological	мифологи́ческий *aj*
Namibian	намиби́йский *aj*
napalm	напа́лмовый *aj*
naphthalene, of	нафтали́нный *aj*
narcotic	нарко́ти́ческий *aj*
narcotization	наркотиза́ция *nf*
nasalize	назализи́ровать *impf, pf*
nationalist(ic)	националисти́ческий *aj*
nationalize	национализи́ровать *impf, pf*
NATO	нато́вский *aj*
naturalize	натурализова́ть *impf, pf*
navigational	навигацио́нный *aj*
nazalized	назализи́рованный *aj*
Nazi	наци́стский *aj*
Neanderthal	неандерта́льский *aj*
Neapolitan	неаполита́нский *aj*
Negro	негритя́нский *aj*
Nenets	не́нецкий *aj*
neo-fascist	неофаши́стский *aj*
neo-Nazi	неонаци́стский *aj*
neoclassical	неоклассиче́ский *aj*
Neolithic	неолити́ческий *aj*
neon	нео́новый *aj*
NEP, of	нэ́повский *aj*
Nepalese, Nepali	непа́льский *aj*
nerves, to get on someone's	нерви́ровать *impf*
nervous, to feel	не́рвничать *impf*
nervously	не́рвно *av*
Netherlandish	нидерла́ндский *aj*
neuralgic	невралги́ческий *aj*
neurogenic	нейроге́нный *aj*
neuroleptic	нейролепти́ческий *aj*
neurologic(al)	неврологи́ческий *aj*
neuropathic	невропаталоги́ческий *aj*
neurotic	невроти́ческий *aj*
neutralize	нейтрализова́ть *impf, pf*
neutralizing	нейтрализу́ющий *aj*
neutron	нейтро́нный *aj*
New York	нью-йо́ркский *aj*
New Zealand	новозела́ндский *aj*
Nicaean, Nicene	нике́йский *aj*

Nicaraguan	никарагу́анский *aj*
nickel	ни́келевый *aj*
Nietzschean	ницшеа́нский *aj*
Nigerian	нигери́йский *aj*
nihilistic	нигилисти́ческий *aj*
Nile, Nilotic	нило́тский *aj*
nitrify	нитрифици́ровать *impf, pf*
nomenclature, of	номенклату́рный *aj*
nominal [value]	номина́льный *aj*
non-party	неparти́йный *aj*
non-political	неполити́ческий *aj*
non-Russian	неру́сский *aj*
noncommercial	некомме́рческий *aj*
nonmaterial	нематериа́льный *aj*
nonnreligious	нерелигио́зный *aj*
normalize	нормирова́ть *impf, pf*
normalize *vt(i)*	нормализова́ть(ся), *impf, pf*
normally	норма́льно *av*
Norman	норма́ндский *aj*
North Atlantic	североатланти́ческий *aj*
North American	североамерика́нский *aj*
Norwegian	норве́жский *aj*
nostalgic	ностальги́ческий *aj*
notarial	нотариа́льный *aj*
note	но́тный *aj*
notify	нотифици́ровать *impf, pf*
noumenal	ноумена́льный *aj*
November	ноя́брьский *aj*
Nubian	нуби́йский *aj*
number, numbered	номерно́й *aj*
number	нумерова́ть *impf,* пронумерова́ть *pf*
numbered	нумеро́ванный *aj*
numismatic	нумизмати́ческий *aj*
nylon	нейло́новый *aj*
objectification	объектифика́ция *nf*
objectify	объективи́ровать *impf, pf*
objectively	объекти́вно *av*
objectivization	объективиза́ция *nf*
observatory	обсервацио́нный *aj*
obstructionist	обструкцио́нный *aj*
obstructiveness	обструкцио́нность *nf*
occult	окку́льтный *aj*
occupation	оккупацио́нный *aj*
occupy	оккупи́ровать *impf, pf*
oceanograpic	океанографи́ческий *aj*
ochreous	охря́ный, охро́вый *aj*
octane	окта́новый *aj*
October	октя́брьский *aj*
Odessan	оде́сский *aj*
off-center	не по це́нтру *nm*
office	о́фисный *aj*
officer	офице́рский *aj*
officially	официа́льно *av*
ohmic	оми́ческий *aj*
oleographic	олеографи́ческий *aj*
oligarchic	олигархи́ческий *aj*
olive	оли́вковый *aj*
Olympian, Olympic	олимпи́йский *aj*
onomastic	ономасти́ческий *aj*
ontological	онтологи́ческий *aj*
oogenetic	оогенети́ческий *aj*
oolitic	ооли́товый *aj*
oological	оологи́ческий *aj*
opalesce	опалесци́ровать *impf, pf*
opera, operatic	о́перный *aj*
operate	опери́ровать *impf, pf*
operating	операцио́нный *aj*
operative	операти́вный *aj*
operetta	опере́точный *aj*
ophthalmic, ophthalmological	офтальмологи́ческий *aj*
opium	о́пийный, о́пиумный *aj*
oppose	оппони́ровать *impf*
opposition(al)	оппозицио́нный *aj*
optimistically	оптимисти́чно *av*
optimization	оптимиза́ция *nf*
optimize	оптимизи́ровать *impf, pf*
orate	ора́торствовать *impf*
oratorical	орато́рский *aj*
orbital	орбита́льный *aj*
orchestral	оркестро́вый *aj*
orchestrate	оркестрова́ть *impf, pf*
orchidaceous	орхиде́йный *aj*
order	о́рденский *aj*
organ	орга́нный *aj*
organic	органи́ческий *aj*
organically	органи́чески *av*
organizational	организацио́нный *aj*
organize *vt(i)*	организова́ть(ся) *impf, pf*
organized	организо́ванный *aj*
organizing	организа́торский *aj*
organogenetic	органоге́нный *aj*
orgasmic	оргазми́ческий *aj*
Oriental	ориента́льный *aj*
Orkney	оркне́йский *aj*
ornament	орнаменти́ровать *impf, pf*

ornamental	орнамента́льный *aj*
ornithological	орнитологи́ческий *aj*
orographic(al)	орографи́ческий *aj*
orthodox	ортодокса́льный *aj*
orthoepic	орфоэпи́ческий *aj*
orthopedic (BR orthopaedic)	ортопеди́ческий *aj*
oscillate	осцилли́ровать *impf*
Osmanli	осма́нский *aj*
osmotic	осмоти́ческий *aj*
osteological	остеологи́ческий *aj*
osteopathic	остеопати́ческий *aj*
Ostrogothic	остго́тский *aj*
otological	отологи́ческий *aj*
ottoman	оттома́нский *aj*
ovular	овуля́рный *aj*
ovulate	овули́ровать *impf, pf*
Oxford	оксфо́рдский *aj*
oyster	у́стричный *aj*
ozone	озо́нный, озо́новый *aj*
ozonize	озони́ровать *impf, pf*
ozonized	озони́рованный *aj*
pacifist	пацифи́стский *aj*
pack, package	пакова́ть *impf*, запакова́ть *pf*, упакова́ть *pf*
Pakistani	пакиста́нский *aj*
palatalize	палатализи́ровать *impf*
palatalized	палатализиро́ванный *aj*
Paleocene	палеоце́новый *aj*
paleographic	палеографи́ческий *aj*
paleontological (BR palaeontological)	палеонтологи́ческий *aj*
Palestinian	палести́нкский *aj*
palindromic	палиндроми́ческий *aj*
palliative	паллиати́вный *aj*
palm	па́льмовый *aj*
palpate	пальпи́ровать *impf, pf*
Pan-American	панамерика́нский *aj*
Panamanian	пана́мский *aj*
pancreatic	панкреати́ческий *aj*
panegyrical	панегири́ческий *aj*
panel	пане́льный *aj*
Panhellenic	panэ́ллинский *aj*
panic	паникова́ть *impf*, запаникова́ть *pf*
panic-stricken, panicky	пани́ческий *aj*
panoramic	панора́мный *aj*
pantheistic	пантеисти́ческий *aj*
pantomime	пантоми́мный, пантомими́ческий *aj*
papal	па́пский *aj*
papist [pej]	папи́стский *aj*
Papuan	папуа́сский *aj*
papulose	папулёзный *aj*
papyrology	папироло́гия *nf*
papyrus	папиру́сный *aj*
parachute	парашю́тный *aj*
parade	пара́дный *aj*
paradigmatic	парадигмати́ческий *aj*
paradoxical	парадокса́льный *aj*
paradoxically	парадокса́льно *av*
paraffin	парафи́новый *aj*
Paraguayan	парагва́йский *aj*
parallactic	параллакти́ческий *aj*
paralytic	паралити́ческий *aj*
paralyze (BR paralyse)	парализова́ть *impf, pf*
paralyzed	парализо́ванный *aj*
paramagnetic	парамагни́тный *aj*
parametric	параметри́ческий *aj*
paranoid, paranoiac	параноичес́кий, парано́идный *aj*
paraphrase	перефрази́ровать *impf, pf*
paraphrasing	перефразиро́вка *nf*
paraphrastic	перефрасти́ческий *aj*
parcel out (land)	парцелли́ровать *impf, pf*
parcelling out (land)	парцелля́ция *nf*
parietal	париета́льный *aj*
Parisian	пари́жский *aj*
parity	парите́тный *aj*
park *vt(i)*	паркова́ть(ся) *impf*, запаркова́ть(ся) *pf*
parking	парко́вочный *aj*
parody	пароди́ровать *impf, pf*
parody, of	пароди́йный *aj*
paronymous	пароними́ческий *aj*
parthenogenetic	партогенети́ческий *aj*
partisan	партиза́нский *aj*
partnership	партнёрский *aj*
party	парти́йный *aj*
pass [the ball]	пасова́ть *impf*
passport	па́спортный *aj*
pastel	пасте́льный *aj*
pasteurize	пастеризова́ть *impf, pf*
pastoral	па́сторский *aj*
pasture	па́стбищный *aj*
patent	патентова́ть *impf*, запатентова́ть *pf*
patented	патенто́ванный *aj*

pathogenic	патоге́нный *aj*
patrician	патрициа́нский *aj*
patrilineal	патрилине́йный *aj*
patriotic	патриоти́ческий, патриоти́чный *aj*
patrol	патрули́ровать *impf*
patrol	патру́льный *aj*
patronymic	патроними́ческий *aj*
pause	де́лать па́узу *nf*
pedagogical	педагоги́ческий *aj*
pedal	педализи́ровать *impf, pf*
pedal	педа́льный *aj*
pedological	педологи́ческий *aj*
pension, pensionary	пенсио́нный *aj*
percent	проце́нтный *aj*
perceptual	перцепцио́нный *aj*
perfect	перфе́ктный *aj*
perforate	перфори́ровать *impf*
perforated	перфори́рованный
perfumery	парфюме́рный *aj*
periodization	периодиза́ция *nf*
peripheral	перифери́йный *aj*
periscopic	перископи́ческий *aj*
peristaltic	перистальти́ческий *aj*
Persian	перси́дский *aj*
personify	персонифици́ровать *impf, pf*
personnel	персона́льный *aj*
perspective	перспекти́вный *aj*
Peruvian	перуа́нский *aj*
phallic	фалли́ческий *aj*
phantasmagoric	фантасмагори́ческий *aj*
Pharaonic	фарао́н(ов)ский *aj*
pharasaical	фарисе́йский *aj*
pharmacological	фармакологи́ческий *aj*
pheasant	фаза́нный *aj*
philatelic	филатели́ческий *aj*
philharmonic	филармони́ческий *aj*
Philistine	фили́стерский *aj*
Phillipine, Filipino	филиппи́нский *aj*
philological	филологи́ческий *aj*
philosophically	филосо́фски *av*
philosophize	филосо́фствова́ть *impf*
phlegmatic	флегмати́чный *aj*
phosphoresce	фосфоресци́ровать *impf, pf*
phosphorescent	фосфоресци́рующий *aj*
photochemical	фотохими́ческий *aj*
photocopy	фотокопи́ровать *impf, pf*
photograph	фотографи́ровать *impf*, сфотографи́ровать *pf*
phototropic	фототропи́ческий *aj*
phrase [music]	фрази́ровать *impf*
Phrygian	фриги́йский *aj*
phylogenetic	филогенети́ческий *aj*
physically	физи́чески *av*
physico-chemical	фи́зико-хими́ческий *aj*
picket	пикети́ровать *impf*
pictographic	пиктографи́ческий *aj*
pigmented	пигме́нтный *aj*
pilot	пилоти́ровать *impf*
pioneer	быть пионе́ром в чём
Pioneers, of	пионе́рский *aj*
piquancy	пика́нтность *nf*
pirate, piratical	пира́тский *aj*
pirouette	де́лать/сде́лать пируэ́т *impf, pf*
pistol	пистоле́тный *aj*
placental	плацента́рный *aj*
plan *vt*	плани́ровать *impf*, заплани́ровать *pf*
plan *vi*	стро́ить пла́ны *nmpl*
planetary	планета́рный, плане́тный *aj*
planimetric	планиметри́ческий *aj*
planimetry	планиметри́я *nf*
plastic	пластма́ссовый *aj*
platinum	пла́тиновый *aj*
Platonic	платони́ческий *aj*
plebeian	плебе́йский *aj*
Pleistocene	плейстоце́новый *aj*
plenary	плена́рный *aj*
pleonastic	плеонасти́ческий *aj*
pleural	плевра́льный *aj*
plus [advantage]	плюс *nm*
plush	плюшевый *aj*
plutocratic	плутократи́ческий *aj*
Plutonian, Plutonic	плуто́нов, плутони́ческий *aj*
pneumonic	пневмони́ческий *aj*
podzolic	подзоли́стый *aj*
poetically	поэти́чно *av*
poeticize	поэтизи́ровать *impf, pf*
pogrom	погро́мный *aj*
point by point	по пу́нктам
polarize *vt(i)*	поляризова́ть(ся) *impf*
polemic(al)	полеми́ческий *aj*
police	полице́йский *aj*
Polish	польский *aj*
polish	полирова́ть *impf*, отполирова́ть *pf*
polishing	полиро́вочный *aj*

politicization	политиза́ция *nf*
politicize	политизи́ровать *impf, pf*
polyester	полиэфи́рный *aj*
polyethylene	полиэтиле́новый *aj*
polygamous	полига́мный *aj*
polygraphic	полиграфи́ческий *aj*
polymeric	полиме́рный *aj*
polymerize *vt(i)*	полимеризи́ровать(ся)
polymorphism	полиморфи́зм *nm*
Polynesian	полинези́йский *aj*
polyp	поли́пный *aj*
polysemantic	полисеманти́ческий *aj*
polytechnic(al)	политехни́ческий *aj*
polytheistic	политеисти́ческий *aj*
Pompeian	помпе́йский *aj*
popularize	популяризи́ровать *impf*
pornographic	порнографи́ческий *aj*
porosity	по́ристость *nf*
port, portal	порта́льный *aj*
portrait	портре́тный *aj*
Portuguese	португа́льский *aj*
pose	пози́ровать *impf*
positional	позицио́нный *aj*
positive	позити́вный *aj*
post-revolutionary	послереволюцио́нный *aj*
post-Soviet	послесове́тский *aj*
potential	потенциа́льный *aj*
potentiality	потенциа́льность *nf*
potentially	потенциа́льно *av*
powder	пудри́ть *impf*, напудри́ть *pf*
powdered	пу́дреный *aj*
practically [in a practical way]	практи́чески *av*
practice (BR practise)	практикова́ть *impf*
Prague	пра́жский *aj*
pre-Christian	дохристиа́нский *aj*
pre-revolutionary	дореволюцио́нный *aj*
pre-Soviet	досове́тский *aj*
precapitalist	докапиталисти́ческий *aj*
predicate	предици́ровать *impf*
predicative	предикати́вный *aj*
prefixal	префикса́льный *aj*
premenstrual	предменструа́льный *aj*
Presbyterian	пресвитериа́нский
presidential	президе́нтский *aj*
press	прессова́ть *impf*, спрессова́ть *pf*
pressed	прессо́ванный
preterit (BR preterite)	прете́ритный *aj*
principle, in/on	принципиа́льно *av*
principle	принципиа́льный *aj*
privatize	приватизи́ровать *impf, pf*
privileged	привилегиро́ванный *aj*
prize	призово́й *aj*
pro-American	проамерика́нский *aj*
problematic(al)	проблемати́чный, проблемати́ческий *aj*
problems [collectively] *npl*	проблема́тика *nf*
procedural	процеду́рный *aj*
proclaim	проклами́ровать *impf, pf*
productively	продукти́вно *av*
profane	профани́ровать *impf, pf*
professionally	профессиона́льно *av*
professorial	профе́ссорский *aj*
prognosticate	прогнози́ровать *impf, pf*
programmatic	програ́ммный *aj*
progress *vi*	прогресси́ровать *impf*
project	проекти́ровать *impf*, спроекти́ровать *pf*
projected	прое́ктный *aj*
projection	проекцио́нный *aj*
proletarian	пролета́рский *aj*
proliferate	пролифери́ровать *impf, pf*
Promethean	промете́ев *aj*
propagandistic	пропаганди́стский *aj*
propagandize	пропаганди́ровать *impf*
prophylactic	профилакти́ческий *aj*
proportionality	пропорциона́льность *nf*
proscriptive	проскрипти́вный *aj*
prose	прозаи́ческий *aj*
proselytize *vi*	иска́ть прозели́тов
prosthetic	проте́зный *aj*
protectionist	протекциони́стский *aj*
protein	протеи́новый *aj*
protest	протестова́ть *impf*, запротестова́ть *pf*
Protestant	протеста́нтский *aj*
Provençal	прованса́льский, прова́нский *aj*
providential	провиденциа́льный *aj*
provoke	провоци́ровать *impf*, спровоци́ровать *pf*

Prussian	пру́сский *aj*
pseudo-scientific	псевдонау́чный *aj*
psychic	психи́ческий *aj*
psychically	психи́чески *av*
psychoanalytic	психоаналити́ческий *aj*
psychoanalyze (BR psychoanalyse)	психоанализи́ровать *impf, pf*
psycholinguistic	психолингвисти́ческий *aj*
psychoneurotic	психоневроти́ческий *aj*
psychopathic	психопатологи́ческий *aj*
psychotic	психоти́ческий *aj*
Puerto Rican	пуэторика́нский *aj*
pulsate	пульси́ровать *impf*
punch	пу́ншевый *aj*
Punjabi	пенжа́бский *aj*
punk [rock]	па́нковый *aj*
puristic	пуристи́ческий *aj*
Puritan [obs]	пурита́нский *aj*
purple	пурпу́рный, пурпу́ровый *aj*
Pyrenean	пирене́йский *aj*
pyritic	пири́товый *aj*
pyrotechnic	пиротехни́ческий *aj*
Quaker	ква́керский *aj*
qualify (as)	квалифици́ровать *impf, pf*
quantization	квантиза́ция *nf*
quantize	квантова́ть *impf, pf*
quantum	ква́нтовый *aj*
quarter	квартирова́ть *impf* расквартирова́ть *pf*
quartz	ква́рцевый *aj*
Quebec	квебе́кский *aj*
quinine	хи́нный *aj*
quinoid	хинои́дный *aj*
rabbinic(al)	равви́нский *aj*
rachitic	рахити́ческий *aj*
racial	ра́совый *aj*
racist	раси́стский *aj*
racket	раке́тный *aj*
radar	рада́рный *aj*
radial	радиа́льный *aj*
radiation	радиацио́нный *aj*
radically	радика́льно *av*
radio engineering, of	радиотехни́ческий *aj*
radio	ради́ровать *impf, pf*
radiochemical	радиохими́ческий *aj*
radiographic	радиографи́ческий *aj*
radiolocation(al)	радиолокацио́нный *aj*
radiological	радиологи́ческий *aj*
radium	ра́диевый *aj*
rail, railway, railroad	ре́льсовый *aj*
ratify	ратифици́ровать *impf, pf*
rational	рациона́льный *aj*
rationalistic	рационалисти́ческий *aj*
rationally	рациона́льно *av*
rattan	рота́нговый *aj*
reactive	реакти́вный *aj*
readdress	переадресо́вывать *impf*, переадресова́ть *pf*
reanimation	реанима́ция *nf*
rear-guard	арьерга́рдный *aj*
recommend	рекомендова́ть *impf, pf*, порекомендова́ть *pf*
reconnoiter	рекогносци́ровать *impf, pf*
reconstruct	реконструи́ровать *impf, pf*
reduce	редуци́ровать *impf, pf*
reef [sail]	брать ри́фы *nmpl*
refine [sugar]	рафини́ровать *impf, pf*
refined [sugar]	рафини́рованный *aj*
reflex	рефлекто́рный *aj*
reform	реформи́ровать *impf, pf*
reformative	реформа́торский *aj*
reforming	реформи́рование *nn*
reformist	реформи́стский *aj*
refrigerator	рефрижерато́рный *aj*
regenerate	регенери́ровать *impf, pf*
regional	региона́льный *aj*
register *vt(i)*	регистри́ровать(ся), зарегистри́ровать(ся) *impf, pf*
registration	регистрацио́нный *aj*
regress	регресси́ровать *impf*
regressive	регресси́вный *aj*
regroup *vt(i)*	перегруппиро́вывать(ся) *impf*, перегруппирова́ть(ся) *pf*
regularity	регуля́рность *nf*
regularly	регуля́рно *av*
regulate (adjust)	регули́ровать *impf*, урегули́ровать *pf*, отрегули́ровать *pf*
regulated	регламенти́рованный *aj*

regulation регламента́ция *nf*
regulatory регули́рующий *aj*
rehabilitate реабилити́ровать *impf, pf*
relativistic релятиви́стский *aj*
relay реле́йный *aj*
relevance релева́нтность *nf*
religiosity религио́зность *nf*
religiously религио́зно *av*
remilitarize ремилитаризи́ровать *impf, pf*
renegade ренега́тский *aj*
rent арендова́ть *impf*
rental ре́нтный *aj*
renter (payee) аренда́тель *nm*
reorganization реорганиза́ция *nf*
reorganize *vt(i)* реорганизова́ть(ся) *impf, pf*
repatriate репатрии́ровать *impf, pf*
report рапортова́ть *impf*, отрапортова́ть *pf*
repress репресси́ровать *impf, pf*
reproduce репродуци́ровать *impf, pf*
reptilian репти́льный *aj*
republican республика́нский *aj*
requisition реквизи́ровать *impf, pf*
reserve резерви́ровать *impf*, зарезерви́ровать *pf*
resonate резони́ровать *impf, pf*
restore реставри́ровать *impf, pf*
result, as a в результа́те *nm*
results, without безрезульта́тно *av*
retouch ретуши́ровать *impf, pf*
retrospective ретроспекти́вный *aj*
retrospectively, in retrospect ретроспекти́вно *av*
revanchist реванши́стский *aj*
revise ревизова́ть *impf, pf*
revising ревизио́нный *aj*
revisionist ревизиони́стский *aj*
revolutionary революцио́нный *aj*
revolutionize революционизи́ровать *impf, pf*
revolver револьве́рный *aj*
rhapsodic рапсоди́ческий *aj*
rheumatic ревмати́ческий *aj*
Rhine, Rhenish ре́йнский *aj*
Rhodesian [obs] родези́йский *aj*
rhythmic(al) ритми́ческий, ритми́чный *aj*
rhythmically ритми́чно *av*
rickety, rachitic рахити́чный *aj*
ricochet рикошети́ровать *impf, pf*
Riga ри́жский *aj*
risk, risky риско́ванный, ри́сковый *aj*
risk рискова́ть *impf*, рискнуть *pf*
riskiness риско́ванность *nf*
ritual ритуа́льный *aj*
ritualistic ритуалисти́ческий *aj*
ritually ритуа́льно *av*
rococo *aj* в сти́ле рококо́
roentgen рентге́новский *aj*
Roman Catholic ри́мско-католи́ческий *aj*
Romanian румы́нский *aj*
Romanize романизи́ровать *impf, pf*
romantic quality романти́чность *nf*
romanticize романтизи́ровать *impf, pf*
rudimentary рудиме́нтный *aj*
Russian ру́сский, росси́йский *aj*
Russianize, Russify русифици́ровать *impf, pf*
sabbatical суббо́тний *aj*
Sabine саби́нский *aj*
sable собо́лий *aj*
sabotage саботи́ровать *impf, pf*
saddle седе́льный *aj*
saffron шафра́нный, шафра́новый *aj*
Saharan са́харный *aj*
saline соляно́й, солево́й *aj*
salt соли́ть *impf*, посоли́ть *pf*
saltiness солёность *nf*
salute *vi* салютова́ть *impf*, отсалютова́ть *pf*
Salvadoran сальвадо́рский *aj*
Samaritan самаритя́нский *aj*
Samoan самоа́нский *aj*
sanatorium, sanitarium санато́рный *aj*
sanction санкциони́ровать *impf, pf*
sanforize санфоризи́ровать *impf*
sanitary санита́рный *aj*
Sanskrit санскри́тский *aj*
Sapphic сафи́ческий *aj*
sapphire-like сапфи́рный *aj*
Saracen сараци́нский *aj*

sarcastically	саркасти́чески *av*
Sardinian	сарди́нский *aj*
sardonically	сардони́чески *av*
sateen, satinet(te), satiny	сати́новый *aj*
satiric(al)	сатири́ческий *aj*
satirically	сатири́чески *av*
Saudi-Arabian	сау́довский *aj*
Saxon	саксо́нский *aj*
scalp [Indian trophy]	скальпи́ровать *impf, pf*
scan [process]	скани́рование *nn*
scan	скани́ровать *impf, pf*
scandalize	скандализи́ровать *impf, pf*
Scandinavian	скандина́вский *aj*
scanning	скани́рующий *aj*
scenic	сцени́ческий, сцени́чный *aj*
schematic	схемати́ческий *aj*
schematize	схематизи́ровать *impf, pf*
schizophrenic	шизофрени́ческий *aj*
scholastic	схолисти́ческий *aj*
school	шко́льный *aj*
Scottish, Scotch	шотла́ндский *aj*
sculptural	скульпту́рный *aj*
Scythian	ски́фский *aj*
secret	секре́тный *aj*
secret, to keep a	секре́тничать *pf*
secretarial	секрета́рский *aj*
secretly, in secret	секре́тно *av*
sectarian	секта́нтский *aj*
secularize	секуляризи́ровать *impf, pf*
selective	селекти́вный *aj*
self-critical	самокрити́ческий *aj*
semasiological	семасиологи́ческий *aj*
seminal [fluid]	семенно́й *aj*
senate	сена́тский *aj*
senatorial	сена́торский *aj*
Senegalese	сенега́льский *aj*
sensory	сенсо́рный *aj*
separability	сепара́бельность *nf*
separatist	сепарати́стский *aj*
Sephardic	сефа́рдский *aj*
September	сентя́брьский *aj*
sequester	секвестрова́ть *impf, pf*
Serbian	се́рбский *aj*
serge	са́ржевый *aj*
serialization	сериализа́ция *nf*
serialize	издава́ть се́риями
seriously	всерьёз *av*
serve (food)	сервирова́ть *impf, pf*
shamanistic	шама́нский *aj*
Shiite	шии́тский *aj*
shock	шоки́ровать *impf, pf*
shock	шо́ковый *aj*
Siamese [obs]	сиа́мский *aj*
Siberian	сиби́рский *aj*
Sicilian	сицили́йский *aj*
signal	сигна́льный *aj*
signal	сигна́лить *impf*, просигна́лить *pf*
Sikh	си́кхский *aj*
silhouette	силуэ́тный *aj*
silicone	силико́новый *aj*
simulate	симули́ровать *impf, pf*
Singaporean	сингапу́рский *aj*
Sinhalese, Singhalese	синга́льский *aj*
sisterly	се́стринский *aj*
skeletal	скеле́тный *aj*
skeptical (BR sceptical)	скепти́ческий *aj*
skeptically (BR sceptically)	скепти́чески *av*
Slavic, Slavonic	славя́нский *aj*
Slovak, Slovakian	слова́цкий *aj*
Slovene, Slovenian	слове́нский *aj*
socialist(ic)	социалисти́ческий *aj*
solo [alone]	со́ло *av*
solo	со́льный *aj*
Solomonic	соломо́нов *aj*
Somali, Somalian	сомали́йский *aj*
somnambulistic	сомнамбули́ческий *aj*
sophistic	софисти́ческий *aj*
soprano	сопра́новый, сопра́нный
soup	супово́й *aj*
South African	южноафрика́нский *aj*
South American	южноамерика́нский *aj*
sovereign	сувере́нный *aj*
Soviet	сове́тский *aj*
soy, soybean	со́евый *aj*
Spanish	испа́нский *aj*
Spartan	спарта́нский *aj*
spasmodic	спазмати́ческий *aj*
specialize *vi*	специализи́роваться *impf, pf*
specially	специа́льно *av*
specific	специфи́ческий *aj*
specify	специфици́ровать *impf, pf*
spectroscopic	спектроскопи́ческий *aj*
speculate	спекули́ровать *impf*
speculative	спекуляти́вный *aj*
speleological	спелеологи́ческий *aj*
spinal	спинно́й *aj*

spiritualistic	спирити́ческий *aj*
sponsoring	спо́нсорский *aj*
sponsorship	спо́нсорство *nn*
sporadically	споради́чески *av*
sport(s), sporting, sporty	спорти́вный *aj*
sprint	спринтова́ть *impf*
spy (on) *vi*	шпио́нить *impf*
spy	шпио́нский *aj*
St. Petersburg	санкт-петербу́ргский *aj*
stabilize *vt(i)*	стабилизи́ровать(ся) *impf, pf*
stabilized	стабилизи́рованный *av*
stabilizing	стабилизи́рующий *aj*
Stalinist	сталини́стский *aj*
stamp	штампова́ть *impf,* проштампова́ть *pf*
standardization	стандартиза́ция *nf*
standardize	стандартизи́ровать *impf, pf*
start	стартова́ть *impf, pf*
starting	ста́ртовый *aj*
static	стати́ческий *aj*
station	станцио́нный *aj*
stationary	стациона́рный *aj*
stearin	стеари́новый *aj*
steel	стально́й *aj*
stenographic	стенографи́ческий *aj*
steppe	степно́й *aj*
stereographic	стереографи́ческий *aj*
stereotype	стереотипи́ровать *impf, pf*
stereotyped	стереоти́пный *aj*
sterilize	стерилизова́ть *impf, pf*
sterling	сте́рлинговый *aj*
stimulate	стимули́ровать *impf, pf*
stoically	стои́чески *av*
storm [assault]	штурмова́ть *impf*
strategically	стратеги́чески *av*
stratospheric	стратосфе́рный *aj*
stressful	стре́ссовый *aj*
stroboscopic	стробоскопи́ческий *aj*
strophic	строфи́ческий *aj*
structured	структури́рованный *aj*
stucco	штукату́рный *aj*
stucco, to apply	штукату́рить *impf,* оштукату́рить *pf*
student, student's	студе́нческий *aj*
studio	студи́йный *aj*
Stygian	стиги́йский *aj*
stylistic	стилисти́ческий *aj*
stylization	стилиза́ция *nf*

stylize	стилизова́ть *impf, pf*
stylized, styled	стилизо́ванный *aj*
subjectively	субъекти́вно *av*
sublimate	сублими́ровать *impf, pf*
subsidize	субсиди́ровать *impf, pf*
substantive	субстанти́вный *aj*
subtext	подтекст *nm*
Sudanese	суда́нский *aj*
Suez	суэ́цкий *aj*
suffixal	суффикса́льный *aj*
sum up	сумми́ровать *impf, pf*
Sumatran	суматри́йский *aj*
Sumerian	шуме́рский *aj*
surrealistic	сюрреалисти́ческий *aj*
suzerain	сюзере́нный *aj*
Swedish	шве́дский *aj*
Swiss	швейца́рский *aj*
syllogistic	силлогисти́ческий *aj*
symbolic	символи́ческий *aj*
symbolize	символизи́ровать *impf*
symmetrically	симметри́чно *av*
symmetrization	симметриза́ция *nf*
sympathize (with) *vi*	симпатизи́ровать *impf*
symphonic	симфони́ческий
symptomatic	симптомати́ческий *aj*
synchronically	синхро́нно *av*
synchronizing	синхронизи́рующий *aj*
synclinal	синклина́льный *aj*
syncopate	синкопи́ровать *impf, pf*
syncopated	синкопи́рованный *aj*
syncretic	синкрети́ческий *aj*
syndicate	синдици́ровать *impf, pf*
syngenetic	сингенети́ческий *aj*
synodal	синода́льный *aj*
synonymous	синоними́ческий, синоними́чный *aj*
synoptic	синопти́ческий *aj*
syntactic	синтакси́ческий *aj*
syntagmatic	синтагмати́ческий *aj*
synthesize	синтези́ровать *impf, pf*
syphilitic	сифилити́ческий *aj*
Syrian	сири́йский *aj*
systematic	системати́ческий *aj*
systematically	системати́чески *av*
systematization	систематиза́ция *nf*
systematize	систематизи́ровать *impf, pf*
systolic	систоли́ческий *aj*
tabular	табли́чный *aj*
tabulate	табули́ровать *impf*
tactfully	такти́чно *av*

tactical	такти́ческий *aj*
tactically	такти́чески *av*
tactlessly	беста́ктно *av*
taffeta	тафтяно́й *aj*
Tahitian	таитя́нский *aj*
Taiwanese	тайва́ньский *aj*
talc(um)	та́льковый *aj*
Tallin(n)	та́ллинский *aj*
Talmudic	талмуди́ческий *aj*
Tamil	тами́льский *aj*
tank	та́нковый *aj*
tantalic	таntали́ческий *aj*
Tanzanian	танзани́йский *aj*
tariff	тари́фный *aj*
Tartar, Tatar	тата́рский *aj*
Tasmanian	тасма́нский *aj*
tattoo	татуи́ровать *impf, pf*
tattooed	татуиро́ванный *aj*
tautological	тавтологи́ческий *aj*
teak	ти́ковый *aj*
technically	техни́чески *av*
technocratic	технократи́ческий *aj*
technological	технологи́ческий *aj*
telegraph	телеграфи́ровать *impf, pf*, протелеграфи́ровать *pf*
telegraphic	телегра́фный *aj*
telemetric	телеметри́ческий *aj*
teleological	телеологи́ческий *aj*
telepathic	телепати́ческий *aj*
telephone, telephonic	телефо́нный *aj*
telephone	телефони́ровать *impf, pf*
telephoto	телефото(графи́ческий) *aj*
telephotographic	телефотографи́ческий *aj*
telescopic	телескопи́ческий *aj*
television	телевизио́нный *aj*
tellurous	теллури́ческий *aj*
temper	темпери́ровать *impf, pf*
tendentiousness	тенденцио́зность *nf*
tender	те́ндерный *aj*
tennis	те́ннисный *aj*
tenor	теноро́вый *aj*
teratogenic	тератоге́нный *aj*
teratological	тератологи́ческий *aj*
termite	терми́тный *aj*
terra-cotta	террако́товый *aj*
terrace	терраци́ровать *impf, pf*
terraced	терра́сный *aj*
terrorist(ic)	террористи́ческий *aj*
terrorization	терроризи́рование *nn*
terrorize	терроризи́ровать *impf, pf*
test	тести́ровать *impf, pf*
tetrarchic	тетрархи́ческий *aj*
Teutonic	тевто́нский *aj*
textile	тексти́льный *aj*
textual	текстово́й, тексту́альный *aj*
Thai	та́йский *aj*
Theban	фиви́йский *aj*
theistic	теисти́ческий *aj*
theocratic	теократи́ческий *aj*
theological	теологи́ческий *aj*
theoretically	теорети́чески *av*
theorize	теоретизи́ровать *impf*
theosophical	теосо́фский, теософи́ческий *aj*
therapeutic(al)	терапевти́ческий *aj*
thermoscopic	термоскопи́ческий *aj*
thermostatic	термостати́ческий *aj*
throne	тро́нный *aj*
Tibetan	тибе́тский *aj*
tiger	тигро́вый *aj*
Tik, Tiki	таджи́кский *aj*
Titanic	титани́ческий *aj*
titled	титуло́ванный *aj*
titrate	титрова́ть *impf, pf*
tobacco	таба́чный *aj*
Togolese	тоголе́зский *aj*
toilet	туале́тный *aj*
Tokyo	токи́йский *aj*
tomato	тома́тный *aj*
tonal	тона́льный *aj*
tone up	тонизи́ровать *impf, pf*
tonic	тони́ческий *aj*
topaz	топа́зовый *aj*
topographic(al)	топографи́ческий *aj*
toroidal	тороида́льный *aj*
torpedo	торпе́дный *aj*
totalitarian	тоталита́рный *aj*
totem	тоте́мный *aj*
tourist	тури́стский *aj*
tournament	турни́рный *aj*
toxicological	токсикологи́ческий *aj*
tracheal	трахе́йный *aj*
tractor	тра́кторный *aj*
traditionalism	традицио́нность *nf*
traditionally	традицио́нно *av*
tragically	траги́чески *av*
tragicomic	трагикоми́ческий *aj*
train *vt(i)*	тренирова́ть(ся) *impf*, натренирова́ть(ся) *pf*

trained	тренирóванный, натренирóванный *aj*
training	тренирóвочный *aj*
tramway	трамвáйный *aj*
trans-Caucasian	закавкáзский *aj*
trans-Siberian	транссибúрский *aj*
transatlantic	трансатлантúческий *aj*
transcendent(al)	трансцендентáльный, трансцендéнтный
transcontinental	трансконтинентáльный *aj*
transcribe	транскрибúровать *impf, pf*
transform	трансформúровать *impf, pf*
transformational	трансформáторный *aj*
transistor	транзúсторный *aj*
transit	транзúтный *aj*
transliterate	транслитерúровать *impf, pf*
transport	транспортúровать *impf, pf*
transport, transportation	трáнспортный *aj*
transport	транспортúровать *impf, pf*
transportable	транспортáбельный *aj*
transporter	транспортёр *nm*
transpose	транспонúровать *impf, pf*
Transylvanian	трансильвáнский *aj*
traumatic	травматúческий *aj*
traumatize	травмúровать *impf, pf*
tref	трефнóй *aj*
trepan	трепанúровать *impf, pf*
tricot	трикóвый *aj*
triumphal	триумфáльный *aj*
trivia *npl*	тривиáльности *nfpl*
triviality	тривиáльность *nf*
troglodytic	троглодúтский *aj*
Trojan	троя́нский *aj*
trolleybus	троллéйбусный *aj*
tsarist, czarist	цáрский *aj*
tubercular	туберкулёзный *aj*
tulip	тюльпáнный *aj*
tulle	тю́левый *aj*
tundra	тýндровый *aj*
Tunisian	тунúсский *aj*
tunnel	тýннельный *aj*
turbine	турбúнный *aj*
Turkish	турéцкий *aj*
Turkmen	туркмéнский *aj*
tweed	твúдовый *aj*

typhoid	тифóзный *aj*
typically	типúчно *av*
typify	типизúровать *impf, pf*
typographic(al)	типогрáфский *aj*
typological	типологúческий *aj*
tyrannize	тирáнить *impf*
Tyrolean, Tirolean	тирóльский *aj*
Ugandan	угáндский *aj*
Uighur	уйгýрский *aj*
Ukranian	украúнский *aj*
ultramarine	ультрамарúновый *aj*
unaggressive	неагрессúвный *aj*
unanalytical	неаналитúческий *aj*
unannotated	неаннотирóванный *aj*
unassorted	несортирóванный *aj*
uncatalogued	некаталогизúрованный *aj*
uncemented	нецементúрованный *aj*
unceremoniously	бесцеремóнно *av*
unchristian	нехристиáнский *aj*
uncivilized	нецивилизóванный
unclassified	неклассифицúрованный *aj*
uncrowned	некоронóванный *aj*
uncultivated, uncultured	некультýрный *aj*
underprivileged	лишённый привилéгий *aj*
undramatic	недраматúческий *aj*
unhygienic	негигиенúчный *aj*
Uniat(e)	униáтский *aj*
unification	унификáция *nf*
unify	унифицúровать *impf, pf*
Unitarian	унитáрный *aj*
unitary	унитáрный *aj*
university	университéтский *aj*
unmusical	немузыкáльный *aj*
unnatural	ненатурáльный *aj*
unnerve, to	нервúровать *impf*
unofficial	неофициáльный *aj*
unorganized	неорганизóванный *aj*
unorthodox	неортодоксáльный *aj*
unphilosophical	антифилосóфский *aj*
unpoetic	непоэтúчный *aj*
unprecedented	беспрецедéнтный *aj*
unprivileged	непривилегирóванный *aj*
unproductive	непродуктúвный *aj*
unreal	нереальный *aj*
unrhythmical	неритмúчный *aj*
unsanitary	антисанитáрный *aj*

unsterilized	нестери́льный, нестерилизо́ванный *aj*
unsystematic	несистемати́ческий, несистемати́чный *aj*
unventilated	невентилиро́ванный *aj*
uranium	ура́новый *aj*
uremic (BR uraemic)	уреми́ческий *aj*
urological	урологи́ческий *aj*
Uruguayan	уругва́йский *aj*
usurp	узурпи́ровать *impf, pf*
utilize	утилизи́ровать *impf, pf*
Utopian	утопи́ческий *aj*
Uzbek	узбе́кский *aj*
vacant	вака́нтный *aj*
vaccinate	вакцини́ровать *impf, pf*
vanilla	вани́льный *aj*
vary *vt(i)*	варьи́ровать(ся) *impf*
vassal	васса́льный *aj*
Vatican	ватика́нский *aj*
vector, vectorial	ве́кторный *aj*
veil	вуали́ровать *impf*, завуали́ровать *pf*
velour	велю́ровый *aj*
velveteen	вельве́товый *aj*
venereal	венери́ческий *aj*
Venetian	венециа́нский *aj*
Venezuelan	венесуэ́льский *aj*
venous	вено́зный *aj*
ventilate	вентили́ровать *impf*, провентили́ровать *pf*
ventilated	вентилиро́ванный *aj*
ventilation	вентиляцио́нный *aj*
vertically	вертика́льно *av*
veterinary	ветерина́рный *aj*
vibrating	вибри́рующий *aj*
vibrate	вибри́ровать *impf*
Viennese	ве́нский *aj*
Vietnamese	вьетна́мский *aj*
Vilnius	ви́льнюсский *aj*
vinyl	вини́ловый *aj*
viral	ви́русный *aj*
virulence	вируле́нтность *nf*
visa	визи́ровать *impf, pf*
viscose	виско́зный
viscous	вя́зкий *aj*
Visigothic [obs]	вестго́тский *aj*
visit	визи́тный *aj*
vitamin	витами́нный, витамино́зный *aj*
vocalize	вокализи́ровать *impf*
vocally	вока́льно *av*
Volga	во́лжский *aj*
volitional	волево́й *aj*
vulcanize	вулканизи́ровать *impf*
vulgarize	вульгаризи́ровать *impf, pf*
Walloon	валло́нский *aj*
waltz	вальси́ровать *impf*
Warsaw	варша́вский *aj*
Washingtonian	вашингто́нский *aj*
Welsh	уэ́льский *aj*
West Indian	вест-и́ндский *aj*
Westphalian	вестфальский *aj*
wine	ви́нный *aj*
xerographic	ксерографи́ческий *aj*
xerophilous	ксерофи́льный *aj*
xerox	ксерокопи́ровать *impf, pf*
Yakut	яку́тский *aj*
Yalta	я́лтинский *aj*
Yemeni, Yemenite	йе́менский *aj*
Yugoslav(ian)	югосла́вский *aj*
Zairean	заи́рский *aj*
Zambian	замби́йский *aj*
zenith	зени́тный *aj*
zeugmatic	зевмати́ческий *aj*
Zimbabwean	зимбабви́йский *aj*
zinc	ци́нковый *aj*
Zionist(ic)	сиони́стский *aj*
zodiacal	зодиака́льный *aj*
zone, zonal	зона́льный *aj*
zoogeographic(al)	зоогеографи́ческий *aj*
zoological	зоологи́ческий *aj*
zoomorphic	зооморфи́ческий *aj*
Zulu	зулу́сский *aj*